Ideology and the Microfoundations of Conflict

SERIES IN POLITICAL PSYCHOLOGY

Series Editor
John T. Jost

Editorial Board
Mahzarin Banaji, Gian Vittorio Caprara, Christopher Federico, Don Green, John Hibbing, Jon Krosnick, Arie Kruglanski, Kathleen McGraw, David Sears, Jim Sidanius, Phil Tetlock, Tom Tyler

Image Bite Politics: News and the Visual Framing of Elections
Maria Elizabeth Grabe and Erik Page Bucy

Social and Psychological Bases of Ideology and System Justification
John T. Jost, Aaron C. Kay, and Hulda Thorisdottir

The Political Psychology of Democratic Citizenship
Eugene Borgida, Christopher M. Federico, and John L. Sullivan

On Behalf of Others: The Psychology of Care in a Global World
Sarah Scuzzarello, Catarina Kinnvall, and Kristen R. Monroe

The Obamas and a (Post) Racial America?
Gregory S. Parks and Matthew W. Hughey

Ideology, Psychology, and Law
Jon Hanson and John Jost

The Impacts of Lasting Occupation: Lessons from Israeli Society
Daniel Bar-Tal and Izhak Schnell

Competing Motives in the Partisan Mind
Eric W. Groenendyk

Personalizing Politics and Realizing Democracy
Gian Vittorio Caprara and Michele Vecchione

Representing Red and Blue: How the Culture Wars Change the Way Citizens Speak and Politicians Listen
David C. Barker and Christopher Jan Carman

The Ambivalent Partisan: How Critical Loyalty Promotes Democracy
Howard G. Lavine, Christopher D. Johnston, and Marco R. Steenbergen

Disenchantment with Democracy: A Psychological Perspective
Janusz Reykowski

Hot Contention, Cool Abstention: Positive Emotions and Protest Behavior During the Arab Spring
Stephanie Dornschneider

Divided: Open-Mindedness and Dogmatism in a Polarized World
Victor Ottati and Chadly Stern

Hope Amidst Conflict: Philosophical and Psychological Explorations
Oded Adomi Leshem

Ideology and the Microfoundations of Conflict: From Human Needs to Intergroup Violence
Veronika Müller and Thomas Gries

Ideology and the Microfoundations of Conflict

From Human Needs to Intergroup Violence

Veronika Müller and Thomas Gries

OXFORD
UNIVERSITY PRESS

Oxford University Press is a department of the University of Oxford. It furthers
the University's objective of excellence in research, scholarship, and education
by publishing worldwide. Oxford is a registered trade mark of Oxford University
Press in the UK and certain other countries.

Published in the United States of America by Oxford University Press
198 Madison Avenue, New York, NY 10016, United States of America.

© Oxford University Press 2024

All rights reserved. No part of this publication may be reproduced, stored in
a retrieval system, or transmitted, in any form or by any means, without the
prior permission in writing of Oxford University Press, or as expressly permitted
by law, by license, or under terms agreed with the appropriate reproduction
rights organization. Inquiries concerning reproduction outside the scope of the
above should be sent to the Rights Department, Oxford University Press, at the
address above.

You must not circulate this work in any other form
and you must impose this same condition on any acquirer.

CIP data is on file at the Library of Congress

ISBN 978–0–19–767018–7

DOI: 10.1093/oso/9780197670187.001.0001

Printed by Sheridan Books, Inc., United States of America

Contents

Acknowledgments ix

1. Motivation and Introduction 1

2. From Individual Psychological Needs to Social and Political
   Conflicts: The General Framework 12
   - 2.1 Fundamental Human Needs [Layer i] 15
   - 2.2 Ideologies and Belief Systems [Layer ii] 18
   - 2.3 Ideological Organizations [Layer iii] 27
   - 2.4 Implications for Conflict Resolution and Conditions for Peace 32

PART I: FUNDAMENTAL HUMAN NEEDS, THREATS, AND NEED DEPRIVATION

3. Fundamental (Psychological) Human Needs 47
   - 3.1 Existential and Epistemic Needs and Need Deprivation 47
     - 3.1.1 Existential Threat, Competition, and Poverty 48
       - 3.1.1.1 The Resource Curse: The Resource Scarcity Approach 49
       - 3.1.1.2 The Resource Curse: The Resource Abundance Approach 50
       - 3.1.1.3 Poverty and Absolute Deprivation 55
       - 3.1.1.4 Relative Deprivation 58
     - 3.1.2 Threats to One's Own Social Group 61
       - 3.1.2.1 Polarization and Intergroup Threat 63
       - 3.1.2.2 Minorities 66
   - 3.2 Psychological Implications of Threat 69
   - 3.3 Existential and Epistemic Needs and Need Deprivation 76
     - 3.3.1 The Existential Need for Safety/Existential Security 76
     - 3.3.2 The Existential Need for Control 80
     - 3.3.3 The Epistemic Need for Ambiguity Avoidance/Cognitive Closure 84
     - 3.3.4 The Epistemic Need for Consistency 89
     - 3.3.5 The Epistemic Need for Predictability 93
     - 3.3.6 The Epistemic Need for Order 96

4. Relational Needs and Need Deprivation 101
   - 4.1 The Concept of Identity 102
   - 4.2 Identity Formation 109
   - 4.3 Relational Human Needs 115
     - 4.3.1 The Relational Need for Identification 116
     - 4.3.2 The Relational Need for Belongingness 121

vi Contents

	4.3.3 The Relational Need for Social Approval	127
	4.3.4 Is There a Fundamental Human Need for Pro-sociality?	133
	4.3.4.1 Empathy—The Source of Pro-sociality?	*134*
	4.3.4.2 The Empathy–Altruism Hypothesis	*138*

5. Agency Needs and Need Deprivation — 143
 5.1 The Intrapersonal Process—The Self-Concept — 144
 5.2 Personality — 154
 5.3 Agency Needs — 160
  5.3.1 The Agency Need for Self-Esteem — 160
  5.3.2 The Agency Need for Self-Determination — 168
  5.3.3 The Agency Need for Self-Efficacy — 175

PART II: IDEOLOGIES AND NEED RECONCILIATION

6. Belief Systems and Ideologies as Psychological Need Reconciliation — 185
 6.1 The Concept of Ideology — 188
 6.2 The Concept of Reconciliation — 194
  6.2.1 Ideological Reconciliation in a Nutshell — 194
  6.2.2 Ideological Reconciliation—The Underlying Psychological Mechanism — 196
  6.2.3 Ideological Reconciliation—Why and How — 200
 6.3 The Impact of Personality Traits on Ideological Orientation — 209

7. Right, Left, and Religious Ideologies—Their Need-Serving Capacities and Potential for Conflicts — 217
 7.1 The "Traditional Ideological Right" — 217
  7.1.1 Racism — 218
  7.1.2 Nationalism — 230
  7.1.3 Ethnic Nationalism — 240
  7.1.4 Fascism — 248
 7.2 The "Traditional Ideological Left" — 254
  7.2.1 Socialism/Communism — 254
  7.2.2 The New Left — 270
 7.3 Religious Ideologies — 278
 7.4 Are All Extremists the Same? Ideological Differences and Similarities — 290

PART III: EXTREMIST ORGANIZATIONS, IDEOLOGIES, AND REAL CONFLICT

8. Extremist Organizations—Their Network and Structure — 303
 8.1 Extremist Organizations from the "Need-Serving" Perspective — 305
 8.2 The Traditional Criminal Organization—The Mafia — 307
 8.3 The Radical Right Organizations — 311

8.4	The Radical Left Organizations	323
8.5	The Radical Religious Organizations	335

9. Extremist Organizations—Their Recruitment and Mobilization Strategies   348
   9.1 Recruitment and Mobilization from the Need-Serving Perspective   348
   9.2 Recruitment and Mobilization in Traditional Criminal Organizations   359
   9.3 Recruitment and Mobilization in Radical Right Organizations   367
   9.4 Recruitment and Mobilization in Radical Left Organizations   376
   9.5 Recruitment and Mobilization in Radical Religious Organizations   385

10. Real-life Cases and the Link between Needs, Ideology, and Conflict   398
   10.1 Case: FARC in Colombia   400
   10.2 Case: Sri Lanka and LTTE   406
   10.3 Case: Boko Haram   412
   10.4 Case: Niger–Delta Resource Abundance, Grievance, and Conflict   417
   10.5 Case: Muslim Youth in Europe and the Islamic State   422
   10.6 Case: Right-Wing Populism in (Post-Soviet) Eastern European Nations   428

Notes   435
References   443
Index   517

Acknowledgments

We are exceptionally grateful for the input we received at various conferences, notably the Jan Tinbergen European Peace Science Conference and the International Max Planck Research School on Adapting Behavior in a Fundamentally Uncertain World, where we presented our first ideas. We are also very grateful to the members of the Social Justice Lab at New York University, which was an opportunity for a thorough discussion of the book's fundamental premises. The members' critical but constructive feedback allowed us to rethink certain ideas, especially from a psychological point of view, and helped broaden our perspective. Special thanks also go to the School of Advanced International Studies at John Hopkins University that not only provided extensive resources to finalize the book, but also an opportunity to discuss the final project with scientists from various academic disciplines. Here, particular thanks are due to Thomas Homer-Dixon for his extremely valuable insights and inspiring thoughts. However, our most heartfelt thanks go to John Jost for his constant openness to discussing our ideas, and for being so open-minded, supportive, and thoughtful. Thanks to his guidance, we could focus on a particular direction and make the book far better than it would have been without him. Finally, we want to thank our family and friends, whose unwavering support allowed to us write—and finish—this book. We are grateful to everyone who supported us on this extraordinary journey.

1
Motivation and Introduction

After the end of the East–West conflict in 1990, a major global source of conflict appeared to have disappeared. The East–West conflict was an ideological conflict that was fought out globally. It often took the form of numerous proxy conflicts around the world. With the collapse of the Soviet Union in 1990, one of the main protagonists of this conflict vanished. A significant decrease in the number of conflicts was expected in the aftermath. As can be seen in Figure 1.1, this expectation initially appeared to be correct because, after 1990, the total number of conflicts indeed significantly declined. However, this decline did not last long. Since 2005, the number of conflicts has been trending upward again, reaching an all-time high in 2020.

Between 1946 and 2020, not only were intrastate conflicts the dominant type of conflict in terms of pure number; also, more external conflict parties were involved, and conflicts became more internationalized. A similar picture emerges for battle-related deaths. Figure 1.2 indicates that the number of casualties, too, has substantially increased during the last decade. However, the figures also indicate that while interstate wars were less frequent, when interstate wars do break out, casualties can increase sharply, and fighting may spread to a larger territory such that entire systems of allied states can be affected. With Russia's attack on Ukraine in February 2022, interstate war, which at least in Europe was no longer considered a meaningful means of shaping interstate policy, is once again being implemented as a real option for action. Although human history is beset by suffering due to violence and disastrous wars, including two devastating twentieth century world wars with more than sixty million dead after WWII alone, conflicts and violence within societies, cultures, and nations, but also between religions and countries, are more present than ever.

Against this background, the question arises as to the underlying base and motivation of individuals to participate in (violent) conflicts, either individually or in concert with conflict groups. The sometimes-popular idea that "crazy," "psychopathic," "megalomaniac," or just "greedy" leaders with a hunger for power force individuals into fighting, violence, and wars is insufficient and is not the focus of our analysis. Neither are we necessarily interested

2 Ideology and the Microfoundations of Conflict

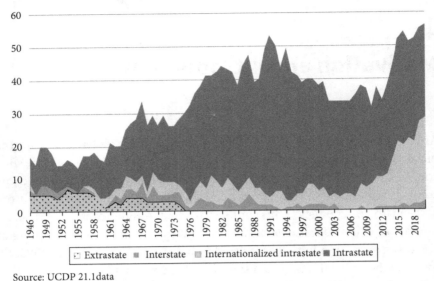

Source: UCDP 21.1data

Figure 1.1 Armed Conflicts, Total Number and by Type, 1946–2020

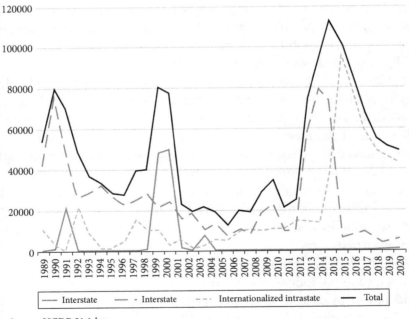

Source: UCDP 21.1data

Figure 1.2 Number of Battle-Related Deaths, 1989–2020

in understanding why conflict parties fight for resources, power, or territory, or why institutions fail to settle a conflict. All these reasons for conflict or conflict onset exist, but there is more. In most conflicts, we see a significant number of supporters without whom a major conflict cannot be launched in the first place. Major conflicts only exist provided both conflicting parties find sufficient supporters. So, what we need is a better understanding of the motivations to engage in conflicts on an individual level. What are the motivations of individuals to follow warring leaders and support an often-violent conflict? In other words, why are people willing to fight for a particular group, support a conflict party, and invest a considerable share of their personal resources in participating in intergroup violence? If we understand more about the motivations behind the conflicts then we can improve our analysis of conflicts and perhaps defuse them before they descend into violence, war, and disaster.

Our aim is thus to combine (and reconcile) insights from various disciplines, such as social and political psychology, economics, and political science, to understand the microfoundations of (violent) conflicts. In economics, "The quest to understand microfoundations is an effort to understand aggregate economic phenomena in terms of the behavior of individual economic entities and their interactions. . . . The quest for microfoundations grew out of the widely felt, but rarely explicitly stated, desire to stick to the position of methodological individualism (see Agassi, 1960; 1975; Brodbeck, 1958) [. . .] Methodological individualism is the view that proper explanations in the social sciences are those that are grounded in individual motivations and their behaviour" (Janssen 2008, 600).

In this book, we look at such individual motivations and behavior and identify ideologies as an extremely important ingredient in human behavior and motivation to support or participate in conflicts, and we explain why and how ideologies are so important. We point toward ideologies, although there is an influential view that after the collapse of the Soviet Union ideologies would disappear as an important reason for conflict and war. Yoshihiro Fukuyama, writing in *The End of History and the Last Man* (1992), was one of the most prominent representatives of this idea. During the Cold War different world views led to different ways for societies and economies to organize. So, when the ideology that opposed the western political and economic world view disappeared, there was a convergence toward one world view only.

However, today it is rather obvious that this interpretation is not borne out by reality. Among many others, we observed the 9/11 attacks; religiously motivated terrorism; intra-religious civil wars (e.g., in Yemen, the Taliban in Afghanistan, Al-Qaeda); the rise of the Islamic State in various countries; nationalist, right- and left-wing terrorism; and, most recently, a nationalistic-imperialistic attack by Russia on Ukraine. As Nobel laureates Esther Duflo and Abhijit Banarjee write in *Good Economics for Hard Times*, "we live in an age of growing polarization. From Hungary to India, from the Philippines to the United States, from the United Kingdom to Brazil, from Indonesia to Italy, the public conversation between the left and the right has turned more and more into a high-decibel slanging match, where harsh words, used wantonly, leave very little scope for backtracking" (Duflo and Banarjee 2019, 11). So not only was Yoshihiro Fukuyama's interpretation of history an overoptimistic narrative; in particular, it did not account for what ideologies are, what their role is, and how they function.

The discussion of ideologies has a long tradition in political science and builds upon several conceptions. Putnam (1971) identified fourteen main (political) elements in the definition of the term, while Gerring (1997) proposed focusing on a single attribute that describes ideology in an appropriate manner, namely *coherence*, referring to a set of idea elements that are bound together. Knight (2006, 619) defines ideology as "the way a system—a single individual or even a whole society—rationalizes itself." Knight recoded 1,148 articles on ideology and its definitions that were published in the *American Political Science Review (APSR)* over the years. She identified five broad categories that were used to define the concept of ideology. The first is based on references to particular individuals or politicians that are identified as ideological (e.g., Hitler, Stalin, Mao) or to personality traits and emotions. The second refers to ideology as a characteristic of a group (national character, "racial components"), while the third refers to ideology as "parties" or abstract political tendencies, such as communism, liberalism, or nationalism. Most definitions, however, conceptualize ideology in spatial terms—the fourth category—which still dominate in political science literature and unify ideology on a left-to-right continuum. The most familiar unit of analysis is hence the liberal-to-conservative, or left-to-right, continuum used in mass surveys, followed by the analysis of elite behavior and the ideological inclinations of a collective. Twenty-eight percent of all research articles published in the last decade before Knight's study adopt such a spatial conceptualization of ideology. The fifth and most abstract category includes theoretical and philosophical discussions of ideology that neither conceptualize it in spatial terms nor subject it to empirical tests (e.g., Marxist ideas). The author concludes that although more than half of the research articles in the *APSR* over the last five decades before the analyses use the term "ideology," there is no common understanding of it. However, almost all definitions appear to imply coherence, contrast, and stability, an interpretation that has remained constant over time.

However, conflict analysis that includes ideologies mostly relates only to the traditional controversy of communist versus capitalist views. When debating recent conflicts, ideologies and belief systems typically do not figure large. In terms of today's civil wars, groups conflicts, or terrorism, Leader Maynard (2019) suggests that ideology "remains a relative theoretical newcomer in recent conflict research. By comparison with ideational phenomena like identity, norms or ethnicity, conflict scholars do not possess a well-developed theoretical literature to inform analysis of ideology, and rarely reference specialist work from other fields, such as political psychology, social movement research, and intellectual history. In consequence, debates in conflict research are characterized by considerable uncertainty over the microfoundations of political ideology: exactly what ideologies are and how they can influence political outcomes (see also Kertzer, 2017)" (Maynard 2019, 635). Our aim is thus to build on insights from various disciplines to understand why individuals adopt particular ideologies, how ideologies function on an individual level, and how they can influence individual and collective behavior.

Understanding these microfoundations of ideologies allows us to explain how they can influence political outcomes and exacerbate violence and conflict. Established explanations in this regard vary from the use of ideology as a strategic instrument by elites to recruit and mobilize individuals (e.g., Walter 2017) to the "true believer" who is willing to invest their personal resources in supporting a conflict faction (e.g., Gutierrez Sanin and Wood 2014). None, however, answer the fundamental question of how exactly ideologies shape behaviors and choices and why individuals follow a particular belief system. At this point we will discuss the microfoundations of ideologies and belief systems and how they are also microfoundations of conflicts.

Figure 1.3 indicates that, statistically, belief systems, or ideologies, play a significant quantitative role within the conflict nexus. Data on national and international conflicts provide evidence that ideologies were the main driver of seventy-five violent conflicts in 2018 and sixty-nine conflicts in 2019, causing more fatalities than any other conflict item (Heidelberg Institute for International Conflict Research [HIIK] 2018, 2020).

Other sources show that ideologically driven conflicts have increased tremendously in number in the last decades, reporting a rapid growth since the turn of the century, as shown in Figure 1.4 (Schwank 2014).

Significant research articles confirm this development, reporting that, since 2001, more ideologically based terrorist groups have formed than before (Jones and Libicki 2008). Most of these newly established groups after 2001 are religious fundamentalist groups, whose number began to rise in the

6 Ideology and the Microfoundations of Conflict

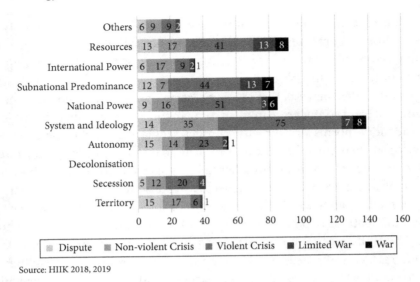

Figure 1.3 Frequency of Conflict Intensities by Conflict Item, 2018

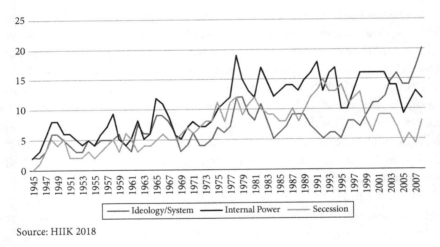

Figure 1.4 Intrastate Conflicts by Conflict Item and Year, 1945–2007

early 1990s. Other ideological groups, too, such as left-wing and nationalist groups, grew more numerous post-2001. However, the average number of newly formed religious radical groups has more than tripled in recent years, most of them located in low- and middle-income countries with a partly free democratic or autocratic political system. Most religious groups formed in the Middle East and North Africa (MENA) region and in South Asia, while nationalist groups mostly emerged in Europe and Central Asia. Table 1.1 shows

Table 1.1 Distribution of Terrorist Incidents by Group Ideology, 2002–2007

Ideology	Number of Groups	Number of Incidents	Number of Casualties
Left Wing	29	322	919
Right Wing	3	12	11
Nationalist	30	124	2,415
Religious	41	216	3,482
All	103	674	6,827

Data are taken from Table 3 in Gaibulloev and Sandler (2019) p.281

that leftist terrorist groups account for the highest number of incidents, while religious and nationalist groups were responsible for the highest number of casualties and are thus far deadlier (Gaibulloev and Sandler 2019).

An example of a specific country is given in Figure 1.5. According to Center for Strategic and International Studies (CSIS) data on terrorist attacks in the United States, most perpetrators had a far-right-wing orientation, with religious and far-left-wing orientation playing a significant role, too.

Despite this evidence, most influential theories on conflict (e.g., Le Billon 2001; Collier and Hoeffler 2004; Fearon and Laitin 2003; Ross 2004; Humphreys 2005; De Soysa 2002) pay little attention to the comprehensive significance of ideologies, presenting them either as a strategic instrument for radical groups to mobilize individuals and pursue their objectives or as a

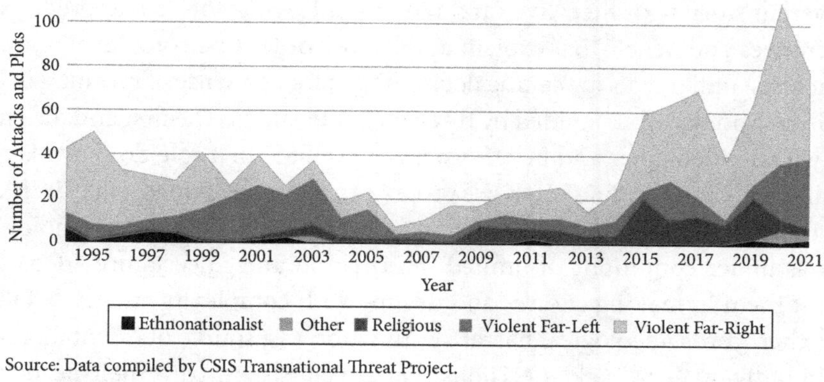

Source: Data compiled by CSIS Transnational Threat Project.

Figure 1.5 Number of US Terrorist Attacks and Plots by Perpetrator Orientation, 1994–2021
Source: CSIS Transnational Threat Project (Doxsee et al. 2022), retrieved from CSIS website, June 1, 2022.

source of normative commitment (Gutiérrez Sanin and Wood 2014). While this line of argumentation is certainly reasonable, psychological literature, in particular, argues that ideologies are adopted for psychological reasons.

In recent years, a growing body of literature has thus identified the motivational, social, and cognitive underpinnings of ideologies (e.g., Jost 2006, 2021) and emphasized their impact on individual behavior and decision-making. Although some researchers have begun to explore the link between ideology and conflict, they have yet to find clear explanations of how ideologies may shape conflict. This book contributes to this effort by providing an interrelated multidisciplinary framework to explain the multidimensional functions of ideology. Ideologies are not only capable of shaping conflictual behavior or mobilizing political actors; they can also address human needs, desires, and preferences. However, this book does not merely seek to explain the instrumental value of ideologies and the functioning of armed groups, it also examines the psychological appeal of various belief systems.

But what do we mean by the term "ideology"? The common and normative concept of ideologies as adopted by Steger (2013), Freeden et al. (2013), or Heywood (2017) defines belief systems as a (usually consistent) set of beliefs, narratives, and attitudes that provides interpretations and explanations of reality, visions, and/or utopias of what an idealized society should look like, and suggests strategies to achieve such a desired vision of society. While we fully agree with this concept, we go further and integrate the view of ideologies proposed by MacKenzie and Baumeister (2014). Thus, we suggest that ideologies are mental meaning-making systems that offer individuals narratives, enabling them to link the past, present, and potential future and align this coherent story with their lives and identities. Having consistent, predictable narratives and beliefs that explain and restore order to a complex world and that assist individuals in making decisions generates a sense of meaning in life.

In this book, we are guided by three main questions. The first and foremost is: why do ideologies and belief systems exist and what role do they play for individuals and conflicts? Here we propose that human beings make decisions in a complex environment primarily to serve their physical and psychological needs under conditions of limited information and uncertainty. Ideologies assist them in making choices and dealing with complexity and uncertainty. In other words, ideological narratives function as a source of orientation and help individuals to make decisions that are consistent with their needs and preferences. But how can ideologies address human needs—needs that go beyond the drive to secure one's physical existence? This is possible because ideological narratives, interpretations, evaluations, and strategies provide a view of the world that enables the individual to imagine a world that functions and can be shaped in accordance with their own individual needs. Yet why should we even focus on this seemingly "blurry" concept of needs? Considering human needs is of utmost importance because they provide a basis for understanding human behavior in general, particularly during conflicts and conflict onset. Human needs define important elements of humanity ("what it means to be a human being"). Four clusters of needs are fundamental to human existence: needs to secure one's existence, needs to process information and understand one's environment, needs to form social relations, and needs to make autonomous decisions. All these needs can be addressed by ideological narratives so that these narratives are able to reconcile such individual needs. Variations of ideologies address different human needs and preferences. For instance, individuals with a greater need for order, stability, and ambiguity avoidance and a preference for social cohesion and traditional role abidance will lean more toward ideologies that can reconcile these needs and preferences (here, ideologies with a traditional conservative appeal). By contrast, individuals with a greater need for autonomy, freedom, and self-efficacy who prefer weak governmental control and less group coherence will find libertarian ideologies more appealing.

However, these needs may be thwarted. Individuals may feel threatened in their existence, cannot make autonomous choices, do not feel they belong to a group, and do not feel approved by their group or society, or even feel rejected because of their identity. If society and its dominant ideological narratives and institutional and organizational structures fail to reconcile these needs, individuals will search for alternative options. In doing so, they may find other belief systems and ideologies that reconcile their needs and thus become attracted to them. This means conflicts are not only an expression of unresolved interests between two political actors striving for power, sovereignty, or territory, but they can also be an expression of inappropriate social structures and political institutions to which individuals have problems adjusting. If we can identify the social and political conditions that deprive individuals from reconciling their fundamental needs, conflict resolution and prevention can provide viable solutions, such as adjusting institutions to the needs of individuals (Burton 1990). However, if society and policymakers fail to provide conditions or resources to reconcile individuals' needs, individuals will search and possibly find belief systems and ideologies that do. Even extreme ideologies may become a viable reconciliation option.

The second question guiding our discussion is: How do ideologies function? Having understood the role of ideologies and their need-serving tendencies, let us explore how exactly they function. Belief systems consist of an interrelated set of norms, values, and attitudes that is shared by an identifiable group and has palliative and ontological functions. They provide alternative explanations and interpretations of the social environment, a view of the world, and narratives that enable individuals to identify and connect with social others. Because we propose that individuals adopt ideologies that resonate with their needs and desires, they rely on those ideologies to make decisions, process information, address life's problems, and manage threatening or uncertain situations. Ideologies support individuals in organizing their values and beliefs (e.g., Jost 2006; Jost et al. 2008). However, ideologies also have the capacity to influence collective behavior and choices, including conflict-related choices and actions.

This may also lead us toward the answer to our third and final question: How do groups or organizations use ideologies and belief systems to reach their objectives and to recruit and mobilize individuals? We propose that ideological organizations use ideological narratives or instrumentally provide services to address human needs, desires, and preferences. Then, the internalized world views not only provide individuals and groups with a clear and reliable guidance system, but they are also a basis for forming and sharing a group identity, and they may foster the development of the individual self.

To summarize, we propose that in our complex world in which we as humans do not have the resources and capacities to be perfectly informed and perfectly understand the reality of the world, belief systems and ideologies are suitable substitutive instruments for the incompleteness of information and understanding. Because the incompleteness of information and understanding is an important problem for beneficial decisions, belief systems and ideologies play an important role in a human's life. The adoption of a specific ideology is based on the specific physical and psychological need system of each individual. As different ideologies address different needs, individuals with different expressions of needs will choose different ideologies that help them reconcile these. Adopting a particular ideology, with its propagated values, narratives, and beliefs, is a viable option for need reconciliation. So, the world view that individuals adopt match and serve their need system such that the ideological narratives provide a view of the world that enables them to imagine a world that corresponds to their own needs. Ideologies and their narratives provide orientation and have a significant influence on individuals and the values they adopt. Once an individual trusts their adopted belief system, it guides them—through rules and advice—through everyday decisions, as well as in situations of conflict. Organizations that shape an ideology are aware of these mechanisms. They are able to guide individuals either into violent conflict or into compromise and peaceful conflict resolution. Major conflicts require a larger number of supporters on either side, many of whom were attracted by ideological narratives. Thus, ideological narratives are either the vehicle of the conflict—if their narratives address supporters' real or perceived deprived needs (base of the conflict)—or they are combined with organizational instruments for mobilization and recruitment. Finally, organizations and leaders who actively shape the conflict environment can either find compromises or lead their followers in violence and war.

The message, in a nutshell, is that ideologies and belief systems play an important role for human beings under both normal and conflict conditions. Ideologies address and serve fundamental human needs. Deprived needs are not the immediate and direct drivers of conflict. However, organizations and their leaders can use the narratives of belief systems or ideologies to address such (perceived or real) deprived needs and mobilize supporters. Thus, major and/or violent conflicts are the result of an interaction between fundamental human needs, the narratives offered by belief systems and ideologies, and organizations and leaders who actively shape the conflict environment. To address the complex interrelation between human needs, ideologies, and extremist organizations, this book is organized into three main parts: Part 1 focuses on human needs, Part 2 on ideologies, and Part 3 on extremist organizations. The introductory discussion and the main findings are condensed and summarized in Chapters 1 and 2. Part 1, consisting of Chapters 3 to 5, provides insights from various academic disciplines to address the concept of human needs. In this regard, Chapters 3, 4, and 5 discuss the role of socioeconomic and political conditions, as well as individual dispositions, which may deprive individuals from serving their fundamental human needs—needs that can be classified into existential, epistemic, relational, and agency needs. We introduce and discuss each of these need categories while presenting valuable theoretical and empirical findings which reveal the biological-evolutionary foundation of these needs. Part 2, consisting of Chapters 6 and 7, discusses the role of various belief systems or ideologies, and their need-reconciling abilities. And Part 3, consisting of Chapters 8, 9, and 10, explains how extremist groups or organizations use particular belief systems to recruit and mobilize individuals and decide between violent and nonviolent options. Here, we rely on theoretical and empirical findings to understand how ideologically motivated groups are structured and managed and how they provide viable reconciliation options to serve human needs in particular. In the final chapter, Chapter 10, we apply our framework to analyze and explain in a compact manner real-life ideological conflicts that happened in the past. The goal here is to explain consistently why individuals adopt certain ideologies, how ideologies function on an individual level, and how they can influence or degenerate into violent behavior.

2
From Individual Psychological Needs to Social and Political Conflicts
The General Framework

Throughout history, people have always faced extensive social and political conflicts; that is, struggles between two or more contesting groups over territory, resources, or political power, but also over values, a shared identity, or faith. The basic approach in economics toward explaining the motivations behind and conditions for such conflicts is based on the concept of choice. Choice, from an individual perspective, can be described as a process in which different desires, needs, and preferences are reconciled and culminate in a decision or action that is subject to external conditions and constraints (such as social pressure, norms, resources, or information). Because conflict involves choosing a conflict-resolving option, but also making a choice between nonviolent and violent alternatives, it is sometimes perceived as a pure outcome of a strategic choice; that is, calculated, rational thinking with the aim to achieve a profitable end. Hirshleifer (1994) postulates that individuals face a choice between production and acquisition. If the opportunity cost of acquisition (e.g., through violence or conflict) is tolerable, then violence will occur. In other words, individuals will choose violence and join radical groups if this is more profitable at the margin than economic exchange and cooperation.

While the economic approach has received much appreciation in conflict literature, psychologists argue that these assumptions alone do not provide a sufficient basis for explaining and predicting individual choices and behaviors. Individuals may also join groups and opt for violent alternatives for (non-materialized) psychological reasons, such as group belongingness, threat, uncertainty, identity, or self-esteem, which are often deemed irrational. While various empirical studies, interviews, and governmental communiqués reveal that individuals indeed join radical groups in the hope of economic gain (e.g., Ewi and Salifu 2017; Moir 2017), they also show that group dynamics and ideologies play a significant role in recruitment and mobilization.

Considering these findings and looking simultaneously at the empirical evidence that ideologies play a significant role, the main question that arises here is, why do normal individuals follow, support, or join radical groups—even if they provide radical or violent narratives—and accept a high level of personal risk to participate in ideological conflicts? And how can we explain this choice from an interdisciplinary perspective?

The main idea we explore in this book is that ideologies, or belief systems in general, have the capacity to help reconcile individuals' fundamental human needs that vary on both a situational and dispositional level. We combine economic and psychological approaches to explain the underpinnings of choices of ideologies and the function of ideologies and their organizations to recruit and mobilize followers. This interdisciplinary approach allows us to understand and conceptualize belief systems as the social and psychological products of individuals' internal needs, motives, and desires. Accordingly, our main argument is based on the insight that human beings have fundamental physical and psychological needs and are thus driven to reconcile these needs (i.e., to find means and ways to serve or satisfy their particular set of needs).

In other words, individuals' choices and behaviors can be understood as originating in an attempt to serve their needs. Belief systems, or ideologies, can help to reconcile these needs because they provide a psychological framework. Such a framework, irrespective of its ideological content, first and foremost provides orientation and guidance on how to process information, to evaluate events and circumstances, and to perceive oneself and one's environment. There is substantial evidence that individuals differ in their need manifestations and that their ideological proclivities stem from these basic differences (Jost et al. 2008). Individuals choose the ideology that best matches their underlying needs, desires, and preferences, given external conditions and constraints. Following the rules, norms, and values imposed by their ideology not only helps individuals to make consistent decisions and understand their social environment, but it also generates meaningful and reliable patterns of social reality. This psychological and social mechanism of ideology is used (and often misused) by radical groups or organizations to recruit and mobilize new members. In turn, adhering to a group's ideology, behavioral norms, and rules can have a palliative effect on individuals, which may explain, at least partly, the viability, success, and intensity of its operations.

Figure 2.1 explains our interdisciplinary approach in the form of an interrelated framework. To understand violent conflicts and the role of ideology in conflicts, three layers must be considered: (i) fundamental (psychological) human needs, (ii) belief systems/ideologies, and (iii) the (mostly radical and

14 Ideology and the Microfoundations of Conflict

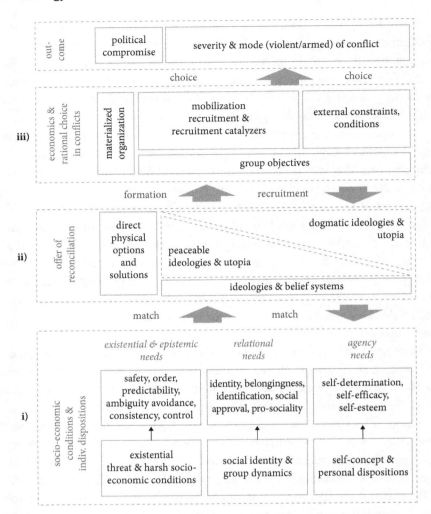

Figure 2.1 Layers of Violent Social and Political Conflicts: Psychological Human Needs, Ideologies, Ideological Organizations, and Political Conflict

dogmatic) groups or organizations that disseminate ideological narratives, recruit and mobilize individuals, control the mode of conflict, and decide between violent and nonviolent alternatives. Each layer defines an important ingredient of (violent) conflicts. The motivation to engage in conflict can arise from each layer individually, yet they are also interrelated and can reinforce a willingness to opt for violence.

When we analyze a real-world conflict, we should look not only at the conflict-driving organization, but also at its supporters and ask the following questions:

1. What are the underlying psychological needs in a particular conflict? What are the external conditions and constraints that deprive individuals of resources and opportunities to serve their needs?
2. What ideological narratives are disseminated by particular groups or organizations that aim to address these thwarted needs? Why and how do these narratives and their implications motivate or fuel conflict?
3. What are the objectives and motivations of the ideology-promoting organizations that decide between violent and nonviolent alternatives?
4. How do they recruit, mobilize, and address the needs of the deprived?

These fundamental questions address all three layers. If we discard one of these layers, we may not understand why and how a conflict occurs and how it can be resolved.

2.1 Fundamental Human Needs [Layer i]

The first layer of this framework focuses on the role of socioeconomic and political conditions, centralized as exogenous factors, as well as the collective and individual mechanisms which may deprive individuals from serving their fundamental (physical and psychological) human needs. Deprivation implies a denial of or a reduction in access to resources or opportunities to satisfy one's needs. These can range from physiological needs that secure one's existence and materialistic and consumption preferences to psychological needs that assure mental well-being. But why is it so important to serve these needs, and what role do they play within the conflict nexus?

Various disciplines, including psychology, economics, philosophy, and political science, postulate that all human beings seek to understand and actively shape their own environment and live a meaningful life (e.g., Baumeister 1991). In this process, individuals are confronted with complex conditions, such as ambiguous information, unpredictable circumstances, unstable socioeconomic and political conditions, and threatening events, amidst which they must make appropriate choices. Individuals strive to reduce this complexity to understand their existence, to identify their own role within the social context, and to make autonomous and effective decisions that are consistent with their goals, preferences, and needs. Accordingly, we postulate that aside from physical needs individuals have fundamental psychological human needs which can be classified into three interrelated subgroups:[1] (i) existential and epistemic needs, (ii) relational needs, and (iii) agency needs. Each of these needs is shaped by internal determinants, such as an individual's disposition, and by external determinants such as economic, social, political, or environmental factors.[2]

Existential and epistemic needs encompass a variety of needs that imply a safety-seeking mechanism. Individuals have a fundamental need to understand the unknown and complex environment, to process incoming stimuli, and to search for reliable and consistent patterns of reality. They do so not only to avoid threats and secure their existence, but also to understand the given reality and their own role in it. Individuals are hence driven by the motivation to reduce complexity, to understand, to acquire knowledge, and to attain control over their own environment. In this context, we identify the human need for (existential) safety and security, order, control, ambiguity avoidance, consistency, and predictability. These needs encompass the human need to secure one's existence; to feel that one is able to control and affect one's life; and to live in an ordered, predictable, and consistent environment.

However, to survive and to maintain mental health, human beings also need social relations. The second subgroup of needs, *relational needs*, describe the human drive to form relationships and to connect with significant others. They focus on the formation of social identity, social belonging, and pro-sociality. Individuals aim to maintain a sense of belonging; to share their identity, values, and ideas with significant others; and to feel loved and approved by other members of their group. In this regard, we consider the need for belongingness, identification, and social approval, but also the human need for pro-sociality—the innate human drive to care, help, and feel empathy for others.

However, individuals are not only social beings. They also have distinct personal dispositions, desires, and preferences. All individuals thus strive to develop a self-concept—a distinct description and positive evaluation of oneself that is made up of one's physiological and psychological characteristics, interests, goals, skills, roles, and so forth. Individuals want to make autonomous choices, feel efficacious in their aspirations and decisions, and maintain a positive self-view. Beyond the need for survival and sociality, then, individuals also have *agency needs*, which relate to their needs for high self-esteem, competence, and a self-determined and meaningful life (i.e., a need for self-esteem, self-efficacy, and self-determination). These needs are related to the desire of individuals to act freely and autonomously.

These human needs are fundamental, meaning they are universal and can be explained and reasoned in evolutionary-biological terms. They can be applied to every human being to varying degrees, with the manifestation of a particular need varying from person to person. Serving these fundamental needs is a premise for sound mental health and healthy environmental adjustment (Baumeister and Leary 1995). Depriving individuals from serving these fundamental human needs can have adverse physiological and psychological effects and may lead to social maladjustment. Take the need for belongingness, for example. If the need to belong (to society, to a particular group, to significant others, etc.) is deprived, that is if certain conditions such as an exclusionary social environment deprive the individual from serving this fundamental need, the activity of their anterior cingulate cortex (dACC) increases, an area associated with regulating the experience of physical pain (Eisenberger 2011). Our bodies and brains therefore react to an unmet need, which gives rise to internal drive states that push us to find ways to cope with the arousal to remain physically and mentally healthy (Deci and Ryan 2000).

Accordingly, individuals search for reconciliation options to satisfy their fundamental human needs. "Reconciliation" is commonly used to describe a process of conflict resolution between two parties. In our approach, however, we use it to refer to an internal psychological process of reducing tension within the individual, "tension" referring here to that between a need and the satisfaction of the need. We propose that individuals try to find ways to reduce the inner arousal (internal tension) that arises when their needs are thwarted (Max-Neef 1992). In this regard, economic literature (e.g., Sambanis 2002; Østby 2008; Pinstrup-Andersen and Shimokowa 2008) argues that a lack of resources and opportunities to satisfy these fundamental needs can lead individuals to seek violent or antisocial alternatives. However, this "direct" link between deprivation and conflict has been questioned due to its empirical discord. Several papers, including the popular studies of Collier and Hoeffler (2004) and Fearon and Laitin (2003), argue that grievance over endured mistreatment or serious deficits faced by individuals or groups has no explanatory power compared to the prospective material gain of rebellion. While both studies use different methods and assumptions, they both come to the same basic conclusion: the opportunity and feasibility of rebellion; that is, certain conditions that favor insurgency and the prospective gain of rebellion, have a stronger explanatory power than poverty, ethnicity, or political repression. While this indicates that conflict parties that address deprived needs do not opt for violent conflicts at all costs, it does not mean that deprived needs are irrelevant. Deprived needs define latent conflicts; however, needs deprivation alone normally does not directly turn into open or even violent conflict, but it can motivate individuals to search for viable need reconciliations. Only if conditions seem favorable can a latent conflict turn into open, or even violent, conflict. However, while external conditions and prospective personal enrichment certainly play an important role in explaining violence and conflict, it is also evident that a large number of individuals join groups, support conflict parties, and risk their lives for psychological rather than materialistic reasons (e.g., Gurr 1970; Muller and Seligson 1987; Basedau and Lay 2009). Evidence shows that in Nepal more deprived regions also had a higher number of Maoist sympathizers and were thus more drawn to rebellion (Murshed and Gates 2005).

2.2 Ideologies and Belief Systems [Layer ii]

Following the previous discussion, we propose that individuals are driven to find reconciliation options to serve their needs so they can remain physically and mentally healthy. In Figure 2.1 we emphasize the role of belief systems, or "ideologies" in political terms, which play a significant role within the conflict nexus. In our framework we thus introduce a second layer to explain how belief systems can be a viable reconciliation option to serve individuals' fundamental needs. Traditionally, belief systems have been regarded as a collection of ideas and narratives to win votes, influence people, and gain political support. While some sociologists and political scientists have declared that belief systems or ideologies have lost their significance (e.g., Bell 1960; Fukuyama 1992), psychologists such as Jost (2006) have emphasized their social, motivational, and cognitive underpinnings. This means that ideologies do have an impact on individuals' lives and "are not merely a passive reflection of vested interests or personal ambition, but have the capacity to inspire and guide action itself and so to shape material life" (Heywood 2003, 2). Hence, psychologists and cognitive scientists argue that belief systems grow out of individuals' attempts to serve their psychological human needs (Jost et al. 2003; Jost 2017). But what exactly makes belief systems so important?

The Functions of Belief Systems and Ideologies
Belief systems in general provide six important functions in human life. They are also relevant for conflicts and are briefly introduced in the following.

1. Belief systems help to "*solve the human problem of imperfect information.*" Belief systems are a consequence of the fact that humans have incomplete information about and an imperfect understanding of their environment. Humans are able to think logically, to collect information, to theorize, and to potentially understand the mechanisms that shape their environment. This capacity enables them to develop technologies and improve their living conditions. However, while science has helped to reveal some of the mechanisms at play here, we are still far from a

real understanding of our complex environment. This holds particularly true with respect to our complex social and economic systems, although we have certainly come some way in explaining the underlying mechanisms. Although humankind's information problem is severe, we still try to make decisions that help improve our living conditions and well-being. But how can we make beneficial choices under conditions of incomplete information and imperfect understanding? We search for instruments that can help solve this information problem. As the costs of information and real knowledge are high, we believe in plausible narratives and rely on heuristic rules (Burs and Gries 2022). Available ideological narratives substitute for the large efforts and high costs involved in a complex real analysis of social and economic systems. When "rational choice" models in economics often assume perfect information, they neglect the human information problem and hence discard a function that beliefs may provide. This simplification in rational choice models is indeed a very fundamental assumption. Omitting this information problem could be methodologically valid if it made no material difference to the decision (e.g., when information costs are close to zero). However, in a world with complex alternatives and high information costs, this must be doubted. For complex decisions, a real "rational choice" has to involve solving the information problem (Burs and Gries 2022). Thus, the first function of a belief system is that it provides support for solving the persistent human information problem. This means that ideologies provide a low-cost solution for an otherwise unsolved information problem (i.e., a set of norms, values, and narratives that help individuals to process incoming information, explain circumstances, and make decisions accordingly).

2. Belief systems *generate a coherent world view*. Belief systems consist of an interrelated set of norms, values, and attitudes that is shared by an identifiable group and that has palliative and ontological functions. The ontological function implies that ideologies provide alternative interpretations and explanations of reality (i.e., the social, political, and economic environment and of human existence). In other words, belief systems provide narratives that enable individuals to understand and link the past, present, and potential future and integrate this coherent story with their own life (and existence). Such an integration and understanding of (life) events, circumstances, and information form coherent patterns of reality, which generates stability and a sense of meaning.

3. Belief systems *provide a viable reconciliation option to serve psychological human needs*. Ideologies and belief systems provide mental meaning

systems that address individuals' existential, epistemic, relational, and agency needs. They explain why these needs are important and how humans can reconcile them. However, belief systems do not address and serve psychological human needs in a symmetrical manner (for an extensive discussion see Jost 2017). Ideologies that are usually termed "conservative" or assigned to the "traditional right"[3] of the political spectrum emphasize the core values of tradition, social order, status quo conservation/preservation, role ascriptions, and acceptance of inequality (upholding the organic structure of society). Conservative belief systems thus defend established institutions, social orders, and values, hence giving especially safety-seeking individuals (with strong existential needs) a sense of stability, order, consistency, and control over their lives. Empirical studies show that individuals who opt for a conservative belief system have stronger needs for order, control, consistency, and ambiguity avoidance (e.g., Jost et al. 2003). They also perceive the environment or the unfamiliar as dangerous, and consider individuals or events that destroy the traditional social order as highly threatening. Furthermore, conservatives place significantly greater emphasis on tradition, conformity, loyalty, and group cohesion and are thus argued to have a stronger need to "share reality" with like-minded others.

Looking at belief systems that are commonly termed "liberal" or assigned to the "traditional left" of the political spectrum, it becomes clear that they serve different psychological needs. The central theme of a liberal belief system is formed around the individual (i.e., the aim to construct a society in which individuals are free to choose and shape their lives as they wish). In doing so, individuals are endowed with equal rights and opportunities. However, there are significant differences between classic and modern liberalism[4] in this regard. Classic liberalism (or libertarianism) rejects governmental support and aims to limit the role of the state, while modern liberalism accepts the necessity to support individuals in promoting their personal development (welfare provision). The core values of modern liberal belief systems are thus formed around freedom, justice, individualism, diversity, and tolerance, which seems to appeal more to individuals who want to lead an autonomous and "socially unconstrained" life. Empirical studies thus show that individuals who prefer a liberal belief system score lower on the need for order and stability but higher on integrative complexity, uncertainty tolerance, and cognition (e.g., Jost et al. 2003; for a comprehensive discussion, see Jost 2021). In contrast to conservative belief systems, liberal belief systems do not favor a homogeneous, traditional society but rather support a diverse, open-minded, and tolerant society.

However, we note that this collection of ideas in a bipolar ideological system is probably the result of the majority voting system in the US and the UK. Faced with just two choices, voters need to integrate a multi-dimensional system of needs and need reconciling narratives into the two ideological camps of the respective parties. That is, a multidimensional system is pressed into a single left–right dimension. The multidimensional nature of this system can be more easily observed in Europe. Many democratic countries in Europe operate according to proportional representation, so there we see a more differentiated representation of the various need dimensions. In these systems, conservative ideologies and parties focus on preserving existing (cultural) patterns, and they also promise safety and security. There are also liberal parties which focus on civil rights, individual freedom, and economic deregulation, which in turn address self-determination and agency needs. Finally, there is clear evidence of social democratic ideologies which focus on solidarity and prosocial issues. Ideologies mirror individuals' needs and their need manifestation. So, different ideologies appeal in different ways to different individuals, with human beings drawn to the belief systems or ideologies that best match their needs and preferences.

In general, in a society we find a broad variety of individual need profiles. For some individuals, existential needs such as safety are fundamentally important, while others have a stronger need for autonomy. Yet others may be more focused on belongingness and identity. Each individual is hence unique with respect to their needs, and we may describe a whole distribution of individuals with various need dimensions. Every belief system offers a particular mental meaning-making system that addresses a particular set of underlying needs, and individuals adopt the belief system that best matches their underlying need structure.

4. Belief systems *provide a foundation for identifying with significant others*. For example, if all individuals share the same historical narrative that explains their cultural or religious existence, they may form a shared identity. Sharing similar values, norms, beliefs, and attitudes, and adopting similar narratives concerning one's own identity generates a sense of belongingness and unification. Thus, belief systems can help unify individuals into a community and shape collective thinking, which at one extreme can descend into ingroup favoritism and outgroup hostility.

5. Ideologies *establish/destroy* interpersonal and/or intergroup *trust*. In a complex world with imperfect and incomplete information, trust is an effective way to reduce complexity and information costs. The difficulty of assessing unknown situations and persons makes it necessary to accept information whose truth content is unclear. For example, a party to a transaction may or may not have been correctly and truthfully informed about the characteristics of the good to be exchanged. If this individual has been deceived, the complexity of the transaction increases significantly due to the resulting conflict. The information and transaction costs become considerable. The trusting party now behaves as if they do not expect any deception and they reduce complexity. In this step, the trusting party must take a risk because they have neither sufficient information about nor control over future events. However, taking this risk is rewarded because trust reduces complexity and thus reduces information and transaction costs (risk premium). Thus, belief systems can convey a general attitude toward trust, but also in particular an attitude toward which groups can be trusted. The way trust is handled between ingroup and outgroup individuals is significantly influenced by their belief system.
6. Belief systems *provide guidance for everyday decision making*. Complementary to the second point, not only do ideologies provide a general and sometimes abstract orientation and understanding of the world, but they also often give very concrete detailed rules and recommendations for everyday behavior. Belief systems hence support individuals in processing information, understanding reality, and organizing their values and beliefs. They help explain why people do what they do and how to evaluate when making everyday decisions. Individuals can thus rely on their belief system to guide them how to behave, address life's problems, and manage threatening and uncertain situations (e.g., Jost 2006; Jost et al. 2008).

Ideologies are most often linked to organizations that claim to have the sole ability and power to correctly interpret a particular ideology. These organizations announce behavioral rules in accordance with their interpretation. Followers are willing to follow these rules because they want to be consistent with their beliefs (Burs et al. 2022). Take the simple example of a consumption decision. An individual who subscribes to ecological narratives is guided by the recommendation to consume organic food. As they make their everyday shopping decisions, they will try to scale back the purchase of conventionally produced food and instead buy more organic products—even if they cost more. Another example related to the topic of this book is occupational choice. With respect to conflicts, an individual may decide to join a militia because they are committed to an ideological narrative and the representing organization has called to arms. The individual will follow this call even if they are badly paid and take a high personal risk. Both examples show that decisions are co-determined by psychological effects which guide our everyday behavior. Individuals not only decide according to purely physical preferences. Their choices are also influenced by rules and evaluations of their adopted ideology. Following the rules and norms of a particular ideology when making decisions generates consistency, order, and a sense of meaning in life.

Considering these attributes and functions of belief systems, it becomes clear that belief systems and ideologies seem to be a natural part of our psychological functioning. Therefore, let us take a closer look at the question of how humans adopt an ideology.

Adopting an Ideology

How do people arrive at a particular ideology that best matches their needs and preferences? We suggest that individuals engage in a process of information searching and Bayesian learning. They must find out which ideology best serves their specific set of needs. In Burs et al. (2022) this process is formally described. Typically, it starts at a young age. In such Bayesian learning processes, young people start at a prior belief that a particular belief system and the associated narratives may match their needs. This prior belief may be influenced by their parents, family, or the general environment. However, at a certain age they start questioning their original (prior) belief system and searching for alternatives. During a certain stage of personality development, the individual is more open to developing their own view of the world. They search for more information and examine to what extent various belief systems match their needs and preferences. In this search process, certainty about the match improves. At some point, the benefit of accumulating more information is no longer greater than the information costs this incurs. The orientation process then terminates, and a particular belief system is adopted. They choose the belief system which at that moment is on offer in their informational environment and which they perceive to best serve their underlying needs. Individuals hence adopt those belief systems that are consistent with their needs and preferences. However, in some disciplines the choice of belief system seems to be linked to irrationality. Motivational biases, cognitive incapability, resource limitations, or informational complexities have all been attributed to biased and irrational ideological choices (e.g., Heath 2000). There is no doubt that individuals may also choose a belief system based on irrational factors such as prejudice, hatred, or informational bias. However, we consider that choosing a belief system can reflect a fully subjectively consistent decision in a purely logical sense.[5] In particular, we argue that the choice of belief system depends not only on individual needs and preferences, but also on the informational environment and individual constraints. In other words, finding a potential match between an ideology and one's needs depends on both an individual's acquisition of information and on the external constraints. The more information an individual collects and processes about a particular belief system, the better they are able to predict the probability of a potential ideological match. So, a choice of a belief system is considered optimal—conditional upon the incomplete set of information—if there is no other alternative that improves reaching the individual's objectives (i.e., satisfy their human needs).

An important implication of such a choice is that behaving and making decisions based on a chosen belief system not only serves one's individual needs but also generates a sense of coherence (meaning) in life. At the most basic level, coherence, or meaning, emerges when reliable patterns exist in the environment that help individuals to understand and evaluate incoming stimuli (e.g., information). Meaning connects ideas, things, and information in a predictable and consistent way and it can be thus defined as a collective, organized network of (reliable, and relatively stable) patterns (Baumeister 1991; MacKenzie and Baumeister 2014). Ideologies provide such meaning systems; that is, predictable, reliable, and relatively stable mental representations of reality. This (ideological) mental representation helps an individual to understand the environment, to process information, to integrate their own self into this environment (perceived reality and their own role in it), and to make choices accordingly.

This mental representation of reality can be corrected and updated by empirical evidence. Individuals are capable of processing new information to update, or even change, their beliefs in a manner that will result in a relatively accurate representation of reality. We can hence argue that individuals collect and process information about particular belief systems to assess how well they serve their most important needs. This process is determined by various conditions and constraints, such as deliberation and information costs, availability, and feasibility of a particular belief system, and whether the social and political environment allows or restricts the exercise of it (e.g., in a country with an authoritarian government). Once a choice has been made, the individual will rely on the belief system to process information and make consistent decisions. However, if the chosen belief system repeatedly fails to provide good service (in terms of bad decisional outcomes, inaccurate representation of reality [due to changed circumstances], or lack of meaning), the individual will re-evaluate or even reject it and then search for a new belief system. In other words, individuals compare their own beliefs with new experiences and information and with the beliefs of other individuals and thus re-evaluate and even change them if necessary.[6]

An example of such a change in circumstances and ideological preferences is currently observable. In recent decades, many people experienced rapid economic change, the disappearance of well-paid and stable jobs, and increasing uncertainty. Low-status individuals in particular saw their jobs disappear due to technological innovations, automation, and increasing globalization. They also belong to the most fragile groups because they live in poor socioeconomic conditions and have less access to resources and opportunities to fully serve their underlying needs. Living under constant existential stress creates an image of the world as a threatening and uncontrollable place. However, the existing narrative, in particular in Western societies, has been long dominated by the capitalist-meritocratic belief that one's status in society is based on merit (i.e., on individual talents and efforts alone).[7] In her empirical study, Mueller (2021) explains that this strong narrative, which dominates in particular in the US, provides a basis for a shared social identity, offers a vision of how society should be structured and portrays, and integrates individuals into the social environment. Based on this narrative, individuals are able to understand the structure of the social environment and their own role in it. This integration and understanding of circumstances (e.g., understanding of poverty and social inequality in the country), the social environment ("all individuals have the opportunity to succeed on the basis of their own will and effort"), and one's own role in it ("I can be whatever I want, I only have to make an effort") creates a consistent pattern of reality and generates a sense of purpose and meaning in life. However, empirical evidence shows that the US has the highest inequality level of all industrialized countries, with sixty percent of the population living in either majority rich or poor neighborhoods (Bartels 2005; Bischoff and Reardon 2014), indicating a rapidly shrinking middle class. Based on these developments, the narrative of equal opportunity for all has begun to dissolve, especially among fragile low-status groups (Page and Jacobs 2009). Mueller (2021) hence shows that lack of identification with the socially shared belief system, paired with enhanced frustration about economic disadvantages of some groups (group grievance), increases the willingness of certain individuals to actively search for alternative worldviews to reconcile their psychological needs. This search can culminate in ideological extremism, leading to extraordinary attacks on the democratic norms and social values prevalent in the United States.

This means that extremist ideologies, too, can address people's needs. However, while dogmatic and radical narratives may serve the needs of some, they can be very harmful to society, especially when they are discriminative, xenophobic, racist, antisemitic, or violent in nature. Their ideological underpinnings are not neutral and amplify the attitudes, emotions, and behavior of individuals. Therefore, ideologies must be ethically evaluated. Even though an ideology serves certain needs, it can be ethically bad.[8] Talking about violent conflicts, in this book we focus on ideological narratives that conceptually imply and provoke conflict, such as racism, fascism, nationalism, right-wing and left-wing extremism, and many more.

We also want to point to another interesting implication of our concept. Looking at populist narratives, including fake news and disinformation, we can observe that many of them address fundamental needs no matter whether these narratives are "good," "bad," "true," or "fake." An ideological organization (group) may design a set of narratives that is full of unprovable, incorrect, and fictitious statements or it may even create a full-fledged conspiracy theory. If these narratives are capable of addressing certain human needs, they will find support from people looking for a way to reconcile those needs. In a world of incomplete information, even crude ideologies may perform the functions we just discussed. The success of such ideologies increases the less individuals feel they can trust established institutions and ideological narratives. Should they be disappointed by the established explanations and systems of guidance and if they cannot identify with the social values and belief systems prevalent in their society, they become open to alternatives, even if these appear unconventional. Thus, we should not be surprised that under conditions of higher complexity, threat, uncertainty, and a partial failure of existing dominant narratives, simple populist explanations and narratives are in greater demand because they address the (seemingly) deprived needs of the individuals. However, the function of populist ideologies to serve needs is not the only reason why these narratives are so successful. Organizational structures, leaders, or political elites that represent and disseminate particular ideologies, along with group dynamics and recruitment and mobilization techniques, play a significant role in conflict onset. The last layer in our framework thus represents the radical groups and organizations in question.

2.3 Ideological Organizations [Layer iii]

Having considered the ability of ideologies and belief systems to serve individuals' psychological human needs, we now translate this function into the conflict scheme and enlarge our framework to include the role of groups and organizations. Accordingly, the third layer in our framework in Figure 2.1 describes how groups disseminate their beliefs and ideas to recruit and mobilize individuals and make strategic choices. Accordingly, an ideological organization is an entity that has a strong influence on the ideological narratives, and simultaneously represents the ideology as an institution determining strategic and operational actions.

In the context of conflicts, need deprivation is often a reason why people subscribe to certain ideologies and adopt particular belief systems. Factors such as resource scarcity, discrimination, inequality, poverty, as well as modernization and socioeconomic change (e.g., transition from a medieval clan system to modern institutions and governance) can thwart individual existential, epistemic, relational, and agency needs, which can motivate individuals to search for viable means for need reconciliation. This mechanism is different from that of the direct/shortcut link, perhaps expressed as "Because I am poor, I will directly support a violent conflict/insurrection to fight for more income." (It is rarely observed that poor people directly organize violent insurrections just to obtain more income.) Therefore, we emphasize the more "indirect" path from need deprivation to need-serving belief systems and onward to violent conflict. Further, sometimes it is argued that radical organizations strategically use ideologies for their own purposes which in fact have little to do with the ideological narrative. Ideological organizations understand the bad socioeconomic conditions in which people live and misuse their deprived needs to recruit and mobilize them for their own purposes. They often provide material resources and social goods in a move to attract people to them and encourage them to follow their ideological orientation. We refer to this phenomenon as the instrumental use of measures to address human needs. Such a scenario is possible, but it does not reflect the full picture. Ideological organizations can only use these instruments strategically if there is a target group that feels aligned with the ideas and beliefs in question. So matching need deprivation and reconciliation through ideological narratives—even if it is done strategically—is still active.

Thus, we argue that organizations which disseminate ideologies and belief systems recruit followers in two ways (see Figure 2.2). Both are related to the need system of individuals: (i) ideology as a viable form of need reconciliation,

28   Ideology and the Microfoundations of Conflict

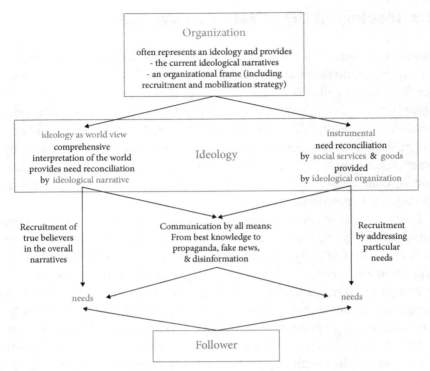

Figure 2.2 Channels of Recruitment by Ideological Organizations: Needs Reconciliation of True Believers versus Needs Reconciliation Is Instrumentalized

and (ii) an instrumental need reconciliation provided by the ideological organization. Both strands deserve a closer look.

Ideology as a viable form of need reconciliation. Individuals typically do not create their own belief systems (although some do), but rather turn to preassembled belief systems as provided by society or ideological organizations. Thus, the organization that shapes the ideology addresses the need system of individuals by providing consistent interpretations and narratives of the world, as well as problem resolution. Individuals follow the belief system that matches their needs, desires, and preferences and are committed to its beliefs, norms, and values. Its adherents take the ideology very seriously, shape their lives according to its norms and values, and make decisions based on its principles. This is the mechanism which was previously introduced by the match of needs and ideologies.

A historical example would be West Germany's Red Army Faction, a group of young individuals from socially and economically stable backgrounds whose ideological ideas were based around a harsh criticism of capitalism, materialism, and imperialism, and who called for revolutionary revolts of the masses. Such revolutionary ideologies are usually underpinned by an abstract, utopian understanding of an idealized society and state. Another example is religious belief systems. The Taliban take the Quran literally and they seek to establish a Muslim theocracy. Ideological mobilization is possible because their ideological narrative is able to address the underlying needs of individuals who live in that particular environment.

Instrumental need reconciliation by ideological organizations. The second way in which ideological organizations address the need system is "instrumental." It is not only the abstract ideological narrative that appeals to or matches individuals' underlying needs and preferences. Here, the ideological organization recruits individuals or groups by serving (or promising to serve) their deprived needs directly by providing them materialistic goods, financial resources, or social services. An example would be individuals from Western nations who join foreign Jihadist groups. They may have no deep religious or political commitments yet join the groups anyway because this allows them to reconcile their thwarted needs (e.g., the need for belonging and social approval that remains unmet because of social rejection, and/or the need for self-efficacy and self-esteem that has been thwarted due to [assumed or real] discrimination or exclusion from the job market, and so forth). Individuals may also join radical groups out of retaliation or due to a feeling of collectively experienced injustice or threat. In this regard, they identify with the goals of a particular group or organization without being fully committed to its ideology.

However, ideologies can be combined with instrumental mechanisms, particularly in situations where societies and states failed to reconcile individuals' basic needs. Extremist groups such as Islamic State, al-Qaeda, Hamas, or Boko Haram provide a full range of services to their adherents and address various fundamental needs of these individuals, who either truly adopt the belief system (and follow the religious dogmas) or, according to the interpretation of Lister (2014), accept the established mode of governance in return for the benefits. Especially in environments with a failing government that only follows parochial interests and neglects the interests of society in general or discriminates against minority groups, extremist organizations can attract quite a following from among the deprived. Political and economic corruption; lack of social and educational opportunities; inequality; lack of vital resources such as water, gas, food, and healthcare; and environmental degradation and human insecurity deprive individuals from serving their fundamental human needs (Iannaccone and Berman 2006). Extremist organizations, in particular those who can provide such "state-based" goods and services, are more likely to be accepted among the broader public. Moreover, increased rivalry between groups or regions enhances the likelihood of ideological extremism: in Iraq, Sunnis living under Shia-led governments; in Nigeria, Northern Muslims against Southern Christians; in the Middle East, Palestinians against Israelis. All these rivalries are backed by religious extremist organizations, such as al-Qaeda, Islamic State, Boko Haram, or Hamas, whose ideology, organizational structure, and "state-based" goods and services respond to the needs of their adherents. Individuals join them not always because of their deep ideological commitment, but also because the organizations offer structural opportunities to reconcile their fundamental needs, along with economic incentives. However, radical groups, organizations, or political leaders can only be successful in their ideological mobilization to the extent that their ideological narrative is able to address the underlying needs and preferences of individuals who live in a particular environment under certain conditions and constraints.

This implies that individuals join groups or organizations not predominantly because of impulsiveness, emotional breakdown, or mental illness, but because of enduring need deprivation. Starvation, poverty, and lack of opportunities in life, but also self-uncertainty, alienation, and lack of meaning all tend to be absorbed by radical groups or organizations. These groups disseminate certain belief systems that are appealing to or that match certain needs of individuals, who are either passively or actively recruited.[9] This explains why normal individuals join a radical group or organization and conform to its collective rules, goals, and interests. Although political scientists such as Della Porta (1988) argue that radical groups and organizations recruit individuals who already share a strong political identity and who are politically predisposed to violence, we argue that these are not necessarily a precondition for being recruited by a group or organization. Any individual, even one without any previous political commitment, knowledge, or criminal or violent history, can actively reach out to radical groups or organizations, leaning toward those whose belief system best matches their individual needs and preferences. Serving the needs that are important for the individual enhances the value of the group, and thus increases the willingness of a given individual to protect what is a valued source of reconciliation.

While individuals can certainly join groups and organizations that are moderate and peaceful, groups with a radical or extremist appeal and belief system have particular characteristics that serve individuals' human needs in a different manner. Uncertainty–identity theory (Hogg 2007) argues that uncertainty about one's self and a sense of disintegration from society (feeling of nonbelonging) can motivate individuals to identify in particular with radical groups that provide a distinct and clearly defined identity, an unquestionable representation of reality, and strict behavioral rules. Individuals without the resources or opportunities to be integrated into society and resolve feelings of uncertainty may suffer feelings of anxiety, powerlessness, and threat. Radical groups that present themselves as powerful, strong, and assertive absorb such negative feelings and replace them with a sense of certainty, power, and control. The mostly hierarchical structure and direct leadership of such groups or organizations relieve individuals of the responsibility to make decisions and actions and provide instead orientation and guidance. Conforming to these norms, values, and beliefs, and obeying the orders imposed by group authorities not only provides stability and certainty, but it also generates predictable and consistent patterns in life (Jenkins 2008). This means that both the structure and the belief system of a group or organization play an important role when it comes to recruiting individuals. Yet again, different groups with different belief systems imply different organizational structures. While right-leaning or conservative groups follow a hierarchical and strictly ordered organizational setup with directive leadership and command, left-leaning or liberal groups have a rather horizontal structure and decentralized decision-making. Those on the traditional right usually form their organizations or groups based on prescribed roles, norms, and rules. They have a homogeneous group identity, clear goals, and direction of actions, and demand strict compliance and conformity from all adherents. Furthermore, they form and maintain close connections to other right-leaning groups and create dense internationalized networks that enable them to recruit and mobilize members from abroad, secure funding, and share information. Such an organizational setup is especially attractive to individuals with a stronger need for order, stability, consistency, and predictability (Hogg 2014; Hogg and Adelman 2013). However, relational needs can be well served in terms of a homogeneous and distinct group identity, prescribed roles within the group, and narratives that portray the distinctiveness and superiority of the group (basis for identification). These reliable and prescriptive group patterns provide individuals with coherence and meaning in life.

By contrast, groups or organizations usually classified as belonging to the traditional left display a rather fragmented order and a diffuse, heterogeneous identity (no prescriptive and distinctive group characteristics). Research shows that left-wing groups organize themselves in a rather "underground military" fashion, are not restrictive or prescriptive, and have a polycentric network structure in which various groups with similar beliefs follow their own intentions and ideals (heterogeneity). In other words, left-leaning groups are more inconsistent and ambiguous, without dogmatic leadership or clear group identities and structures. Such groups are potentially more appealing to individuals with a stronger need for autonomy and self-efficacy. Relational needs are addressed in terms of shared ideals and visions and a diversified communal structure (diversity, acceptance, and equal rights as a basis for identification). However, both left- and right-leaning groups can assume radical forms and then display similar organizational structures. Post-war communist groups clearly had a vertical and hierarchical group structure, a centralized decision-making system (hegemony), and a dogmatic world view, and they called for strict conformity—all hallmarks of right-leaning groups. This means that different organizational forms and belief systems address individuals' psychological human needs in a different and distinct manner. The formal construction of these groups, their decision-making bodies, clear belief systems and goals, and networking strategies seem to determine how well they can ultimately recruit and mobilize individuals, to survive, and to make strategic choices as a collective entity.

2.4 Implications for Conflict Resolution and Conditions for Peace

While this book focuses on violent conflicts and the role of ideologies in such conflicts, it is also an opportunity to briefly describe the implications of our findings for achieving consensual relations or even peace. To search for conflict resolution, we must refer to all the layers in Figure 2.1 and the role they play in conflicts. To recall: the *underlying base* of a conflict are often perceived or objectively thwarted physical or psychological needs (Layer i). As long as this need deprivation remains, the source of conflict sustains and the conflict remains latent. However, real or perceived need deprivation is normally not the direct cause of starting or continuing a violent conflict. The ideology is the *vehicle* for identifying and describing the lines of conflict (the ideologies, Layer ii). Ideological narratives can suggest conflicting positions, explanations, and solutions. Generally, these narratives can be best knowledge and realistic, but they can also be misconceptions illusions and deliberate misdirection based on fake information. Finally, the ideological organization is the *driver* of the conflict (the organizations, Layer iii). It determines the current narrative the intensity of opposing interpretations or agreeable views and decides about the future path of the conflict. Ideological organizations either drive into conflict or allow for a compromise. They determine dogmatism or compromising strategies.

Interpretation of Ideological Conflict Emergence

The point of departure is the idea that individuals are heterogeneous, each with their own set of needs. This diversity is one of the most important ingredients for understanding conflict. If individuals are diverse, not only do they have different interests and demands, but they also have different desires and unique perceptions of the environment and themselves. Ideological narratives reflect this diversity of needs and play a major role in addressing these needs and discussing them in a social discourse. A variety of individuals requires a variety of ideologies that serve their needs. As a specific ideology resonates with a specific need structure, the ideological narrative will mostly serve its followers' need structure. Other ideologies have followers with a different need structure. Consequently, ideological conflicts are a natural result of the diversity of humans and their need structures. However, conflicts need not turn into hostile, violent, or even deadly conflicts. Humans have the ability to resolve conflicts peacefully.

To illustrate, let us take the example of two ideologies. Ideology A promises clear rules, a stable order, a hierarchic structure, and little change. Individuals who support this ideology have strong needs for safety, control, uncertainty avoidance, etc. It is apparent that the way ideology A provides need reconciliations is opposed to that of ideology B, which promises to allow for unconventional actions, to overcome existing hierarchies and rules, and to promote change. Ideology B is supported by individuals with strong needs for self-determinacy, self-efficacy, etc. Each ideology largely reflects the underlying needs of the two groups of individuals. The narratives of these two ideologies and their organizations promise competing or contrasting solutions and answers, so the adherents of the respective narratives gather around them, and a conflict emerges between them. Thus, the ideological conflict is the result of contrasting responses to two questions:

1. Which needs are relevant and must be served and reconciled?
2. How (through which ideological narrative) can need reconciliation be obtained?

Various ideological narratives may answer both questions, and these answers can be proposals open to compromise or controversial and confrontative views. First, as soon as ideologies, as proposed by their organizations, begin to regard the needs they serve as exclusively and solely authoritative, a claim arises to the absoluteness of one's ideology. This claim inevitably conflicts with other ideologies that serve other needs. Moreover, adherents of each ideology consider exclusively their own need structure. They know they lack something, but do not realize that others, too, have unconsidered needs and want to bring them to bear. Thus, from the perspective of each ideological organization and their followers, it seems "just" to fight for their own solution that serves their particular needs. Each group believes they have good reasons to fight, and violent attacks or even war is regarded as "justified." So, when each group's answer to the first question is that "only my needs are relevant," then each group fights—from their respective point of view—a "just" war. War is the only way to assert one's exclusively legitimate needs. Second, similarly, if each group (in response to the second question) believes that its ideological narrative is the only true solution that leads to need reconciliation—even if it happens to address the same needs as another ideology—then this belief in their own solution is another reason for a "just" fight. In other words, for the followers of an ideology, a strong belief in just one exclusive solution, without considering other possibilities or compromises, is thus the second reason that justifies a fight. Consequently, if both conflict parties believe they are fighting for a "just" cause, it is obvious why such conflicts are so severe, long-lasting, and devastating.

Interpretation of Conflict Resolution
This understanding of conflicts has an important implication for their resolution. We again start by looking at the (potentially thwarted) needs of groups of individuals. When different ideologies reflect the needs of the groups that support them but only one ideology dominates the political decision-making process, the needs of the other groups are not considered. Therefore, there can be no sustainable peace without considering the needs of all groups. Dogmatic insistence on exclusive attention to the needs of one's own group makes peaceful coexistence between opposing groups impossible. Therefore, to resolve conflict, ideological organizations must be willing and able to adopt the perspective of the other, opposing organization, even if they have opposing ideological narratives. This process is sometimes referred to as mentalization. As Zick (2021) explains, "Mentalization is interpreting and understanding one's own behavior and the behavior of others through the attribution of mental states (e.g., intentions, desires, needs). The ability to reach consensus in conflicts revolving around interests, identity, and values and to recognize the harm done to others early on is fundamental" (Zick 2021, 31, own translation). Transferring this concept to the context of this book, the mentalization process will only be successful if the conflict parties find a way to serve the essential underlying needs of their adherents in a reasonable and acceptable manner.

Even more sustainable than a temporary compromise between different opposing ideologies, however, would be a self-commitment of society to the peaceful coexistence of its members and groups, as well as the establishment of institutions that enable and promote this objective, even if said society is aware of the heterogeneity of the need structures of the individuals.

What elements would a societal system need to have to help society achieve sustainable peace?

1. *A consensus on basic values and assessments.* People must have an awareness that the variety of needs at stake can best be met under peaceful conditions. Peace is a public good, and its provision is a key benefit for everybody. A consensus on the value of a peaceful and empathetic society is therefore a first element of such a societal system. Peace must be understood as an important value in a value system.
2. *Human needs and the value system.* Because the needs system is at the heart of individual prosperity and well-being but is also a cause of conflict, there also needs to be a consensus that these diverse needs are considered in society in an appropriate manner. This requires a corresponding value system that relates to these needs. A first expression of such a consensual value system are universal human rights. They already reflect some of the needs described above and derive rights from them. Furthermore, prosperity and well-being must be measured by including the various elements of the need system. Prosperity and well-being require more than the serving of physical needs (consumption, GDP, etc.). Thus, any society's value system would have to find a measured way to balance the different needs and determine what weighting should be assigned to them. Such a balanced weighting scheme should be perceived as just by all groups.
3. *Credible institutions as guardians and developers of the value system.* The term "public institution" is usually associated with public administrations, legal regulations, or governmental decision-making mechanisms. In our context, however, we need to go beyond this first apparent concept. A little-discussed but important implicit institution of a society is trust. Trust is another public good. Consensus concerning a value system is an important step in building trust—trust between individuals, but also trust in established administrative institutions, democratic institutions of decision-making, and the government. Only when government and institutions act in accordance with an agreed value system can trust emerge and be reaffirmed repeatedly. This means the government follows the democratically agreed objectives and runs

the institutions according to evidence-based, best-knowledge policy instruments and a sustainable resource use, instead of following ideological beliefs or the claims or views of particular groups. Further, there must be congruence between a society's belief and value system and a government's actions and plans. Only then can lasting trust develop between individuals and the government and its institutions. Only then can individuals be sure that government institutions are acting in accordance with agreed-upon values. When this process is in place, public institutions fulfill the function of guardians and developers of the value system and make a lasting contribution to averting major conflicts.

4. *Identification and identity*. On the basis of shared basic values and constructive narratives, members of a society can develop a social identity and identify with the value system and their society at large. This identity and identification strengthens the concept of peaceful coexistence with one's fellow group members, including individuals with different need structures and preferences.

If these elements are brought together in a consistent comprehensive narrative, a society that follows this narrative can lay the foundation for peaceful and prosperous development. However, considering the different needs does not mean that this society would be conflict-free. There would still be conflicts, but they would revolve around a balanced and consensual set of policies that balance the different needs. This narrative of a sustainable peaceful design of society could be called the path of a "just peace."

Is such a narrative a utopia? Maybe at first glance, but it is a (positive) orientation, and that is what belief systems and world views are all about. It contrasts with the polarized societies that exist today, not only in the many autocracies. Formerly consensual democracies, such as the US and some European countries, are currently maneuvering themselves into polarized conflicts—and that is indeed a dystopia. Part of this global dystopian picture is that ideologies that conceptually attack the basic needs of other groups or even of sovereign countries and their populations are re-emerging in the current reality. Ideologies such as racism, antisemitism, fascism, anti-feminism, and imperialism are obvious examples. For instance, racists do not accept the needs and human rights of the groups they attack; instead, they claim systematic domination of their own group over others as their narrative. Imperialist narratives, such as European Imperialism in the nineteenth and first half of the twentieth century, or, most recently the Kremlin's narrative around the attack on Ukraine, claim supremacy and dominance over a sovereign country and its people. While these destructive and disruptive ideologies are also capable of addressing and serving certain needs of their adherents, it is clear by their very nature that these ideologies disregard the needs and human rights of the groups subject to the aggression, and thus lead directly to conflict and violence.

To illustrate how our approach and the related reasoning works, we suggest applying it to a conflict related to The Social Question in Box 2.1. While this interpretation is extremely condensed and simplified, it outlines our line of argumentation. It can also be applied to future conflicts in our increasingly polarized societies, given that The Social Question is starting to reappear.

Box 2.1 Interpreting a fundamental conflict: The Social Question

Moving away from abstract considerations, let us examine a historical example and its interpretation from our perspective, when applying this approach. A historical example of deprived needs is The Social Question. While there is a broad discussion among historians about various specific time periods relating to The Social Question, there is no need to dive into them here. For simplicity, we suggest that The Social Question arose during the first half of the nineteenth century out of mass poverty and hence the need deprivation of wage earners. Among other factors, population growth and labor-substituting technologies resulted in an oversupply of workers during industrialization in Europe and an economic policy of laissez-faire allowed for the emergence of mass poverty. The government policy of not intervening in markets or the economy meant that, for example, child labor and long working hours were widespread, as was asymmetric market power in local labor markets. In these local labor markets, a small number of well-organized factory owners often profited from downward competition of wages paid to an unorganized labor force. As a result, many industrial workers and their families were extremely poor and struggled to survive. Existential needs such as safety, control, and predictability were massively deprived at the individual level. While the capital-owning bourgeoisie and high-ranking civil servants grew more prosperous as the result of industrialization, capital formation, and technical progress, workers were unable to participate either economically or politically. However, what was not observable at the time is that these miserable conditions directly led to frequent and widespread uprisings of the working population, even though they faced existential threats. While there was ample reason for struggle and a latent conflict caused by poverty, an ideological narrative was necessary to generate the social controversy which then defined the dominant conflicts of the nineteenth and twentieth centuries. According to Marx's analysis of social conditions, a class struggle would eventually overthrow capitalism and lead to a communist utopian society. He introduced a system of narratives and (often utopian) beliefs that fulfilled the functions of ideologies and served the various needs of laborers. These narratives gave laborers a group to identify with (the working class), which served their need for belonging and identification, explained to them their situation and conditions that served epistemic needs, and showed them a future path into a better life. These prospects served various existential needs. It was this ideological narrative that, in the nineteenth century, gave rise to a strong communist and general workers' movement. The ideological narrative was the vehicle for developing a common view and interpretation of the world.

Communism was not the only ideology that suggested an explanation or even solution to The Social Question. Social democracy, too, sought to improve the rights and living conditions of the working class in an evolutionary reform process. The idea was not to overthrow capitalism but to continuously promote an increase in participation and move toward improving conditions for the working class, both politically through democratization and economically through labor unions claiming higher wage participation in value added. This ideological narrative also attracted a large number of workers and became a significant ideology. While it addressed the same need, its narrative competed with that of communism. The third ideological narrative that deserves discussion is the capitalist-meritocratic narrative, which stipulated that even workers and the poor could achieve income and wealth if only they worked hard enough given the opportunities. This ideology introduced yet another idea for possible need reconciliation that resonated with many believers. So, there are even historical examples to show that ideologies transport a set of narratives which form the mindset that people gather around. While all these narratives address the same problem—deprivation of physical existential needs (poverty)—we find that the ideologies offer very different explanations, interpretations, and solutions. In fact, at some point in the twentieth century they were even so opposed that they triggered the east–west ideological conflict.

The Social Question emerged in the nineteenth century, yet in the twentieth century the most important related events were the foundation of the Communist Soviet Union (1922) and the Great Depression in the 1930s. The latter, which led to devastating poverty among large parts of the population in Western capitalist-meritocratic economies, brought The Social Question to the forefront once again. While deprived needs were the underlying base, a conflict developed around incompatible ideological narratives and their suggestions. Until the disaster that was the Great Depression, societies and their different strands of ideologies were unable to agree, or even compromise, because the respective narratives were so contradictory and conflicting. What is more, some ideologies even suggested ideas that led to new need deprivation. Soviet-style Communism was not only physically suppressive, but its ideological narrative also deprived agency needs such as that for self-determination or self-efficacy.

Thus, Soviet-style Communism was clearly unable to compromise with ideologies built upon agency needs such as the capitalist-meritocratic narrative. A conflict between these two ideologies was inevitable. By contrast, two other ideologies were able to compromise at least for a while. In the 1950s, 1960s, and 1970s, social democratic and meritocratic narratives jointly succeeded in finding ways to serve the existential needs related to The Social Question without jeopardizing agency needs. In the US, the New Deal and legislation adopted around World War II, along with similar developments in Europe, produced a compromise-based policy that combined social democratic with capitalist-meritocratic ideas. Governments introduced policies to address hitherto existing massive inequalities of opportunity, lifting large numbers of previously (during the Great Depression) poor families out of poverty and enabling them to earn a reasonable income. A broad middle class developed during the 1950s, 1960s, and 1970s. This was a golden age of economic prosperity and growth coupled with a decline in income inequality, an episode that was particularly favorable for middle-class families. Ideologically, to a certain extent governments followed a meritocratic approach offering incentives for economic efforts in markets and combined this with social democratic ideas supporting more education for all, stronger labor unions, and instruments for more labor participation in income growth, as well as stronger social security and progressive tax schemes. These policies generated social mobility opportunities for those who were less privileged in terms of socioeconomic status.

On balance, what this interpretation suggests is that a society which is guided by ideologies that allow all categories of needs to be considered and served, and that seeks compromise between need structures, avoids costly conflicts and is hence successful not only with respect to individual well-being.

PART I
FUNDAMENTAL HUMAN NEEDS, THREATS, AND NEED DEPRIVATION

Introduction and Guidance through the Chapter

In the previous chapter we outlined our framework and its underlying mechanism. The first element of this framework considers the role of socioeconomic and political conditions, centralized as exogenous factors, and individual dispositions, which may deprive individuals from serving their *fundamental human needs*. The deprivation of a need implies a denial of or a reduction in access to resources or opportunities to serve one's own fundamental human needs. Needs that range from physiological, materialistic needs to secure one's existence and security, to psychological needs to assure one's mental well-being. This is discussed in the current chapter. Second, to meet the needs that are vital for survival, well-being, and personal fulfillment, individuals search for *reconciliation strategies*. Here, we propose that various *ideologies*, mindsets, and belief systems tend to represent viable reconciliation options that absorb negative emotions and deliver narratives for evaluation and identification with like-minded individuals. While they can incorporate moderate and peaceful ideas, belief systems can also be aggressive and radical and involve irrevocable and static dogmas. The last element therefore considers the radical belief systems that are disseminated by *groups or organizations* to recruit and motivate individuals and to pursue a particular set of objectives. It is clear that this framework provides a dynamic pattern. An individual's needs are neither static nor predetermined; instead, they can change and manifest in different ways. A reconciliation option in the form of a belief system is a possible strategy, which, however, does not apply to every human being. Groups and organizations with a certain ideology do not necessarily become radical and aggressive, but some do; and when they do, they become the drivers of often violent conflicts. However, to contain the scope of this book and the framework, we focus on the three elements mentioned above and elaborate the underlying mechanism explicitly.

The first part focuses mainly on the first element which looks extensively at the external and internal factors that deprive individuals from serving their fundamental human needs. Having reviewed a vast body of theoretical and empirical interdisciplinary literature, we identify three interrelated dimensions (or clusters) of fundamental human needs that are worth to consider: (i) We start with *existential and epistemic needs* that are driven by conditions of threats, uncertainty, and the struggle for survival, which drive human beings to attain a sense of security, mastery of circumstances, and control over their own environment. Here we identified needs for safety/existential security, for control, order, ambiguity avoidance, consistency, and predictability. These needs, as discussed in Chapter 2, imply the human necessity to secure one's own existence; process information and understand circumstances; feel that one is able to control and affect one's own environment; and to live in an ordered, predictable, and consistent surrounding. But to survive and be mentally healthy, human beings also need social connections. Here we identified (ii) *relational needs* that focus on identity, social belonging, and pro-sociality. Pro-sociality refers to behaviors that intend to help and benefit others. Individuals aim to maintain a sense of belonging; to share their identity, values, and ideas with significant others; and to feel loved and approved by other members of their group. In this regard, we consider the need for belongingness, identification, and social approval, but also the human need for pro-sociality—the innate human drive to share, help, and feel empathy for others. Beyond the needs for survival and sociality, individuals have also (iii) *agency needs*, which imply individuals' striving for a positive self-view, competence, and an autonomous and meaningful life (i.e., needs for self-esteem, self-efficacy, and self-determination).

These mental needs belong to an entire system of needs and demands that includes more than a desire for physical and intangible consumables. To understand the severity and the various manifestations of these needs, we first have to identify factors and conditions that may deprive individuals from serving these needs. But before going into detail, we provide a potential answer to the question of: What is a need?

What Are Fundamental Human Needs?

Our framework is built around the identification of fundamental human needs—needs that can be understood as a condition or internal state in an organism that when activated or aroused, directs human behavior. In this context, deprivation of needs, or deviation from desired states, play a central role

(American Psychological Association 2019c). There is no doubt that humans have physical needs and demands (e.g., the need to eat and drink), and—while not fundamentally necessary for survival—they have a desire for goods they would like to consume. The question of how to serve these consumption needs in the best possible way is all about traditional economics. While in standard economic analyses, these consumption needs involve physical goods, such as apples, bananas, or cars—in particular in the contributions by Becker (1965) and others—these models have been extended by time allocation and even by more "abstract" desires such as health, education, or leisure time. Also, models which have appeared bizarre to non-economists (and sometimes also for economists), such as the economics of marriage (Becker 1973, 1985), fertility (Becker and Barro 1986), or the choice of spouse (Keeley 1977), have been developed in a move to extend the theory of consumer behavior.

There is no doubt that intangible goods such as education, health, relationships, or leisure are important elements in our system of wishes and demands. They complete our needs system and determine eventually how we process information and make economic decisions. In this regard, the psychological literature goes further and postulates that there are more aspects of human behavior—the internally driven aspect of behavior that derives in part from internal tensions or arousals in an organism. However, some motivational analyses do not necessarily include the concept of human needs in their assumptions, nor do they emphasize need deprivation as possible internal drives of behavior (Gollwitzer and Moskowitz 1996; Bandura 1997). Others (Ryan and Deci 2000; Baumeister and Leary 1995) postulate that fundamental human needs indeed energize and direct human behavior.[1] This approach, which is central to our analysis, perceives needs as variable internal states that go beyond physical needs and demands. When social psychologists talk about human needs, they emphasize needs related to social relations, self-esteem, and control. This implies that there are dimensions to needs and demands that go beyond the necessity to preserve human (physical) existence. We refer to these needs as psychological or mental needs which, if appropriately served, lead to well-being and psychological thriving. Having reviewed more than fifteen thousand academic articles and theoretical and empirical studies from various academic disciplines, we identify three dimensions of psychological human needs that have been already mentioned above: (i) *existential and epistemic needs*, which imply needs for safety/existential security, for control, order, predictability, consistency, and ambiguity avoidance; (ii) *relational needs*, which focus on the needs for belongingness, identification, social approval, and pro-sociality, and (iii) *agency needs*, which include needs for self-esteem, self-efficacy, and self-determination.

These mental needs belong to an entire system of needs and demands that include more than a desire for physical and intangible consumables. However, these needs are neither static, nor do they function in isolation. Take the example of the need to belong (Baumeister and Leary 1995). At the beginning of life, a newborn cannot survive without the involvement of significant others or a group of people who take care of the infant and ensure its basic sustenance. At such a young age, social support and prosocial cooperation is just as vital to survival and identity formation as physical goods such as water and food. Beyond feelings of existential certainty and safety, belonging to a group and forming positive relationships with significant others generates also greater self-esteem and a positive self-perception (Pittman and Zeigler 2007).

"Inadequate degrees of satisfaction of these basic needs may not lead to premature death but instead are revealed in the failure to achieve one's potential or to function as well as one might under more optimal conditions of need fulfillment" (Pittman and Zeigler 2007, 475). According to psychologists, serving these basic needs appropriately would thus contribute to enhanced psychological health and general well-being. In our analysis we provide evidence that these psychological needs are fundamental, which implies that the origin of these needs can be explained or reasoned in evolutionary-biological terms. Fundamental human needs are universal; that is, they can be applied to every human being to varying degrees. They lead to ill effects when thwarted (e.g., poor mental health, low adjustment to environment), and elicit goal-oriented behavior designed to serve these needs. They are not derivatives of other motives, but they represent the foundation from which various preferences, wishes, and goals may depart (Baumeister and Leary 1995). As discussed in Chapter 2, consider again the example of the need to belong: if the need to belong is deprived; that is, if certain conditions, such as an exclusionary environment, deprive the individual from serving his need to belong, then the activity of the anterior cingulate cortex (dACC) increases, an area associated with regulating physical pain experiences (Eisenberger 2011). This means that our body and our brain react to an unmet need to belong, which gives rise to internal drive states that push the individual to find means to cope with the arousal to remain physically and mentally healthy (Deci and Ryan 2000). However, the intensity of a need differs from personality to personality. Also, the manifestation of a particular need can be determined by external factors including threatening situations, socioeconomic conditions, political change, or terrorist attacks (Jost 2009; Kay and Friesen 2011).

How Is Part I Organized?

Part I focuses extensively on fundamental human needs; that is, on their origin, manifestation, and the possible sources that deprive individuals from serving these needs. To clarify these assumptions, we include theoretical and empirical studies focusing especially on need-depriving outcomes: how can experiences of threat, existential uncertainty, and competition (among others) deprive existential and epistemic human needs, which in turn may induce conflictual behavior? How can social exclusion, ostracism, or identity confusion deprive relational needs and potentially lead to adverse, or even violent, behavior? And how can depriving individuals from opportunities to make autonomous choices, to feel good about oneself, and to reach subjective goals (i.e., thwarting agency needs) potentially direct individuals toward radicalization? In the course of Part I, we explain how certain conditions, whether induced by real-threat scenarios, subjective ostracism, or intergroup disputes, can lead to need deprivation. Although we clearly emphasize the severest outcomes of need deprivation, such as violence, conflict, or individual radicalization, we should think of need-depriving situations and circumstances also in moderate terms. Not every individual will employ radical means to serve their needs, and not every need-depriving circumstance leads to radical outcomes.

However, to provide consistent guidance for the reader, the part is structured as follows. We start with the first need dimension, (i) *existential and epistemic needs*. Before we go deeper into the biological/evolutionary sources of such needs, we examine various (external) factors that can deprive individuals from serving their existential and epistemic needs. These sources, such as resource scarcity or abundance, marginalization, or severe poverty, can threaten individuals' existence and long-term survival, but they can also encourage individuals to protect their privileges, the status quo, and wealth. Intergroup and intragroup factors can pose threats to one's own social group and cause individuals to secure the survival and viability of that group. These threats have a severe impact on both the physical existence and psychological states of individuals. This means that beyond the need to be safe and protected, individuals can also have the need for a predictable and consistent environment that can be ordered and controlled. After identifying and discussing the origin and various manifestations of existential and epistemic needs, we proceed in the same manner with the second and the third need dimensions of (ii) *relational needs* and (iii) *agency needs*.

3
Fundamental (Psychological) Human Needs

3.1 Existential and Epistemic Needs and Need Deprivation

In the following section, we discuss how various kinds of states and conditions, whether intergroup threats, economic threats, uncertainties, denial of basic resources, or harsh competition, can have devastating repercussions on individuals' physical and psychological well-being. These conditions can deprive individuals from serving their existential and epistemic needs, which in turn drives them to find ways to serve these needs. While we propose that belief systems can be a viable reconciliation option and may indirectly lead to severe outcomes, we also discuss how needs deprivation can directly conclude in violent outburst. This direct mechanism is a major assumption in the economics conflict literature. However, we later introduce alternative and extending theories that are common in other social science disciplines.

A highly debated condition that tends to deprive individuals from serving their existential and epistemic needs is threat. Threats can assume various forms. Individuals can experience genuine threats that harm their subsistence, such as war, resource deprivation, natural disaster, or poor primary care. But they can also experience perceived threats, which can stem from subjective feelings of being discriminated or socially rejected by a majority group. In general terms, a threat can be defined as a condition, information, or event with the potential to affect people adversely. Threats can have several consequences and may deprive individuals from serving their fundamental human needs (Koomen and Van Der Pligt 2016). Threats can increase individuals' feelings of being in an uncontrollable, uncertain, and unpredictable environment and thus have a severe impact on their attitudes, perceptions, and behaviors. Threats can change how individuals perceive their environment, their group, and themselves and can lead to deviant, aggressive, or even violent behavior. In the following we discuss the various forms of threats and their implications on fundamental human needs. Of notable interest are instances that may conclude in violence, radicalization, or even social conflicts and wars, which can imply severe material and non-material costs, and have implications for individuals and society at large.

3.1.1 Existential Threat, Competition, and Poverty

Various disciplines agree that the most basic premise in human life is to secure one's own existence. It is an instinctive desire, a biological drive to avoid threatening situations to safeguard the future. Thus, biologists and evolutionary psychologists, among others, postulate that the most basic of all human needs is the maintenance of one's own existence and a continued security (Doyal and Gough 1991). To ensure this state of survival, biological necessities (food, water, air, etc.) must be safeguarded (Pyszczynski et al. 1997). However, to survive and do well in life people must maintain not just their physical but also their mental health. This means that certain conditions must be given to enable individuals to understand their environment, to socialize, to be proactive, and to feel secured and approved by society. Individuals must be able to exercise autonomy and formulate their consistent goals, to participate in society, and to connect with significant others (Doyal and Gough 1991). In this vein, some economic studies (e.g., Østby 2008) argue that socioeconomic conditions play a significant role in explaining why particular groups or individuals seek to realize certain goals through violence. For example, individuals who experience persecution and poor living standards may rise up and fight an existential threat. A lack of fundamental resources to secure one's own physical and mental health can motivate individuals to resort to violent measures to access these resources. To analyze the relationship between resources and conflict, two contending schools of thought have been elaborated in the conflict literature: the resource scarcity approach and the resource abundance approach. The feature of this strand of literature that sets it apart from the later discussion is that it essentially originates in economic and political science. It draws a direct line from fundamental needs and threats to resulting aggression and conflicts, and thus assumes a very straight causality. Psychological mechanisms are not explicitly accounted for. However, this strand is an important part of the scientific literature and it can be taken as a point of departure when we later turn to mechanisms that include more complex psychological items.

3.1.1.1 The Resource Curse: The Resource Scarcity Approach

The *resource scarcity*[1] approach postulates that the competition for access to vital but scarce resources can increasingly drive violent conflict. Lack of access to renewable resources generates frustration and grievances against the state, weakens the state, and increases opportunities for insurrection (Theisen 2008). Thus, resource scarcity is perceived as one of the main drivers in conflicts such as the Rwandan genocide (Olson 1995), clashes in Kenya (Kahl 2006; Theisen 2012), the civil war in Sudan (Suliman 1998), and rebellion in South Africa (Homer-Dixon and Blitt 1998) or Chiapas (Homer-Dixon 1999). Empirical evidence shows that factors such as deforestation, land degradation, and clean water shortages increase the risk of armed civil conflict (Hauge and Ellingsen 1998). Such environmental scarcity factors can be categorized as supply-induced, demand-induced, or structural scarcity. Supply-induced scarcity describes a failed adjustment to resource degradation and regeneration. Demand-induced scarcity emphasizes the consequences of increased consumption and population growth. Structural scarcity emerges as a result of unequal resource distribution (Homer-Dixon 1999). Interaction between these three categories can result in resource capture and ecological marginalization. Resource capture results when powerful elites bar weak groups' access to scarce resources. They manipulate state policies to serve their own interests, which weakens institutions and dampens political responses to social grievances and deprivation. Thus, resource capture tends to induce frustration and protest that may lead individuals to employ violence to gain access to deprived resources (Theisen 2008). The literature describes a number of cases. Resource capture has been observed in Zimbabwe, where a major clash concerning the unequal distribution of land and natural resources occurred. Colonial expropriation of agricultural land and natural resources produced a situation in which, even after colonial independence, a small, mostly white elite joined forces with the government to control most of the lucrative sectors of the economy, like agriculture and tourism, in turn barring access for 1.5 million families and other subaltern classes to vital resources. This created a country-wide, low-level violent uprising which led to the adoption of a radical land redistribution program in 2000 (Moyo 2005). Denying individuals access to vital resources implies, among others, a deprivation of their existential human needs—needs such as existential security and the mastery and control of their environment.

Similar to resource capture, ecological marginalization describes how unequal access to resources and population growth cause resource depletion and degradation. The interaction between deprivation and population growth can trigger migration to ecologically fragile regions. The accrued high population density, combined with weak human capital and financial capabilities to protect and cultivate local resources, causes severe poverty and environmental depletion (Theisen 2008). Thailand is a good example of ecological marginalization. Unequal access to resources among hill tribe farmers and a region-wide population increase across Northern Thailand forced marginalized farmers to live on less land with few off-farm options. Soil degradation in these regions led to enhanced demand for land rental outside their own territories and for fertilizer, driving up costs and lowering profit margins. This insecure and unstable situation, which led *inter alia* to a decline in land productivity, income, and health, has triggered conflicts over resources between the hill tribe farmers and government elites (Crooker 2007). Similar disputes have occurred in the Philippines, where forced migration to degraded upland areas due to high population growth and insufficient rural development spurred rebellion and violent insurgencies among economically deprived farm workers and landless peasants (Homer-Dixon 1994).

Although some empirical studies have found a direct relationship between resource scarcity and conflict onset, especially in developing countries (e.g., Raleigh and Urdal 2007), other empirical findings suggest a more indirect link, arguing that it is rather the relationship between environmental shortages, population density, and state fragility that increases the risk of conflict (Gurr 1970; De Soysa 2002). From a different perspective, studies on political ecology question the relationship between resource scarcity and conflict by postulating that state weakness, bad governance, corruption, and low investment in rural areas are the real causes of environmental degradation and conflict onset (Peluso and Watts 2001). Further, they argue that severe resource scarcity and lack of financial opportunities decrease the feasibility and effectiveness of a rebellion against the state, even if the grievance-based motivation is high (Klare 2001). In their famous empirical study, Collier and Hoeffler (2004) found that financial opportunities, rather than objective resource deprivation, determine the outburst of civil conflict.

3.1.1.2 The Resource Curse: The Resource Abundance Approach

In contrast to the resource scarcity approach, the *resource abundance* theory postulates that resource abundance and possible resource dependence provide both funding and motivation for armed conflicts (Collier and Hoeffler 2005; Fearon 2005). Although the classic economic view regards resource abundance as advantageous for economic growth and development, a number of empirical studies since the 1990s have taken an opposite perspective. These studies and the growing literature on the "resource curse" and the "paradox of plenty" postulate that resource abundance slows down economic growth while increasing the risk of conflicts and authoritarian and corruptive political regimes (Basedau and Lay 2009). Empirical studies support this theory and provide evidence that natural resource-rich countries seem to be more prone to conflict and violent insurgencies (Ross 2004). Abundant primary commodities and the "booty" character of natural resources tend to provide opportunity and motive for "greedy rebels," which increases the likelihood of conflict onset (Collier and Hoeffler 2004). Beyond "internal greedy rebels," "greedy outsiders," such as external states or corporations, can also engage in or foster the escalation of wars and conflicts, with the aim to gain access to raw materials (Dashwood 2000). Once certain access to resources is established, elites, groups, or individuals are willing to protect their source of wealth and privilege, even with violent measures. The threat of losing those privileges becomes a great source of motivation and causes hostility to the source of the realistic threat. Such realistic threats include any (tangible) threat to the survival, physical integrity, social status, or welfare of an individual or their group, not just the competition for resources (Stephan et al. 2008).

Box 3.1 Example of resource abundance: Congo-Brazzaville

The former French colony Congo-Brazzaville became independent in 1960, and four years after independence turned into a one-party state under a Marxist-Leninist ruling party. After a period of political instability and the assassination of then-president Marien Ngouabi in 1977, Denis Sassou-Nguesso, an army colonel, came to power in 1979. Sassou-Nguesso established stable relations with the former colonial power France and presided over the rapidly growing oil industry, which was mainly dominated by the French oil company, Elf. By 1984, minerals accounted for ninety percent of export earnings while mining contributed forty-three percent of the country's GDP (Bazenguissa-Ganga 1998). To keep the system stable, Sassou-Nguesso incorporated elites from the south, the north, and the central region of the country by redistributing oil profits to allies and potential enemies. While the president was northern in origin, southern elites held several powerful positions in the government, civil service, and the army. However, Sassou-Nguesso's regime came under scrutiny in the early 1990s, following francophone Africa's wave of democratization. "Political pressure from southern elites, labor parties, intellectuals, and French officials forced Sassou to relinquish his hold on power. The country held multiparty presidential elections in 1992, sparking competition for the apex of Congo's patron-client pyramid and giving southern elites a legally sanctioned chance to control the country's oil wealth" (Englebert and Ron 2004, 64).

Sassou-Nguesso's two main opponents were Bernard Kolelas and Pasacal Lissouba, the latter, a former prime minister, who at the end assumed the presidency in 1992 that was invariably backed up by the dominant provinces in the south. During his presidency, Lissouba allocated key positions in the government to southern elites, which were vital sources of oil rents and patronage. This regional favoritism was criticized by non-southern elites and oppositions who feared losing their once-established social, political, and economic privileges. Despite his introduced nepotism, Lissouba struggled to assert political power and control due to Sassou-Nguesso's former established tied networks of allies, patrons, and clients who continued to support him. As a result, Lissouba created an independent security force, mainly consisting of men from the south, which led to the formation of other militia groups: three other groups that backed Lissouba (the Zoulous, Mambas, and Cocoyes); the Ninjas, a militia led by police and military officers who supported Kolelas; and Cobra, Sassou-Nguesso's militia that was established in 1992 with members of his old presidential guard (Bazenguissa-Ganga 1998).

All groups were formed to secure the power, privileges, and control enjoyed by the three main political parties and their leaders. The control over Congo's capital Brazzaville was one major strategic goal, which assured access to oil revenues and international recognition. Lissouba's presidency was strongly contested by powerful opposition parties and the public, who questioned his regional favoritism (the south), economic decentralization, and cuts in public spending. His unpopularity and Sassou-Nguesso's defection led to the dissolution of parliament and new elections in May 1993. This uncertain political situation and the paramilitary mobilization of private militia groups led to the first civil war in the second half of 1993, which ended in January 1994. By 1996–1997, the three main militias—Lissouba's Cocoyes, Kolela's Ninjas, and Sassou-Nguesso's Cobras—had divided the capital city into three control zones (Englebert and Ron 2004). As new elections approached in 1997, political rivalries between the three main militia groups led to a second civil war, this time pitching Cobras against the unified Cocoyes and Ninjas. With the intervention of Angolan troops, Sassou-Nguesso claimed military victory in October 1997 and banished Lissouba, Kolela, and other southern elites (Bazenguissa-Ganga 1998). However, a third round of violent fighting took place in the rural south, which ended in late 1999 with a deal that guaranteed amnesty to Ninjas and Cocoye commanders and a reintegration in their former privileged public sector jobs.

The example of the Congo in Box 3.1 shows how the threat of losing one's own privileges and resources can deprive individuals from serving their existential needs, such as the need to secure one's own existence and maintain control over one's own environment, which, in some cases, can lead to greed, violence, and civil conflict. However, in contrast to the often-cited greed argument, the grievance hypothesis emphasizes severe resource deprivation and real existential threat. "Perceived deprivation of producing regions and social groups or indirect negative economic consequences of resource wealth, such as the 'Dutch disease', price shocks or uneven distribution of revenues, create 'grievances' and trigger violent uprising, especially secessionism in producing regions" (Basedau and Lay 2009, 759). This implies that economies that are highly dependent on natural resources may be more vulnerable to trade shocks that can cause instability, uncertainty, and stress of survival for those affected. Furthermore, resource extraction can lead to forced migration, which in turn produces grievances, loss of land rights, environmental damage, and ecological marginalization. Whether resources involve production and extraction can determine the nature of violent insurgencies. Resource extraction (e.g., of minerals) tends to trigger physical violence with the aim to achieve territorial or state control, as was the case in Congo-Brazzaville over oil rents in 1997. Resource production (e.g., crops) involves more structural forms of violence, such as forced labor or control over trade (Le Billon 2001). This structural violence may have secondary effects, such as violent uprisings and low-key resistance as an expression of grievance and exploitation. "In Chiapas, the rebellion by self-defense groups and the Zapatista movement mostly served to respond to the violence of a local political economy of neglect and marginalization, to challenge the neo-liberal political economic order which supported it, and to attract the attention of the government and media to improve their negotiating position" (Le Billon 2001, 568).

A further aspect concerns unequal natural resource wealth distribution, as has been observed in Nigeria or Sierra Leone (Humphreys 2005). Northern Nigeria suffers from a lack of support from the political center in the south, which exploits the north's rich uranium deposits with no visible returns. As a result, communities in the north suffer from chronic poverty, severe youth unemployment, non-functioning institutions and infrastructure, an educational deficit, and weak economic production (Agbiboa 2013).

Despite its broad acceptance in the literature, the nature of the resource curse and the causal mechanisms linking natural resources to conflict onset has not gone unchallenged. While one side criticizes the validity of data and methodology (Brunnschweiler and Bulte 2008), the other points out that the resource curse is mainly a political problem, not an economic one (Karl 2007). Further discussions refer to the neglected differentiation between the synonymously treated variables of a country's dependence on and its abundance of resources. Dependence on resources implies that rents from resources are the most important source of a country's income relative to other variables, while abundance of resources refers to the absolute amount of resource rents. Such a differentiation has further implications for the analysis, indicating that the lack of alternative revenue sources in the dependence case can fuel grievance-based conflict, while "greedy rebels" can be attributed to the abundance variable (Basedau and Lay 2009). Some empirical studies go further and suggest that only a certain subset of natural resources fuels conflicts and violent insurgencies, namely lootable resources and oil (Ross 2004). "The exploitation of so called 'distant' and 'diffuse' resources such as alluvial diamonds, timber or drugs can hardly be controlled by the central government—hence, rebels can 'loot' them more easily than deep shaft gems or off-shore oil production, which in addition require sophisticated technical know-how" (Basedau and Lay 2009, 759). By contrast, others insist that there is no correlation between conflict and diamonds (Lujala et al. 2005) and instead emphasize the significance of oil and mineral resource trading in explaining conflict onset (Fearon 2005; Ross 2006; De Soysa and Neumayer 2007).

However, critics postulate that not only the specific resource characteristics or the type of resource extraction play a key role, but also the quality and strength of state institutions (Snyder and Bhavnani 2005). They argue that resource-rich economies tend to suffer from a weak and corrupt leadership or even oppressive and authoritative regimes (Brunnschweiler and Bulte 2008). This implies that it is not only the presence of natural resources that leads to the resource curse, but also the political, economic, and social institutions and the governance structures around the extraction and management of these resources (Idemudia 2012). Cases such as Norway, Chile, or Botswana show that resource-rich countries can be capable of successfully managing their resource wealth. The quality of resource governance and the weakness of state structures hence seem to depend on country-specific characteristics, such as socioeconomic development, intergroup relations, integrity of state institutions, and so on (Basedau and Lay 2009). Especially in resource-rich states in Africa, colonialization, political instability, environmental degradation, and ethnic cleavages (triggered by the creation of artificial borders) can deprive individuals from serving their existential needs. Resource-induced conditions, either lack or abundance, enhance the threat and uncertainty of not being able to secure one's existence, or to control and to live in an ordered and (economically, politically, and socially) predictable environment, which must be taken into full account when explaining the outburst of resource-based conflicts (Fosu and Collier 2005).

3.1.1.3 Poverty and Absolute Deprivation

Despite the existence of empirical evidence, the resource–conflict link is still under debate. While some studies postulate that resource dependence, rather than abundance, increases the likelihood of conflict onset—even attributing the latter to peace—others argue that resource scarcity and accompanying severe socioeconomic conditions fuel violent insurgencies. In this context, the risk factors of economic fragility are perceived as a significant determinant of violence and conflict. "According to the World Health Organization (WHO), violence also includes deprivation and neglect. Such violence, often termed structural violence, includes any form within a social structure that prevents some of its members from meeting basic needs" (OECD 2016, 86). Such economic risk factors include unemployment, poverty, migration, economic closure, or educational backwardness. Empirical evidence supports the link between economic fragility and conflict and demonstrates that countries with high poverty, high child mortality and malnutrition, high undernutrition, and limited access to water sources are more prone to armed civil conflicts. Especially the lack of appropriate nutrition and health care tends to significantly increase the risk of armed conflict onset (Nafziger et al. 2000; Pinstrup-Andersen and Shimokawa 2008).

In much of the existing literature, the concept of poverty is considered in terms of income alone while neglecting its multidimensional nature. This leads to a one-sided focus on economic incentives and opportunities for rebellion (Collier and Hoeffler 2004). However, Sen (1992) initiated a critical discussion of the economical concept of poverty and developed a comprehensive approach which goes beyond economics. At the heart of his theory is the notion that all individuals have the needs and the capabilities to achieve something valuable and meaningful in life. "Thus, living may be seen as consisting of a set of interrelated 'functionings', consisting of beings and doings" (Sen 1992, 38). Such interrelated functionings may include both physical elements, such as housing and nutrition, as well as more complex social achievements, such as social and political participation, ingroup identification, social approval, and self-esteem. Accordingly, the perception of poverty has been extended in the development literature to include the concept of deprivation of opportunities, information, freedom, and services (Braithwaite et al. 2016). According to this concept, the term "poverty" is defined as a condition characterized by severe deprivation of basic (existential) human needs, including nutrition, water access, sanitation, safe shelter, and the possibility of access to health care, education, and information. The basic human needs perspective goes beyond the purely economic income perspective to include the needs for community, information, and social services (UNESCO 2018). Deprivation of basic human needs and a weak socioeconomic position constitutes a severe existential threat to individuals or social groups, which in turn increases uncertainty, frustration, stress, and anxiety.

The concept of *deprivation* has been widely examined in social science studies as a significant contributing factor concerning conflictual human behavior in society (Silke 2008). Here, deprivation can be defined in either absolute or relative terms. *Absolute deprivation* expresses the average level of poverty or human well-being within a population, whereas *relative deprivation* is a subjective perception of unequal treatment and defines poverty from a comparative point of view (Baten and Mumme 2013).

Considering *absolute deprivation*, a low level of physical (ownership of goods and land), human (education, health, and employment), social (community, information, participation), and environmental (resource availability) capital denies individuals or groups the possibility of reinvestment and development (Eyber and Ager 2003). Accordingly, poor economic conditions provide no options or resources for the poor to obtain optimal health and educational standards (Thorbecke and Charumilind 2002), which in turn reduces educational attainment, economic activity, and overall social and political engagement in society (Easterly 2007). Examining the causal relationship between conflict and absolute poverty—where poverty is measured in terms of infant mortality—an empirical study by Braithwaite et al. (2016) shows that countries with higher levels of absolute poverty tend to be more prone to conflict onset. Once a country has experienced a conflict, it faces negative repercussions for its economic development, which in turn increases the likelihood of future insurgencies (Braithwaite et al. 2016). This reinforcing relationship between conflict and poverty has become known as the "conflict trap"—a vicious cycle of conflict and underdevelopment. Hence, the outbreak of a civil war in poorly developed countries causes economic devastation, which in turn increases the likelihood of further insurgencies (Collier 2003). For example, "Burundi has experienced multiple, separate conflicts over the last four decades (in 1972–1973, 1988, and between 1991 and 2005). As a result of these recurrent civil wars, GDP per capita fell by half in the 1990s, from $211 in 1991 to $110 in 1999. Angola has similarly experienced multiple conflict onsets—in 1991, 1994, 1996, 1998, 2002, 2004 and 2007. These conflicts precipitated a decrease in GDP per capita from in excess of US$1000 in 1989 to US$954 in 1991 and US$630 in 1994" (Braithwaite et al. 2016, 46).

Despite this evidence, some studies have failed to find evidence that poverty is a significant contributor to conflict onset. Public opinion polls, obtained from Palestinians living in the West Bank and Gaza, show that it was not the poor, but rather the well-educated and affluent respondents who supported armed attacks on targets in Israel (Krueger and Maleckova 2003). Further studies argue that participation in terrorism is associated rather with lack of civil liberties, political freedom, and oppression than with average national income (Abadie 2006; Piazza 2006). A similar study of fourteen African and South Asian countries with a majority Muslim population also turned up contradicting results, namely an association between less poverty and greater support for terrorism (Fair and Shepherd 2006). Further evidence is provided by a large empirical study in London and Bradford that questioned men and women of Muslim heritage on their attitudes toward violent conflicts and terrorism. The results show that sympathy for violence and terrorism is particular high among well-educated, young, affluent, and British-born individuals (Bhui et al. 2014). One possible explanation could be that support for terrorism and political engagement, even if violent, requires resources and a certain amount of knowledge—all of which is available to individuals in better economic positions (Krueger and Maleckova 2003).

However, a study predicted changes in global and regional events of armed conflict for the period 2010–2050 by using exogenous variables such as population size, poverty level (infant mortality rate), demographic composition, education level, oil dependence, ethnic cleavages, and neighborhood characteristics. The simulated predictions conclude that over the next few decades a large number of conflicts will occur in eastern, central, and southern Africa, as well as in eastern and southern Asia—regions with the highest poverty rate. For many countries, the strongest driver of increased conflict risk is strong population growth. "According to the medium UN population projections, 29 countries are estimated to at least double their populations between 2009 and 2050, 24 are in Sub-Saharan Africa. The population of the fastest growing country, Niger, is estimated to increase by close to 250% in this period, from less than 16 million to more than 53 million people" (Hegre et al. 2013, 264). Accordingly, the predicted results assume that an increase in population size in poorly developed countries, with a shortage of existential resources and lack of education, may increase the risk of civil conflict. Especially scarcity of food-related resources, as seen in Somalia, Chad, or Mali, increases the risk of food insecurity and existential threat. The Sahel region in Africa, extending from Mauritania and Senegal in the west to Eritrea, Ethiopia, and Sudan in the east, where droughts and famine are ubiquitous, has faced a particularly large number of conflicts in the last decades (Hendrix and Brinkman 2013). In Niger and South Sudan, farmers fight herders over land, a conflict that is fueled by ethnic and religious rivalries and scarce livelihood opportunities. Beyond tremendous poverty and limited access to minimum subsistence means, Sudan is facing high food prices, violent conflicts between farmers and pastoralists, depletion of food stocks, and a strong migration flow from South Sudan (WFP 2018). But conflict-prone countries, such as Venezuela, Yemen, Iraq and Afghanistan, are also facing high levels of hunger and misery, with millions of people in need of immediate assistance to survive (HIIK 2019). The previous theoretical and empirical considerations and case studies show the complexity of the link between poverty, food insecurity, and conflict. The difficulty of assigning conflicts to categories shows that poor developmental conditions, hunger, and conflict form vicious cycles that are hard to control. All this implies that severe socioeconomic conditions and denied access to education and services deprive human beings from serving their existential needs, which include both physical elements, such as housing and nutrition, as well as more complex psychological factors, such as having the perception of control over one's own life, being able to affect one's environment, and receiving valuable information to form a consistent world view.

3.1.1.4 Relative Deprivation

Another plausible explanation for the correlation between poverty and conflict is the *relative deprivation* hypothesis—the subjective perception of one's own economic position relative to that of others. This means that dissatisfaction and frustration with one's situation arise due to subjectively set standards and comparisons with others. Theories of relative deprivation often contrast between comparison types. Personal comparison describes the case where one person compares oneself to other similar individuals from the same group. For example, a Palestinian living in Germany would compare themselves to other Palestinians living in the same country. By contrast, group-based comparison means comparing one's own deprived situation (or the deprived situation of one's own ingroup) to the situation of other outgroup members. For instance, a Palestinian individual living in Germany would compare themselves to the German majority (Koomen and Van Der Pligt 2016). These two forms of deprivation and comparison have different repercussions at the macro and individual levels. There is some evidence that personal deprivation enhances subjective grievance, frustration, and feelings of exclusion, whereas group deprivation strengthens support for violent protest and increases the propensity toward group militancy (Burraston et al. 2018). A large meta-analysis supports this hypothesis and shows that group-based relative deprivation increases collective action and generates negative attitudes toward outgroup members, whereas subjective relative deprivation predicts distinct responsive behavior, such as drug abuse, self-evaluation, suppression, or aggression (Smith et al. 2012). Koomen and Van Der Pligt (2016, 31) suggest that "such comparisons can easily lead to realization that, in various ways, they are not receiving all that they feel they are entitled to. This awakens a sense that they are being discriminated against, a feeling of injustice that would not have been evoked had they not made the comparison in the first place." This may imply that relative or subjectively perceived deprivation has stronger implications than absolute or real deprivation. A consistent problem in this regard is the level of measurement for empirical analysis. Across studies, relative deprivation has been measured among others in terms of income inequality (Pridemore 2011), health care, access to electricity (Saito et al. 2014) or the perception of one's own social status (Zhang and Chen 2014). Economic literature in particular uses income inequalities on a community and country level to examine the impact of relative deprivation on violent behavior. The empirical results suggest that income disparities are a reliable measure of insurgencies at the macro level (Ward et al. 2010). A study on income inequality shows that youths with a low socioeconomic position but living in affluent communities tend to be more aggressive and prone to violent behavior than poor youths living in impoverished communities (Jarjoura and Triplett 1997). A cross-section study of seventy-one developing countries confirms these results, finding that income inequality is highly correlated with socio-political instability because persistent social discontent and grievances about one's own situation can fuel rebellion and conflict (Alesina and Perotti 1996). Although some scholars question the relationship between income inequality and conflict due to the lack of adequate income inequality data (Collier 2000), a vast number of researchers take a contrasting position. They argue that income disparities may also lead indirectly to social or political disintegration, which exacerbates grievances and political strife. Thus, socioeconomic and political isolation and lack of governmental support can increase competition for regional resources and reinforce the risk of conflict (Nafziger and Auvinen 2002). A further factor that can contribute to conflict and violent disputes is social provision, defined *inter alia* as welfare and unemployment benefits and state-funded provisions for health and education. A study by Burgoon (2006) provides evidence that in more than ninety countries, better social provision has had a dampening effect on violent insurgencies and conflict due to its partial role in reducing poverty and relative deprivation (Burgoon 2006). Using disaggregated data on welfare and socioeconomic inequalities between and within subnational regions in twenty-two countries in Sub-Saharan Africa, a study provides evidence that conflict onsets are more likely in regions with (i) high levels of relative deprivation regarding household assets, (ii) low levels of education, (iii) high intraregional inequalities, and (iv) relative deprivation in regard to natural resource deposits (Østby et al. 2009). According to that, we may contend that denied access to vital resources, political and social isolation, and high inequality lead to competition and need deprivation (i.e., individuals are deprived from the opportunity to secure their existence, to control their surroundings, to feel integrated and approved by society, and to receive all the information to form consistence and order in their lives, which can lead directly to violence and conflict).

Box 3.2 Nepal: Poverty, relative deprivation, and the People's War of 1996–2006

Nepal is a land-locked country located between India and China that has few natural resources. With a population of twenty-eight million and per-capita income of $340 in 2007, it still lags behind most other south Asian countries. Although its position on the Human Development Index (HDI) has improved gradually since 1990, the Inequality-adjusted Human Development Index (IHDI) falls below the HDI, which indicates a high level of inequality, especially in regard to income (UNDP 2018). Looking at the purchasing power parity (PPP) GDP per capita across regions, its far- and mid-western regions have far lower incomes per head compared to other parts of the country, even worsening in the period 1996 to 1999 (Murshed and Gates 2005). These far-reaching inequalities can be explained by political, economic, and social transformations in the past, which, in the end, led to the outbreak of the civil war in 1996.

From a political perspective, Nepal was ruled by a monarchy until 1990, when widespread protests led to the abdication of the king and the establishment of a multiparty democracy (Do and Iyer 2010). Democratization brought high expectations of greater political freedom, social inclusion of rural areas, and economic growth, which were dampened by political instability, corruption, and a lack of appropriate democratic institutions. In fact, political elites have maintained their power by providing political and social participation opportunities to the middle class and their supporters, while excluding political opponents and marginalized groups (Deraniyagala 2005). Economically, in the 1950s the country embarked on an import substitution policy that focused solely on urban-based, non-agricultural activities. This strategy failed to benefit fifty-six percent of the population living in rural mountainous areas that rely heavily on subsistence farming and agricultural production. In addition, foreign investment flows targeted mainly the garment and carpet industries located in urban areas, while fully neglecting the farming-dominated mountain regions. This unequal economic growth pattern contributed to high poverty, high unemployment, and income disparity in the mid-1990s. The percentage of the population living below the poverty line rose from thirty-three percent in 1976 to forty-two percent in 1996, which hit the rural regions in particular. Cuts in development expenditure as a part of an austerity policy further exacerbated the problem in non-urban areas" (Sharma 2006).

Rising grievances, frustration, and lack of perspective drove especially poor and disadvantaged young adults to join the Maoist movement and fight against the unjust economic and political system. The Maoists clearly demanded an end to corruption and to racial, sexual, and caste discrimination, and they advocated for land reforms, drinking water provisions, a proper infrastructure, and electricity for all rural areas. Furthermore, they aimed to dampen the established privileges of the royal family, to form a new constitution, and to nationalize the property of capitalists. Due to governmental neglect of the rural regions, Maoists could claim high support in these deprived areas (Deraniyagala 2005). Their beliefs about a social community based on equality, solidarity, and ethnic inclusion were appealing to many individuals who felt left behind by the governmental elites.

However, the political situation changed in 2001, when King Gyanendra came to power and took up a more aggressive stance toward the Maoists. Three rounds of talks between representatives of the government and Maoists failed to reach an agreement due to contrary demands and interests of both sides. In February 2005, in the face of increased attacks by Maoist activists in urban areas, King Gyanendra dismissed the political ruling elite and seized power. In response, the Maoists declared a unilateral ceasefire and initiated talks with seven major political parties to establish a common front against the monarchy. In the face of this growing political pressure and public protests, King Gyanendra resigned in April 2006 (Sharma 2006). In the months that followed, a peace agreement was signed that enabled the participation of the CPN-Maoist party in the government, which in turn led to the abolishment of the monarchy in 2007 and the electoral victory of the party in April 2008 (Do and Iyer 2010).

*These political and economic inequalities were additionally worsened by the social hierarchical caste system. The upper castes (Bahun-Chetri-Newar), which constitute only thirty-seven percent of the whole population, enjoyed high social status and privileges, whereas over sixty percent of the lowest caste, the Dalits, live below the poverty line. The support of the Maoist movement was therefore particularly strong among the most disadvantageous castes (Deraniyagala 2005). Because the links between ethnicity, caste, and conflict are very complex in Nepal, we refrain elaborating extensively on this issue.

3.1.2 Threats to One's Own Social Group

The previous paragraph has shown that conditions of existential threat, competition over scarce resources or one's own privileges, discrimination, and poverty can deprive individuals from serving their existential needs and can, in direct forms, even lead to violent conflict. However, psychological literature postulates that the most basic premise in human life is indeed to secure one's own existence, as well as that of one's own social group. Evolution reveals that resource-sharing, cooperation, and socializing within a group all tend to enhance individuals' survival and continued existence. Individuals strive to improve their fitness through collaboration and affiliation with significant others. Belonging to and identifying with a group enables individuals to sympathize with fellow members, understand their behavior, and develop their own identity (de Waal 1996, 1998). The importance of the group in terms of identity formation and relational human needs is thoroughly examined in the next chapter. In this section, we instead focus on the stress induced by conditions of threat, competition, or exclusion of the group as a whole. Realizing that one's group is subject to negative evaluation, structural deprivation, or to existential threat can engender a sense of frustration, grievance, uncertainty, and aggression. Intergroup threats, whether realistic or symbolic, can induce negative feelings about oneself and one's own group and can easily foster anger and outgroup hostility (Koomen and Van Der Pligt 2016). Factors such as intergroup threats, deprivation, or discrimination can increase cognitive discrepancies, uncertainty, and perceived lack of control over outcomes and the environment, which deprive individuals from serving their existential needs as a group.

This can enhance individuals' willingness to protect and fight for the existence and survival of their own group, which may even degenerate into violence and war.

The most common and widely accepted concept in this regard is Ted Gurr's (1970) aggression–frustration theory, which argues that the primary source of human capacity for intergroup violence is relative deprivation. In other words, higher levels of frustration and subjective feelings of discrimination increase the probability of deprived individuals or groups turning to illegal means to achieve certain goals. This aggression–frustration theory emphasizes the interrelation between relative deprivation, emotions, and the ideological value attached to the goods one is deprived of. The scale of the deprivation tends to increase frustration, especially when one's own identity is attached to it (Bartusevicius 2014). In this context, existing literature highlights the concept of horizontal, or intergroup, inequality.

Horizontal inequality is defined as inequalities in economic, political, and social terms between culturally defined groups (Østby 2008). Especially in countries where ethnicity and religion seem to determine resource allocation and social power structures, horizontal (or intergroup) inequality can fuel violent conflicts. In this regard, more severe grievances and accrued frustration may enhance mobilization capacities in countries where cultural groups are socially clustered and group cohesion is strong (Gubler and Selway 2012). Possible examples to support the frustration–aggression link are the insurgencies in Iraq, where Shiite Muslims revolted against the Sunni regime; the

Syrian civil war, through which the Sunni majority expressed their grievances toward the dominant Alevi regime (Basedau et al. 2017); and the ethnic and religious cleavages in former Yugoslavia, the USSR, Northern Ireland, and the Basque Country. Such ethnic or religious-based intergroup conflicts are fought especially in less developed countries that face resource scarcity, poor governmental institutions, and vulnerable environmental conditions (Stewart 2008). In Sudan, the highly violent conflict in the Darfur region between various armed ethnic African groups and the Arab-affiliated Sudanese government, entered in 2017 its fifteenth consecutive year as a war. Also, in the Central African Republic, the Anti-balaka, a militia group composed primarily of Christians, fights against ex-Séléka, a predominantly Muslim militia group, over land, resources, and state power (HIIK 2018).

3.1.2.1 Polarization and Intergroup Threat

Although there is empirical evidence that economic grievances can motivate rebels to engage in violence (Krieger and Meierrieks 2011), unequal income distribution is perceived as providing little statistical evidence to explain the outbreak of group-level phenomena (Collier and Hoeffler 2004; Fearon and Laitin 2003). Accordingly, theories like horizontal inequality and polarization emphasize the role of a threatened identity in explaining conflicts within national boundaries. While horizontal inequality refers to multidimensional differences, polarization measures social "antagonism." Social "antagonism" is fueled by two factors: (i) alienation, felt between members of different groups; and (ii) identification with one's own ingroup (Esteban et al. 2012). The degree of polarization increases when members of a homogeneous and cohesive group feel socially or ideologically separated from members of other groups. Accordingly, the level of conflict increases with the magnitude of polarization. "This notion of polarization is particularly relevant to the analysis of conflict, because it stands for the idea that the tensions within a society of individuals or states result from two simultaneous decisions: identification with other subjects within the own group of reference and distancing oneself from one or several other competing groups" (Esteban and Schneider 2008, 133).

An empirical study combines the argument of economic disparity and polarization—where identification is measured in terms of similar income levels—by arguing that the dynamics of intragroup homogeneity and intergroup heterogeneity in terms of income increase the probability of social riots (Esteban and Ray 1994). This assumption has been challenged by the suggestion that economic polarization becomes insignificant when testing cross-sectionally, while social horizontal inequality contributes to the outbreak of civil conflict (Østby 2008). According to this, ethnic groups with a shared and stable group identity who find themselves oppressed and discriminated by the government or other dominant ethnic groups tend to turn to violent means to voice their discontent and stand up for their rights. "Unequal access to political/economic/social resources by different cultural groups can reduce individual welfare of the individuals in the losing groups over and above what their individual position would merit, because their self-esteem is bound up with the progress of the group. But of greater consequence is the argument, that where there are such inequalities in resource access and outcomes, coinciding with cultural differences, culture can become a powerful mobilizing agent that can lead to a range of political disturbances" (Stewart 2002, 3). According to this, identity-related issues based on religion, ethnicity, language, or region, which foster group identification and group cohesion, are perceived to have a larger impact on the outbreak of intergroup civil conflict than economic factors alone (Østby 2008).

The intergroup threat theory extends the concept of horizontal inequality and postulates that realistic or symbolic threats are experienced when one group realizes that another group is in the position to cause it harm. Physical injury, loss of resources or power, and deprivation of existential livelihoods pose realistic (tangible) threats to a group, while the concern about the integrity of the ingroup's identity or belief system is a symbolic (intangible) threat (Riek et al. 2006). The often-cited conflict between Israelis and Arabs illustrates these types of threat. The enduring conflict involves realistic struggles over land, resources, and power, as well as symbolic threats in regard to religion, cultural world views, and language (Stephan et al. 2009). But intergroup threats alone are insufficient to explain conflict onset; they largely depend on whether or not political elites have strong incentives to mobilize groups for violent conflict "along cultural group lines" (Langer and Brown 2008). However, the experience of severe deprivation, discrimination, and resource competition as a group does not just deprive individuals from serving their existential needs; it also prevents them from securing the subsistence of the group. Doubts about the group's self-concept and identity feed hesitation about one's own self and thus contribute to negative self-evaluation. Being subject to negative stereotypes; to a lack of possibilities to change the group's own situation; and to an uncertain, inconsistent, and unpredictable environment deprives group members from serving their existential and epistemic needs—needs for order, certainty, predictability, consistency, safety, and control.

Box 3.3 Intergroup threat and violence in Central African Republic

In 2018, the war over resources and national power between Anti-balaka and ex-Séléka militias in the Central African Republic (CAR) continued to involve serious human rights abuses. Both groups expanded their power and control to cover an estimated seventy percent of the country, while the central government, led by President Faustin-Archange Touadéra, only controlled the capital Bangui. Despite his being elected president in 2016, violence continued to escalate in 2017, with the number of displaced individuals reaching a record high of 1.1 million (HRW 2018).

Despite gaining independence from its former colonial ruler in 1960, CAR remained politically, socially, and economically vulnerable. Although the country's first democratic and peaceful elections took place in 1993, the absence of state security forces and reliable governmental institutions generated an uncertain and inconsistent environment that facilitated the formation and achievements of independent militia groups. In addition, political elites used ethnic and religious identities as political means to create a clustered power structure and strengthen their own political positions. "Domestic and international pressure on [then-president] Patassé increased and culminated in a successful coup in March 2003, led by the former army chief of staff, General François Bozizé. In the course of Bozizé's rise to power, the CAR's bush war started" (Welz 2014, 602).

Bozize's autocratic leadership and the use of the national army FACA to assert power and control generated a fertile ground for the formation of armed opposition groups. In particular, the north and east of the country, where the majority is of Muslim origin, was marginalized and neglected by the central government, which failed to serve the citizens' basic existential needs. The lack of schools, hospitals, businesses, and general infrastructure fueled grievances and enhanced social antagonism (Siradag 2016). In response, various predominantly Muslim armed groups, such as the Union for Peace in Central Africa (UPC) and the Patriotic Rally for the Rebirth of the Central African Republic (RPRC), formed the Séléka in 2012, led by Michel Djotodia, which aimed to overthrow the then-president François Bozizé and seize state power. Despite the signing of a peace agreement between the Séléka and Bozizé's government in January 2013, the continued neglect of the region led to renewed fighting. In March 2013, Bozizé was overthrown, and Djotodia declared himself the new President of CAR. In response to Séléka activities, predominantly Christian self-defense militias had formed the Anti-balaka movement with the backing of FACA, the former national security force. The main aim of the movement was to dampen the power of Séléka and the Muslim population in order to protect their Christian identity and maintain the group's existence and national control (Welz 2014). Mainly poor and unemployed young adults from rural areas joined the rebel group to fight along ethnic and religious lines. Following international pressure and the forced resignation of Djotodia in January 2014, the National Transitional Council of CAR set up a temporary parliament with Catherine Samba-Panza as interim president. Nevertheless, violent confrontations between the Séléka and Anti-balaka have since continued* (Weyns et al. 2014).

According to reports by Amnesty International (2014), both militias are responsible for committing severe human rights abuses, including war crimes and crimes against humanity in CAR. Despite its resource wealth, the country is classified as one of the least developed nations in the world and is among the poorest countries in Africa. Seventy percent of the population lives below the poverty line and CAR is one of the few countries in the world where almost every second individual depends on aid to survive (FAO 2018). The example of CAR shows that perceived realistic or symbolic intergroup threat, competition, and deprivation (governmental neglect of rural areas) can deprive individuals from serving their existential and epistemic needs—needs for control, order, safety, certainty, consistency, and predictability. The experience of an inconsistent and unpredictable environment, fueled with grievances, discrimination, governmental neglect, and threats related to one's own group identity may lead to anger, fear, and an enhanced subjective willingness to fight.

*The Anti-balaka groups are the main perpetrators of abuses committed against Muslims, while Séléka forces are responsible for serious human rights violations and war crimes against, but not limited to, Christians. Such atrocities still continue given an unstable, corrupt, and poorly managed environment and persistent severe poverty across the country (Amnesty International 2014).

3.1.2.2 Minorities

Considering the theories on horizontal inequality, polarization, and intergroup threat, further theories and empirical studies have shifted their focus to minority groups (e.g., Cederman et al. 2010). Beyond poor economic conditions, a discriminatory social environment can induce stress of survival, where ethnic, religious, or social minorities are confronted with hostile stereotypes, prejudice, and ostracism. Under these circumstances, feelings of threat in interpersonal, intergroup, and social domains may occur, which in turn can trigger violent countermovements (Koomen and Van Der Pligt 2016). The frustration–aggression argument and Gurr's ethnic-based models of conflict have contributed to an influential body of literature on group-level grievances and insurgencies by identifying a connection between perceived deficiency, negative emotions, and the propensity for collective violence (Basedau et al. 2017). The "perceived discrepancy between expectations and capabilities [. . .], the number of other satisfactions to fall back and the quantity of the alternative ways to satisfy one's discontent" play a significant role in determining the level of frustration (Shaykhutdinov and Bragg 2011, 143).

Following this assumption, an empirical study (Cederman et al. 2010) examines a set of mechanisms to explain the effect of deprived minorities and collective negative emotions. The results show that economic and political grievances have an impact only in combination with ethnicity, which serves as a mobilizing factor for conflict outbreaks. The authors conclude that economic and political factors cannot be separated from frustration-driven ethno-nationalist mobilization and violent conflict. Another analysis confirms these results by showing that major domestic disputes can also occur in countries with high national income if some minority groups feel deprived of their share of the national economic wealth (Koubi and Böhmelt 2014). Evidence is provided by the example of the government-sponsored cultural, religious, and social deprivation of Muslim minorities in the poorest regions of southern Thailand. Numerous obstacles and severe exclusion, ranging from denied educational opportunities to social subordination, have intensified the ethnic awareness and identity of Malay Muslims. Consequently, Wahhabi doctrines have been disseminated with the aim to recruit discontented young adults as spearheads of the Islamist movement in the south. This example suggests that cultural, ethnic, or religious deprivation, which leads to social isolation and marginalization, can reinforce perceived threats associated with one's own identity. Feelings of rejection engender a sense of injustice, frustration, uncertainty, and anger. Such feelings can induce civil uprisings against the government by deprived minority groups who aim to protect their group identity or bring about major changes to their social status (Croissant 2007).

The struggle to preserve one's cultural and ethnic identity is linked to political and civil rights rather than to economic opportunities. This could explain why rebels are often willing to fight for their group without any expected economic gains, and why sustained and highly violent ethnic conflicts have arisen in developed countries (e.g., former Yugoslavia, Israel, Northern Ireland, Cyprus) (Sambanis 2001). Hence, beyond reducing poverty and improving overall national economic wealth, government policies should also focus on providing equal opportunities, enabling political participation, and including ethnic groups to curb civil strife. Discriminative policies toward minorities can cause severe frustration, anger, and eventually political unrest (Østby 2008). Similar factors explain major social conflicts in north-east India. The land-locked region—home to more than seventy ethnic groups with close to four hundred languages and dialects—has been disregarded by the Indian government, which ignored burgeoning grievances and the demands of the local population. As a result, there was a spate of long-lasting conflicts ranging from rebellion to achieve autonomy (Bodos) and riots to achieve secession (e.g., Nagas in Nagaland), all the way to terrorist incidents (United

Liberation Front of Asom) and ethnic clashes (Manipur and Nagaland) (Vadlamannati 2011).

Although ethnicity has been identified as the main cause of civil conflicts since 1945—including conflicts in Congo, Sudan, Pakistan, and Georgia, among others—the role of ethnicity remains a complex subject of discussion (Denny and Walter 2014). Observing the relationship between ethnic discrimination, grievances, and conflict onset, a large empirical study (Basedau et al. 2017) found no significant relationship between grievances, ethnicity, and conflict involvement. Apparently, grievances and ethnic discrimination do not seem to be the primary drivers of conflict engagement, especially for religious groups. Only for twenty out of the 433 examined groups—such as Christians in Azerbaijan, India, Indonesia, and Sudan; Buddhists in Bangladesh; Muslims in Ethiopia, India, Israel, the Philippines, Cote d'Ivoire, and Uganda; and Sikhs in India—was the causal chain of discrimination, grievance, and armed conflict confirmed. By contrast, more than 150 aggrieved groups that experienced severe discrimination did not choose to engage in violence. One possible explanation provided by the authors (Basedau et al. 2017) is that it could be that countries in which deprived groups do not engage in violent protest are under either authoritarian Muslim or Communist rule. These restrictive regimes are assumed to curb violent uprisings. Furthermore, most aggrieved minority groups are small in size, which indicates that minority group size (relative to population size) has an impact on conflict involvement. Especially for non-state conflicts, and also partly for armed conflicts with theological contradiction, the authors (Basedau et al. 2017) found robust and significant evidence of a relationship between size and conflict. They argued that the opportunity for rebellion in the form of domestic armed conflicts depends on both group size and state capacity, meaning that greater state capacity—measured in terms of GDP—decreases the opportunity for rebellion. In sum, the empirical evidence suggests that opportunity and feasibility of rebellion seem to play a greater role in conflict onset than deprivation and religious grievances.

However, given the controversies in the economic literature, psychological studies insist that intergroup threat and ethnic deprivation can reinforce uncertainty and inconsistency with one's own identity. Feelings of rejection engender a sense of injustice, frustration, fear, and anger. Such feelings can induce civil insurgencies between the government and deprived minority groups who aim to protect their group identity or bring about major changes in their social status (Koomen and Van Der Pligt 2016; Croissant 2007). While we do not disagree with economic studies which emphasize the importance of structural factors in enabling conflict onset, we also support the psychological assumptions on cognitive and emotional effects of experienced group threat. Anger and uncertainty, for example, have a detrimental effect on how we process information and make decisions. Thus, experiencing negative emotions and cognitive ambiguity (e.g., stereotypes, negative evaluative judgments) toward one's own group can lead to the severe deprivation of the need for order, safety, ambiguity avoidance, control, predictability, and consistency. We therefore discuss in the following section the psychological implications of threat, and consequently move on with a thorough examination of each of the prior mentioned existential and epistemic human needs.

3.2 Psychological Implications of Threat

A deeper insight into threats in interpersonal and intergroup domains is provided by social psychology. Social identity theorists argue that intergroup tensions occur due to the assessment of psychological benefits of a group membership—namely acceptance; belonging; social orientation; and a system of rules, values, and norms—which guide behavior and provide a purpose in life. Furthermore, stable group cohesion boosts self-esteem, provides dependability and consistency, and increases the sense of distinctiveness. Because humans are "tribal" in nature, membership in particular groups is essential for the basic subsistence and identity formation of each individual. Therefore, individuals strive to preserve their social status as much as they strive to preserve their physical existence, a process referred to social self-preservation (Dickerson et al. 2004). Accordingly, a perceived threat to a group implies a threat to each member of that group, who fears losing his stable social system and, in turn, his own identity.

But also, subjectively perceived threats, such as feelings of discrimination, negative evaluation by others, or prejudice, increase uncertainty, self-doubt, and perceived loss of control (Stephan and Stephan 2000). The experience of social exclusion and socioeconomic deprivation raises doubts about one's own identity, status, and social belonging. Such threats can affect individuals from minority groups, in particular, who feel threatened by the majority, but also subgroups within the majority who feel threatened by minority groups. In the latter case, notably groups with low socioeconomic status may feel left behind and under threat from "elite" sections of society, such as politicians, the government, and other institutions, but also from minorities such as immigrants or refugees. This can generate uncertainty, perceived competition, and feelings of exclusion. Thus, beyond existential threats (concerning material assets, resources, food, shelter, etc.), individuals can be threatened by ambiguity, inconsistency, and cognitive uncertainty (e.g., possible acts of terrorism, ambiguous information, different cultural or religious values) (Koomen and Van Der Pligt 2016), all which create uncertainty and a perceived loss of control.

Research on threats and discrimination shows that individuals who experience discrimination and social rejection due to their culture, religion, or ethnic background are particularly vulnerable to depression, uncertainty, and decreased self-esteem (Bhugra and Becker 2005). "Targeted exclusion," which involves an active and intentional rejection of a certain group or individual, tends to enhance the risk of depression. Such obvious rejection may elicit negative self-referential cognitions concerning one's own self-worth, beliefs, values, and ways of thinking and behaving, which raises severe doubts about one's own role and place in society (Vedder et al. 2007). "These cognitions, which are hallmarks of many depressive episodes, may in turn give rise to self-conscious emotions like shame and humiliation, which are associated with biological processes (e.g., inflammation) that support behavioral disengagement and withdrawal" (Slavich et al. 2010, 3).

Likewise, individuals who are rejected by society due to their low socioeconomic position—not necessarily because of their religion or ethnicity—suffer stigmatization, depression, and negative self-image. "A lot of research in the U.S. (cf. Lott 2002; see also Lott 2012), for instance, indicates that members of the lowest social classes are widely regarded as having failed to seize the opportunities available to them because they lack initiative and enthusiasm. They are also viewed as dishonest, dependent, lazy, uninterested in education and promiscuous. Wider society considers the fact that they are poor as an individual problem, and as result far more attention is paid to the behavior of the poor than the social and economic conditions and circumstances that perpetuate poverty, inequality and exclusion" (Koomen and Van Der Pligt 2016, 43). Such prejudice, stigmatization, and ostracism decrease one's own self-confidence and self-efficacy, which in turn reduces trust in one's own abilities and future opportunities.

A growing body of psychological research shows that experiences of discrimination, rejection, and social isolation tend to have severe repercussions for individuals' mental well-being (Cacioppo et al. 2003). Deprivation and discrimination in the area of education, housing, labor, healthcare, political representation, or public policy can lead to long-term structural processes of social and political disintegration. This causes psychological damage, expressed in feelings of inferiority, shame, powerlessness, and apathy (Chow et al. 2008; Dickerson 2011). Consequently, feelings of being left behind and disintegration tend to generate, in the long run, a reluctance to adapt to social circumstances and to show consideration for other social members (Anhut 2005). Perceived loss of control reinforces strong feelings of uncertainty, fear, anger, and impuissance (Kay and Eibach 2013). A neuroimaging study shows that the pain felt upon social exclusion is similar to the pain experienced upon physical injury. This implies that the experience of exclusion activates the same neural region that is responsible for assuring survival (Eisenberger et al. 2003). These regions include the anterior insula and dorsal anterior cingulate cortex (dACC)—the latter perceived to represent "a neural alarm system" that can detect and react to threatening environmental stimuli. Here, the hypothalamic-pituitary-adrenal (HPA) axis and sympathetic-adrenal-medullary (SAM) axis are particularly responsive and release cortisol and epinephrine in times of stress. "Specifically, stressful conditions characterized by low controllability and high social-evaluative threat were associated with the greatest cortisol responses and slowest recovery of cortisol to baseline levels" (Slavich et al. 2010, 4). An experiment provides evidence that social-evaluative threat conditions tend to release greater cortisol and exhibit an increase in negative self-perception and lower self-esteem (Gruenewald et al. 2004). Especially in conflict-prone regions, the permanent experience of instability, inconsistency, and threats can have a severe impact on need satisfaction and subjective mental well-being, as portrayed in the subsequent case.

Box 3.4 Psychological implications of existential threat and conflict

In conflict-affected regions, individuals are greatly exposed to repeated and enduring existential threats, which means that they live in a state of pervasive insecurity and anxiety. Such conditions of terror, instability, torture, and violence have an immense impact on the psychological states of those involved. Especially in developing, conflict-prone regions, individuals face a severe loss of resources, which translates into unstable and uncertain future prospects (de Jong et al. 2001). Field surveys and empirical investigations on the psychologically detrimental effects of potentially traumatic events (such as natural disaster, conflict, or torture) have observed high rates of post-traumatic stress disorder (PTSD)[*] and depression among affected populations (e.g., Johnson and Thompson 2008). A review of 161 articles that included 81,866 respondents from forty countries, with 122 surveys conducted in low- and middle-income countries, confirms that potentially traumatic events are associated with mental disorder. The traumatic events that conflict-affected individuals experience often lead to severe resource loss and deprivation, which in turn leads to negative self-appraisal and high levels of depression. PTSD arises not simply as a condition triggered by life-threatening events, but it can also be a condition that is shaped by enduring existential threat and insecurity (Steel et al. 2009). Especially in low-income war-prone regions, the rates of depression and PTSD within communities are high. For example, studies on 993 Cambodian refugees living in Thai-Cambodian border camps observed a fifteen percent PTSD prevalence rate (Mollica et al. 1993), a twenty percent PTSD rate was found among 550 survivors in the Gaza Strip (El Sarraj et al. 1996), and 14 percent rate of PTSD was noted in a random community sample in northern Sri Lanka (Somasundaram and Sivayokan 1994).

Other studies show that ongoing exposure to threat and traumatic events involve higher levels of psychopathologic conditions (e.g., Green et al. 2000). An epidemiological study conducted between 1997 and 1999 in Algeria, Cambodia, Ethiopia, and Gaza—all of which experienced high-intensity conflicts and violence within the last decades—found high levels of PTSD among the surveyed individuals: 15.8 percent in Ethiopia, 17.8 percent in Gaza, 28.4 percent in Cambodia and 37.4 percent in Algeria. In Ethiopia, 25.5 percent of respondents reported to have experienced torture in life, while 59.3 percent of Palestinians and 91.9 percent of Algerians reported having experienced conflict-related events. While 25.7 percent of Cambodians stated that their parents had a history of mental disorders, in Ethiopia (88.6 percent) and Algeria (78.3 percent) individuals claimed to struggle for daily survival. The high rate of PTSD prevalence in Algeria (37.4 percent) is explained by the persistent conflict and terrorist attacks by Islamic fundamentalists, and in Cambodia (28.4 percent) by the violent history during the Pol Pot era, the Vietnamese invasion, followed by long decades of political and economic instability (de Jong et al. 2001). A similar study conducted by Médecins Sans Frontières (MSF) in Freetown, Sierra Leone, after a period of intense violence in January 1999, revealed that all 245 respondents reported having experienced violence, destruction, and torture in the previous years. Almost all participants (99 percent) showed very high levels of mental disorder, indicative of severe PTSD, and physical disturbances (de Jong 2002).

A social psychological framework of war and trauma (Janoff-Bulman 1992) claims that post-traumatic symptoms result from an individual's attempt to cope with loss of meaning and of their self-worth. "When one's basic assumptions of the construction of the world and its reality are in mismatch with perceptions following exposure to potentially traumatizing events, the result is a disorganized memory structure as manifested in PTSD" (Kanagaratnam et al. 2005, 512). In other words, life-threatening and traumatic experiences destruct individuals' cognitive assumptions about themselves and their environment, and this psychological inconsistency or "disconnection" leads to mental maladaptation in the form of PTSD or depression. Rebuilding these shattered assumptions about oneself and the world into a consistent and stable set of beliefs helps to adapt to the new circumstances and cope with the threatening experiences (Janoff-Bulman 1992). Other psychological studies show that rejecting information or downplaying conflictual circumstances may also serve as a cognitive coping mechanism. For example, perpetrators may downplay or justify their behavior and the overall system (Sommer et al. 2001), while victims compensate their suffering by engaging in prosocial, antisocial, or socially avoidant behavior (Richman and Leary 2009). In case of a possible social reconnection, individuals tend to adopt prosocial behavior to "re-affiliate" with significant others (Williams 2007; Riva et al. 2014). At the opposite end of the scale, experiences of threat and deprivation can lead to self-destructive and antisocial behavior. Anger and aggression can decrease empathy for other victims (Chow et al. 2008) or may even increase the propensity to engage in extreme violence, such as mass shootings or terrorism (Hartling 2007; Knapton 2014; Wesselmann et al. 2015).

Economic studies support this approach and demonstrate that socioeconomic exclusion (deprivation) increases survival stress by generating feelings of grievance, frustration, and anger. This can result in aggressive behavior, rejection of social norms and values, or attachments to political extremes (Gurr 1970; Østby et al. 2009; Stewart et al. 2006; Cederman et al. 2013).

Post-traumatic stress disorder is a mental disorder that develops when individuals experience extremely traumatic events. Trauma involves circumstances and events that pose a significant threat (physical, psychological, emotional) to the survival and safety of a person. Individuals with PTSD have intense, disturbing thoughts and feelings related to their experience, but also about themselves or their environment. Emotional arousals, angry outbursts, reckless social behavior or self-destruction are also symptoms that vary in severity (American Psychological Association 2019e).

Box 3.5 Socio-economic status (SES) and the perception of threat

Interdisciplinary research—ranging from psychological neurocognitive to economic and political disciplines—has discussed at length the impact of individuals' socioeconomic position on their cognitive and affective behavior. An integrative framework that differentiates between a large number of social classes shows that low socioeconomic status reinforces feelings of threat and the feeling of having less control over own life and social environment (Stellar et al. 2012). The authors argue that low-status individuals often live in environments that are more vulnerable to external threats. Poor economic and social circumstances do not provide appropriate coping resources for resistance and protection against external threats. Such individuals are thus perceived to be at higher risk of depression, anxiety, and substance abuse (Johnson et al. 1999). A longitudinal study shows that low-status children are far more vulnerable to stressful and unpredictable life events, which in turn are linked to negative psychological and physiological outcomes. Lower socioeconomic status

(SES) is associated with increasing daily cortisol release over time, which in turn increases vulnerability to stressful and threatening events (Chen et al. 2010). These results support the assumption that SES has an impact on individuals' ability to process and evaluate information and life events (Chen et al. 2004). Individuals from a low socioeconomic background tend to draw more negative inferences from certain situations and interpret ambiguous situations as far more threatening than high-SES individuals (Gump et al. 1999). The authors suggest that low-status individuals tend to experience more negative life events with unpleasant outcomes, which leads them to develop adaptive behavioral and cognitive patterns to deal with adverse circumstances in the future. This negative perception of life situations in turn affects their overall attitude toward society and external events. Another study reveals that low-status individuals tend to perceive the world as a hostile place and society and its members as dominant and controlling (Gallo et al. 2006).

Further studies (see review of Brito and Noble 2014) on socioeconomic disparities and neurobiological development show that low socioeconomic conditions tend to affect brain development, socio-emotional processing, and cognitive control (self-regulation). These aspects are relevant to how humans process emotionally salient environmental stimuli. Using structural magnetic resonance imaging (MRI) in a sample of children, a study (Noble et al. 2012) shows that a poor socioeconomic background tends to have an impact particularly on the development of the hippocampus and amygdala, which are both responsible for cognitive and emotional processing (social cognition). Memory skills are dependent on the hippocampus while the processing of social and emotional information relies on the amygdala. The results indicate that experiencing stressful events and the income-to-needs ratio* are responsible for the smaller size of the hippocampal volumes. A similar study on pre-school children supports the assumption that exposure to poverty during early childhood is associated with changed hippocampal and amygdala volumes, as well as white and cortical gray matter volumes. Poverty not only increases stress, but it also interferes with the mechanisms that enable children to cope with their social environment. Thus, increased amygdala volume is associated with greater vulnerability to external stressors and a diminished capacity to process information and to assess one's social and physical environment (Luby et al. 2013).

Although one of the most ubiquitous findings in psychological literature suggests that stressful and vulnerable situations undermine children's cognitive abilities, recent studies insist that these children develop problem-solving behaviors enabling them to adapt to risky environments. Life history theory provides a heuristic measure to observe how harsh environmental conditions shape human development. "Thus, within harsh rearing contexts characterized by limited caregiver investment and resources, individuals are likely to shift toward here-and-now survival and early reproduction strategies" (Suor et al. 2017, 902), which includes, among others, pronounced risk-taking behavior, aggression, or greater orientation toward immediate rewards. The results show that early experiences of environmental harshness predict enhanced reward-oriented problem solving. Resource deprivation may adapt individuals' mindsets such that they favor small immediate rewards over larger future rewards, which are perceived as less probable. This implies that children in their early developmental stage learn to adopt a strategy which is consistent with their environment so as to ensure survival and secure resources (Suor et al. 2017). Despite the limitations and inconsistent results, neuroimaging analyses provide evidence that resource deprivation and harsh socioeconomic conditions have an impact on subjective information processing and the perception of one's social environment. Such conditions deprive children, and individuals in general, of serving their foremost existential needs. The world is perceived as threatening, insecure, and unpredictable. The lack of opportunities to improve one's state increases one's perception of an uncontrollable and uncertain environment, which may decrease one's subjective willingness to adjust to it in a socially accepted way.

Considering the theories and empirical results discussed above, we can summarize that life-threatening events and potentially traumatic experiences, such as conflicts, natural disasters, or resource loss, have a devastating impact on the mental and physical needs of individuals—needs for an ordered, safe, and predictable environment, for an unambiguous and consistent perception of the world and oneself, and for (the perception of) having control in life. Poverty, deprivation, and discriminatory living conditions generate persistent distress and grievances, which in turn reinforce feelings of instability, anxiety, and loss of control (Doosje et al. 2013). The perception of an uncontrollable and ambiguous environment following exposure to traumatic events leads to psychological disequilibrium, severe self-doubts, and confusion (Kay and Eibach 2013). The lack of orientation and opportunities to improve one's own situation enhances the perception of an uncertain and unstable social environment. Decreased self-worth and personal significance, as well as the meaning of personal existence, can lead to severe mental disturbances and negative emotional processing (Kruglanski et al. 2014). Consequently, existential stressors that trigger feelings of grievance, threat, and uncertainty increase the demand for managing these conditions and re-establishing a positive and consistent self-view (Deci and Ryan 2002). This implies that beyond physical or existential needs, such as the need for safety, survival, and nutrition, there are also psychological needs that help individuals to cope cognitively and emotionally with threatening, uncontrollable, and ambiguous situations. Thus, individuals strive to establish a sense of meaning in life and to form a consistent and reliable world view about themselves and their social environment. This produces enhanced needs for uncertainty and ambiguity avoidance (or cognitive closure) (Jost 2009), consistency (Haidt and Graham 2007), predictability (Pyszczynski et al. 1997), order (Brandt and Reyna 2010), and control (Kay and Eibach 2013). All these needs are covered by a safety-seeking mechanism, which is explained in greater detail in the following section.

*A family's income-to-needs ratio is defined as total family income divided by the federal poverty threshold for a family of that size in the year the data were collected.

3.3 Existential and Epistemic Needs and Need Deprivation

3.3.1 The Existential Need for Safety/Existential Security

The theories and empirical studies previously discussed provide evidence that the most basic of all human needs is the need to secure one's own existence. Individuals strive to mitigate threatening and uncertain situations to feel secured and safe. As Maslow (1943) has indicated, a fundamental and biologically settled motivation, beyond all physiological needs, is to maintain existential safety. The need for safety can be understood as a human motivation to feel protected from environmental threats and to have sufficient material resources to ensure basic survival. Maslow proposes that this need can be efficiently observed and fully understood by studying infants who haven't yet learned to inhibit reactions to dangerous, unpleasant, or threatening situations. Infants react immediately if they feel threatened or if their surroundings are inconsistent and disrupted, which makes them feel anxious and unsafe. Perceived threats make the world look unreliable, unpredictable, and unsafe (Evans et al. 2005). Thus, young children, according to Maslow, need an organized and rigid environment with routines and schedules which produce feelings of reliability, consistency, and safety. As with infants, adults also seek to create an ordered, predictable, and safe environment, as reflected in their very common preferences for familiarity, consistency, and the tried-and-trusted. Existential safety and security needs simply represent the human desire to remain alive (which means having sufficient resources to assure basic survival) and to avoid threatening situations and death-related thoughts (such as about one's own mortality, existential anxiety, etc.).

The need for safety/security is strongly determined by ecological conditions and external events. Climate change, pollution, diminishing water supplies, and other forms of ecological degradation, but also economic shocks, terroristic attacks, or natural disasters have clear ramifications for the potential fulfillment of this need. "[Finally] If resources such as clean water and sufficient food do indeed become scarce, history suggests that aggressive battles for those resources may soon follow. Clearly, any of these circumstances is likely to decrease the felt safety and security of a substantial portion of humanity (especially the poor), resulting in decrements to their personal well-being" (Kasser 2009, 176). Beyond physical and materialistic safety, individuals also have a need for subjectively perceived feelings of safety. Unlike physical safety, perceived feelings of existential insecurity can arise even if no real danger is encountered. Thus, psychologists tend to differentiate between the physical and psychological need for safety (Ryan and Deci 2000; Andersen et al. 2000). Feelings of personal unsafety have been linked to decreased psychological well-being, lower quality of life, and higher levels of mortality. Mental disorders such as anxiety, phobia, or depression have also been associated with unmet safety/stability needs (Zheng et al. 2016). Empirical studies show that economic and financial insecurity, in particular, decrease subjective well-being and undermine psychological needs, such as the need for safety, which can result in harmful and risky behavior (Weinstein and Stone 2018).

Experiments with nonhuman organisms provide evidence that threatening information is processed faster than rewarding information, which may be attributed to an evolutionary survival strategy. Feelings of personal insecurity, like anxiety or uncertainty, dampen the need for safety. In other words, when the need for safety is deprived, increased feelings of threat and anxiety initiate approach or avoidance behavior. Appraisal theory proposes that emotions related to harm, or threat, are activated faster and more automatically than the emotions that are triggered when experiencing blame or anger. When something uncontrollable or unexpected happens, the individual will first perceive it as a threat (fear/uncertainty) and next evaluate its hedonic value (sad/happy). This implies that the need for safety is an evolutionary adaptation that helps individuals to cope with unexpected events and an uncertain environment (Zheng et al. 2016).

One prominent approach asserts that when survival and sustenance are threatened, individuals search for means or material resources to feel safe and secure. "Having a steady job and money in a savings account makes people feel more secure and thus fulfills the same needs that drove our ancestors to store dried meat for another long winter" (Kasser 2002, 29). This approach is backed up by experimental studies which postulate that consumption and financial prospects tend to serve subjective psychological needs. Higher income is associated with higher social status and enhanced social belongingness (Diener and Biswas-Diener 2002) and a greater feeling of control and self-esteem (Howell and Hill 2009, Deci and Ryan 2008). Accordingly, low-status individuals are perceived to have a vulnerable internal buffering system for coping with threatening situations because they have limited access to appropriate resources (Cummins 1998). An empirical study provides evidence that increased income and decreased personal debt lead to greater feelings of safety and existential security, which in turn serves further psychological needs and increase psychological well-being (Howell et al. 2013). Others reveal that materialism and consumption help to construct and maintain the personal self. Objects, services, products, and experiences that individuals consume help them to form an identity that is perceived to be distinctive and valuable (Shrum et al. 2013).

However, opposite assumptions claim that beyond physical objects, non-materialistic means, such as social ties, the possibility to make decisions, and a cognitively consistent environment, also play a significant part in serving psychological needs and contributing to one's subjective perception of existential safety (De Donder et al. 2012). Individuals strive to understand and control their social environment, to avoid threatening and ambiguous situations, and to live in consistent and predictable surroundings. Accordingly, they search for ways to buffer against mortality, inconsistency, threats, and death-related concerns (e.g., thoughts about a possible illness). To find "cognitive safety" and to buffer against death-related thoughts, psychologists assume that individuals seek to create a meaningful and eternal universe. Terror management theory (TMT) "has demonstrated that concerns about human mortality affect a broad range of socially significant behaviors that are unrelated to the problem of death in any superficial, semantic, or logical way, including interpersonal evaluations, judgments of moral transgressors, stereotyping, ingroup bias, aggression, social consensus estimates, and conformity to personal and cultural standards" (Pyszczynski et al. 1999, 1). TMT proposes that individuals are highly motivated to establish a (cognitively) safe and eternal environment to cope with their anxiety about mortality. This can be done in the shape of a dual-component anxiety buffer consisting of "(a) a cultural worldview—a humanly constructed symbolic conception of reality that imbues life with order, permanence, and stability; a set of standards through which individuals can attain a sense of personal value; and some hope of either literally or symbolically transcending death for those who live up to these standards of value; and (b) self-esteem, which is acquired by believing that one is living up to the standards of value inherent in one's cultural worldview" (Pyszczynski et al. 1999, 2). To provide "real-life evidence" of such a dual-component anxiety buffer, consisting of a cultural component that generates self-esteem and safety, we take a short look at gun culture in the United States.

Box 3.6 Gun culture in the United States

As a nation, the United States has a profound connection to guns, not only on a social or political level, but also as something that is deeply ingrained in the cultural identity of American society. Whether for protection, hunting, or sport shooting, gun owners consider gun ownership a form of personal freedom. Being able to defend themselves and to control their own environment generates a feeling of personal security and existential safety. According to the PEW Research Center, two-thirds of surveyed gun owners claim that protection is their main reason for owning a gun. The survey also shows that especially white male adults who live in rural areas and have low educational attainment are more likely to be gun owners. From a political perspective, more than four in ten Republicans and Republican-leaning independents are gun owners (forty percent), compared to twenty percent of Democrats. Republican gun owners are also much more resistant than Democratic gun owners to establishing a database for tracking gun sales and to banning high-capacity magazines; instead, they are more supportive of extending gun ownership rights. Ninety-one percent of Republican gun owners claim that owning a gun is essential to their freedom and safety (PEW 2017) and that gun control would deprive them of the opportunity to protect themselves from violent criminals (Lott 2000). In this regard, a psychological study assumes that this "white male effect" is derived from differences in cultural orientation. Individuals of "hierarchical and individualistic orientations should be expected to worry more about being rendered defenseless because of the association of guns with hierarchical social roles (hunter, protector, father) and with hierarchical and individualistic virtues (courage, honor, chivalry, self-reliance, prowess)" (Kahan et al. 2007, 474). By contrast, egalitarian and communitarian individuals are assumed to worry more about uncontrolled gun violence and its association with patriarchy, racism, and aggression. A gun may "fill" a social identity with a particular male role—a symbol of white male dominance and status. Therefore, the authors argue, it is these individualistic, hierarchical, white men whose identities are threatened by gun regulation and who reject the assertion that guns are dangerous (Kahan et al. 2007). The cultural theory of risk postulates that individuals form perceptions of threat that reflect their "cultural way of life." Individuals living in competitive, individualistic environments believe that they have to protect themselves without collective assistance or governmental support (Kahan 2012; Celinska 2007). Accordingly, gun ownership tends to provide a viable means of self-reliance, and thus serves the psychological need for "existential safety," self-efficacy, and control.

3.3.2 The Existential Need for Control

Alongside the human need to feel safe and secure, the human need for control displays a further important internal driver within the safety-seeking mechanism. The central assumption in modern cognitive psychology is that individuals actively seek to understand the social environment and their place within it. They aim to find explanations for unexpected events and to understand the system and their own position within that system. Believing that a particular situation can be fully understood, influenced, and managed has significant implications for one's mental and physical health. A sense of control, regardless of its true extent, has a tremendous impact on the mental and physical functioning of individuals and helps them to cope with existential anxieties (Kluegel and Smith 1986). Individuals exercise control over their environment by making decisions that express preferences and allow them to assert themselves. Having the possibility to make choices, no matter how small, reinforces one's perception of control and self-determination. According to the assumptions of Julien Rotter (1966), every individual has an internal and external locus of control. The internal locus of control describes the subjective belief that life events are within one's personal control, as opposed to the belief that events are uncontrollable (external locus of control) (Leotti et al. 2010). The more a person perceives having control over a situation, the less threatening the situation and the environment appear to them. Empirical studies reveal that humans and animals prefer choice over non-choice, even when the choice option does not imply an improvement in the expected outcome. In economic terms, the preference for choice and control in such conditions may be perceived as irrational. However, studies show that even the mere possibility to exercise control over a situation tends to be rewarding for the individual, leading to better physical and psychological conditions (Steptoe and Appels 1989) and even greater feelings of confidence and self-efficacy. "The benefits of perceived control can exist even in the absence of true control over aversive events, or if the individual has an opportunity to exert control but never actually exercises that option" (Leotti et al. 2010, 459). Both clinicians and researchers agree that psychological well-being is associated with the feeling of being able to control one's internal mental state and external environment. It has been shown that individuals with a physical illness who feel they have control over their disease or the stress resulting from the disease tend to have a more positive psychological adaptation, better moods, and higher life satisfaction. Individuals' sense of control can also have severe effects on mortality and morbidity. Often-cited studies on nursing-home residents provide evidence that those who were given control over external variables (such as the type and timing of meals and entertainment) or who were taught internal self-control practices tended to live longer than those in the control group (e.g., Rodin and Langer 1977). Similar studies of cancer patients support these results, showing that low perceived control and desperation about one's health tend to increase the probability of relapse and death (Shapiro et al. 1996).

This implies that perceived lack of control tends to increase feelings of helplessness and self-uncertainty, which appear to predict reduced somatic and psychological functioning (Gebhardt and Brosschot 2002). Observations of humans and animals in case of absent control reveal increased cortisol release, immune system suppression, and maladaptive behaviors. Experimental studies show that removing the possibility to exert control enhances feelings of anxiety, reinforces negative perceptions of the stimulus, and increases efforts to regain control (Leotti et al. 2010). Such negative responses have been observed in all age groups, ranging from four-month-old infants to adult to senior citizens (Sullivan and Lewis 2003). Accordingly, preference for control is perceived as a core intrinsic motivation and one of the strongest fundamental human needs. Individuals' ability to gain and maintain a sense of control thus seems to be essential to evolutionary survival (Bandura 1977; Deci and Ryan 2000).

Consequently, the threat of losing control increases levels of distress, which in turn boosts efforts to regain control. Such efforts can result in conformity, aggression, violence, and attitude change, or, if the attempt to regain control fails, in helplessness and withdrawal (Friedland et al. 1992). Self-blame or denial, for example, can provide an illusion of control. Studies show that low-income individuals attribute negative outcomes to their lack of ability, rather than to external conditions, because doing so allows them to sustain a sense of personal control. Attributing negative outcomes to uncontrollable external conditions (e.g., discrimination) implies that one cannot change or influence the environment and future outcomes, whereas self-attribution indicates that a person can potentially affect the outcomes (Kluegel and Smith 1986). Further assumptions indicate that attributing negative outcomes to external events, such as discrimination, tends to decrease individuals' self-esteem, self-efficacy, and social standing and is thus associated with high social costs (Kaiser and Miller 2001; Sechrist et al. 2004).

Distinguishing between "normal" and more pathological cases, individuals may also try to compensate for lack of control by asserting it in a different manner. Psychological studies show that behavioral and mental disorders can be partly explained by the need to restore control. *Anorexia nervosa* and *bulimia nervosa* are major eating disorders that are perceived as a mechanism to cope with problems involving personal control. By refocusing one's attention on weight, disciplined food consumption, and body shape, the individual gains emotional and physical control over their own body, eating habits, and the biological need for nutrition (Polivy and Herman 2002). Experimental evidence confirms that induced loss of control leads patients with an eating disorder to report feeling fatter, undisciplined, and more pessimistic (Waller and Hodgson 1996). Other mental disorders are also linked to a low sense of control and the inability to cope with potential threats. "Individuals suffering from anxiety and related disorders process failures or perceived deficiencies as an indication of a chronic inability to cope with unpredictable, uncontrollable, negative events, and this sense of uncontrollability is associated with negatively valenced emotional responding. Functional or "normal" individuals, on the other hand, seem to manifest what has been described as an *illusion of control* in which response deficiencies are attributed to passing external causes or trivial and temporary internal states" (Barlow 2000, 1254). Obsessive-compulsive disorder (OCD), for example, is an anxiety disorder that is characterized by obsessive, persistent thoughts and ritualized behavior. Obsession may be reflected in constant fears of contamination, pathological doubts, need for symmetry and order, or fears of inappropriate behavior. To deal with these fears and to reduce the distress associated with these obsessions, OCD individuals act compulsively. Such acts include repetitive washing, checking, and counting, which tend to provide perceived reassurance or symmetry attainment. Experimental evidence shows that such obsessive-compulsory symptoms in both clinical and non-clinical groups are observed in individuals who recently experienced uncontrollable stressful life events. This suggests that exogenous stressors dampen individuals' sense of control, which in turn increases their attempts to restore control—in the OCD case, through obsessive thoughts and rituals (Moulding and Kyrios 2006).

As we have seen, theoretical and empirical studies provide evidence that the perception of control is adaptive, that individuals strive to make choices, and that perceived loss of control causes stress for individuals. This implies that the perception of control affects cognition and behavior by regulating individuals' affective and cognitive processing. "Although the affective experience of choice itself has not been examined directly, there is converging evidence that implicates a corticostriatal network as the neural substrate for perceiving control. The prefrontal cortex (PFC) and striatum are highly interconnected and have been consistently implicated in affective and motivational processes. Certain regions within this corticostriatal network explicitly code for actions that are most adaptive in a given context" (Leotti et al. 2010, 460). That means that both animals and human beings desire to make active choices rather than being passive observers of their interactions with the environment. The possibility to make choices, and thus to influence the environment, recruits the neural circuitry involved in reward and cognitive processing. Neurocognitive studies show that rewards following choice activate the striatum to a greater extent than the same rewards that are passively received (no-choice option). Participants reported higher perception of control over monetary outcomes when the choice option was available, which indicates that choice itself is inherently rewarding (Tricomi et al. 2004). Other studies show that in stressful and threatening situations, perceived control can dampen and regulate negative emotions. In this context, the prefrontal cortex tends to play an important role in the top-down adjustment of emotional responses. Experiments show that rats responded stressfully to escapable and controllable shocks when their medial prefrontal cortex was deactivated. By contrast, when the medial prefrontal cortex was stimulated during uncontrollable shocks, rats demonstrated a reduced stress response (Amat et al. 2005). Even the perception of control, not actual control, leads to increased activity in the medial prefrontal cortex that moderates negative emotional responses in threatening situations. Accordingly, it is assumed that disruptions to the perception of control may occur as result of a malfunctioning medial prefrontal cortex. The apathy accompanying Alzheimer's disease, or the delusions of control observed in schizophrenic individuals, are associated with reduced metabolic activity in the (ventral) medial prefrontal cortex. This indicates that the need for control is an essential and biologically manifested component for survival (Leotti et al. 2010).

> **Box 3.7 The neural basis of the need for control**
>
> Individuals make decisions every day, ranging from the mundane (such as what to eat for lunch) to the difficult (such as the choice of a field of study). The ability to make such decisions generates a sense of self-efficacy and agency, which in turn refers to the perception of one's own ability to exercise control over the environment. "Such beliefs in personal control are known to be highly adaptive, for their presence or absence can have a profound impact on the regulation of behavior, emotion and physiology" (Leotti et al. 2015, 145). As we have seen, several studies provide evidence that the subjective sense of control can have palliative and rewarding effects, while control deprivation can lead to either compensatory or maladaptive behavior (Karsh and Eitam 2015). The opportunity to make choices and to reveal one's own preferences reflects one's own ability to exert control over the subjective environment. Individuals feel more confident and competent through their engagement with the environment and the expression of their choices, and thus preferences and

feelings (Leotti et al. 2015). While there is a rich history of research on the subjective belief of control (see, e.g., Leotti et al. 2010; Kay et al. 2009), the neural mechanisms of the need for control are still unexplored. However, the identification of neural mechanisms underlying control shows how the sense of control, even if illusionary, can have beneficial and adaptive effects. "Specifically, one can hypothesize that if expectations of control, via choice, are valuable and exert a rewarding feeling, then anticipation of choice opportunity should recruit brain structures involved in reward-related processes. A highly interconnected cortical-striatal network, modulated by dopaminergic neurons, has been implicated in processing reward information and fostering goal-directed behavior" (Leotti et al. 2015, 149). Brain regions that support such reward processes include the cortical and subcortical regions. Especially the striatum, which is responsible for instrumental learning, has been shown to play an important role in the processing and anticipation of rewards (O'Doherty et al. 2003). Empirical studies found increased striatal activity in response to the receipt of rewards, such as food or money, as well as to the anticipation of incoming rewards (e.g., Kirsch et al. 2003). Here, the dorsal striatum is perceived to be activated by stimuli with motivational incentives (rewards conditional upon behavior), whereas the ventral striatum responds to rewarding stimuli irrespective of the actions leading to rewards. Experimental studies show that individuals respond to rewards that are contingent upon behavior with enhanced activity in the striatum. Exerting control through choice seems to be more rewarding than passively receiving rewards (Leotti et al. 2015). One of the first neuroimaging studies that supports this assumption was conducted by Tricomi and colleagues (2004). In three experiments, the authors showed that participants reported perceiving greater control over outcomes that were "dependent" on their actions (even if illusionary). Here, the dorsal striatum was activated only for the "choice" condition, when participants believed that the outcomes were dependent on their decisions. This implies that the belief of having control over a situation (here, via choice vs. non-choice) induces higher rewards and is associated with greater activity in the striatum.

3.3.3 The Epistemic Need for Ambiguity Avoidance/Cognitive Closure

Box 3.8 What is ambiguity and why do we want to avoid it?

Suppose a patient must decide between two potential treatments: treatment A and treatment B. Treatment A is a standard method and has been used extensively. It therefore provides information on the probabilities of potential outcomes. Treatment B is a new method that has barely been used so far. There is little information on probabilities because no observations have been made about potential outcomes. While the probability of treatment A can be judged from relative frequencies or event histories, the probability of success of treatment B lacks considerable information. This decision problem implies two types of uncertainty: risk, or expected uncertainty; and ambiguity, or unexpected uncertainty. Risk, or expected uncertainty, is present where probabilities are objectively given, known, or observed thanks to past events (treatment A). Ambiguity, or unexpected uncertainty, implies that observers have incomplete knowledge about the environment (treatment B). The latter type of uncertainty can be reduced by accumulating information, e.g., by increasing the number of observations. Ambiguity generally increases when the environment changes to a new state (because there are relatively few observations of the new state) (O'Reilly 2013). Experiments in different disciplines showed that individuals are more willing to bet on risky options than on ambiguous ones (Hsu et al. 2005), which enhanced researchers' interest in studying people's subjective aversion to ambiguity. The difference between risk and ambiguity is best described using the well-known Ellsberg paradox. Consider two urns—A and B—each containing one hundred red and blue balls. The composition of the red and blue balls in urn A is not known, whereas urn B contains exactly fifty red and fifty blue balls. An individual is now asked to first choose an urn, and then to bet on a color to obtain a monetary reward. A bet on a color pays a fixed sum (e.g., $1) if a ball with the chosen color is pulled, and zero otherwise. Because individuals are free to choose which color is the winning one, the probability of a win for urn A is fifty percent. The same is true for urn B, with the only difference that the probability distribution for urn B is given. In such ambiguous situations, individuals must make a subjective estimate of the absent probabilities to make decisions. Consider the case where the individual guesses that urn A contains n red balls (and thus $100 - n$ blue balls). Because the individual is free to choose on which color to bet, the likelihood of winning is the average of the likelihoods of winning with red or blue balls, which would be the same as the unambiguous urn. However, in Ellsberg's experiment, as in many subsequent studies, most individuals preferred to avoid the ambiguous urn A and instead chose urn B, despite the potentially higher rewards associated with urn A (Hsu et al. 2005). This choice pattern corresponds to our first example, with the majority preferring treatment A over treatment B (Curley et al. 1986). Ambiguity can be thus defined as an unknown probability; that is, a decision-maker is aware of possible future events that may occur but does not have appropriate information to make subjective estimates (Weber and Tan 2012).

This raises the question of why individuals strive to reduce or even avoid ambiguous situations. Psychological studies reveal that most individuals tend to interpret an ambiguous situation as threatening (see, e.g., Campbell and Tesser 1983; Majid and Pragasam 1997). Ambiguity involves complexity, novelty, unpredictability, and uncertainty, which induces certain cognitive, emotional, and behavioral reactions enabling individuals to cope with the unknown. A cognitive reaction may include the tendency to assess an ambiguous situation rigidly in black or white; emotionally, individuals may respond with discomfort, anger, or anxiety; and a typical behavioral reaction refers to the tendency to reject or avoid ambiguous situations (Grenier et al. 2005). The motive to not choose the completely unknown option, which is perceived as potentially threatening, may be equally important as survival. Neurocognitive studies provide evidence that, under uncertainty, the brain is alerted to the fact that information is missing. The options based on this lack of information carry more unknown (and possibly dangerous) consequences. Therefore, the amygdala is encoding ambiguity by sending "fear signals" that help individuals to adapt and react to threatening environmental stimuli* (Payzan-LeNestour and Bossaerts 2012).

Psychological literature differentiates in this regard between intolerance of ambiguity and intolerance of uncertainty. Intolerance of ambiguity "refers to a static component embedded in the present. Individuals who are intolerant of ambiguity are unable to tolerate a 'here and now' situation characterized by equivocal or ambiguous features. In fact, these individuals interpret the present situation as a source of threat. On the other hand [intolerance of uncertainty] refers to an unpredictable component that is future oriented. Because future is characterized by uncertainty, these individuals interpret the future as a source of discomfort. Thus, those individuals who are intolerant of uncertainty will consider it unacceptable that a future and negative event may occur, however small the probability of its occurrence" (Grenier et al. 2005, 596). This time-oriented distinction in psychology implies that ambiguity avoidance refers to avoiding a threatening situation and uncertainty avoidance refers to avoiding potential negative events in the future.

This crucially raises the question of why certain individuals seek to avoid ambiguity while others strategically explore the unknown options.

But let's start from the beginning.

*We refrain from going deeper into the neurobiological foundation of ambiguity aversion. For more information see Hsu et al. (2005), Huettel et al. (2006), or Levy et al. (2010).

The epistemic need for ambiguity avoidance dates back to the work of Frenkel-Brunswik (1949) who defined intolerance of ambiguity as "a tendency to resort to black-white solutions, to arrive at premature closure as to evaluative aspects, often at the neglect of reality, and to seek for unqualified and unambiguous overall acceptance and rejection of other people" (Frenkel-Brunswik 1949, 115). According to this definition, ambiguity avoidance is a personality characteristic that tends to affect subjective psychological functioning in the cognitive, emotional, and behavioral domains. While the majority of researchers confirm that an intolerance of ambiguity is part of a cluster of subjective traits, alternative approaches consider exogenous factors, too. They argue that vast information, time pressure, or uncertain events or situations tend to reinforce feelings of threat. These in turn lead to increased uncertainty and anxiety, a rejection of the unknown, and a tendency to insist on predetermined conceptions, inter alia (Lauriola et al. 2016). Recent research on ambiguity avoidance has reconceptualized this definition by putting more emphasis on information processing and cognitive judgment. Accordingly, the desire for a definite answer to a question, the avoidance of uncertainty and confusion, and the inclination to use simpler cognitive structures to process information is summed up by the need for cognitive closure (Webster and Kruglanski 1994).

As a dispositional construct, the need for cognitive closure is manifested in the desire for predictability, order, and a stable cognitive structure. Information processing is seen as costly and effortful, which may induce uncertainty, confusion, and vacillation (Webster and Kruglanski 1997). The foregoing discussion suggests that the need for closure may vary depending on the situation at hand. Experimental evidence shows that time pressure increased subjects' tendency to draw on primed impressions and stereotype-driven judgments and to base appraisals on initial estimates (Kruglanski and Freund 1983; Sanbonmatsu and Fazio 1990). By changing the effort (costs) involved in information processing, subjects were more likely to show an over-attribution bias. Over-attribution bias describes the tendency of "attributors to overestimate the causal role of dispositional relative to situational factors when explaining an actor's behavior" (Webster 1993, 261). This means that individuals with a strong need for closure tend to judge faster (by generalizing and adopting a quick hypothesis on the basis of a person's disposition rather than the situation) when information processing is effortful and costly. Stereotype-driven inferences also arise if the information is inconsistent, which can lead to a rejection of the information source. Similar psychological studies on information processing postulate that subjects with a strong need for closure tend to prefer flat information sources (e.g., websites with fewer hyperlinks and less information), while those with a lower need for closure tend to prefer exhaustive information sources (e.g., interactive websites with vast information). Thus, strong-need-for-closure individuals tend to reject or avoid large amounts of information that may imply ambiguity, instead preferring to base their decisions on predetermined judgments, heuristics, or theory-driven anecdotes. Relying on a consistent and reliable set of knowledge that can be generalized across situations reduces ambiguity and enhances the perception of a certain and predictable environment (Amichai-Hamburger et al. 2004).

Standard economic theory on individual behavior assumes that individuals prefer more information to make better decisions. Although there are countless situations where individuals seek out or even pay for useless information (Powdthavee and Riyanto 2015), contrary evidence shows that individuals also prefer to avoid receiving information (Golman et al. 2017). Laboratory and field research shows that investors, for example, avoid looking at their financial portfolios when the stock market is down (Sicherman et al. 2016), or that individuals with higher health risks often reject medical tests even if the information could improve their decision-making. Active information avoidance is characterized by two criteria: awareness of the available information, and free and effortless access to this information. "In most situations information is costly to obtain (carrying an opportunity cost, at least) . . . If a medical test is expensive, an individual who foregoes the test may do so due to its cost, a preference to not find out the information . . . Indeed, it is even possible that people could use the cost to justify, to themselves or to others, a decision to avoid getting tested that actually had other motives" (Golman et al. 2017, 97). Accordingly, information avoidance can have personal and economic consequences. It prevents individuals from making appropriate decisions and receiving potentially valuable feedback, and it can lead to political polarization and media bias. However, information avoidance can also have positive utility effects. Economic-theoretical models on belief-based utility (e.g., Köszegi 2010; Caplin and Leahy 2001) assume that individuals derive their utility not only from their objective reality but also from the beliefs and information they obtain about that reality. Thus, information avoidance can occur if individuals hold favorable beliefs about reality that they do not want to dilute (Golman and Loewenstein 2018).

In an experimental study, subjects either took an IQ test or had their attractiveness rated by other subjects. Before receiving the final results, participants obtained confidential preliminary feedback that hinted at their possible final results. Subjects who initially received information about their IQ rating or attractiveness that was unfavorable relative to their expectations were less likely to prefer receiving full information, or were even willing to spend money on avoiding that information (Eil and Rao 2011). Other studies found similar results, showing that some individuals were willing to invest money to avoid obtaining test results for HSV-1 and HSV-2, an incurable herpes simplex virus (Ganguly and Tasoff 2017). This implies that individuals derive utility from avoiding unfavorable or threatening information. "A number of studies in both psychology and economics find that people weigh and interpret evidence in a fashion that supports what they are motivated to believe, and that they tend to denigrate the quality of evidence that contradicts beliefs that they hold or would like to hold" (Golman et al. 2017, 101). Thus, individuals strive to reject information that implies threat, negative emotions such as anxiety and uncertainty, a high probability of a negative outcome in the future, and a negative self-concept. Receiving information about one's bad health may increase utility gains from receiving medical treatment in the future, but it also causes disutility from accrued negative emotions and changed attitudes about one's own personality and lifestyle.

3.3.4 The Epistemic Need for Consistency

The need for ambiguity avoidance (or cognitive closure) is associated with the epistemic need for consistency and predictability. Research in the area of cognitive consistency first appeared in psychological literature during the 1950s. Initially described under various names (balance, dissonance, symmetry, congruency, etc.), the terms "had in common the notion that the person tends to behave in ways that minimize the internal inconsistency among his interpersonal relations, among his intrapersonal cognitions, or among his beliefs, feelings and actions" (McGuire 1966, 1). Festinger's (1957) theory on cognitive dissonance is one of the most recognized theories in social psychology. He postulates that cognitive inconsistencies induce a state of arousal (dissonance) which in turn produces the need to reduce such contradictions and to restore a state of consonance (Gawronski 2012). Inconsistency may arise when an individual holds two or more elements of knowledge (ideas, beliefs, values) that are relevant to each other but contradictory—a cognitive conflict between the already held belief and the truth or newly acquired evidence. These cognitive inconsistencies may generate uncertainty, anxiety, self-doubts, and confusion. To minimize the accrued negative feelings and the contradictions between one's own perception and acquired evidence, individuals tend to respond by changing their cognitions (McGuire 1966). The need for consistency has been found to be as important and basic as the need for survival and water. The fundamental nature of the need arises because it signals potential "errors" in one's system of beliefs. These "errors" or inconsistencies require a reassessment of one's beliefs because cognitive inconsistency may disrupt context-appropriate behavior and lead to inadequate courses of action. Thus, the state of arousal which is triggered by inconsistencies serves as a signal that one's own current belief system has to be revised to deal with the environment (Gawronski 2012).

However, a large body of research suggests that individuals are more often concerned with their emotions than with accuracy. It is argued that restoring consistency is not the fundamental motive but instead the accrued affective consequences of inconsistencies (Kruglanski and Shteynberg 2012). Newly acquired information, for example, may appear threatening because it conflicts with one's existing belief system. Thus, individuals may accept inconsistencies in their beliefs because restoring consistency requires great cognitive effort or even a change in attitude (Kluegel and Smith 1986). Empirical research shows that individuals often resort to stereotypes or heuristics instead of rationally considering all relevant information to acquire complete consistency in their beliefs and opinions (e.g., Degner and Wentura 2010). Searching for shortcuts as efficient and fast solutions to problems, or using categorizing methods, helps subjects to cope with inconsistencies. Instead of questioning their predominant belief system, individuals tend to "ignore" cognitive arousal and instead use ready-made explanations to defend their interpretation of the environment. Furthermore, individuals may eliminate the information that leads to cognitive inconsistencies by rejecting or degrading the mediator. Other methods to evade cognitive inconsistencies include searching for congruent information and substitution or changing one's set goals. Empirical studies show that individuals tend to prefer information that coincides with their attitudes, beliefs, and actions over dissonant and contradictory information (Schultz-Hardt et al. 2000; Jonas et al. 2001). A prominent example of the reduction in cognitive inconsistencies is a habitual cigarette smoker who is told that smoking is unhealthy. According to the theoretical approach, the smoker intends to reduce the dissonant information by changing their habitual pattern. So, they change their cognition about their behavior by changing their actions. Quitting, or no smoking at all, is consistent with the information (new knowledge) that smoking impairs one's health. Although this sounds plausible, in reality individuals tend to adopt other methods to dampen this cognitive arousal. This means that the smoker may adjust their knowledge about the effects of smoking by rejecting the received information. Because cognitive inconsistency implies uncertainty and negative feelings about oneself, the smoker may reject the received information or try to find facts or opinions that support their smoking behavior (Festinger 1957).

Finding alternatives to eliminate contradictions and reach cognitive consistency is part of the self-affirming and image-maintaining approach. The goal of the rationalization and justification process is to maintain overall self-integrity. Faced with a threat to one's own self, the subject can also accept the threat without countering it by instead emphasizing some other important aspects of their self. The habitual smoker, for example, having realized that every rationalization for smoking is socially disqualified, still copes with the cognitive arousal and self-threat by emphasizing other personal traits (e.g., a strong work ethic, to sustain their sense of self-worth). Personality research postulates that individuals with high self-esteem and a positive self-image feel less threatened by dissonant information and thus feel less pressure to rationalize the self-implications of this perceived threat (Steele et al. 1993). The preference-for-consistency scale shows that individuals with a strong preference for consistency also have high preferences for preservation, compliance, uniformity, and coherence (Cialdini et al. 1995).

Cross-cultural psychology studies show that cultural differences, too, determine how cognitive inconsistencies and self-related threats are perceived and processed. Individuals with North American cultural backgrounds construct their autonomous selves independently from others and their environment. The independent self is characterized by personal attributes, and individuals' behavior corresponds to their attitudes, emotions, and judgments. By contrast, the interdependent self of individuals from Asian cultural backgrounds is characterized by a subjective effort to connect to others. The behavior of individuals is governed by constraints and obligations and is not implicitly viewed as a reflection of individuals' inner thoughts and perceptions. This suggests that individuals who base their identity on internal attributes, such as their own attitudes and opinions, experience any dissonance involving these attributes as a self-related threat. "Viewing one's attitudes as inconsistent with one's behaviors, or one's decisions as unsound, then, may pose a significant threat to North Americans' self-integrity. Such attributes are not likely to be easily compromised and individuals should be motivated to go to great lengths to reduce the dissonance. [. . .] In contrast, the core of the identity of the interdependent self (the Asian) lies more within the individual's roles, positions, and relationships. Internal attributes are patently less relevant to such persons' identities. Hence, inconsistencies between one's attitudes and behavior, or thoughts that one may have made a poor decision, are likely to be relative tangential to such an individual's self-identity" (Heine and Lehman 1997, 391). Their behavior is mainly determined by the obligations and responsibilities assigned by the individual's social roles and statuses. Subjective behavior is thus less attributed to the actor's dispositions than to situational demands (e.g., an obligation to make a decision in accordance with social requirements), whereas in North American cultures, subjective decision-making and behavior is more likely attributed to the actor's dispositions than to situational factors. In other words, in North American cultures the possibility to exercise one's freedom of choice is a way to define oneself. Being told that one has made a bad choice would thus generate cognitive inconsistency for a North American individual because it is directed at the core of their own self. Conversely, being told that one has made a bad choice would not pose a self-related threat to Asian individuals because they define their identity not on internal attributes but on social factors (e.g., relationships, roles, and status). The cultural concept of an interdependent identity is rather grounded in belongingness, interconnectedness, and interpersonal harmony with significant others than in subjective thoughts, beliefs, and perceptions (see review Heine and Lehman 1997).

> **Box 3.9 "Shattered Assumptions" and the need for consistency after life-threatening and traumatic events**
>
> "At the core of our internal world, we hold basic views of ourselves and our external world that represent our orientation toward the 'total push and pull of the cosmos,'" (1992, 4) writes Janoff-Bulman in her book, *Shattered Assumptions*. These basic views, beliefs, or assumptions form a conceptual system that enables the individual to interact with and adapt to the external environment. The author proposes that almost all individuals strive to perceive the environment they live in as just and benevolent. The world and one's personal existence must appear meaningful and the self as worthy and impactful. Individuals need a stable and reliable conceptual system to deal with the complex world and thus strive to maintain cognitive consistency. However, violent assaults, conflicts, natural disasters, or terrorist attacks, all which threaten individuals' physical and psychological existence, tend to "shatter" these fundamental assumptions of a meaningful and benevolent world. The self is perceived as helpless and fragile, the environment as dangerous and life-threatening. Such a cognitive disturbance or "disconnection" from oneself and the environment (because the traumatic events cannot be easily integrated with previously held world views) gives rise to anxiety and mental disorders (Edmondson et al. 2011). After such threatening events, individuals tend to engage in strategies to decrease their accrued negative feelings and resolve the contradictions between their own perception and acquired evidence. Janoff-Bulman argues that such (mostly unconscious) strategies are essentially natural products of a human organism seeking "mental equilibrium" after a life-threatening event.
>
> Psychotherapeutic research on potentially traumatic events suggests that trauma-induced cognitive inconsistency creates a sense of adversarial tension in an organism and helps revise one's previously held assumptions. "When the assumptive world is revised to take into account the trauma-related information, people are said to have accommodated their experiences. In contrast, when the trauma-related information is perceived in such a way as to be consistent with preexisting beliefs, they are said to have assimilated their experiences" (Payne et al. 2007, 76).* Assimilation is mostly achieved by downgrading or rejecting negative (threatening and traumatic)

information and reaffirming, or even rigidly defending, previously held beliefs (e.g., endorsing own faith, supporting a certain political leader or party, justifying the system or certain circumstances, and engaging in self-blame). Accommodation, in turn, involves questioning one's previously held beliefs and attitudes which can take both a negative and positive direction.[**] Negative accommodation may produce negative and depressive assumptions about one's self and the environment (e.g., the world as a hostile and unfair place, one's own helplessness, meaninglessness of life, low self-worth), while positive accommodation may trigger a positive outlook and personal growth (e.g., life appreciation, using one's own experience to help others, etc.) (Joseph and Linley 2008).

[*]*The* authors provide an analogy: Imagine a vase has been shattered. Someone wants to restore it and has several ways to do so. One would be to put the pieces back together exactly as they were (assimilation), but that would make the vase fragile and marred by fractures. Alternatively, the individual can put it in the trash (negative accommodation) or use the fragments to build something new (positive accommodation).

[**]*How* individuals deal and cope with traumatic and life-threatening situations is influenced by personality, available resources, the social environment, and memory representations (Joseph and Linley 2008).

3.3.5 The Epistemic Need for Predictability

Ignoring, rejecting, or re-interpreting information using heuristics and stereotypes or searching for shortcut solutions are all viable techniques for coping with one's social environment. A clear and meaningful cognitive structure with predominant views, explanations, stereotypes, and categorizations provides order and predictability. Early theories on the need for predictability appeared in the psychological literature during the 1950s (Pervin 1963). They assumed that subjects' belief in a predictable social environment increased their perceived safety, self-certainty, and comfort. Experimental studies have shown that both animals and humans prefer to have information about the onset of aversive stimuli, even if that information has no significant value. Being able to receive information about a possible event reduces stress because it allows humans and nonhumans to predict important aspects of the situation and thus to better adjust to the given circumstances (for a review see Miller 1979). The ability to self-administer and predict electric shocks, rather than having them administered by the experimenter, reduces stress and results in less physiological arousal (measured by galvanic skin response). The possibility to predict electric shocks enables individuals to react according to the significance of the received stimuli, while an inability to predict the shocks enhances the perceived importance of all stimuli. This means that having predictable information about events helps individuals to experience and react appropriately to stressful events. It reduces their subjective feelings of helplessness, cognitive tension, and confusion (Staub et al. 1971).

Personality research assumes that anxious-ambivalent and avoidant individuals, who prefer order and cognitive closure, also tend to have a greater need for predictability. Especially uncertain individuals seem to be less tolerant of ambiguity, unpredictability, and disorder and hold dogmatic pre-defined beliefs that can be relied on in any situation. However, research indicates that uncertain subjects do not reject new information per se, but do feel uncomfortable when presented with new evidence if it induces confusion and ambiguity. By contrast, certain open-minded personalities tend to maintain a positive attitude toward unpredictable information. They are confident in their ability to deal with any stressful or threatening situation and have a high tolerance for unpredictability, disorder, and ambiguity. Also, self-assured individuals tend to reject rigid and dogmatic beliefs by integrating new information to make decisions and social judgments without relying on predefined cognitive systems. This suggests that certain individuals are cognitively flexible, which allows them to adjust easily to new situations and environmental changes (Mikulincer 1997).

Other studies show that people with a high need for predictability tend to adhere to social norms and rules which provide a predictable form of behavior and social interaction (Kiesler 1973). Norm violators or individuals who do not comply with pre-defined role models are perceived as a threat and are thus rejected by individuals with a strong preference for predictability. An empirical study using community samples from the United Kingdom and Belgium showed that individuals with a high need for predictability, order, and cognitive closure tend to reject individuals who do not conform to social conventions and predefined social roles (e.g., gender). Obedient individuals adhere closely to social rules, respect authority, and endorse traditional gender roles and prescribed social hierarchies. A predictable social structure generates certainty and order and guides behavior and information processing. The results of the study revealed that participants who prefer predictable social structures tend to reject especially individuals who are perceived as violating society's traditional social roles and expectations of gender because they do not correspond to the cognitively consistent and predictable social structures they tend to rely on (Makwana et al. 2018).

Using functional magnetic resonance imaging (fMRI), a neurocognitive study measured the effect of predictability on human brain responses to sequences of pleasurable stimuli. In the experimental setting the participants received small amounts of orally delivered water and juice in either a predictable or unpredictable sequence. During the predictable sequence, the order of juice and water was alternated at a fixed interval of ten seconds, while in the unpredictable sequence the order and the stimulus interval were randomized. After the scan session, subjects were asked to state their preferences for water or juice. The results show that the activity in the reward system correlated more with the predictability of a sequence of the pleasurable stimuli than with stated preferences. The brain response to the previously stated preferred beverage showed little differential activity relative to the nonpreferred beverage. The main effect of predictability was greater than the main effect of stated preference (Berns et al. 2001). Another study provides evidence that individuals search for predictability in the shape of rules that govern decision-making even in the presence of randomness (Paulus et al. 2001). A common claim in neuroscience is that the brain actively predicts upcoming stimuli to code information efficiently. The predictability of sensory input alters the processing of upcoming stimuli and is efficient "in the sense that the brain does not need to maintain multiple versions of the same information at different levels of processing hierarchy" (de-Wit et al. 2010, 8702). Consequently, predictable stimuli require less neural activation to be transferred from lower to higher cortices and thus influence the representation of the subjective experience of the stimuli. Another study reports correlations between risk prediction and the physiological arousal of financial traders, while yet another finds that identical pain stimuli are rated as more painful when they are unpredictable rather than predictable. Unpredictable pain stimuli result in increased ratings of anxiety and uncertainty, whereas predictability allows subjects to conceptualize a response to an external aversive event, which results in lower anxiety and fear ratings (Carlsson et al. 2006).

> **Box 3.10 Can the ability to predict the likelihood of an aversive event reduce subjective pain and anxiety?**
>
> As we have seen, the ability to make predictions reduces uncertainty and threat, but it also tends to reduce pain. Recent neuroimaging studies have attempted to differentiate between brain responses associated with the expectation of pain and those associated with a direct experience of pain. This separation is important because both processes imply distinct adaptive processes and consequences. In an fMRI study, twelve healthy participants were presented with a pseudo-random sequence of two levels of thermal stimulation. Colored lights informed them beforehand whether a nonpainful warm or painful hot thermal stimulation was induced. Hence, during the imaging sessions subjects learned about the relationship between the light color and the intensity of the stimuli. The authors identified three brain regions (medial

frontal lobe, insular cortex, and cerebellum) where responses to direct pain could be segregated from those to predicted pain. This implies that the neural substrates of the experience of pain and its prediction can be separated by the involvement of different brain regions. Activation in the "usual pain regions" was consistent from trial 1 while the activation in the distinct "prediction regions" increased through a learning process. Based on this learning process, a schematic model of pain was developed enabling individuals to make predictions about future pain events (Ploghaus et al. 1999). Early predictions of pain tend to make pain less threatening and direct one's appropriate pre-emptive behavior (adaptation). In other words, predicting incoming pain generates subjective certainty that a negative event is imminent, which enables the organism to "prepare" and adjust. The release of fear mobilizes the organism to take action (fight or flight) or, if this option is not available, to minimize the impact of the incoming stimuli (e.g., by cognitive distraction). "In contrast, uncertainty about the nature of the impending event ('uncertain expectation') has very different consequences. It is associated with the emotional state of anxiety (rather than fear) which is characterized by risk assessment behavior or behavioral inhibition, and by increased somatic and environmental attention (rather than by distraction, as in the case of fear). Compared with fear, anxiety has the opposite effect on pain perception: it has been shown to lead to increased pain sensitivity or hyperalgesia"[*] (Ploghaus et al. 2003, 197). These findings may lead us to assume that predictability enables individuals to "effectively" process incoming information and (mentally) adjust to certain circumstances even if they cannot be avoided. It generates subjective certainty and the perception that "one can control the situation." The possibility to "predict" future events or incoming information reduces the perception of threat and stress, because it allows the individual to foretell some important aspects of a situation. This, in turn, provides existential safety because individuals "know" when the next negative stimuli are imminent, which reduces cognitive overload (permanent evaluation of incoming stimuli).

[*]*Hyperalgesia* is an increased perception of pain (see for more information, see Purves et al. 2001).

3.3.6 The Epistemic Need for Order

Box 3.11 Individual differences in the personal need for structure and order

"Each person, each stimulus that meets our senses changes our environment, at times challenging our sense of knowing what to expect from the environment. Without structuring this array into coherent units that provide meaning, the world would be experienced as chaos" (Thompson et al. 2013, 19). Individuals strive to reduce chaos and disorder in their lives. But why? First, to ensure survival individuals try to "structure" the incoming stimuli into coherent units to avoid danger and approach potential rewards. This enables them to determine which stimuli in the environment are pleasurable (and thus species-promoting) and which are troublesome. Categorization, for example, is one cognitive tool that can be used to structure and predict stimuli and shape subsequent actions. It produces meaning behind every stimulus that allows individuals to predict, act, and react. This suggests that humans generally have a need to establish a set of causal explanations that account for environmental stimuli. Organizing the environment into coherent meaning reduces uncertainty and self-doubt and generates a sense of control. This, in turn, helps to reduce the feeling of living in a random universe, which is essential for avoiding feelings of helplessness and uncontrollability. However, psychological literature assumes that individuals differ in terms of their subjective tolerance for indeterminacy. An individual with a high need for structure and order prefers a structural categorization of the social environment, clarity in most situations, and reduced ambiguity. To them, an ordered environment is a place where they can make consistent decisions and act confidently (Thompson et al. 2013). Accordingly, such individuals dislike unpredictable environments or individuals who do not conform to the predefined social order or who even disturb or threaten established settings. They are thus rejected in an effort to protect the certainty and stability provided by the established order (e.g., Brand and Reyna 2010). Personality studies using the personal need for structure scale (PNS) have shown that individuals high in the need for structure tend to apply stereotypes and rely on social categories to make judgments and decisions. Furthermore, they are more likely to apply predefined attitudes and beliefs to new situations, rely on stereotypical notions to evaluate other people, and have simpler ways of organizing social information (Moskowitz 1993). Behaviorally, such individuals establish daily routines and rely on predefined roles and schemata, or even prefer hierarchical structures, that reduce the amount of information they must process on a daily basis. Such a cognitive order enables individuals to draw inferences about new events and thus to understand the world without expending a lot of cognitive resources (Neuberg and Newsom 1993). Other studies go further and show that social conformity and the need for structure positively interrelate with right-wing authoritarian attitudes (RWA), which involve submissiveness vis-à-vis authorities, aggressiveness against norm violators, and adherence to traditional norms (Jugert et al. 2009).

These individual differences in the need for order show that individuals strive to understand their social environment and find coping mechanisms so they can deal with complexity and indeterminacy. Here, psychologists suggest that to cope with negative emotions, self-uncertainty, and cognitive confusion, individuals may adopt problem-focused and emotion-focused coping strategies. Problem-focused coping strategies are a direct way to attack an uncertain and ambivalent situation, which involves much cognitive effort and a change in attitude. Revising one's own perceptions and expectations to make them consistent with one's experiences is referred to as accommodation. The individual accepts the ambivalent or uncertain situation and adapts their own attitudes to achieve cognitive consistence. By contrast, emotion-focused strategies are more indirect and focus rather on reducing the negative emotions associated with ambiguity or uncertainty rather than on the attitude per se (van Harreveld et al. 2014). Threats to one's own self-esteem and meaning in life, cognitive confusion, or uncertainty trigger a demand for cognitive and mental compensation. Assimilation, as discussed before, involves reinterpreting experiences to make them consistent with one's beliefs and expectations. Individuals tend to create their own perspectives and an ordered conceptual system of reality and of themselves, which they use to understand events, cope with unexpected circumstances, and construct future plans. Such a system is composed of basic assumptions and principles that are abstract enough to be applied to any event or situation and thus make life more comprehensible. It guides and reflects social interactions and provides an ordered cognitive structure. This ordered cognitive system reduces ambiguity and provides a reliable tool for adjusting rapidly to given circumstances (Proulx et al. 2012).

A suitable example observed in empirical studies is that individuals generally believe that one gets what one deserves. When this "cognitive order" is violated, individuals tend to assimilate the event to restore cognitive consistency (e.g., blaming victims for their own misfortune). Such cognitive categorizations influence how the perceiver interprets incoming stimuli. One important theoretical framework for explaining victim-blaming is the deservingness model. This model has been used, for example, to account for how individuals react to penalties that are imposed if someone commits an offense. Empirical studies show that individuals' need for order and the offender's perceived responsibility ultimately determine the degree to which the offense is perceived as serious (Feather 2006). Such a crime or offense may be perceived as a violation of legitimate authority such as the rule of law or social order. However, "when people are confronted with others (such as innocent victims) who get something that they do not deserve, people's principles of deservingness are violated. As a result, people need to restore their belief that the world is a just place in which good things happen to good people and bad things to bad people. Especially when the events that have happened cannot be changed, people often tend to come to the conclusion that victims somehow deserved their ill fates and are to be blamed for what happened to them" (van den Bos and Maas 2009, 1567).

Some psychological researchers claim that when individuals are confronted with ambivalence or perceived loss of control, the need for order becomes affirming (van Harreveld et al. 2014). This need can be served, for example, by social hierarchies that reflect a form of social structure and interpersonal organization. Empirical studies show that after external shocks such as economic crises or terrorist attacks, individuals tend to adhere more strongly to hierarchy-promoting social structures because they provide order, certainty, and consistency in their lives (Friesen et al. 2014). Giving the world a simplified and manageable form reduces threats and generates the illusion of a controllable environment. Empirical studies provide evidence that individuals with a strong need for order/structure are more likely to organize information in simpler ways and to apply previously formed social categories to new and ambiguous situations (Neuberg and Newsom 1993).

Relying on predefined social and cognitive structures (e.g., stereotypes) generates a clear, predictable, and unambiguous environment. Unlike egalitarian structures, hierarchies offer rules about who should be doing what, about interpersonal patterns, and about one's role in the system. Thus, hierarchies appear to provide a cognitive sense of order and structure, especially for low-status individuals who appear to have a low sense of personal control (Friesen et al. 2014). Order is generated by restrictions, obligations, prescribed roles, norms, and rules that dictate what kind of behaviors are permitted or prohibited. This social order implies certain expectations and actions that guide appropriate social behavior (Cummins 2000).

Evolutionary biologists and neuroscientists provide evidence that social hierarchies are deeply rooted in the biology and evolutionary history of our brains. Social interactions, adaptations, and behaviors are formed and learned in social groups and hierarchies. Neuroimaging studies show that the brain uses different learning algorithms when absorbing social hierarchies in competitive versus non-competitive situations (Chen et al. 2017). Yet others show that ventral striatal responses to social status information depend on the subjective socioeconomic situation. Nonhuman primates high in the hierarchical order preferentially associate with other high-order primates, whereas low-status primates attend to both high- and low-status primates. Similar results have been found for human participants, with the exception that low-status individuals tend to put slightly more value on higher-ranked individuals than on low-status individuals (Ly et al. 2011). Another fMRI study shows that subjective social rank tends to determine how individuals process and perceive their environment. Low-status individuals show greater neural activity in a brain region of the mentalizing network (including DMPFC, MPFC, and precuneus/PCC) which indicates that lower-status subjects are more social group-oriented. A subsequent study reveals that low-status individuals show higher amygdala activity during threat processing (Muscatell et al. 2012). This suggests that they experience higher levels of stress and increased cortisol release.

A pharmacological experiment with male rats showed that those with stronger amygdala activity became subordinate in the hierarchy that was formed. Exposure to different types of emotional or physical stress released oxytocin and arginine vasopressin in different brain areas, which seems to be a mechanism for dynamic changes in social behavior. In other words, the rats with a stronger release of stress hormones in a stressful or threatening situation became subordinates in the established hierarchy and adhered to the hierarchy longer than non-stressed rats (Timmer et al. 2011). This means that hierarchically induced order tends to reduce stressful reactions to threat, providing instead predictable and reliable guidance on how to process information and act in a given setting. Another neural study provides evidence that "individuals who indicated greater desire for social [dominance] hierarchy showed less response when perceiving pain in others within fronto-insular regions critical to the ability to share and feel concern for the emotional salience of another person's misfortune" (Chiao et al. 2009, 180). This implies that social hierarchies and structured organizations serve the need for order and help individuals to restore structure and meaning in their lives. Furthermore, they tend to reduce uncertainty and increase one's sense of personal control, especially (but not limited to) for those individuals who feel socially low-ranked.

4
Relational Needs and Need Deprivation

The previous chapters identified crucial socioeconomic mechanisms and exogenous conditions that can deprive individuals of serving their existential and epistemic needs. Our bodies and brains react to an unmet human need, which gives rise to internal drive states and pushes individuals to find ways to cope with the arousal. Threats, uncertainty, and lack of opportunity to serve one's own needs can, in extreme cases, lead to aggression, rioting, and conflictual human behavior. However, besides threatening, stressful, and uncertain factors, inherent aspects related to identity formation, social identification, interaction, and cooperation contribute toward explaining human behavior. Evidence of human evolution shows that cooperation, socializing, and pro-sociality are all factors which tend to enhance individuals' survival and continued existence. Individuals enhance their fitness through cooperation, resource-sharing, and affiliation with significant others. Identification enables individuals to sympathize with ingroup members, to understand their behavior, and to develop and show empathy (de Waal 1996, 1998).

In the following section we thus discuss the significance of social identity and how social interaction, identification, and cooperation with significant others form our self-concept and assure psychological well-being. We explore the effects of group membership and explain why identification, social approval, and cooperation play a significant role in the human need system. We discuss the processes of identity formation, social categorization, and identification and show how they influence the way individuals perceive themselves and their environment. In this regard, we also focus on aspects that can accentuate intergroup differences and enhance intergroup rivalry and conflict. Despite our emphasis on the conflictual and negative outcomes of need deprivation, we also show that human beings have an innate drive to behave in a prosocial manner; that is, to benefit others in an unselfish way. For better guidance, we start with a discussion of identity in general and show how identity formation can instigate a number of processes and affect individuals' perception of reality and the self. Here, innate conflicts which can arise during identity formation, and which can certainly be triggered by external factors (e.g., social exclusion, identity confusion, perceived threat, or traumatic events), can lead to severe need deprivation. We therefore discuss the fundamentality of these relational human needs and explain how need deprivation can lead to both antisocial and social behavior.

4.1 The Concept of Identity

The concept of identity has a rich tradition in scientific research and offers a multidimensional variety of meanings and interpretations from philosophers, anthropologists, sociologists, psychologists, and recently also from economists and neurobiologists. In general terms, identity has been referred to an individual's sense of self that is defined by multiple variables, such as physical, psychological, and interpersonal characteristics that are distinct to the individual, as well as a range of affiliations and social roles (American Psychological Association 2019b). Personal identity, in this sense, consists of various features that can change over time. In philosophy, these features, or "identifiers," are perceived to be unique in nature and distinguish one subject from another. Thus, identity is embraced in the first place predominantly as a sense of individuality and as a non-given construct that must be formed and accepted by every human being (Staub 2001). It is not physical appearance that is regarded as a major characteristic of the self, but rather the creations, actions, and self-expressions of the individual. Kant goes further and postulates the significance of self-awareness and cognitive reflection, known as the consciousness of the self (Sollberger 2013). Being aware of oneself and having the feeling that one's memories, goals, and preferences belong to oneself provides a sense of continuity and consistency (consistent and stable self) (Schwartz et al. 2017).

While in philosophy identity is perceived as the uniqueness of the concerned object (the persistent sameness of the self) (Sollberger 2013), in social psychology it is defined as a dynamic expression and perception of oneself and one's identification and affiliation with significant others (the persistent self within a social context). "The term identity expresses such a mutual relation in that it connotes both a persistent sameness within oneself (self-sameness) and a persistent sharing of some kind of essential character with others. [...] At one time, it will appear to refer to a conscious sense of individual identity; at another to an unconscious striving for a continuity of personal character; at a third, as a criterion for the silent doings of ego synthesis; and finally, as a maintenance of an inner solidarity with a group's ideals and identity" (Erikson 1956, 57). Accordingly, identity is shaped by both self-awareness and an interaction with one's external environment. Identity is thus a synergy between the inner coherence of mental states and the social environment, which can generate subjective conflicts between acceptance vs. expression, adaptation vs. individualism, social dynamic vs. old traditions, and solidarity vs. egoism (Erikson 1968). This implies that individuals are faced with the task of forming a coherent and "balanced" identity, characterized by a clear and stable self-definition with an inner continuity of values, attitudes, and beliefs.

Although personality psychologists argue that social tightness and stigmatized role ascriptions dampen the formation of a distinctive self or even harm the dynamic evolvement of a personal identity (Alarcon and Foulks 1995), social psychologists insist that social interaction, cooperation, and affiliation are inevitable factors in identity formation (Simon and Hamilton 1994). According to the self-categorization theory (Turner 1987) and social identity theory (Tajfel and Turner 1979), affiliation and group belongingness represent crucial internal parts of the subjective self. A social identity is a person's awareness that they belong to a particular group or social category, which induces self-categorization and social comparison processes (Stets and Burke 2000). In the self-categorization process, individuals perceive similarities between themselves and other ingroup members and differences between themselves and outgroup members. Ingroup categorization can be emphasized in terms of shared attitudes, norms, values, affective reactions, styles of speech, and other properties that are perceived to be specific to the ingroup (Hornsey 2008). The social comparison process implies an evaluation of the ingroup and the outgroup on dimensions that lead to a positive rating of the ingroup and a negative rating of the outgroup—resulting in self-enhancing outcomes for oneself. This suggests that individuals derive their sense of self from the social categories to which they believe they belong.

The idea of social identity was first framed by an experiment in which participants were assigned to groups on the basis of redundant and random criteria. Having been told their group membership, participants had to allocate points to their ingroup and to the outgroup. Despite the random group allocation, the lack of interaction within the group members, and the level of anonymity, participants allocated more points to "their" ingroup—even if this had no personal benefits (Billig and Tajfel 1973). This has been explained by the intergroup interaction approach, where individuals relate entirely as representatives of their groups by deriving their self-image from the social categories to which they belong (Hornsey 2008). Interacting, cooperating, and identifying with significant (social) others generates feelings of self-confidence and self-worth and has significant effects on one's subjective mental well-being (Usborne and Sablonnière 2014). A study with 2,109 Filipino Americans provides evidence that both affiliation and identification with a social group increase one's mental well-being and serve as a buffer against negative and discriminatory events (Mossakowski 2003). Another survey shows that stroke patients who identified with and belonged to a particular group prior to the stroke were more likely to report higher levels of psychological well-being and a faster recovery after a stroke (Haslam et al. 2008). Other studies assert that individuals with greater social connectedness are better able to manage their resources, have higher self-esteem, and are less prone to mood disorders. They are also more capable of adapting to new social situations, entering new groups, and starting conversations easily (Lee and Robbins 1998).

> **Box 4.1 Social identity, ingroup favoritism and conflict**
>
> The experiment of Billig and Tajfel (1973) shows that despite the random group allocation and the lack of interaction within and between the groups, clear group preferences were formed. This led to increased interest in the study of ingroup favoritism and outgroup ostracism. Individuals often make comparisons between their own ingroup and an outgroup and are concerned to promote their attitude that "we" are better than "them." Thus, intergroup comparisons are usually characterized by ethnocentrism and outgroup antagonism. The term ethnocentrism was introduced in an early theory on intergroup relations (Sumner 1906). It describes the belief in the superiority of one's own group. The belief in one's own superiority includes positive attitudes and evaluations of one's own social group and its distinctive properties and negative attitudes, or even hostility, toward outgroups (Brewer 2001a). "Members strive for evaluatively positive intergroup distinctiveness because the self is defined and evaluated in group terms and therefore the status, prestige, and social valence of the group attaches to oneself" (Hogg 2016, 9). As individuals strive to form a positive self-image, intergroup comparison represents a functional tool for receiving information about the relative value of one's own group and thus one's social identity. Being part of a "superior" group with high social status, power, and recognition enables individuals to have positive self-views. On the downside, ingroup favoritism can also have negative cognitive, affective, and behavioral dimensions (Lüders et al. 2016).
>
> From this perspective, intergroup categorizations can lead to the formation of stereotypes that provide a clear framework for the interpretation of outgroup members. Stereotypes help individuals to process information and to predict and evaluate the behavior of others (Koomen and Van Der Pligt 2016). In a study, Bodenhausen (1988) asked participants to assume the role of judge and rule on the guilt or innocence of a suspect in a case of armed robbery. Some participants were told the suspect was called "Carlos Ramirez," a name expected to evoke stereotypes of an aggressive Latin American, while to others the suspect was presented

as "Robert Johnson." The results show that the stereotyped suspect with the Latin American name was more likely to be found guilty, regardless of other information presented about the robbery. Such negative stereotypes can also have a severe impact on the behavior of individuals. In another experiment, participants were asked to make a fast decision whether to shoot a figure in a computer game who was suspected to be armed. The results indicate that individuals were more likely to shoot when the targets were wearing an Islamic head covering (*hijab*) (Unkelbach et al. 2008). Accordingly, ingroup favoritism can lead to depreciation of outgroup attributes; to negative associations and emotions, such as threats or hate; and aversive behavior, such as discrimination, aggression, and violence. Historic and recent examples* provide evidence that a strong group identity, paired with a sense of superiority, can lead in extreme cases to dehumanization, genocide, and intergroup conflict (Haslam 2006).

Severe cases, such as intergroup conflicts in Rwanda and Northern Ireland, Germany's Nazi regime, or the religious extremist group ISIS, are all examples of perceived superiority of one group and the resulting dehumanization, mass killing, and genocide of opponents and outgroup members (Haslam 2006).

Beyond self-awareness and feelings of belongingness, social interaction, communication, and subjective experiences define the concept of identity. Clinical psychologists put emphasis on such interactions and transactions with oneself and others: namely, the experiences we have and the awareness of our ability to interact and influence our social environment. However, negative social interactions and destructive experiences (e.g., traumatic events, social rejection, economic/political discrimination), but also dysfunctional and abusive environments (e.g., an abusive parental home) can result in identity disorders—a disruption of identity characterized by two or more personality states.[1] Such negative experiences and environments can change how individuals perceive themselves and their environment. Facing permanently destructive situations or constantly receiving negative social feedback (e.g., in abusive relationships or a rejective social environment) can lead to a discontinuity in one's sense of self. First, it transforms the individual's self-view and reflects confusion about the perception of their own personal self. Second, it implies disturbances of the social self—one's relational interactions with significant others and one's self-view (Feinberg 2009).

Population studies in North America, Turkey, and Europe have found that dissociative identity disorder[2] (DID) is a relatively common psychiatric disorder that affects between one and three percent of the general population. Individuals with DID report multiple forms of sexual, physical, and emotional abuse in early childhood or adulthood, traumatic experiences of violence, early maltreatment, and neglect. "DID is conceptualized as a childhood-onset posttraumatic developmental disorder in which the traumatized child is unable to complete the normal developmental processes involved in consolidating a core sense of identity. Instead repeated early trauma disrupts unification of identity through creation of discrete behavioral states [. . .], and it disrupts the development of normal metacognitive processes involved in the consolidation in a unified sense of self across different contexts, for example with parents, peers and others" (Brand et al. 2014, 440). Neurobiological studies confirm that severe stress and abuse in early childhood are associated with changes in the structure of the hippocampus, the area of the brain responsible for learning and stress regulation. Thus, patients with identity disorder and a history of early childhood mistreatment tend to have lower amygdala and hippocampus volumes, which can result in maladaptive stress responses in late adulthood (Vermetten et al. 2006). Negative experiences and a destructive environment can thus have severe repercussions on individuals' perception and development of the self and can lead, in case of permanent exposure, to personality disorders and maladjustment.

All these findings imply that the self is perceived as an inner center that organizes and manages social interactions, self-perceptions, subjective experiences, expectations, and self-image. Knowing who I am, who they are, how I perceive myself, and how they perceive me is an essential part of the self—a classification of the world and one's own place within it. Thus, sociologists perceive identity as a conscious state of existing as a unique individual with a distinct biography who is aware of their roles, attitudes, and behaviors, and their societal and environmental consequences (Abels 2006). A positive self-concept emerges through a successfully established intersection between the collective and the individual self (Gaertner et al. 1999). Identity cannot therefore be built in isolation because a consistent self-image and self-perception require constant feedback from one's social environment (Taylor 1997).

Accordingly, identity is a dynamic and constantly evolving construct that is dependent on permanent inner evaluation and feedback from one's external environment. The (organizational) economic perspective thus views identity as a dynamic property which is constituted relationally through a social system. This constant dynamic transformation is essential to understanding how networks and groups are formed and how individuals shape divergent but interdependent institutions (Cilliers 2010). Subjective interaction and decision-making are integral parts of a system of decisions which constitute the environment of any individual. That means that the behavior of others represents feedback on one's own behavior or decisions that either reinforces that behavior or restricts it. The structured, ordered, and mutually interdependent behaviors of interacting individuals are institutions that, in turn, shape individual actions. "It keeps the idea of individual choices while making them part of a social system. The individuals are who they are because of their interactions, and their opportunities are shaped by what others do" (Schmid 2004, 9).

The norms that govern how to behave and how to make decisions depend on an individual's position within the social context. Thus, it is argued that peoples' preferences for, for example, fairness and justice, depend on who they feel they are, on external feedback from others, and on social interactions in a particular social setting (Akerlof and Kranton 2010). The general belief in traditional economics is that individuals are exogenous to economic processes and that subjective preferences are independent of a social context. However, recent economic theories and studies suggest that subjective preferences and decision-making are indeed dependent on social context and social evaluation (Davis 2003). Thus, economists argue that a person's identity defines their social category. Identities influence decisions because different norms that govern behavior are associated with different social categories. For example, a woman may see herself as a mother at home but as a professional at work, and these two social categories determine how she perceives herself at a given time. Each social category implies particular norms and ideals which, in turn, influence her preferences and decision-making. "Identity utility," which is the gain or loss when subjective actions conform or do not conform to norms, changes not only because of subjective choices, but also because of the choices of others. Thus, identity economics suggests that individuals have individualistic tastes in their utility functions, but that social norms, which are internalized through social interactions, also add to this. An individual can increase their utility when they adhere to the norms of their social category, but they can also do so when they do something that allows them to fit into a group. Differentiating one group from another is another utility gain that is derived from group processes. From an organizational perspective, identity economics argues that the most significant determinant of whether an organization functions well or not is not its monetary reward system, as standard economic theories would assume, but whether it has a strong organizational identity that is shared by its employees (Akerlof and Kranton 2010). The authors thus argue that economists should include identity-related variables in their analyses to better understand individuals' motivations, decision-making, and behaviors.

Subjective motivations, attitudes, beliefs, and behaviors are largely determined by the character of one's social interactions, which are subject to the dynamic and constantly changing environment to which they are exposed and from which they emerge (Cilliers 2010). Subjective decision-making, then, is driven not only by subjective tastes, but also by internalized social norms and values. Social norms provide a sense of belonging and guide individuals as to how to behave within the social strata. Individuals with preferences for group consonance may receive social approval through norm adherence, which enhances their subjective utility (Akerlof and Kranton 2010). Shared norms, values, and attitudes provide benchmarks through which individuals evaluate themselves, which in turn forms their sense of self-worth. Actions motivated by one's sense of self-worth are thus perceived as rational and are an important factor in economic behavior (Hargreaves Heap 2001).

> **Box 4.2 Identity economics, decision-making, and utility**
>
> Identity economics is a relatively new research field in economics that provides a framework for analyzing subjective decision-making about individuals' identity as the primary motivation for choice. Because identity is formed through social interactions, subjective decision-making is driven not only by subjective preferences but also by the social context. The internalized norms and values of one's own ingroup, the perceived intergroup differences, and the information received from the external world in regard to one's own identity and group tend to determine individuals' perception of themselves and their social preferences (Huettel and Kranton 2012). Besides resource competition in developing countries, even in modern democracies, resource redistribution and provision of public goods are often affected by ethnic and group divisions. A study by Alesina et al. (1999) shows that in US cities, preferences for public goods are inversely related to the cities' ethnic fragmentation. This means that in cities where ethnic groups are polarized ("by racial segregation"), spending on public goods, such as education, roads, and trash collection, is low. The results show that voters tend to reject public goods provision when a significant fraction of tax revenues collected on one ethnic group are used to finance public goods shared with other ethnic groups.
>
> Another survey in the Unites States, using self-reported attitudes from the General Social Survey (GSS), provides evidence that preferences for resource redistribution are not only determined by financial self-interest but also by the social context. Thus, individuals prefer resource redistribution to their own ethnic, racial, or religious group, but reject it when members of their own group constitute a smaller share of beneficiaries (Luttmer 2001). Along these lines, a vast number of experimental studies in social psychology, and recently also in economics, provide evidence that social divisions affect subjective decision-making. The 1954 pioneering *Robbers Cave Experiment* by Sherif et al. (1961) separated eleven- and twelve-year-old boys into

two groups for a week and brought them together in the second week to play competitive games at the Robbers Cave State Park in Wilburton, Oklahoma. During the first week, the "ingroup formation phase," the boys developed positive attitudes toward their ingroup and developed a sense of affiliation and belongingness. In the second week, in which the two distinct groups met and entered in competition for resources, both groups developed a stronger sense of ingroup favoritism and outgroup hostility. The experimenters describe an outburst equivalent to war with flag-burning, name-calling, and aggressive attacks. This phenomenon has been replicated across a wide range of settings, showing that *a priori* social divisions lead to a strong group identity and thus ingroup favoritism, which in turn may result in intergroup conflict.

However, economic studies provide evidence that beyond self-regarding or ingroup-regarding preferences, individuals may also have other-regarding preferences and thus may derive utility from altruistic behavior. An economic experiment shows that the majority of participants were willing to donate over seventy percent of their endowments to suffering strangers, due to their enhanced empathic concern for others (Klimecki et al. 2016). Other experiments, usually modeled in public goods games, in which individuals must decide whether to invest their endowments in a project that is beneficial for all or to keep them for themselves, provide similar results: a considerable number of participants are willing to contribute between forty and sixty percent of their endowments (Ledyard 1995; Fehr and Rockenbach 2004). This implies that individuals may have an innate need to contribute to society, not just to their own ingroup, and are willing to invest resources to enhance the welfare of others, even if reputation gains are small or absent.* For our discussion we can conclude that identity is fundamentally relational—that is, entangled with significant others. In the following section we thus explain how the social environment influences identity formation and shape individuals' self-perception, self-definition, and self-regulatory processes.

*A more detailed discussion on altruism, reciprocity, and a potential human need for pro-sociality is provided in the section on relational needs.

4.2 Identity Formation

As we have seen, the dynamic concept of identity has several meanings and multidimensional understandings, implying (i) a sense of self-perception; (ii) social embeddedness in the shape of commitment, goals, and norms; (iii) subjective behavior and decision-making in accordance with such commitments; (iv) a synergy between distinctiveness and group belongingness; and (v) the evaluation of one's own options, choices, and preferences. The basic assumption in identity formation is that individuals are faced with the developmental task to form a coherent identity, which is characterized by a clear self-view with an inner consistency in values, beliefs, and interests. A stable and coherent identity is described by the subjective feeling of self-continuity across situations and time. A unified and consistent self dampens uncertainty, anxiety, and confusion and is vital for mental health. Erikson (1956) argues that individuals have to overcome role ambiguity and identity confusion to explore their own interests, preferences, attitudes, and beliefs, whereas Marcia (2002) states that identity is formed through exploration and commitment. Both theories postulate that individuals move through a series of psychosocial crises that must be overcome. The turbulent state of adolescence, in particular, is perceived as a crucial period during which one establishes a sense of one's own meaning in life. A consistent and stable sense of self serves as a defense mechanism against exogenous shocks, rapid changes, risks, traumatic experiences, and meaninglessness (Wheeler 2017).

The Meeus-Crocetti model (Mercer et al. 2017) puts more emphasis on the synthesis between exploration and commitment. Commitment refers to firm choices that individuals make; in-depth exploration "refers to the extent to which adolescents actively explore their commitments, gather new information about these commitments, and discuss their commitments with others; and reconsideration of commitment refers to the comparison of current commitments to possible alternatives, and adolescent's efforts to change their current commitments when they are no longer appropriate or satisfactory" (Mercer et al. 2017, 2183). In other words, the development task is to find out who one is and where one belongs, to explore one's own interests and beliefs, and to find (and reconsider) commitments that satisfy one's own needs and desires.

Already in infancy, children start to understand that they are unique and separate individuals, form a sense of self, and develop cognitive abilities and an awareness of their own limits. Contemporary psychoanalysis reveals that intrapsychic factors emerging from earlier developmental experiences, but also external factors such as family background, parental control, or a safe environment, tend to be important for personal development (Blustein and Palladino 1991). One of the widely accepted theories in this regard is Kohut's theory of self-psychology. "At the heart of the theory lies the self, conceptualized as a mental system that organizes a person's subjective experience in relation to a set of developmental needs. Kohut (1971) called these needs 'self-object needs' because they are associated with sustaining the self and are satisfied (or not) by external figures in a person's life" (Banai et al. 2005, 224). The cohesive self is the initiating center of personality that consists of feelings, attitudes, and thoughts about oneself and one's social environment. It is formed along three axes: (i) the grandiosity axis, (ii) the idealization axis, and (iii) the alter ego-connectedness axis. The first axis, grandiosity, refers to the establishment and retention of positive self-esteem, ambitions, goals, and meaning in life. The idealization axis refers to the development of an individual's ideals and values. The third axis describes their ability to interact with significant others, form relationships, and become a member of a social group or large organization. Along these three axes, a psychologically healthy and cohesive self must ideally be formed that consists of positive self-esteem and the ability to influence one's own social environment, to have values and goals in life (meaning), and to experience a sense of belongingness, connectedness, and social approval (Kohut 1984).

Confidence about the social approval of one's personality, skills, and ideas contributes to a consistent self-structure that provides a sense of stability, unity, and certainty. It serves as a bulwark against threatening and stressful situations and generates a sense of consistency and inner security. Difficulties along the axes can result in disorders of the self, which are characterized by lower self-esteem, lack of meaning in life, doubts about one's self-efficacy, and sense of continuity. Consequently, individuals with a disordered self tend to be vulnerable to criticism and failure, are pessimistic, have negative emotions, and feel isolated and estranged (Banai et al. 2005). To establish and maintain a cohesive self, interpersonal relations with significant others are of utmost importance, according to Kohut. The major function of significant others appears to serve the developmental needs of the individual—specifically their need for mirroring, idealization, and twinship. To form a self-perception that is in line with reality, individuals need relationships with significant others who provide constant feedback about the self and who facilitate permanent self-reflection (mirroring). Furthermore, relationships with other people, especially one's parents, who serve as role models, help to internalize values, goals, and morality (idealization). Feeling similar to others and being part of a group (e.g., one's family or peers) that surrounds and protects the individual, serves the need for twinship. This enables individuals to feel connected and to easily adopt the norms and values of their social community. Accordingly, individuals who lack such relationships suffer from damaged self-representation, loss of reality, and a fragile sense of self (Klafter 2015).

Box 4.3 Identity formation in a globalized modern world

Throughout the developmental process, individuals receive information about themselves and their environment that they must understand and evaluate in a self-consistent way. In a globalized, modern, and constantly changing environment, where ideas, goods, cultures, and people are moving at an unprecedented speed and scope, individuals find it difficult to form persistent and stable identities. Media, such as search engines, social networks, television, or music contribute to a massive information access and a rapid exchange of ideas, attitudes, and world views. Individuals, at least in the Western world, may follow the same consumption patterns, have similar preferences, and similar beliefs that they share through the social web. This "cultural" assimilation may make it more difficult to form a distinct and autonomous self, individual preferences, and a unique self-representation. In addition, the declining importance of cultural traditions and role ascriptions, which are supposed to provide guidance and consistency, increases subjective vulnerability and confusion. Traditional institutions, such as church, family, or community, initially provided orientation for decision-making, which decreased decisional uncertainty and risk. However, today enhanced autonomy and self-responsibility result in a vast number of opportunities to form one's identity (Zhou and Kam 2018). On the one hand, enhanced freedom of choice may serve the human needs for self-determination and self-efficacy; on the other, it can increase uncertainty and the fear of making wrong decisions. The expansion of possibilities, global mobility, and consumption options, paired with disappearing barriers to the creation of one's own life and gender variety, in religious issues and class affiliation, puts strong pressure on individuals to achieve economic, social, and private success. Excessive emphasis on self-determination and self-expression has created unrealistic expectations of life, education, work activities, relationships, and consumption, which is supposed to be the best of its kind (Schwartz 2000).

Accordingly, psychopathological studies (e.g., Hermans and Dimaggio 2007) assume there may be a link between globalization and identity disorders and substance abuse, which is explained, at least partly, by the confusion that results from the absence of consistent and stable values, norms, and roles. Using the 2001–2002 National Epidemiologic Survey on Alcohol and Related Conditions (NESARC), with a sample of 43,093 US citizens aged 18 and over, a clinical study finds that in the period under review, two percent of adult respondents experienced a drug use disorder, whereas 10.3 percent developed a drug use disorder at some time during their lives. Drug abuse and drug dependence have been observed to begin at a very young age, with higher rates greater among men than women. Onset of drug abuse has been observed during late adolescence or early adulthood, with the authors arguing that this developmental period is subject to strong vulnerability and uncertainty (Compton et al. 2007).

Further data on children's mental health in the United States show that attention deficit hyperactivity disorder (ADHD), anxiety, depression, and behavioral problems have increased over time: among children aged four to seventeen, ADHD (parent-reported diagnosis) increased to eleven percent, a forty-one percent increase relative to prevalence in 2003;* anxiety and depression among children aged six to seventeen increased from 5.4 percent in 2003 to 8.4 percent in 2011. One in six US children aged two to eight (17.4 percent) had a diagnosed mental, behavioral, or developmental disorder and approximately 20.1 million people aged twelve or older had a substance use disorder in 2016. Furthermore, in 2016, 12.8 percent of young adolescents aged twelve to seventeen (3.1 million) had severe depression or another mental illness, indicating a higher number than in previous years (NSDUH 2016).

Although research postulates that poor economic and familial conditions have an impact on the mental development of children and young adults, psychosocial studies suggest that increased stress, expectations, and pressure to perform also have negative impacts on their mental state (e.g., Wiklund et al. 2012). In Europe, in 2013–2014, the National Society for the Prevention of Cruelty to Children (NSPCC), the UK's leading children's charity, reported a two hundred percent increase in requests from young people for counseling for exam stress, depression, and family issues. Its ChildLine service received a record number (approximately 280,000) of calls in 2017–2018 over issues related to mental and emotional health, family relationships, and suicidal thoughts (NSPCC 2019).

*Despite this evidence, we are skeptical of these numbers because other studies (e.g., Cosgrove and Krimsky 2012) reveal that over three-quarters of the Diagnostic and Statistical Manual of Mental Disorders (DSM-IV) working group members for ADHD and other behavioral disorders had ties to the pharmaceutical industry. It is argued that the pharmaceutical industry may influence recommendations in review articles and clinical practice guidelines, which can lead to overdiagnosis and over-prescription. Several studies question the high diagnosis and drug prescription rate and argue that there may be social and economic incentives (e.g., special educational service, additional time for tests, additional security income) that encourage an ADHD diagnosis (see Hinshaw 2018; Fulton et al. 2015; Bui et al. 2017).

A series of empirical studies support these assumptions and developments, showing that a tight social network, parental assistance, and social connectedness, in particular, have a positive impact on mental well-being and the successful formation of a stable self. Mirroring, supportive, and conciliatory relationships buffer against external stressors, unpredictable shocks, and personal failures (Baumeister and Leary 1995). A lack or loss of connectedness has severe repercussions for the self, leading to feelings of isolation, helplessness, lack of meaning in life, or even to mental disorders (Townsend and McWhirter 2005). Using multiple, large, population-based samples, a study has shown that social integration, or the quality of social relationships, produces better physiological functioning and lowers the risk of physical disorders (Yang et al. 2015). Beyond physical health, connectedness and group belongingness shape a person's mind, cognitive self-awareness, and cognitive capacity to engage effectively with their social environment. From the neurobiological perspective, the development of the self implies an increase in complexity of the maturing brain systems that adaptively regulate the interaction between organisms and the external environment. The experiences needed for this brain maturation are shaped in the attachment context, where the infant, securely attached to its caregiver, learns how to regulate its emotions and elicit emotional responses. Such stable attachment bonds are vital for the infant's neurobiological development because they expand its coping, interactive, and adaptive capacities. By contrast, several developmental studies show that attachment dysfunctions have devastating repercussions for a child's mental health, and even affect the way they form social relationships later in life. "Because attachment status is the product of the infant's genetically encoded psychobiological predisposition and the caregiver experience, and attachment mechanisms are expressed throughout later stages of life, early relational trauma has both immediate and long-term effects, including the generation of risk for later-forming psychiatric disorders" (Shore 2001, 206).

Empirical studies provide evidence that maltreatment and emotional neglect by parents undermine children's cognitive functioning, physical development, and problem-solving skills. It has also been established that emotional abuse or destructive relationships in general have similar repercussions on infant's development as physical or sexual abuse (Pears et al. 2008). Emotional abuse in early childhood tends to predict psychological distress in adulthood (Wright et al. 2009) or can even lead to post-traumatic stress disorder symptoms and violent behavior. "In emotional abuse, the victim is made to feel non-valued and their thoughts, feelings, and behavioral choices are not validated or are actively condemned. Emotional abuse creates a climate of fear and uncertainty, limiting confident exploration and personal assertion" (Wekerle et al. 2009, 47). In other words, destructive relationships in early childhood and the lack of social connection and positive feedback from significant others tend to have greater psycho-pathogenic risks than any other physical or environmental stressors. Relational trauma dampens the development of the cognitive, emotional, and physical self by depriving the infant of a safe and caring environment (Shore 2001).

However, adolescence, too, involves similar developmental risks and identity diffusions. This phase is marked by the exploration of one's own choices and alternatives, of finding commitments, engaging in relationships, and searching for goals and meaning in life. Identity development is the key concern during adolescence. The individual must form a stable and coherent self and simultaneously reconsider and question their existing commitments. This involves making several choices in different social domains, as well as defining oneself and one's own social group, and finding a purpose and orientation in life. Adolescents are members of various social groups, among which peer groups tend to be a place for self-discovery. Among peers, individuals learn how to interact and to compare themselves with significant others. Identification and assimilation with a peer group promotes their ability to cope with developmental problems and adjust psychologically to their external environment (Albarello et al. 2018).

During adolescence, peer relations become more salient and complex. Individuals learn how to adapt and assimilate, and also how to form a distinctive self. They learn how to socialize within a given group, to initialize or conform to group norms, and to categorize and differentiate between ingroup and outgroup members (Chung-Hall and Chen 2010). This development phase is also marked by the need for self-determination, which can also involve the urge to rebel, especially against adults. Several studies show that adolescents strive to be liked by their ingroup members, acquire a certain status, and be socially approved (Brown and Larson 2009). Those who assimilate successfully with their groups' ideals and norms are more liked and accepted by others (Nangle et al. 1996). Empirical studies on the heterogeneity of popularity provide surprising evidence that, regardless of socioeconomic background, those who exhibited aggressive and rebellious behavior toward others were mostly admired (Becker and Luthar 2007). While one study shows that strong academic skills are positively rated by significant others (Graham et al. 1998), another demonstrates that high-achieving individuals who belong to an ethnic minority group are rejected by their own group because they are perceived to "deviate from the group standard" (Tyson et al. 2005). Group norms shared by ingroup members provide orientation for interaction and shape the personality of members in a norm-consistent way. This suggests that norm violations and deviations are strictly prohibited and that, if they do occur, they can lead to punishment or rejection by other group members (Reitz et al. 2014).

4.3 Relational Human Needs

So far we have seen that social contact is of utmost importance for individuals. A lack of emotional and interactive relationships, whether during early childhood, adolescence, or adulthood, has devastating consequences for one's subjective development, health, and mental well-being. Social relationships play a key role in supporting individuals in overcoming threatening situations, external stressors, and personal failures. Individuals define themselves in terms of group membership, while the norms and values of that group affect individuals' behavior, decision-making, thoughts, and information-processing. Social identification is the basis for various forms of social interaction, including empathy, reciprocity, trust, and mutual commitment. Social belongingness is a basis for self-formation, assimilation and differentiation processes, and orientation and stability. Social approval forms and reinforces individuals' self-esteem, self-efficacy, and self-assurance. A stable personal and social identity is vital when it comes to managing and combating threatening situations, being self-aware and self-reflective, making consistent choices, and staying cohesive in terms of change. All this suggests that human beings have fundamental needs for a prosocial co-existence, identification, social belongingness, and social approval, which allows them to form stable, positive, and coherent identities.

4.3.1 The Relational Need for Identification

As we have seen, individuals strive to develop a personal and social self by defining and evaluating themselves in group terms. This means that individuals associate their selves with other individuals and their characteristics or attitudes—the infant identifies with its parents, the adolescent gradually adopts the views and characteristics of the peer group, and the adult identifies with a particular profession or a political party. Identification and affiliation of this kind play an important role in how individuals perceive themselves and their environment, and how they interact with others. In general, individuals strive to portray their own ingroup in a positive and distinct way, and thus make intergroup comparisons to differentiate their ingroup from outgroups. A positive conception of one's own group leads to a positive view of oneself and plays an important role in sustaining one's self-esteem (Koomen and Van Der Pligt 2016).

Social psychologists thus postulate that self-enhancement induced by group comparisons is underpinned by the fundamental human need for self-esteem. "The implication is that low self-esteem motivates social identification and intergroup behavior, and social identification elevates self-esteem" (Hogg 2000, 225). Besides positive self-esteem, identifying with a group, with its shared norms and values, world views, attitudes, and symbols, results in feelings of certainty. As described in the previous chapter, individuals have a strong need for reassurance about their social environment and their place within it. This certainty provides them with a meaningful existence and with confidence in how to behave and to evaluate and what to expect from one's environment. Uncertainty about oneself and one's attitudes, behavior, values, and perceptions reduce the feeling of control over one's life (Fiske and Taylor 1991). Thus, uncertainty-reduction theories postulate that individuals strive to identify with a well-defined, consistent, and prescriptive group because it provides orientation and thus certainty in their lives. Empirical studies support this view and show that individuals with strong self-doubts and self-uncertainty tend to identify more strongly with their ingroup and value their ingroup more than individuals with a certain self. This confirms the notion that individuals identify with a social category if they are uncertain about something that is relevant to their self-definition (Hogg 2000).

Box 4.4 Muslim immigrants in Europe—Uncertainty, self-esteem, and strong identification with their Muslim heritage

Because groups are fundamental to identity and social life, individuals strive to belong to and be accepted by a certain group. Naturally, individuals like to perceive themselves in a positive light and thus prefer it if their group reflects positively on themselves. Identification processes have important intragroup implications because the own ingroup serves as a key reference point in everyday life—it guides how to perceive oneself and others, how to act, and how to evaluate and process information (Verkuyten and Martinovic 2012). However, immigrants with different cultural backgrounds often face uncertainty and negative appraisal about their groups and thus their social identity. Accordingly, members of such groups tend to search for psychological ways to reduce uncertainty and maintain their sense of self-worth and that of the group as a whole (Koomen and Van Der Pligt 2016). A study on Dutch citizens with a Turkish background shows that these individuals identify more with their Turkish identity than their Dutch identity and more with their Turkish culture and its values, beliefs, and norms. They were also found to put more emphasis on their cultural ethnicity than the ethnic Dutch citizens on theirs (Verkuyten and Reijerse 2008). A similar study on 602 Turkish Muslims living in Germany and the Netherlands examined ingroup pressure to maintain one's ethnoreligious culture and identity. The more the Muslim individuals felt this ingroup pressure or norm, the stronger they identified with their cultural and religious group, regardless of outgroup behavior (such as discrimination). This finding confirms research that shows that within ingroups and ethnic communities, there is often normative pressure to sustain the ingroup culture, values, and norms, and to adapt to given roles and customs (Martinovic and Verkuyten 2012). Identifying with and adhering to ingroup traditions, cultural values, and customs generates a sense of security, consistency, and stability. It reduces self-uncertainty because it guides the individual as to how to perceive the self and others (due to formed social categorizations) and how to behave and interact with one another. "Social categorization of self and others generates a sense of ingroup identification and belonging, and regulates perception, inference,

> feelings, behavior, and interaction to conform to prototype-based knowledge one has about one's own group and relevant outgroups. Furthermore, because group prototypes are shared ("we" agree "we" are like this, "they" are like that) one's world view and self-concept are consensually validated by the overt and verbal behavior of fellow group members. Social categorization makes one's own and other's behavior predictable, and allows one to avoid harm, plan effective action, and know how one should feel and behave" (Hogg and Adelman 2013, 439). Regarding immigrants living in Europe, a clear self-definition comprising the values, beliefs, and goals to which an individual is committed helps to form a consistent self-image and adapt fast to given circumstances. The received support and permanent reassurance from their own ingroup endows the individual with confidence and self-esteem. However, strong ingroup identification can also result in ethnic separation, which involves rejecting the mainstream culture or dominant ethnic group (Berry 1990). An empirical study on second-generation Indian and Pakistani adolescents living in Britain shows that those who feel socially rejected by society tend to identify more strongly with their ethnic identity. Mainly Pakistani adolescents reported that they felt discriminated against in British society, which in turn had a negative impact on their willingness to adapt (Robinson 2009). This implies that feelings of rejection, discrimination, or non-acceptance by society or the major ethnic group strengthen identification with highly entitative, or in severe cases with extreme, groups (Hogg and Adelman 2013).

Social identification is a two-sided process that reflects the shared aspects of ingroup members on the one hand and the differences between the ingroup and the outgroup on the other. It is a statement about categorical membership that forms and encourages a collective identity that is shared with other ingroup members who seem to have common characteristics. The group and the collective identity provide a home in a social world, common identifiers, and a distinctive sense of self. Common identifiers may be based on ascribed characteristics like ethnicity or gender, or on external states like political convictions, occupations, or ideologies. Sharing characteristics or beliefs does not require direct contact with other members. Forming a group identity is first and foremost a subjective mental process that involves identification, cognitive evaluation, emotional attachment, and ideological adoption. Identifying as a member of a particular social group, finding perceived similarities, and reassuring oneself that one shares the group's characteristics are the first steps in this process (Ashmore et al. 2004).

Humans, along with (several) nonhuman species, are highly adaptive when it comes to group-living and collaboration and are neither physically nor mentally well-equipped to survive alone (Brewer 1991). Identifying with a group and its norms, values, and rules enables individuals to reduce conflict, overcome competition, and establish cooperation and mutual reciprocity. In a group, we learn to trust, how to behave, and how to evaluate and perceive the world—and the social identifiers provide a stable background to do so. Trust enables cooperation and intensifies social behavior, leading to benevolence and social awareness. Accordingly, heightened social identification encourages humans to contribute to a public good to sustain social welfare. Empirical studies have shown that social identification has a positive effect on group members' contributions to the common good, with increased identification even dampening selfish behavior. This suggests that "increasing the group salience encourages people who are normally only focused upon their personal outcomes to make efforts in obtaining good outcomes for the group even when it runs against their direct self-interest" (De Cremer and Van Vugt 1999, 887).

Evolutionists and historians show that individuals strive through cooperation, but that nonhuman species, too, evolve through ingroup interaction. Observations of orangutans have shown they imitated humans with whom they lived because of emotional closeness and identification. "The capacity to identify with others is widespread in the animal kingdom, as are basic forms of sympathy and empathy" (de Waal 1998, 689). Identification enables individuals to sympathize with ingroup members, understand their behavior, and develop and show empathy. Animals with strong attachments identify with one another and are sensitive to others' emotions. To develop empathy, one must differentiate between the self and the other (de Waal 1996). An experiment with capuchin monkeys provides evidence that subjects correctly distinguished ingroup members from outgroup members when shown touchscreen images. Ingroup/outgroup distinctions are critical for the survival of many species because an outgroup poses a threat to a group's resources. The capuchin monkey study supports this view, showing that the animals were able to distinguish between ingroup and outgroup members by recognizing the former on the basis of personal knowledge gained through interactions. Personal interactions within the ingroup strengthens one's identification with its members, which in turn encourages intragroup collaboration (Pokorny and de Waal 2009). This implies that human and nonhuman species both have a fundamental need for identification with significant others because it enables them to form groups, develop empathy, and value mutual cooperation. Clear identification and differentiation enhance the group's identity, ensure loyalty, and provide clear boundaries for action, thinking, and decision-making (Brewer 1991).

Empirical studies show that strong ingroup identification can lead to activism and collective behavior, reinforced especially by feelings of fraternal deprivation (Becker and Wagner 2009). Feelings of group discrimination, or the realization that one's group faces a disadvantage relative to an outgroup, has significantly stronger effects on the likelihood of conflict than feelings of personal deprivation. "Specifically, perceptions of discrimination might strengthen identification with those who share the stigma. When taking this more group-based approach, members of devalued groups are likely to engage in social creativity by rejecting dominant group standards and instead placing greater emphasis and value on how they differ from the dominant group" (Jetten et al. 2001, 1205). Discrimination represents a tremendous threat, not only to one's group identity but also to one's personal identity, because it implies social devaluation. Empirical studies assure that group members react to threats to their group identity in the form of increased ingroup identification and cohesion (Branscombe et al. 1999). The perceived significance of one's ingroup and one's efforts to ensure the distinctive characteristics of that group increase when individuals believe that their identity, and thus their self-esteem, is under threat (Dovidio et al. 2007). Emphasizing one's own social identity supports individuals in threatening situations. Threats heighten the importance of one's ingroup because group membership offers safety, security, and "protection" for one's self-esteem in a hostile environment and help individuals to cope with possible stressful situations in the future. Cases from Europe, North America, and other parts of the world show that minorities, in particular, tend to identify strongly with their group, especially when the perception of threat is pervasive (Koomen and Van Der Pligt 2016). Experiments show that identification among minorities or low-status groups was stronger especially when social barriers were perceived as impermeable. Accordingly, it is argued that devalued individuals who perceive social mobility as impossible tend to endorse their ingroup identification to increase their feeling of belongingness, acceptance, and self-esteem. Inclusion and identification with one's minority group may serve as a strategy for protecting one's psychological well-being. Several empirical studies have found that minority group identification increases mental health and positive self-esteem and decreases self-related uncertainty and negative feelings. They also show that devalued individuals with non-significant ingroup identification or a weak sense of self are more likely to suffer from drug abuse, depression, hopelessness, or even suicide (Branscombe et al. 1999).

However, socially dominant groups can also feel threatened by minorities, for example, immigrants, who are perceived as abusing the system, competing for resources, or threatening traditional values. Such perceived threats can lead to dehumanizing beliefs which legitimize intergroup inequality and social discrimination (Haslam and Pedersen 2007). Experiments show that in case of threat, legitimizing myths are endorsed and stereotypical and prejudiced thinking increases (Kay et al. 2009). Perceptions of an "immigration threat" can lead to severe anti-immigration attitudes by rationalizing fairness perceptions (Louis et al. 2013). Furthermore, nationalistic thinking increases, while one's own national identity, culture, and traditional values receive more appreciation. An empirical study based on German survey data reveals that several multidimensional factors tend to predict anti-foreigner attitudes. Factors like economic deprivation, conservatism, high perception of threat, and higher endorsement of national identity tend to lead to negative attitudes to immigration. In particular, perceived threats to one's own ethnic or national group, rather than threats to one's own personal identity, tend to increase opposition to immigration (Pettigrew et al. 2007).

However, the perceived threat of immigration depends also on the various ways in which national identity is defined (Pehrson et al. 2009b). A survey of English adolescents provides evidence that negative attitudes toward asylum-seekers were pervasive only among participants who defined their national identity in ethnic terms (Pehrson et al. 2009a). This implies that different definitions of group identity predict the degree to which one perceives threats, prejudice, and opposition toward outgroups. A cross-national study reveals that in countries where national identity is understood in terms of citizenship, the identification–prejudice relationship is negative or close to zero. By contrast, where it is defined in cultural terms (e.g., language or religion) the relationship becomes positive (Pehrson et al. 2009b). These findings imply that the perception and definition of one's own social identity determine how individuals perceive and evaluate the environment and social others. Social identity and belonging to a certain group, whether defined by nationality, ethnicity, gender, or religion, influences the way individuals define and evaluate themselves, the way they view ingroup and outgroup members, and the way they behave toward them. This can potentially lead to an ingroup bias and an accentuation of intergroup differences, which can enhance "us-versus-them" attitudes. In the following we examine how belonging to, not just identifying with, a particular group can have palliative effects, as well as the potential of destructive tendencies.

4.3.2 The Relational Need for Belongingness

Identifying as a member of a particular social group, finding perceived similarities, and reassuring oneself that one shares the characteristics common to the group, is the foundation for group belongingness (Ashmore et al. 2004).

Belonging to a social group and forming attachments and social bonds are innate human tendencies that are crucial to survival. The need to belong describes a fundamental need of individuals to form close relationships and stable and reliable attachments (Baumeister and Leary 1995). The need to belong encompasses two important criteria: continuity and mutual interactions. Individuals strive for non-negative interactions that are filled with mutual concern and empathy and are long-lasting (Baumeister 2012). "Close relationships offer a symbolic promise of lastingness and continuity that provide individuals with a sense of symbolic immortality [...]. They allow people to feel a part of a larger symbolic entity (e.g., couple or group) that transcends the limitations of their own body and expands the capacities and boundaries of their own self" (Lambert et al. 2013, 1419). Group belongingness reduces self-uncertainty, provides stability, and increases positive self-esteem. A social group provides a platform for sharing, communication, and affection, which helps the individual to form a social identity and pursue collective goals (Haslam et al. 2009). From a biological and evolutionary perspective, humans build groups and communities to sustain their existence. They were, and still are, dependent on mutual cooperation, cohesion, and the exchange of goods, services, and knowledge. Without exchanging information and maintaining secure bonds, early hominids would not have been able to survive and adapt to changing environments. This implies that all humans are predisposed to attach to others and to experience mental distress when social relationships dissolve. Forming and maintaining social relationships increase life satisfaction, happiness, and mental health (Carvallo and Gabriel 2006).

Belongingness also appears to be relevant to the feeling of meaningful existence. Four studies provide evidence that being part of a group and having a strong sense of belonging both increase meaning in life and promote psychological health (Lambert et al. 2013). Failure to form close relationships can lead to feelings of isolation, alienation, and lack of meaning in life. The absence of positive and stable interpersonal relationships tends to elicit adverse emotions like anxiety, depression, and mental distress. Being isolated or excluded from a group or society has devastating repercussions on one's physical and mental state. A vast amount of research has shown that such negative feelings of non-belongingness can lead to antisocial behavior, crime, and violence (Sampson and Laub 1995); substance abuse (Sprunger et al. 2020); poor academic performance; and the sense of lost control (Williams et al. 2000). Researchers postulate that individuals' self-esteem, in particular, tends to be directly related to belongingness (Baumeister 2012). Strong self-esteem evolves from social interactions and feelings of belonging and identification. These social experiences form the cognitive awareness of the self in relation to others. Continuous and stable relationships provide individuals with a social lens through which they perceive the social world in which they live, how to behave, and how to evaluate information. Hence, it is argued that people with high levels of social belongingness are more confident in their evaluations and perceptions. These "back-up" resources increase their self-esteem and interpersonal trust and make them better able to manage negative emotions and experiences (Lee and Robbins 1998). Therefore, self-esteem is perceived as an indicator of the degree of belongingness because it rises and falls in accordance with one's acceptance or rejection by a group (Williams 2007).

Lack of belongingness and group support represents an identity threat, which diminishes a person's sense of self-worth and self-confidence. Unmet needs for belongingness, and resulting low self-esteem and identity threat, can lead to antisocial or deviant behavior. An empirical study shows that, in organizations, unmet belongingness needs and lack of support from leaders can lead to low self-esteem and increased organizational deviance. Behaviors and actions by others that suggest that an individual is not a valued member of the group produce low self-esteem and identity threats, which in turn increases the probability of deviance (Ferris et al. 2009). Perceived self-devaluation or non-belongingness can lead to severe identity threats that, in turn, may trigger aggressive and derogatory behavior. The level of aggression has been shown to be even higher when rejected participants are unable to control the aversive situation (Warburton et al. 2006). The World Health Organization reports that youth violence and homicides have increased worldwide. Two hundred thousand homicides occur among young adults aged ten to twenty-nine each year, which represents forty-three percent of the total number of homicides globally. One risk factor for adolescent violence has been found to be social isolation. Weak attachments to significant others, social deprivation, and low levels of social protection, rather than gang membership, are strong predictors of propensity toward violence (WHO 2018).

Neuroimaging studies provide evidence that some of the same neural structures underlie both social and physical pain. They show that the activity of the dorsal anterior cingulate cortex (dACC), which is associated with the affective component of pain, correlates with perceived pain emotions. Participants who reported feelings of social exclusion showed increased dACC activity. "The magnitude of dACC activity correlated significantly with self-reports of social distress felt during the exclusion episode, such that individuals who showed greater dACC activity in response to social rejection also reported feeling more distressed by the rejection episode. In response to social exclusion (vs. inclusion), participants showed increased activity in the right ventral prefrontal cortex (RVPFC), a region of the brain typically associated with regulating physical pain experience or negative affect" (Eisenberger 2011, 232).

However, research also shows that it is not social contact per se that is important, but rather the existence of stable, continuous, and positive relationships which provide a buffer against stress and loneliness. Continuity, reliability, affection, and stability are essential factors to meet this belongingness need. Interaction, mutuality, and interdependence are the hallmarks of affectionate, close relationships that provide a social compass (Baumeister and Leary 1995). An empirical study shows that the quality of relationships plays a significant role when it comes to meeting the need for belonging. Even individuals with many friends and relationships, or who live with others instead of alone, may still feel lonely if their needs are less satisfied (Mellor et al. 2008).

As a result, it should be borne in mind that individual differences are associated with this need. It is assumed that individuals with a strong need to belong will put more effort into forming and sustaining relationships than individuals with a lesser need. These individuals are perceived to have a strong social monitoring system which helps them to monitor the social environment and process information in a targeted fashion. This integrative mechanism supports individuals in meeting their need for belongingness by guiding them as to how to process external information that is relevant for inclusion in a group. This means that an individual with a strong need to belong tends to have higher interpersonal sensitivity—the ability to sense and process verbal and nonverbal social cues (Pickett et al. 2004). Further research that uses the Need to Belong Scale[3] indicates that individuals with a strong need to belong are characterized by a strong need for acceptance and for the physical presence of others (Leary et al. 2001). Some researchers suggest that narcissistic personalities tend to have a strong need to belong and be accepted and are more sensitive to socially adverse situations (Casale and Fioravanti 2018). By contrast, individuals with a dismissive-avoidant personality tend to disregard emotional attachments and have no interest in forming close relationships. Instead, they maintain high levels of self-esteem by putting effort into their accomplishments and abilities. Achievement and skill, rather than personal attachments, deliver a positive image of oneself and increase one's self-confidence and self-reliance. Although it is assumed that such individuals have a weaker need to belong, it is also possible that they have a strong fear of rejection, which would explain their inhibited attachment need. Indeed, empirical studies show that a dismissive-avoidant attitude may be a mechanism to guard against the negative experience of social exclusion. This implies that dismissive-avoidant individuals have a different strategy to cope with social exclusion, but still need to belong and to be accepted by others.

Such empirical investigations on personality traits and disorders provide evidence that a strong and fundamental need for belongingness and affiliation is present in all human beings, even if its intensity varies from person to person (Carvallo and Gabriel 2006).

From an economic perspective, feelings of group belongingness, solidarity, and cohesion determine the willingness of individuals to adhere to social norms and to contribute to social welfare. A society is composed of individuals with subjective preferences and attitudes. Feelings of belonginess to a particular group or a nation determine how individuals make choices, how they perceive their environment, and how they consume and invest (Sen 2017). Being accepted and approved by friends, colleagues, or society as a whole increases one's self-esteem and encourages individuals to put more effort into sustaining this condition. We work, consume, and obey social norms so that we are liked and approved by others and can maintain a stable socioeconomic status. Compliance with group norms is rational in this regard, as it helps individuals to coordinate actions, exchange information, and cooperate with each other. "Individual motivation and beliefs are influenced by values and the practice of norms, and they in turn are influenced by the products of society, such as institutions, artefacts and technologies" (Dasgupta 2005, 9). The formation of social networks and interpersonal relationships enables individuals to share values, manage resources, build trust, and invest in the future. Social capital, which is defined as an aggregate of social networks, is thus perceived to be indispensable for economic development and civic engagement (Putnam 1993).

Box 4.5 Group belongingness, survival, and morality among primates

"In no society worthy of the name do the members lack a sense of belonging and a need for acceptance. The ability and the tendency to construct such associations, and to seek security within them, are products of natural selection found in members of species with better survival chances in a group than in solitude" (de Waal 1996, 9). Belonging to a group has several advantages, the most important being increased chances to find food and shelter from enemies. Acting in accordance with a group gives strength in numbers against competitors, and the "aggregated" knowledge of all group members can have comparative advantages for survival. However, belonging to a group can have, beyond securing one's livelihood, also moral implications for human and nonhuman beings. Living and acting within a group means adapting to the norms, values, and beliefs of that group. Like human beings, primates act in conformity with their group, adhere to a hierarchical order, and engage in mutual cooperation. In his book *Good Natured* (1996), Frans de Waal, a Dutch primatologist, describes the behavior and attitude of macaque monkeys living in Jigokudani Park in Japan toward a handicapped monkey named Mozu. Mozu looks like any other Japanese monkey except she has no hands or feet, which makes it harder for her to keep up with the group. Despite the harsh natural conditions in the mountainous region, Mozu survived in the park for two decades because she was tolerated and accepted by her groupmates despite her inability to provide great advantage to the group. In the spring of 1991, the troupe of monkeys in the park increased in number and thus split in half. In macaque society, groups are usually divided according to a matrilineal hierarchy. Female Japanese macaques remain with their kin for life while males leave the group before sexual maturity. One part of the troupe consisted of dominant matriarchs and the other of subordinate matriarchs, to which low-ranked Mozu and her offspring belonged. Despite the natural ties with her kin, Mozu decided to leave her offspring and switch groups to secure her survival. She actively established contact with other females in the dominant group, who, after initially rejecting her, accepted her presence and accepted her invitation to cooperate. "Mozu's case teaches us that even though primate groups are based on such give-and-take contracts, there is room for individuals with little value when it comes to cooperation. The cost to the others may be negligible, but their inclusion is remarkable, give the realistic alternative of ostracism" (de Waal 1996, 9).

Further observations reveal that, for example, chimpanzees show sensitive, humanlike expressions in response to distress in others. They actively seek contact and reassurance and when upset, they make noises to make clear to others that they urgently need the calming contact. If all else fails, chimpanzees resort to temper tantrums, lose control, and scream pathetically to reveal their emotional distress and outrage over a lost fight or misbehavior of other group members. These examples provide evidence that the need to belong to a particular group is not restricted to humans but is rooted in every human and nonhuman being.

From a neurocognitive perspective, interactions in social networks and interpersonal relationships enable individuals to understand the behavior, intentions, and attitudes of others as well as their own. Individuals use reflected appraisals, which involve their ideas of another person's opinion about them (or, in other words, "What do I think they think of me?"), or they consult their theories of themselves to understand themselves and others. Judging or observing significant others tends to activate regions in the medial prefrontal cortex (mPFC), the region responsible for self-reflective processes (Lieberman 2007). Such processes allow individuals to recognize similar others who tend to share the same beliefs, feelings, and desires. "This unique awareness that the inner workings of other's minds overlap meaningfully with one's own allows humans to use their own thoughts and feelings as a guide to those of others" (Mitchell et al. 2006, 655). This strategy is useful only to the extent one can assume the similar other is likely to experience the same feelings and thoughts as oneself. If someone is perceived to be different from oneself (e.g., from a different culture or social or ethnic group), using self-knowledge to make inferences about others may be less useful. Using fMRI data, a study shows that distinct dorsal and ventral sections of the mPFC are activated when another person is perceived to be similar to oneself. A ventral region of the mPFC (self-reflection region) shows higher activation during judgments about the potential mental state of similar others, whereas higher activation in the dorsal region of the mPFC (the mentalizing region) is observed during judgments of dissimilar others. This implies that a distinct neural region that is usually active during self-reflection is also activated when individuals think about similar others. Mentalizing of similar others in terms of one's self promotes understanding and enhances feelings of identification (Mitchell et al. 2006). Sharing one's ideas, beliefs, and attitudes with others means providing insights into one's own behavioral biases and prospective reactions to different attitude-relevant situations.

Knutson et al. (2006) show that the amygdala is more responsive to perceived threats, such as other ethnic group members, than to objects that are associated with positive attitudes. The study confirms that the ventromedial prefrontal cortex (vmPFC) is activated when evaluating attitude-based objects and revealing one's preferences. Individuals draw on their own preferences and stereotyping knowledge when evaluating politicians, suggesting that specific brain areas are activated when a social task involves attitudes and beliefs about persons with whom one has strong associations (Knutson et al. 2006). Neuroimaging studies show that when individuals see a person with whom they maintain a friendship or who they love, the basal ganglia are activated, which is associated with dopamine release and reward and motivation systems (Aron et al. 2005).

4.3.3 The Relational Need for Social Approval

Social identification and the formation of intimate consistent relationships are not the only important factors when developing a stable self-concept and subjective self-esteem—social approval is also relevant. The need for social approval corresponds to the desire for validation and appreciation from significant others regarding one's personality, actions, and achievements. It can manifest itself in compliments, kind gestures, praise, statements of approbation, and so on. Receiving social approval is important not only for the individual but also for social interactions. An economic model suggests that individual cooperative behavior depends not only on material gain but also on the strength of the approval incentive. The model assumes that subjective preferences are based on utility not only from private and public goods, but also from social approval, and that the latter can have an impact on one's cooperative behavior in social dilemma environments (Holländer 1990). Empirical research (partly) supports the notion that social approval or social punishment may affect cooperative behavior, the efficiency of teamwork, and decision-making in various areas. Unlike pure economic exchange, social exchange also involves the exchange of social rewards, which are not based on contractual obligations but are rather expressed by spontaneous positive or negative emotions. One possible example of the effect of social (dis)approval is the recruitment of volunteer soldiers during World War I. The British government used large-scale posters to state that non-participation was an instance of free-riding and that such behavior would be socially disapproved and despised by British society (Gächter and Fehr 1999). Public disapproval and loss of social reputation are social (identity) threats to individuals. Disapproval, especially of loved ones or people with whom one constantly interacts, tends to be more hurtful and threatening than if it comes from strangers (Grasmick and Green 1980). "If the social distance between subjects is somewhat reduced by allowing the creation of a group identity and of forming weak social ties, approval incentives give rise to a large and significant reduction in free-riding. It seems that group identity is like a 'lubricant' that makes social exchange effective" (Gächter and Fehr 1999, 362). Other related experiments show that indirect social approval, meaning a person's belief that someone dislikes their behavior, tends to incite cooperation in a public good game among strangers (Rege and Telle 2004), and that the cue of being observed by others enhances prosocial behavior (Kurzban et al. 2007; Bateson et al. 2006). Even a random (costless) opportunity to approve or disapprove of another's decisions (without a direct effect on earnings) increases contributions significantly (Masclet et al. 2003).

A study involving fMRI examined the neural correlates of reward valuations, with individuals deciding in the presence or absence of observers whether or not to donate money. The presence of observers tended to increase their willingness to donate, which increased the activation of the ventral striatum. High striatal activations were observed especially when a high social reward was expected (observed donation), but also when the possibility for personal enrichment was given without social costs (self-enrichment in the absence of observers). Among subjects who decided to donate, the activation of the left striatum was significantly higher when the donations were observed. This suggests that the extrinsic reward of social approval is processed in the same striatal region as monetary rewards. Both rewards, social and monetary, thus increase the subjective utility of individuals (Izuma et al. 2010).

The human striatum is the input unit of the basal ganglia, a region that is relevant for social information processing, learning, and decision-making. It is especially involved in reward-related processing, where rewards are measured by blood oxygen level-dependent fMRI signals. Rewards thus increase striatum activity, which tends to correlate with social rewards in a similar way as monetary or material rewards (Bhanji and Delgado 2014). This suggests that individuals also derive utility from social approval, which tends to influence their behavior and thinking. Receiving positive or negative feedback determines an individual's perception of themselves and others, influences social learning, and shapes social preferences. A neurocognitive study provides evidence that prior positive interactions with others shape individuals' expectations of future interactions. In other words, individuals who provide constant positive approval are perceived as more likeable and receive a faster response in the course of future interactions (Jones et al. 2011).

Further research shows that striatum activity is greater when an individual's evaluation of an object conforms to the opinion or attitude of others (Izuma and Adolphs 2013). Receiving advice from an expert and evaluating this advice increases activity in the ventromedial and dorsomedial striatum, reflecting the social reward gained by agreeing with the expert or by placing high value on their opinion (Campbell-Meiklejohn et al. 2010). Positive social feedback and general social approval increase striatum activity and tend to have a significant impact on neural, affective, and behavioral responses. In such cases, social rewards (in terms of social approval) are valued to such an extent that they offset the loss of other valued resources (e.g., in the case of a monetary donation). It is also assumed that individuals gain higher rewards by cooperating with others instead of acting alone. "Earning a reward by cooperation with a partner elicits greater ventral striatum activity compared to earning an equivalent reward in a non-social context and even compared to earning a larger reward by not cooperating at the expense of one's partner" (Bhanji and Delgado 2014, 7). All these findings suggest that approval from significant others tends to generate the same (neural) rewards as physical goods such as food or money. Positive interactions, pleasant feedback, and affiliation with others encourage individuals to create and maintain intimate and social relationships. Norm compliance, conformity, cooperation, and reciprocity all help to fulfill approval-oriented goals.

Cross-cultural studies show that in collectivistic cultures, individuals are more inclined to conform to group norms, base their decisions on the actions of their peers, and define their identity in terms of their relationships than members of individualistic cultures (Middleton and Jones 2000). Yet even in individualistic cultures, the intensity of affiliation and social approval correlates with self-image enhancement goals. Fitting into a group and receiving positive feedback from one's ingroup members reinforce not only an individual's self-esteem but also their perception of self-efficacy (Cialdini and Goldstein 2004). An empirical study shows that individuals who view themselves as sociable, physically attractive, or competent have higher self-esteem only when they believe that these characteristics are approved by society. This implies that subjective self-esteem, at least in this study, depends strongly on how people believe their attributes affect other people's approval of them. Also, believing oneself to be moral and ethical has a significantly higher effect on one's self-esteem if one's morals and beliefs are shared within a social context (MacDonald et al. 2003).

Having strong skills or ethics indeed form one's self-image, but receiving appreciation for one's achievements, thoughts, or beliefs reinforces one's own self-esteem and enables individuals to see themselves through the eyes of others. Receiving positive or negative feedback from significant others gives orientation on how to behave, to process information, and to perceive oneself and others. Thus, the need for social approval is not only significant in terms of self-esteem or self-efficacy but is also relevant to social orientation and environmental adaptation. Although the need for social approval is personally shaped, external factors tend to have an impact, too.

One study (Twenge and Im 2007) examined the change in the need for approval between 1958 and 2001. The authors define the need for social approval as the concern for other people's viewpoints and the desire to be accepted by others (formed cohesiveness). The results show that between 1950 and 1960 the need for social approval was very high but had declined significantly by the late 1950s, with a turning point around 1980. These changes significantly correlate with social indicators. In the 1950s and 1960s the crime, divorce, and suicide rates were low and the birthrate high, indicating a socially cohesive society. This cohesiveness relates positively with the need for social approval; that is, the desire to be approved (and accepted) by such a cohesive society. By contrast, in a less integrative and cohesive society the need for social approval appears to be mitigated. Including personality factors in the analysis, the typical college student in 1960 was described as non-anxious, with moderate self-esteem and a strong need for social approval, whereas students in 1993 were described as high on self-esteem and extraversion, but very anxious and with a weak need for approval. These results indicate that, in 1960, individuals lived in a cohesive society with a strong focus on conformity, belongingness, and congruence of shared beliefs and attitudes, which also enforced their need to be approved by society. By contrast, in 1993 there was greater emphasis on individualism, creating a more disconnected and alienated society which promotes self-reliability and unconventional values rather than traditional norm compliance (Twenge and Im 2007). Interestingly, a similar study found that the number of nervous breakdowns and mental problems in the US increased just as the need for social approval leveled off. A possible interpretation is that cultural values and social norms in a modern society promote and encourage self-reliable, independent, and socially "uprooted" individuals rather than cohesive and conformable subjects. Such a "modern and individualistic" lifestyle may decrease the need for approval from society or one's own group. However, while individuals may gain high self-esteem and question authoritarian systems, an incohesive society and disintegration may also increase confusion and mental distress, which can potentially explain the higher number of mental breakdowns (Swindle et al. 2000).

Box 4.6 Social (dis)approval and aggressive behavior

Social approval has been found to be an effective reward that tends to promote prosocial behavior. Several experiments in economics and psychology show that individuals tend to donate more if they are praised for donating (e.g., Gelfand et al. 1975), are more likely to provide help in a future situation if they are thanked for their assistance in a previous situation, and are even willing to bear hurtful stimuli after receiving expressions of gratitude (Deutsch and Lamberti 1986). Clearly, social approval tends to increase individuals' subjective willingness to invest in and to sustain the social community, and to be cooperative and prosocial to make sure to receive positive appraisal in the future. Being accepted for one's own identity, choices, thoughts, and beliefs not only provides self-assurance, but it also has a positive impact on one's subjective mental health. By contrast, being rejected or disapproved by society or a group has a strong impact on the mental health of individuals. Social disapproval threatens the social self because it implies high levels of negative evaluations (Slavich et al. 2010). To dampen the negative self-referential cognitions, individuals adopt coping self-preservation strategies to preserve their social identity and self-esteem (Gruenewald et al. 2004). While some subjects tend to show prosocial behavior to be socially re-approved by society or a group, others engage in aggressive and conventional-violating behavior (Twenge and Campbell 2003). Case studies on school shootings in the United States provide evidence that most school shooters experienced rejection and disapproval by their peers. Teasing, bullying, and ostracizing individuals, which often happens in public, sends a clear message that the subject is not valued, accepted, and liked by others (Leary et al. 2003). However, not every individual who is socially rejected responds in the same way. Beyond (active) prosocial or aggressive behavior, socially rejected individuals may adopt (passive) coping strategies that are directed toward themselves such as self-blame, substance abuse, or enhanced anxiety and self-doubt (Twenge and Campbell 2003). A neurocognitive study, using fMRI, shows that individuals who scored higher on a measure of rejection sensitivity exhibited greater dorsal anterior cingulate cortex activity in response to disapproving facial expressions. The stronger activity in the amygdala implies that individuals who are sensitive to rejection tend to perceive disapproving faces as more threatening than other negative emotional expressions such as anger or disgust (Burklund et al. 2007). Clinical analyses indicate that individuals who are highly sensitive to rejection are likely to suffer from mental disorders because they perceive every kind of ambiguous social stimuli as a form of rejection and pay more attention to social cues that may result in social disapproval. They constantly feel insecure in social relationships and fail to actively regulate emotional distress in disapproving situations. Rejection sensitivity is thus linked to mental disorders, such as depression, anxiety, or borderline disorder (Sun et al. 2018; Staebler et al. 2011).

Looking at real-life cases, medical data show that social disapproval and race-based discrimination tend to have negative repercussions on the mental state of African Americans in the United States. Sixteen percent of the 45.7 million Black/African Americans living in the US had a diagnosable mental illness in 2014 (MHA 2019). Empirical studies reveal a significant and positive correlation between perceived racial discrimination and impaired psychological well-being (Watkins et al. 2011; Hudson et al. 2016). Everyday racial discrimination also correlates with psychotic disorders and substance abuse as well as social anxiety disorder among African Americans. Furthermore, permanent exposure to social exclusion and discrimination has adverse psychological effects, such as the internalization of negative racialized stereotypes. "Much like the pervasive effects of material hardships (e.g. enduring poverty, nutritional deficits), the chronic nature of everyday discrimination represents a persistent challenge to the emotional well-being of African Americans" (Mouzon et al. 2017, 181). Being disapproved of and not accepted by society provides a negative feedback to individuals that they are not welcome in society, and that their identity, behavior, and beliefs do not conform of the dominant social group. This negative appraisal can lead to severe self-doubt and low self-esteem and in extreme cases, to an increased readiness to resort to aggression and violence.

4.3.4 Is There a Fundamental Human Need for Pro-sociality?

The previous chapter described how social belongingness, identification, and social interactions with significant others are important for subjective identity formation. Cooperation, resource sharing, and communication with others form our self-perception and assure our psychological well-being. Individuals develop a personal and social self by defining and evaluating themselves in group terms. Depending on the value individuals attach to their group, they make an effort to ensure the continued existence of that group, but they also strive to enhance its fitness through cooperation and prosocial behavior. Pro-sociality, or prosocial behavior, can be defined in general as a voluntary behavior that is adopted with the intention to benefit others, including cooperating, sharing, helping, or caring. "Prosocial behaviors may be enacted for many different reasons, including concern for another, anticipation of approval or rewards, the desire to conform to norms or felt duties, or due to a sense of fairness or justice" (Eisenberg et al. 2015, 114). Altruistic behavior is a subtype of prosocial behavior that is motivated by a concern for others rather than by an expectation of rewards or the avoidance of social punishment. Researchers argue that empathy-related processes may induce altruistic behavior (Batson and Shaw 1991; Hoffman 2008; Eisenberg et al. 2006), and that children start to develop a sophisticated form of empathic response aged around two to three years (Hoffman 2008).

However, nonhuman species, too, evolve through cooperation and prosocial interaction. "The capacity to identify with others is widespread in the animal kingdom, as are basic forms of sympathy and empathy" (de Waal 1998, 689). Identification enables individuals to sympathize with ingroup members, to understand their behavior, and to develop and show empathy. Animals with strong attachments identify with one another, are keen to cooperate, and are sensitive to others' emotions, all of which is necessary for survival and reproduction (de Waal 1996). Although research assumed for a long time that animal life and also human nature are based merely on competition and ingroup favoritism, extended studies in psychology, neuroscience, economics, and animal behavior show that both humans and nonhumans strive for pro-sociality (Fehr and Rockenbach 2004). Caring for others and desiring to contribute to society or one's own group is argued to be the main reason why human and nonhuman groups continue to exist. Caring appears to be universal to human (and nonhuman) existence and can be thus assumed to be a fundamental need (Leininger 1984).

In primatology, for example, scientists observed that chimpanzees often kiss and embrace shortly after a fight within their group and return rapidly to preexisting levels of tolerance, affiliation, and reciprocity. Such post-conflict reconciling behavior has been observed in macaques, gorillas, golden monkeys, capuchins, and many other primates, but also in non-primates such as dolphins, wolves, and hyenas (de Waal 2012). However, while researchers claim that nonhuman societies differ from human cooperation in terms of kinship (Fehr and Rockenbach 2004), "this claim has not held up on the basis of DNA extracted from chimpanzee feces in the wild. Males without genetic ties make up the majority of mutually supportive partnerships. The same seems to apply to bonobos. Female bonobos maintain a close social network that allows them to collectively dominate the majority of males despite the fact that females are also the migratory sex, which means that they are largely unrelated within each community. Both of our closest primate relatives are marked, therefore, by high levels of non-kin cooperation" (de Waal 2012, 874). This evidence of non-kin cooperation has sparked long and controversial debates in various academic disciplines. Why do humans and nonhumans cooperate with genetically unrelated subjects, even when there is no prospect of future reciprocity? Why do they care about and help each other and feel compassion for unrelated individuals? Is it really possible to feel empathy for strangers and to have another person's welfare as an ultimate goal? This constitutes an evolutionary puzzle because reciprocal altruism, kin selection, and reputation-based models have provided no clear evidence to explain these patterns of behavior (Fehr and Rockenbach 2004). Therefore, in the following we aim to discuss and understand these forms of affection, cooperation, and caretaking, and emphasize the evidence that indicates there is indeed a universal human need for pro-sociality (and caretaking). We begin with the most basic form of "prosocial" expression, namely empathy.

4.3.4.1 Empathy—The Source of Pro-sociality?

Empathy is, on the one hand, a naturally used term in everyday life, but on the other hand it remains scientifically elusive. It has many definitions derived from its complex theoretical conceptions, which alternate between affective and cognitive components. The affective component implies an emotional response to the emotional display of another person (facial, bodily, or vocal expression), which often, but not always, includes sharing that subject's emotional state. The cognitive element entails an individual's cognitive capacity to understand and mentally represent the feelings, thoughts, and the perspective of another person, while keeping self and other differentiated. It is clear from this distinction that empathy encompasses both an awareness and comprehension of other subject's experience, as well as the ability to vicariously share the subject's emotional experience (Reniers et al. 2011). Research efforts have thus focused for a long time on either the affective or the cognitive aspect of the empathic process (Fuchs 2014) and discussed whether empathy evolves in recognizing emotion or experiencing it, or even both. However, at its core, empathy allows individuals to understand, share, and relate to the emotional states of others and is thus perceived to include both the affective and cognitive components (Zahn-Waxler and Radke-Yarrow 1990). It implies a combination of observation, memory, knowledge, and reasoning that enables the observer to obtain an insight into the other's thoughts and feelings (Jackson et al. 2005).

Experiencing another's emotional or psychological state, to understand it and to respond to it, appears essential for cooperation and the regulation of social interactions among individuals (de Waal 2008). "Evolutionary, developmental, social and neuroscience perspectives stress the importance for survival of investing positively in interpersonal relationships and understanding one's own as well as other's emotions, desires, and intentions" (Jackson et al. 2005, 771). Scientists assumed for a long time that empathy involved merely a cognitive capacity to perceive and understand the thoughts, perspectives, and emotions of others. This view focused on the subjective act of constructing for oneself another person's mental state without being affected by it (Hogan 1969). Later, researchers (Hoffman 1987; Batson et al. 1981) emphasized the affective side of empathy, which is the (instinctive) capacity to feel and share the emotional state of others. The focus shifted to the other person's mental state and involved a change of perspective. In some conceptualizations of the affective component, it was even assumed that individuals adjust their emotions to the emotional state of others (e.g., sadness in response to another's sorrow, anger in response to another's anger, etc.). This emotional contagion—emotional state-matching between a subject and an object—was perceived as developing early in life and was first observed in the mother-child dyad, where small infants displayed an ability to pick up on the emotional state of their caregiver (Zahn-Waxler and Radke-Yarrow 1990).

Indeed, empirical studies in developmental psychology found that affective empathy can already be observed in two-year-old children, who are able to show empathic concern for the mental state of others (Zahn-Waxler et al. 1983). This is explained by the fundamental human need to be connected to others and to sustain emotional communication. An often-cited example is a room full of human newborns who start crying because one of them begins to cry, indicating an automatic contagion of distress (de Waal 2008). Other developmental studies have found that newborns imitate the body language of adults, such as mouth opening, tongue outstretching, or eyebrow motion, to form a connection between themselves and the other. This early connection may lay the foundation for a more sophisticated form of cognition (i.e., the perception and understanding of the intentions or dispositions of others) (Jackson et al. 2005).

Primates, too, have a capacity to be affected by and share the emotional state of others. Mice tend to intensify their own response to pain when perceiving other mice in pain (Langford et al. 2006). A similar behavior has been found in rats and pigeons who displayed greater distress when perceiving distress in conspecifics (Watanabe and Ono 1986). These findings have been confirmed by further experiments showing that, for example, "monkeys refuse to pull a chain that delivers food to them if doing so delivers an electric shock to and triggers pain reactions in a companion" (de Waal 2008, 283). Such studies demonstrate that many animals show sympathetic concern toward distress or danger of conspecifics and even aim to ameliorate their situation. This implies that nonhuman beings are not only able to show emotional contagion, but they can also evaluate and react appropriately to others' emotional state. Such behavior has been observed in, for example, infant rhesus monkeys who reacted emotionally to the continued screams of a punished peer, causing them to embrace and mount of the victim (deWaal 1996). This has been interpreted, on the one hand, as other-oriented altruistic behavior, and on the other hand as an attempt to reduce one's own negative arousal. Such personal distress, which arises when a subject is affected by the emotional state of another, leads the affected subject to selfishly seek to ameliorate their own situation, and is thus not concerned with the other (Batson and Shaw 1991). Cialdini et al. (1987), for example, argue that all prosocial behaviors can be explained by self-based motives; that is, by a desire for reward, social approval, fear of punishment, or the need to reduce negative arousal in response to the distress of another. Another team of researchers, however, argues that prosocial behavior is a multidimensional concept and can thus also result from altruistic and other-regarding motives, as well as an empathically based concern for the welfare of the other (Batson et al. 1989).

While studies were initially dominated by self-report procedures in which individuals had to indicate their feelings and thoughts in response to another's experiential state, recent studies have applied more objective measures to assess empathic arousal (Zahn-Waxler and Radke-Yarrow 1990). It is now possible to code facial affect and brain responses underlying empathy and prosocial behavior using neuro-anatomically based systems (Tusche et al. 2016). One of these studies assumes that the observation and imagination of another in a given emotional state induces shared states in the observer (Brothers 1990). According to that, the simulation theory proposes that the observer understands the emotional and mental state of an object through their own cognitive, emotional, and neural representations (i.e., by simulating the object's state internally) (Davies and Stone 1995). "The discovery of mirror neurons (di Pellegrino et al., 1992) prompted a series of papers extending the possible function of these cells from the coding of simple motor acts, to the coding of other's mental states and these cells were suggested to provide evidence for the simulation theory of empathy" (Preston and de Waal 2002, 10). The mirror neurons alone cannot induce empathy; however, they are assumed to provide a neural mechanism for shared representations of perception and action (Gallese et al. 2004; Keysers and Gazzola 2007; Rizzolatti et al. 2001), which enable human and nonhuman beings to understand and imitate the behavior of others.

Studies in this regard that merely used fMRI focused specifically on empathic brain responses for a variety of observing and experiencing states such as pain (Morrison et al. 2007), disgust (Benuzzi et al. 2008), anxiety (Prehn-Kristensen et al. 2009), or sadness (Harrison et al. 2006). Especially studies on pain-induced empathy received strong attention because they revealed that humans and nonhumans showed the same neural response in the pain area when observing a painful reaction of an object. "The more similar and socially close two individuals are, the easier the subject's identification with the object, which enhances the subject's matching motor and autonomic responses. This lets the subject get 'under the skin' of the object, bodily sharing its emotions and needs, which in turn may foster sympathy and helping" (de Waal 2008, 286). An empirical study observed the brain responses of women who were accompanied by their romantic partners while receiving painful shocks via electrodes attached to their hands. In one condition, the female, lying in the scanner, received a painful impulse, while in another condition the romantic partner of the female received the shock, which the female could observe via a mirror. In both conditions, abstract visual cues demonstrated to the female who would receive the next painful impulse—her or her partner. Hereby, the authors observed enhanced activation of the anterior insula (AI), dorsal anterior cingulate cortex (dACC), brain stem, and cerebellum when the female received the shock herself but also when she observed her partner receiving the painful stimulation. This implies that the female felt the pain through her direct experience, but also vicariously felt the pain of her partner (Singer et al. 2004).

These results indicate that human beings have a natural motivation to respond to and feel vicariously the emotional state of another, especially to connect and identify with significant others. Neural studies provide evidence that individuals assess and perceive the actions and feelings of their own ingroup members differently to those of outgroup members (Molenberghs et al. 2012; Gutsell and

Inzlicht 2010). Other studies even demonstrate greater activation in the fusiform face area in response to ingroup faces than to outgroup faces, implying greater awareness and motivation to process the facial expressions of significant others (Van Bavel et al. 2008). This divergent perception-action coupling also extends to feelings of empathy. An fMRI study on how race and group membership affect empathy-related responses revealed that activity in the bilateral anterior insula and autonomic reactivity were greater for the pain experienced by own ingroup than to that experienced by the outgroup. This effect increased with the level of racial bias and prejudice toward the outgroup (Azevedo et al. 2013). Similar studies show greater response and faster autonomic reactivity (measured by heartbeat and skin conductance response) when seeing various stimuli induced to same-race individuals (Avenanti et al. 2010; Xu et al. 2009).

Do all these results imply that the more a subject identifies with an object, the higher their motivation to process and understand the emotional state of that object? Does our group membership and the magnitude of identification ultimately determine our subjective level of empathy? Does this level of empathy, in turn, affect subjective decision-making? Can it even lead to antisocial, aggressive behavior toward outgroup members? If so, how can we explain the willingness of individuals to understand the emotional state of strangers and, in economic terms, our subjective preference for increasing the welfare of others? Pro-sociality is among our species' most vital, universal, and widespread features. Millions of individuals worldwide donate enormous sums to charitable causes and produce a similar value through volunteer labor. And yet humans' prosocial tendencies remain puzzling. Why should individuals give up part of their resources to increase the welfare of others—typically strangers they will never meet? Given the omnipresence and ambiguity of pro-sociality, it is unsurprising that there is a vast body of research on this question.

4.3.4.2 The Empathy–Altruism Hypothesis

As mentioned before, the formation of empathy is assumed to go back to mammalian maternal care. Whether mouse, elephant, or human, a mother has to be receptive to the needs of her offspring, a response that is stimulated by oxytocin, a neuropeptide that has been found to be relevant to social affiliation and prosocial behavior (de Waal 2008). Several empirical studies reveal that oxytocin promotes various forms of social behavior in both humans and nonhumans, relating to reproduction, bonding, and social interaction (Bosch et al. 2005; Argiolas and Melis 2004). Intranasally administered oxytocin has been shown to affect many aspects of human behavior, such as trust, empathy, and pro-sociality. In humans, enhanced oxytocin tends to increase inference of emotional states as well as generosity toward others, while decreasing social anxiety and threat in regard to fearful faces (Kirsch et al. 2005). This suggests that oxytocin has empathogenic properties and could thus influence prosocial behavior (Baumgartner et al. 2008; Zak et al. 2007). A double-blind experiment on healthy adult males explored whether intranasal oxytocin could increase cognitive and emotional empathy and found that it greatly increased emotional, but not cognitive, empathy in response to both positive and negative valence stimuli (Hurlemann et al. 2010). Similarly, some studies show that especially affective empathy tends to induce prosocial and even altruistic behavior (Nichols 2001).

However, the question whether empathy enhances altruistic motivation and other-related behavior or is rather a self-related motivation to reduce one's own feelings of distress, is heavily debated across all scientific disciplines. Developmental studies assert that empathy and prosocial behavioral patterns are present very early in development, well before children are able to control their behavior and differentiate between the self and others (Zaki and Mitchell 2013). These patterns first appear in the reflexive crying of babies who respond to the cries of other infants. As they continue to develop and form a perception of others as separate beings, children tend to reveal a stronger preference for agents who act in a more prosocial manner toward others over antisocial individuals (Hamlin et al. 2007) and start to engage in spontaneous prosocial behavior (such as helping others in need or sympathizing with a victim). This pattern of behavior holds even if children are neither asked to display prosocial behavior nor are rewarded for doing so. In fact, small children (e.g., an experiment with twenty-month-olds) even reduce helping or stop being prosocial when they are provided with rewards for prosociality (Warneken and Tomasello 2008).

During the second and third year of life, children learn to differentiate between themselves and others, develop a sense of self, and start to identify with significant others (e.g., family members). They learn how to express themselves and talk about their emotions and needs, as well as how to understand the internal state of others. During this period, children are keener to share resources with their own ingroup members (parochial altruism) and cooperate with those who appear more promising for their future utility (reciprocal altruism) than with those who do not. Parochialism—the preference for one's own group members—evolves even more strongly during norm internalization. Experiments provide evidence that "impartial" observers tend to punish outgroup members more than ingroup members for violating norms (Bernhard et al. 2006). In the course of socialization and social norm integration, around the age of eight, children start to show parochial or reciprocal altruism and are more willing to punish deviant behavior (Zaki and Mitchell

2013). These developmental stages support an intuitive model of prosocial behavior because children produce generous behavioral patterns before they are able to control their actions and to differentiate between themselves and others and before they internalize social norms.

However, later in life, too, young adolescents often display altruistic and other-regarding behavior. In an experiment, forty-four undergraduate students observed a young woman receiving an electric shock. After the observation, the students were given a chance to help the woman by taking the remaining shocks for her once, or they could "escape." If the students chose not to help, they either continued to observe the woman receiving the shocks (difficult-escape condition) or not (easy-escape condition). The results show that the number of individuals who were willing to help was high under both conditions. Based on these results, the authors conclude that individuals are not always motivated by self-interest (to reduce their own distress) but instead feel empathy with a distressed person and seek to reduce their suffering (Batson et al. 1991). An economic experiment provides similar results. Here, participants were willing to give over seventy percent of their endowments to suffering recipient and this willingness to contribute was explained by an increase in empathy (Klimecki et al. 2016). This implies that human prosociality extends far beyond reciprocity and parochialism; that is, humans are willing to invest resources to enhance the welfare of others without expecting something in return. Such a nonreciprocating, non-kin, prosocial behavior has been also observed in nonhumans. "The importance of mammalian prosocial tendencies is backed by experiments that range from demonstrating that rats give priority to the liberation of a trapped companion over eating chocolate to those showing that apes are prepared to assist others even in the absence of incentives, go out of their way to give others access to food, or choose shared benefits over selfish ones" (de Waal 2008, 875).

However, this line of argumentation has been strongly criticized by philosophers, economists, and social psychologists, who clearly differentiate between different kinds of pro-sociality. "Economic experiments with humans show the importance of strong reciprocity in cooperation and the enforcement of norm abiding behavior in social dilemma situations" (Fehr and Rockenbach 2004, 784). Such social dilemma situations are usually modeled in public good games that have a certain number of players endowed with a lump sum payment which they can either invest in a project that is beneficial for all (the public good) or keep for themselves. The social dilemma arises because all agents profit equally from the public good irrespective of their subjective contribution, and each player receives a lower amount when investing in the project than if they choose to keep the payments for themselves. This implies that a selfish player refuses to contribute and free-rides on the investment of others, although each contribution would be in the joint interest of the whole group. Decades of experiments with such public good games with one-shot interactions have shown that a considerable number of agents are willing to contribute (between forty to sixty percent) (Falkinger et al. 2000). Based on these results, economists assume that reciprocity plays a significant role for subjective cooperation in groups. A subject who is making an appropriate return for a benefit or harm received from another, even if it is often quite costly and provides no material gain for the subject, is referred to as a strong reciprocator (Fehr and Rockenbach 2004). If, however, effective punishment opportunities are given, a higher level of cooperation can be reached (Fehr and Gächter 2000). Yet the punishment of free riders and the reciprocal form of cooperation would imply that individuals are not purely altruistic, but instead base their decisions on certain conditions, such as subjects' expectations about other subjects' behavior, social approval, fear of punishment, etc. Psychological studies support these results and show that individuals are either guided by social or cultural norms or by self-centered vicarious arousal that tend to determine their helping or non-helping behavior (Schwartz and Fleischman 1982; Piliavin and Charng 1990). In this regard, Cialdini et al. (1997) argue that altruism is not always selfless, but it is also directed toward the self, such as the egoistic desire to relieve one's personal distress, to identify with others, to receive gratification, or enhance one's own self-esteem.

However, despite the controversy, there is longstanding evidence that portrays humans as a remarkably generous species. Spontaneous helping tends to override calculating self-interest. Does this mean that there is indeed an innate, intuitive human need to be altruistic, to care, and to behave prosocially; that is, to invest one's own resources to enhance the welfare of others? Or are such motivational and behavioral patterns not grounded in evolution but rather developed in the social context? Evolutionary theory assumes that prosocial behavior persists in humans because it has proven advantageous for survival and communal benefits (Preston and de Waal 2002). Socio-biologists support this view and show how other-regarding behavior can improve genetic survival, providing further support for a genetic predisposition for prosocial behavior (Hastings et al. 2005). While behavioral genetics emphasizes genetic factors that tend to strongly contribute to prosocial characteristics (Hur and Rushton 2007), developmental psychology postulates that social communities, peers, and the family structure have a strong impact on empathy and altruistic behavior in children (Hastings et al. 2007). However, this would imply that both genetic and environmental factors contribute significantly toward an individual's prosocial tendencies.

This also seems to hold true for empathy. Theoretical and empirical accounts suggest that especially nonpunitive parenting "that deemphasized firm parental control in favor of inductive reasoning, and particularly other-oriented reasoning focused on needs of others, were seen as conducive to prosocial development" (Hastings et al. 2007, 640). However, some twin studies argue that a shared environment, which includes all the variables that children raised in the same family have in common, tends to play only a minor role in the development of prosocial or antisocial behavior of children (Plomin et al. 2001). Instead, they assume that genetic factors and non-shared environmental influences, such as personal experiences or peer groups, have a greater impact on children's prosocial tendencies (Rhee and Waldman 2002). Accordingly, behavioral genetics assume that empathy, which is argued to be a prerequisite for pro-sociality, is an innate disposition that remains stable over time (Knafo et al. 2008). In this regard, an empirical study of 409 pairs of monozygotic and dizygotic twins examined the environmental and genetic impact on empathic development and the relationship between empathy and prosocial behavior. The study found support for the role of an empathic disposition, which was initially greater for the significant other (the mother) but became more generalized with age. The increased self-regulation that develops around the age of two allows children to not only empathize with the victim but also act upon these feelings. Although other field and laboratory experiments show that an empathic or altruistic disposition predicts prosocial behavior (Bierhoff and Rohmann 2004), the current study (Knafo et al. 2008) suggests that the prosocial behavior–empathy relationship accounted for mainly by environmental factors. These findings support a large body of research suggesting that empathic response develops and changes over time and that prosocial behavior increases with age (Eisenberg et al. 2015).

This brief discussion of pro-sociality and the empathy–altruism mechanism shows that there are still inconsistencies in the literature which need to be resolved. However, there is also strong evidence in favor of the existence of a natural drive to care for others and to behave pro-socially. This natural drive, which can be assumed to be a fundamental human need, is universal and transcultural (i.e., prosocial responses are present in all human beings across all cultures). Caring for others and contributing to one's own group or society not only ensures survival and produces common good, but also enables individuals to identify with significant others and understand their mental states. A caring, prosocial society based on cooperation, resource sharing, and helping enables efficient interaction and the development of mutual trust. While many questions remain regarding the origins of prosocial and altruistic behavior, the empirical evidence found so far leads us to conclude that there is indeed a universal human need to care for others and to be prosocial.

5
Agency Needs and Need Deprivation

The previous chapters have identified crucial social mechanisms and exogenous conditions that induce the emergence of fundamental human needs—needs that address individuals' survival, understanding, and social behavior. We have seen external factors, such as lack of substantial resources, harsh competition, or severe poverty, can threaten individuals' existence and long-term survival, but can also urge them to protect their privileges, status quo, and wealth. However, intergroup and intragroup factors can generate threats to one's own social group and trigger individuals to secure the survival and long-term viability of their group. These sources of threat have severe repercussions on the physical and psychological well-being of individuals, and in extreme cases can lead to violence, aggression, and conflict. Further, we have discussed how interpersonal factors have a significant impact on individuals' fundamental human needs. Biological and evolutionary evidence shows that cooperation, resource sharing, and group belongingness not only assure individuals' continued existence, but they also tend to play a significant part in identity formation. Identification and affiliation with significant others enable individuals to form a social identity, sympathize with ingroup members, understand their behavior, and develop and show empathy. Group belongingness influences the way people perceive themselves and their environment. However, individuals not only tend to favor their own ingroup, but they are also willing to invest their resources to increase the welfare of insignificant others. This means that beyond intergroup differences and intergroup rivalry, individuals as social beings also strive for pro-sociality, mutual solidarity, and understanding. Interpersonal relationships, social interaction, and cohesion are thus of utmost importance for the concept of the social self.

However, individuals derive their identity not only from social belonging and affiliation, but also from personal achievements and capabilities. They strive to develop and use their skills to the fullest, to achieve goals, and to live a self-determined and meaningful life. Being able to create and determine one's own environment generates a positive self-view and increases self-confidence. High self-esteem has thus often been found to increase psychological well-being and to relate to more effective behavior and better adjustment to the environment than low self-regard. However, excessive or unstable self-esteem and illusionary perceptions of one's own capabilities can also have detrimental effects and may lead to antisocial, aggressive, and selfish behavior. Self-esteem can be fragile or secure depending upon the extent to which it is authentic or defensive, consistent, or in conflict with implicit feelings of self-worth. It is a central component of individuals' daily experiences and reflects and affects their transactions with the environment.

In the following chapter we therefore focus extensively on the formation of the self-related, intrapersonal construct. We seek to better understand why individuals strive to develop and exploit their potential to the fullest and, in turn, to achieve positive and consistent feelings about oneself. We seek to understand how opportunities to explore and achieve goals enhance individuals' willingness to adjust to their environment, to contribute to and to be an active part of it; how feelings of a self-determined life can significantly contribute to psychological well-being; and how the perception of mastery and self-efficacy can enhance subjective resilience. In this regard, we also explore the factors that can harm the formation of a positive self-concept; that is, factors which deprive individuals from serving their agency needs: the need for self-esteem, self-efficacy, and self-determination. Depriving individuals of the possibility to develop a positive self-view, to lead a meaningful and self-determined life, and to achieve goals can lead to unsuccessful coping and adaption to adversities, which in extreme cases can result in aggression and violence.

5.1 The Intrapersonal Process—The Self-Concept

Social identity theory reveals that belonging to and identifying with a certain group, defined among other things by nationality, ethnicity, gender, profession, or sport team affiliation, form individuals' perception of oneself and the environment (Tajfel 1982). People derive their sense of self-esteem and self-confidence not just from their own personal characteristics but also from the membership of a particular group. However, to better understand how people form their self-concept requires a deeper understanding of interpersonal and intrapersonal factors. Interpersonal processes involve interactions, events, and feelings between two or more individuals through which they become able to interact with others and form social relationships. Intrapersonal factors operate within the individual, such as the subjective desires, attitudes, perceptions, and decisions they make. So the self-concept—an idea or a set of ideas of who we are—is subject to social-contextual influences and developmental roots (Moller et al. 2006). In the previous chapter we extensively observed the interpersonal, social-contextual influences on identity formation, which may turn us to the question of how intrapersonal factors matter. While one strand of psychological literature argues that individuals' self-concept is mainly derived from the active appraisal of our social environment (e.g., Leary and Baumeister 2000), others argue that it is difficult, if not impossible, to distinguish between interpersonal and intrapersonal factors (Swann and Seyle 2005).

While we agree that the formation of an individual's self-concept is based on the interplay between their innate growth-oriented strivings and the social environment that either supports or reject these strivings, we focus in the following on the former. Intrapersonal components determine how people think about themselves and how they develop the capability to make choices and to participate in society. There is a rich literature in psychology that discusses why all individuals have a universal, fundamental need to act volitionally without interference from others (need for self-determination), to feel meaningful and effective (need for self-efficacy), and to have a positive self-evaluation (need for self-esteem) (for a review see Kernis 1995, 2006). Having a positive view of oneself can help individuals to master difficult tasks and adjust to ambiguous situations and events, which has a significant impact on their subjective psychological well-being.

While there is clearly a self-concept that provides an answer to "Who am I?," what is actually meant by self-concept in research is still ambiguous. However, psychological researchers agree that self-concept can be understood in terms of cognitive self-evaluation and memory structure. It depicts one's description and assessment of oneself, including one's psychological and physiological characteristics, qualities, skills, roles, and so forth. This means that self-concept refers to individuals' distinctive self-representations and self-evaluations—their distinctive thoughts, feelings, perceptions, and beliefs about their own self (Epstein 1973). Psychologists thus assume that "the self-concept is, in content, a representation of an individual's personal identity; each self-concept is a unique or idiosyncratic property of the perceiver, belonging to only one individual and not shared with others" (Tyler et al. 1999, 12). This means that a self-concept is an individual's implicit and (relatively) stable knowledge of their own personality; it functions as the cognitive-structural aspect of personality (Oyserman 2007). Personality refers to the dispositions and behaviors that characterize an individual and their unique adjustment to life. It is a complex, dynamic system shaped by many factors, including heredity, physical development, social relations, cultural influences, and formative experiences in life. Personality helps to determine individuals' preferences and behavior, and it lays a foundation for identity[1] (McCrae and Costa 1982; Baumeister 2010).

In the previous chapter we extensively discussed a range of social affiliations, identification, and social relations that determine an individual's identity. To provide a full picture of our need system, we need to understand the role of an individual's dispositions, experiences, and self-perception. However, it seems clear that the self-concept cannot be understood without the social context because the self-concept "influences what is perceived, felt, and reacted to and the behavior, perceptions and reactions of others. It can be thought of an information processor, functioning to reconfigure social contexts, diffuse otherwise negative circumstances, and promote positive outcomes for the self" (Oyserman 2007, 502). It is, therefore, "a theory" about oneself that represents current self-knowledge and guides how new, incoming information about the self should be processed (Epstein 1973). This implies that the self-concept can change as individuals' subjective experiences, observations of their own behavior, and knowledge of others' opinions can vary over time. In this sense, the self-concept has been perceived as multidimensional and dynamic. It can adjust to challenges from the social environment; it processes and interprets self-relevant information, experiences, and actions; and it provides incentives, guidelines, and rules for behavior (Markus and Wurf 1987). A self-concept can thus contain a variety of self-representations: representations of the self can be positive or negative; they can be cognitive and/or affective; they can be in verbal, pictorial, or neural form; they may represent the self in the past, present, and future; and they may portray the actual and the desired self. For example, a person may think of themselves as an empathic human being, an intellectual, a father, with preferences for wine and books. Not all of these representations are important or based on behavioral evidence, and not all can be held in mind at once (Thagard and Wood 2015). Such self-representations differ also in their origins. Some result from inferences that individuals make about their attitudes and perceptions while observing their own behavior, while some result from the feedback received from one's social environment.

Although psychologists argue that the self-concept is dynamic and multidimensional, developmental psychologists assume that, at some point during maturation, the self-concept may become stable (Mortimer et al. 1982). Having a positive and cognitively consistent view of oneself contributes to a stable and clear personality. This view corresponds to the trait model, widely adopted in personality research and social psychology, which postulates that personality traits are stable over time and account for behavioral consistency across different situations. Others, in turn, argue that in different situations and environments, different selves may emerge. This means that individuals can vary in their thoughts, feelings, beliefs, and perceptions of their own selves under different conditions and events (Markus and Kunda

1986). Accordingly, psychologists argue that the self-concept can imply both dynamic and stable components and suggest that the (variable) part of the self-concept that is present in one's awareness at a given moment should be called "the working self-concept." The working self-concept is the concept or self-view that the individual experiences at a given time, and which is elicited by a certain social situation. It thus represents only a subset of an individual's set of self-conceptions.[2] A person may have different working self-concepts at different times and in different situations without changing their actual self-knowledge stored in their long-term memory (Thagard and Wood 2015).

Research on self-concept and self-representation thus seeks to explain how and when the working self-concept is susceptible to change. Psychological studies have shown that individuals selectively interact with those who support and confirm their self-view; that they choose roles and social environments that are consistent with their self-concept; and that they re-interpret, devalue, or reject discrepant feedback (Demo 1992). Other experiments show that individuals usually prefer to engage in tasks that comply with their self-assessed abilities, especially when they are uncertain about these abilities (Trope 1983). Individuals may also differ in terms of willingness to receive potentially threatening information about themselves and reject information when it contradicts their own self-concept (Taylor et al. 2007). As a result, it is argued, the self seeks to protect itself from threat and change. In this regard, economic studies (Shein 1992; Rousseau 1998) show that individuals are only willing to accept (social or organizational) change to the extent it is consistent with their self-concept. Individuals will thus support change if it reinforces their own self-concept but resist changes that threaten their self-concept (Eilam and Shamir 2005).

Self-concepts are also influenced by culture. Looking at individualistic and collectivistic countries, Markus and Kitayama (1991) propose that individuals living in individualistic, Western cultures have more "independent self-concepts" in which the self is perceived as an autonomous force that is guided by one's own attitudes, thoughts, feelings, and so on. By contrast, in collectivistic cultures the self-concept is based more on interdependence, which means that the self is connected to others and guided by social norms, obligations, and others' thoughts and feelings. Although social psychology assumed for a long time that people come to see themselves as others see them, empirical studies have concluded differently: people cannot perceive and assess very clearly how others see them; instead, people assume that others see them as they see themselves. This means that others' perceptions do not influence one's self-view; instead, one's self-view determines how one thinks others view oneself (Thagard and Wood 2015). However, within close relationships individuals tend to integrate the reflected self into their self-concept. Two longitudinal studies provide evidence that individuals' self-concept changes or enlarges when they fall in love or form new affiliations. Individuals even tend to adopt some characteristics of others as their own and show the same preferences and behavioral patterns over time (Aron et al. 1995). Other studies provide evidence that individuals also form their self-concept based on social roles, norms, and others' expectations (Darley and Fazio 1980). In fact, social factors are as important to understanding the formation of self-concepts as factors involving the operation of mental representations in individuals' minds.

Box 5.1 The impact of the self-concept on subjective decision-making

In economic literature, theories and conceptions on self-concept did not receive careful consideration. However, several marketing studies have shed light on the relationship between individuals' self-concept and the consumer choice process. Theories initiated by Levy (1981) or Douglas et al. (1967) assume that consumers prefer products that are consistent, or in line, with their own self-concept. This implies that goods and services have other dimensions beyond functional utility. The first empirical study (Birdwell 1968) on this relationship revealed that car owners chose the brand of car that was congruent with their own self-concept. The findings were stronger for luxury brands than for economy compacts, which was explained by the better opportunities that higher-income individuals have for self-expression through a purchase. In another survey, 352 students at the University of California were asked to rate their self-concept, desired self-concept, and purchase intentions for a list of products. Self-concept was measured in relation to consumer goods on a nine-point scale ranging from "very strongly like me" to "very strongly unlike me." Desired self-concept was measured on a similar nine-point scale ("very strongly like I want to be") and purchase intentions were measured on a five-point scale (indicating a buy-or-reject decision). The results show that one's own self-concept and desired self-concept tend to correlate with purchase intentions, indicating a preference for a match between product and self-concept (Landon 1974).

This matching preference has been explained by the desire of individuals to express themselves in a favorable way. Materialistic goods support and guide individuals in viewing and evaluating themselves ("I'm more worthy because I'm wearing luxury clothes which only few can afford") and influencing how they want to be perceived by others. Buying an item, using a service, or choosing a job that is consistent with one's own self-concept can, from an economic point of view, reduce information

> and deliberation costs. Because gathering and evaluating all the information that is potentially relevant to a given decision is effortful and costly, relying on one's self-related beliefs and perceptions may help to make faster decisions. If, for example, individual X views themself as a social human being who strongly cares for humans and nature and wants to be perceived this way by others, they may choose a job in social care and purchase more sustainably made products. Individuals may hence be more consistent in pursuing a course of action (such as buying only sustainable products even if more expensive), if the psychological benefits of this outweigh the monetary costs (Larrick 1993).
>
> However, psychological research also shows that individuals tend to perceive and evaluate themselves in a biased or unrealistic way. Such over- or underestimation can lead to decisions with a possibly bad outcome for the agent. Studies show that if individuals perceive themselves as healthy although they are not, they tend to reject medical tests or seek out ways to discount them (Dunning 2007). Several lines of evidence suggest that individuals make decisions to protect the view they hold of themselves. Even if they have made choices with a bad outcome, individuals tend to find ways to rationalize them to protect their self-concept. Other studies show that people aim to protect their self-concept by avoiding feedback on their decisions, or they reject a comparison between their decisions and those of others (Larrick 1993). In sum, these studies support the claim that individuals tend to make decisions that are congruent, or aligned, with their self-view. In particular, individuals may use the decision process to enhance or support their self-concept. However, individuals who are vulnerable to threats to their self-concept may also behave in ways that protect them from unfavorable information about their decisions. Economic literature should thus integrate the self-concept into decision theories because it is a potentially important variable in subjective decision-making.

However, many theories and studies on the self-concept lack any reference to the process of self-evaluation, especially the difficulties individuals may encounter when trying to form a concept of themselves. The creation of a clear and consistent picture of one's own self is no simple and unambiguous cognitive process. "In the process of collecting knowledge, [the individual] may meet with different pictures of himself which are more or less analogous to the different theoretical points of view and he may be anxious to discover which of them is the true one. 'Which are my really essential characteristics?'; 'Am I authentically what I pretend to be, or am I only a set of masks?'; 'Am I what I think I am, or what other people think about me?'"(Werff 1990, 18). During this process, the individual may encounter different and even conflicting perspectives about themselves, yet they must choose who they want to be. This process, characteristic of adolescence, contributes to a stable and self-certain identity. However, knowing and conceptualizing the self is not easy. The individual must deal with a variety of possible answers that may be contradictory and incompatible. Over time, societal structures have developed from personal situations where individuals were embedded in traditions and role prescriptions with hardly any choices to situations with many options in which individuals are forced to make choices on their own (Baumeister 1997). Facing these many options to form one's own self-concept without any guidance from society or traditional institutions can lead to severe self-concept problems, especially in adolescence. Adolescence is a period full of changes: cognitive development reaches the final stage, the body modifies, and great changes in individuals' social status occur. These changes shape the way individuals process self-relevant information and generate a basis for the formation of self-knowledge; that is, the beliefs and ideas an individual holds about themselves (Werff 1990). In this regard, Erikson argues that in adolescence individuals begin to ask questions pertaining to who they are, where they belong, and where their lives may be heading. "The timing of this initial foray into matters of crises and commitments is manifest when the burgeoning cognitive sophistication of the young person in question is met with the increased societal expectations that he or she demonstrate to some degree of purpose and direction in life" (Dunlop 2017, 30). During adolescence, individuals may rethink their previous beliefs and ideas about themselves and experiment with new roles and life plans to find new goals and values that fit their sense of self.

In this regard, developmental psychologists argue that self-continuity and self-concept clarity are crucial for identity formation. Self-continuity implies a sense of persistence through time and across situations (Chandler et al. 2003). Having a strong sense of self-continuity—a clear sense of how one's own past, present, and future are linked to form a coherent sense of self is linked to self-concept clarity. Self-concept clarity means that the knowledge of the self is clear and consistent (i.e., self-beliefs are clearly and confidently defined, stable over time, and internally consistent) (Campbell et al. 1996). In other words, self-concept clarity refers to the structure of the self-concept regardless of content (e.g., positive or negative self-attributes). To form clear and consistent beliefs about the self, a process of self-reflection is required. According to several psychological studies (Van Dijk et al. 2014), the consistence of the self is positively related to narrative construction. "Sharing stories is the mechanism through which people become selves" (McLean et al. 2007, 275). Self-reflective talking and sharing of stories about themselves help individuals to adjust to the social environment and to form a clear concept of the self.

A longitudinal study of adolescents provides evidence that open communication within the family and the possibility to share narratives with significant others predict higher self-concept clarity. By contrast, a lower self-concept clarity predicts higher levels of anxiety and depression. For adolescents who are self-uncertain and who have an unstable self-concept, self-reflective talking and narrative sharing may provide a basis to develop clear beliefs about themselves (Van Dijk et al. 2014). By contrast, experiences of threats to one's self-concept (e.g., through social rejection) can harm the development of consistent self-beliefs, especially if there is no room for self-reflection and reprocessing of such negative events (Heppner et al. 2015). Further studies confirm that the lack of options to form consistent and stable beliefs about oneself is strongly and negatively related to internalizing symptoms, such as depression and anxiety (Campbell et al. 2003; Constantino et al. 2006). A study with 923 Dutch adolescents reveals that individuals are more likely to reconsider or change their commitments if they are dissatisfied with their self-concept clarity.

Reconsidering one's commitments implies that individuals may question or reject choices/options that are no longer functional or do not fit in with their present or desired sense of self.[3] This means that the structure of the self-concept—represented by making commitments and maintaining an integrated and coherent sense of self—is reconsidered when it appears inconsistent. In other words, if adolescents' self-concepts are perceived to be clear and stable and their commitments are viewed as functional, reconsideration is unlikely to occur. However, recent findings indicate that self-concept clarity may first decrease and then increase during the transition from adolescence to early adulthood. This is explained by the many transformations faced by young individuals especially during late adolescence (e.g., transition from school to higher education, from familial embeddedness to autonomous living), which are typical of the transition to early adulthood. In this developmental stage, individuals explore alternative ways to live and who to be and thus reconsider their prior commitments and beliefs about themselves, which may lead to a temporary drop in self-concept clarity (Lodi-Smith and Crocetti 2017).

However, it is also worth considering that social and cultural environments constrain the choices that adolescents are able to make. Individuals living under uncertain socioeconomic conditions may face severe constraints to exploring all alternatives to construct a consistent and stable self-concept. Psychological studies show that young urban adolescents did not consider university or professional occupations to be viable options corresponding to their socioeconomic and cultural realities. They thus formed their self-beliefs according to the circumstances that they perceived as consistent with their own self-concept (Oyserman and Destin 2010). A similar scenario has been observed for girls or women living in patriarchal societies, where many options are not available to be selected. They must therefore make choices and create their self-concept based on the given conditions and constraints, or even adjust their self-beliefs to the expectations of their social environment (Bosma and Kunnen 2001). Here, psychological studies indicate that an individual's self-concept is bolstered if their self-beliefs are socially approved by others, which may induce individuals to form their self-beliefs according to the attributes of a certain group or environment (Slotter et al. 2015). Threats to one's own self-beliefs in shape of a negative feedback received from one's social environment enhance self-uncertainty and lead to self-concept inconsistency. However, receiving social support that affirms one's self-beliefs enhance self-certainty and, in turn, self-concept clarity (Slotter and Gardner 2014). Other studies show that alterations or limitations to social roles (e.g., lost job, retirement) are associated with a decrease in self-concept clarity, which implies that social roles help to form beliefs about oneself and that every human being wants to take a certain role in society (Lodi-Smith and DeMarree 2017; Light and Visser 2013).

On the other hand, psychologists argue that experiences of threat, uncertainty, and anxiety can lead to self-concept clarity. Four studies provide evidence that the experience of mortality salience produces anxiety which in turn may enhance self-concept clarity. Confrontation with death induces the need to protect the self and one's self-beliefs, especially for those with a stronger need for order and cognitive consistency. Experiencing death-related thoughts may trigger some individuals to protect themselves against such potential existential threats by maintaining and emphasizing a clearly defined self-concept (Landau et al. 2009). These results thus imply that a clear and consistent self-concept and structured self-knowledge can serve to protect individuals against the threatening thoughts of death's inevitability (McGregor and Marigold 2003). By contrast, the uncertainty-identity theory postulates that personal uncertainty and mortality salience undermine self-concept clarity (Hohman and Hogg 2015). Although these findings appear inconsistent, all these studies have observed a connection between situational uncertainty and self-esteem. Trait self-esteem implies a personal characteristic that appears to be stable over time, while state self-esteem is defined as event-related self-esteem that is subject to temporary fluctuations. This means that individuals' self-esteem can change in a self-relevant situation (state) without having a strong impact on dispositional self-esteem (trait). Therefore, all authors argue that situational death-related thoughts would result in self-concept clarity among those with high trait self-esteem and a strong need for order and structure. However, when there is a boost of state self-esteem (e.g., through positive feedback at that moment), anxiety and uncertainty fail to affect self-concept clarity (Hertel 2017).

The relationship between self-esteem and self-concept clarity has been examined extensively in psychological literature. We cannot undertake a detailed review here, but we return to this matter later in this chapter. Self-esteem is perceived as one of the most important aspects of individuals' self-concept (Baumeister 1997). It is defined as "a self-reflexive attitude that is the product of viewing the self as an object of evaluation" (Campbell and Lavallee 1993, 4). This indicates that the self-concept implies both self-knowledge and self-evaluation, and that both factors can be treated as traits or states (as discussed previously).[4] Self-evaluation (self-esteem) can thus fluctuate across situations, events, and roles, but it can also remain stable over time.

Similarly, self-knowledge can refer to the configuration of currently available self-beliefs, but also to a set of stable self-beliefs about one's central attitudes. Here, psychologists (Campbell 1990) assume that knowledge (self-concept) and evaluation (self-esteem) of the self relate to each other. Individuals with high self-esteem, it is argued, have positive, well-articulated descriptions of the self, whereas those with low self-esteem have more poorly defined self-concepts. While it is wrongly assumed that individuals with low-self-esteem have negative or destructive beliefs about themselves, researchers postulate that they have rather neutral self-beliefs yet experience higher levels of instability and uncertainty. The authors continue to argue that individuals with low self-esteem and poorly defined self-concepts tend to be more reactive to external cues from the social environment and are more conservative in their adjustments to this environment. Because low self-esteem individuals are more uncertain and inconsistent in their self-views, they have a greater need for self-enhancement and approval and tend to react more affectively to negative social stimuli (negative feedback). They also tend to react more cautiously and conservatively to the social environment, which is explained by their perception of themselves as realistic and less optimistic or excessive. Further, it is argued that low- and high-self-esteem individuals tend to adopt different self-presentational styles. Individuals high on self-esteem tend to employ self-enhancing styles, characterized by a willingness to take risks, to achieve something strategically, and to focus on their outstanding qualities. By contrast, individuals with low self-esteem draw rather on self-protective measures, characterized by a low willingness to take risks, by the avoidance of strategic ploys, and a tendency to focus on masking their negative qualities. This means that the self-presentational style of low-esteem individuals is not derogative but self-protective (Campbell and Lavallee 1993). These findings may suggest that having a clear, consistent, and stable self-concept provides self-certainty, structure, and cognitive consistency (of oneself) and may thus generate positive self-evaluation. However, there is also evidence that both causal directions of the relationship between self-concept and self-esteem are plausible, which we will not amplify here.

5.2 Personality

What is of greater interest for our concept is self-concept clarity regarding personality. Personality refers to an enduring formation of subjective characteristics and behaviors that comprise an individual's distinctive adjustment to life. It is viewed as a dynamic and complex integration of various factors, such as heredity, physical training, parenting and social environment, interaction with significant others, and culturally induced norms and values (APA 2019d). Various researchers in personality psychology refer to different measures and assumptions to explain the structure and development of personality. One framework, McAdams' (1995) multilevel conception of personality, has been widely used in personality psychology because of its conceptual breadth and academic acceptance. His model proposes that personality can be best understood in terms of three levels: (i) dispositional traits, (ii) characteristic adaptations, and (iii) integrative narratives of the self.

The first level refers to dispositional traits, which are recurring (mostly stable) patterns of behavior, cognition, and affect. Researchers who are interested in assessing these traits usually refer to different scales, such as the Big Five or the Five Factor Personality Model (FFM). The Big Five Model describes five basic personality dimensions, namely Extraversion, Neuroticism, Agreeableness, Conscientiousness, and Openness to Experience. Individuals who score strongly on Extraversion are perceived to be sociable, talkative, energetic, and gregarious, while traits associated with strong Agreeableness include cooperation, trust, generosity, and lenience. Strong Neuroticism describes individuals who are emotionally unstable, worried, anxious, and uncertain, whereas individuals who score highly on Conscientiousness are assumed to be well-organized, punctual, ambitious, and responsible. Openness to Experience describes individuals who are broad-minded, flexible, curious, and creative (Okun and Finch 1998). The Five Factor Model (FFM) is an alternative instrument for assessing personality traits and is composed of the same five personality dimensions as the Big Five Model (Dunlop 2017). The HEXACO model (Honesty–Humility, Emotionality, Extraversion,

Agreeableness, Conscientiousness, and Openness) refines the FFM by including a sixth dimension (Honesty–Humility), which considers traits such as fairness, greediness, sociality, and modesty. Unlike the Neuroticism factor in the FFM or Big Five models, the HEXACO model focuses on emotions rather than neurotic tendencies and aims to measure the individual responses to emotional content. Furthermore, here the Agreeableness dimension focuses more on altruistic manifestations, embodying traits such as tolerance, forgiveness, and cooperation (Chirumbolo and Leone 2010). Personality psychologists rely on these instruments to measure dispositional traits, which are perceived to have a genetic component and remain stable over the lifespan, although several studies revealed that they may also change across adulthood (e.g., Lodi-Smith et al. 2009).

The second level of personality describes characteristic adaptations and includes factors such as personal strivings, life goals and tasks, subjective coping strategies and adjustment mechanisms, and a wide range of other developmental and motivational constructs that are conceptualized in time, role, and place. In other words, it focuses more on individuals' goal-directed behavior and motivations but also on self-evaluation and the formation of one's own self-concept. Other factors, such as cultural and ideological variables and attachment and coping styles, have been also considered in regard to characteristic adaptation (Dunlop 2017). In a study, Matsuba and Walker (2004) examined personality differences in terms of pro-sociality among young adults and included variables such as social role and time in their analysis that capture individuals' personality otherwise disregarded with a sole focus on traits. Their results reveal that prosocial individuals scored higher in moral reasoning than the comparison group, were more religious, had a clear and consistent self-concept, and were more willing to form close relationships. The authors assume that certain personality types are more prosocial and are initially attracted to prosocial behavior than others, and that participation in social acts may facilitate the development of young adults. We may add, from our own interpretation, that their social role in a religious community, too, helped those young adults to develop a certain and consistent self. Adopting a belief system provides guidance, stability and certainty, and supports individuals in developing a self-certain personality.

The third level of personality is composed of a narrative identity, where individuals try to understand who they are and where they belong to by constructing a consistent life story. "Through the construction of such a story, the narrator is provided with a mechanism to explain how his or her past fits together, has led to present circumstances, and will likely extend into the future. As a result, this story works to bring the many varied ways in which the self is understood across contexts and through time into a broader unifying and coherent framework" (Dunlop 2017, 26). To summarize, this would imply that individuals create identities based on consistent, reliable, and guiding narratives that integrate individuals into society in a self-productive way, by providing guiding principles for a meaningful and coherent life. Such narratives seek to explain the purpose of one's own self in life, and how one's past self, the present self, and the anticipated or even desired future self, are linked with each other in a consistent way.

Relating these three levels of personality to the construction of a self-concept, and especially to self-concept clarity, empirical studies provide evidence that self-concept clarity corresponds to each of these levels. At the dispositional trait level, studies (for a review, see Dunlop 2017) have found that self-concept clarity correlates positively with extraversion, agreeableness, and conscientiousness, but negatively with neuroticism. At the level of characteristic adaptations, self-concept clarity has been found to relate positively to self-esteem, meaning in life, and active coping mechanisms, but negatively to uncertainty, anxious, or avoidant attachment styles. At the level of narrative identity, self-concept clarity tends to correspond with the degree of clarity and details regarding autobiographical reproduction. According to these theories, we may conclude that individuals who have high self-esteem, a purpose in life, clear goals and visions, and an integrated and coherent image of their own past, present, and future (and of how this all relates to each other) tend to have a stable, certain, and consistent self-concept and personality. Individuals need to be able to create and achieve something, to explore their own self autonomously (independently of significant others and their social embeddedness), and to feel effective and productive in their life creation. Hence, all individuals have fundamental needs for self-esteem, self-efficacy, and self-determination, which we address in detail in the following. However, before focusing on these fundamental human needs, we make a brief detour to explore a concept that is frequently discussed in conflict economics but also has important implications for personality psychology—namely the concept of greed.

Excursion: Greed in Personality Psychology and Conflict Economics

Greed has been a topic of discussion for as long as humanity has existed. From the earliest ideas, it became apparent that the excessive desire to acquire and possess goods represents two sides of the same coin. On the one hand, it is argued that greed is part of human nature that promotes progress and motivates better self-performance; on the other, greedy behavior has destructive features which can trigger wars and immoral behavior (Sutherland 2014). In conflict economics, a highly debated article by Collier and Hoeffler (2004) postulates that greed plays a significant role in explaining conflict onset. The authors understand greed as the opportunity, or incentive, for individuals to participate in rebellion for private gain. Violence thus becomes a viable instrument for wealth accumulation. In their strong greed assumption, the authors offer a rational actor account that focuses on the motives of individuals, arguing that greed or loot-seeking, rather than grievance or justice-seeking, is the key determinant in conflict onset. This greed motive has drawn attention to the importance of conflict resolution that aims to identify which actors benefit from conflicts and hence who may prevent their peaceful resolution. "Yet the assertion that contemporary armed conflicts are predominantly caused by greed rather than grievance, and in the ways postulated by some of its proponents, has provoked an ongoing, sometimes heated debate and raised a number of important analytical and normative questions. While there is growing agreement that economic factors matter to conflict dynamics, there is little consensus as to how they matter, how much they matter, or in what ways. In part, this disagreement has stemmed from the loaded normative connotations of the terms 'greed' and 'grievance', the stark opposition in which they were presented, and a continued lack of clarity as to what variables these terms are meant to capture" (Ballentine and Sherman 2003, 5).

But what exactly is greed and how is this term understood in other disciplines? While some definitions emphasize the social harm of greedy behavior (Mussel et al. 2015), others suggest that greed does not necessarily lead to harmful outcomes, but is rather associated with individuals' desire "to always want more" and "never being satisfied" (Seuntjens et al. 2019). This led psychologists to ask whether greed is a pathological, genetic, and instinctive trigger for boundless and risky behavior or rather a "personality disorder" resulting from various conditions during infancy. Also, questions of external/cultural influences and environmentally created impulses have stimulated the quest for explanations (Seuntjens et al. 2015).

Psychoanalysts declare that greedy behavior is the result of a disturbed emotional development of impulses in early childhood. The first impulse of an infant is based on oral saturation through the mouth (e.g., sucking), which is the first part of the body vested by the libido. If the libido is denied satisfaction and pleasure, feelings of anxiety and frustration are compensated by excessive oral ingestion so to keep as much as possible for oneself. If this anomaly is not resolved in the early stages of development, emotional disturbances can persist into adulthood, where an excessive desire for possessions is a symbolic substitute for the need for secure attachment (Wachtel 2003). Psychoanalysis thus argues that a greedy character can evolve if a child's needs for emotional security, belonging, and affiliation are not met. "Thus, attachment to inanimate possessions becomes more important than recognizing and fulfilling inner emotional and authentic needs and deeper longings. [. . .] These possessions serve as substitutes for an inner void and as a defensive screen that prevents recognition of the negative experience of distressful emptiness and loneliness. Thus, the obsession with amassing wealth is symptomatic of a concealed, unverbalized fear of nonexistence. Possessing valued objects compensates for the lack of self-worth, bestows the hope of fulfillment, and restores a sense of having power, being alive, and feeling real" (Nikelly 2006, 69). Using the Aspiration Index questionnaire, an empirical study (Kasser 2002) assessed how individuals' value orientation relate to their mental wellbeing. Subjects who considered financial success and material possessions to be central values reported significantly lower levels of self-realization and joy of life and higher levels of depression and anxiety than individuals who placed a higher value on community, affiliation, and self-acceptance. Using a different sample and method, namely interviews with adolescents, the same authors showed that those who were focused on financial gain found it more difficult to adjust to society, were more antisocial and destructive, and showed signs of behavior disorder. Clinical data support these results and shows that greedy individuals who focus strongly on wealth accumulation, social status, and power tend to show signs of a narcissistic and schizoid personality disorder, involving features of permanent dissatisfaction, impulsivity, difficulties of emotional self-expression, and low self-esteem (Waska 2003).

Accordingly, the psychoanalytical strand perceives greed as a pathological appearance of social maladaptation with severe self-doubts and inner emptiness. Exorbitant wealth accumulation and the possession of certain objects of interest mask vulnerability and negative emotions about the self through feelings of superiority and self-righteousness (Nikelly 2006). This would correspond to Kohut's (1971) psychoanalytical theory of self-psychology (an extension of traditional psychoanalysis), which postulates that positive self-esteem can only be formed through adequate relationships that allow mirroring and self-idealization. To form a self-perception which is in line with reality, individuals need relationships with people who provide constant (emphatic) feedback about the self and who facilitate permanent self-reflection. Furthermore, relationships with people who serve as role models help to internalize values, goals, and morality. Accordingly, individuals who have no such relationships suffer from a damaged self-concept, a loss of reality and a fragile sense of self. Consequently, deprived individuals develop a compensatory self-object relationship with their wealth and possessions in order to create a positive self-image (Klafter 2015).

A different explanation of greed is provided by personality psychology. It argues that greed is a personality trait based on individual differences in environmental adjustment rather than a pathological condition resulting from early childhood traumata. Although a vast amount of psychological literature examines the notion of greed, empirical research on this topic in personality psychology is scarce. Five different self-report instruments exist in order to measure greed as a subjective trait: the Greed Trait Measure (Mussel et al. 2015), the subscale Greed from the Vices and Virtues Scale (VAVS) (Veselka et al. 2014), the Dispositional Greed Scale (Seuntjens et al. 2015), and the GR€€D Scale (Mussel and Hewig 2016).[5] The HEXACO personality model examines greed in its Honesty–Humility dimension, which consider factors such as sincerity, greed avoidance, fairness and modesty, and measures destructive and antisocial tendencies of individuals. These scales define greed as a state of insatiability, except VAVS, in which greed is perceived as manipulation and betrayal of others for personal gain, and HEXACO, in which the focus lies more on measuring greed avoidance (low interest in possessions) (for a more detailed discussion, see Mussel et al. 2018).

Several studies using these self-reporting instruments show that high scores point to a manipulative and pretentious personality that aims to accumulate wealth and privilege by cheating, steeling, and taking advantage of others (Hare 1999). However, some studies also reveal that individuals who exhibit stronger tendencies toward greed and unfairness are also more uncertain and anxious and score low on self-esteem, pro-sociality, and optimism (Rolison et al. 2013). Further, dispositional greed has been associated with high impulsivity (no self-control, emotional instability), a higher propensity to spend money (irrational buying decisions), lower-self-esteem, lower satisfaction with life, and low levels of empathy (Seuntjens et al. 2015).

Considering these diverse theories, methods, and empirical findings from different psychological disciplines, we may conclude that there seems to be more behind greed than the mere desire to enrich oneself, as assumed by conflict economics. Individuals may act greedily to secure their physical existence, dampen uncertainty, enhance their self-worth, or gain social approval. Although experiments showed that greedy individuals consume more or are not willing to share with others, psychoanalysis and personality studies postulate that greed is a broader construct that goes beyond materialistic preferences. The results indicate that individuals who focus extensively on materialistic possessions usually have lower levels of self-worth, do not feel part of society, and find it difficult to adjust to their environment.

Accumulating possessions thus serves as a substitute for social recognition, self-acceptance, and meaningful existence. Thus, for our purpose we may assume that the greed argument, led by Collier and Hoeffler (2004), must be extended to include psychological factors to explain conflict onset. Greedy behavior, insatiability, or the desire to acquire more may be an indicator of deprived psychological needs; that is, the need to feel belonged and approved by society, to feel worthy, efficacious, and self-certain, and to have a meaningful life.

5.3 Agency Needs

5.3.1 The Agency Need for Self-Esteem

Self-esteem is perceived as one of the most important aspects of an individual's self-concept (Baumeister 1993). It refers to the assessment of one's self-worth and can be defined as "a self-reflexive attitude that is the product of viewing the self as an object of evaluation" (Campbell and Lavallee 1993, 4). This means that individuals evaluate their qualities and characteristics, contained in one's self-concept, in a self-reflexive manner. It reflects individuals' physical self-image, their view of their capabilities and achievements, their values and beliefs, and their perceived success in living in coherence with them. The more positive the cumulative evaluation of the self-concept, the higher the self-esteem (Campbell 1990). While some psychologists argue that self-esteem remains stable over time (Hertel 2017), others insist that it can fluctuate across situations, events, and roles, and is thus better conceived of as a dynamic pattern than a passive state or dispositional trait (Lodi-Smith and Crocetti 2017). Trait self-esteem implies a personal characteristic that appears to be stable over time, while state self-esteem is defined as event-related self-esteem that is subject to temporarily fluctuations (Hertel 2017). This implies that self-esteem is a dynamic characteristic that can change over time and situations while exhibiting a certain level of continuity. "Indeed, a remarkable variety of research is addressable when self-esteem is conceptualized in active and dynamic terms, rather than merely as an outcome or resultant state of mind, that is, as something that people seek or strive for, rather than as something people passively 'have' or 'end up with'" (Sheldon 2004, 421). It is apparent that individuals strive for positive self-evaluation and in general want to think well of themselves. Studies show that individuals strive to form consistent self-beliefs and reject information that tends to contradict these beliefs (such as negative feedback) (Slotter et al. 2015). Others reveal that individuals alter their self-evaluations to maintain their self-esteem when it is threatened (Greenberg and Pyszczynski 1985). In this regard, research shows that individuals tend to underestimate or overestimate their performance, especially when the performance is relevant to their self-concept. In other words, when individuals perform poorly in a self-related task, they tend to overestimate the number of individuals who also did not do well; when individuals perform well they tend to underestimate the number of individuals who also performed well (Campbell 1986). Favorable self-belief and positive self-evaluation enhance happiness and mental well-being and may also predict a variety of positive outcomes, such as better adjustment to the environment, better coping with challenges in life, or even better physical health (Leary and MacDonald 2003). Self-esteem also guides individuals as to how to perceive themselves and their social environment and generates a foundation for information processing and behavior. Such findings thus suggest that individuals indeed need self-esteem for healthy psychological functioning.

A natural question that is overtly debated across disciplines is why individuals vary in their levels of self-esteem. Psychological researchers consistently agree that individuals with low self-esteem do not invariably possess negative self-views, but that their descriptions of themselves are rather neutral (Tice 1993). These individuals have a higher need for certainty and ambiguity avoidance; that is, they act to minimize potential losses, avoid risky choices and behaviors, set unchallenging goals to avoid failure, and are motivated to protect themselves from possible threats (Tennen and Affleck 1993). While a vast number of researchers agree that individuals low on self-esteem appear more sensitive and reactive to their social environment (e.g., Campbell and Lavallee 1993), they also indicate that among high self-esteem individuals, high levels of instability also exist. This means that individuals can have high self-esteem and, at the same time, reflect fragility in their positive self-feelings and self-beliefs (Greenier et al. 1995). These fluctuations have been observed especially in individuals who constantly base their self-worth on evaluative information (either externally received or internally generated), which can be potentially inconsistent. In other words, the more weight individuals place on information received about their self to determine their self-worth, the more likely the self-worth will fluctuate. Given that subjective self-evaluation is affected by various forms of information, Greenier and colleagues (1995) suggest the following patterns: "(1) The greater the importance that people report placing on specific self-evaluations as determinants of their global feelings of self-worth, the more these feelings should fluctuate; (2) greater fluctuations in specific self-evaluations should relate to more unstable global self-esteem; and (3) the combination of placing high importance on, and experiencing considerable fluctuations in, specific self-evaluations should relate to especially unstable global self-esteem" (Greenier et al. 1995, 55).

Another factor related to unstable self-esteem is a poorly developed self-concept. It is argued that an inconsistent and fragile self-concept leads to a higher susceptibility to evaluative information. This means the less individuals know about themselves (i.e., their individual characteristics, strengths, weaknesses, or preferences, etc.), the less stable their feelings of self-worth may be. If unstable self-esteem is associated with a poorly defined self-concept, it should also reflect diminished functional flexibility and enhanced dependence on events. This implies a decreased capacity to adjust easily to certain situations because one is less sure of one's own capabilities and self-image, and a dependence on external, situational information to form beliefs and perception of oneself (Dunlop 2017).

But what are the sources of a poor self-concept? Most studies on this issue have examined the effects of approval, anxiety, and uncertainty on self-concept stability. Slotter et al. (2015), for example, show that group identification, belongingness, and approval tend to contribute strongly to a stable self-concept. In an experiment, subjects were asked to imagine they were no longer a part of a group with whom they strongly identified with. Their clear view of themselves decreased. Another study reveals that consistency between self-beliefs reflecting relational value and information about being approved and valued by others leads to higher self-concept stability (Stinson et al. 2010). Considering situational anxiety and uncertainty, several studies (e.g., McGregor and Marigold 2003) provide evidence that threatening events, circumstances, and thoughts about one's own mortality enhance self-uncertainty and trigger self-defense mechanisms. While some studies postulate that especially low self-esteem individuals draw on self-protective measures in case of threat and uncertainty (Baumgardner 1990), others show that individuals with a high but unstable self-esteem tend to be highly threatened by negative self-relevant events. One possible way for them to cope with self-threatening events or information is to locate the source of the threat as external and to attack it. This means that high-but-unstable self-esteem individuals will be highly defensive and actively attempt to derogate the source of the threat (Greenier et al. 1995). They may even become aggressive or hostile and direct their negative feelings toward an unrelated object (Kernis et al. 1989). By contrast, low self-esteem individuals reveal uncertain and cautious behavioral patterns and rather adopt "indirect" self-enhancement and self-protection measures. Accordingly, some psychologists assume that low- and unstable-self-esteem individuals have a greater desire to avoid negative feelings about themselves but lack the internal resources to protect themselves from negative information (Greenier et al. 1995).

However, others (e.g., Baumeister 1993) argue that what distinguishes individuals with low self-esteem from those with high self-esteem is not their negative view of themselves or their greater need to think well of themselves, but the deprivation they experience in serving this need. Certain conditions may deprive them of being able to form a basis for thinking well of themselves. This makes them more vulnerable to threats when they experience events that threaten their self-worth; they are less able to emphasize positive characteristics of the self. Psychologists (e.g., Baumeister 1993; Spencer et al. 1993) thus argue that individuals low on self-esteem are more uncertain and fragile, which enhances their emphasis on self-certainty, order, and safety. To understand the sources of deprivation, psychological research has thus aligned their focus on the self-conceptions of individuals with low self-esteem. As mentioned above, Campbell and Lavallee (1993) argue that individuals low on self-esteem tend to experience self-concept confusion, which means that their self-concept is not stable but subject to permanent changes and fluctuations. Their beliefs and perceptions about the self may contain contradictions and inconsistencies, which enhance uncertainty and ambiguity about their self. But what leads to self-concept confusion and which factors tend to deprive individuals from developing stable self-esteem? Despite the rich psychological literature on self-esteem, these questions are still under debate.

While cognitive psychologists (e.g., Greenier et al. 1995) focus on internal determinants (e.g., ego involvement), developmental psychologists insist that external factors should also be taken into consideration. Childhood experiences that involve substantial amount of inconsistency, threat, and unpredictability are likely to promote the formation of unstable self-esteem. Receiving inconsistent feedback from significant others may enhance ambiguity and vulnerability about one's self because it prevents individuals from developing a clear understanding about their own capabilities and limitations (Greenier et al. 1995). Especially during adolescence, individuals start to become more self-aware and are facing the tasks of exploring and committing to form a distinctive identity. During this developmental stage, they are confronted with new developmental tasks, adopt new roles and responsibilities, form other goals, and gain alternative beliefs and insights, which, in the end, make earlier self-definitions obsolete. Self-esteem drops and fluctuations in self-perception occur. A vital element of the developmental changes occurring during adolescence is the acquisition of new cognitive, emotional, and social skills that enable the individual to form a new relational definition of themselves. The individual learns how to better interact with significant others, how to express their own emotions and desires, and how to process evaluative information relating to themselves. "The adolescent begins to perceive aspects of his own psychological self from the point of view of others (Selman, 1980; Broughton, 1981), a development which is frequently linked with a period of extreme sensitivity and self-relatedness (Elkind, 1967). At the same time, self-consciousness begins to differentiate between private and public aspects of self, while a corresponding shift in disclosure partner, usually from parents to peers, can be observed" (Seiffge-Krenke 1990, 49).

In this process, it is important that individuals develop a stable, clear, and consistent self-concept which enables them to cope appropriately with critical life events or unexpected circumstances. Measuring possible coping strategies by a two-dimensional matrix consisting of twenty coping strategies applied to eight problem fields in a sample of five hundred respondents, a study identified three main modes of coping. The first dimension involves an active information search and coping by means of social resources (e.g., getting advice from parents); the second dimension emphasizes cognitive processes, such as evaluation of the problem and internal reflection of possible solutions; and the third, which may be regarded as dysfunctional, entails denial and repression of the problem, which may lead to withdrawal or defense. The study showed that those who were dissatisfied with themselves and indicated having low self-worth were particularly likely to adopt dysfunctional coping strategies (Seiffge-Krenke 1984).

Similar studies agree that certain internal and external resources are necessary to buffer against environmental stressors. These resources, whether internal, like strong self-esteem, or external, like a supportive social environment, have an impact on the adoption of certain coping mechanisms. Receiving emotional, informative, and instrumental support that is consistent, reliable, and guiding, provides a basis for a successful mastery of life. Therefore, individuals require appropriate resources to develop a certain and stable self-concept, a consistent and predictable environment, and possibilities to form relationships, to control their environment, and to participate in society. This strengthens their self-esteem and enables them to develop a consistent self (Dumont and Provost 1999). By contrast, individuals who are deprived of the resources they need to form a stable self-concept and develop strong self-esteem exhibit less stable development over time. They tend to be more vulnerable, and also differ in their choice of coping strategies. While adolescents with a stable self-concept and strong self-esteem adopt active coping mechanisms, individuals in deprived situations with an unstable self-concept resort less readily to active coping and social support. They were more likely to adopt defensive, antisocial, and avoidant coping mechanisms, such as denial or withdrawal (Seiffge-Krenke 1990).

Internal and external factors can dampen the development or maintenance of strong and stable self-esteem during adulthood as well. A study using 2-wave data from the population-based NorLAG study in Norway (N = 5,555) examines the impact of external and internal factors on the development of and change in individuals' self-esteem. The results show that a low SES, unrelatedness, and lifetime experiences of existential stress and uncertainty (long-term unemployment, physical disability) were associated with low self-esteem and/or a decline in self-esteem over the five-year observation period. But also dispositional traits tend to play a role, with high levels of emotional stability, openness, extraversion, and conscientiousness all relating to higher self-esteem (von Soest et al. 2018). Although the examination of individuals' SES and self-esteem is particularly important, empirical findings on the relationship between these two variables are still very unclear. Some studies find a positive relationship, others a negative, and yet others find no relationship at all. In a meta-analysis Twenge and Campbell (2002) summarized all the findings from 446 studies on self-esteem and SES, with a total number of 312,940 participants. The authors identified three models they assume are most relevant to explain the relationship between self-esteem and SES: (i) social indicator or salience, (ii) reflected appraisals, and (iii) self-protective mechanisms. The social indicator/salience model has been used to explain the link between social status and self-esteem. It is argued that an individual's self-esteem rises if they achieve their goals in the form of wealth and social status but decreases if they fail to do so. The reflected appraisals model or the "internalization of stigma," suggests that individuals living in low socioeconomic circumstances perceive themselves as "lower class," which may have an effect on their self-esteem. Finally, the self-protective mechanisms model assumes that individuals use (biased) strategies to protect their own self-concept from negative external feedback or evaluation due to their SES (i.e., they may take credit for high SES, but blame external factors for their low SES). The meta-analysis reveals that there is a small but significant positive relationship between self-esteem and SES. However, the authors (Twenge and Campbell 2002) indicate that the summarized data are very heterogeneous, so that the effect size varies greatly between groups. While the link between SES and self-esteem is not strong during childhood and adolescence, it enhances significantly in young adulthood and middle age, and decreases after retirement age. Considering other moderators, Asian and Asian American samples showed larger effect sizes, suggesting that in Asian cultures SES is perceived as more salient to self-esteem. Among socioeconomic variables, education and occupation showed the largest correlations, while income had the smallest effect. The overall positive effect size was most consistent with the social indicator/salience model. This means that individuals' self-esteem is significantly linked to their achievements and social status, which seems to be more salient in some cultures (e.g., Asian).

These findings suggest that self-evaluation depends on the beliefs held by individuals about the factors they consider important to their self-esteem. Some individuals place more value on economic success and material gain, others value social relations and cultural goods more, and yet others rely on inner harmony to define their self and feel worthy. Some cultures, such as Japan, endorse self-criticism rather than self-evaluation, which means that self-esteem depends less on positive self-appraisal and more on self-criticism as a functional means to achieve social harmony. A cross-cultural study provides evidence that despite cultural differences, self-esteem is indeed a fundamental, universal human need that each individual—irrespective of cultural background—wants to achieve. The study uses the Rosenberg Self-Esteem Scale in fifty-three countries with 16,998 participants and shows that most individuals have an internally consistent concept of self-esteem and can rate, whether they are in the West or the East, their position on the self-esteem scale. Further, the results show that across all nations, individuals with a high self-esteem score low on neuroticism, which indicates that strong self-esteem serves as a natural buffer against anxiety and provide emotional stability (Schmitt and Allik 2005). While a vast number of researchers emphasize the advantages of high self-esteem, others insist that an overtly positive self-evaluation can also be detrimental. We examine this perspective in the following case study.

Box 5.2 The darker side of the self-esteem

In their influential article, Crocker and Park (2004) advance two main arguments which sparked a debate within the psychological discipline. First, they endorsed that self-esteem is a fundamental human need and not just a state of mind or a feeling; second, they posit that self-esteem can be harmful in some fundamental ways. The authors argue that when individuals want to protect, maintain, and enhance their self-esteem, they constantly face stress, anxiety, and self-uncertainty because failure to achieve that goal leads to a decrease in self-esteem. Accordingly, several studies show that individuals who tie their self-esteem to their academic achievements experience strong pressure to succeed, more stress, conflicts with professors and teaching assistants, and pressure to make consistent academic decisions (Deci and

Ryan 2000; Crocker and Luhtanen 2003). Further studies argue that when individuals have a higher need for self-esteem, they tend to validate mistakes, failures, and criticism as a threat to their own self. "Because negative self-relevant information in domains of contingent self-worth implies that one is lacking the quality on which self-esteem is staked, people resist and challenge such information" (Sheldon 2004, 400). Baumeister and colleagues (1993) even argue that an experienced threat to one's favorable self-evaluation can cause violent aggression. In their view, it is not low self-esteem, that is the root of violence, aggression, and antisocial behavior, as is often argued, but threatened egotism (favorable self-view). The term "egotism" refers to favorable self-evaluation and a stronger preference for a positive self-view. Any beliefs that support the view that one is a superior human being, especially in comparison with others, are relevant. If these beliefs are threatened, individuals tend to react aggressively toward the source of the threat (Baumeister et al. 1996).

A long tradition in psychology regards low self-esteem as a potentially harmful and dangerous cause of violence. It has been interpreted as the most "pervasive characteristic" of terrorists, armed robbers, and murderers, and an important trigger of hate crimes (Long 1990). However, Baumeister and colleagues argue that such studies suffer from several ambiguities and inconsistencies (for their arguments, see Baumeister at al. 1996; Baumeister and Boden 1998). Low-self-esteem individuals have no negative or even destructive beliefs and views about themselves; instead, they are characterized by high levels of uncertainty and instability (Dunlop 2017). While it is true that they tend to be more reactive to external cues from the social environment, it is also evident that they are more conservative in their adjustments to this environment. Because low-self-esteem individuals are more uncertain and inconsistent in their self-view, they are assumed to have a greater need for certainty, stability, and approval, and they tend to react more cautiously and engage in more risk-avoidant behavior (Baumgardner 1990; Campbell 1990). In this context, Baumeister and colleagues (1996) postulate that unlike low-self-esteem individuals, high-self-esteem individuals tend to have more favorable, even superior, views of themselves and may feel entitled to receive more resources and opportunities for personal gain. Also, many violent acts require high risk-taking and strong self-esteem may provide the necessary confidence and self-assurance for taking such risks.

However, their main argument does not portray strong self-esteem in isolation as the main cause of violence, but in combination with perceived threat. When favorable views and beliefs about the self are questioned, criticized, challenged, or devalued, individuals may react aggressively toward the source of the threat. Unrealistically positive or inflated views of the self, and favorable self-evaluations that are uncertain, ambiguous, or heavily dependent on external validation, are perceived to be especially vulnerable to such threats. They often elicit negative emotions when an individual refuses to thoroughly process, accept, and internalize the negative information they receive about their self. This is in line with the vast amount of research on the stability of self-esteem, which argues that high, but unstable, self-esteem individuals tend to react especially aggressively to negative self-appraisals (Kernis 2005).

Accordingly, when seen in isolation, the level of self-esteem (whether high or low) is not enough to enable a complete understanding of its role in aggressive and antisocial behavior. Unstable self-esteem, irrespective of its level, is not well anchored and requires constant validation and approval. This means that individuals with unstable self-esteem tend to be more vulnerable, uncertain, and inconsistent in their views, attitudes, and behavior. They show a heightened reactivity and defensiveness in response to self-evaluative information and events, which often has adverse consequences such as an increase in violence, hostility, or depression (Franck and De Raedt 2007; Paradise and Kernis 2002). Unstable self-esteem reflects a self-worth that is more vulnerable to threats because it requires constant validation and protection through self-protective or self-enhancing strategies. Several studies have found that individuals with unstable self-esteem tend to be more reactive toward self-related threats and are thus more likely to exhibit aggressive or antisocial behavior (Lee 2014). For our general analysis, these findings suggest that self-esteem instability is an important aspect to consider when examining violence and conflict. Individuals with unstable and fragile self-esteem tend to be more reactive to threat, are more vulnerable toward ambiguous information (more affected by daily evaluative events and information), tend to take a more self-protective strategy than a mastery-oriented strategy, and have more inconsistent self-concepts.

5.3.2 The Agency Need for Self-Determination

Self-determination is a highly debated concept across various academic disciplines. While we refrain from outlining the historical uses of this term in philosophy and psychology, this section focuses on the universality of this concept from a human need perspective. In other words, we will discuss why individuals strive for self-determination (or the alternatively used term, autonomy); that is, to act volitionally based on their own will, and why it is regarded as a fundamental human need.

Considering various definitions of self-determination, the philosophical discourse discusses whether human behavior is predetermined or the result of free will, while psychology focuses more on the internal and external factors that determine human behavior. In philosophy, determinism implies that human behavior is the effect of preceding causes. Here, the discourse differentiates between hard and soft determinism. Hard determinism postulates that every action and event is caused in accordance with causal laws, while soft determinism argues that an act can be both free (not compelled) and caused. Hard determinism infers that when human actions are assumed to result from implicit determinants or causes, such as feelings, needs, or desires, those same feelings, needs, or desires are themselves caused by certain conditions that induce their appearance. Unlike hard and soft determinism, anti-determinist positions insist that human behavior results purely from free will (with no causes for actions or events). This debate on free will versus determinism is said to be one of the most enduring philosophical problems of all time (Wehmeyer et al. 2017).

John Locke, a soft determinist, argues that human behavior is guided by human thought that is shaped by experience and reflection. Self-determination, in his view, is a developmental process. Human actions encompass the ideas of power, volition, and freedom. Power is the ability to influence the environment (make change) and the human mind has the power to induce human actions. Volition is the exercise of that power. Freedom, in turn, is the power to execute volition without any external force or constraint. It is thus the agent, not the will, who is free to act on volition (Wehmeyer et al. 2017). Human beings act freely to the extent they are able to translate their psychological preferences into performance. In other words, as far as an agent has the power to think and act according to his mental preferences, so far is he free (Locke 1690). For our purposes, this would imply that the agent is free to act, but the action itself is "caused" by numerous "determinants." These physiological, psychological, economic, and environmental determinants have an impact on the agent's mental preferences and the agent is free to choose a course of action according to these preferences.

While such a philosophical discussion focuses on the question whether human behavior is the effect of human thought and free will or if human actions are predetermined, psychology emphasizes the internal and external determinants of human action. Skinner (1971), a hard determinist, rejects the idea of autonomy and that human behavior is a function of free will. Instead, he postulates that all human actions are caused by laws of operant conditioning. However, personality psychologists insist that an "essential feature of a living organism is its autonomy" and that "the science of personality is, in essence, the study of two essential determinants to human behavior, autonomous-determinism (or self-determination) and heteronomous-determinism (other-determined) (Wehmeyer et al. 2017, 9). One of the most influential works on self-determination is that of psychologists Edward Deci and Richard Ryan (1986, 2008, 2012). In his early writings, Deci (1980) argued that self-determination is the basic human need to feel competent and autonomous of using will to choose how to serve one's own preferences. Self-determination theory thus postulates that human beings are active organisms that are motivated to adapt and integrate their experiences, knowledge, and abilities into their environment. Human beings are perceived to be proactive and growth-oriented (Deci and Ryan 2012). Further, the theory argues that constructive and destructive sides of human behavior can be explained as outcomes of the interaction between individuals' basic psychological needs and the sources of need satisfaction or thwarting (Vansteenkiste and Ryan 2013). These assumptions correspond to our framework where we argue that certain external and internal factors are important sources for need "deprivation"—the denial of or reduced access to the resources or opportunities needed to serve one's own existential, relational, and self-related needs. To serve these needs that are vital for survival, well-being, and personal fulfillment, individuals search for reconciliation strategies, which can also result in antisocial and destructive human behavior.

Self-determination theory, however, focuses on the satisfaction of three basic needs (need for autonomy, competence, and relatedness)[6] which is assumed to energize the development of self-determination, the autonomous motivation consisting of intrinsic and extrinsic motivations. The interaction between people striving to meet these needs and the resultant autonomous motivation stimulates causal action. The theory thus emphasizes the intrinsic, autonomous motivation for producing healthy adjustment and the negative consequences that can arise if individuals are deprived of the opportunity to act autonomously (and the perception that one is driven mainly by external forces or rewards) (Shogren et al. 2017). In this regard, Deci and Ryan (2012, 85) argue that "to be autonomous means to behave with a sense of volition, willingness, and congruence; it means to fully endorse and concur with the behavior one is engaged in. Autonomy—this capacity for and desire to experience self-regulation and integrity—is a central force within [. . .] the life span development of individuals [. . .]. In healthy individual development, people move in the direction of greater autonomy. This entails internalizing and integrating external regulations over behavior and learning to effectively manage drives and emotions. Additionally, it means maintaining intrinsic motivation and interest, which are vital to assimilating new ideas and experiences."

Various empirical studies thus postulate that satisfying the need for autonomy enhances subjective mental well-being and supports the development of a consistent and stable self-concept. A true self develops as one acts autonomously and consistently according to one's own preferences, and as one is socially accepted for who one is rather than for matching some external requirements. Being able to act freely according to one's own preferences, desires, or attitudes (perceived locus of causality) enables one to develop a true and consistent sense of self and a stronger sense of self-worth. Being autonomous is both an input to and a manifestation of a high and stable self-esteem (Deci and Ryan 1995). However, if individuals feel the obligation to assume a certain role or comply with certain social standards and thus feel forced to give up autonomy and their true sense of self (and thus one's own "true" preferences, desires, attitudes, etc.), their self-concept becomes contingent on following these implanted roles or rules. Clinical studies have shown that being deprived of the need for autonomy (i.e., the lack or denial of resources or opportunities to serve this need), this can even result in personality or behavioral disorders. In this regard, an empirical study argues that individuals with an eating disorder report difficulties in defining and controlling themselves. One possible explanation for this, it is argued, could be an overtly controlling parenting style, which left individuals with no opportunities to make decisions that were consistent with their needs and desires. Controlling one's own eating behavior and weight can be thus perceived as a compensating factor to regain control over one's body and mind (Wechselblatt et al. 2000).

Further studies examine the relationship between socioeconomic factors and the subjective ability to feel autonomous. They assume that socioeconomically disadvantaged individuals have mostly physically demanding jobs with limited opportunities to express their autonomy, and also fewer resources to make choices that are consistent with their needs and desires (Poleshuck and Green 2008). Having little access to socially valuable resources which allow the individual to serve their own needs, and thus make autonomous decisions according to their own preferences and goals, is perceived to dampen the development of a self-regulatory mechanism that helps them manage various tasks and challenges in life. In other words, the lack of environmental support and opportunities to make decisions according to one's preferences and goals can have a detrimental effect on individuals' psychological and physical well-being (Shogren et al. 2017; Little et al. 2002).

However, the interaction between individuals' striving to act volitionally and the given context or environment is complex, but, in essence, it reflects individuals' coping with threat and opportunities in the environment. "Opportunity," here, refers to situations or circumstances that allow individuals to make decisions so they can achieve the desired outcome. These situations and circumstances provide individuals a chance to be active members of their environment, to induce change and make something happen by means of their subjective causal capabilities. However, opportunities are also bound up with individuals' causal capabilities (i.e., the mental or physical resources that enable a person to cause something). If an individual has limited causal capabilities, their opportunities are few and far between. "The second challenge condition, threat, involve situations or circumstances that threaten the organism's self-determination and provoke the organism to exercise causal action to maintain a preferred outcome or to create change that is consistent with one's own values, preferences, or interests, and not the values, preferences or interests of others" (Shogren et al. 2017, 23).

Considering this interaction between the two challenge conditions—opportunity and threat—and an individual's need for autonomy, it becomes clear that the development of autonomy is a complex process. Especially during adolescence, individuals strive to develop a stable self-concept and a consistent sense of self; that is, the perception that they are able to act according to their own preferences, desires, or goals. Experiencing oneself as the originator of one's actions and decisions enforces self-worth and increases self-confidence (Hansen and Jessop 2017). Therefore, developmental psychologists emphasize that self-determination is achieved if the individual identifies and reaches goals based on the foundation of knowing and appreciating oneself (Field and Hoffman 1994). Because volition and choice are instrumental to experiencing and developing autonomy, an important question is how constrained resources and environments dampen this development (Hansen and Jessop 2017). The self-determination model of Field and Hoffman (1994) postulates that self-determination is promoted or thwarted both by internal (e.g., individuals' values, knowledge, skills) and external (e.g., opportunities for choice making, social support from others, etc.) variables. The authors argue that to be self-determined, one must have both a foundation of self-esteem and self-awareness as well as the ability to act on this foundation. Especially during adolescence, individuals learn to be aware of their own capabilities, skills, attitudes, and preferences and strive to develop personal independence. Because acting on one's own behalf always involves risk, individuals learn how to make risky choices to reach their goals and how to cope with potentially negative outcomes. Learning how to tolerate uncertainty and the consequences of risky choices helps adolescents to develop self-confidence and trust their own decision-making. Developing the ability to make plans, to think more abstractly, and to control impulses enhances their ability to anticipate potential consequences of their choices and actions, which is also a key ingredient of self-determination (Field et al. 1997).

However, cross-cultural psychologists insist that the manifestation and endorsement of autonomy (or self-determination) differ across cultures that hold different values. Self-determination is, they argue, characteristic especially of individualistic Western societies that promote subjective independence over social interdependence. Therefore, the need for autonomy conflicts with the need for belongingness and interdependence, both which are highly valued in collectivistic societies. Yet others argue that the need for autonomy is universal and present in every human being, although it may be reflected on different levels. In collectivistic cultures the need for autonomy can be served by internalizing the choices made by significant others. A study with Chinese children showed that those with a close relationship with their mother had a lower need for autonomy but were still intrinsically motivated to complete a task chosen by their mothers. By contrast, autonomy was an important factor for children with no close relationships. The authors concluded that the effect of freedom of choice no longer prevailed when the relationship was intimate and positive (Bao and Lam 2008). Another study with Chinese students showed that the need for autonomy was strongly linked to the need for belonginess, revealing that the more autonomous support they received from their parents, the greater a connection they felt with their parents (Hui et al. 2011). The authors of the previous study assume that "the issue of autonomy is concerned with the extent to which one fully accepts, endorses, or stands behind one's actions. If Chinese children have internalized the choices made by trusted others, they might experience autonomy although they did not make the choice" (Bao and Lam 2008, 280). Individuals who base their self-concept on interdependent relationships perceive themselves as a part of a social system and may thus perceive close individuals as a part of their own selves (Markus and Kitayama 1991). These findings and assumptions confirm that the need for autonomy is a fundamental human need that seems to hold across cultures and values.

Box 5.3 Overemphasis of self-determination and potential negative implications

Considering the various theories and empirical findings on self-determination, we can surely agree that the need for self-determination is universal, and that the freedom to choose and act according to one's own preferences and goals can lead to greater physical and psychological well-being. However, developmental studies also provide evidence that to develop the capacity to act autonomously, individuals, especially during adolescence, require close and positive attachment relations. Such early adolescent attachment relations with parents provide a stable foundation from which young people can develop their self-view, self-trust, and self-competence, which are necessary to successfully exercise autonomy. Such intimate and positive relationships have been also found to buffer against stress and uncertainty in decision-making (Papini and Roggman 1992). All this may suggest that self-determination can only develop if individuals experience secure, consistent, and stable relationships that support them in forming a consistent self-concept and positive self-awareness.

Accordingly, sociologists argue that due to the continued disintegration of social systems and communal bonds and the overemphasis on autonomy and individualism especially in Western societies, individuals face greater vulnerability and uncertainty in their decision-making. In his famous book *Risikogesellschaft* (*Risk Society*), the German sociologist Ulrich Beck (1986) postulates that, in the modern-era, individuals are increasingly exposed to various threats, such as environmental disasters, terroristic attacks, economic downturns, or social inequalities, but also to great personal risks, such as the augmented responsibilities to make choices and to embrace opportunities to create their own concept of life. While previously traditional social structures, cultural norms, and role ascriptions "limited" the range of possible decisions and provided guidance on how to perceive one's environment and make decisions, the modernization process uprooted the individual from "these bonds and limitations" and expanded their possibilities for choice and self-expression. While we agree that enhanced freedom of choice and autonomy can contribute significantly to psychological well-being, it can also enhance decisional anxiety and indecisiveness. Several clinical studies show that especially in Western, individualized societies, individuals tend to suffer increasingly from cognitive and mental overload, burnout, depression, and substance abuse (Carod-Artal and Vazquez-Cabrera 2013). The World Health Organization (WHO) warns that by 2030, mental ill-health (such as burnout or depression) will be the most frequent disease problem in the developed world (WHO 2008). Maslach and colleagues (2001), for example, postulate that burnout can result from enhanced subjective responsibility to make decisions at work (overload), but also from lack of identification and belonging to one's own working environment.

In modern societies, the enhanced emphasis on self-determination and individualism has created, on the one hand, more opportunities for developing one's own self-concept, but on the other hand, it has provided no guidance how to do so. Individuals are confronted with an overwhelming amount of information and options for forming their self, their personal and professional life, and their relationships. They are perceived as independent entities, and the boundaries between the self and the others are distinctly shaped (everyone tries to be unique and independent) (Inglehart and Oyserman 2004).

The psychologist Berry Schwartz (2000) refers to this daunting multitude of options in life, estrangement from oneself and society, and the personal task of "fulfillment" as "the tyranny of self-determination." He argues that "most of us now live in a world in which we experience control [and autonomy] to a degree that people living in other times and places would think quite unimaginable. Extraordinary material wealth enables us to consume an astonishing quantity and variety of goods, and the magical mechanism of the market allows us an almost limitless array of choices. Further,

> this autonomy and control extend beyond the world of material goods. In careers, there is an enormous degree of mobility, both in career type and in geographical location. People are not constrained to do the work their parents did in the place where their parents did it, nor are people constrained to have only a single occupation for their entire working lives. Therefore, almost anything is possible. In personal life, religious, ethnic, racial, class, geographic, and even gender barriers to mate selection are rapidly disappearing. Moreover, one is free to choose whether to have kids or not, whether to have them early or late, whether to bear them or adopt them, whether to have them as part of a traditional marriage and family or as part of any of a host of nontraditional family arrangements" (Berry 2000, 85). He argues that for the very first time in history individuals can live the lives they always wanted to and thus must be mentally healthy. Instead, the number of individuals with mental health issues, such as depression, is rising exponentially.
>
> Schwartz (2000) explains this growth in terms of rising expectations: everything we do or choose must be the best of its kind. An overemphasis on self-determination has contributed to these unrealistic expectations, while the culture of individualism promotes the idea that individuals must create everything on their own. Yet if they fail to achieve these unrealistic expectations, they tend to make causal attributions that focus on internal factors ("it's my own fault") rather than on external factors (e.g., social barriers). This kind of causal attribution may promote negative self-perception in case of failure and can be thus a potential source of mental disorders.

5.3.3 The Agency Need for Self-Efficacy

The previous sections have shown that the development of a true, stable, and consistent self is assured if individuals act autonomously; are accepted for who they are (feel like they belong and are approved by significant others); and learn to appreciate and be aware of their own capabilities, skills, attitudes, and preferences. A further significant aspect of true self-development is the ability to experience an inner sense of self-efficacy; that is, the perception of the individual to have the capacity to create, achieve, and produce something of subjective significance and to achieve the desired results. Individuals strive to feel competent and to make decisions, solve problems, and overcome challenges effectively (Gecas 1989). Albert Bandura (1977, 1986), the pioneer of self-efficacy theory, postulates that self-efficacy is the primary determinant in behavioral change and successful environmental adjustment. "The initiation of and persistence at behaviors and courses of action are determined primarily by judgments and expectations concerning behavioral skills and capabilities and the likelihood of being able to successfully cope with environmental demands and challenges" (Maddux 1995, 4). In this regard, Bandura (1977, 1986) distinguishes between efficacy expectations and outcome expectations. Efficacy expectation is a subjective belief that one is capable of successfully performing an action, while outcome expectation is a subjective belief that an action will lead to a desired outcome. The former is a subjective belief about one's skill, while the latter is a belief about one's environment. Bandura argues that this distinction is important in case of subjective feelings of meaninglessness in life, which can be then explained either by a low sense of self-efficacy or by lack of opportunity or responsiveness in one's own social environment. To decrease efficacy-based meaninglessness requires individuals to develop their own abilities and an awareness of their personal effectiveness. To change the outcome-based meaninglessness requires changing the prevailing environmental structures (e.g., social barriers). Thus, Bandura differentiates between the perception of the self and the perception of the self in relation to the social environment.

This concept of self-efficacy has been expanded to refer to the subjective belief that one is able to mobilize one's resources to reach certain outcomes. Self-efficacy judgments in this regard are not concerned with individuals' skills but with the evaluation of what they can do with their resources and skills. In this process, individuals weigh up, evaluate, and integrate information from various sources concerning their capabilities (i.e., given skills, resources, knowledge, etc.), and regulate their choices, actions, and effort expenditure accordingly. In experiments, self-efficacy expectancy has been observed to be a viable and reliable measure to assess individuals' success in reaching certain outcomes. One study shows that the best way to predict the success of a smoker's attempts to give up is to assess their self-efficacy expectancy. In other words, measuring a smoker's perception of their own ability and eagerness to quit smoking under specific environmental conditions will provide better results than measuring their self-esteem or self-confidence (Maddux 1995). An individual who believes that they can abstain from smoking or other form of drugs, and thus to produce a desired outcome through their own personal resources can pursue a more active and self-determined life course. In this regard, several abstinence self-efficacy scales have been developed to measure the role of self-efficacy in treatment outcomes. A study with 2,967 participants in fifteen residential substance-abuse disorder treatment programs assessed the relationship between abstinence self-efficacy and treatment success. Abstinence self-efficacy was measured with a questionnaire asking participants to indicate on a ten-point scale how confident they were about their ability to become completely abstinent within a year. Further, they were asked to rate their ability to refrain from substance use in specific tempting situations (e.g., stress, emotional or physical negative states, interpersonal conflict). The results show that an enhanced belief in one's own self-efficacy was the strongest predictor of abstinence after one year (Ilgen et al. 2005).[7]

The findings may indicate that self-efficacy can induce change in one's own behavior, actions, and value priorities. If individuals believe that they have the ability to achieve certain outcomes, and thus to promote change, it can enhance their willingness to adjust to their given environment. Self-efficacy thus plays a crucial role in psychological adjustment. Studies show that individuals with low self-efficacy are more likely to suffer from depression because they often believe they are not able to behave effectively and to reach the desired outcomes. But also, dysfunctional anxiety and avoidant behavior are often assumed to be a direct result of low self-efficacy. Individuals who lack confidence in their abilities and agency are more likely to avoid difficult and stressful situations and tend to react more uncertainly and anxiously to threats and unpredictability. By contrast, individuals with strong self-efficacy are assumed to be more capable of managing threatening and uncertain situations and of reacting more calmly to stress and unexpected events (for a review, see Maddux 2002). Some researchers even argue that self-efficacy is crucial to mental and physical health and to coping and successful environmental adjustment (Bandura 2000; Maddux 1995). It influences a number of biological processes that support individuals in coping with illness and stress, such as an enhancement of components of the immunological system (Wiedenfeld et al. 1990) or the activation of catecholamines, a family of neurotransmitters important for managing stress and threat (O'Leary and Brown 1995).

However, there is also a long and rich tradition in sociology which deals with self-efficacy. Marx, for example, argues that the subjective self can only be developed through efficacious actions in the context of work. If individuals receive the opportunity to create or achieve something of subjective significance, their self is created and affirmed. By contrast, individuals who feel estranged and alienated from their social and work environments suffer from a frustrated need for self-efficacy. Depriving individuals of the opportunity to perform in a given setting, to be effective, and to attain desired results will lead in the long-term to an enhanced perception of powerlessness and meaninglessness in life. Another perspective in sociology on self-efficacy provides the theory of symbolic interactionism. It perceives the individual as an active member of their environment who is able to shape, change, and influence their world, as well as being formed and created by it. In this process, the "true self" evolves if the subject receives the opportunity to act authentically and impactful; that is, according to their desires and goals (Gecas 1989).

To develop an ability to act in an impactful, efficacious, and authentic manner, developmental psychology assumes that certain socioeconomic factors must be present. Among the scarce studies on this issue is Bandura et al. (2001), who examined the multifaced socio-cognitive origins of children's self-efficacy beliefs and their impact on their career-related choices. The proposed conceptual model tested the influence of socioeconomic, familial, and self-related factors on self-efficacy and career choice. It was shown that familial SES tends to influence parents' self-efficacy and their aspirations to achieve certain goals, which in turn affected their children's perceived efficacy and academic aspirations. This then shaped their perceived efficacy about career choice. In other words, familial SES and parents' perception of their own efficacy and goal achievements shape children's personal efficacy which, in turn, determines their decision-making regarding potential career paths. The first link in the proposed model refers to the impact of the SES. Various studies (e.g., Elder 1995; Bandura 1997) reveal that socioeconomic factors, such as income and parental education level, tend to affect children's developmental courses through their influence on familial processes. Another study (Boardman and Robert 2000) shows that even the socioeconomic level of the neighborhood, such as high levels of unemployment or public assistance, tend to have an impact on individuals' self-efficacy. In some cases, the results show that neighborhood socioeconomic background appears to reinforce this relationship over and above an individual-level SES. This means that individuals with a similar SES will report different levels of self-efficacy depending on the socioeconomic conditions in the neighborhoods they live in. The authors explain that due to limited resource flows into low socioeconomic neighborhoods, an individual with a low SES, living in such an environment, will have fewer resources to draw on. Living in a social context where opportunities and resources are limited lowers one's perception that one can achieve something and act according to one's own desires and goals. This means that the individual has less exposure to other individuals who engage in efficacious actions and achievements, which lowers his or her perception of one's own efficacy.

However, other studies have shown that it is not a SES per se that tends to dampen individuals' level of self-efficacy, but the deprived social context. A pilot study (Ali et al. 2005) examined the impact of contextual support, barriers, and SES on the vocational/educational self-efficacy of a group of a lower SES adolescents. The results indicate that peer and sibling support, but not parental support, was an important contributor to the vocational/educational self-efficacy expectations of low SES youth. Especially the support of peer groups was found to be an important predictor of adolescents' self-efficacy. Siblings and peers at the same age are regarded as role models and better sources of encouragement and career information than parents in the low SES sample, who most often had a low education level which may have reduced their ability to give appropriate career advice. However, receiving general support from the social environment decreased individuals' perception of social barriers and enhanced their self-efficacy beliefs, irrespective of the SES background.

Contrary to these results, the study of Bandura et al. (2001) mentioned previously argues that parental support does play a significant role in children's self-efficacy beliefs, but is mediated by their own efficacy beliefs. If parents believe in their own efficacy and ability to achieve subjectively set goals, they are more likely to support their children's engagement in academic pursuits. Such parental influence promotes the development of children's beliefs in their social and self-regulatory efficacy. Other empirical findings show that parents with strong self-efficacy beliefs who believe they can influence the development of their children in a positive and constructive way are more proactive, supportive, and successful in cultivating their children's competencies than parents with low self-efficacy and strong self-doubt (Coleman and Karraker 1997; Elder 1995; King and Elder 1998). Especially academically aspiring parents tend to promote not only their children's self-efficacy beliefs and academic achievements but also the development of their social and self-management skills. This parental support in turn helps children to develop a strong sense of efficacy for self-regulation and mastery of academic requirements. If children or adolescents believe they can master the complex cognitive tasks on their own, be efficacious in their actions, and impactful in their choices, it encourages the formation of a consistent and stable self-concept. Acting autonomously and authentically according to one's own desires, preferences, and goals and receiving opportunities and active encouragement from one's social environment will generate a self-determined, stable, and consistent identity. Depriving individuals of all these resources, options, and mental support will lead to maladjustment, frustration, and the formation of an inconsistent self-concept.

> **Box 5.4 Self-efficacy and meaning in life**
>
> Each individual seeks to actively shape and construct their own environment. In doing so they are confronted with a complexity of conditions, such as ambiguous information, unpredictable circumstances, uncertain outcomes, and adverse events, under which they must make appropriate life choices. Individuals aim to order and interpret their existence, find their role within the social context, and make

consistent decisions according to their preferences and goals (Baumeister 1991). To be able to act autonomously, impactfully, and consistently with one's "true self" generates feelings of power, mastery, and meaningful existence. Self-efficacy, as discussed previously, has been found to be a significant factor in overcoming various negative health-related behaviors, such as anxiety and depression, alcohol and drug abuse, eating disorders, smoking, and socially avoidant behavior. Having strong beliefs in one's own efficacy and abilities helps individuals to overcome difficult life situations and to better adjust to changing environmental conditions. Acting upon one's preferences and goals and receiving the opportunity to achieve something and express one's potential also fosters the perception of a meaningful self. Although psychology has only just started to examine the concept of meaningfulness in individuals' lives, existing studies portray it as one of the central factors for happiness and life satisfaction (MacKenzie and Baumeister 2014).

But what exactly does it mean to have meaning in life, and why is it even important to search for it? Throughout the history of mankind, individuals have been searching for answers to explain their existence and purpose in life. These universal questions address the core concerns of humanity and have inspired many ideologies, philosophies, arts, and narratives in various cultures around the world. The concept of meaning carries multifaceted functions and manifestations, such as cognitive (a sense of consistence), motivational (having a purpose and goals), and the search for or awareness of meaning, as well as sources of meaning. Baumeister (1991) argues that the basic human need for self-efficacy guides individuals to create sense in their lives. Having a meaningful life refers to a subjective sense of significance, direction, and purpose. The opportunity to fully explore one's potential, to act upon one's desires and goals, and to create and achieve something subjectively meaningful generates a sense of continuity and trust in life. The lack of meaning awareness, by contrast, has been found to have a major impact on mental health issues ranging from depression, substance abuse disorders, anxiety and compulsive disorders to adjustment difficulties (Batthyany and Russo-Netzer 2014). Sociologists argue that especially the modern and fast-changing environment challenges the existing patterns of continuity, social embeddedness, and traditions. An overabundance of choice has turned out to be frightening rather than liberating, often leading to uncertainty, frustration, and a sense of powerlessness and dissatisfaction (Schwartz and Ward 2004). Thus, psychologists argue that the search for meaning has intensified in the last decades. "In the face of the uncertainties and instabilities of our times, failing to respond to the inner voice of meaning may lead to boredom, anxiety, disengagement, and an existential vacuum" (Batthyany and Russo-Netzer 2014, 3).

Today, many young people lack a clear direction and purpose in life, which in the long run can lead to emptiness and destroy the foundation of a fulfilled life (Damon

2008). Meaning can be seen as an important psychological resource that guides individuals' decision-making and behavior and points toward a valuable future. "Eliminating the meaning people perceive in their lives would seem to dismantle the interconnecting filament on which are hung the most savory and desirable qualities of a full life. Life without meaning would be merely a string of events that fail to coalesce into a unified, coherent whole" (Steger 2009, 685).

PART II
IDEOLOGIES AND NEED RECONCILIATION

6
Belief Systems and Ideologies as Psychological Need Reconciliation

In the previous Part we identified fundamental human needs—needs that refer to a safety-seeking mechanism, to identity and group formation, and to a consistent and stable self-concept. In our analysis we gathered evidence that these needs are fundamental; that is, the origin of these needs can be explained or reasoned in evolutionary-biological terms. Accordingly, we identified three interrelated "categories" of fundamental human needs, as shown in Figure 6.1.

(i) Existential and epistemic needs are driven by conditions of threat, complexity, uncertainty, and the struggle for survival, which drive human beings to seek a sense of security, mastery of circumstances, and control over their own environment. Here we identified needs for safety, for control, order, ambiguity avoidance, consistency, and predictability. These needs originate in the human necessity to secure one's own existence, to feel that one is able to control and affect one's own environment, and to live in an ordered, predictable, and consistent environment. However, to survive and remain mentally healthy, human beings also need social connections. In this context, we identified *(ii) relational needs* that focus on identity, social belonging, and pro-sociality. Individuals aim to maintain a sense of belonging; to share their identity, values, and ideas with significant others; and to feel loved and approved by other members of their group. In this regard, we consider the need for belongingness, identification, and social approval, but also the human need for pro-sociality; that is, the innate human drive to share, help, and feel empathy for others. Beyond the needs for survival and sociality, individuals have also *(iii) agency needs*, corresponding to individuals' striving for a consistent and stable self-concept, a positive self-view, and an autonomous life; that is, a need for self-esteem, self-efficacy, and self-determination.

Further, we emphasized that depriving individuals from serving these fundamental human needs tends to produce tension in an organism (Staub 1993). If, for example, the need for safety is not met, neurocognitive functions of the brain support the threatened individual to process negative information faster than rewarding information. This can be attributed to a survival strategy and environmental adaptation that helps individuals to cope with unexpected

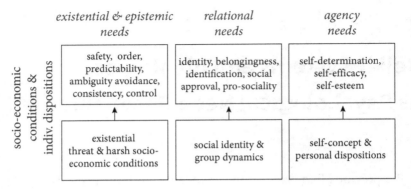

Figure 6.1 Fundamental Human Needs

and uncertain situations (Zheng et al. 2016). If the need for belongingness is not met—fueled by feelings of rejection—the activity of the anterior cingulate cortex (dACC) increases, an area that is associated with regulating the physical experience of pain (Eisenberger 2011). This implies that our body and our brain react to needs deprivation, which gives rise to drive states and which pushes individuals to find a way to cope with the arousal in order to remain physically and mentally healthy. "Human needs specify the necessary conditions for psychological health or well-being and their satisfaction is thus hypothesized to be associated with the most effective functioning" (Deci and Ryan 2000, 229). The need strength differs from personality to personality, while the manifestation of a particular need can be determined by external factors, including threatening situations, socioeconomic and political change, or terrorist attacks (Jost 2009; Kay and Friesen 2011).

Accordingly, we propose that individuals are driven by an "inner tension" to find ways to manage their unmet or threatened needs (deprivation). This is what we refer to here as reconciliation. The term "reconciliation" has been mainly used in religious discourse to describe the act of salvation but it has increasingly become a subject of discussion in social science. Here, reconciliation is understood as a process of conflict resolution between two parties. "It explores the causes of the conflict, particularly causes in the form of threatened and unmet needs for identity, security, recognition, autonomy [. . .]. It seeks solutions responsive to the needs of both sides through active engagement in joint problem solving" (Kelman 2008, 17). Although in this context the use of reconciliation focuses on the transformation of the conflictual relationship between two parties, our analysis puts more emphasis on the internal psychological process of conflict resolution. We propose that every individual tries to find ways to reduce the inner tension (inner conflict) due to threatened or unmet needs (Burton 1990; Max-Neef 1992; Deci and Ryan 2000). This implies that the failure to meet these fundamental needs tends to cause psychological, or even physiological, suffering, which in turn urges the individual to reduce the resulting inner tension or negative arousal. Successful reconciliation, that is, finding ways to satisfy one's own fundamental needs, can thus lead to enhanced well-being and the perception of a meaningful existence. Human beings strive to find meaning in life, where the essence of meaning can vary on the individual level. Finding a connection, starting a family, or achieving financial success or autonomy can all guide individuals to make sense of their lives. Although Baumeister (1991) argues that the quest for a meaningful life can be understood in terms of four fundamental human needs (for purpose, values, self-efficacy, and self-worth), we argue that individuals can find meaning in life by satisfying the needs that are most important for them. Individuals who do so are likely to regard their lives as valuable and meaningful. We will return to the relationship between reconciliation and meaning in life later in greater detail.

In psychological literature, human needs are defined in a two-process model "as both behavioral motives that are inborn within everyone (although people may develop variations in the strengths of these motives) and as experiential nutriments that everyone requires in order to thrive and experience wellness (although people may vary in how well these needs are satisfied). The two aspects of psychological needs serve as part of a coupled motivational system that functions by prompting people to pursue (typically) adaptive behavioral motives and also reinforces them when successful need-relevant behavior occurs" (Sheldon 2011, 522). The experience of need deprivation motivates individuals to search for coping mechanisms to adapt to the given circumstances and resolve the inner tension. In biology, this can be referred to homeostasis: a self-regulating process of biological systems to adjust to conditions to maintain survival, personal development, and self-determination (Burton 1972).

Experiencing need deprivation, and thus a negative arousal, the individual can search for possibilities to reduce the state of arousal and find means to serve one's own needs. Possible reconciliation options can range from direct physical solutions to indirect mental strategies. Choosing a direct physical option for reconciliation, the individual must actively evaluate and understand the source of arousal, search and process information needed to find a solution, and adjust his attitudinal and behavioral patterns. However, such a deliberation process incurs high costs. Questioning and changing one's own behavior and prevalent attitudes requires much effort and can even lead to uncertainty, self-doubt, and confusion (Gawronski 2012). An alternative to a direct physical reconciliation can be an indirect, mental reconciliation. A mental reconciliation provides means to understand and evaluate the given circumstances, information, and events, which can be consistent to one's (self-consistent) ideas and attitudes. In other words, it requires neither a vast information search nor the questioning of one's prevalent attitudes and behaviors. Such a feasible mental reconciliation can be provided by ideologies, narratives, and belief systems, which form a mental framework that helps individuals to interpret social reality and to deal with inconsistencies, uncertainty, and threatening situations. While individuals can either choose a direct or indirect reconciliation option (or both), in the following we focus only on indirect, mental reconciliation options in the form of belief systems and their need-serving faculties. A belief system is thus a system or accumulation of beliefs that provides a mental framework which guides individuals in processing information, interpreting, and evaluating various life events and making consistent decisions. As a function of their personal history, personality traits, and exogenous conditions, individuals seek to choose a belief system that best serves their relational, existential, epistemic, and agency needs. This means that an individual chooses the belief system that is consistent with his individual needs and preferences, and that adhering to a certain belief system is, to some extent, rational (even if it may produce self-defeating outcomes). In the forthcoming chapters we will thus focus on the concept of beliefs and ideologies and their reconciling features. For simplification, we focus on ideologies that can also be found in popular political discourse. After outlining our working definitions and conceptions of ideology and reconciliation, the greater part of this chapter addresses in detail the ontological, social, and psychological function of beliefs and ideologies.

6.1 The Concept of Ideology

The concept of beliefs and ideologies has been discussed for over two hundred years in various disciplines, ranging from philosophy and political science to psychology and sociology, and, in the last decade, also in economics. Despite their prevalence in everyday life, the role of ideologies, narratives, and belief systems is still under debate. Especially in political science, ideologies are merely perceived as a tool for propaganda, basically as a collection of ideas and narratives designed to win votes and gain political support. Yet opposing voices argue that beliefs and ideologies "are not merely a passive reflection of vested interests or personal ambition, but have the capacity to inspire and guide [political] action itself and so to shape material life" (Heywood 2015,

2). However, beliefs and ideologies do not evolve from nowhere—they are shaped by social, cultural, and historical circumstances. We refrain from analyzing the historical roots and developmental stages of ideologies and beliefs, and instead focus on their social, ontological, and psychological functions (their need-serving faculties).

So, how can we define a belief and ideology, and what is our understanding of them? In the *Encyclopedia Britannica*, the *Oxford Dictionary of Philosophy*, and the *APA Dictionary of Psychology*, for instance, a belief is defined as the acceptance of a proposition being true on the basis of inconclusive evidence. Here in the first stance, we are concerned with the state of believing, without asking what exactly is believed. Various debates on beliefs are led in philosophy, cognitive psychology, and economics. Philosophers distinguish between the mental state of believing and the propositional content itself. In the former sense, two individuals hold the belief that grass is green; however, due to their subjectively different mental states, their perception/belief of the grass is not the same. The latter sense implies that the propositional content— grass is green—is the same for both individuals (Oxford Companion to Philosophy 2005).

Psychologists and cognitive scientists agree that beliefs do not rely on general assumptions and logical reasoning but are rather subject to individuals' cognitions and representations of reality. Belief formation is not primarily guided by accuracy, but by self-serving and identity-maintaining motives (Benabou 2015). This means that individuals form and hold beliefs that generate a positive self-view and are even willing to invest resources to avoid information that contradicts their beliefs (Eil and Rao 2011; Ganguly and Tasoff 2017; Golman et al. 2017). They may invest heavily in certain beliefs that have an emotional and instrumental value for them. Holding positive beliefs about oneself and one's environment can thus have palliative (Jost and Hunyady 2005) and utility-maximizing effects (Benabou 2015). People want to believe that they can have success and positive opportunities in the future, that they are skilled and liked by others, and thus (often, but not always) deceive themselves to achieve such beliefs. This assumption concerning motivated beliefs implies that beliefs shape information-processing and decision-making in the context of goal-directed individual behavior (Benabou and Tirole 2016).

In contrast to the motivational approach, economists process beliefs in respect to Bayesian updating. In the Bayesian framework, data are perceived as a fixed set of additional information that is used to update prior beliefs. Such cognitive processes pertaining to the formation of beliefs about the external environment (and the given facts) differ from those pertaining to beliefs concerning one's internal motivations. The reason for the difference is that internal motivations cannot be considered on a factual basis because self-related convictions cannot be objectively quantified or predicted on the basis of some probability distribution. Bayesian beliefs, in turn, are determined and adopted on the basis of available information in light of Bayes' rule. So, Bayesian beliefs are "evidential beliefs" because they can be corrected or updated by empirical evidence. This implies that individuals are capable of processing new information to update their beliefs in a manner that will result in a relatively accurate representation of reality, which tends to decrease uncertainty and indeterminacy (Khalil 2010, 2011). However, as previously discussed, individuals are usually inclined to hold beliefs about themselves and their future that are often biased and non-warrantable (e.g., Pronin, Lin, and Ross 2002). Experimental studies demonstrate that individuals tend to update their beliefs asymmetrically by underestimating negative evidence relative to positive evidence, even when they are explicitly given an incentive to report accurate beliefs (e.g., Eil and Rao 2011; Möbius et al. 2014).[1]

However, in our analysis we depart from these two approaches and argue that individuals not only hold (and update) beliefs to reduce complexity and to pursue self-interested goals, but they also use them to reconcile needs. To recall, by reconciliation we mean a subjective process aimed at reducing inner tension arising from need deprivation. From our perspective, we thus use the term *need-serving beliefs*, which can be both motivated and Bayesian. Such need-serving beliefs provide a mental framework that leads individuals to serve their fundamental human needs, such as identification, social approval, certainty, ambiguity avoidance, or self-esteem. Subscribing to one's own beliefs and a subjective sense of reality, or processing information in a biased, self-relevant way, may appear logically and objectively irrational. However, from a subjective perspective such actions may be considered reasonable, even if they are sometimes self-defeating. We address the concept of reconciliation in the forthcoming chapter and describe the need-serving process in greater detail.

For now, it is enough to keep in mind that a belief is defined here as a subjectively consistent presumption, or even a narrative in which we have specific confidence. It is a mental guide that addresses the self and how the self can cope with uncertain states of the world.[2] Beliefs can be also self-defeating, but we focus here on mind-independent (Bayesian) beliefs that are not subject to self-deception or self-illusion. Rather, they are based on real empirical evidence that can be updated, revised, or even replicated. Take individual A, who is very confident, or even purports to know, that ghosts do not exist. They believe this because there is no evidence (for now) that ghosts may indeed affect our experiences. However, we could also be provocative and say that we also do not have proof that ghosts do exist. So, it remains a belief that can be updated with empirical evidence: if we receive evidence that ghosts do exist, then we can update, or revise, our belief accordingly.

A further aspect mentioned in our definition is the concept of narratives. A narrative is an instrument used to understand and construct social reality (Benabou et al. 2018). Narratives can be life stories, objectively given facts, or cultural myths that people tell themselves or each other to understand a situation or a series of events. Ideologies provide such coherent narratives that explain the origin of a given problem or circumstance and show how to resolve them within the ideological context. These narratives are usually constructed by starting with an initial state ("once upon a time," "back then," etc.), containing protagonists, describing a problem or obstacle, portraying enemies, a clash, and a potential (or desired) outcome. "Ideological narratives incorporate a reconstructed past and imagined future, often telling a story of progress or of decline [. . .]. They are successful only to the extent that large numbers of people accept the same ones (although they may edit their own versions to better complement their personal life stories). These ideological narratives are usually grander than life stories, often reaching back centuries or millennia for their "once upon a time," casting larger groups and forces as the actors, and justifying epic actions, reforms, and even violence as the way to reach the dénouement" (Haidt et al. 2009, 115). In other words, ideologies provide narratives that enable individuals to understand and link the past, present, and potential future and to integrate this coherent story in their own life. Such integrations and understanding of events, information, and circumstances form coherent patterns of reality in terms of a given ideology, which generate stability and meaning for individuals' lives. Furthermore, ideological narratives are shared with social others and can be thus seen as a significant source of identification and belongingness.

Accordingly, we can define a belief system as a system or accumulation of beliefs that provide a mental framework which guides individuals in processing information, interpreting, and evaluating various life events and making (consistent) decisions. Despite the fact that ideologies are constructed within a particular cultural and social setting, we refrain from outlining the anthropological view of ideologies. Instead, we look at belief systems in a broader, more dynamic context and propose that individuals choose a belief system from a set of existing options, and revise or even change it under certain conditions. This means that individuals evaluate and choose a belief system that "best" serves their needs and preferences subject to given constraints (e.g., deliberation and information costs, time, environmental restrictions, etc.). Further, we assume that once an individual has adopted a certain belief system, they do not really think much about these beliefs because they have "provided good service" in the past (helped to evaluate information and events, to make decisions, or to act based on these beliefs). If an individual has succeeded in making certain decisions by relying on their beliefs (and belief-based rules, heuristics, etc.) in the past, they will continue using this kind of mental framework also in the future (without thinking much about it). Relying on the belief system means not evaluating it permanently. Only if the adopted beliefs repeatedly failed to provide "good service" (in terms of bad decisional outcomes) will individuals re-evaluate or even reject them and search for a new belief system. That means that individuals compare their own beliefs with new experiences and information and with the beliefs of others, thus re-evaluating and even changing them if necessary (Bayesian updating). To limit the scope of our analysis, we focus in the following discussion on the more political conceptualization of belief systems, namely on ideologies. Originally, the term "ideology" was developed in the late eighteenth century when it was used to describe the science of ideas and thoughts. The concept was later adopted by Marx and Engels and has since been used in two different explanatory approaches: one, as an abstract and symbolic meaning system that provide explanations (or justifications) of reality and two, as a set of ideas that are blurred, incoherent with reality, and subject to "false consciousness" (Jost 2006). False consciousness can be defined as the holding of false or inaccurate beliefs that are inconsistent with one's own social interests, and which can lead to the preservation of the disadvantaged position of the self or the group. The concept of false consciousness plays a significant role in the Marxian concept of ideology, as it was used to describe ideological domination. "Because of ruling class ideology (defined as a system of ideas or beliefs that serve the dominant group's social interests at the expense of other groups), Marxists have argued that most people's understandings of social and political reality are distorted. Significantly, however, mainstream social science came to drop the negative evaluation associated with ideological thinking (Allport 1954; Mannheim 1936), and the search for ideology became not a search for false or distorted conceptions of the political world (the effects of ideology), but the search for coherent [and] consistent belief-systems" (Jost 1995, 413).

We depart from the concept of false consciousness and define ideology as an interrelated set of norms, values, and attitudes that is shared within an identifiable group and that involves cognitive, affective, and motivational components. It provides alternative interpretations of the social, political, and economic environment, as well as prescriptions on how the world should be (Jost et al. 2009). Ideologies help individuals to process information, to understand reality, and to organize their values and beliefs. It helps to explain why people do what they do and to understand and evaluate outgroup and ingroup related behavior. It guides them as to how to behave, how to address life's problems, and how to manage threatening situations (Jost 2006; Jost et al. 2008). Considering all these attributes, it may be clear that ideologies seem to be a "natural" part of our psychological functioning and thus seem to represent a viable reconciliation strategy that serves human psychological needs.

It is worth mentioning that in some scientific disciplines the adoption of ideologies seems to be linked to self-deception or cognitive limitations. Motivational biases, cognitive incapability, resource limitations, or informational complexities have all been linked to ideological adoption. In particular, the assumption of false consciousness implies that individuals make irrational choices that contradict their self-interest (Heath 2000). There is no doubt that such inconsistent decisions are made without reasoning; however, in our elaboration we explain that choosing an ideology is consistent with subjective needs and preferences. Empirical tests provide evidence that individuals who reject, for example, climate change or gun control, mainly supporters of the Republican party in the US, did not score better or worse on the Cognitive Reflection Test, an objective measure of information-processing dispositions associated with cognitive biases (Kahan 2014). Other studies show that racial prejudice cannot always be explained by a low SES or education (cognitive limitation) because well-educated individuals with a high SES, too, tend to adopt racist ideas (Manstead 2018). Accordingly, it is argued that when individuals face economic threats or social risks, it can be subjectively reasonable for them to process information in a manner that reliably connects them to the positions that dominate in their identity-defining groups (Kahan 2014). Relying on consistent and predictable ideas, values, and norms that are supported by other ingroup members can provide, from a psychological perspective, feelings of certainty, stability, and control, and, from an "economic" perspective, can be an optimal (cost-)efficient way to manage threats and risks.

Hence, we argue that finding reconciliation in belief systems to manage external threats or uncertainties is not always linked to self-deception or destructive behavior. Adopting a particular ideology can be perceived as an individual's attempt to deal with the complex reality based on subjective needs and preferences. However, particular ideologies can surely have devastating implications on a social and collective level. We refrain from going deeper into this discussion and focus rather on the reconciling functions of ideologies.

6.2 The Concept of Reconciliation

In our conceptual framework, we use the term reconciliation to describe the resolution of a subjective inner conflict, or tension, that arises due to threatened or thwarted human needs. We propose that every individual tries to find solutions to reduce this inner tension (inner conflict) and to find a way to serve their own (unmet) needs (Burton 1990; Max-Neef 1992; Deci and Ryan 2000). Deprivation of these fundamental needs tends to cause psychological or even physiological suffering, which in turn leads the individual to reduce this negative arousal. This implies that finding ways to satisfy one's own needs can enhance one's physical and psychological well-being. One of the central factors associated with psychological well-being is the experience or sense of a meaningful life and existence. "At the most basic level, meaning is about the shared association and distinctions of particular pieces of information. One definition could be that meaning is a shared mental representation of possible relationships among things, relationships, and events. Thus, meaning is the basis of a collective, organized network of concepts" (MacKenzie and Baumeister 2014, 26). Ideologies provide such meaning systems and guide individuals as to how to process information, behave, and make decisions within a social context. This means that individuals do not create their own meaning systems but select those that society has to offer (the preassembled mental frameworks like ideologies). Psychologists like Baumeister (1991) argue that meaning can be achieved by satisfying four fundamental human needs (for purpose, values, efficacy, and self-worth). While we agree with this approach, we go further and argue that individuals can make sense of and find meaning in life by satisfying the needs that are most important to them. Further, we argue that ideologies provide viable reconciliation options to serve these fundamental needs of individuals and can be thus understood as significant meaning systems.

6.2.1 Ideological Reconciliation in a Nutshell

But how do ideologies (or belief systems in general) serve these needs? First and foremost, belief systems deliver guidance on how to interpret and evaluate information and provide principles for judgment, decision-making, and action. The formed perceptions, roles, and attitudes support individuals in dealing with social reality, uncertainty, and threatening situations (Knight 2006). The values, beliefs, and norms (that are shared within a group) supply a construct of how the (idealized) world should be by emphasizing the deficiencies of the current social, political, or economic system. Furthermore, belief systems deliver narratives for identification and group identity, provide group reassurance, and support the formation of positive self-esteem. All this forms a concept of (perceived) coherence, consistency, and meaning. The shared framework explains, guides, unites, and reacts appropriately to burgeoning emotions. But beyond peaceful ideas, ideologies can be aggressive and totalitarian, covering irrevocable and static dogmas. In this case, an ideological framework presents a clear and orderly image of the world in that it provides stereotyping images of "good and evil," with the aim of shaping a social pattern of coherence and contrast. Radical ideologies can provide a stable structure, perceived certainty, and control. They often incorporate strong (superior) moral principles that help individuals to differentiate between "the bad and the good" and between opponents and sympathizers. They offer adherents clarity and consistence in a "threatening," unpredictable, and uncertain world, often combined with static ideas about how things ought to be and little tolerance for those who do not agree with them (Koomen and Van Der Pligt 2016).

In fact, belief systems, whether dogmatic, moderate, or peaceable, tend to serve an ontological, social, and psychological function. They provide answers about human existence, reality, meaningfulness, identity, and belongingness. They include representations of alternative worlds and help individuals understand what the idealized world should look like based on guiding categories of concepts defined in one way or another as "good" or "bad." These polarities have a strong organizing function by providing guiding insights about the self and the others. The practicability of belief systems, or ideologies, means they can be used in everyday life to answer everyday questions and to direct the everyday behavior of their members (Uso-Domenech and Nescolarde-Selva 2016). This implies that the general beliefs, values, and norms of ideologies are "made" to serve individuals' needs and can be applied to their experiences, circumstances, and dispositions. In other words, "all ideological practices of group members are based on specific mental models that feature a subjective representation of events or actions observed or participated in" (van Dijk 2013, 180). It is therefore important to observe not only the overall group-based appearance and operation of ideologies, but also the subjective application, effects, and role of ideologies for their individual members.

The following subchapters aim to provide a deeper insight into the mental framework of ideologies and their capacity to serve existential, epistemic, relational, and agency needs. "The possibility that ideological preferences are derived partly from the psychological needs of individuals and groups has been neglected by social scientists for decades, apparently because they have discounted the possibility that individuals have genuine ideological preferences and constraints" (Jost et al. 2008, 132). But we argue that psychological human needs, which are derived from situational and dispositional factors, determine individuals' ideological preferences. This implies that individuals adopt the ideologies that best serve their psychological states. For example, individuals with a stronger need for order, consistency, and control may find structure and closure in hierarchy-based and rigid ideologies, because ideas of social equality, tolerance, and divergency imply rather greater unpredictability and structural inconsistency. While psychological theories, such as motivated social cognition, argue that individuals adopt belief systems due to their motivation to reduce uncertainty and threat (Jost and Amodio 2012), we argue that individuals adopt the ideologies that tend to best serve their needs and preferences. Given an uncertain and indeterminate environment, ideologies can be a viable option for dealing with these environmental constraints to process information and make consistent decisions (here, consistent with one's own needs and preferences). Thus "individuals gravitate toward those ideologies that are present in the informational environment and that appeal to them, given their own psychological needs, motives, and desires" (Jost et al. 2013, 235). To give a simple example, let us assume that individual A has a stronger need for order, control, and cognitive consistency. They prefer a stable and consistent environment and reject rapid changes, ambiguity, and divergency. Imagine that due to severe socioeconomic or political changes the environment becomes uncertain and unpredictable. Individual A feels threatened, insecure, and out of control over their environment (i.e., their needs for control, safety, order, and consistency are thwarted). They may now find reconciliation by choosing a belief system that appeals to them given their preferences and needs. Considering all belief systems that are present and feasible in their environment, they will adopt that which is perceived to best serve their deprived needs; that is, an ideology that supplies order, a consistent world view, and guidance on how to deal with the threat and the changed environment. In the following, we examine the psychology behind this mechanism.

6.2.2 Ideological Reconciliation—The Underlying Psychological Mechanism

Several psychological theories and studies reveal that, especially, perceived threat and uncertainty tend to determine ideological orientation. According to the uncertainty-identity or uncertainty-reduction theory (Hogg 2010), uncertain feelings about the personal self and about one's perceptions, attitudes, and values can be experienced as a significant psychological threat that the individual strives to reduce by all available means. One way to reduce self-related uncertainty is group identification because identifying with clearly defined groups and ideological belief systems delivers feelings of belonging and distinction and a definition of the self in terms of shared ingroup attributes (Hogg et al. 2007). Beyond the reduction of a self-conceptual uncertainty, devotion to a particular ideology supplies simple explanations about the social world and one's own place within it, which allows individuals to adopt appropriate behavior toward ingroup and outgroup members, plan actions, and regulate perceptions and feelings (Jost et al. 2007). Especially strong groups with clearly defined boundaries and a clear internal structure, internal homogeneity, common goals, and ideals tend to attract a lot of supporters. The rationale is that identification with a strong group diminishes self-uncertainty, and that prototypes which are simple, focused, distinct, and prescriptive are more effective than ambiguous and unemotional ideas (Hogg 2010). Accordingly, empirical research (Hogg et al. 2010; McGregor, Prentice, and Nash 2013) reveals that increased feelings of threat and uncertainty result in a tendency to identify more with radical groups and radical belief systems than with moderate ones. Dominant, homogenous, and action-driven groups provide a clear internal structure and explicit guidance for orientation and offer social order, stability, and perceived consistency, unlike their inoffensive and peaceable counterparts. Furthermore, extreme ideologies respond to various emotions by creating frameworks for feelings like fear, anxiety, desperation, and hope. "This package of assorted cognitions (the interpretative framework) and affect (the various emotions) provides extreme ideologies with some of their magnetic appeal" (Koomen and Van Der Pligt 2016, 150).

To shed light on the control mechanism of ideologies, a new compensatory control model (CCT), derived from psychological, social, and clinical personality research, explains the variability of ideologies in terms of their control function (Kay and Eibach 2013). The model postulates that all ideologies, irrespective of their divergent content, function to serve the fundamental human need for control. Extreme events, such as economic crises, terrorist attacks, or political turmoil, trigger widespread uncertainty which in turn can propel individuals toward radical ideological positions. "CCT proposes that people defensively embrace ideologies that emphasize personal, societal, or religious control in order to alleviate anxieties they experience when they perceive randomness and disorder in their lives. Thus, according to CCT, the need to perceive the world as controllable, nonrandom, and orderly is a latent human need that is commonly fulfilled by social and political ideologies that differ in their manifest contents" (Kay and Eibach 2013, 566). Therefore, it is hypothesized that individuals who either temporarily or chronically have a stronger need for order, control, or certainty tend to adopt rather conservative ideologies, which are characterized by a consistent and predictable world view and a hierarchy-based order (Jost et al. 2013).

As mentioned in Chapter 5, many cognitive studies (e.g., Rodin and Langer 1977; Gebhardt and Brosschot 2002) support the existence of a fundamental need among people to believe that they can control and determine their personal environment. Believing the opposite can lead to disturbed psychological outcomes and negative emotional processing (Kruglanski et al. 2014). The belief of personal control varies across individuals, cultures, and socioeconomic conditions. In some cultural contexts, endorsing beliefs in the power of social institutions, the ruling elite, or supernatural agents can give individuals the perception of a controllable and consistent environment. Threatened personal control or the lack of possibilities to exercise personal control can be compensated by external sources of control, which can manifest in religious or political ideologies (perceived control by group leaders, divine figures, etc.) (Kay and Eibach 2013). The motive to adopt a certain ideology also depends, beyond the cultural context, on personal socioeconomic conditions. People who suffer poor living conditions or live in a politically unstable environment are less inclined to trust and believe in their government, which is perceived to be too unstable or untrustworthy to provide social order and stability. Consequently, individuals living in an environment that restricts their ability to exercise personal control and limits their faith in the power of the government tend to search for alternative coping mechanisms, such as ideologies (Ottaway and Hamzawy 2011). But even in wealthy countries, members of deprived communities who feel left behind by the government and suffer from low personal significance tend to support alternative belief systems in an attempt to control these threats (Koopmans 2013).

Psychological studies on counterterrorism show that individuals join extreme groups not due to idealistic motives, deeply held faith, or personality disorders, but rather to acquire a sense of control, structure, and certainty in their lives (Webber et al. 2018). Recent numbers suggest that, since 2015, more than forty-two thousand individuals traveled from at least eighty-six countries to Syria and Iraq to join the Islamic State and other violent Salafist groups (MMP 2021). Empirical investigations, ranging from laboratory experiments to field surveys of imprisoned extremists (e.g., Jasko et al. 2017; Webber et al. 2016, 2018), provide evidence that radicalization and extremism is driven—beyond a need for control, stability, and order—by the need for self-significance and meaning in life. The significance quest theory indicates that "extremist behavior is seen as a means to gaining or restoring an individuals' sense of personal significance, importance, or effectiveness; that is, the sense of mattering in the eyes of oneself and others who matter" (Webber et al. 2018, 271). Increased feelings of self-insignificance, social disapproval, and personal randomness can be triggered by shattering events which may entail social rejection, discrimination, humiliation of one's own social group, or the denigration of personal characteristics that define one's own identity. Such incidents can lead to social disintegration and identity vulnerability and induce negative feelings about oneself (Anhut 2005; Sageman 2008). Ideologies, in this context, can be viable reconciliation options to satisfy one's own needs and thus provide a sense of meaningful existence.

Negative experiences, such as ostracism, a perception of self-insignificance, or disintegration, deprive individuals from serving their existential, epistemic, relational, and agency needs. Such need thwarting in turn drives individuals to reduce the inner tension and to find viable reconciliation options (McGregor et al. 2001). The results of four empirical psychological studies, conducted either with detained former extremists or with students in experimental manipulations, show that increased feelings of personal insignificance increased individuals' propensity toward radicalization. Individuals who experienced self-uncertainty, lack of meaningful existence, or feelings of social rejection reported a significantly stronger need for cognitive closure, which was subsequently related to enhanced support of extreme political beliefs (Webber et al. 2018). The endorsement of extreme beliefs shared within a strong group provides feelings of certainty, self-esteem, and control. Individuals who experienced rejection, powerlessness, and anger receive mutual respect, social approval, and solidarity in a given group, generating a sense of a meaningful existence and enhancing their self-esteem (Koomen and Van Der Pligt 2016).

Empirical studies on terrorism and radicalization provide evidence that poor socioeconomic conditions and the experience of relative deprivation can enhance the tendency of individual radicalization (see, e.g., Piazza 2011; Mousseau 2011). Others, however, find the opposite. Analyzing data on terrorism in the Middle East, a study (Krueger and Maleckova 2003) revealed that higher levels of education and better economic conditions correlated positively with support of terrorism. The researchers argued that participation in politics and society requires cognitive and financial resources that are only available to a limited group of privileged individuals. A reexamined study (Testas 2004) with extended data confirms the positive relationship between education and terrorism, which remains stable even after controlling for GDP or the impact of political repression. The author reasons that almost seventy percent of countries that experienced at least one civil war within the last decades were also the most politically repressive. This implies that in a repressive and authoritarian socio-political environment, individuals do not have the power and control to express themselves and to experience self-efficacy. The failure of a (mostly corrupt or illegitimate) government to integrate an emerging and educated social class may lead them to search for alternative (even violent) means to express their political voice and thus experience self-significance.

The rise of ideological radicalism can be thus explained on the one hand as a consequence of uncertainty and threat (e.g., systemic instability, economic inequality, anxiety due to system breakdown, political insecurities) and, on the other hand, as an enhanced need for stability, self-esteem, and orientation (Jost et al. 2007). Sociological studies postulate that young adolescents are particularly vulnerable to ideological frameworks due to their undergoing a turbulent process of self-discovery. The process of identity formation is marked by self-doubt, confusion, and the search for answers, meaning, and stability. Young adults are confronted with permanent changing socioeconomic and political conditions, which force them to respond autonomously to the conditions and challenges they encounter (Heitmeyer 1991). An empirical sociological study of 1,257 German adolescents aged sixteen to seventeen found that those who suffered from feelings of self-insignificance (lack of perspective) and negative self-image tended to seek affiliation and social approval from an alternative community. The analysis shows that the interaction between various elements—including the individual process of identity formation, personal resources, and an awareness of societal requirements and contradictions—can result at worst in subjective feelings of social alienation, identity confusion, and severe self-uncertainty. Young adults who feel socially disintegrated tend to seek guidance from radical groupings that propagate disparity and exclusion. Young male adults are especially prone to adopt radical authoritarian-nationalistic views that provide strict order, stability, and guidance, and that legitimize the use of violence as a means of self-expression and problem-solving (Heitmeyer 2005b).

6.2.3 Ideological Reconciliation—Why and How

In light of the theoretical and empirical evidence, it becomes clear that ideologies provide viable reconciliation options to serve human needs in terms of alternative mental meaning-making systems. The wide range of ideologies covers different paradigms and provides different moral models, which form attitudes toward issues related to the social, economic, and political system, but that are also related to the self. We learned in the previous chapter that ideologies provide a viable reconciliation option and respond to different kinds of needs. In political science, but also in other social disciplines, it is quite common to divide ideologies along a liberal/conservative or right/left political spectrum. The terms "left" and "right" first emerged during the French Revolution in 1789, reflecting the seating arrangements of radicals and aristocrats at the first meeting of the Estates-General and thus the choice between revolution and reflection.[3] Since then, the terms have been used to describe contrasting attitudes to political change (Heywood 2017). While left-leaning, or liberal,[4] ideologies are said to support change and progressive policies in terms of democracy, resource redistribution, and environmental protection, right-leaning, or conservative, belief systems tend to oppose change and policies directed at redistribution and climate change (Jost et al. 2013). Such divergent attitudes and perceptions toward society and environment determine the way individuals act and exercise power and control. However, this traditional ideological divide also has its drawbacks. All ideologies, whether they lean left or right, contain contradictory elements that make it difficult to place them clearly along a linear political spectrum. Anarchism, for example, can be located at either the far left or far right end because it contains elements of both. Furthermore, ideologies can manifest differently in different cultural and geographical contexts, which makes it even more difficult to clearly assign them to the right or left (Heywood 2017). In light of this fluidity, we refrain in the following discussion from employing a distinct left–right ideological divide and focus instead on the mental frameworks of ideologies and their need-serving tendencies.

Ideologies do not just serve as "organizing devices" or as a "processing mechanism," but also as a cognitive, emotional, and motivational device for justifying or rationalizing ideas about the past, present, and future (meaning-making system). They provide narratives that enable individuals to understand and connect past events with the present status quo and to integrate this coherent story with their own life. Such integration and understanding of events, information, and circumstances form consistent and unambiguous patterns of reality (in terms of a particular ideology), which generate stability and meaning in individuals' lives. Furthermore, ideological narratives are shared with social others and can be thus seen as a significant source of identification and belongingness. In other words, ideologies have the capacity to influence and structure social, economic, and political understanding in order to motivate, set goals, and connect individuals with each other. They provide a sense of certainty and stability in times of threat and uncertainty;

order, consistency, and guidance in times of chaos or disorientation; shared values, beliefs, and identity as a basis for identification and belonging; and a sense of self-significance in the presence of disintegration and a low self-regard. Ideologies can thus be perceived as a viable reconciliation option for satisfying individuals' existential, epistemic, relational, and agency needs.

Empirical studies show that individuals with a stronger need for order, certainty, social approval, or belongingness are more motivated to perceive the social environment as fair, legitimate, orderly, and stable, and to aim to maintain the status quo. Justifying the system can have positive short-term effects, such as reducing feelings of uncertainty, unpredictability, anxiety and the lack of control over the environment, but also negative long-term consequences when issues such as climate change and social inequality remain unchallenged (Jost et al. 2009). System justification theory suggests that socially disadvantaged individuals, in particular, are motivated to support societal systems and to perceive them as fair and legitimate because this reduces uncertainty and creates the illusion of control. A paradoxical consequence of suffering is that individuals prefer to increase their commitment to their own social position over pursuing clear actions to reduce their disadvantage (Kay and Jost 2003).

Further studies in this direction showed that individuals lower in SES were more likely to support civil rights restrictions, were more likely to trust and less likely to question the government, and more likely to adopt beliefs that justify social inequality (Jost et al. 2012; Osborne and Sibley 2013). Furthermore, a stronger endorsement of meritocratic beliefs (the non-egalitarian "deservingness" principle) was found to be associated with greater life satisfaction and made people feel better about their own situation, which in fact satisfied the need to explain and justify their actions and those of others (Jost et al. 2013). A survey experiment in low-income South African townships showed that perception about the inevitability/changeability of the status quo tends to determine demand for social change. More than half of respondents underestimated the extent of inequality in their community and believed that strong social inequality was inevitable, while more than half believed that South Africa's rich deserved their high incomes. Accordingly, "high and persistent inequality may breed a sense of inevitability, resignation and system justification which may depress demand for redistribution, thus consolidating the high and persistent levels of inequality" (Pellicer et al. 2016, 5).

A similar survey of 356 Bolivian school children aged ten to fifteen showed that those living in the poorest areas, mainly Indigenous peoples, were more likely to support the Bolivian government and to believe that political dissent should be oppressed, compared to their high-status Hispanic counterparts. The lower-status children also felt less alienated by the government and supported political attitudes that in fact were less advantageous for them. The results were all the more surprising given that there were no significant differences in political knowledge between low- and high-status groups, and the fact that the government was run by a high-status Hispanic leader (Henry and Saul 2006). Both studies suggest that low-status individuals supported the status quo not because of their limited political knowledge but because of the perception of invariability. "Their motivation to attain a state of firm, secure and unambiguous knowledge may lead to less information processing, so that they see the world and others in a more simplistic way. Disposition to preserve what is established, to stress continuity, to prefer existing or traditional situations and institutions may be the outcome of a tendency to avoid a state of epistemic ambiguity that change always entails" (Chirumbolo 2002, 608). This strand of literature shows that individuals with a low SES tend to search for ways to serve their deprived existential, epistemic, relational, and agency needs. In this context, ideologies that provide narratives to justify the status quo and thus explain the present state of the adherents provide such a viable reconciliation option. System-justifying, social order-advocating ideologies provide a way to understand the social environment and one's own role in it, providing a sense of stability, consistency, and predictability. Perceiving the social environment as fair and legitimate, orderly, and stable, creates a sense of control and a positive self-image. Especially when individuals value their situation and status as unchangeable, reappraising the system in a more positive (even if self-defeating) way can have palliative effects. However, adhering to a particular ideology not only serves one's own needs but can also shape one's social, political, and economic understanding and attitudes. A much-debated issue in this regard is redistribution. We therefore now discuss how various ideologies shape individual preferences regarding redistribution and show, based on this example, their need-serving capacities.

Excursion: Political Ideologies and Redistribution Preferences

One much debated economic topic, especially in the United States, is the attitude toward redistribution policies that seem to be influenced by certain belief systems. One theoretical study in economic research (Giuliano and Spilimbergo 2008) suggests that the personal experience of threat, frustration, and misfortune tends to increase risk averseness and make individuals less optimistic about their future upward mobility. These negative perceptions in turn tend to increase the support of equal wealth distribution. Accordingly, the POUM (Prospects of Upward Mobility) hypothesis assumes that voting behavior on redistribution is determined not only by current income but also by expected future income (Benabou and Ok 2001). A similar economic analysis shows that beliefs about individuals' responsibility to influence their income tend to influence redistribution preferences. Believing that effort alone determines individuals' current and future income had a negative impact on redistribution preferences, whereas the belief that family background influences income differences was associated with stronger support for redistribution (Isaksson and Lindskog 2007).

A similar economic survey, using General Social Survey data for the United States and World Value Survey data to measure cross-country differences, attempted to explain divergent preferences for redistribution by means of individual characteristics (such as income, race, education, age, employment status, etc.); personal values; and the political, historical, and cultural environment. Looking at the results for personal characteristics, factors such as income, education, and race have a strong impact on the preference for redistribution. In the US sample, the white, rich, and well-educated were shown to be highly averse to redistribution. Furthermore, having a middle-to-upper class background therefore increased options for upward mobility and also decreased one's preference for redistribution. The picture changes when controlling for political ideologies. Adherents of the ideological left who are well-educated and have a middle-to-upper class background were shown to support redistribution of wealth, as opposed to ideological right-loyalists. This implies that ideological beliefs indeed have an impact on redistribution preferences (Alesina and Giuliano 2011).

Ideologies on the left advocate the right of the individual, each of equal worth, to receive equal opportunities to make decisions and pursue goals. Ideologies on the right, by contrast, draw on a social and political order grounded in law and tradition and seek to preserve the continuity of society's structures and institutions. Individuals who prefer a more ordered and traditionally shaped society, more consistency, predictability, and control choose ideologies at the right end of the political spectrum, thus rejecting the ideas of equality and wealth redistribution. On the other hand, individuals who prefer an equal and caring social system and have a stronger need for pro-sociality, change, cognitive complexity, and tolerance rather choose ideologies on the left and demonstrate a stronger preference for resource redistribution (enabling equal opportunities for all members of society) (Carney et al. 2008).

Testing for personal values and experiences, the study mentioned above finds that the experience of unemployment and personal trauma has a positive and strong effect on attitudes toward governmental intervention. Moreover, a religious background tends to increase support for redistribution, as does racial, ethnic, or language group belongingness. In this regard, the study shows that individuals are more generous to those who are similar to them and who belong to their own (religious, cultural, ethnic, etc.) group (Alesina and Giuliano 2011). These findings have important consequences for the relationship between immigration and redistribution. Various sociological studies suggest that especially lower-educated individuals tend to dislike welfare support for ethnic minorities or immigrants because they feel threatened in their own economic status (Van Oorshot 2006). From a classical ideological "left vs. right" perspective this seems paradoxical because it assumes that especially those who are socially deprived will adopt left-oriented ideas that strive for policies aimed at egalitarianism, social equality, and economic redistribution (Achterberg and Houtman 2009). Yet empirical evidence suggests the opposite.

One possible explanation addresses the idea that lower-educated individuals have "limited cognitive structure" to understand the complexity of politics and to deal with ambiguous information. So, it is assumed that the ability to understand and evaluate political information leads to a preference for left-wing oriented ideas. A further approach rejects the theory of political competence and suggests that the economically deprived and low-educated individuals have enough insight into social policy, but feel powerless, unequally treated, and left behind. The ethnic competition theory thus argues that resource competition among ethnic groups and scarce welfare provisions can explain the rejection of redistribution for socially disadvantaged groups (van der Waal et al. 2013). An empirical study of 1,972 individuals in the Netherlands tested these explanatory approaches and found that the association between egalitarianism (governmental intervention) and welfare universalism (welfare support for ethnic minorities) is conditional upon the level of education. While an economically insecure position leads individuals to support economic egalitarianism, it does not influence welfare universalism. This means that those with low socioeconomic status potentially support governmental aid but reject the idea that this aid is offered to all individuals in need, such as immigrants or ethnic minorities. On the contrary, higher-educated individuals tend to support both economic egalitarianism and welfare universalism. These attitudes can be explained by the resource competition theory. Those with a low SES, and thus few possibilities to accumulate resources, feel under threat and risk to secure their existence. By contrast, those with a high SES do not have to compete with other minority groups for resources. The analysis also indicates that attitudes toward welfare universalism/chauvinism also tend to be shaped by individuals' cultural position—those with strong cultural participation (reading books, attending cultural events, etc.) and low cultural insecurity (pessimistic world view, social insecurity, negative perceptions of the future) tend to adopt ideas of welfare universalism. Tests regarding the explanation of political competence showed no significant effects (Koster et al. 2013).

The link between socioeconomic conditions and redistribution preferences has been extensively analyzed in the United States. Although the United States has the highest inequality level of all industrialized counties, several sociopsychological surveys have revealed that the majority of Americans tend to support tax cuts and reduced spending on social services and redistribution policies (Bartels 2005). To deal with this paradoxical implication, several psychological studies have tried to find possible explanations by identifying two frequently cited factors: (i) ideology and (ii) economic self-interest. The ideology assumption suggests that the attitude toward redistribution is driven mainly by a coherent system of principles concerning how resources should be distributed. Egalitarian/liberal[5] ideologies define fairness as a state in which all individuals should be treated equally, and thus favor governmental intervention when it comes to social justice. By contrast, conservative ideologies support the idea that only individuals' effort and talent will lead to a good economic outcome and thus reject redistributive policies (Brown-Iannuzzi et al. 2015).

This means that ideologies shape the understanding of the social, political, and economic system and provide a means to justify or reject the existing redistribution policies. These differences are also formed by cultural factors, such as images of public target groups or deservingness perceptions. Especially in the US, various studies have demonstrated that images of people in need play an important role in the support of welfare policy. "There is very low support for the highly selective American "welfare" scheme (now TANF), because people perceive that it is mainly used by teen and single mothers ("welfare queens"), who are morally looked down upon, and by those people who are assumed to be lazy, unreliable, and/or addicted to drugs and alcohol. Programs targeted at groups with no negative images—such as widows, elderly people, and physically disabled people—are well supported by the American public" (Van Oorshot 2006, 25).

Racial stereotyping tends to also play an important role in forming Americans' opinion on welfare. Americans perceive black people as lazy and less responsible and thus reject additional governmental support for them (Alesina and Glaesser 2004). Accordingly, individuals tend to support welfare schemes based on the "deservingness principle," which consists of five criteria. The "control over neediness" criterion states that people who are seen to be personally responsible for their neediness are considered less deserving (e.g., teen mothers [Rein 2001], black people in the US, or the unemployed in Europe [Halvorsen 2002]). Secondly, "level of need" refers to the fact that people in greater need are seen as more deserving. Thirdly, the "identity" criterion implies that people support those who are similar (ethnicity, "race," nationality, etc.) to them. A fourth criterion is "attitude," which states that "needy" people who are likeable, grateful, and conform to social standards are perceived as more deserving. And the final "reciprocity" criterion describes the attitude that individuals who have contributed to society in the past are considered more deserving. In this context, several empirical studies have shown that of these criteria, the control over neediness factor (personal responsibility) seems to be most dominant, closely followed by identity (Osborne and Weiner 2015).

In the European context, a Dutch study provides evidence that especially older individuals with less education, lower SES, and stronger right-wing orientation tend to be more judgmental (deservingness perception), believe that welfare benefits are misused, and that the social security net triggers laziness and irresponsibility. This indicates that deservingness perceptions tend to coincide with personal self-interest. Less educated older people with low SES perceive themselves to be in a risky and uncertain position, which may induce them to reject social provisions they may need in future when targeted at people who "do not really need it" (Van Oorschot 2000). Adopting a more conservative ideology enables them to serve their existential, epistemic, relational, and agency needs; that is, to protect themselves from "potential threats" and defend the status quo and their own social status. Accordingly, political preferences and ideologies are chosen on the basis of momentary motivations, psychological needs, and self-serving preferences.

Economic studies support these findings and assert that ideological inclinations determine attitudes toward redistribution (Alesina et al. 2012; Van Oorschot 2006). Using detailed, quantitative, animated, or interactive survey questions in five different countries in 2016, an economic analysis (Alesina et al. 2018) showed that attitudes toward social mobility, government, fairness, and redistribution policies are strongly determined by ideological preferences. Left-leaning individuals are more pessimistic about social mobility and the fairness of the economic system, and hence do not agree that only hard work can increase an individual's social status. These pessimistic perceptions in turn generate increased support for governmental intervention and greater redistribution of wealth. This, however, does not hold for conservatives, who reject governmental intervention despite maintaining a pessimistic attitude toward mobility and social fairness. This can be explained by the fact that supporters of the ideological right tend to have a negative attitude toward the government (low trust), while leftists have a much more favorable opinion about the government's role and capacities. Furthermore, conservatives believe that less government intervention in economic issues can improve unequal opportunities. By contrast, liberal respondents support progressive tax systems and government spending on schooling and higher education.

"However, right-wing respondents' policy preferences do seem to be correlated with their beliefs conditional on effort. The key belief for them that is most strongly correlated with redistributive preferences seems to be whether one can make it to the top quintile conditional on effort: respondents who hold stronger such a belief want significantly less progressive taxation (higher taxes on the bottom 50 percent), support significantly less equality of opportunity policies and significantly less spending on the safety net (social insurance and income support programs)" (Alesina et al. 2018, 27). Testing for cross-country differences, especially in the United States, conservatives tend to have low trust in government and thus reject redistribution policies. While in all European countries, public spending on opportunity policies is not conditional on individuals' roles, in the US upward mobility is perceived to depend on an individual's responsibility and effort. Hence, right-leaning respondents in the US believe much more in the impact of effort and "self-infliction."

Considering research on personality differences, the social dominance theory postulates that individuals who score high on Social Dominance Orientation (SDO) endorse the belief that some groups deserve more than others. Empirical studies assert that individuals who hold such beliefs tend to oppose governmental and nongovernmental redistributive acts. This opposition is tied to the idea of an essentialist attribution of poverty—the belief that poor people are themselves responsible for their low SES. These findings underline the role of ideology, which indicates that ideological ideas about social structure and its causes can influence the way how individuals perceive and evaluate social reality (Rodriguez-Bailon et al. 2017).

To extend the understanding of redistribution preferences, psychological studies analyze the relationship between personality traits, needs, and ideologies, and suggest that especially open-minded individuals who tolerate complexity and encourage innovations tend to support liberal economic policies and aim to change the status quo, such as reducing income inequality. By contrast, individuals with a conscious personality act in an intentional, disciplined, and achievement-oriented manner. They have a stronger need for order, compliance, and stability—all of which they can find in a conservative economic ideology (individual attribution to economic success). Agreeable individuals are prosocial, altruistic, and tender-minded, and thus may respond positively to liberal economic ideologies. Emotionally unstable individuals who are anxious, vulnerable, and prone to worrying tend to support liberal economic policies that "create safety nets and reduce exposure to market risks" (Gerber et al. 2010, 116). In this context we may assume that individual dispositions have a strong impact on a person's ideological preferences, whatever they may be. Although we do not focus extensively on this line of argumentation, in the following discussion we illustrate the main assumptions made in this regard.

6.3 The Impact of Personality Traits on Ideological Orientation

While psychological and sociological studies consider socioeconomic conditions and social networks as dynamic catalyzers for ideological adherence, personality studies reveal that certain personality dispositions also tend to play a significant role in ideological orientation. Although there is no universal agreement on what personality actually is, most research views personality traits as a cluster of personal experiences, genetic (biological) mechanisms, and environmental adaptations. In this view, it is argued that many personality traits can be assessed early in life and that they remain relative stable across time (Roberts and DelVecchio 2000), which implies that personality traits precede other social tendencies, such as political orientation. This concept has been criticized for ignoring exogenous factors and situational circumstances to explain response tendencies and environmental adaptation, such as the adoption of a certain political ideology. Despite their limitations, personality studies have emphasized the relationship between subjective dispositions and social attitudes (Verhulst et al. 2012). Our aim is therefore not to extensively focus on this research field, but to review the broad conception behind it. In Chapter 7 we thus present the different models and measures used in personality studies, without going into excessive detail, and explore how they are used to explain subjective ideological orientations.

In an effort to provide an extensive overview of the current research in regard to personality and ideology, a study (Carney et al. 2008) listed the traits that have been assumed to be relevant in explaining the differences in ideological orientations and that have been analyzed extensively in different psychological theories since 1930 (Table 6.1). The general idea was to create relationships between general psychological characteristics and the specific contents of ideological ideas and beliefs, and more widely to construct personality profiles of liberals and conservatives in a broader sense. The authors drew on conceptual

Table 6.1 Personality Traits and Political Orientation (extracted from Carney et al. 2008, 816)

Liberal/Left-Wing	Conservative/Right-Wing
Slovenly, ambiguous, indifferent[1] (C−)	Definite, persistent, tenacious[1,2,5] (C+)
Eccentric, sensitive, individualistic[1,3] (O+)	Tough, masculine, firm[1,2,3,18] (C+, A−)
Open, tolerant, flexible[2,3,9,20] (O+)	Reliable, trustworthy, faithful, loyal[1,4,5] (C+, A+)
Life-loving, free, unpredictable[7,8] (O+, C−, E+)	Stable, consistent[1,2] (C+, N−)
Creative, imaginative, curious[9,10,11,20] (O+)	Rigid, intolerant[2,3,5,7,8,15,18,20,22] (O−, A−)
Expressive, enthusiastic[9,22] (O+, E+)	Conventional, ordinary[2,3,5,18] (O−, C+)
Excited, sensation-seeking[9,10,11,20] (O+, E+)	Obedient, conformist[2,3,18] (O−, C+, A+)
Desire for novelty, diversity[9,20] (O+)	Fearful, threadful[2,15,18,20,22] (N+)
Uncontrolled, impulsive[9,12,13,22] (C−, E+)	Xenophobic, prejudiced[2,3,15,18,19] (O−, A−)
Complex, nuanced[16,17,18,20,21] (O+)	Orderly, organized[4,5,7,8,12,13,14,20] (C+)
Open-minded[20,21] (O+)	Parsimonious, thrifty, stingy[4,5] (C+)
Open to experience[10,11,20,23,24,25] (O+)	Clean, sterile[4,5,7,8] (C+)
	Obstinate, stubborn[4,5] (O−, C+, A−)
	Aggressive, angry, vengeful[2,3,4,15] (A−)
	Careful, practical, methodical[5] (O−, C+)
	Withdrawn, reserved[5,9] (E−)
	Stern, cold, mechanical[5,7,8,9] (O−, E−, A−)
	Anxious, suspicious, obsessive[5,6,15] (N+)
	Self-controlled[7,8,9,12,13,14] (C+)
	Restrained, inhibited[7,8,9,22] (O−, C+, E−)
	Concerned with rules, norms[7,8,9] (C+)
	Moralistic[9,15,18,28] (O−, C+)
	Simple, decisive[19,20,21] (O−, C+)
	Closed-minded[20,21] (O−)
	Conscientious[25,26,27] (C+)

Sources: [1]Jaensch (1938); [2]Adorno et al. (1950); [3]Brown (1965); [4]Freud (1959/1991); [5]Fromm (1947); [6]Kline & Cooper (1984); [7]Maccoby (1968); [8]bem (1970); [9]Tomkins (1963); [10]Levin & Schalmo (1974); [11]Feather (1984); [12]Milbrath (1962); [13]St. Angelo & Dyson (1968); [14]Constantini & Craik (1980); [15]Wilson (1973); [16]Tetlock (1983, 1984); [17]Sidanius (1985); [18]Altemeyer (1998); [19]Van Hiel, Pandelaere, & Duriez (2004); [20]Jost, Glaser, Kruglanski, & Sulloway (2003a, 2003b); [21]Kruglanski (2005); [22]Block & Block (2006); [23]McCrae (1996); [24]Barnea & Schwartz (1998); [25]Gosling, Rentfrow, & Swann (2003); [26]Caprara, Barbaranelli, & Zimbardo (1999); [27]Rentfrow, Jost, Gosling, & Potter (2009); [28]Haidt & Hersh (2001)

Note: O = "Openness to Experience"; C = "Conscientiousness"; E = "Extraversion"; A = "Agreeableness"; N = "Neuroticism"; + = "High"; − = "Low"

and empirical contributions of the Big Five Model of personality to classify distinct, relatively nonoverlapping personality dimensions. For each of the descriptive traits listed in Table 6.1, they identified which of the five basic personality dimensions—Extraversion (E), Neuroticism (N), Agreeableness (A), Conscientiousness (C) and Openness to Experience (O)[6]—best capture the ideological differences. The results reveal a remarkable consensus that has existed for more than seventy-five years that two personality dimensions in particular, namely Openness to Experience and Conscientiousness, play a significant part in explaining ideological orientation. "In this sense, the liberal preference for social change and equality both reflects and reinforces motivational needs for openness, creativity, novelty, and rebelliousness, whereas the conservative preference for social stability and hierarchy both reflects and reinforces the opposing motivational pull toward order, structure, obedience, and duty" (Carney et al. 2008, 817). The table shows that individuals who score high on Openness to Experiences (O+), for example, show characteristics of an open, tolerant, flexible, sensitive, and individualistic individual, which are associated with a more liberal political orientation. On the other hand, individuals who score high on Conscientiousness (C+) tend to be more definite, persistent, firm, tenacious, stable, and consistent, which rather seems to correspond to a conservative ideology.

Individuals who score high on Neuroticism have been found to prefer moderate policies, on both the right and the left of the political spectrum. Hence, it has been shown that neurotic individuals seem more likely to support redistribution policies that provide aid to the economically disadvantaged (Van Hiel et al. 2007; Verhulst et al. 2012) and are generally more likely to adhere to ideologies or policies that tend to provide "a certain amount of security," such as social security but also supervision and armament. Because neurotic individuals are rather inconsistent and emotionally unstable, their ideological choice may reflect the same inconsistent pattern. However, further analyses have been unable to find consistent evidence that Neuroticism, Extraversion, or Agreeableness are reliably correlated with ideological orientation, arguing that external environmental conditions and circumstances account for a significant amount of variance in the ideological dimensions (Verhulst et al. 2012).

Another piece of research relying on the Five Factor Personality Model (FFM) agrees that Openness to Experience tends to correlate with ideological orientation. Specifically, Openness to Experience has been found to be negatively related to conservatism, right-wing authoritarianism, and social dominance orientation, with researchers arguing that individuals who are open to new experiences tend to oppose strict conventions and rigid rules (Jost et al. 2013; Van Hiel et al. 2004). A consistent, positive, but weaker relationship between personality and ideological orientation has been found to exist between conservatism and Conscientiousness, a dimension focusing on factors like order and discipline (Van Hiel et al. 2004). The HEXACO model (Honesty-Humility, Emotionality Extraversion, Agreeableness, Conscientiousness and Openness) refines the FFM by including a sixth (Honesty–Humility) dimension, which considers traits such as fairness, greediness, sociality, and modesty. Unlike the Neuroticism factor, the HEXACO model focuses more on emotions than on neurotic tendencies, aiming to measure individual responses to emotional content. Furthermore, the Agreeableness dimension focuses here on altruistic manifestations, embodying traits such as tolerance, forgiveness, and cooperation. From the HEXACO perspective, liberal voters tend to score high on the Honesty–Humility and Agreeableness dimension because they favor fairness, social cooperation, social equality, solidarity, and mutual altruism, whereas conservatives are prone to tolerating social inequality and opportunistic behavior. The model also revealed that individuals scoring high on Honesty–Humility scored low on status-seeking, hierarchical orientation, and self-enhancement, which are usually linked to a conservative ideological orientation (Chirumbolo and Leone 2010).

A longitudinal study (Block and Block 2006) revealed that such personality differences that predict political attitudes in adulthood tend to be already present when children are of nursery school age. Specifically, preschool children who later adopted liberal ideologies were perceived by their teachers as self-reliant, energetic, emotionally expressive, sociable, and impulsive. By contrast, children who later identified themselves as conservative were seen to have been rigid, indecisive, anxious, and inhibited. This implies that factors such as a preference for hierarchy, leadership roles in play, equity versus equality, allocation of given resources, and sharing seem to be present already in early childhood (Carney et al. 2008). Previous research goes one step further by suggesting that genetic factors play a vital role in political orientation and participation in the future. A study found that heritability accounts for a large proportion of the variation in political participation and turnout. It is argued that citizens who have a strong preference for civic duty tend to pass civic values to the next generation (Fowler et al. 2008). Indeed, a body of research has provided evidence that genetic dispositions have an impact on individuals' level of tolerance, social trust, altruism, or political violence (Eaves and Hatemi 2008; Hatemi and McDermott 2012). However, political participation has also been linked to subjective propensity to participate in collective actions, which is also determined by multifarious factors such as patience, socialization, and political environment (Fowler et al. 2011).

A study with twelve thousand sets of twins, gathered from nine different studies and five democratic countries over four decades, found a common genetic influence on ideological orientation across all samples and measures, with the exception of the "Left–Right" association. The traditional terms

"Left" and "Right" are understood differently in European countries than the terms "liberal" and "conservative." "Indeed, the phrase 'Left– Right' appears highly subject to local and cultural definitions and may indicate group identification more than ideological position [. . .]. Outside of the phrase 'Left–Right,' the influence of genetic factors on the development of political ideology appears to be reasonably uniform across time, measure and country, while the influence of common and unique environmental factors differs with the shifting political and social factors in various circumstances" (Hatemi et al. 2014, 291). In this regard Australia, the US, Denmark, Sweden, and to a slightly lesser degree Hungary tend to share similar genetic ancestry but are marked by completely different cultural, political, and social environments. The authors state that although genetic markers remain similar across those countries, the manifestations of divergent cultures and the external environment also have a strong impact on ideological orientation. Hence, models of genetic and environmental variation should be merged to provide a more comprehensive notion of ideological orientation.

Although a variety of genetic studies claim a causal relationship between genetic variance and ideological orientation, arguing that neurobiological factors are the primary contributors to an individual's personality, none has provided definite evidence of a specific genetic marker being related to ideological orientation (Kandler et al. 2012). Instead it is argued that parenting and extreme childhood experiences such as traumata, wartime events, or formative indoctrinations tend to have a direct effect on one's future ideological orientation (de Neve 2015). Several interviews with individuals who were children during the Nazi regime, showed that they connect the Nazi ideology with happy childhood memories rather than with racism and authoritarianism. Some children who were intensively formed and indoctrinated by the ideology of the Third Reich had difficulties adjusting to life after the war. Rather than abandon their identities, indoctrinated individuals avoided a closer examination of the past and preferred to simply get on with their lives by holding on to their beliefs, identity, and the good memories of a prosperous and happy childhood (Shay 2015). A further study on the long-term effects of ideological indoctrination and wartime exposure to political attitudes provides evidence that young men (from the annexed Eastern Borderland region in France) who were forced to serve in the Wehrmacht during the Third Reich maintained their radical right-wing ideas and political attitudes until old age (Vlachos 2016). This implies that ideological indoctrination, group loyalty, identification with community values, and group identity seem to have a significant impact on ideological persistence, maybe even more than certain dispositional aspects.

Despite the empirical evidence on the impact of strong group dynamics, personality psychology insists that certain personality types determine specific ideological inclinations. The most popular work in this regard is on the concept of an authoritarian personality, proposed by Adorno et al. (1950), as a possible explanation for the rise of fascism during World War II. The theory suggests that individuals who score high on authoritarianism are more likely to accept and adhere to authority and hierarchical structures, tend to be more aggressive to outgroups, and to support traditional norms and values, especially when they are endorsed by authorities. Although this concept and the measures of authoritarianism have received both praise and substantial criticism, the study of authoritarian dispositions seems to have made a comeback. The newly constructed validated instrument that is used in this arena to assess a right-wing authoritarian personality is the Right-Wing Authoritarianism Scale (RWA) by Altemeyer (1981). The RWA seems to focus mainly on prejudice proneness, hostility, and discrimination against outgroup members. For example, studies show that people who score high on the RWA tend to be highly prejudiced against African Americans, women, homosexuality, and the disabled (see, e.g., Altemeyer 1998; McFarland et al. 1993). The prejudices are perceived to be indicative of a high need for cognitive closure—the need to organize the world in patterns, in ingroups and outgroups, in good or bad, and in enemies and companions. Outgroup members, or those who are "disobedient" or derogate from traditional values and norms, are perceived as a threat to the established value system. Further, prejudices are perceived to be a cause of strong self-righteousness. Individuals with a high RWA score perceive themselves as morally superior to others, which seems to justify the aggressiveness, intolerance, and devaluation of "dissidents" or deviants (Whitley 1999).

In the 1990s, Sidanius and Pratto (1993) developed a second instrument to measure individual differences in prejudice, authoritarian submission, and social hierarchy preferences, namely the Social Dominance Orientation (SDO). SDO describes "a general attitudinal orientation toward intergroup relations, reflecting whether one generally prefers such relations to be equal, versus hierarchical, that is, ordered along a superior–inferior dimension" (Pratto et al. 1994, 742). The theory argues that individuals who are more oriented to social dominance tend to favor hierarchy-enhancing ideologies and policies, while those who are not tend to prefer the attenuation of hierarchical structures. This difference determines individuals' dispositions to prejudices and hostile or even racist attitudes toward outgroup members, rejection of social equality and redistribution policies, and a sense of (ingroup) superiority. Furthermore, SDO has been linked to various ideological orientations, such as conservatism, just-world beliefs, nationalism, militarism, meritocracy, sexism, and many more hierarchy-endorsing beliefs. But also, to group-relevant social policies, such as adherence to the hierarchical social order, support for the death penalty and torture, or the rejection of social welfare and redistribution (Ho et al. 2015). Recent research has provided a new concept to differentiate between various personality forms and preferences along the SDO scale. It forms subdimensions within the SDO, namely SDO-D (-Dominance) and SDO-E (-Egalitarianism), which assess different dispositions and preferences. SDO-D represents a preference for group-based dominant hierarchies in which group members oppress subordinate groups, are hostile toward them, and justify aggressive behavior to sustain the dominant hierarchy and to control low-status groups. SDO-E refers to the preference for maintaining social inequality and an affinity to ideologies and policies that preserve group-based societal differences (ingroup privileges), but it does not explicitly involve group domination. This means that individuals scoring high on SDO-D are more aggressive and hostile toward outgroups, while SDO-E individuals are less aggressive and dominant but still prefer an ordered hierarchical social structure. Empirical studies show that high-SDO-D individuals endorsed masculinity, torture, and hierarchy-enhancing beliefs about citizenship (see, e.g., Hindriks et al. 2014), whereas high-SDO-E individuals had negative attitudes toward immigrants and multiculturalism and believed that undemocratic governmental attitudes are fair (e.g., Ellenbroek et al. 2014).

Although both the RWA and SDO are perceived to measure similar personality dispositions, research has shown considerable independence between the two. However, the issue of what exactly they both measure has sparked a debate. The assumption that they measure generalized behavioral dispositions (without any external influences) has never been empirically supported (Duckitt and Sibley 2007). Instead, it has been argued that the scales measure social attitudes and values rather than personality traits. In addition, it has been shown that both scales are highly sensitive to situational manipulations and primes, which indicates that individuals' attitudes tend to interact with (and can be thus influenced by) the external environment (Duckitt and Fisher 2003). Accordingly, a dual process approach argues that the RWA and SDO underlie different motives and needs. "This model proposes that the RWA scale measures ideological attitudes that express the threat driven motivational goal of maintaining and establishing group and societal order, cohesion, and security and SDO measures ideological attitudes that express the competitively driven goal of establishing and maintaining ingroup dominance, power and superiority" (Duckitt and Sibley 2007, 115). Empirical studies show that the RWA, but not SDO, predicted negative attitudes toward groups or individuals who are perceived to be socially deviant (e.g., drug dealers) and to pose a threat to established norms and values. Here, perceived threats played a stronger role than subordination or competitiveness (Duckitt 2006). In contrast, SDO, but not the RWA, predicted negative attitudes toward disadvantaged groups (e.g., immigrants, the unemployed, housewives), which enhanced individuals' competitive motives to maintain their subordination. Here the desire to maintain ingroup privileges outweighed perceived threats or social deviance.

Although personality studies support the view that such preferences remain stable over time, opposing studies provide evidence that threats tend to boost individuals' preference for conservatism and authoritarian policies (Chowanietz 2010). This implies that threatening events and negative emotions, such as anxiety and anger, make nonauthoritarians and liberals more prone to endorsing policies they would normally oppose (Jost et al. 2004). A two-wave panel study with French subjects, undertaken both before and after the terrorist attacks in Paris in January 2015, indicates a moderate yet significant authoritarian shift. Here, fear, rather than anger, played an important role in the public's authoritarian shift; in other words, individuals who felt fear rather than anger after the attacks were more likely to change their ideological orientation. The authors suggest that anxious voters on the left are more likely to abandon their ideological convictions, while anger tends to encourage ideological adherence. Consequently, angry individuals on both the left and the right of the political spectrum stick more strongly to their ideological convictions. The impact of anger was found to be even stronger on the political right (Vasilopoulos et al. 2018). These results imply that although individual dispositions tend to determine ideological preferences, the impact of situational or exogenous factors should not be ignored. Threatening events, harsh socioeconomic conditions, or the political climate can change individuals' attitudes and needs and hence their preferences for ideologies and policies. The following chapters are thus designated to explain the interaction, or "match," between underlying psychological needs and ideologies without focusing extensively on individual dispositions. The aim is to provide an overview of ideological mental frameworks and their viable need-serving functions. Specifically, we emphasize various belief systems and their organizing, affective, and motivational, as well as palliative and need-reconciling, effects.

7
Right, Left, and Religious Ideologies

Their Need-Serving Capacities and Potential for Conflicts

As we have seen, much research on belief systems and ideologies relies on the classification of the ideological stance of political parties, and this is usually measured along a more or less well-defined Left–Right ideological scale. Abstract principles like the Left–Right dimension, or the similar liberal–conservative scale that dominates more in the United States, are generally seen as an instrument to guide ideological orientation and self-identification in a complex political environment. However, such classifications can be misleading because ideologies can manifest themselves differently in various cultural, social, and geographical contexts, which makes it more difficult to assign them a clear left–right categorization (e.g., feminism and ecologism can be found on both sides of the political spectrum). Although we do not fully agree with the traditional left–right ideological classification, we stick to it in the following discussion for simplicity's sake as we discuss the various mental frameworks provided by a variety of ideologies. We focus in this regard on the capacity of ideologies typically found on the traditional left–right political spectrum to match and serve individuals' fundamental human needs. This wide range of ideologies covers different paradigms and provides different moral models, which form attitudes toward social, economic, and political issues, but are also related to the self. From this point of departure, we start to examine various belief systems; their narratives, ideas, values, and norms; and how these can serve specific human needs.

7.1 The "Traditional Ideological Right"

We start with the manifestation of ideologies usually found on the far right of the political spectrum. Here, the focus is not on their developmental dimension and historical roots, but rather on their social, cognitive, and psychological functions.

7.1.1 Racism

Racism is foremost a socially constructed belief that characteristics and abilities are determined largely by race. The term "race" implies a social classification system used to divide humans according to real or imagined descent. Such divisions are usually based on "naturally perceived" biological and genetic differences and physical appearance, such as skin color, face shape, or body type (Oxford Dictionary of World History 2015). This classification leads to a "justified" discriminatory treatment of certain groups and ranking of populations based on inherent and/or biological characteristics, usually accompanied by the belief that some races are "better" than others. This superiority thinking and formed prejudices lead to a denigration of individual characteristics and differences and a reluctance to perceive individuals based on their subjective capabilities and merit. Instead, classifications based on subjective belonging to an exogenously determined group provide stereotypical ideas and orientations on how to perceive and evaluate a human being (Farfan-Vallespin and Bonick 2016). There is a grounded consensus that racism is an ideology that can manifest itself in various forms, ranging from a set of prejudices and attitudes found in everyday life to exclusionary practices, such as exclusion from the labor market or the political sphere, or as a political instrument. In this regard, racism as an ideology addresses systematic segregation, denigration, and ostracism, which can enforce feelings of hate, repugnance, and even disgust that are felt and expressed by one group for another (Dalal 2006). Racist narratives generally attribute individual characteristics to biology, which are mainly used as an argument to establish a hierarchy among ethnic groups and to maintain permanent inequalities between individuals. Such clustering, which ascribes certain devaluing and revaluing characteristics to certain groups of people, generates a mental order and enable categorized thinking (compartmentalization). These formed categories and stereotypes in turn provide guidance on how to process information, evaluate events, and deal with unpredictable circumstances, which is assumed to provide a sense of certainty and cognitive consistency (Baldwin 2017; Koomen and Van Der Pligt 2016). In the following we discuss in detail how these racial narratives, and the ideology of racism as a whole, provide a mental framework to serve individuals' existential, epistemic, relational, and agency needs.

Experimental evidence has shown that systemic or institutional racism exists in almost every social domain, expressed *inter alia* in education (McCarthy 2003), the labor market (Bertrand and Mullainathan 2004), the real estate market (Beatty and Sommervoll 2012), and the mortgage market (Williams et al. 2005). Systemic racism implies institutionalized discriminatory practices, unjustly allocated power between groups, resource inequalities along racial divides, and the rationalization of institutionalized privileges of one group (Feagin and Hohle 2017). Sociological data on several generations of families of color and White families provide evidence that, among these groups, enormous differences persist in the acquisition and intergenerational transfer of wealth and social networking capital. White families experienced more than six times as many cash inheritances than families of color, and possessed unequally more land, properties, businesses, and government-derived assets (Mueller 2013). To understand these conceptual differences, vast research has been undertaken, triggering various empirical and theoretical debates to understand the concept of racism.

In political science, it is argued that the concept of race was created "artificially," rationalized by "biological race theories" to form social categories and justify unequal resource allocation (Banton 1998). Although several theories claim that the change in the political and economic sphere after WWII restructured society and thus dissolved arguably predefined social categories, there is ample evidence that racism continues to be present in Europe and the United States. The evidence ranges from incidents in schools and on college campuses and the burning of synagogues, Black churches, or refugee hostels, to vitriolic radio shows and marches that call for killing Muslims (Macedo and Gounari 2016). The old colonial model of "racial" exploitation and cultural oppression is indeed losing ground, yet resurfacing again in ethnic and nationalistic forms (Essed 1991). However, the notion of racism as a political instrument disregards the concept of "race" as a principle of social organization, identification, and identify formation. Racial bias does not just appear on the institutional surface, it is also deeply ingrained in the psyches of individuals (Dalal 2006).

In this regard, sociological and psychological studies have focused on prejudice, psychological mechanisms, and group dynamics to shed light on the attitudes, beliefs, and perceptions that generate and sustain racial stereotyping and discriminatory behavior. From the early to mid-twentieth century, psychological research portrayed prejudice and racial bias as a "psychopathology," suggesting that only authoritarian personalities or individuals with low self-esteem were biased against racial/ethnic groups in ways that led to aggressive and violent behavior (Dovidio and Gaertner 2004). "However, stimulated by developments in the area of social cognition, by the mid-1960s and early 1970s, much more attention was devoted to examining how normal, often adaptive, cognitive (e.g., social categorization), motivational (e.g., needs for status), and sociocultural (e.g., social transmission of beliefs) processes can contribute to the development of Whites' biases toward Blacks"

(Pearson et al. 2009, 315). Accordingly, various empirical studies from the US show that prejudices and stereotypes of Black individuals as violent and hostile are deeply ingrained. Eight out of ten individuals still believe hostility and brutality to be typical characteristics of Black people as a "racial" group (Devine and Baker 1991) and perceive criminal justice as fair and legitimate, while the majority of African Americans are skeptical about the fairness and colorblindness of the system (Pew Research Center 2019).

While the majority of Whites in the Unites States perceive themselves as nonprejudiced on self-report measures, the same percentage shows typically aversive racial behavior (Greenwald et al. 2009). Aversive racism implies that the simultaneous existence of conscious egalitarian beliefs and nonconscious negative affect can produce the ambivalence that characterizes a subtle form of racial prejudice. It is assumed that individuals often face a discrepancy between nonprejudiced beliefs and automatic negative reactions to stigmatized groups (Gaertner and Dovidio 1986). Surveys provide evidence that most White Americans automatically and unconsciously activate stereotypes of Whites as being intelligent, educated, and high-achieving and of Blacks as being violent, lazy, aggressive, and impulsive (Blair 2002).

Cognitive and social psychology argues that such racial categorizations and narratives provide guidance on how to process information, how to perceive oneself and the social environment, how to evaluate unpredictable events and circumstances, and how to behave toward others (Hamilton 1981; Dovidio et al. 1986). Such a social structure with perceived sameness and differences can also generate a sense of meaning—meaning in terms of consistent, reliable, and comprehensible social patterns (Hirschfeld 1996). Relying on racial stereotypes, norms, and beliefs to process information and make decisions allows individuals to perceive the environment as stable and predictable. It provides order and a sense of a controlled and consistent social environment. In this regard, social dominance theory (SDT) suggests that such group-based hierarchies create "legitimized and institutionalized" narratives based on prejudice, stereotypes, and racial discrimination to justify social inequality (Sidanius and Pratto 1999). According to SDT, the degree of group-based social hierarchy in a given social system is formed by two opposing forces: hierarchy-enhancing and hierarchy-attenuating forces. Hierarchy-enhancing forces are represented by individuals who prefer social order and hierarchical structures by their dominant attitudes and behavior, superior beliefs, and stereotypes. By contrast, hierarchy-attenuating forces imply preferences for social equality, welfare institutions, and egalitarian beliefs promoting global human rights (Sidanius et al. 2017).

Accordingly, SDT assumes that individuals scoring high on social dominance orientation tend to favor hierarchy-enhancing policies. However, empirical evidence shows that disadvantaged individuals, too, such as African Americans who are more often affected by systemic racism, may also reveal a preference for establishing and maintaining a hierarchical social structure (Ho et al. 2012). This can be explained by our need-serving approach, in particular that the concept of race can serve individuals' fundamental human needs. Social categorizations and a predetermined social order based on racial segregation meet not only the need for order, control, predictability, and consistency, but also the need for belongingness and identification. Identifying with and belonging to a racial group, even if it is low status, generates stable and reliable patterns in life and provides a basis for identity formation. Forming one's own self-concept according to the concept of race generates a consistent image of oneself and guides how to perceive oneself and the other within the social environment. Being in a disadvantaged position and facing prejudice and stereotypes can have devastating consequences for oneself, but it can also provide a cognitively ordered narrative of the social environment and guidance on how to behave and process information. Holding positive beliefs about one's ingroup and maintaining negative attitudes toward an outgroup can become an organizing framework for the construction of intragroup and intergroup interactions. Such mental frameworks, such as racial categorizations, stereotypes, or superior/inferior thinking, provide guidance on how to perceive oneself and others and help to maintain a positive self-image. Hierarchy-legitimizing ideologies like racism indicate how individuals and institutions should allocate resources and how they should process and evaluate information on ingroup and outgroup members (Baldwin 2017). The central component of any dominant racial ideology is thus to frame or provide guidelines for processing information, constructing and maintaining social order, and making decisions, all of which are based on the concept of race.

Sharing the same race and the attendant beliefs, thoughts, and attitudes generates a sense of mutual understanding and reinforces affiliation and coherence. A group of individuals who share the same racial beliefs and attitudes creates group norms that are used to evaluate social reality and outgroup members. Belonging to a "racially superior" group helps to reduce uncertainty, to elevate self-esteem, and to enforce the perception of control (Koomen and Van Der Pligt 2016). Superior thinking enables individuals to exert and justify control over valuable resources, social positions, and privileges and to reduce perceived intergroup threats. The belief that one belongs to a highly valuable group who seem to deserve more than others enforces positive feelings about oneself. The self-enhancement motivation underlying intergroup comparisons serves the fundamental human need for self-esteem that has a significant impact on all social identity processes. Social categorizations transform individuals' self-conception by assimilating all aspects of their feelings, perceptions, behavior, and attitudes to the ingroup prototype. Prototypes define the distinguished characteristics of ingroups and outgroups and prescribe attitudes, perceptions, and feelings based on these characteristics. These prescriptions and categorizations reduce subjective uncertainty about the self and one's attitudes and beliefs and reinforce the perception of having control over one's social environment (Hogg 2004). "Pointing to minorities as the cause of social problems, however falsely, provides a facile avenue for problem resolution through concerted action against the scapegoat, and provides psychological reaffirmation for those banding together" (Kly 1998, 49).

Surveys of Dutch youth, regarding their perceptions and attitudes of other ethnic groups residing in the Netherlands, show that individuals, regardless of their positive or negative attitudes toward immigration, tend to hold similar (socially) predefined stereotypes about immigrants and preferences about a "racial" hierarchy. Surprisingly, individuals who scored high on racial prejudices shared the same preferences concerning a "racial-based" social order with individuals who scored low on racial beliefs. The authors argue that these preferences were most probably shaped by cultural or social beliefs, rather than subjective attitudes and biases (Hagendoorn 1995; Verkuyten 2004a).

Further experimental studies reveal that prejudiced attitudes of college students are influenced strongly by the "racial" behavior and attitudes expressed by members of a broader social reference group (Blanchard et al. 1994). This means that individuals adjust their own racial attitudes and thinking to conform to those held by the main social reference group. Several studies provide evidence that students assimilate, and even change, their racial beliefs and attitudes to those held by a broader student population once they realize their reported stereotypes and prejudices are not in line with those of the majority group (Sinclair et al. 2005; Sechrist and Stangor 2001). This may indicate that some individuals prefer belief consonance; that is, a preference to hold and share similar beliefs with others. This preference can motivate individuals to change their own beliefs so as to conform to those held by (self-relevant) others (Golman et al. 2016). In particular, ideologies to the right of the political spectrum, such as racism, demand conformity within the ingroup and aim to construct a homogeneous society. Sharing the same (racial) social identity, values, and beliefs generates consistent and reliable patterns in the environment and thus coherence in life. Adhering to the prescribed norms and roles satisfies the need for social approval and belongingness and enhances one's sense of self-worth (belonging to the superior race). Individuals in such a racial category process and evaluate themselves and the social environment based on this category and derive their understanding and decision-making from it. This, in turn, serves the need for consistency, order, and control, while making decisions according to social category generates self-certainty and a consistent and positive image of oneself.

Thus, ideological beliefs held by significant others, such as peers or fellow students as in the example above, significantly shape and influence the attitudes and beliefs of those around them. This effect has been found to be stronger for authoritarian peer groups and for individuals with a non-diversified social environment (e.g., primarily White friendships) (Poteat and Spanierman 2010). Personality research suggests that especially individuals with a strong need for conformity, social approval, and identification with intragroup members tend to adopt generalized outgroup prototypes that are held by the main group (Dunn 2004). Further, individuals who have strong preferences for a homogeneous society, who adhere to societal conventions and norms, and who reject a pluralistic society (e.g., who reject those who do not have similar beliefs and attitudes), direct their discriminative and aggressive behavior toward outgroups and ethnic minorities (Duckitt et al. 2002).

If beliefs can be changed, should all political and social measures be geared to eroding the concept of race? A longitudinal study with 857 White participants observed the changed patterns of color-blind racial ideology over time. Color-blind beliefs imply that the concept of race and associated racial group memberships and race-based differences should be ignored when processing information and making decisions. The rationale behind this is the belief that if individuals or institutions are not confronted with the idea of race, they cannot act in a racially based manner. However, critics argue that avoiding talking about racism does not prevent the formation of prejudices and stereotypes. Rather, it affects disadvantaged individuals in a negative way. The belief that no racism exists prevents legal and political integration and affirmative action, which are needed to provide equal opportunities (Carr 1997). Thus, it implies a rather subtle and implicit racism where people of color, especially African Americans, are subject to unequal legal protection, excessive surveillance, and unequal opportunities in the labor or mortgage market—all of which is in the name of security and crime control (Spanierman et al. 2008; Mazzocco and Brunner 2012). One study found that especially women and individuals who were more open to diversity in their first year at college were more likely to report lower levels of racism-justifying beliefs. Specifically, college diversity experiences as well as close friendships with especially Black individuals were associated with decreased levels of color-blind racial ideologies over the four-year period of observation (Neville et al. 2014). If this implies that racial beliefs can be changed in response to new subjective experiences and conditions, an important question arises: what conditions can lead individuals to choose a racist ideology?

Theories of modern racism postulate that the conflict between individuals' egalitarian attitudes and their feelings about outgroup members is best resolved by denying the existence of racism-based discrimination. "Although they endorse equality (of opportunity) as an abstract principle, modern racists also see their hostility to antidiscrimination policies (such as affirmative action) as being based on rational grounds (such as issues of fairness and justice). The rationalization process builds on a series of interrelated arguments, namely, that prejudice and discrimination are things of the past, that any subsisting inequality is a consequence of the character of the victims, that protest about contemporary disadvantage is unjustified, that victims seek special favors, and that a number of benefits are illegitimate" (Yzerbyt and Demoulin 2010, 1044). Such justifying beliefs are held especially by individuals who favor traditionalism, reject diversity, and have strong feelings of ingroup belongingness (Sears and Henry 2003). However, a preference for racist beliefs is not always reflected in feelings of hostility or hate, but could rather be a subjective expression of fear, anxiety, uncertainty about otherness, contempt, or unease (Dovidio and Gaertner 1998).

Personality psychology seizes on this notion by postulating that individuals who score high on the RWA scale have an especially strong ingroup identity and are thus motivated to "protect" the perceived threat stemming from outgroup members (Petersen and Dietz 2006). Theoretical assumptions claim that authoritarian-prone personalities who express racial animosity tend to have lower incomes, are less educated, and live in small urban centers with a low and undiversified quality of institutions (Farfan-Vallespin and Bonick 2016). Although self-reported surveys report that higher levels of formal education tend to reduce racial prejudice, other empirical studies suggest that well-educated individuals may not be less xenophobic but simply more likely to give xenophile and socially desirable answers in self-reported questionnaires (Ostapczuk et al. 2009). Other experiments support these assumptions, showing that among the well-educated, aversive racism seems to be more prevalent, which suggests that despite their egalitarian beliefs, educated individuals still experience, possibly unconsciously, negative affect toward immigrants or ethnic minorities. They do not exhibit explicit discriminative behavior but still seem to have ambiguous attitudes toward ethnic minorities (Kuppens and Spears 2014). An empirical study examined the effects of formal education on ideology and racial prejudices against immigrants in Norway by testing six competing hypotheses. The results provide strong empirical support for only one hypothesis, namely that high education generates a higher social status and improves job opportunities, which in turn means that there is no direct competition with immigrants in the labor market (Jenssen and Engesbak 1994). This implies that well-educated, high-status individuals do not directly compete with immigrants or ethnic minorities over resources or job opportunities, which undermines their race-based comparison and decreases perceived group-threat.

Further theories declare that low access to socially valuable resources and perceived deprivation in cultural, intellectual, and social domains prevent working-class individuals, in particular, from improving their social cognition (i.e., how they perceive, think about, interpret and understand their own social behavior and those of social others) (Carvacho et al. 2013). This information processing is vital to understand the social environment, to be able to adjust to unexpected events, and to make appropriate decisions. An adaptive mind enables individuals to override automated responses and categorical social perceptions by producing new behavioral outputs and ideas (Macrae and Bodenhausen 2000). According to this idea, most working-class individuals lack the resources to expand their understanding of diverse groups and ideas and to adjust flexibly to a constantly changing environment. Instead, they may develop social categories and stereotypes, expressed through racial prejudices, which help them to reorder the world meaningfully (Carvacho et al. 2013). Overall, empirical studies show that prejudices and racial behavior decrease with higher income, although the effect is stronger if the general economic conditions are favorable. A cross-national study examined the relationship between anti-immigration attitudes and socioeconomic indicators (labor market position, education, and income) in seventeen European countries. The results confirmed that the self-employed, the blue-collar workers, the unemployed, and those not in the labor force are more likely to adopt racial behavior than white-collar workers; that students are less prejudiced; and that education and income decrease racist ideas. However, the analysis suggests that national economic conditions have a divergent effect on advantaged and disadvantaged groups. Poor economic conditions do not alter the level of prejudice among individuals, whereas prosperity tends to reduce prejudices among the advantaged while promoting anti-immigrant attitudes among the disadvantaged (Kunovich 2004).

However, several contributions on this issue agree that individuals who objectively or subjectively compete with an outgroup react with discriminative and hostile outgroup attitudes (Küpper et al. 2010). A recent econometric analysis using microdata from the German Socio-Economic Panel (SOEP) found that individuals, independent of their social status, with low life satisfaction and a high level of bitterness are more likely to adopt anti-immigration ideas (Poutvaara and Steinhardt 2018). The authors argue that life satisfaction is not merely an outgrowth of material well-being and business success, but of personal meaning in life, social engagement, and the feeling of being able to act autonomously (Headey et al. 2010); in fact, being able to satisfy one's fundamental relational, existential, epistemic, and agency needs. In this regard, failed choices, a lack of perceived meaning in life, and unfulfilled goals can lead to bitterness—an emotional complex incorporating frustration, helplessness, anger, and severe self-doubt. Such individuals often feel unjustly treated by society or fate and feel they are neglected by the political establishment. Consequently, the lack of opportunity to satisfy one's own needs generates a negative image about oneself and one's social environment, which is then projected onto certain objects or individuals. Individuals use projection as a psychological defense to manage self-doubt, anxiety, and frustration, and to sustain a positive self-image (Rasmussen and Salhani 2010). Specifically, the construction of social clusters with stereotyping images helps to reduce self-uncertainty and provides a viable option for evaluating the self. Perceiving that one belongs to a superior "race" and defining oneself according to these characteristics not only forms a consistent self-concept based on this identity narrative but also serves one's need for higher self-esteem.

Further, "the organization of the social environment in meaningful categories allows people to construct and organize knowledge about the surrounding social world, enabling them to deal with its complexity" (Roets and van Hiel 2011, 54). Especially racial categorizations, implying "inalterable and natural" characteristics, are easily understood and can be applied to everyday decisions. They enhance the perception of a valuable self and generate self-consistency and group homogeneity. In this regard, psychological research shows that individuals with a need for cognitive closure are particularly likely to demand clear world views, avoid ambiguity, and call for predictability and order in their lives—reflected in the desire for secure and stable knowledge that is unchallenged and reliable in all circumstances. Empirical studies show that individuals with a strong need for cognitive closure tend have more prejudices and adopt more social evaluations based on race and ethnicity (Roets and van Hiel 2011).

Given these assumptions and the empirical evidence, we can state that racism is a viable reconciliation option to serve existential, epistemic, relational, and agency needs. The ideology generates foremost social clusters and (identity) narratives that enable fast, efficient information processing in everyday life and in a variety of settings. The formation of ingroups and outgroups along racial lines creates a social order and guides individuals in perceiving and evaluating themselves and their social environment. These predictable, reliable, and stable social categorizations generate cognitive consistency and certainty because they can be easily applied to events and individuals. This decreases uncertainty and offers a sense of control and meaning; that is, reliable social patterns that help individuals to recognize and interpret a state of arousal (information, event, stimuli, etc.). Racism as an ideology thus provides reliable social and mental patterns that help individuals to understand the environment, to find answers and explanations for life events, and to recognize their social roles. However, beyond serving such existential and epistemic needs, racism also generates a sense of identification and belongingness. Identifying as a member of a particular "race" generates a sense of belonging and enables individuals to perceive and define themselves. A predefined order and a hierarchical social system provide members of the "advantaged race" in particular with a sense of superiority and righteousness ("we deserve more and have more rights"). Identification with the "favored and superior race" creates a positive self-image and, hence, enhances one's self-esteem. Sharing the same beliefs, narratives about (racial) identity, values, attitudes, and norms within a group serves individuals' relational needs. They feel accepted, belongingness, and socially approved. Maintaining a strong group identity that is reinforced and preserved through racial segregation has a positive impact on individuals' self-esteem and self-perception. The mission to protect one's own racial group and its interests, aims, and status against a perceived threat from outgroup members or foreigners represents an important goal in life, which serves one's need for self-efficacy. In this context, dogmatic racial segregation, paired with static beliefs and conservative values, and the use of fake news and crime statistics to legitimize the preservation of the system, increase individual self-opinionatedness. Accordingly, the demand for a consistent and hierarchical social order, the preservation of a strong group identity, and a strong sense of self-significance indicate a need structure that can be linked to racism. People want to find quick answers and to protect the static world views that help them deal with social complexity and resolve problems. The identification with a superior and immutable group essence, based on the perception of a "legitimized" genetic and biological supremacy, guarantees the allegedly unchangeable status of social groups in a reliable and consistent social structure.

7.1.1.1 Case: An Extreme Form of Racism—The Ku Klux Klan

Beyond "everyday" structural racism, racism can also assume an extreme form that can lead to severe aggression and violence against outgroup members. One well-known, extremist, and highly violent group is the Ku Klux Klan (KKK), a white supremacist movement in the United States. Since 1945, no regime or a political movement has called itself "fascist," although white supremacist thinking, neo-Nazism, and radical right movements persist to this day. The oldest and most widespread white supremacist movement in the United States is the Ku Klux Klan, which was formed in 1866 by six veterans of the Confederate Army. The name is derived from the ancient Greek word *kuklos* (circle), while its distinctive uniform (white robes and hoods) represents the ghosts of the Confederate soldiers. The hierarchical structure of the Klan is based on race and power. It transformed from a social club in 1866 to a paramilitary racial and extremely violent movement in 1867. Southerners used the Klan to preserve the Southern white power structure by suppressing the Black population. By the end of 1867, the movement had spread to other states that aimed to prevent social equality and social integration of Blacks by all available means. The violence and brutality of the Klan soon spiraled out of control, and in 1871 President Ulysses Grant used the US Army to crack down on it. The Klan re-emerged in 1915 and lasted into the late 1920s. This time, the Klan's role was to enforce nationalism and patriotism and to defend the US against foreign and national deviants (alien enemies, ethnic outgroups, "immoral women"). Its success in the 1920s can be attributed to a combination of high-pressure recruitment, the fear of losing privileges, nativism, and the attraction of mystical fraternalism. Furthermore, the Klan offered order, a consistent world view, brotherhood, and a position in a hierarchical system that appeared to provide alienated men structure and certainty in their lives. It received strong support from political leaders and fundamentalist clergy as its aim to purify America and to restore the traditional Protestant way of life was very much *en vogue*. The Klan promised to restore order in the streets; to dampen the Catholic, Jewish, and African American impact; to enforce morale and protect homes; to provide self-efficacy to its members; and generally to promote a "new era of life." Despite rumors and scandals, which weakened the popularity of the Klan, by the end of the 1920s it had more than six million members (a modest estimate).

Researchers consider the KKK to be similar to European fascist movements that emerged at the same time. "Both the Klan and the fascists responded to industrial era social change with a combination of nostalgia and forward-looking appeals. Both used mass marketing, propaganda, and elaborate ritual to mobilize a broad following into a hierarchical organization. Both developed as a backflash against the Left and against supposed moral and cultural decay within society at large. Both promoted social oppression but appropriated some elements of anti-elitism and liberatory politics, such as feminism and labor activism. And at least, in some cases, both used violence and intimidation against political opponents and scapegoats" (Atkins 2011, 12).

An offshoot of the KKK was the Black Legion, which was formed in 1931 by a former Klansman from Ohio. The majority of its members came from Detroit, Michigan; most were unskilled workers. The name is a reference to the black clothing that members wore during meetings or attacks on those they perceived as enemies, such as Blacks, Jews, communists, immigrants, or trade union members. The Black Legion aimed to control the automotive factories and dominate state policy in Michigan and other midwestern states in a violent and aggressive way. It was a secret society that operated as a radical guerilla army in opposition to the Democratic and Republican parties. "The legion appealed to unskilled and semiskilled workers migrating to the auto center from the South, small-town men stranded in the city at the center of the Depression's worst economic devastation. The Black Legion modeled the Klan's ideology: it was virulently anti-Catholic as well as anti-Semitic, anti-communist, and anti-Negro" (Bennett 1988, 247).

Even after the Second World War, these Klan groups remained supportive of white supremacy and nativism. The increase in Black voters and the perceived change in the political power structure posed a threat to Klan members, which led to a series of lynchings of Black people in the late 1940s. The empowerment of the KKK lasted until the late 1970s, out of which further neofascist and right-wing movements arose. The most significant of the militant Klan groups was the United Klan of America (UCA), which advocated racial segregation, racial homogeneity, and an authoritarian hierarchical regime. It rejected communism, liberalism, dissidents, and elitists. The use of conspiracy theories and violence set the agenda. An even more violent group was the White Knights in Mississippi, founded in 1964, which used radical and violent means to fight social integration, civil rights, Black people, and Jewish people, even with support from the state and local governments (Atkins 2011). The violent Klan groups committed 225 bombings and one thousand acts of racial violence and murder between 1955 and 1965 alone. Law enforcement (even the FBI), especially in the South, was in the hands of authorities that either belonged to one of the Klan groups or supported their ideology. This enabled the KKK to re-emerge as late as in the 1980s and 1990s with new leaders and new ideas about how to maintain white supremacy. However, in the 1990s, several scandals and financial instability meant the Klan lost its appeal and members began to drift to other right-wing extremist groups (e.g., Aryan Nations, Christian Identity, or Militia Movement) (Wade 1998).

In general, research on various Klan groups, their members, and the ideology behind them reveals that their success and power can be explained on the basis of perceived threat and uncertainty. Most of the (largely male) members belong to the White working classes, where feelings of alienation, disintegration, of despair, fear, insecurity, and threat reside. The average Klansman is a day laborer, mechanic, or factory worker who faces job insecurity and direct competition with the Black workforce. He was raised in the countryside but had to move to a city to find work, where he never felt welcomed and integrated. Although generally perceived as less educated, some members, among them businessmen or politicians, have college educations and occupy high-status positions. However, the average Klansman does not belong to the white power structure and his actions and frustrations tend to reflect the grievances held by other deprived groups. Accordingly, the lack of opportunities to secure one's existence, understand the complex environment and social change, feel belonging and accepted in society, and form a consistent and positive self-view (i.e., to satisfy one's fundamental human needs) can enhance the willingness of deprived individuals to search for alternative options to serve their needs. Racism and Klan membership provide such alternative reconciliation options, which form, based on the concept of race and exclusion, reliable and consistent patterns of reality. The excluded and left-behind individuals apply exclusionary means and beliefs to reject those below them (outgroup members) and those above them (elitists) in a move to restore a sense of high self-worth, belonging, and control (Atkins 2011).

7.1.2 Nationalism

A further ideology to consider is nationalism. The term "nation" derives from the Latin terms *nasci* (to be born) and *natio* (origin), which refer mainly to people who are related or who belong together by (place of) birth. The focus on the biological form of belongingness (birth) implies the concept of "natural attachment" that cannot be acquired by choice. This biological reading of nationalism has induced many theories of survival, competition over resources, and natural selection, which in turn sparked many debates about imperialism, colonialism, civilization, and the idea of superior or inferior racial groups (Vincent 2013). However, during the twentieth century, and especially post-1945, the term "nationalism" went through a range of interpretations, variously being defined as an emotional and conscious attachment to a nation, as a symbol or human artefact, as a sociopolitical movement, as an expression of a rationally liberal normative culture, or as a doctrine and organized ideology (see, e.g., Tamir 1993). These concepts must be carefully distinguished because individuals can possess considerable nationalistic feelings in the absence of any symbolism, political movement, or ideological doctrine. A group can also have a strong national consciousness and strong group identity based on national affiliation without pursuing ideological or organizational goals. On the opposite, nationalism can also assume radical forms and culminate in violent fanaticism (Vincent 2013).

Yet it is clear from many historical and ethnographical studies that nationalism is a comparatively modern human idea, a phenomenon of the late nineteenth and twentieth centuries. In principle, nationalism reinforces "popular sentiments evoked by the idea of a nation; in this ideological discourse, the nation is a felt and lived community, a category of behavior as much as imagination, and it is one that requires of the members certain kinds of action" (Smith 2010, 11). The substance of a nation consists of the formed community of people living in a political system with a shared language, territory, history, and cultural values. This nation is bound together by the idea and power of nationhood that creates feelings of identity, mutual affiliation, and solidarity, seeking to achieve (or sustain) political self-determination. Thus, the ideology of nationalism can be understood in general as a political sentiment to establish national sovereignty, as a social movement to perceive and defend one's own national community, as passionate loyalty and devotion to a nation, and as a shared identity that creates a sense of coherence and distinction (Langman 2006). This implies that nationalism provides a mental framework that serves fundamental human needs—needs that involve a safety-seeking mechanism, understanding, group belongingness, and individual self-concept. Before analyzing how nationalism serves individuals' relational, epistemic, existential, and agency needs, we briefly examine the historical roots of the ideology.

Most researchers now agree that the concept of nationalism is a modern phenomenon. Before the Enlightenment and the French Revolution, the political, social, cultural, and economic environment was hierarchically divided between the privileged groups and the illiterate masses who were socially and geographically immobile. The distinct worlds of the ruling elite and the ruled were underpinned by the belief in the monarch's right to reign on the basis of warfare and the divine. In the course of socioeconomic transformations—which led to the formation of bureaucratic institutions, the introduction of mass education, and secularization and democratization of the social realm—peasants became citizens with social, civil, and political rights (Malesevic 2006a). Beyond these positive impacts, the conversion from traditional socioeconomic systems to modern societies dissolved traditional structures and patterns of interaction. Patriarchal and oligarchic networks were challenged by ideas of democracy, social equality, and civil participation, while indigenous cultural values and religious beliefs collided with liberal and secular socio-cultural thinking. Furthermore, tight familial and communal bonds, cultural traditions, and role ascriptions lost value and were transformed into autonomous social subsystems, isolating the individual from communal patterns and interpersonal bonds (Gelfand et al. 1996). The literature argues that such socio-cultural and institutional transformations generate tensions between the public and the private, because they remove the subject from the previously established collective bonds. Therefore, "more than any other ideology, nationalism was able to articulate a narrative bent on reconciling the public and the private, the institutional and the communal, the political and the cultural, utilizing the most egalitarian and democratic expression—'we the nation'. [It is seen as] a phenomenon of Gesellschaft [society] using the idiom of Gemeinschaft [community]: a mobile anonymous society simulating a closed cozy community" (Malesevic 2006b, 309).

From a psychological point of view, these transformations, which decreased social ties and formed autonomous subjects, have generated uncertainty and vulnerability among the public. Increased ambiguity and emerging demands for affiliation, meaning, and social identification have led to the adoption of retrograde nationalistic ideas, propounded by "powerful leaders" (Vincent 2013). Psychoanalysis goes further by postulating that the modern individual is a vulnerable, anxious, and isolated figure that constructs the self based on ambiguity and compulsion. By identifying with superior and powerful images of the nation, the subject can find stability and integrity. "While people regard the state as a machine, the nation can be regarded as something transcendent, with a place and a role for all its members. Nationalism fulfils a utopian function both retroactively in terms of a past golden age, and for the future that awaits the people who seize their 'natural' inheritance" (Finlayson 1998, 152). This belief in common ancestry forms a collective national identity, which is reinforced by the creation of boundaries between the "national self" and "the others." The formation of a distinct national identity is a continuous process of affiliation and identification which involves aspects of exclusion and inclusion, and which is linked to a shared common culture, history, fate, and destiny. Anthems and flags, celebrations, and rituals enforce the feeling of a shared identity and inflame pride in, and loyalty to, the nation (Edensor 2002). All this provides a foundation for serving one's needs for belongingness, identification, and mutual affiliation. The strong and consistent narrative of a shared and national identity increases individuals' self-esteem and generates a sense of meaning (i.e., reliable, stable social patterns of reality). Sharing the same national beliefs, attitudes, and values can enhance the sense of approval and acceptance and can emphasize the shared goal to protect, serve, and be proud of the nation one belongs to. "The nation is regarded as sovereign over any other groups and is thus the ultimate ground of legitimacy and loyalty" (Vincent 2013, 464).

In 1996 and 2006, the General Social Survey measured the significance of national identity in the United States. In 1996, fully forty-five percent indicated that being American was the most important thing in their life and over eighty percent said they were very proud of America's achievements and history. Compared to 1996, when the majority of respondents indicated that national defense spending was appropriate or even excessive, in 2016 the majority (63.6 percent) thought that the defense budget should be increased (Smith and Son 2017). This may indicate that awareness of a national identity or national beliefs, in general, has strengthened due to a perceived threat to the nation. The 2004 National Election Study found that eighty percent of respondents highly appreciated the national symbols of America, and the Roper Center for Public Research revealed that in 2006 over one-half of the population had an extremely patriotic mindset. However, these nationalistic feelings can change over time. During the 1991 Gulf War and after the 9/11 terrorist attacks, nationalism peaked in the US, having been at record low levels in 1989 and 2006 over negative reactions to the war in Iraq. However, Americans are not unique in their nationalistic sentiments. The World Value Survey during the period 1999 to 2004 revealed that in forty out of seventy countries, more than eighty percent of the population claimed to be very proud of their nation. The United States, besides twenty-eight other countries, including Canada, Poland, Nigeria, Iran, etc., achieved the highest score, with ninety percent of the population indicating they were highly patriotic (Schildkraut 2011). Recent surveys show that populations in most European countries, too, have strong beliefs in a superior nationhood. Six out of ten EU citizens feel that being born in a country and having family in that country are important factors when it comes to truly sharing the national identity. Populations in some EU member states have even stronger nationalist beliefs: eight in ten Czechs state that they would not accept a Muslim as a family member; while two-thirds of Romanians believe their culture is superior to others. The results for the UK are mixed: forty-three percent of less educated respondents reject other cultures and religions and fifty-one percent believe that the UK is a superior nation, while sixty-three percent of college-educated respondents believe that having a UK family background is very important to be truly British. These beliefs prevail especially among the older population, while young adults (aged eighteen to thirty-four) have stronger anti-immigrant attitudes (Joshi and Evans 2019).

Although social psychology indicates that sharing such strong national beliefs and a national identity has positive implications for a country and its population, the other side of the coin points to processes of discrimination and segregation due to a belief in "naturalistic" belonging (Spears 2011). Social identity theory suggests that people are driven to maintain positive group identities to enhance their self-esteem. The motivation to sustain a superior and positive national image can encourage a denigration and rejection of individuals who do not seem to meet the "criteria" of national belongingness. Research has repeatedly shown that the collectively shared definition of nationality has significant effects on prejudice toward immigrants. Empirical results demonstrate that individuals who feel more affiliated with their country were more hostile toward asylum seekers and immigrants. Furthermore, the results show that strong national identification increases the tendency to take threats directed toward the nation personally (i.e., threatening one's own identity), which in turn promote individuals' willingness to draw on and support defensive measures (Barnes et al. 2014). Thus, strong nationalism is considered to promote, in radical terms, xenophobia, anti-immigrant attitudes, a superior national identity, and the desire for strong defense (Licata et al. 2011).

Although nationalism could be perceived as deeply embedded in the psyche of the masses that satisfies individuals' need for belongingness and identification, in particular, alternative approaches perceive nationalism as a political instrument that appeals at different times to different groups and serves different needs. The concept of nationalism has been embraced by various divergent ideological movements that adopted national beliefs in a different manner. Liberals, for example, view nations as moral entities that are endowed with human rights, especially with the right to self-determination, while socialists tend to view the nation as an artificial division of humankind that aims to enforce social order. Conservative ideologies perceive the nation as an organic and continuous entity, bound by a common ethnic identity of a culturally and historically unique community. It is a source of social cohesion, mutual solidarity and loyalty, and group identification (Heywood 2017). While all ideologies agree that nations are formed by cultural and psychopolitical factors, they strongly disagree about its dissociation. "On the one hand, 'exclusive' concepts of the nation stress the importance of ethnic unity and a shared history. By viewing national identity as 'given', unchanging and indeed unchangeable, this implies that nations are characterized by common descent and so blurs the distinction between nations and races" (Heywood 2017, 170). The national community in this sense is formed on the premise of "naturalistic" order and obedience, articulated through ethnic/racial claims. This organically pre-established order forms national identity and artificial unity that need to be protected.[1] The nation is thus held together by "innate" bonds which are fostered by emotional attachments to a shared history, culture, language, religion, and traditional way of life (Vincent 2013). "On the other hand, 'inclusive' concepts of the nation, as found in civic nationalism, highlight the importance of civic consciousness and patriotic loyalty. From this perspective, nations may be multi-racial, multi-ethnic, multi-religious and so forth" (Heywood 2017, 170). This "inclusive" view of the nation tends to blur the lines between nationality, citizenship, and belonging, and is more likely adopted by liberal and socialist belief systems that endorse the nation as a community, which bases their existence on normative beliefs such as human rights, liberty, and democracy (Vincent 2013).

Despite these different manifestations of nationalism, the mental framework of the belief system provides a viable way to serve relational, existential, epistemic, and agency needs. The belief in a strong and superior nationhood provides consistent, reliable, and meaningful social patterns that help individuals to label and evaluate incoming stimuli. Processing information, evaluating events, and making decisions based on the concept of a nation satisfies the need for certainty, stability, and control. Relying on nationally shared norms, values, and attitudes generates a sense of order and consistency in life, while the powerful image of a superior and "invincible" nation reinforces a positive image of oneself and of society. Narratives of familial background, identity, and cultural inheritance serve the needs for belongingness and identification. National characteristics (e.g., flags, anthems, special dishes, history, etc.) are symbols that are shared with significant others and that generate a sense of mutual affiliation and acceptance as well as loyalty and pride. Based on these narratives and symbols, individuals form an understanding of themselves and their social environment. They provide a basis for self-definition and support individuals in forming their self-concepts. Having the goal to protect the nation (e.g., by joining the army) or serve it (e.g., by working for the government) can induce strong feelings of self-efficacy and a meaningful existence, but also a sense of responsibility and care.

But beyond positive and prosocial, communal feelings of national belonging, nationalism can lead to outgroup derogation, aggression and, in severe cases, to international conflicts. Hence, external events, circumstances and changed conditions can generate a major shift in nationalist sentiments and beliefs. Looking, for example, at nationalist movements in Brazil between 1889 and 1930, the ideology was adopted by middle-class movements yet for substantially different reasons. While the Brazilian Jacobins, formed in 1889, did so to denounce the weak position of the working class, the Ação Social Nationalista, established post-WWI in 1920, collaborated with the ruling elite to dampen the revolution of the working class by praising Catholicism and the preservation of the traditional agrarian economy and hierarchical social structure. Nationalism, in this sense, was converted from a progressive force to a regressive and defensive instrument—a radical shift triggered by changed socioeconomic conditions that demanded a new response from an uncertain middle class (Topic 1978).

Similar shifts in nationalism are evident in US history, with Americans reaffirming and renewing their national consciousness and identity during periods of crisis and transformation—from the establishment of the colonies to militant foreign policy and the war on terrorism (Hixson 2008). But the recent presidency of Donald Trump and his aim to "Make America Great Again" also renewed the country's enthusiasm for reviving the nation's former glory. Presenting himself as the antithesis to the typical politician, Trump proposed a "new form" of nationalism—an anti-globalization and anti-immigration protectionist form of nationalism. Accordingly, social scientists proposed various explanations for his triumph, including economic grievances, sexism, racism, Islamophobia, and social disintegration. Election data show that the White working class in America's Rust Belt (Ohio, Wisconsin, Pennsylvania, Michigan) was the strongest supporting group of Donald Trump. This support has been mainly explained in terms of this group's increased insecurities and the feeling of being left behind (Berezin 2017).

Other sociological studies provide evidence that cultural factors played an even larger role in the rise of Trump's nationalistic appeal. Sexist attitudes, in particular, were a stronger predictor of support for Trump than ethnocentrism or economic dissatisfaction (Schaffner et al. 2017). Blaming African Americans for societal problems or the impression that they have too much influence in society were other strong reasons for vote for Trump (McElwee and McDaniel 2017). Dampening the impact of other ethnic groups and restricting immigration, especially from Muslim countries, were further concerns among Trump supporters (Ekins 2017). Furthermore, using data from a probability sample of American adults who were surveyed soon after the November 2016 election, a study found strong evidence that Christian nationalism played a strong role in the triumph of the Republican agenda, despite the anti-Christian attitudes of its leader. Christian nationalism represents a stable set of beliefs and ideals that merge American and Christian group identities and aim to protect the distinctly Christian heritage, values, and its future. Both groups present a narrative of a superior and strong national identity, of a shared origin and values, which unites those who belong to it. The myth of a Christian nation functions as a symbolic boundary that is a source of identification, belonging, and purpose in life (such as to protect the Christian heritage). Trump's Christian nationalist rhetoric also responded to the threat and disintegration that the American nation and Christian identity are facing, and the appeal to use "this last chance" to "restore" America and to "regain control" (Whitehead et al. 2018). Trump's nationalistic ideology thus provided a viable option for individuals to reconcile their relational, existential, epistemic, and agency needs.

Yet in Europe, too, Euroscepticism, economic insecurity, perceived threats, and social disintegration played a role in the rise of radical nationalist sentiments. The Eurosceptic far-right nationalist movement arose in response to individuals' demand for a strong nationhood that serves their need for stability, control, and existential certainty—a collective defense against real or imagined external threats. Individuals demanded for a powerful and consistent nation state that can protect its citizens against global forces such as terrorism, immigration flows, or economic crisis, and can thus control external and internal fluctuations. "Where globalization establishes cosmopolitan heterogeneity as the norm, the neo-nationalist impulse is to compel fear of a lost identity. At the core of nationalist sentiments is the need for society to preserve its identity and tradition" (De Matas 2017, 25). While not all forms of nationalism are destructive and regressive, in extreme cases nationalist beliefs can help justify using violence against those who do not share the same national identity. Especially political science and sociology examine the relationship between nationalism and violence, focusing on authorities that use nationalistic rhetoric to trigger an aggressive and exclusionary behavior in public. Here, the intentionalist approach in sociology assumes that most forms of organized nationalistic violence can be traced back to the intentions and actions of powerful individuals (Malešević 2013). Critics of this approach argue that it considers foremost motivations and dispositions of only one individual (the leader) while ignoring the conditions and historical processes that laid the foundation for nationalism. Without denying the culpability of individual leaders, a number of recent studies have revealed that social processes also play a crucial role in the outbreak of nationalistic sentiment. "In contrast to the popular views that see revolutions, wars, and genocides as calculated and well-planned events, many macro-sociological studies show otherwise. [. . .] Revolutions are rarely the product of deliberate, predetermined, planning; instead they are caused by dramatically changed geopolitical conditions" (Malešević 2013, 14). Thus, the top-down approach that focuses on the motives of national leaders does not consider the complexity and intangibility of modern warfare.

In contrast to the intentionalist approach, the naturalist approach devotes more attention to the ancient and cultural nature of nationalism that, in itself, is capable of inflaming large-scale violent incidents. Several historians argue that the cultural foundation of nationalism accounts for the birth of violent confrontations as seen in the Ancient Greco-Persian wars, the violent disputes in Northern Ireland, or the war in former Yugoslavia. The naturalist approach adopts a neo-Darwinian stance that proclaims the biological entrenchment of nationalism and violence because all animal and human beings are biologically programmed to favor kinship over distant relations. In this context, nationalism is understood as a superior form of kinship that requires defensive measures to ensure the chance for survival and to win the competition for scarce resources. However, these biological theories of nationalism and organized violence have been strongly criticized for their tendency to create boundaries and exclusion, and they have been thus rejected due to their dogmatic determinism (Malešević 2013).

Other than the intentionalist and naturalist approaches, the formativist perspective has been widely embraced in social science discourse. The main idea of formativism is that violent experiences and threatening confrontations drive the outburst of nationalism, and not vice versa. Thus, nationalism is not the cause of violence but a byproduct of circumstance, changed environments, perceived or real threats, and social conflicts. One approach focuses on geopolitical instability, suggesting that nationalism arises from changed social conditions that create insecurity and uncertainty, which may, in turn, trigger a collective response. The deprived subjective need for security, control, certainty, and safety may enhance the demand for a strong national power. The continuous perception of threat and uncertainty fosters the rise of strong national ideologies. Other assumptions put more emphasis on individuals' needs for emotional attachment (i.e., a strong unity, common myths and memories, and a shared national identity). Shared cultural interpretations of sacrifice or martyrdom on behalf of the nation create a strong national feeling and enforce national consciousness (Malešević 2015).

However, all these perspectives, which aim to explain the causal relationship between nationalism and violence, are not exempt from criticism. They appear mainly in extreme cases and severe circumstances, and not all security dilemmas lead to national extremism. A direct experience of conflict and deprivation does not necessarily create strong national solidarity, while not all violent confrontations of the past have enhanced national identification and nationalistic sentiment (Malešević 2013). Despite a prevailing assumption that nationalism and violence correlate, empirical evidence is scarce on this topic. A quantitative study, using data on state-level nationalism from 1816 to 1997, revealed that nationalism significantly increases the probability of an interstate war. That said, not all forms of nationalism have the same impact. According to the study, ethnic nationalism tends to promote war to a greater extent while civic, revolutionary, and counterrevolutionary nationalism tends to have a weak, or almost non-significant, effect. Ethnic nationalism arises when a government stresses the significance of one common culture, religion, language, or ethnicity through laws, education, labor market, and other means by excluding and oppressing those who lack the "appropriate ethnic attributes" (Schrock-Jacobson 2012).

All in all, this discussion illustrates that nationalism promises to protect individuals from external threats, to guarantee safety and sovereignty, and to provide a means for identification and belongingness. Nationalism serves the desire of being part of something larger and more powerful—a strong community that shares the same values, goals, and beliefs. The protection of one's own cultural heritage and the survival of the nation demands subjective action against threatening and hostile surroundings, which provide individuals with a sense of meaningful existence and self-efficacy. National beliefs do not invariably lead to ostracism or aggression, but they can also give rise to positive inclusionary attitudes, such as multiculturalism, cooperation, and care for others. In extreme cases, though, the belief in a superior nation that has the power to control resources, people, and events can result in internal divisions based on innate and "natural" characteristics. This segregation then generates an immutable group essence and a shared idea of a "natural" ancestry, which generates a strong group identity and group cohesion. Such consistent beliefs in a strong nation provide stability and the feeling that one can rely on the nation's sovereignty and power (security). It decreases the perception of threats and enhances one's sense of a controllable environment. This in turn strengthens individuals' self-esteem and self-significance. Shared national beliefs, values, identity narratives, symbols, and history provide a means for identification paired with a taste of pride and solidarity. The perception of a strong and unified nation reduces feelings of uncertainty, inconsistency, and disintegration because it transforms the world into an orderly, meaningful, and predictable place.

7.1.3 Ethnic Nationalism

As mentioned in Schrock-Jacobson (2012), among all forms of nationalism, ethnic nationalism is most likely to significantly increase the probability of conflict onset. Ethnic nationalism, as said before, arises when a government stresses the significance of one common culture, religion, language, or ethnicity through laws, education, labor market, and other means by excluding and oppressing those who do not have these "appropriate ethnic attributes." The concept of ethnicity arose to replace the undesirable term "racism" in everyday discourse. While racism points to the biological differences between individuals, such as skin color or physical appearance, ethnicity places more emphasis on historical, cultural, and linguistic characteristics. But the term "ethnicity," too, can become the basis for segregation, group categorization, oppression, and exploitation (Essed 1991) and has been argued to be a defining criterion in conflicts between various groups (Esteban et al. 2012). In the following, we thus consider ethnicity a belief system and a potential source for reconciliation, which can, in extreme cases, lead to intergroup conflict.

The concept of ethnic categorization underlines "the ways in which ethnic boundaries, identities and cultures, are negotiated, defined, and produced through social interaction inside and outside ethnic communities" (Nagel 1994, 152). Social categories are formed out of (1) restricted boundaries that stress who is and who is not a member of a given category, and (2) a specific content that covers the beliefs, thoughts, moral commitments, and physical attributes that unite the members of this category, but also expected behavior and social evaluation of ingroup and outgroup members (Fearon and Laitin 2000). Ethnicity is thus constructed out of shared language, religion, cultural values, appearance, ancestry, and historical myths—all of which create boundaries (identity) and meaning (culture). Ethnic identity is formed of a subjective belief in a common ancestry and shared origin that creates the idea of belongingness in the present and continuity with the past (Verkuyten 2004b). Group identity is shaped in the process of individuals' self-identification with the significant ethnic characteristics and the outsiders' perception of that group (i.e., how you perceive your ethnicity and what others think your ethnicity is) (Nagel 1994). Membership of an ethnic group provides alternative ways to interpret, perceive, and represent the social world. "These include 'ethnicized' ways of seeing (and ignoring), of construing (and misconstruing), of inferring (and misinferring), of remembering (and forgetting). They include ethnically oriented frames, schemas, and narratives, and the situational cues—not least those provided by the media—that activate them. They include systems of classification, categorization, and identification, formal and informal. And they include the tacit, taken-for-granted background knowledge, embodied in persons and embedded in institutionalized routines and practices, through which people recognize and experience objects, places, persons, actions, or situations as ethnically [...] marked or meaningful" (Brubaker 2004, 17).

Empirical research shows that identification with a particular ethnicity is inevitable and central to the development of a stable identity (Phinney and Alipuria 1990). A study among Black female adolescents revealed that participants regarded ethnicity as the most significant attribute of self-definition. Other interviews with adolescents from different ethnic groups (Asian American, White, Black, and Mexican American) showed that all participants were aware of their ethnic characteristics and their obligation to commit to their own ethnic group (Aries and Moorehead 1989). Ethnicity not only forms the basis for group identification and belongingness, but it is also considered to play a significant role in psychological well-being. Psychological studies demonstrate that positive identification with an ethnic group enhances the value of the own self and thus generates higher self-esteem (Phinney and Chavira 1992). Research on self-esteem thus argues that self-efficacy and interpersonal experiences provide the foundation for self-esteem and that both can be successfully developed through (ethnic) group membership (Verkuyten 2001, 2009). Although social identity theory assumes that membership of a low status or disadvantaged social group diminishes the self-esteem of its members, empirical investigations show the opposite (Phinney et al. 1997). There is strong evidence that African Americans or Latin Americans value their ethnic identity more than White adolescents (Bowler et al. 1986; Martinez and Dukes 1991). This is explained by the assumption that group identification and strong group cohesion provide a basis for a consistent self-concept, even if one's own group has a low social standing. Belonging to and identifying with a specific ethnic group generates a meaningful and consistent place in the social environment, as well as order, stability, and certainty in life (Verkuyten 2004b). Understanding oneself and one's social surroundings from the perspective of one's own ethnic group and making decisions and behaving accordingly generates consistency and predictability in life. Following shared values, norms, and goals enhances one's self-assurance and generates higher self-esteem.

A survey of Dutch citizens of Turkish descent found that these individuals highly appreciate their Turkish identity and identify more with their Turkish culture than the ethnic Dutch majority with their Dutch culture (Verkuyten and Reijerse 2008). This implies that a strong ethnic identity offers ethnic minorities valuable resources to cope with challenges and risks they must face. Experiences of discrimination and ostracism can trigger individuals to cope with such distress also in a more productive way. A study with African Americans found that students who identified strongly with their ethnic group and who expected to experience ethnic discrimination in the future responded with more confidence and academic engagement (Eccles et al. 2006). This suggests that ethnic minority groups with a lower status than the majority will go to great lengths to restore control and maintain their sense of self-worth and that of the group as a whole. "Members might seek to increase their self-esteem [or to contrast to the majority group] by, for example, shifting their focus to new or different group qualities ('Money is not that important, what matters are happiness and good relationships with other people'), ascribing its situation to discrimination ('We simply aren't given a fair chance to prove ourselves') or making specific social comparisons (Romanians are at least as criminal as we are')" (Koomen and Van Der Pligt 2016, 119).

Although viewing one's own ingroup in a positive light is an important contributor when sustaining strong self-esteem, various studies show that the positive evaluation of the group *per se* is not the most important point, but rather the simple fact of belongingness and identification (Knowles et al. 2010). Experiments demonstrate that the feeling of being socially rejected, even by strangers, triggers a decline in psychological well-being. Rejection is thus linked to psychological pain, disappointment, and sorrow. A series of meta-analyses of experimental research on rejection, covering eighty-eight studies with a total of 3,692 participants, found that the severe form of rejection, namely ostracism, has a considerable effect on individuals' mental well-being. When experiencing ostracism, people are disappointed and feel worthless and incompetent. This "social pain" can be perceived as analogous to physical pain—the same neural circuits activated during an emotional reaction to rejection are triggered when experiencing environmental threat. This in turn generates an "alarm" signaling that something must be done to deal with the threat. Furthermore, the emotionally distressing experience of rejection is perceived to affect the state of an individual's needs; that is, the need for belonging and control (Williams 2001; Gerber and Wheeler 2009). An experiment shows that those individuals who were ostracized and who could not control the situation responded more aggressively, while those who could control it were no more aggressive than participants who were included. The authors argue that ostracism and a diminished opportunity to control the negative situation enhance individuals' perception of powerlessness, which undermines their feeling of self-worth and self-efficacy (Warburton et al. 2006).

While one strand of research shows that people tend to react aggressively when rejected, another provides evidence that this is only the case for those with weak ingroup identification. A study of Syrian refugees in Turkey found that individuals who derived a meaningful existence, self-certainty, and distinctiveness from their Syrian identity were not affected by discrimination. This implies that identification with an ethnic group not only provides a basis to form one's identity, but it also serves various psychological human needs, such as the need for consistency and order, belongingness, social approval, and self-esteem. This source of reconciliation helps individuals to cope with external events, negative experiences (such as social rejection) and negative feelings of uncertainty, helplessness, and loss of control (Celebi et al. 2017). However, the protective function of one's own ethnic identification could depend on the extent to which one's group membership satisfies fundamental psychological needs (Greenaway et al. 2015). If group membership does not serve basic psychological needs—such as social approval, feelings of acceptance and self-esteem, and safety and consistency in life—then group identification would have little to no impact on individuals' well-being (Verkuyten 2004b).

Accordingly, positive ingroup identification and strong (ethnic) group identity serve fundamental psychological needs and offer stability, consistency, and a shared interpretation of reality by diminishing uncertainty, self-doubt, and feelings of disorientation. The emphasis on one's own ethnic group provides support in threatening situations because the group can offer security and refuge in a perceived hostile environment. Furthermore, group identification has a strong influence on the perception of oneself, others, and social reality: perceived ingroup similarities and shared ethnic characteristics are emphasized and displayed outwardly, while the willingness to defend one's own group increases (Koomen and Van Der Pligt 2016). An empirical study on the indigenous Mapucho people in Chile showed that discrimination by the White majority caused the minority group to put greater emphasis on their own ingroup identity, which in turn made the negative experience of prejudices and discrimination more bearable for them (Mellor et al. 2009). Focusing more on the positive characteristics and emphasizing the strengths of one's own ethnic group decreases feelings of powerlessness and self-worthlessness. The culture, norms, and ingroup characteristics of the ethnic group are valued and defined as good and desirable, while the characteristics of the reference group are rejected (e.g., "our culture and values are more moral," "we are friendlier and more family-oriented"). Although favoring one's own ingroup and emphasizing its positive characteristics moderately can have palliative effects on the ingroup members, radical forms of ingroup assimilation and outgroup derogation can lead to ostracism of and radical behavior toward outgroup members (Verkuyten 2004b).

A study by Maoz and McCauley (2008) on public support in Israel for retaliatory actions against Palestinians showed that perceived ethnic identity threats experienced by Israelis enhanced their support for aggressive attacks. A further significant factor that influenced their adverse attitude toward Palestinians was dehumanization. This was explained by the fact that enhanced identity threat increases group cohesion, by making group members feel a greater sense of attraction and engagement toward their own group and the opposite toward the source of threat (the outgroup). Dehumanizing outgroup members helps the threatened group to increase the distance between them and the outgroup from which the threat is perceived to emanate (Koomen and Van Der Pligt 2016).

Both enhanced ingroup assimilation and outgroup derogation have been observed especially among members of minority groups who base their preferences and identity heavily on their own group (Simon and Brown 1987). However, such strong cohesion and conformity can also have adverse effects on the behavior and self-perception of ingroup members (Christakis and Fowler 2007). An empirical psychological study examined how group similarity and dissimilarity in strengths-based intervention programs for young male detainees changed their behavior and belief system. Similarity among participants is considered on the basis of self-reported demographics, such as age, ethnic identity, and previous living situation, but also behaviors and belief systems. It is assumed that greater similarity between individuals contributes to the formation of groupings and thus to changes in behaviors and belief systems. The findings confirmed that participants' cooperative behavior increased within a similar group setting by changing their attitude to the benefits of education and of criminal activity in an opposite direction. In other words, close identification with the minority subgroup increased ingroup assimilation but decreased individuals' motivation to achieve educational goals and to stay away from crime. This means that greater homogeneity among participants enhances assimilation and conformity with the dominant group but decreases individualistic needs for self-determination, with individuals indicating they were willing to use violence to protect or benefit the group (Viola et al. 2015). The reason behind this is that ethnic minorities feel threatened by the dominant majority and are constantly concerned about the existence of the group and their identity. This anxiety leads to efforts to enhance the group's position, to highlight its unique characteristics, and to sustain the own self (Wohl et al. 2010).

Various studies on ethnic minorities in Europe support these assumptions by showing that minorities prefer multicultural integration over holistic assimilation to maintain their own ethnic identity (Verkuyten and Reijerse

2008). On the contrary, ethnic majority members who think in terms of social assimilation express more negative and even hostile feelings toward ethnic minority groups. They perceive social assimilation—which emphasizes a dominant one-group representation, conformity, cultural homogeneity, and social cohesion—as identity-conforming and as a justification of their dominant world view. In this view, ethnic minorities are obliged to conform to dominant values and abandon their own ethnic identity (Koomen and Van Der Pligt 2016). Four studies in the Netherlands found that a belief in holistic assimilation was important for those who strongly identified with the ethnic majority group and who wanted to protect the shared values, norms, and heritage of the dominant social group (Verkuyten 2011). Further empirical studies provide evidence that readiness for social integration can be increased if ethnic minorities believe in viable upward social mobility. The existence of opportunities to serve one's needs and change one's social status can alter one's attitude and behavior toward society and can thus enhance one's willingness to adapt. If individuals believe they can escape deprivation and become fully recognized members of society, their propensity toward conflict decreases. However, if individuals perceive their situation as unjust and immutable, non-normative actions such as crime, violence, or fraud are seen as a possible last resort (Koomen and Van Der Pligt 2016). Accordingly, members of ethnic minority groups must be given the opportunity to maintain and emphasize their own ethnic identity without being rejected or disapproved of by the major ethnic group. Belonging to and identifying with one's own ethnic group has a palliative effect on individuals and can enhance their psychological well-being. Experiences of rejection or discrimination because of one's ethnic belonging can deprive individuals from serving their human needs and can lead to decreased willingness to cooperate and invest in the common good.

Especially immigrants with a dual identity are prone to adopting radical belief systems or displaying anti-social behavior (Glasford and Dovidio 2011). Perceived unfairness paired with a strong ingroup identification tends to enhance political mobilization among dual identifiers, yet not among those without a dual identity (Simon and Grabow 2010). Eagerness to engage in normative action or adopt extreme beliefs is thus perceived to be even stronger in case of a dual-identity conflict. A dual-identity conflict arises if both ethnic identities are perceived as incompatible or contrasting. Identity incompatibility implies that different identities, such as the identity one forms in a traditional familial setting or culture and the identity one develops in a non-ethnic-related environment, encompassing divergent beliefs, norms and customs, are contradictory (Spiegler et al. 2019). Such an identity conflict can lead to alienation and anomie, which paves the way for more oppositional, destructive, or even radical reactions (Verkuyten 2004). This means that individuals experiencing dual identity conflicts search for reconciliation to reduce this inner conflict and serve their fundamental human needs. Their own ethnic group, with its norms, beliefs, and traditions, is a viable reconciliation option which provides individuals a way to belong and form their identity. Adhering to the conventions and behavioral norms of the group not only serves individuals' need for certainty and consistency, but it also serves their need for social approval and high self-esteem.

A study on Turkish and Russian immigrants in Germany provides evidence that those who experienced a strong identity incompatibility (a dual-identity conflict) had more sympathy for radical beliefs. Neither grievance nor group-based anger nor lack of opportunity fostered political radicalism among the respondents, but only perceived identity incompatibility (Simon et al. 2013). Another empirical study examined changes in dual identities during adolescence in a sample of 2,145 Muslim adolescents in four western European countries. The results show that those with an assimilated dual identity scored higher on psychological well-being, socio-cultural adjustment, and health. Higher levels of intergroup contact (assimilation) help to develop a national identity without negatively affecting ethnic identity. By contrast, identity separation (identity incompatibility) was linked to more delinquent and aggressive behavior, while full assimilation (abandonment of one's own ethnic identity) was linked to reduced psychological well-being (lower life satisfaction, lower meaning in life, lower self-esteem, etc.) (Spiegler et al. 2019).

In this context, recent German government data on 910 individuals who traveled to Syria and Iraq to join ISIS show that the majority (seventy-eight percent), aged eighteen to twenty-five, had German or a dual citizenship. Two-thirds were the subject of criminal investigations, with a significant increase in criminal activity and violent attacks post-radicalization. The radicalization process was triggered by like-minded ingroup members (fifty-four percent), contact with extremist mosques (forty-eight percent), online contacts (forty-four percent), or Islam seminars (twenty-seven percent). During the process, the importance of close social contacts increased, with the most significant impact coming from like-minded peers and the mosque community. However, changes in subjective needs also fueled the radicalization process, especially among those who radicalized in a very short time (departure within six to twelve months after the process began) (Heinke 2017). Hence, several factors must be carefully considered when explaining the process of radicalization given the absence of interlinking and causal levels of explanation. A review of 16,582 empirical studies on radicalization found that social networks, moral vulnerability (non-adherence to a conventional moral framework), and adolescence—a transition phase—are significant factors in the radicalization process. Furthermore, the authors argue that the process can be triggered by a "turning point," a negative subjective experience or external event that changes an individual's needs and preferences, which in turn leads an individual to dedicate time and energy to finding ways to serve these changed needs. Belief systems and particular group membership, irrespective of type and setting, can provide reconciliation to reduce need-thwarting and provide stability and coherence in life. Belonging to and identifying with a group serves individuals' relational needs to the extent that they experience companionship, loyalty, and moral support in such groups, which emphasizes their feeling of being heard, accepted, and understood. Such groups do not always have to have radicalizing features, yet if individuals are cognitively and morally vulnerable, experience identity confusion, and do not know where they belong, radicalization can occur (Bouhana and Wikstrom 2011).

These studies provide evidence that the concept of ethnicity can be a viable source of need reconciliation. Belonging to and identifying with an ethnic group generates reliable patterns of reality; that is, individuals evaluate and understand themselves and their social environment in terms of their ethnic belonging. They form their identity based on shared group norms and values and behave and make decisions that conform to them. A strong ethnic identity can enforce one's own self-esteem, as individuals can take pride in the fact that they are English, American, or Pakistani, and can enhance consistency, as it generates congruence with their self-view. Especially ethnic minorities emphasize the positive characteristics of their group to feel appreciated and valuable. Identifying with one's own ethnic group, even if socially disadvantaged, can thus provide stability and predictability (ethnic identity as an innate continuum), while strong attachment and belonging can generate a sense of power and control. However, extreme forms of ingroup favoritism can also lead to outgroup derogation and dehumanization. In such cases, some ethnic groups tend to perceive themselves as more moral, intelligent, superior, or valuable, and may start to feel they are entitled to more resources than others. This kind of awareness of one's ethnicity—the perceived superiority of one's ethnic culture, history, values, language, etc.—and the awareness of other ethnic groups may trigger conflict onset. In extreme cases, this can lead to outgroup hostility, violence, and conflict. Therefore, we can expound upon our argumentation that ethnicity is one of the most important and fundamental aspects of social structures, especially regarding intergroup conflict.

7.1.4 Fascism

As we have seen, ideologies like nationalism, racism, and ethnicity can provide viable reconciliation options to serve psychological human needs. Belonging to and identifying with a nation, "race," or ethnic group can have a strong palliative effect on group members. However, radical manifestations of ultra-nationalistic or racist movements can result in totalitarian belief systems such as fascism. Fascism is difficult to define because the ideology implies various meanings,[2] but it typically rests on aspects of "blood-and-soil" nationalism, racist attitudes, generic ethnic pride, and the idea of a community led by a strong leader (Mudde 2000). The aspect of "community" is perceived to form the core of the belief system, which holds that states should be inhabited by members of the "organic native" group, embodied in a belief in "strength through unity" (Mudde 2002). "The individual, in a literal sense, is nothing: individual identity must be entirely absorbed into the community or social group. The fascist ideal is that of the 'new man', a hero, motivated by duty, honor and self-sacrifice, prepared to dedicate his life to the glory of his nation or race, and to give unquestioning obedience to a supreme leader" (Heywood 2017, 194).

Historians argue that Italian fascism, first introduced by Mussolini in 1919, differed from race-based German fascism, which portrayed the Aryan people as a superior race and advanced a brutal form of antisemitism. That said, both manifestations implied a "palingenetic" form of ultra-nationalism, which mainly referred to the quest of "national rebirth" (Eatwell 2013). The ideas of fascism have been perceived to serve individuals' psychological need for stability, consistency, shared identity, and social attachment and thus had an appeal akin to that of a "political religion" (Heywood 2017). Hitler's first speech to the German nation as Chancellor contained words like "salvation," "mission," and "resurrection," and it stressed the impact of the economic and social crisis on the working and middle classes. Mussolini, too, spoke about the integrity, religiosity, and the fighting spirit of the common man. Both leaders promised to dampen the repercussions of World War I, eliminate economic vulnerability, and create a strong, national community that would unite the people and end "collective isolation." The people were hence unified through a form of activism—absorbed by a variety of organizations such as factory, youth, and women's groups (Eatwell 2013).

Fascism is a particularly male-oriented ideology, which perceives the ultimate role of women as bearing and raising a healthy new generation. The nation and its empowerment are at the heart of fascist thinking and the idea of organic unity is taken to an extreme. The national community, formed in Mussolini's fascism on the basis of "cultural heritage" and in Nazism on biological racism, was regarded as an indivisible whole that was destined for a higher purpose. The strength of the nation was therefore perceived as reflecting the population's integrity, morale, and willpower, which created the duty to dissolve one's own personality in the social whole (Heywood 2017). "Fascist myths [about the nation, race and the organic community] were not designed simply to mobilize people for production of war. Exemplar or identity myths, like the cult of Romanitá, told Italians that they were not a divided, mongrel nation, but the proud descendants of ancient Rome. Such myths were also about the importance of great leaders and fulfilling one's duty, and of the dangers of decadence and miscegenation" (Eatwell 2013, 482). All fascist movements thus highlighted the superiority of the national identity and proclaimed the resurrection of the state as a phoenix rising from the ashes. They fused myths about the glorious past with the image of a future reawakening of a sovereign nation and "a new man." "Influenced by Social Darwinism and a belief in national and racial superiority, fascist nationalism became inextricably linked to militarism and imperialism. Nazi Germany looked to construct a 'Greater Germany' and build an empire stretching into the Soviet Union. Fascist Italy sought to found an African empire through the invasion of Abyssinia in 1943. Imperial Japan occupied Manchuria in 1931 in order to found a 'co-prosperity' sphere in a new Japanese-led Asia" (Heywood 2017 204).

Although the fascist ideology rejected materialism, liberalism, and Marxism, economic success and development was central to forming a powerful nation and securing popular support. Yet economic power had to be achieved solely through the capacity of the autarkic nation and its resources, expansionism, and military power. Both Italy and Germany advocated a corporatist economy with an apparent "socialist" appeal. But organizations, such as the German Kraft durch Freude (Strength through Joy) or the Italian Dopolavoro, did not question nor monitor companies' activities, but offered instead a place for identification, joint leisure activities, and indoctrination. Similarly, the factory programs were established to decrease workers' alienation while neither raising wages nor improving working conditions (Roberts 2005). The people were unified in a more spiritual manner that was designed to transcend social and political divisions and link individuals closely to the nation state. The core "fundamentalist" aspect of fascism was therefore in the idea to merge state and civil society in such a way that the "strong leader" had the command, and every individual must make sacrifices for the common good (Griffin 2018).

These beliefs, attitudes, and norms thus addressed several human needs: the patriarchal and elitist ideology provided order and guidance on how to perceive the environment and the self and prescribed social roles, duties, and norms which in turn generated a consistent and predictable environment. The predetermined social order, which was based on subordination, patriarchy, and group segregation, produced meaningful social patterns that guided individuals as to how to process and evaluate information, events, individuals, and behavior. The narrative of a strong man with a strong body and mind who had to commit to and defend the national community created a source of identification. The myth of a strong nation led by a strong leader and the creation of communities and traditional familial patterns served the subjective needs for certainty and belonging by offering a sense of power and coherence. Individuals made choices and acted as subordinates in a hierarchy, whether human or mythical, which absolved them of personal responsibility and helped them believe they were fulfilling a higher (collective) purpose in life.

Given the seemingly appealing character of fascism, psychological studies have tried to explain why the totalitarian belief system attracted so many supporters and was so successful in its implementation. It has been assumed that fascism arose as a consequence of system instability, uncertainty, and perceived threat (e.g., economic inequality, anxiety owing to system breakdown, political insecurities) (Jost et al. 2003) and as an enhanced demand for moral authority (a strong leader), stability, and orientation (Haidt and Graham 2007). Other studies stress the importance of external rather than individual factors and argue that (socioeconomic) crises enhanced the subjective need for a strong national leader (Eatwell 2006). However, some emphasize that threat to identity, rather than the political and economic impact, tended to enhance demand for perceived certainty, control, and "salvation." The "Führer" (leader) was seen as an anchor that would solve the crisis and provide stability and meaning (Griffin 2018). "Underlying such approaches is usually a variation on mass society theory, which stresses the impact of the rise of anomie and 'automised' individuals" (Eatwell 2006, 149). But empirical studies which support these approaches and assess individual support for fascism are scarce in nature. However, historical case studies postulate that the totalitarian ideology and regime, the authoritarian operations, the constant portraying of an enemy, the community work, and the shared national/ethnic identity reacted to the unmet psychological human needs and provided a mystified form of attachment, which seemed to reduce the subjective sense of self-inefficacy, loss of control, and disintegration (Copsey 2018).

To provide more empirical evidence and to support historical case studies, several studies have examined why some individuals support totalitarian regimes and adopt fascistic ideologies. However, due to missing data and empirical research during the fascist era in the 1920s and 1930s, scholars have focused more on recent electoral data, starting in the 1980s, to explain the success of the radical right (Arzheimer 2018). Although some political scholars differentiate between fascism and the radical right, others challenge this distinction, arguing that the old fascism paved the way for the modern radical right. We refrain here from discussing the historical relation between the radical right and fascism and focus instead on the empirical findings that explain individual's inclination to the radical right.

Throughout the post-war era, there were periodic outbreaks of extremist activities around the globe. Significant new radical right-wing parties in Europe were not just copies of the old fascist right of the interwar years, they actually formed a new party family. However, the new parties proposed similar ideas about nationalism, ethnic/cultural pride, enemies (anti-immigration sentiment), threat, and anti-establishment attitudes. In this regard, charismatic leaders, such as those in Jörg Haider's Austrian Freedom Party or Jean-Marie Le Pen's French National Front, have been associated with greater electoral support (Oesch 2008). According to several political science and political psychology studies, dominant and masculine leaders are preferred under conditions of threat and intergroup conflict, whereas feminine and less dominant leaders are preferred in times of peace and cooperation (Little et al. 2007; Spisak et al. 2012, Laustsen and Petersen 2016).

Using nationally representative surveys of 2,009 Poles and Ukrainians fielded during the 2014 Crimean crisis, a study (Laustsen and Petersen 2017) found that the subjective preference for a strong and dominant leader increases under a conflict condition. That is, preferences for leader dominance are driven solely by the perception of threat and the contextual need for collective action against the enemy (e.g., in terms of war or intergroup conflict). Further, the study reveals that individuals with aggressive tendencies prefer dominant leadership the most. Using the Social Dominance Orientation (SDO) scale, the Right-Wing Authoritarianism (RWA) scale, and the Hawk–Dove game,[3] the study confirms that those who scored high on SDO but not on RWA and who are behaviorally predisposed to follow aggressive and dominant rather than submissive and avoidant strategies in the game have a significantly stronger preference for dominant leaders. The authors argue that these findings challenge the traditional ideas in the literature that propose the subjective preferences for a dominant leader come from defensive reasoning. In this regard, RWA ought to outperform SDO scorers and Dovish (submissive, risk-avoidant) subjects ought to show stronger preferences for dominant leadership. However, the results across the three tests show that subjective preferences for a dominant leader are mainly "a product of (1) contexts characterized by intergroup conflict and (2) predispositions for valuing group-based conflict and dominance in society and following aggressive and offensive strategies rather submissive and defensive strategies" (Laustsen and Petersen 2017, 1098).

Evolutionary theories of leadership emphasize the dual role of aggression and intimidation coupled with respect and admiration. While some leaders assert authority using threats and physical aggression (the dominance model), others rely on profound skills, competence, and generosity to lead a group or large community (the prestige model) (Garfield et al. 2019). Using three large-scale tests, a study provides robust evidence that enhanced perception of threat and the psychological sense of loss of control increases the subjective preference for a dominant and aggressive leader. The authors explain that to reduce these perceptions of threat, personal uncertainty, and loss of control, individuals prefer a leader who is perceived to be decisive, authoritarian, dominant, and assertive over a leader who is respected for their knowledge, decision-making skills, tolerance, and generosity. Looking at the United States, the study shows that individuals faced with uncertainty stemming from enhanced economic struggles showed stronger preferences for dominant and authoritarian leaders in their personal environment. This relationship has been confirmed across sixty-nine countries spanning twenty years: when individuals face (economic) threat, uncertainty, and lack of personal control, they prefer dominant and authoritarian leaders over prestigious leaders (Kakkar and Sivanathan 2017).

Another strand of literature in political science emphasizes the argument of a "protest vote." Individuals vote for authoritarian leaders and radical parties because they feel alienated from the political elites and frustrated about the in which system they live (Arzheimer 2018). "Mainstream parties, the argument runs, have effectively lost touch with 'the man on the street' and they have not responded sufficiently—or even quickly enough—to the concerns expressed by a 'forgotten working class'" (Odmalm and Hepburn 2017, 3). The radical parties and the dominant leader promise to offer viable solutions to dampen rising threats (such as immigration) and revive the national identity (and what it means to be a national citizen) (Mudde 2007). Empirically, however, the protest vote assumption remains elusive. Electoral data provide evidence that rather than pure protest, an enhanced perception of threat (immigration) is the most significant driver of the radical right vote (Van der Brug et al. 2000; Mughan and Paxton 2006; Cutts et al. 2011). This means that individuals adopt radical right-wing and fascist beliefs because these provide viable options to reduce perceived threat and hence serve their need for certainty, stability, order, and control. Authoritarian beliefs provide orientation in terms of prescribed roles, behavioral norms, and a hierarchical and ordered structure. Following authoritarian leaders and conforming to rules and norms generates stability in life and helps form coherent patterns of reality. Individuals can rely on a non-ambiguous and cognitively consistent world view, which serves their need for ambiguity avoidance, predictability, and control (existential and epistemic needs). Adhering to group norms and roles emphasizes their feelings of communal belonging, approval, and acceptance (relational needs) while providing them an enhanced sense of self-worth and self-significance (agency needs).

Combining these empirical results about individuals' preferences for authoritarian leadership with the psychological structure of fascism, we can summarize that fascism indeed serves individuals' existential, epistemic, relational, and agency needs. The creation of a strong and homogeneous community unifies individuals and provides a source of identification and belongingness. Within this community, social interactions and behaviors are regulated under the authority of the state and sustained by fixed norms and rules. Following these, and thus sharing the national ideal of an appropriate member (such as strong masculine men and feminine submissive women), not only provides a sense of coherence, order, and meaning in life, it also enhances social approval and an individual's self-esteem. Thus, the preservation of homogeneity, unity, and adherence to prescribed norms and rules which sustains a community is seen as a major goal by all social members. Dissidents and critiques of social homogeneity and the state are regarded as a threat to and dissociation of the organic community. Protecting the national community from enemies inside and outside the state provides a sense of self-efficacy (to serve and protect the superior nation and culture) and guidance in life (Kallis 2004). The narratives and myths of strong and exceptional ancestors who fought for the nation, and words used like "superiority," "noble," "exalted," and "sovereignty," provide a justification for dominating and even oppressing ingroup and outgroup members owing to their age, physical weakness, national status, etc. This "natural" appeal of authority and dominance serves the psychological needs for control, order, and cognitive consistency. Fascism, therefore, can be perceived as a "unifying" ideology that transcends social and political divisions and links the individual closely to the nation state. This link and relatedness to an "organic" community, strong nation, and a strong leader generates existential certainty, stability, and meaning in life.

7.2 The "Traditional Ideological Left"

As we have seen, various ideologies provide (i) an account of the existing order (evaluation and critique of existing society), (ii) offer a vision and shared beliefs of future society, and (iii) explain how political action can trigger desired outcomes. The descriptive understanding of what is and what should be has a powerful emotional character because it expresses hopes and fears, hate and affection. Beyond the descriptive feature, ideologies comprise fundamental and operative levels which trigger their proponents to take deliberate action (Heywood 2017). Although ideologies on the political left have been regarded as a complete opposite to right-leaning belief systems, it is argued that the mental frameworks of socialism, communism, and left-wing extremism provide similar ways to serve fundamental psychological human needs. This means that all ideologies, irrespective of their content, reveal critique of the current social, economic, and political system, show alternatives to it, and provide a theory of transition and change. The relative manifestation of these attitudes varies of course according to distinct belief systems, and it may even have different characteristics. In the following section, we will thus focus on the mental framework of socialism and communism to gain insight into how these distinct ideologies serve psychological human needs.

7.2.1 Socialism/Communism

Socialism is perceived to be one of the core traditional ideologies within the political spectrum. It goes back to the nineteenth century, when the exploitation of labor and the misery of large population groups under capitalism created demand for an alternative belief in social existence (Singer 2020). Despite its long history and rich tradition in political thought and action, the ideology of socialism incorporates a vast number of utopian views and theories, often differing in their conceptions and norms, which makes it difficult to provide a precise and orthodox definition of it. While one version propagates the abolition of political power and the establishment of a social order based on cooperation, altruism, and interdependence, another dreams of the formation of communes, in which familial roles, private property, and the division of labor are fractured, to instead create a society without barriers of any kind (Freeden 2003). However, the basic assumption of socialism is directed against capitalism, its dominant role of capital ownership, and its individualistic-liberalist market structure. Each version of socialism provides its own suggestions for overcoming the capitalist system and replacing it with a social order based on solidarity, equality, and justice (Geoghegan 2003). It describes a democratic society without social classifications, where the government is a representative of the people and all citizens have the same rights and duties, as well as equal access to vital resources.

What traditional socialism generally postulates is a society where the means of production are not the private property of a minority elite while the majority suffer from deprivation and are dependent on the owners of the means of production to assure their survival (Singer 2020). "The character of early socialism was influenced by the harsh and often inhuman conditions in which the industrial working class lived and worked. The laissez-faire policies of the early nineteenth century gave factory owners a free hand when setting wage levels and factory conditions. Wages were typically low, child and female labor were commonplace, the working day often lasted up to twelve hours and the threat of unemployment was ever-present. In addition, the new working class was disorientated, being largely composed of first-generation urban dwellers, unfamiliar with the conditions of industrial life and work and possessing few of the social institutions that could give their lives stability or meaning" (Heywood 2017, 85). The core of socialist ideology is therefore the perception of capitalism as the main driver of social and economic inequality, concentrating wealth and power in the hands of a minority while condemning the majority to a deprived, powerless, and alienated state of subsistence. Socialists therefore criticize the unequal living conditions and opportunities in such polarized societies, contrasting the capitalist notions of constitutional and market equality with the evident unequal conditions found in everyday life. The institutions and values formed by the capitalist system are regarded as creating isolated, consumption-oriented, and selfish individuals who neither cooperate nor care for others. As a result, capitalism forms individualistic societies encapsulating alienated individuals who bear the brunt of the work in isolation (Geoghegan 2003).

The ideology of socialism, by contrast, refers to the idea of a powerful community based on mutual cooperation and collective action to pursue collectivistic goals rather than individualistic self-interests. Socialism is characterized by a belief in social and economic equality which implies justice and egalitarianism and fosters identification and solidarity within society. From a socialist point of view, private property and unequal wealth accumulation are the source of class divisions that deliver a privileged status for some people while condemning others to poverty and powerlessness. These social inequalities are perceived to create grievances, social instability, and conflict. Accordingly, socialists aim to create a state that distributes wealth and power more equally. All of society, not only private individuals, ought to control and regulate resources and properties for the benefit of all (Ball et al. 2019). "The socialist economy will then be market-based but not free-market based. The state will have to intervene in the market functioning to redistribute income, taking from those who earn more and providing everybody with a minimum income that ensures that nobody is deprived of consuming essential goods and services" (Singer 2020, 150). These beliefs in a free, equal, and altruistic society generate a sense of a stable and continuous community that promises their members equal opportunities for self-realization and social approval. The state provides protection and enhances the sense of a secured existence. The mental framework of socialism therefore attracted many adherents who dreamed of a liberal, altruistic, and equal society which aimed to provide a sense of meaning, communality, and opportunity. Socialism promised to reduce the misery of the working class and instead establish a state that assured opportunities for self-realization and productivity (Lott 2016). Accordingly, we can argue that socialism clearly provides a viable option to serve individuals' human needs. In particular the need for belongingness, identification, social approval, and pro-sociality are served by the core belief that a society, based on mutual cooperation, care, and solidarity, can be established through communal living and working. This community, or society as a whole, unified by social principles, tolerance, and mutual altruism, provides guidance on how to process information, how to understand the social environment, and how to behave. The belief in equal opportunity and resource redistribution forms the attitude that every individual can reach their full potential, achieve their goals, and be self-efficacious. The ban on social categorizations and class divisions promotes the idea that every human being is equal and accepted in society, which elevates individuals' sense of self (high self-esteem and self-worth). Not only does socialism hence satisfy relational human needs, but the belief in equal opportunities for self-realization and social participation also serves the need for self-efficacy and high self-esteem. All this should not be accomplished through individual responsibility but collectively, within a unified and caring community. This means that individuals were not supposed to act in isolation to pursue their goals and interests but were embedded in a social and caring community. This community, and the state as a whole, ensured (economic) existence and provided vital resources for individuals to explore their full potential.

In Marx's early writings, the capitalist system, with its ideas of a self-interested, profit-seeking individual, were strongly criticized because it produced socially alienated and depersonalized human beings. Therefore, the ideas of socialism aimed for a re-devotion of the individual to himself, a re-creation of a collectivistic culture and a regained identification and solidarity with society. The goal of full employment and economic security associated with "the ideology of the working class" were designed to provide stability and diminish uncertainty. A shared collectivistic identity and the shared vision of a future ideal society created hope and meaning while re-enforcing confidence and self-esteem of the grieved working population (Heywood 2017). The core values of equality, community, and liberty were deemed to be both goals to be achieved and individual attributes to be desired. In arguing this way, socialists deploy a variety of propositions and moral characteristics. While few argue that all individuals possess similar characteristics regarding ability or character, the majority insist that humanity is shaped by distinct human capacities, needs, and entitlements that society must care for. Despite the divergent ideas, Marx's core position on capitalism came to be shared by all socialists, irrespective of the variety of their arguments (Giddens 2008). Although socialism seeks to call out the limitations of capitalism, its subdivisions—communism and social democracy—assume different opinions in this regard. While communism clearly rejects private property and class division and prefers common ownership, social democracy supports a compromise between the market and the state rather than a complete abolition of capitalism. In other words, traditional social democracy does not neglect the negative effects of free market capitalism but believes these can be overcome by government intervention. Instead of providing a dogmatic and ultimate solution of salvation or prescribing behavioral norms and values to reduce the suffering of the working class, social democracy offers ideas on how to regulate the market and thus reduce social and economic inequalities. At its core, social democracy can be understood as the application of democratic collective action to implement the principles of equality and freedom; that is, to create a balance between state and market, and between individual and community, without resorting to violence and revolution. Early social democratic parties, such as the Germany's SPD,[4] Britain's Labour Party, Canada's NDP, Sweden's SAP, and France's Socialist Party, enjoyed considerable success in implementing it (Jackson 2013). "The attraction of social democracy is that it has kept alive the humanist tradition within socialist thought, offering an alternative to the dogmatism and narrow "economism" of orthodox Marxism" (Heywood 2015, 276). Social democracy and its advocates aimed at pursuing a peaceful middle course by implementing a form of socialism that addresses all people rather than as an ideology focusing on only one group (cross-class coalitions) (Jackson 2013). Despite its appeal in north-western European countries, the end of the Cold War, the decline of industrial labor, the rise of neoliberalism, and the political agenda against communism/Marxism (especially in the United States) have reshaped the beliefs and behaviors of many social democratic parties (Oxford Dictionary of the Social Sciences 2002).

Despite its diversity, all forms of socialism favor resource redistribution and the regulation of private property as means to overcome social and economic inequality, various forms of cooperative production or community-building to overcome subjective isolation and harsh competition, and favorable conditions of work and education to enable growth of free human beings. Here, democracy is seen as embodying the unity of community, equality, and liberty, grounded in the free choice of every individual. Only through legislation and governmental policy can an egalitarian society be realized (Jackson 2013). However, beyond its democratic appeal, socialism has also induced democracy with more authoritarian elements (dictatorship), as reflected in the Marxist-Leninist principle of "democratic centralism" (Geoghegan 2003). As we focus on the more radical appeal of ideologies, we continue with a discussion of the revolutionary and dogmatic form of socialism—communism.

Looking first at historical trajectories, the distinct variations of socialism emerged mainly in the nineteenth century—one version at the beginning of industrial capitalism, others in response to sharp ideological polarities later in the century. However, the idea of a socialist society where property is shared and divisions based on rank and privilege are abandoned long preceded the writings of Marx and Lenin. Around the fourteenth century, British precursors rejected hierarchical authority and social inequality and proclaimed common ownership, which was linked to the Peasants' Revolt of 1381 and the complex resolution of English feudalism (Brown 2013). By the sixteenth century, the capitalist structure of the agricultural sector had stimulated Thomas More's critical work *Utopia* (1516), in which he questions private property and pictures a society in which the common good is equally shared, distribution is based on need, and opportunities are generated for all (Geoghegan 2003). In the centuries that followed, the French Revolution in 1789 inspired the principles of socialism, and especially the founders of communism, Marx and Engels, and all those who believed in passing power from monarchs to citizens. However, the term "socialism" first appeared in Britain and France in the late 1820s, first used by Robert Owen in an issue of *Co-operative Magazine*. Owen, considered the founder of British socialism, attempted to put socialistic ideas into practice by ameliorating working and living conditions at his mill and more or less successfully establishing a new form of cooperative existence.

Britain, hence, became home to the most influential theorists of socialism, Karl Marx and Friedrich Engels, who produced a new, complex theoretical system of critique on capitalism (Heywood 2017). Their most memorable and influential work was the Communist Manifesto of 1848 that exclaims understanding history (why capitalism was an inevitable step of development), while simultaneously urging the working class to fulfill its revolutionary task of overthrowing the capitalist system. In his writings, Marx differentiated between "revolutionary communism" and "utopian socialism," with the former a more realistic step toward a societal state. Communism has been thus regarded as an ideal state, characterized by classlessness (common ownership of productive wealth), rational economic organization (production-for-use replaces production-for-exchange), and statelessness (Heywood 2017). Although Marx's theory suggested that the "places ripest for revolution and the transition from capitalism to socialism were the most advanced industrial countries in the nineteenth century—Britain and Germany[5] [. . .], Communism's first and most momentous victory was in Russia" (Brown 2013, 368).

Inspired by the Marxist philosophy of revolutionary communism, the well-planned and organized Bolshevik Revolution in 1917, which was led by the most important of Russian revolutionaries, Vladimir Lenin, was the first to succeed in overthrowing the existing capitalist class and replacing it with the "rule of the proletariat." As the revolution occurred in a preindustrial, semi-feudal, and largely agricultural country, it was expected to catch up with the economic and material progress achieved in the West and to establish socialist structures in the Russian economy. The Bolshevik leaders had to promise the peasantry peace, land redistribution, and adequate resource allocation once they had abolished the Tsarist Empire (Dowlah 1993). They believed that private property should be abolished and replaced by common ownership. Beyond economic and political factors, the Bolsheviks dreamed of transforming the social and cultural field into "the culture of masses." But by 1919, fighting and restructuring had brought poverty and hunger to Russia, including painful struggles against internal and external Anti-Bolshevik forces (Von Geldern 1998). Throughout this period of upheaval, the new state was constantly under threat and was attacked and occupied by foreign Allied forces, internal pro-Tsarist White generals, and anti-Bolshevik and pro-nationalist groups. The needs and concerns that emerged from such internal and external threats induced the formation of the Communist Party and called for centrally controlled management of scarce resources in war-devastated Russia. These factors—including a shortage of resources, ongoing threats, economic uncertainty, and armed opposition to the government—had all contributed to the formation of a centralized and authoritarian political system. The burden of rebuilding a devastated economy with a conflict-torn population led to stricter laws and order in the country, which in turn resulted in the consolidation of a one-party dictatorship and the nationalization of industries and factories (Dowlah 1993).[6]

During the nineteenth century, revolutionary movements were attractive for two reasons. The early stages of industrialization produced poverty and unemployment among the working class, which had few political rights of co-determination. The traditional patterns of family and community that were disrupted by economic transition and the cultural implications of capitalism created physically and psychologically uprooted individuals. As a result, belief systems, especially those with a radical and dogmatic appeal such as communism, religious fundamentalism, or fascism, attracted millions of people because they addressed unmet psychological human needs, reduced perceived threats, and promised material wealth. Furthermore, these consistent and rigid belief systems offered mental stability in form of a closed meaning system and guidance on how to understand social reality and make decisions (Salzman 2008). Communism, in this regard, provided a closed world view that guided people on how to end class division, exploitation, and alienation, and proclaimed itself the only way to escape misery. The teachings of Marx have been regarded as the true values that have to be achieved, even if that meant removing critical voices and opponents. The only state that was desired was the revolutionary "Dictatorship of the Proletariat," which promised to give power and control back to the working people, unite them, and generate opportunities to reach their full potential. However, as Lenin proclaimed, to reach this desired state the power of the proletariat must be centralized and combined with spiritual leadership (the Communist Party). In other words, order, unity, compliance, and discipline were important conditions for the victory against the bourgeoisie (Bernholz 2017).

Accordingly, twentieth century communism, especially in Asia and Russia, differed significantly from the ideas of Marx and Engels. In Russia, communist rule became the rule of the Communist Party and leaders, which was crucially shaped by the contributions of Lenin and Stalin. In Asia, the Chinese Revolution of 1949, led by Mao Zedong, represented an impressive success of the Communists against both Japan and the Chinese Nationalists, the Kuomintang. In both countries, the Communists believed that only a "revolutionary party" could lead the working class and was able to understand the true meaning of Marxist ideas. This belief implied the existence of a monopolistic party which enjoys sole power to decide and carries sole responsibility for reaching the goals and serving the needs of the proletariat (Heywood 2017). The success of communism in Russia and China was determined by several factors, such as the symbolic power of the ruling party, its organizational structure, the Communist ideology, and most of all the shared feeling of belongingness and attachment. Both the translation of radical ideas into action and the creation of an emotional attachment based on mutual commitment, a passionate devotion to the community, and collective solidarity among leaders and followers were key ingredients in the successful campaigns against rival groups. "The millions who enlisted on the side of the Red Army were probably motivated less by some abstract affinity for the principles of nationalism or land reform than by heartfelt allegiance to a highly charged crusade" (Perry 2002, 112). Further revolutionary movements, including the 1975 Vietnamese uprising against France and later against the United States; the 1959 Cuban revolution, led by Che Guevara, which overthrew the U.S.-backed Batista regime and brought Fidel Castro to power, and various other movements in Africa (e.g., Algeria against the domination of France), demonstrated the political necessity, but also the psychological and emotional desire of the masses, to trigger political and social change (Heywood 2017).

However, distinctive characteristics clearly set communism apart from democratic socialism. While in theory, communism adopted similar conceptions as socialism and postulated an ideal, caring society without a ruling class, in reality it became an elitist and totalitarian state, first emerged in the Soviet Union, and more severe under Stalin and Mao Zedong. After World War II, the ideology spread to Eastern Europe and developed a more bureaucratic and conservative appeal (Freeden 2003). The most distinctive characteristic of communism is hence the necessity to give the Communist party the monopoly on power. Although in some communist states, the existence of other political parties was not forbidden, they were denied power and autonomy. The Communist Party alone was perceived to have the knowledge and sovereignty to guide the working class, build a socialist society, and become the institutional embodiment of "the dictatorship of the proletariat." In reality, what ensued was a party dictatorship over the proletariat and society as a whole. The second ideological distinction is democratic centralism, which calls for subordination of the individual to the collectivity and strict compliance with decisions made by the leading party. Although in theory discussions among parties were generally accepted, in practice the strictly centralized and hierarchical Communist Party tolerated no dissent on major issues. The third feature of a communist ideology is the fundamental belief that state ownership of the means of production is inevitable to dampen capitalistic development. This is linked to a further distinction based on the idea that a centrally planned economy is more efficient and only then a market economy. This ideological premise guided the nationalization of industry and the collectivization of agriculture, especially in the early years of communist rule, by failing to adjust to questions regarding technological innovation, foreign investment, and product quality. Instead, it presented orthodox communists with a compelling list of restrictions. Those who dared propose modifications to the established economic, social, and political system were condemned as "revisionists," or, in China, as "capitalist roaders." Further distinctions of the communist ideology are assumed to be the sense of belonging to an International Communist Movement and the ambition to build a stateless and classless future society. The international doctrines that inspired many individuals and nations were regarded as a fellowship of faith, shared by many with a common goal and vision (Brown 2013).

This implies that communism and its doctrines and narratives were able to serve individuals' psychological needs. The need for order, certainty, stability, and control, in particular, could be met by the rigid and restrictive social, political, and economic system. The monopolistic power of the Communist Party generated a sense of control, sovereignty, territorial integrity, and the ability to address the needs of the people on condition of their subordination and compliance (Bernholz 2017). The narratives of communism also responded to the need for belongingness, identification, and social approval. The unification of an alienated working class and the erosion of class divisions provided a narrative of social cohesion and a collectivistic working class that shared the same values, norms, and social identity (Kolar 2012). Analyzing the diary entries of young adults in the Stalinist Soviet Union, Jochen Hellbeck (2009) found them to express the needs and desires of these young adults to belong to communist society and contribute to the "big story" of the Soviet revolution. From the 1970s onward, most young adults were embedded in authoritative social groups, such as schools, universities, sports clubs, and especially the well-known youth organization Komsomol. "The Komsomol organization was responsible for organizing much of the youth activities of that generation, from strictly ideological activities—those linked to reading party texts, performing various political assignments, participating in meetings, parades and elections—to various cultural, social, musical, and sporting events and other activities" (Yurchak 2006, 81). The hierarchical organization not only provided stability and orientation for young individuals by serving their need for certainty, stability, consistency, and order, it also offered a place for social identity formation which strongly addressed their need for identification, belongingness, and social approval. Every individual was obliged to demonstrate service and loyalty to the youth organization and to subordinate and comply with the norms, rituals, and values as directed by the organizational leaders (Komsorgs and secretaries). Every member of the youth organization received a subjective task that was supposed to be socially meaningful and personally fulfilling, and whose fulfilment was controlled by higher-ranking members (Yurchak 2006). Young members hence received an opportunity to prove themselves and achieve something, but only if they submitted to subordination and collectivity. Following the values, rules, and behavioral norms of the youth organization and adhering to their assigned tasks and roles generated reliable and consistent patterns of the environment and gave them meaning in life.

Although there is scarce empirical research on communism in the former Soviet Union, two studies from the mid-1950s have shown that communists and fascists—extremists on the left and right—tend to have similar psychological human needs while sharing a core personality trait akin to authoritarianism (Eysenck 1954). However, critics insist that the perspective of authoritarianism differs between communist and non-communist countries. While in Western countries authoritarianism was linked to political conformity and obedience, in Soviet communist nations authoritarianism was viewed as a central feature of conventionalism, which involves an adherence to cultural norms and own group values (Duckitt 1989). During Perestroika in the Soviet Union, further empirical psychological studies on ideology and personality became viable. A study using a 1989 sample of 340 Russian and 463 American adults confirmed that both cultures, while divergent, had similar perceptions of authoritarianism, which included opposition to democratic ideals and civil liberties. Nevertheless, an extended analysis on this issue revealed that even after the collapse of the Soviet Union, individuals from former Soviet states linked authoritarianism mainly to the idea of conventionalism and loyalty to one's own cultural values. However, this loyalty was coupled with outgroup ostracism and hostility toward dissidents and an endorsement of violence against those who were perceived as threats to the accepted order, values, and lived stability (McFarland et al. 1992).

Despite their loyalty, subordination, and belonging to the Communist state in the past, empirical studies on post-communist nations reveal that post-communist citizens tend to show weak trust in the government and are less likely to regard the political and social system as just and legitimate than their capitalist counterparts (Cichocka and Jost 2014). More detailed comparisons of post-communist and capitalist societies, among them large-scale social surveys in the UK, the US, West Germany, the Netherlands, and Japan that contrast the attitudes and beliefs of citizens in Russia, Bulgaria, Hungary, East Germany, Estonia, Slovenia, and former Czechoslovakia, showed that individuals in post-communist societies have a negative attitude toward material wealth, which is strongly associated with corruption, dishonesty, and exploitation of personal connections instead of hard work and personal ability (Kluegel et al. 1995). Furthermore, post-communist societies tend to believe that justice (equal outcomes for all) and security can only be provided and sustained by a strong government that is able to directly address individuals' human needs. This belief results from the prevailing attitude to the state in a former socialist system that promised full employment and equal pay (none of which were tied to individual effort or skill) (Flanagan et al. 2003). This implies that the communist state was seen as a caregiver and authority that provides guidance, orientation, stability, and certainty to its members and thus serves their fundamental human needs.

In this regard, a 2005 economic study compared the different preferences for resource redistribution and state intervention between East and West Germans after reunification. The results show that East Germans indeed had significantly stronger preferences for state intervention and redistribution than did West Germans, which held especially true for older and poorer individuals. The authors argue that East Germans more strongly believed that social conditions, rather than personal effort, determine subjective welfare (Alesina and Fuchs-Schündeln 2005). Another study (Schwartz et al. 2014) examined the relationship between personal values and core political values in different country-specific political contexts. The eight core political values are blind patriotism (no questioning and adherence), traditional morality (preservation of traditions in society and family), law and order (the government should provide rules and order), free enterprise (no state intervention in the economy), equality (equal opportunities and resources for all citizens), civil liberties (freedom of speech and action), foreign military intervention (use of military power to deal with global problems), and accepting immigrants. The basic personal values are cognitive representations which support individuals in evaluating and understanding different situations, behaviors, or people. Personal values are represented in terms of power (control and dominance over resources or people), achievement, hedonism (pleasure and gratification for oneself), stimulation (excitement and novelty in life), self-direction (autonomy), universalism (welfare for all people and nature), benevolence (reciprocal altruism), tradition, conformity, and security. The authors argue that individuals' personal values should match political values consistently; that is, military intervention for example correlates with the personal values of power, security, and achievement, but less with benevolence and universalism. The results show clear and significant differences between formerly communist and non-communist countries. Universalism, for example, correlated with traditional morality positively in post-communist countries, but negatively in non-communist countries. Caring for the community and nature is perceived as a traditional and moral value in post-communist but not in non-communist countries. Communism, as stated above, generated a sense of belonging to and identifying with society, the party and other related organizations, with each individual responsible for caring and acting on behalf of the ideology. The three conservation values (security, conformity, tradition) correlated positively with military intervention and equality and negatively with free enterprise in post-communist countries. In this regard, the authors reason that governmental intervention (military power, equal opportunities for all, and intervention in the economy) enhances the sense of security and certainty in post-communist countries, while the negative correlation in non-communist countries implies that they prefer a rather limited role of the government. The authority and strong role of the government, which is perceived as the main caregiver and supplier of social and economic security, thus correlates positively with conservation values in post-communist countries. Based on these results, we can argue that communism clearly serves individuals' needs for security, stability, order, and ambiguity avoidance because it guides individuals how to think, to act, to perceive the social environment (us vs. the enemies of communism), and to process information about themselves and the social, political, and economic environment. The state apparatus is seen as a moral authority, a source of security, and a social caregiver—a strong and powerful unit that produces and sustains security, conformity, and tradition.

A similar multilevel analysis (Barni et al. 2016) reveals that conservative values strongly relate to the left–right political dimension in non-communist countries, but not in countries with a communist past. In non-communist countries the authors observe a clear relationship between conservative values and the political right. On the contrary, in former communist countries they find no clear relationship between the left–right political division and conservative values, but a positive link between conservative values and preference for economic redistribution (which is usually observed on the political left). They reason that in the context of transitioning to a free market economy, "leftist" parties in post-communist nations also adopted features of the political "right," pursuing, on the one hand, "liberal" fiscal and social policies such as austerity, and, on the other hand, principles of democracy and equity. These findings correspond with various other studies that have found that in post-communist countries, individuals with conservative values and who are less educated, older, and less democratically oriented have a stronger preference for preserving their political past (Pop-Eleches and Tucker 2010). This means that conservatives support established policies because they generate a sense of stability, certainty, order, and control in life (Barni et al. 2016).

In this context, various surveys provide evidence that nostalgia and positive attitudes toward the old Communist Party system have not entirely disappeared in post-communist nations. A Polish survey in 2010 found that sixty-four percent of respondents evaluated their lives before the transition to capitalism more positively, whereas only seven percent indicated the opposite (Prusik and Lewicka 2016). In several political surveys in Romania, in 1999, 32.6 percent of respondents indicated they preferred a communist leader and, in 2007, the results remained unchanged. Similarly, four political barometers between 2002 and 2006 showed that between fifty-two and sixty percent of respondents had a positive attitude toward communism. These nostalgic sentiments about the former social and political system tend to be strongest among those with a lower economic and social status. While in Western countries the responsibility for economic prosperity is attributed to individuals rather than the system, in post-communist nations most people still consider the system to be responsible for citizens' economic situation, job status, and welfare of each citizen (Cernat 2010).

After the collapse of the communist system, numerous scholars assumed that the shift to democracy and capitalism would effect a change in the general belief system from egalitarianism to meritocratic, market-based principles. However, the negative implications of the economic transition, including high unemployment and high inflation, dampened the enthusiasm for the new system. Instead, increased perception of economic inequality, corruption and market unfairness arose, which in turn led to the resurgence of populist and "ex-communist" parties in many post-communist nations (Smith and Mateju 2012). In line with this trend, empirical studies in Poland and Ukraine in 2014 showed that enhanced perception of social conflicts and threats increased subjects' preference for dominant leaders and offensive, aggressive measures (Laustsen and Petersen 2017). Thus, research on long-term social development insists that the transformation of belief systems, values, and attitudes is long-lasting and proceeds at a slow pace between one generation and the next (Inglehart and Baker 2000). Consistent with this view, some empirical surveys have found that especially older generations still express positive feelings for the communist era (Ekman and Linde 2005), while other studies state that despite a system change, younger generations, too, have a strong preference for communist beliefs and ideas (Krauss 2002). To explain these preferences, research on post-communism suggests that the harsh political and economic transition in post-communist countries and the fragile governments that were unable to provide citizens stability, certainty, and a shared identity increased their doubts about the new path of development (Mason 1995). Communism, by contrast, was experienced as a stable system that united the people and generated certainty and order in their lives. It created an environment in which individuals shared moral values, traditions, festivities, thoughts, and most important social identities—all of which generated a perception of unity and equality.[7]

A large cross-national survey, conducted in a period of political and economic turmoil between 1989 and 1991, showed that individuals from post-communist countries stated they had never personally experienced discrimination or injustice due to race, age, gender, or social background, but did experience it for their political or religious beliefs during the communist period. It is surprising that there is no difference between answers provided by democratic and post-communist countries, and that individuals in post-communist nations indicated they experienced more justice than those in democratic ones. The majority of respondents from post-communist countries who were asked about their attitude toward socialism and the state still attribute a high role to the government in providing stability and security and were still skeptical about a distributive system based on merit rather than need (Mason 1995). Surveys conducted before the collapse of communism found a high degree of social and economic egalitarianism in the population (Mason 1985). After the breakdown and the restructuring phase, which brought economic inequality and deregulated employment, communist values remained ingrained in the population. The overwhelming majority of Eastern Europeans felt that differences in income were too large, and that the government had a strong responsibility to guarantee security and employment. In both East and West, but more in the East and least in the United States, individuals highly valued the principles of a welfare state, equality of opportunity, and strong governmental support which regulates the market, provides social stability, and protects the weak and the poor (Kluegel and Mason 2004).

This strand of economic egalitarianism and governmental role is linked to a popular conception of justice that calls for resource distribution based on need rather than merit. For example, in Poland sixty-six percent of low-income individuals but also forty-eight percent of high-status individuals agree that resource allocation should be based on need. Almost eighty percent of respondents in post-communist countries endorse a strong government, while capitalist societies, especially the United States, reject a strong governmental role. This indicates that all post-communist nations score higher on socialist orientation than capitalist countries, except for Japan and, more or less, Germany, which are closer in terms of attitudes to socialist ideas. Despite economic and political reconstruction in these post-communist countries, individuals still have an egalitarian and statist orientation that works against the decentralized loose reforms implemented by the new governments (Mason 1995).

Recent studies show that for many Eastern Europeans, the reality of system transformation and democratization did not meet their expectations, which enhanced frustration and distrust in the new political and economic system (Rose 2008). Data from the New Europe Barometer and the Global Corruption Barometer show that individuals perceived an increase in injustice and corruption in their societies. People who hold a positive view about the fairness and non-corruptibility of authorities and officials in their country tend to be more supportive of the new democratic system. Although the subjective perception of injustice increased, on average fifty-nine percent of the people from ten former communist countries reject non-democratic alternatives, except in Bulgaria and Poland, where the majority supports authoritarian alternatives (Linde 2012). Using data from the 1996 and 2006 International Social Survey Program (ISSP), an analysis provides evidence that citizens in post-communist countries feel alienated and have less confidence in their political leaders. However, the most significant difference between post-communist and democratic countries is the perceived lack of self-efficacy—a subjective belief that one can influence the political and social environment. Individuals living in former communist countries indicate a low sense of self-efficacy and self-determination, but an enhanced perception of a distrustful and uncertain environment. But citizens from Spain, Portugal, Chile, and Taiwan, all countries that have experienced totalitarian regimes, also demonstrate a high level of political alienation (Mierina 2014). This may suggest that communist regimes, despite their authoritarian appeal, generated a sense of self-significance because individuals were embedded into a collectivistic system, each with a certain socially meaningful role and task. Post-communist regimes failed to provide such a meaningful (collectivistic) system and assign their citizens social roles and duties.

Further studies have found that especially younger people feel more alienated or have dissident attitudes than those aged over fifty-five. The reason behind this is that increased individualism, consumerism, self-responsibility, and declined significance of traditional communities and families may cause alienation and lost orientation. The resulting feelings of uncertainty, powerlessness, and frustration about the system can trigger either passivity or increased engagement in unconventional political activities (Mierina 2014). This development in post-communist countries may suggest that communism, despite its dogmatic tendencies, indeed served individuals' particular psychological needs such as order, certainty, stability, control, and ambiguity avoidance (guidance, orientation by the state, prescribed world view, thinking and behavior) but also a sense of belonging (community, conformity, tradition), identification (shared communist identity, values, norms, morality), and social approval (social role, subjective contribution to society), and to some extent the need for self-esteem and self-efficacy (feeling of self-significance, meaningful contribution to society and the state). The theoretical background of and empirical evidence on socialism and communism show that the primordial "utopian" ideas of an egalitarian and altruistic community that is based on freedom, equality, and cooperation has been dissolved in reality into various versions with different outcomes. While one version propagates the abolition of political power and the establishment of a "social order" based on cooperation, altruism and interdependence, another dreams of the formation of communes, in which familial roles, private property and the division of labor are fractured, creating instead a society without barriers of any kind (Freeden 2003). These beliefs aimed to provide a source of belongingness and meaningful existence, stability, consistency, and predictability. Socialism propagated benevolence, equality, and cooperation, which was expected to provide isolated and alienated human beings hope and a sense of a collective co-existence. It served their need for a strong and stable community and a state that promised to generate security and equal opportunities for all citizens, decreased threats, and reduced their anxiety about an uncertain future. However, beyond peaceful ideas of an egalitarian society, radical views concerning the abolishment of private property, individualism and democracy called for a revolution and a radical change in society. While Marx and Engels called for abrogating class divisions and for an organized working-class political party, more radical appeals, mainly from Russia under Stalin or China under Mao, propagated strong one-party leadership and unquestioning obedience.

One of the major differences between socialism and communism was therefore the emphasis, especially in the latter, on the need for a strong state that assures stability, security, and order for all citizens. In contrast to the utopian ideas of an equal, egalitarian, and liberal state, the elitist and totalitarian leadership of the Communist Party seized absolute power and controlled all citizens and resources, which seemed to serve individuals' psychological needs for stability, order, and certainty in life. The Communist Party provided various social organizations, such as sport clubs or Komsomol for young people, which were a source of belonging, identification, and orientation in life. But beyond pleasure, identity formation, and commitment, the state-controlled organizations with their rules and norms were established to assure conformism and absorb every individual into the communal whole (Riordan 1980). They shaped and regulated individual preferences and basic attitudes toward the self, the community, and the state and they helped to reduce uncertainty by providing dependable and efficient frameworks for social, economic, and political exchange. Communist parties, such as those in China or Russia, portrayed themselves and were regarded by citizens as the only legitimate ruling power in the country, representing the most advanced culture, production unit, and the interest of the people. Government-endorsed beliefs, norms, and values directed citizens how to behave, evaluate, and understand information. Those who complied were rewarded, while those who were critical of the regime were punished and ostracized from society (Yongnian 2009). This radical from of "institutionalism" and one-party dictatorship provided a sense of order, consistency, and control, guided individuals how to think and behave, and formed a shared cultural identity, which in turn emphasized a sense of a strong and powerful community.

7.2.2 The New Left

While the revolutionary socialist movement in the former Soviet Union and other developing nations formed authoritarian regimes and pretended to address the needs and interests of economically disadvantaged groups, the so-called New Left movements in developed countries were stimulated, in the age of television and industrialization, by perceived social injustice and suppression of the Third World. These idealistic thoughts triggered simultaneous riots in Paris, Berlin, and Washington, where students revolted against social injustice, militarism, and the exploitative character of the capitalist system (Post 2007). The New Left defined themselves as a unique stage in the ambitions of revolutionary movements, by portraying the advantages of communalism based upon social autonomy and individual freedom, a new world society based on international decentralization of political and economic institutions, and a new way of life based on the unification with nature. The individual was perceived as a part of a harmonious, communal, and natural system that does not suppress their freedom of choice and action and that is based on mutual solidarity. The movements rejected the subjective accumulation of wealth and property, which was perceived as a conservative value of the middle class; the social routines, predefined roles, and class divisions that were perceived as the core values of patriarchal domination; and the traditional way of life associated with conventionalism and individual suppression (Katsiaficas 1987).

During the legitimate student protests, voices were raised that peaceful revolts were insufficient and ineffective and that only violent measures could lead to desired outcomes (Koomen and Van Der Pligt 2016). As a result, militant factions split from the legitimate student groups and formed their own violent revolutionary groups, such as West Germany's Red Army Faction, which split from the Socialist Union of German Students; the Japanese Red Army, which emerged from the student group Zenga Kuren; the Red Brigades in Italy; Direct Action in France; the Combatant Communist Cells in Belgium, and so forth. Their ideological ideas centered on harsh criticism of materialism, imperialism, and capitalism, urged revolutionary revolts, and even called for armed and violent social conflicts. Such revolutionary ideologies usually imply a utopian perspective of an idealized state and discuss the deficiencies of the present reality (Abelson 1979). Therefore, the New Leftist fighting organizations share all the following features: "secrecy; the willingness to carry out lethal attacks; adherence to Marxist-Leninist ideology; an urban operating environment; a cellular, compartmentalized organizational structure; and democratic centralism in decision making" (Post 2007, 103).

In the aftermath of 1968, the New Left organizations, formed foremost in Western societies, had reached a large degree of unity that aimed to spark a generational disbanding and awaken a new youth rebellion. The rise in youth movements in western countries, such as West Germany, the United States, Japan, Italy, and France, had several reasons. The bright economic circumstances of the Golden Years gave the young generation increased purchasing power, which extended their options for development and enhancement of the individual self. With increased consumerism, a new and diverse youth culture developed, shaped additionally by the growth of mass media and educational system. Furthermore, the global conditions caused by the Cold War induced a significant background of young people's intellectual abilities and social understanding. In western and northern European countries, in 1970 students and pupils accounted for almost twenty percent of the total population and the number of graduations doubled or nearly tripled (France, Denmark) during this period. Furthermore, the voting age was lowered to eighteen in several countries which enabled young people to influence the political environment and exercise their rights as sovereign legal subjects (Siegfried 2006). These well-educated young intellectuals from respectable middle-class families influenced the political climate in the 1960s and triggered a cultural and generational conflict, which was associated with the attempt to adjust to rapid socioeconomic transformation. The demand for cultural assimilation to constantly changing economic, social, and political conditions and the desire for new patterns of meaning was expressed in revolutionary upheaval. The alienation from and disintegration of established society led to an enhanced search for new patterns of identification and understanding (Lichter and Rothman 1982). The young adults represented new "post-materialistic" values, covering needs for self-realization, self-determination, individualism, and meaning in life, which collided with those held by older generations who had experienced harsh economic insecurity, real threat, and post-war instability (Inglehart 1977).

With the rise of New Left movements, several theories and empirical studies attempted to explain the motives behind political engagement and ideological adherence in terms of psychosocial dynamics. One idea was that political involvement emerges out of personal identity development. Accordingly, surveys found that for some individuals, their experienced feelings within the group were more important than the goals or consequences of political participation. In answer to "Why do you like the Left Movement?" participants stated they had experienced "warm" feelings of belonging, of being a part of something, and of having visions of an "ideal life." Beside these felt emotions, motives regarding increased awareness and information processing played also an important role, with individuals indicating an increased need to understand the complexity of social and political structures and to analyze the environment "properly." The emphasis here is on the need for explanation and understanding, the search for orientation in life, and the meaning for personal existence (Candee 1974). Other psychological studies examined the link between radical Left movements and personality traits. While some scholars (e.g., Rokeach 1960; Van Hiel et al. 2006) argue that right-wing and left-wing radicals share the same dogmatic cognition and an authoritarian character that is derived from the need for order and guidance and the desire for domination and submission, others (e.g., Knutson 1974; Van Hiel 2012) stated that the New Left movement represents a different form of personality. "The most influential studies portrayed youthful radicalism as an expression of 'positive' personality traits, [. . .]. Radicals and protesters were found to be autonomous, self-expressive, non-authoritarian, and morally advanced or 'principled'" (Lichter and Rothman 1982 208). Even the disposition to violence and terror has been explained as a reaction to frustration and inactivity. But these initial analyses were grounded on insufficient data and weak methodologies that render deep interpretations impossible (Van Hiel 2012).

To address these deficits, a survey of 1,195 students at four large US universities assessed the relationship between left-wing radicalism and individual dispositions from 1971–1973. The results indicate that left-wing adherents are characterized by an enhanced need for self-efficacy, self-determination, and self-enhancement (self-esteem), an ambiguous attitude toward power, a self-assertive psychosocial orientation (male-oriented, action-driven, resistant), and a lack of relational needs. The analyzed data show that, among the student samples, the left-wing radicals have a conflictual orientation to power (fear vs. attraction), score high on narcissism, and low on need for social affiliation.

Furthermore, left-wing radicals are strongly self-assertive, react adversely to social authority, and express strong sympathy with opponents of the state (outgroups)—the inverse of the traditional authoritarian personality (Lichter and Rothman 1982). A further study extended the analysis in an attempt to consider the contrastive motivation of politically radical and non-radical American adults. The group was composed of radical leaders of the New Left movement, while the control group included socially active adults who represented the attitudes and orientations of the "average American." In the radical group, ninety-five percent of participants were employed compared to the moderates (eighty-four percent) who, in contrast to the radicals, lived in a more traditional patriarchal family setting (overrepresentation of housewives). More radicals occupied high-skilled positions, such as lawyers and college professors, whereas moderates were mainly employed as salespersons or financial managers. Other results reveal that radical New Left leaders scored high on the need for power (assertiveness, self-efficacy, having an impact on the environment) and less on the need for intimacy (feelings of belongingness and community). In comparison, the moderates scored low on the need for power, but high on the need for intimacy and affiliation with others. In their perceptions and thoughts, left-wing radicals tended to rate interpersonal relations differently than the moderates by focusing more on action-driven and effective personal connections which should have a great impact on society, rather than a friendly, artificial, and simple exchange. These needs for power and self-efficacy are reflected in the ideological principles to act and trigger change. Accordingly, political protests and revolts provided possible arenas to serve the need for self-expression and control of the environment (impact on society) (McAdams et al. 1982).

Similar results have been confirmed in several demographic studies that constructed a profile of the "typical left-wing terrorist" as being a well-educated, single man in his mid-twenties from a middle-to-upper-class background (see Russell and Miller 1977; Strentz 1988 and Horgan 2003). Other psychoanalytical studies claimed that lack of parental guidance and a warm maternal relationship tend to generate a strong distrust toward of society and authority. Lack of attachment and social role models may be compensated with narcissistic self-enhancement and the demand for power so as to rebel against a hostile system (Kernberg 1975). To confirm this psychoanalytical inquiry, the same large student survey mentioned above measured participants' perception of their parents and how they evaluated their parent–child relationship. The results showed that left-wing radicals perceived both parents as cold (uncaring), weak, and incapable, with lack of guidance and authority, in other words as negative and unsatisfying. This negative identification with parental authority and the failure to develop a positive image of authority and adulthood (positive social role models) have been assumed to enhance distrust of and revolt against the government at a later age (Lichter and Rothman 1982).

The fall of the authoritarian communist regimes in Central and Eastern Europe was also devastating for the Western European radical left, causing many parties to leave the political arena and change their names or strategies (Bozoki and Ishiyama 2002). "The vision of a society of equals beyond capitalism that had animated the early labor movement, as well as the radical left movements in the years around 1968, was deemed obsolete or inadequate for the new times by many observers. [However] [. . .], in the aftermath of the 2008 financial crisis new protests arose against the austerity policies that many countries adopted to counteract their rising public debt" (Wennerhag et al. 2018, 2). These protests led to the emergence of new radical left parties, such as Syriza in Greece, Podemos in Spain, the Socialist Party in the Netherlands, or the Red-Green Unity Lits in Denmark. However, anarchist and radical anti-fascism movements in Poland, Russia, and several Scandinavian countries also flooded the political scene, encouraging the success of ideologically diverse radical-left parties (RLPs). Despite this heterogeneity, most RLPs rejected the capitalist socioeconomic structure with its neo-liberal market-oriented policies and advocated for transformative and systemic change (Dunphy 2004).

The way RLPs express their anti-capitalist attitudes differs across parties, ranging from traditionalist (authoritarian) Marxist-Leninist, reform communists (social democrats) and red-green parties (Backes and Moreau 2008). Using Comparative Manifesto Project (CMP) data, a study performed a factor analysis to explore the dimensionality of policy positions of RLPs since 1945. Traditional (authoritarian) Marxist-Leninist parties, such as the KKK in Greece and PCF in France, adopted a more radical anti-imperialist view, while New Left Parties, such as the German Left Party (Die Linke) or the Swedish or Finnish Left (V, VAS) had positive attitudes to democracy, internationalism, and environmentalism. Based on this classification and using European Election Studies (EES) data from 1989–2009, the study formed socio-demographic profiles of RLP voters with the following results: New Left RLP voters do not differ from traditional RLPs in terms of age, residence, class identification, and gender, but do differ in terms of economic success and less significantly in education. Traditional RLPs have a considerable support base among the least-well-educated. Furthermore, New Left RLPs tend to be more secularized and ideologically centrist in relative terms, less Eurosceptic, but more dissatisfied with the current democratic system (Gomez et al. 2016).

Box 7.1 The ideological left in South America and its implications

Such a political "left turn" has been observed especially in South America, where the presidents of Argentina, Bolivia, Brazil, Chile, Ecuador, Peru, Uruguay, and Venezuela led their countries with varying shapes of a leftist ideology. By 2009, nearly two-thirds of Latin Americans lived under a kind of "left-leaning" political regime. But how is the Left conceived in ideological terms across the various South American countries? While Brazilian and Chilean presidents Luiz Inacio da Silva and Michelle Bachelet supported free trade and close international relations, Hugo Chavez of Venezuela rejected the capitalistic mindset of Western societies, especially the United States. These differences reveal the difficulty to range ideologies in Latin American countries along the left–right political spectrum. Finding left vs. right distinctions in major parties in Costa Rica is virtually impossible, while in Nicaragua and El Salvador the political parties display strict ideological splits (Seligson 2006). To understand the differences between leftist ideologies, one must examine and understand the beliefs and attitudes of Latin American citizens. The traditional Left was historically associated with a socialist, Marxist belief system that provided alternatives to a capitalist system and ideas. "By the 1980s, however, the crisis of Marxism as an ideological referent and of socialism as a development model compelled the Left to redefine itself" (Levitsky and Roberts 2011, 4). Many leftists began to transform their public policy toward a more moderate and ambiguous ideas, which diluted their programmatic content and political identity. This diversity of existing left ideologies did not create neat boundaries, and thus allowed for unclear ideological portraits. Indeed, politicians such as Néstor Kirchner (Argentina), Lucio Gutiérrez (Ecuador), Álvaro Colom (Guatemala), and Ollanta Humala (Peru) have raised the debates over their purportedly leftist policies (Seligson 2006).

The Americas Barometer—a survey carried out by the Latin American Public Opinion Project (LAPOP) of the Vanderbilt University and its twenty academic partner institutions—in 2004 and 2006 interviewed more than thirty thousand individuals in nineteen countries. Surprisingly, the survey revealed that most Latin Americans adopt beliefs and attitudes that point clearly toward the right end of the ideological spectrum.* The 2004 survey showed a stronger inclination toward conservatism, which may imply "a slight shift" to the left in 2006. Comparing the 2006 data to that of 2016, the most dramatic downward trends are observed for beliefs concerning fairness and trust. Most Latin Americans do not believe in fair courts or efficient political systems that respects citizens' basic rights, do not trust the current system, and are not proud to live under the current political system (LAPOP 2016/2017). Furthermore, the data (2006) show that those who support left ideologies are less likely to prefer democracy (and the authority of the regime) than those on the right (with exceptions observed in Bolivia and Chile). Looking at recent data from 2016/2017, support for democracy has declined in all Latin American countries. This can be explained by the deprived psychological needs of Latin American people—needs such as (economic and political) stability, order (a fair and non-corrupt system), control (widespread crime and corruption), the need for identification (shared cultural, religious identity), social approval and belongingness, as well as the need for self-efficacy, self-esteem, and self-determination (no governmental support for achieving one's goals, lack of opportunity). Such deprived needs, and the failure of the current political system to address these needs, can lead to a shift in ideological and political preferences, as observed in the case of Brazil.

The Ideological Shift in Brazil

Distrust, perceived unfairness, and lack of order and stability possibly led to an ideological shift and the rise of populism in several Latin American countries. In 2018, Jair Bolsonaro, a far-right candidate, won the presidential elections in Brazil. "Brazil presents a more complex picture which highlights how democratic decay can arise not simply as an executive-led problem, but as a result of multiple forms of populism, different strains of anti-democratic elitism, a constitutional system suffering significant design and implementation flaws, and the lingering legacy of military power. Over a decade of what was often termed left-wing populist governance under Presidents Lula and Dilma [. . .] is viewed in some quarters as having produced not only a revenge of the élites in the 'abusive impeachment' of Dilma Rousseff, but also a wider right-wing populism, and an even wider disenchantment with the political system, which has propelled Bolsonaro to the presidency" (Daly 2019, 2). Looking at the political rhetoric of Bolsonaro, the far-right president takes a radical and conservative position regarding democracy, education, militarism, and ethnic minorities. Political surveys (e.g., Rennó 2020; Daly 2019) show that especially popular disappointment with the system's corruption and lack of safety, security, and control (widespread crime, which was perceived to be out of control) in the country led to Bolsonaro's electoral victory.

Furthermore, the social policies of the former left-leaning government increased the average national income—especially for the poorest and the richest percentiles—but generated least growth for the middle percentiles. Social inclusion policies, including measures in healthcare, education, employment, and housing, increased the prosperity and purchasing power of lower-income groups and enabled previously excluded workers to re-enter the job market. Above all, material poverty declined, and the nationally defined poverty line dropped from thirty to fifteen percent across the period. At the same time, increased federal investments and credit subsidies generated lucrative options for capital owners. The income growth of the affluent was facilitated by the lack of reform of the country's regressive tax system and was reinforced by the upswing in the stock market, consumer credits, and real estate prices. "The middle classes, to a large extent, have been pitted against the least privileged groups in society for their share of the national product, which would become increasingly scarce after 2014. Furthermore, with prices beginning to rise from 2013, following rising labor costs—including for services routinely used by the upper-middle class (e.g., domestic service)—and their acquired entitlements to social insurance coming under increased scrutiny, this cohort would increasingly lose faith in a Workers' Party that was only perceived to be in it for the working poor" (Gethin and Morgan 2018, 4).

In this regard, many Brazilians blamed the Workers' Party (PT) that governed Brazil from 2003 to 2016 for the serious economic downturn after 2013, persistent corruption, and ever-rising levels of crime. These deficiencies were promised to be eroded with "law and order" by the president-elect. This message resonated strongly with the public, while Bolsonaro's military ties shored up his credibility as a strong and powerful leader (Hunter and Power 2019). However, survey polls indicate that the fight against corruption was not the main reason why Brazilians would vote for a party, but rather the supply of health, education, and job security. This would imply that the need for fairness in the system (no corruption) and distributive justice (resource redistribution) was covered by the need for existential security. But these needs differed between respondents with different socioeconomic backgrounds. Poor voters emphasized social and economic issues while the upper and middle classes tended to attach greater importance to public security and corruption. Bolsonaro's electoral victory can be thus explained by his appeal to voters on both types of needs. Especially the needs of the middle classes, who felt left behind by the left leaning Workers' Party, were potentially served by the president's public policy. His clear stance against crime and corruption and his conservative tax reforms, cuts to public spending, and further privatization programs appeased a broad group of middle-class citizens and business owners (Gethin and Morgan 2018).

*The World Value Survey, encompassing more than 280,000 respondents in eighty-four countries, indicates a slight shift to the right worldwide (data from 1981–2004).

The example of Brazil shows how different ideologies can reconcile various needs of voters. The shift from a left-leaning, progressive, social ideology to a far-right conservative belief system indicates asymmetrical reconciliation. The need for existential (economic and social) security and public safety obliterated the need for social and economic equality, justice, and democratic participation. Hence, we argue that Bolsonaro's political appeal and success can be at least partly explained by his ability to address and reconcile individuals' existential and epistemic needs (i.e., for order, control, ambiguity avoidance, consistency, and stability).

Although studies on ideological shifts are relatively scarce, existing research shows that especially threat and fear induced by external shocks, such as economic crises or terrorist attack, lead to changed ideological preferences (Jost et al. 2017). These ideological shifts result due to changed individual psychological needs. Threat, fear, anxiety—all of which are induced by external events and circumstances—tend to elicit a need for security, certainty, control, and an ordered environment. In this regard, studies (such as Jost et al. 2017) show that threatening circumstances which deprive individuals from serving their existential and epistemic needs are more conducive to conservative than to liberal ideological outcomes. A study hence found that after September 11, 2001, American voters were more supportive of the George Bush administration, which promised to restore safety, power, and control (retaliation) (Huddy and Feldman 2011).

Other studies in social and political psychology provide similar results that threatening experiences increase support for conservative, authoritarian, and right-wing belief systems (see Jost et al. 2003 for meta-analytic review). A meta-analysis looked at how experimental manipulations of mortality salience affect ideological variability. The result of thirty-one experiments, with more than 3,162 participants in total, show that mortality salience tends to induce an ideological shift toward conservatism (Burke et al. 2013). Fear plays an especially significant role on the political right because such belief systems offer relatively simple, rigid, hierarchical, orderly, familiar, black-and-white solutions that decrease uncertainty and threat. However, mortality salience also seems to strengthen liberal preferences, observed especially among liberal students and racial minorities. But subjective fears differ between conservative and liberal individuals (in the US): whereas liberals report being more afraid of environmental and political conditions (e.g., climate change, pollution, overpopulation, police brutality), conservatives rather fear personal (restrictive) concerns (e.g., illegal immigration, gun control, corruption, lost subjective privileges, terrorist attacks, the use of drones, governmental monitoring) (Jost et al. 2017). These results seem to suggest that there is indeed an ideological asymmetry with respect to individuals' needs and concerns, which is discussed in more detail in the last section of this chapter.

7.3 Religious Ideologies

As we have seen, ideologies such as racism, right- and left-wing extremism, nationalism, or communism serve fundamental human needs by forming a coherent world view, diminishing uncertainties and cognitive complexity, and providing a sense of belonging, social approval, and enhanced self-esteem. Identification with a particular group and shared beliefs, values, and norms enable the formation of a social identity and shape one's understanding of society and one's own role in it. They guide individuals as to how to process information and react to a range of circumstances. A similar role is played by religious belief systems that, in doing so, serve an extraordinary function. Religion is a complex phenomenon. It includes a range of beliefs, perceptions, and interpretations that vary historically, across nations and religions, and thus cannot be defined in a static and precise manner. The materialist perspective perceives religion as a human-made product of obligations, discipline, and bonds (Vasquez 2011). Psychologists define it as a mental reflection of human desires, wishes, and needs, as a spiritual experience, or simply as a set of values and beliefs, complemented by a series of rules that serve to make life more organized and predictable (Hick 2006). Among the discipline, cognitive psychologists perceive it as a path for meaning and significance that helps individuals overcome existential anxieties (McNamara 2001), while social psychologists consider religion a community's investment in commitment and belonging. The set of beliefs, values, and norms adopted by a certain community or group provides a means for identification and affiliation, for transcendent and shared emotional experiences, and for the endorsement of certain rules to coordinate self-control, discipline, and communal behavior (McKay and Whitehouse 2015).

Although there is agreement that the influence of religion has declined over the years, this applies only to Europe, where the number of self-identified atheists or agnostics has increased, but to lesser extent to North and South America (Pew Research Center 2017). Even if the number of religious individuals has declined in Europe, in Western civilization, and especially in North America (for which the most data are available), religion remains an ever-present aspect of life. For individuals who identify with a particular faith, religion is often an important source of their cultural identity. The ability to practice one's faith freely, without fear of discrimination and ostracism, to provide religious education to the next generation, and to share spiritual experiences with other ingroup members are all important factors that contribute to one's own (cultural) identity (Cohen 2011).

Despite evidence that the five largest religions (Islam, Christianity, Judaism, Buddhism, and Hinduism) incorporate divergent conceptions, beliefs, and norms, their central manifestations generate a similar psychological framework. Religions of all kind offer answers to fundamental questions regarding life, death, suffering, and salvation. Rituals, rules, prayers, or meditation create consistency and stability in life and support believers in increasing self-awareness and building resilience. Established beliefs, values, and norms provide guidance on how to behave, process information, and judge and perceive oneself and one's environment. In this regard, many theories connect religion with morality and argue that moral standards emerge mainly from religious institutions (Zuckerman 2009). According to surveys in thirty-nine countries by the Pew Research Center, many people state that it is necessary to believe in God to be a moral person. In twenty-two out the thirty-nine countries, a clear majority state that believing in God is a precondition for being a good and moral person. This position is highly prevalent in most countries in the Middle East (except Israel), in Africa, and some Asian (except Japan and Australia), and Latin American nations (except Argentina and Chile). Canadians and Europeans fully reject such attitudes, whereas in the United States the position seems to be dichotomous (Pew Research Center 2014). Especially Islam perceives a person as moral and good if they obey to the commandments of God. Islamic ethics are understood in the face of *islam* (submission), *iman* (faith), *ishan* (virtue), *Shar'iah* (law), *Tariqah* (the Path) and *Haqiqah* (the Truth). A good and moral character is expressed by behaving with piety, in the service of God, and in commitment to the Quran. In Buddhism, morality is expressed through self-discipline and a strong will. Although in Buddhist teachings there is no eternal God to obey, who can punish or reward good or bad behavior, the law of Karma is a guiding path for (moral) choices. This means that religions primarily provide orientation and guidance on how to behave and which choices to make (Wade 2010).

Opposite theories argue that culturally constructed moral norms are formed by genetically inherited biological and psychosocial systems rather than through religious internalization. Individuals are social beings that inherit fundamental principles like empathy, fairness, and cooperativeness (de Waal 2009)[8] and may be moral without religious influence. Communication and imitation create shared feelings, norms, and prescribed behaviors to dissociate from and affiliate with significant others (Tomasello et al. 2005). But sociological studies postulate that religion facilitates the establishment of such communities and enables faster information processing within them. Furthermore, religious identification provides stability, orientation, and affiliation within a stable setting of shared "sacred" beliefs and norms that are accepted unquestioningly. Traditional mechanisms in the form of moral frameworks, rituals, symbols, daily practices, and role ascriptions are fostered and preserved (Seul 1999). This compact and reliable network of predetermined world views and clear behavioral guidelines empower individuals to handle change, fear, anxiety, and cognitive ambiguity. On an aggregate level, it serves individuals' psychological needs for order, consistency, belongingness, existential safety (life after death), and meaningful existence. Daily rituals, prayers, and customs generate a sense of consistency, order, and predictability, which in turn provide calmness and a sense of control. (Strict) adherence to these rituals and norms generates a sense of self-certainty and enhances individuals' self-esteem. Religious leaders and divine figures serve as inspiring models that assure emotional security, reliability, and hope (Brandt 2013).

Empirical studies support these assumptions and show that religion tends to increase individuals' mental well-being (Ivtzan et al. 2013) and that religious believers score higher on happiness and life satisfaction than nonbelievers. This is explained by the fact that faith reduces cognitive complexity and feelings of threat and self-uncertainty by providing the possibility to experience community-based feelings of belonging, loyalty, and trust (Graham and Haidt 2010). An empirical study with 433 undergraduate and graduate students from three evangelical Christian colleges in the western and eastern United States investigated the spiritual and psychological development of the participants regarding their relational attachments. The results showed that secure attachments to God and their own religious community contributed to higher levels of spiritual development (e.g., connecting to God, to oneself and others), psychological well-being, life satisfaction, and positive coping. In other words, emotional and cognitive secure attachments (to God and one's religious community) deliver internal resources which allow individuals to absorb negative emotions and to better adjust to negative events and experiences (Augustyn et al. 2017). A similar psychological study on health and religiosity supports the link between religious attachment and mental well-being by comparing somatic symptoms across conservative, moderate, and liberal Christians. Conservative Christians adopt an orthodox world view that posits that humans are subject to the moral authority of God, which implies an unconditional trust in God. Strong feelings of guilt can arise among conservative Christians who fall short of these orthodox expectations, which in turn promotes distress and fear of being rejected by other church members. Accordingly, conservative Christians tend to be more coherent, adaptive, and devoted to the prescribed norms and values of their religious group, largely because they want to avoid sanctions or negative feedback from other ingroup members. Conservative individuals, but not moderate and liberal Christians, are more likely to believe in heaven, which stems from the belief that the main purpose in life is spiritual salvation. Trusting in heaven and in God generates consistency, certainty, and meaning in life, which in turn lead to greater psychological well-being (Krause 2015).

The significance of relational attachment is emphasized by the uncertainty-identity theory, which states that belonging to and identifying with a (religious) group tends to reduce feelings of threat and self-uncertainty. Individuals usually strive to find reconciliation to reduce such negative feelings, shore up their own self-esteem and make their environment more stable and predictable. Religious groups hence provide a shared belief system that addresses existence, causality, and morality issues by prescribing normative practices related to daily life, information processing, and decision-making. "Because there are no objectively correct or scientifically verifiable answers to such questions, religious ideologies invoke a rich symbolic and supernatural universe relating to sacred and sanctified people, places, and objects, with the sacred nature of God and the divine imparting purpose and legitimacy to beliefs, expectations, and goals and prescribing appropriate emotions and behaviors" (Hogg et al. 2010, 76). The unambiguous and clearly defined meaning-making system and moral compass serve basic psychological needs, ranging from belongingness and social approval to existential meaning and a sense of order and control. Empirical studies (e.g., Hogg 2014) confirm that people who feel uncertain about themselves and their social environment tend to identify more strongly with coherent groups that impose strong boundaries, are rigidly structured, propose a clear and prescribed sense of the self, and represent an exclusionary set of beliefs and values. Such highly structured groups provide a sense of power, control, and superiority, and induce the perception of an unquestionable group status (Koomen and Van Der Pligt 2016).

In this regard, many psychological theories argue that the fundamental function of religion is to help individuals to find meaning and purpose in life. Both philosophers and psychologists assume that the search for meaning is universal and ever-present. The struggle with existential questions and the search for corresponding answers is experienced by all individuals at one point or another. People want to understand what life is about, to find their place in the world, and to be aware of their environment and their self (Hood et al. 2018). In essence, people need to understand their environment to "survive" and adapt. The quest for significance theory thus postulates that the search for meaning in life encompasses four fundamental human needs—the need for meaningful existence, the need for self-efficacy, the need for self-esteem, and the need for value (i.e., the belief that one's actions and thoughts are good and justified) (Galek et al. 2015). Empirical evidence confirms that various forms of religion are directly related to meaning and sense in life. For example, the belief in God (Jewell 2010) and the frequency of church attendance, prayers, and Bible study are positively related to the belief in a purposeful life (Francis and Evans 1996). Studies show that people who believe in a divine figure and incorporate spirituality in their lives are more likely to perceive life as meaningful (Jung 2015). The reason for this is that religions provide existential explanations (e.g., concerning death and suffering) and offer ideas and visions about the past, the present, and the future. Religion fills the "gaps" in our knowledge of life and the world and offers a sense of cognitive stability and existential security (life after death). Especially in times of crisis, trauma, or difficult circumstances, religious beliefs provide salvation (through explanations) and offer a guiding path of "healing and enlightenment." In addition, constant and repetitive prayers, church attendance, and norm abidance deliver a predictable and consistent environment (environmental patterns) which also create the perception of a meaningful life.

Making choices and complying with religious rules, norms, and values promise a sense of order and structure in life, a sense of comprehensiveness, and transcendence (Klinger 2012). Religion answers questions related to oneself and one's social surroundings in a cognitively simple way—how to perceive one's environment and significant others, how to behave, how to evaluate circumstances, how to bear existential threat and suffering, and how to make appropriate life choices in an ambiguous and constantly changing environment (Galek et al. 2015). It addresses an extensive range of issues at the descriptive and prescriptive level: beliefs about one's social environment, oneself and human existence, about punishment and reward for good or bad behavior, about goals (e.g., benevolence), actions (e.g., compassion or violence), and emotions (e.g., love or hate). All these beliefs are accessible and cognitively comprehensible. "A belief in a transcendent and authoritative being, especially when complete sovereignty is attributed to that being (as in the case of Western monotheistic religion), is the basis of the most convincing and fulfilling sense of meaning for many. Perhaps more than any other system of meaning, religion provides a focus on that which is 'beyond me'. Thus, many people have 'ultimate concerns' that require some belief in an ultimate authority, be it God or some other conception of transcendence in which higher meaning is found" (Hood et al. 2018, 21). This belief in a transcendent and authoritative being also serves, beyond the need for personal significance, the fundamental human need for control. It refers to the belief that God or an alternative supernatural being empowers individuals to gain control over their lives by "cooperating" (Krause 2011). Especially during traumatic and challenging life events, individuals tend to place their sense of control in the hands of external forces. The compensatory control model suggests that people want to have a sense of personal control to reduce feelings of randomness and chaos, which can induce stress, threat, and anxiety. Therefore, believing in a deity that has some sort of control over the universe, or in a transcendent order, such as karma, may provide a compensatory resource during times of lowered sense of personal control. Experimental studies provide evidence that reminding people of their lack of personal control leads to increased beliefs in the existence of a controlling God (Laurin et al. 2008). This means when dispositional or situational factors dampen their perception of personal control, people can rely on external substitutes such as God or another spiritual force to mitigate negative feelings of powerlessness and uncertainty (Kay et al. 2008).

Further studies show that religious ideologies also play an important role in identity formation. According to identity theory, individuals construct their identity based on the roles they occupy in life. Being a religious person may be a central social role for some individuals, where religious beliefs and values form a coherent concept of understanding and evaluating (Park and Edmondson 2012). Individuals who are strongly committed to their faith and identify strongly with their religious roles experience harsh negative feelings when these identity markers are under threat. The perceived threat to their faith can prompt them to adopt defensive measures to protect their identity (Galek et al. 2015). A study of moderate as well as more fundamentalist Christians showed that the latter group reacted with uncertainty and anxiety when confronted with contradictions and inconsistencies in the Bible. These doubts about their beliefs and about God prompted existential uncertainty and increased their concerns about their identity. This suggests that religious ideologies provide a buffer against anxiety, uncertainty, and unpredictability by absorbing negative emotions about oneself (Friedman and Rholes 2007). A similar study investigates the link between spiritual struggles (e.g., doubts about the existence of God, struggle with certain beliefs, etc.) and aspects of psychopathology (depression, anxiety, etc.). The results show that individuals who base their identity around their faith and identify as very religious experience the strongest negative reaction to spiritual struggles. They have an intimate relationship with their faith and "collaborate actively" with God (e.g., talk to God every day) in an attempt to cope with personal problems, stressful situations, and negative emotions. As a result, the closer examination of divine existence and doubts about one's beliefs tend to have negative implications for mental health, ranging from depression and anxiety to suicidality and lack of self-esteem. One explanation could be that religious certainty is an important cognitive and emotional pillar which facilitates positive social adjustment. In the case of spiritual struggles, this essential mental part dissolves, leading to distress, uncertainty, and inconsistency. Furthermore, a troubled relationship with God and religious doubts may be experienced as threatening to one's sense of self because it induces an incoherent perception of oneself and one's social environment (Ellison et al. 2013).

All these findings are consistent with Evolutionary Threat Assessment Systems (ETAS) theory, which assumes that beliefs serve some sort of defensive and threat-relieving function. Relying on certain religious beliefs, ideals, rules, and norms when deciding about right or wrong not only reduces anxiety and self-related uncertainty, but it also provides a sense of security and higher self-esteem (Flannelly and Galek 2010). Forming and adopting certain beliefs and values is thus an essential criterion for a stable identity and psychological well-being. Cognitive therapists suggest that psychiatric disorders (such as depression or anxiety) are, among others, the product of neural assessments of potential threats (Galek et al. 2015). In their view, a central feature of mental malaise is the steady concern about one's own safety and the dangerousness of the world. Such concerns may involve perceived threats of psychological or physical harm, of one's social status, of the existential and relational self—which, on aggregate, pose a threat to one's identity (Price et al. 2016). Such beliefs may not be reasonable, yet they are useful as heuristics to process information and make decisions. They reflect primitive evolutionary systems that help to make quick decisions about potentially dangerous situations (Gilbert 2001). Psychiatric studies assume that the most common source of psychopathology is perceived social threat. In this regard, the ETAS theory makes three assumptions. First, threat assessments in the brain can lead to mental disorder because different parts of the brain assess threats in different, even conflicting, ways. Second, the same adaptive brain mechanisms that assessed threat in the past may not be appropriate for the modern environment. Third, threats can be falsely perceived as threatening and trigger false alarms in the brain. "For most animals, once a threat no longer exists (or is simply out of sight), the emotional system that it triggered returns to its normal baseline (Panksepp, 1998). But, ever since humans evolved consciousness and the ability to think about the past and future, people have been able to activate their emotional responses to threats when no threat is present" (Flannelly and Galek 2010, 341). These perceived threats are moderated by religious beliefs that provide a sense of security and certainty about oneself and one's social environment, which in turn is associated with lower levels of psychiatric symptoms. An empirical study supports these assumptions and shows that pleasant afterlife beliefs (peace, union with God, paradise after death, etc.) are associated with lower levels of mental disorder and greater psychological well-being (Flannelly et al. 2008). The theory states that religious beliefs reduce concerns about life's unpredictability and uncertainties—the uncertainties that trigger fear in the brain's core region, the amygdala (Flannelly 2017).

Accordingly, recent literature has highlighted the role of religion (as an identity-affirming and threat-avoiding mechanism) in regard to migration (Koomen and Van Der Pligt 2016). Immigrants face severe obstacles in negotiating their heritage and their belonging to a new society and in developing mechanisms to cope with the emotional stress of intercultural interactions. This process of stabilization and reconciliation of the various identities can cause stress, frustration, and personal crisis, especially during adolescence. An empirical study using the Multiple Identities Approach explored how young Australian Muslims overcome difficulties with identification, belongingness, and adaptation. The quantitative analysis revealed that the adolescents felt most attached to their religion, followed by their heritage and culture, and were least attached to their Australian identity. The participants noted that their religious identity was formed mainly by their cultural background as Muslims and their shared faith and religious rituals such as prayers, celebrations, or religious practices (Abu-Rayya et al. 2016). This finding corresponds with similar research, showing that shared religious beliefs, values, and norms provide Muslims a common identity and way of life, and that Islam has a stronger cultural influence in Muslims' lives, behavior, and world views than their national background (Akbarzadeh and Saeed 2001). The weaker attachment to their Australian identity may be explained partly by perceived social exclusion, identity threat, and negative public attitudes that young Muslims indicated they had experienced in Australia. In self-reported interviews the majority of adolescent Muslims noted that the presence of perceived racism and prejudices toward Muslims dampened their affiliation with Australian society (Mansouri 2012). Similar studies show that perceived social exclusion lead to enhancement of and adherence to internalized religious beliefs. A psychological study compared Turkish immigrants living in Germany with a comparable sample of Turkish individuals in Turkey and found that the former group was more religious than the latter. Perceived "social exclusion led to heightened levels of religious affiliation, which buffered the stress caused by rejection, thereby going beyond an initial observation that social exclusion strengthens a belief in supernatural beings including ghosts, angels, and, most importantly for our purposes, God" (Aydin et al. 2010, 750). Accordingly, religious devotion tends to dampen negative feelings of ostracism and identity threat, which lead to decreased self-certainty and self-esteem, disintegration (lack of belongingness), lack of meaning in life, and uncertain feelings about one's role in society (lack of control).

However, feelings of social exclusion and a threatening self can lead, in severe cases, to religious dogmatism and extreme behavior. An extensive study of Turkish immigrants in six Western countries and Moroccan immigrants in four Western countries showed that almost half of participants agreed with radical statements concerning their Islamic faith (e.g., "there is only one right interpretation of the Quran") and adopted radical attitudes toward religious rules (e.g., "Muslims should return to the roots of the Islam") (Koopmans 2014). This implies that beyond beneficial effects—such as guidance, purpose in life, and buffer against anxiety and unpredictability (see, e.g., Phillips and Ano 2015)—religious beliefs can lead to radicalization and extreme behavior such as intolerance, dogmatism, and violence (Bangura 1994). Outgroups and non-believers are cast as evil and immoral, even as subhuman, while one's ingroup is perceived as superior, "chosen" by a higher power, and representing the sole absolute truth (Koomen and Van Der Pligt 2016). Such religious fundamentalism can be perceived as "a discernible pattern of religious militancy by which self-styled 'true believers' attempt to arrest the erosion of religious identity, fortify the borders of the religious community, and create viable alternatives to secular institutions and behaviors" (Almond et al. 2003, 17). Members of these religious movements view themselves as elects of the mission who attempt to defend their internal belief system and superior identity (Waldmann 2005). Sharp boundaries create feelings of coherence and contrast, and hierarchical structures within the ingroup provide members with order, stability, and group affiliation.

Fundamentalist movements are typically controlled and conducted by charismatic leaders who are perceived as a "predestination with supernatural qualities and special insight into the sacred texts." Radical and fundamental movements usually involve hierarchical patterns, role ascriptions, sharp boundaries, and prescribed world views, which generate a consistent environment, especially for young adults, in that they provide social approval, orientation, and guidance in life, all of which seems to dissolve in the context of modern transformation (Emerson and Hartman 2006). The need for belongingness and social approval and the hope for "redemption" indicate a strong need for orientation, identification, and self-esteem. The patterns of religious fundamentalism provide young adults not only simple and unambiguous answers to questions of meaning, the self, and life, but also a daily course of action, a moral compass, and emotional security in an isolated and self-revalued group (Koomen and Van Der Pligt 2016). In this regard, empirical studies confirm that religious fundamentalists are less able to cope with cognitive uncertainty, ambiguity, and inconsistency, and therefore rely strongly on their religious beliefs. This indicates that radically construed beliefs serve the psychological need for certainty, consistency, and predictability, as well as the need for cognitive closure, stability, and control (Brandt and Reyna 2010). Researchers have indicated that religious radicalism often flourishes in times of uncertainty and economic, political, and social instability. They suggest that radical and dogmatic belief systems and world views and their focus on tradition, morality, and norms tend to provide stability, predictability, and order in a perceived instable environment (see, e.g., Huntington 1996, Salzman 2008). The central and defining feature of fundamentalism is its harsh negative attitude toward (Western) modernity, its burgeoning secular values and beliefs, the resulting ambiguity and immorality, and the decreased value of tradition and norms. This rejection of modernity can involve withdrawal from society, increased negative feelings about certain lifestyles (cognitive and emotional segregation from society), or even aggressive and hatred attitudes toward dissidents (Verkuyten 2018).

The main differentiating factor between religious fundamentalism and mainstream faith movements is thus the conviction that religion is under threat. Empirical studies show that perceived threat is one of the most significant pre-conditions for polarization and radicalization (Hogg and Adelman 2013; Maoz and McCauley 2008). A psychological study among Iranian college students showed that confrontation with (identity) threat and one's own mortality led to increased support for suicide bombings directed against the United States (Pyszczynski et al. 2006). Similar studies among fundamentalist Christians in the United States revealed that confrontation with external threats led to increased support for radical beliefs and a greater inclination toward punitive and violent measures (Williamson and Hood 2014). The propensity to use defensive and aggressive measures was explained not by individuals' religiosity per se, but rather by their social identification and group belongingness. Cooperation and communication within their ingroup increased conformity, loyalty, and hostility toward outgroups. In this regard, a large empirical survey across twenty-six countries in 2011 and 2012 with 6,576 Muslim participants examined the effects of religiosity (radical religious beliefs, frequency of Mosque attendance, prayers, Quran study, etc.), demographic variables (sex, age, education, urbanity, etc.), and threat perception (perceived religious suppression, interfaith and intrafaith tension, etc.) on the support for extremist violence. The results showed that only Mosque attendance and all aspects of perceived threat were significant predictors of support for extremist violence, while individual aspects of religiosity (such as fundamentalist beliefs) and demographic variables showed little effect. This implies that collective ritual behaviors, in particular, enhance group solidarity and group commitment, which in extreme cases can lead to a propensity to sacrifice one's life for the group. Perceived threats may be interpreted in terms of group identification and religious (group) identity rather than of personal beliefs (Beller and Kröger 2017). Studies in the UK, France, and the

Netherlands showed a weak but growing fundamentalist orientation among second- and third-generation Muslims, expressed in dogmatic interpretation of religious texts, an emphasis on basic religious principles, and support for Sharia law (Kibria 2008). For example, a survey in the UK provides evidence that forty-two percent of young Muslims (aged sixteen to twenty-four) adhere to the absolute and original interpretation of Sharia law, and thirty-six percent agree that converted Muslims should be punished by death (Mirza et al. 2007). Similar surveys indicate that especially young Muslims tend to have much more fundamentalist beliefs than older Muslim individuals (Koopmans 2015). More than fifty percent of respondents, living all in European countries, agreed that Muslims should return to traditional Islam, whereas seventy percent indicated that there is only one right interpretation of the Quran and sixty-four percent believe that the rules of the Quran are more important than the laws of the country they live in (Verkuyten 2018). These results imply that adherence to radical beliefs can have clear psychological reasons. Intergenerational conflict, identity confusion, disintegration, and self-uncertainty can lead to the endorsement of dogmatic world views. Adopting radical belief systems that contrast with society and the parental home can provide a sense of self-efficacy, meaning in life, and increased self-esteem.

To sum up these theoretical and empirical findings, it is clear that religion plays a significant role in serving psychological needs. Religion, in general terms, provides a stable and coherent mental framework with prescribed beliefs, values, and norms, as well as clear behavioral guidelines and social roles which help individuals to cope with complexity, change, various emotions, and cognitive ambiguity. It provides a way to manage reality in consistent, comprehensible, and meaningful regularities. At the most basic level, meaning emerges when reliable patterns exist in the environment, which help individuals to label and interpret a state of arousal (such as information or stimuli, etc.). Religions provide such reliable and repetitive patterns that help subjects to understand the environment and incoming information, and to find answers and explanations for life events. However, beyond serving existential and epistemic needs, religion provides a basis for social identity formation; that is, it facilitates the establishment of a social community and enables faster identification with significant others. Sharing the same beliefs, values, and norms serves the need for social approval and belongingness and provides significant value for one's own self-perception (self-awareness about the group and the religion). Conformity with and adherence to beliefs and norms not only generates meaning and order in life, but it can also enhance individuals' self-esteem and self-significance (a sense of superiority and greater self-worth due to perceived morality and discipline). On an aggregate level, we may conclude that religion clearly has the capacity to serve individuals' fundamental human needs, which may explain, at least partly, its potential to eventuate in dogmatism and individual radicalization. This leads us to the question whether all ideologies have similar dogmatic and radical tendencies and manifestations, or if there are certain differences between them. Do all right-leaning, left-leaning, and religious individuals have the same psychological needs and dispositions, or can we identify any specific distinctions? And what about extremists? Are their needs and preferences disparate or similar?

7.4 Are All Extremists the Same? Ideological Differences and Similarities

Although extremism theory claims that all extremists, irrespective of their traditional left, right, or religious orientation, have a similar cognition level and are authoritarian, dogmatic and intolerant, some studies show that extremist adherents to various belief systems are not a homogeneous group (Van Leeuwen et al. 2007). Most empirical studies on ideological extremism are conducted in Western nations, especially the United States, where far-right, far-left, and religious fundamentalists are all categorized in the same manner, namely as extremists.[9] Individual and socio-demographic contextual studies attempt to categorize extremists, while psychological studies insist that there is no such thing as a generalizable extremist profile (Chermack and Gruenewald 2015). A study, using combined data from the American Terrorism Study (ATS) and the FBI's Terrorist Research and Analytical Center, provides insight into the "individualistic profiles" of 170 far-right and far-left extremists. In this regard, far-right sympathizers tend to be male, older, less educated, less skilled, and reside more in rural areas (Smith et al. 2006). A similar study collected newspaper clippings compiled by the FBI and find that women were more likely to be involved in left-wing attacks and were more likely to occupy leadership positions in leftist groups. Left-wing extremists were more likely to have a college degree, yet fifty percent of right-wing leaders had higher education compared to only five percent of the ordinary members. Over ninety-four percent of right-wingers were Protestants, while left-wingers were adherents of other religions (e.g., Catholic, Jewish, Baptist, Episcopalian, Methodist, or Lutheran). Furthermore, right-wing extremists were more likely to be White and working in blue-collar occupations, while both left and right-wingers had relatively low incomes (Handler 1990). Recent studies in the US, using ATS and FBI data on one thousand extremists (far-right, far-left, and religious), provide evidence that most right- and left-wingers are White (compared to seventeen percent of religious extremists), on average twenty-eight years old, and have no military experience. Both rightists and religious extremists were mainly male and eight percent had a mental disorder (compared to no mental illness at far-left). Further results show that only twenty-three percent of far-rightists have a college degree, compared to far-leftists (seventy-six percent) and religious extremists (forty-five percent). Most leftists are single, while the majority of rightists and religious extremists are married, in a relationship, or divorced (Chermack and Gruenewald 2015).

Psychological studies focus less on socio-demographic differences and more on cognition and extremists' distinct attitudes and motives. The choice of a far-right belief system is associated with the subjective preference for maintaining the status quo, while left-wing belief systems are perceived as supporting openness to change. Individuals on the ideological "right" tend to attribute more importance to security, conformity, authoritarianism, and power, while the ideological "left" puts more emphasis on universalism, equality, and freedom (Anderson and Singer 2008). Several studies have therefore attempted to understand the underlying psychological motives, needs, and feelings that are connected to the distinct ideas of the right and the left. What is most often studied in this regard are the needs for cognitive closure, structure, order, certainty, and conformity, which are assumed to be significantly more present among proponents of right-wing than left-wing ideology (Thorisdottir et al. 2007). Other psychological studies confirm that individuals who score high on the need for cognitive closure and who prefer order, structure, and stability over change and flexibility are more likely to adopt right-wing ideas. Individuals who attempt to prevent unfavorable outcomes, to reduce anxiety and fear, to avoid disruption and ambiguity, and who are more perceptive of their mortality (terror-management theory) tend to adopt the core values of a right-wing ideology (Jost et al. 2003). However, most of these studies were conducted in the United States, which raises the question if the same psychological mechanisms would hold in nations with different cultural and historical backgrounds.

In this regard, a longitudinal study, based on four waves of European Social Survey data (2002, 2004, 2006, and 2008), showed that in Europe, left-wing groups scored significantly lower on conservation, anti-immigration, and self-enhancement attitudes than right-wing groups. How can these ideological differences be explained? The theory of "personalized politics" states that political beliefs correlate with subjective values and attitudes toward the social system. Thus, individual differences in political orientation can be viewed as the result of different dispositions and subjective world views. Accordingly, the world view of right-leaning and religious individuals is derived from perceived threat and established order—the conviction that society is a dangerous place and that individuals must observe strict discipline, self-reliance, obedience, and respect. Adherents of such world views support the idea of law and order; of a moral, just, and beneficial authority; and of a "natural" social hierarchy (e.g., God is above all humans). For this reason, feminism, atheism, or homosexuality are perceived as a threat to society because they do not adhere to the perceived "natural order" (Strickland et al. 2011). By contrast, adherents of left-leaning values and ideas support the idea of a caring, emphatic, and inclusive society, which enables citizens to live in a mutually supportive community (McAdams et al. 2008). Thus, left-leaning individuals give higher priority to achieving social and political equality, support welfare redistribution, and are less likely to adopt prejudicial attitudes toward ethnic minorities, homosexuals, dissidents, and other deprived groups (Cunningham et al. 2004). Although research has shown that communists have similar psychological needs as fascist right-wingers (e.g., uncertainty avoidance, order, intolerance of ambiguity, etc.), other studies point out that leftists and rightists (especially in relation to the West and East) are not equally dogmatic and close-minded and do not share the same preferences and values (see the related discussion in the section on socialism/communism) (Van Hiel 2012).

In this regard, a study of nineteen different European countries analyzed data from the European Social Survey (ESS) and provided evidence that needs, preferences, and attitudes differ significantly between eastern and western European countries. While traditionalism was associated with right-wing ideology in all nineteen countries, the acceptance of inequality was strongly related to ideological right in all western countries, but not in any of the four eastern nations in scope. This implies that the past socialist authoritarian background in eastern European countries has a direct impact on the relationship between psychological needs, subjective attitudes, and ideological preferences. Accordingly, the need for security is strongly associated with the "ideological right" in the West but with "ideological left" in the East. "This suggests that people in Eastern Europe continue to depend upon socialist forms of government to satisfy their needs for safety and security, more than a decade after the collapse of communism. In many of these countries, the transition to capitalism has led to economic insecurity, fear, and resentment" (Thorisdottir et al. 2007, 198). Furthermore, the openness to change variable, which is associated with greater equality and egalitarianism, correlated with the ideological left in the West, but surprisingly also with right-wing groups in the East. Only the traditionalism and rule-adherence variables were associated in all nineteen nations with right-wing orientation (Thorisdottir et al. 2007).

A similar study, using ESS data for twenty European countries, examined the role of personal values and sociodemographic variables in political orientation (Piurko et al. 2011). Political scientists have largely disregarded the significance of personal values, focusing instead either on attitudes in political domains or on group mechanisms as the major determinants of political orientation (Schwartz et al. 2010). Yet recent investigations have revealed that personal values have a stronger impact on political orientation and voting behavior than sociodemographic variables. The Schwartz Value Theory (1992) identifies ten major personal values: (1) power (need for prestige, control over resources or people), (2) achievement (need for personal success), (3) hedonism (pleasure and gratification for oneself), (4) stimulation (challenge in life, excitement), (5) self-direction (autonomous thinking, acting), (6) universalism (tolerance, protection for people and nature), (7) benevolence, (8) tradition (respect, commitment, acceptance of traditions), (9) conformity, and (10) security. Power and achievement (self-enhancement values) oppose universalism and benevolence ("self-immolation" values), while the stimulation and self-direction (openness values) contrast with tradition, security, and conformity (conservation values). Both self-enhancement and conservation reflect individuals' need to reduce anxiety and threat. This is expressed by individuals' preferences for avoiding change and unpredictability (conservation) and gaining power and dominance in their social environment (self-enhancement). On the opposite, "self-immolation" and openness reflect individuals' need to explore and grow, which is expressed by individuals' preferences for promoting welfare equality and self-determination (Schwartz et al. 2010).

Applying this value theory, the empirical study mentioned previously (Piurko et al. 2011) in twenty European countries, which were split into liberal, post-communist, and traditional nations (strong religious influence), showed that personal values had a strong impact on the adoption of divergent ideologies across nations. In liberal states, a right-wing orientation expresses values of power, tradition, security, and conformity, while the ideological left expresses universalism and to some extent benevolence. In traditional countries, conservative values are associated with religiosity and support for traditional and conservative lifestyles, while a left-wing orientation expresses self-direction and universalism. The results for post-communist studies showed no obvious pattern because the perception and "meaning" of right and left ideologies differ across these countries. Furthermore, the analysis postulates that in economically advanced liberal nations, personal values have a stronger impact on political orientation than do sociodemographic factors, while in post-communist countries the opposite holds (Piurko et al. 2011).

Beyond personal values, the moral foundation theory suggests that individuals construct their attitudes, beliefs, and voting behavior according to moral intuition. In this context, five major moral dimensions have been elaborated. The Harm/Care and Fairness/Reciprocity dimensions imply values of empathy, justice, and altruism; the Ingroup/Loyalty dimension includes ideas of patriotism and self-sacrifice for the group; and the Authority/Respect dimension covers values of obedience, subordination, and hierarchy. The last dimension, Purity/Sanctity, comprises values associated with divinity and religious laws. The last three dimensions have binding components because of their emphasis on groupism, loyalty, commitment, and self-control (Graham et al. 2009). Four empirical studies provide evidence that left-leaning individuals tend to base their judgment, thinking, and perception on individualistic values, which relate to traditional notions of morality in terms of individual rights and social justice, while right-leaning individuals score relatively high across all dimensions. Such findings suggest that traditional (religious) or right-inclined individuals are more attentive to morality and thus derive their thinking and behavior from moral intuition (Haidt et al. 2009; Weber and Federico 2013). The adherence to such "moral codes" is explained by the fact that they imply a clear and prescriptive structure, which does not allow for flexibility and ambiguity. With clear prescriptions for how to live, to act, and to evaluate the social environment, individuals can derive a sense of meaning in life because they have more stability, order, and certainty. Furthermore, individuals with right-leaning tendencies adhere to traditions and group cohesion and define fairness more in terms of equity (return based on contribution) instead of equality (equal outcome regardless of contribution) (Schlenker et al. 2012), which seem to provide them order and consistency (Napier and Jost 2008).

Although all these studies emphasize fundamental psychological and ideological differences between the left, the right, and religious individuals, opposing studies reveal that psychological similarities exist especially in terms of extremism. A large analysis of the Twitter accounts of 355,000 American followers of US extremist organizations and politicians found that all extremist users, irrespective of ideological orientation, show more negative emotions (especially uncertainty and fear) than random users (Alizadeh et al. 2017). "Theories on political extremism emphasize the rigid nature of ideological beliefs at both extremes, which is characterized by black-and-white thinking in which social stimuli are dichotomously categorized as good or bad, positive or negative, and the like. Such rigidity is, for instance, reflected in a belief in straightforward and simple solutions to the problems that society faces" (van Prooijen et al. 2015, 487). These rigid belief systems absorb feelings of uncertainty and anxiety and provide structure and meaning to deal with complexity and unpredictability. It is therefore assumed that negative feelings, such as fear, anger, and anxiety, are compensated by strict ideological adherence (dogmatism) and strong conviction of own political beliefs and world views (Toner et al. 2013).

Further studies reveal that extremists express similar levels of intolerance toward ideologically dissimilar groups and dissidents (Brandt et al. 2014). Testing for coherent psychological dynamics of political extremism, a large-scale study in the Netherlands postulates that especially socioeconomic fear, grievances, and outgroup derogation are addressed by all types of ideological extremism. This suggests that all extreme ideologies, irrespective of the content, tend to address psychological human needs in a similar way (Van Prooijen et al. 2015), such as the need for order, control, ambiguity avoidance, cognitive consistency, and predictability, but also for belongingness, social approval, self-esteem, and self-efficacy. These results are backed up by an extended analysis that found that all ideological extremes imply strong dogmatic intolerance and outgroup derogation (strong ingroup favoritism), which serve all the mentioned needs in a strong manner. Dogmatic, clear, and prescriptive ideas do not allow for cognitive flexibility and interpretation, which in turn generate an increased willingness to defend one's own values and beliefs (Van Prooijen and Krouwel 2017).

One of the most accepted assumptions in psychology argues that ideological extremism is rooted in the psychological need for meaning and personal significance in life; that is, to be accepted, respected, and to matter in the eyes of oneself and one's social others. Experiencing meaningful existence and strong self-significance enhances life satisfaction and personal well-being and is argued to be one of the fundamental aspects in human life (Kruglanski et al. 2014). On the contrary, loss of meaning in life or experiences of self-insignificance due to ostracism, humiliation, or injustice enhance negative feelings about oneself and one's environment, which in turn enhances the need for clear-cut ideologies that help to restore a sense of order (meaningful patterns) and self-worth (Webber et al. 2018). Accordingly, an empirical study argues that enhanced needs for meaning, self-esteem, and personal significance tend to increase the motivation to adopt radical ideologies and engage in violence. A study using data on 1,496 ideologically radicalized individuals in the United States, the descriptive observations showed that only twelve percent of individuals were unemployed, and sixty-five percent were middle-class. However, nearly half of the respondents stated they had failed to achieve life goals, twenty-two percent had relationship troubles, twenty-nine percent experienced a loss of social standing, and thirty-six percent had been dismissed from a social group or organization. Forty-eight percent had experienced traumatic events in the past and thirty-five percent were abused as children, and thirteen percent as adults. Only a small number of respondents had a criminal record, and all were relatively young. Further results show that among ideologically motivated individuals, those who experienced economic failure, relationship trouble, and threatened self-esteem at an early age were more likely to engage in violent extremism. "Because of their counter-normativity and greater visibility violent actions may signal stronger commitment to a cause and leave little uncertainty about the intentions of the actors. Due to these properties, violent means may offer a more direct route to earning significance, which may increase the attractiveness of violence to individuals searching for clear-cut and unambiguous actions" (Jasko et al. 2017, 14).

However, similar studies emphasize that severe needs deprivation in general can enhance individual leanings toward ideological extremism. "SDT (self-determination theory) suggests that need-thwarting contexts readily foster and catalyze self-protective, defensive and aggressive propensities. [. . .] Need thwarting is associated with more competitive interpersonal attitudes and more destructive and reactive forms of aggression. Thus, in the SDT view, the occurrence of these 'dark sides' to human nature is both systematic and predictable, catalyzed by conditions that undermine basic needs satisfactions" (Ryan and Hawley 2017, 209). Accordingly, a growing body of research provides evidence that severe and repetitive experience of ostracism, personal insignificance, and social, economic, and political isolation tends to explain, at least partially, an inclination toward extremism and the motivation to engage in terrorism (Gill et al. 2014). When social identities are threatened or feelings of social disapproval arise, people often react with harsh aggression and are more likely to respond with violence (Jasko et al. 2017; Sidanius et al. 2016; de Zavala et al. 2009). In this regard, strong beliefs, irrespective of ideological content, provide clear prescriptions and call for strict adherence, which promotes dogmatic intolerance toward other world views, denial of free speech, and antisocial behavior (Van Prooijen and Krouwel 2017). "Distressing societal and personal events (e.g., injustices, economic crises, wars) undermine the extent to which perceivers experience the world as meaningful and therefore stimulate people to regain a sense of purpose through strong and clear-cut ideological convictions" (Van Prooijen and Krouwel 2019, 160).

Yet other studies show that the same variables that trigger aggressive behavior may also influence benevolence and empathy. An empirical analysis demonstrates that self-uncertainty and perceived rejection of an ideological group led participants to donate more money to that group than in situations when they felt certain. Furthermore, in some individuals, experiences of suffering and harmful life events lead them to be altruistic and benevolent, which gives them meaning in life (Davis and McKearney 2003). This implies that prosocial and empathic behavior can have psychological benefits and also serve fundamental psychological needs such as social belongingness, social approval, and self-efficacy. Thus, altruistic behavior and prosocial motivations can be, just like aggressive and selfish behavior, a means for adaptations and need reconciliation. In other words, need thwarting and experiences of rejection and disappointment can trigger behaviors from both ends of the aggressive–benevolent spectrum. But what leads individuals to adopt prosocial or aggressive coping mechanisms?

SDT assumes that these different modes of adaptation and needs reconciliation are responses to particular types of environments. Specifically, under generous economic, social, cultural, and familial conditions that allow for the reconciliation of basic existential and mental needs, a healthier social and autonomous self occurs (Ryan and Hawley 2017). By contrast, a destructive social environment which does not provide supportive resources and opportunities for restoring acceptance and integration can enhance the tendency toward extremism and delinquency. Hence, the disintegration approach assumes that the inclination to adopt radical beliefs, to denigrate others, and to use violence increases with the level of social disintegration. Disintegration implies the lack of services of social institutions and communities to ensure existential bases (in our approach, the satisfaction of existential and epistemic needs), social approval and belongingness (relational needs), and personal integrity (agency needs) of all members of a society. The approach seeks to explain how need deprivation and the insufficient integrative measures of modern societies can trigger an inclination toward violence, ideological extremism, and outgroup hostility. A successful holistic integration can be achieved by mastering three coping dimensions: socio-structural, institutional, and personal. The socio-structural dimension describes access to substantive goods of a society, which is objectively satisfied by sufficient access to housing, work, and consumption market, and subjectively satisfied by the social approval of one's own social position and accomplishments. The institutional dimension suggests that conflicting interests must be balanced without violating the integrity of all groups. Here, adherence to democratic and socially moral principles must be ensured (fairness, justice, and solidarity). Finally, the personal dimension describes the formation of interpersonal relations for the purpose of self-efficacy, self-fulfillment, and meaning in life. Emotional attachment to significant others provides security and psychological support that helps to counterbalance identity crises, value diffusions, and impairment to self-esteem or disorientation. A successful integration of these three dimensions leads to an affiliated social being who identifies with the social community and accepts socially ingrained norms and values (Anhut 2005).

At the opposite end, disintegration tends to generate a reluctance to adapt to social instances and show consideration toward other social members. In particular, socially disadvantaged individuals are exposed to unequally distributed risks and opportunities; have insufficient access to housing, jobs, and consumer goods; and lack opportunities for self-accomplishment. These individuals, who feel left behind and unappreciated by government, are less willing to cooperate and to invest in collective goods (Anhut and Heitmeyer 2005). This theory coincides with the assumption that loss of personal significance instills a sense of self-uncertainty which, in turn, fuels an endorsement of extremism (Webber et al. 2017). Evoked feelings of shame, anger, dishonor, and alienation are absorbed especially by national-authoritarian, right-wing extremist, or religious fundamentalist ideologies that provide disintegrated individuals a perceived sense of stability, orientation, and control by means of clear-cut world views and a demonstration of power. Strict adherence to and defense of beliefs, values, and norms of the extremist group enhances their feelings of belonging, approval, and self-significance (Webber et al. 2018). The use of narratives based on hostility (prejudices, scapegoats, dissidents, threatening others) and the formation of dogmatic "exclusionary zones" enforce the perception of regained control, power, and self-efficacy. The denigration of others is a way to cover up one's own inefficacies and to sustain a positive self-image (Kaddor 2017).

The disintegration approach also argues that adolescence is shaped by ambiguous interpretations of social reality and an unstable and constantly changing social environment—all which tend to generate disorientation, ambiguity, and uncertainty. Accordingly, sociological and psychological studies reveal that radical ideologies can absorb this turbulent and emotional stage of development by providing orientation, stability, and a sense of belongingness, appreciation, and companionable solidarity (Toprak and Weitzel 2017). Radical ideas are an option to evaluate and understand reality in a manner that runs counter to mainstream society. It reduces complexity by providing predefined, clear, and focused explanations about the social world and one's own place within it (El-Mafaalani 2017). Empirical findings support this view. A series of studies provide evidence that left- and right-wing extremists perceive the world more simplistically and divide it into sharply distinguished mental categories (Lammers et al. 2017). Such a simple and rigid ideological model does not allow for variable interpretations or misconceptions. Compliance with prescribed norms, values, and roles promises a "postmortem salvation," which reduces the fear of mortality and enforces a positive self-image (Dantschke 2017). Reduced cognitive complexity and a predefined world view increase overconfidence and allow one to believe that one accurately understands reality. This in turn enhances the perception of one's cognitive and moral superiority and judgmental certainty (Van Prooijn and Krouwel 2019).

Furthermore, radical ideologies provide a non-performance-related option for belongingness, which supply especially social disadvantaged individuals with an alternative form of identity and individuality (Anhut 2005). The experiences of exclusion, which can occur in economic, political, social, or cultural dimensions, can lead to long-term social and political disintegration. Disintegration, in turn, causes psychological damage and feelings of inferiority, shame, powerlessness, and apathy. Perceived loss of control generates strong feelings of uncertainty, fear, and impuissance. Consequently, the negative feelings of disintegration and perceived loss of control tend to be compensated in terms of a radical outgroup-derogating belief system, which is the "active inversion of one's own exclusion experiences." One's own negative experiences of social rejection are thus projected onto others (e.g., ethnic minorities, refugees, or dissidents).

PART III
EXTREMIST ORGANIZATIONS, IDEOLOGIES, AND REAL CONFLICT

8
Extremist Organizations
Their Network and Structure

In the previous chapters we discussed (i) the existence of fundamental human needs that are a product of biological evolution but may also be elicited and shaped by external conditions, (ii) the inner tension that arouses when these needs are deprived, and (iii) the subjective search for reconciliation to reduce this inner (psychological) conflict. Following this, we proposed that ideologies tend to provide a viable reconciliation option and showed their palliative and need-serving capacities. In other words, ideologies provide a mental framework that leads people to serve their psychological needs. They help individuals interpret and evaluate information and they provide guidance for judgment, decision-making, and action. When people encounter novel information, including information that is contradictory, ambiguous, or threatening, they use mental frameworks associated with certain belief systems to process it. The values, beliefs, and norms that are shared within a group supply a construct of how the (idealized) world should be—by emphasizing the deficiencies of the current social, political, or economic system. Ideologies deliver narratives for identification and group identity, provide group reassurance, and support the formation of positive self-esteem. All this tends to form a concept of (perceived) coherence, consistency, orientation, and meaningful existence. The shared framework explains, guides, unites, and provides answers to burgeoning emotions and ambiguities. However, we also discussed that ideologies can be aggressive and radical, covering irrevocable and static dogmas. In this case, the ideological framework presents a clear and orderly image of the world by providing stereotyping images of the "good and the evil" with the aim to shape a social pattern of coherence and contrast. Radical ideologies provide a stable structure, perceived certainty, consistency, order, and control. They often hold strong (and "superior") moral principles that guide how to behave and how to differentiate between "the bad and the good" and between opponents and sympathizers.

In fact, belief systems, whether radical, moderate, or peaceful, tend to serve an ontological, social, and psychological function. They provide answers on human existence, reality, meaningfulness, identity, and belongingness. They include representations of alternative worlds and provide guidance what the idealized world should look like based on guiding categories of concepts, defined in one way or another as "good" or "bad." These polarities have a strong organizing function, by providing guiding insights about the self and the others. The practicability of ideologies enables them to be used in everyday life, to answer everyday questions, and to direct everyday behavior of their adherents.

So, what we have discussed extensively so far is the mental framework of ideologies and their capacity to reconcile epistemic, relational, existential, and agency human needs. In the following chapter, our aim is now to understand the functioning of ideologies from a group-based, organizational perspective. How are ideologically oriented groups structured and managed? Are there differences in networking and the organizational structure between secular (mafia), left-wing, right-wing, and religious radical groups? Why is it even important to consider the distinct organizational forms of the groups? By providing real-life examples and empirical evidence (as far as given), we can show that the organizational form of a particular ideological group can also address particular human needs. This means individuals join groups not only because of their ideology but also because of their network and distinct organizational form. In addition, we may understand the different forms of ideologization—the political, secular, and religious belief systems—are not only used for strategic or political reasons, but that they also operate on a psychological and social level. In this regard, the ideological group possesses collective preferences and values and selects a course of action from a range of perceived alternatives to make decisions and reach goals. "Organizations arrive at collective judgments about the relative effectiveness of different strategies of opposition on the basis of observation and experience, as much as on the basis of abstract strategic conceptions derived from ideological assumptions" (Crenshaw 1998, 8). Our aim is thus to combine economic thinking and political science with psychological forces to explain the organizational networks and communication tools of radical groups. These organizational characteristics and networking structures have the capacity to address particular human needs. Understanding this connection enables us to understand the crucial role of human needs and ideologies in collective decision-making, and thus in the development, maintenance, and resolution of conflict.

8.1 Extremist Organizations from the "Need-Serving" Perspective

Empirical studies, but also popular scientific articles and governmental communiques, have shown that individuals join radical groups or organizations for prospective economic incentives. Whether considering Boko Haram's successful recruitment of young adults in Nigeria or the reign of the Islamic State in the southern part of the Philippines—both extremist groups promised excessive financial flows for accession (Ewi and Salifu 2017; Moir 2017). But the same investigations also reveal that need deprivation, group dynamics, and the ideology itself play a significant role in the recruitment and mobilization processes. As mentioned in the previous chapters, ideologies tend to provide a viable reconciliation option to serve fundamental human needs. Adopting certain beliefs or a particular ideology does not only provide guidance and cognitive consistency, but it also secures group belongingness and material existence (in the group). Depending on the group size, complexity, and dynamic interactions, a group can be transformed and extended to a structured organization in which all members are differentiated as to their responsibilities of achieving a shared group objective. Individuals belonging to such organizations receive a certain role, whether as a leader, organizer, coordinator, or operator, and are aware of their expected performance with reference to the common goals. Not all members occupy an active position but may act passively and in response to instructions or actions of others. Usually such organizations are strictly hierarchical, but they also provide the possibility for their members to reach higher positions based on their efficiency and self-assertion (Nance 2016).

While later in this chapter we are going to describe precisely the "technical" organizational structures of extremist groups, it may be important to emphasize first the psychological effects of these structures. Belonging to and identifying with a well-structured and homogenous group or organization provides, in the first step, a sense of order and control. Collective actions and decision-making enhance self-assertion by shifting the responsibility from the subject to the collective group. The uncertainty, groundlessness, possible failures behind self-responsibility, and the vast number of choices in the modern environment are abolished by the group, which gives precise and unambiguous directions of action and choice (Schwartz 2000). Sharing values, ideals, and goals with other group members and accepting the ascribed role within the system increases self-significance and generates a sense of meaning in life. Regardless of the role or the context, group membership in itself serves a palliative function and encourages members to act in a collectively rather than subjectively way. Identification with ingroup characteristics, self-evaluation based on these characteristics, and social interactions within the group form an individual's social identity. In fact, the processes of intergroup comparisons, cognitive simplifications, self-evaluation, and the search for positive self-esteem bring groups into being (Jenkins 2008). But group belongingness does not just form an individual's social identity; it also absorbs upset emotions and cognitive "dizziness" (no meaning and direction in life). Individuals join groups or organizations not because of impulsiveness, an emotional breakdown, or mental illness, but because of enduring need deprivation. Starvation, poverty, and resource deprivation, but also self-uncertainty, alienation, and the lack of meaning in life are all aspects that tend to be absorbed by a radical organization.

These factors explain why normal individuals, with neither mental disorders nor traumatic experiences in life, join an extremist group or organization and make collective choices. It is easier to get people who suffer from fundamental need deprivation and harbor grievances to use violence against hated figures or dissidents. However, to kill innocent victims on the streets, in department stores, or in churches requires more powerful psychological mechanisms of moral disengagement. Available interviews and field data of ISIS-held territories in Syria provide evidence that intensive psychological trainings in moral disengagement, especially of children and young adults, created the capacity to commit atrocities and engage in mass killings (Almohammad 2018). Such disengagement practices and ideological indoctrinations are necessary to justify and moralize the decisions and actions of the group. "In this process, destructive conduct is made personally and socially acceptable by portraying it in the service of moral purposes. People then act on a moral imperative" (Bandura 1998, 163).

This means that extremist groups or organizations neither must change an individual's needs or personalities, nor trigger some aggressive drives to make an individual believe and act. But rather by providing reconciliation for an individual's fundamental needs—be that, for example, existential security that is served by economic resources, or lack of control and meaning in life that are absorbed by the collectively shared ideals and objectives. Serving those needs that are important for the subject enhances the value of the group, and thus increases the willingness of the subject to protect the valued source of reconciliation. The narratives, or ideological indoctrinations, promote a symbolization of the collective identity, which in turn generates a consistent similarity of the group. This imagined similarity, or consistent patterns of the group generate identity boundaries; that is, individuals observe and understand the differences to outgroup members, which in extreme forms can lead to dehumanization (Jenkins 2008). Acting in view of a collective identity displaces self-responsibility such that individuals perceive their actions as orders from above rather than from their own volition. For example, "Nazi prison commandants and their staffs divested themselves of personal responsibility for their unprecedented inhumanities; they were simply carrying out orders" (Bandura 1998, 173).

The hierarchical structure of large organizations, in particular, allows individuals to be relieved from their responsibility to verify information and assess the implications of their decisions and actions. Conforming to norms, values, and ideals, and being obedient to the orders dictated from respected authorities not only guides the individual as to how to think and behave, but it also generates predictable interactions within the group (Jenkins 2008). The social construction of conformity and obedience thus reduces uncertainty and increases self-assertion and a sense of meaningfulness (obeying orders, stick to rules, follow the ideals). This implies that the organizational structure itself tends to serve an individual's subjective needs. Strict and stable patterns, a hierarchical order, and role ascriptions generate functional stability and predictable interaction flows. Therefore, in the proceeding chapter we intend to focus on the construction of radical or terrorist organizations, their networks, and professionally led departments of conduct. Before individuals join radical organizations or are selected to represent the group, they usually undergo a process that brings them officially into the organization. So before understanding the recruiting, mobilization, and indoctrination processes, we rely on available sources to shed light into the functional design, representativeness, and network of such groups.

8.2 The Traditional Criminal Organization—The Mafia

Many old-style criminal hierarchies, like the Italian or Japanese Mafia, were governed and organized in a rational, corporate structure. Organized crime involves planning, structuring, functional role division, and rational decision making, with the aim to maximize profits and to extend control in the environment. These procedures and the organizational order do not differ from the patterns and planning of legal and authorized organizations, with the only exception being that organizations like the mafia provide illegal goods and services and adopt illegal tactics to reach corporate objectives (Catino 2014). La Cosa Nostra ("our thing"), for example, is a collection of Italian American organized crime families that has been operating in the United States since the 1920s. Each of these "families" have a similar vertical organizational structure, entailing a leader, who has executive control; a subleader; senior advisors; and a number of "capos," who supervise active members of the organization. In addition, there are several hundred associate members who work for the families. A commission of the leaders coordinates control of their companies and facilitates communication between the families. This vertical organizational order is characterized by centralized power and systemic decision-making processes, which allows for better control of decisions and actions (Kelly 1999). However, in such hierarchical structures, where decisions are made at the top, the organization becomes too dependent on the knowledge and information processing of top managers and fails to incorporate local subordinate managers into the decision-making process. It is often economically profitable and more efficient to decentralize activities and place strategic decision-making in lower levels of the organization. Such a horizontal organizational order is thus characterized by decentralized governance and local, clan-based decision-making. This has the advantage of minimizing the transaction costs and using the local information efficiently to make fast decisions and to mobilize low-level managers (Catino 2014).

Whether horizontal or vertical, in both organizational forms a system of formal regulations, shared norms, and obligations determine the organizational life. Membership rituals and recruitment processes are strictly regulated with varying degrees of rigidity. Being a member of such an organization, as "a man of honor," implies lifetime obedience, subordination, and loyalty. The mafia brotherhood demands secrecy (omerta), discipline, cohesion, and manhood. It is accompanied by affiliation codes with mystified legends, which serve as symbols to enhance fascination and identification with the group (Ciconte 2014). Narratives about the history and origin of the organizations, ones that have been told to young members in Cosa Nostra, Camorra, or 'Ndrangheta, form the shared identity that must be honored by all members. Interestingly, the stories and legends told incorporate religious symbols and divine figures, which play a decisive role in the construction of the culture and ideology of the organizations. Under the protection of Catholic saints and the divine figure Madonna, the members should gain strength and authority, which has been especially told during the training and indoctrination processes of young boys (Serenata 2014). Similar to their rituals, legends, and the inclination to Catholicism, all three Italian mafia organizations provide protection services through a variety of illegal activities. These activities are either controlled directly by the mafia organization, through outsourced subcontracting groups, or co-partnerships/coalitions with other mafia groups. Organizations like Cosa Nostra and 'Ndrangheta show a vertical organizational order (see Figure 8.1) and centralized control mechanisms, whereas

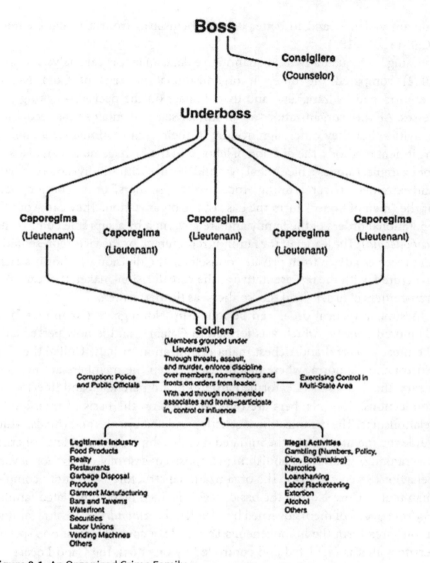

Figure 8.1 An Organized Crime Family
Source: *Task Force Report: Organized Crime*. Washington DC: US Government Printing Office, 1967.

Camorra is characterized by the absence of higher levels of coordination and the presence of clan-based decision-making.

"Mafia groups that are based on a vertical organizational order, thanks to the presence of higher levels of coordination, should, in general, have greater capacity to speak with a single voice, to make collectively biding decisions, and to strategize, compared to mafia groups that present a horizontal organizational order. This should increase their capacity to govern conflicts and contain violence, and to better defend themselves from external enemies" (Catino 2014, 183).

Using both qualitative and quantitative data, an empirical analysis (Catino 2014) compared the different organizational patterns of Cosa Nostra, Camorra and 'Ndrangheta, and their impact on the decision-making processes. All three organizations are of similar size and entail similar economic activities, but they differ significantly in their organizational structure, recruitment methods, the division of labor, and the management. Cosa Nostra, for example, implies a hierarchal pyramidal order with subdivisions of power and extremely strict recruiting processes. The "soldiers," or the "button man," or the "men of honor" form the base of the organization. They carry out the operational orders of the family and are governed by a supreme commander (*capodecina*). The leader of the family is represented by the vice-representative and receives advice from private counselors. The division of labor is strictly structured, with the representative as the core decision-maker, the "capos" as transmitters of orders, and the "soldiers" as the performers.

A similar vertical order can be found in 'Ndrangheta ("manliness"), or "Honored Society," which was formed in Calabria and is now perceived as the most powerful and richest mafia organization in Italy. Unlike the Cosa Nostra and Camorra, where blood-ties between the members are not necessary, the 'Ndrangheta is formed around blood parentage and intermarital connections. The members are thus recruited on the basis of interfamilial relationships. The organization is strictly regulated by rules and rituals, which guide the members from the initiated membership to the next level of criminal ranking, up until the punishment imposed in case of violations or deviant behavior (Serenata 2014). The organizational structure is far more complex than that of Cosa Nostra: the basic level is formed by blood-related families (*'ndrina*), each of them governed by a leader, the *capondrina*. Several families in one area form the homogeneous La Locale, a consortium of one specific territory that is regulated and controlled by one boss, the Capo Locale. He has solitary decisional power and is assisted by the Contabile ("bookkeeper"), who manages the financial department and by the Crimine ("crime"), who is responsible for all illegal activities. The members can reach a higher rank in the hierarchy which increases with the crimes committed (Catino 2014). The 'ndrina distributes the organization's power and control through mergers and acquisitions, by expanding their activities to countries such as, but not limited to, Argentina, Belgium, Canada, Chile, Morocco, Portugal, Spain, Turkey, and the United States. The success of the expansion facilitates the formation of intermediate structures that coordinate local groups and communicate with the main "Crimine" in Calabria (Serenata 2014).

On the opposite, the Camorra, one of the oldest mafia organizations in Italy, is a decentralized consortium of heterogeneous criminal clans that are not formed by familial relations. It is not a unified organization, and it is not governed by a superior leader, which exacerbates the coordination of the entire criminal system. The horizontal organizational form is characterized by distributed power, which leads to severe intergroup competition and violent conflicts. Several attempts in the 1970s and 1980s to implement a vertical order to organize the various Camorra clans and to dampen the permanent conflicts were met with strong disapproval, resulting in bloody conflicts with a high number of fatalities. In fact, Camorra's organizational order remains dynamic, polycentric, and conflictual. "The central unit is made up of the families. Alliances tend to establish confederations between criminal groups and forces, but these alliances are only partial and contingent; they do not give rise to the configuration of a compact organization with a unified, coherent direction. Conflict prevails over agreement, especially during those periods where there are no leaders characterized by special abilities" (Catino 2014, 194). Despite its decentralized order and fragmented power structure, the Camorra is considered an organization by law enforcement agencies. The empirical investigation mentioned above (Catino 2014) provides evidence that the absence of higher-level management and coordinated governance of the Camorra organization leads to violent inter-clan disputes and a high rate of fatalities each year. On the opposite, the hierarchical patterns of the Cosa Nostra and the 'Ndrangheta introduce a higher level of coordination and supervision, which in turn enables the curbing of interclan conflicts and the number of homicides. Centralized decision-making generates stability and continuity in an organization, and it allows an organization to set long-term interests that are pursued by all members collectively. However, vertical organizations are also more visible and vulnerable, which makes it easier for law enforcement agencies to target the main leaders.

8.3 The Radical Right Organizations

Despite the higher vulnerability, vertical hierarchical orders are still adopted by state organizations, such as the military or the police, and by authoritarian and extremist groups. History shows how radical organizations, like the Hitler Youth in Germany or the Ku Klux Klan in the United States, provided, especially to young adults, identification, order, coherence, and group affiliation (Van Leeuwen and Park 2009). The hierarchical patterns of such groups and the obedience to rules, rituals, and collective goals generates certainty and predictability in individuals' lives. Former members of the Hitler Youth, who were asked to reflect on their childhood and early adolescence, remembered the powerful political system of the Third Reich, their pride to be a part of it, the national hymns they sang, and the respect and social approval they received in the group (Kater 2006). The shared experiences in such youth organizations showed them the strength of the community, and the loyalty and respect for each comrade. The strong members would support the weaker fellows and knowledgeable leaders would guide and protect. This mutual reciprocity and group dynamics enhanced the duty, devotion, and sacrifice for the group (Geary 2002). At the same time, the hierarchical youth organizations organized large-scale regional and national sports competitions among its members to prepare them implicitly for war and combat. The drill techniques and the daily sport program were intended to degrade the members to the point that they lost their self-respect and individualism. The principles of Social Darwinism dominated the organizational structure (i.e., the superiority of the fittest), resulting in the legitimacy and encouragement to humiliate weaker members, to use physical and mental torture, and peer-group harassments (Kater 2006).

Similar strategically and hierarchically organized right-wing groups, even if not that size and impact, can be found all around the world. The Ku Klux Klan, by far the oldest right-wing extremist organization in the United States, forms their organizational structure on the basis of race and power. Starting as a social club in 1866 in the Southern part of the US, transforming to a paramilitary racial and extremely violent movement in the 1870s, and extending their actions and ideologies to other states by the end of the nineteenth century, the Klan accounted for more than six million members by the end of the 1920s. The success of the Klan can, at least partly, be explained by the hierarchal structure of the organization, which provided order, certainty, and role assignment in a superior system. All this seemed to provide alienated men, structure, and stability in their lives. The organization had interconnections to political leaders and influential clergymen that seemed to share similar objectives, namely, to restore social order on the streets and to dampen the impact of the Catholics, Jews, and African Americans (Atkins 2011). Compared to European right-wing groups, such as the NPD (National Democratic Party of Germany) in Germany, the BNP (British National Party) in the United Kingdom, or the NSF (National Socialist Front) in Sweden, the American political right-wing groups seemed to play a minor role in the international political sphere. Parties active in the United States, such as the National Alliance (NA) or the NSDAP-AO (the Nazi Party "Foreign and Development Association") are not perceived as significant political organizations, but rather as "hate groups." According to that, little information is available about the organizational patterns and the formal membership arrangements of such groups because their activities are largely secretive (Heitmeyer 2003).

According to the BMI and the German Federal Office for the Protection of the Constitution, in the year 2000 there were more than 144 right-wing extremist organizations in Germany with an estimated membership of fifty-one thousand. While the number of active members had fallen to approximately twenty-five thousand, the numbers of pro-violence right-wing extremists had risen tremendously, from 6,200 in 1995 to 9,700 in 2000, and 12,700 in 2018. These organizations are perceived to be interconnected to other right-wing extremist groups across Europe, such as Sweden or France, or the United States. Within the well-structured international network, members organize and plan yearly events, as well as attract funding and mobilize members to commit collective atrocities (BMI Bund 2018). However, statistics provide evidence that right-wing extremist organizations are rising all over the world. In the United States, for example, 4,420 violent incidents committed by right-wing extremist organizations were counted between 1990 and 2012. Studies in North America show that right-wing terrorism accounted for 31.2 percent of violent incidents and for 51.6 percent of terrorism-related fatalities between 1954 and 2000. Although right-wing groups generate a severe threat to the North American countries, inducing a high number of fatalities and attacks, such attacks, or right-wing organizations in general, receive little media attention compared to those of Islamist groups (Koehler 2016).

All right-wing extremist groups have a similar organizational structure based on hierarchy, obedience, and submission.[1] They usually have a minimalist group structure and induce a centralized top-down decision-making process (De Lange and Art 2011). The individual accepts a subordinate role to the group and obey to rituals, customs, and collective objectives—the subjective identity merges to a social and collective self and provides no room for individual ideas, decision-making, and identity (Heitmeyer 2005b). Psychologists argue that belonging to a powerful, strong, and well-structured organization tends to provide individuals with a feeling of superiority, certainty, and self-significance. Usually for the first time in their lives such individuals tend to experience a sense of importance in a social system (Koomen and Van Der Pligt 2016). Traditional literature on radical groups and terrorist cells argues that radical groups act as a deliberately constructed social unit and make collective decisions to reach specific goals. They use specific ideologies to rationalize their actions and to recruit and mobilize individuals. Such a usually hierarchically organized social unit is perceived to be developed by a circle of sympathizers that participate in political activism. However, such groups or organizations are not characterized by the absence of strategic planning and specialization, but rather by competent members in their particular area of assignment (e.g., recruitment, media, funding) (Wolf 1981). Research on radical right groups and organizations has thus focused on agency to explain the success of certain right-wing groups by arguing that the organizational structure of a group determines its failure or success (Jackson 2019). A strong and well-structured organization is thus able to maintain its coherence and stability, which in turn creates the image of a powerful and reliable group. Institutionalized groups with strong internal and external leadership qualities and well-planned recruitment and training processes are perceived to have a long-term success of existence. Most radical right groups have charismatic leaders who have strong rhetorical skills and know how to present themselves to the outside world. Beyond external qualities, right-wing leaders must provide authoritarian ruling principles and practical management skills to hold the group together and to manage its internal life.

An empirical study (De Lange and Art 2011) compared the organizational structure of two right-wing groups in the Netherlands—the LPF and PVV—and showed that a stable organizational structure, strong leadership, and effective recruitment processes increase the probability of group's long-term success. At sight, both right-wing parties appear to be similar in regard to their campaigns against immigration and their appeal to mostly White and low educated men. However, the organizational structure of both groups differ significantly. LPF was founded in February 2002 by Pim Fortuyn, as a small circle of sympathizers (mostly close friends) and with an absent organizational structure. Despite the assassination of Fortuyn in May 2002, the party won the elections and received an invitation to join the CDA and VVD in government. Without an effective internal and external leadership, a decentralized decision-making, and an absent collective identity shared by its members, the right-wing group could not survive in the long run. Although the LPF established a youth organization and a think tank, the lack of a strong belief system and a shared identity, especially among its executive board members, led to failed identification and enhanced self-interest. Consequently, permanent tensions within the group in the central office (e.g., between the executive board and the parliamentary group, and between various departments in the group), the group in the public office and the group on the ground (such as the regional branches), as well as conflicts between these three groups, led to the breakdown of LPF.

To the contrary, Geert Wilders has built his right-wing party, PVV, which was founded in 2005, slowly and strategically. He rejected his participation in the 2007 provincial elections and focused instead on the 2009 European elections in which PVV became the second largest party. Compared to LPF, PVV has neither regional and local branches, nor additional organizations, but it endorses a strong group identity. The group implies a strong group coherence, unity, and identification, partly because of its exclusive and selective membership that is not available for every possible candidate. Sympathizers and voters of PVV cannot become members of the right-wing group, but they can donate money to the group-based foundation, "Friends of PVV," or they can volunteer during campaigns. The organization is strictly centralized, which means that the decisional power is concentrated in Geert Wilders' hands. This enables him to keep the group clear, to avoid within-group conflicts, and to keep control over his representatives and volunteers. In contrast, the LPF was founded only three months before the 2002 elections. The group had no time to recruit potential candidates, to communicate their shared beliefs, to provide effective trainings, or to establish a strong collective identity. Members of the PVV were selected by Wilders personally, which led to a selective and strict recruiting process. Extensive trainings for PVV members have also been carried out by Wilders himself, which enhanced the attachment to and solidarity with the group. Members received feedback on their performance and were coached and assisted in case of failures. PVV has been thus often been characterized as knowledgeable, cohesive, and disciplined (De Lange and Art 2011).

Similar organizational patterns have been observed in the Dansk Folkeparti in Denmark that endorses a strong group identity, a centralized decision-making, and effective and well-structured recruitment and socialization processes. This implies that the success of right-wing groups is determined not only by a charismatic leader or an appealing belief system, but also by a properly structured organization and a shared group identity. Strong external and internal leadership, effective recruitment processes, and constant trainings within the group have a strong impact on the survival and the persistence of an organization (De Lange and Art 2011). Empirical analyses of far-right groups confirm that strongly organized groups are more successful than less organized ones and are able to sustain their long-term existence (Lubbers et al. 2002).

The far-right group Golden Dawn in Greece provides a further example. Its violent nature and extreme ideology can be compared to those of the neo-Nazi National Democratic Party of Germany (NDP), the neo-fascist British National Party, or the Italian Forza Nuova. The fascist group emphasizes its National Socialist principles and its authoritarian leadership, and it is well known for having committed violent atrocities and hate crimes against left-wing groups, university students, members of Marxist organizations, and trade unions. Violence was also directed toward immigrants of various ethnicities and toward members of pro-immigration and anti-racism organizations. Golden Dawn first appeared in 1980 in the political arena as a circle of former members of the neo-fascist "Party of August 4th," which is associated with the dictatorship of Metaxas (1936–1941) (Vasilopoulou and Halikiopoulou 2015). Despite its long existence, the group first grew in popularity during the 2010 local elections, when the party leader, Nikos Michaloliakos, received 5.29 percent of the votes, followed by seven percent in the national elections in May and June 2012. The group received equal support both in the urban and rural areas and it experienced low levels of electoral volatility despite numerous scandals, court cases, and arrests of its top leadership and management. In May 2014, Golden Dawn received 9.4 percent of the vote and elected three members to the European Parliament (Ellinas and Lamprianou 2017). The main reasons for its electoral success were quoted to be immigration, the support of the group's ideology, and protest and anger against the current regime (especially, resentment against the memorandum). The far-right group criticized the legitimacy of the corrupted government by providing "a nationalist" solution with authoritarian principles to the political and socioeconomic crisis in Greece (Vasilopoulou and Halikiopoulou 2015).

An empirical study observed the group's local organizational activities of sixty-nine branches and shows that their grassroots activities are similar to those of some successful far-right groups in Europe. Like the Front National in France or the Dutch Party for Freedom, the Golden Dawn invested a lot of resources to recruit and train its members through the indoctrination of ideological principles and historical narratives. On the other side, it adopted street-based practices and Nazi-rituals, and drew on violent measures like their radical British, German, and Italian counterparts (Georgiadou 2013). It portrayed an image of a welfare state party by distributing goods and services to the local communities and providing security and protection to older people and shop owners. It acted as "local communal court and police," and it organized social events for Greek people. Although Golden Dawn was centrally and hierarchically organized, it established local branches that provided social services to the communes, which had a strong impact on levels of support for the group (Dinas et al. 2016).

Beyond politically active organizations, militant groups, such as the neo-Nazi comradeships or the Free Forces in Germany, distinguish themselves from their parliamentarian counterparts. Such groups or organizations do not aim to win public office and do not nominate political candidates, but rather they try to mobilize support through the ideological principles with which they identify and which aim to provide guidance for their members.

Comradeship members, for example, include militant neo-Nazis, right-wing rockers, and right-wing youths, who are undeterred in using violence to achieve their ideological means. The local branch in South Germany received media attention when its plot to carry out a bomb attack at the Jewish Cultural Center in Munch came to light. A further militant organization, the Autonomous Nationalists, which first emerged in Berlin and Dortmund, spread their ideological principles within a dense network of the German far-right groups. The members were very young (fourteen years onward), and they were focused on contemporary concerns, such as the economic prosperity and opportunities for the youth in the future. The group tried to reach out to young individuals living in precarious situations and offer them short-term employment and accommodation. Data on such militant organizations provide evidence that right-wing extremism involves not just small, independent groups, but a complex network. This network organizes steadily subcultural events consisting of music, rituals, and clothes, which are designed to appeal, in particular, to frustrated, aggressive, and authoritarian-influenced youth. They sponsor far-right concerts where these young adults can vent their frustrations and racist sentiments (Schellenberg 2013).

Such militant far-right groups, which operate independently of political parties or large social movements, can be found beyond Europe and in the United States. According to the Southern Poverty Law Center (SPLC, 2013), there are more than 1,020 far-right groups operating in the United States. Data show that attacks from these right-wing extremists pose a higher threat to the US than assaults from left-wing or Islamist extremists. Of particular concern are white supremacists and anti-government and anti-immigration extremists who aim to oppose governmental authority, curb immigration, ban abortion, and establish a racial, ethnic, or religious White supremacy (Jones 2018). An empirical analysis, using the Extremist Crime Database (ECDB), shows that far-right militant organizations tend to be formed by mainly male, White, young adolescents who are more likely to have a prior crime history and less likely a college degree (Chermak and Gruenewald 2015). These individuals are perceived to be highly nationalistic, suspicious of governmental authority and globalization, with a high preference for individual liberty (individual right to own guns, be free of taxes) and strong beliefs that one's own identity or "way of life" is under threat. These perceptions of personal or national threats generate the perceived need of militaristic preparation and training to survive in case of attacks.

The ECDB also reveals that, since 1990, such far-right extremist groups have committed 375 homicide delicts, claiming over six hundred lives. More than 140 of these acts were ideologically motivated and more than half were committed by White supremacists (Chermak et al. 2013). Other empirical studies argue that the organizational capacity of far-right groups determines their persistence and violent character. Groups that receive stable funding, that recruit and disseminate their ideology more aggressively, and that adapt easily to changing conditions tend to be more constant (Horowitz 2010). This organizational consistency in turn enhances the group's capacity, knowledge, and willingness to use violent means to reach their goals. In particular, strategically connected far-right organizations that cooperate with other groups in a dense network tend to be more effective. This means that strong intergroup connections enable groups to exchange information and to acquire knowledge in a fast and more effective way, which improves collective decision-making. Groups with more ties imply better logistics, labor divisions, and mutual support. The White Power Movement (WPM), for example, existed for a long time due to its strong ingroup commitment, a strong shared identity, and strong activist networks (Chermak et al. 2013). Empirical studies support these assumptions and show that interconnected far-right groups tend to be more violent, have more financial resources, and have better organizational structures (Horowitz 2010; Caspi et al. 2012).[2]

Anti-immigration groups form one of the strongest and well-connected right-wing networks in the United States. "Today, 35 such groups, with a collective membership of between 600,000 and 750,000, work in research, advocacy, fundraising, and lobbying to influence state and federal policies. Some of the most salient include the Federation for American Immigration Reform (FAIR), the Center for Immigration Studies (CIS), English First, and NumbersUSA. Ten groups channeled $4.2 million into anti-immigration lobbying in 2005, and nine political action committees raised $3.4 million for campaigns in 2006. In Congress, the movement's growth is reflected in the Immigration Reform Caucus, which has grown from 16 members in 1999 to more than 90 today" (Larsen 2007, 14). Not all anti-immigration groups focus solely on the immigration issue, but they all advocate restrictions to legal immigration and deportations of illegal immigrants. These objectives are also shared by the Minutemen and White supremacists, which leads to connections between the US anti-immigrant organizations and extremist groups. Figure 8.2 provides insight into the complex and dense network of anti-immigration organizations, hate groups, far-right extremists, and mainstream conservative politics in the US. FAIR, for example, is one of the largest and most influential anti-immigration think tanks in the United States. It was founded in 1979 by John Tanton and is perceived to be connected to a dozen other large organizations on the right-ideological spectrum. He also established several other influential population control groups, as well as the

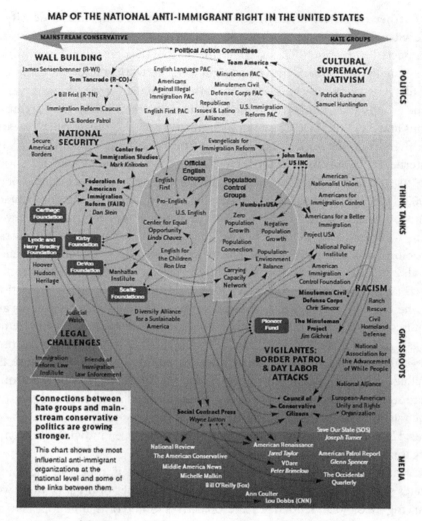

Figure 8.2 Map of the National Anti-Immigration Right in the United States
Source: Taken from Larsen (2007, 17).

Pro-English group, the Center for Immigration Studies (CIS), NumbersUSA, and the Americans for a Better Immigration think tank. These groups or think tanks, in turn, are linked to other conservative or even racial organizations. From 1985 to 1994, Tanton received financial support from the Pioneer Fund, a former Nazi organization that promoted research in eugenics and racial IQ differences (Blumenthal 2004). He also shares an office at Social Contract Press with Wayne Lutton, an editor who is known for his workings at the anti-semitic journal *The Occidental Quarterly*.

Further empirical research (Caiani and Parenti 2013) on the density of the virtual far-right network in the US reveals that 134 organizations are connected with only 173 links, which means that the density of the network is very low. In comparison, the virtual right-wing network in France is composed of fifty-eight organizations with 242 links, the Italian network has seventy-nine groups and 417 links, and the German network has sixty-nine organizations and 389 links (see Caiani and Parenti 2013, 60–63 [figs]). Such research on the virtual network of far-right organizations "has pointed out that the Internet is not only used by these types of groups to spread propaganda, boost the use of violence, and facilitate recruitment of new members (Glaser et al., 2002; Hoffman, 1996; Mininni, 2002), but also to find and maintain contacts with other extremist groups, both at the national and international levels, thus forming dense networks of organizations that can potentially sustain mobilizations and facilitate the construction of collective identity" (Caiani et al. 2012, 54). Empirical analyses thus provide evidence that German neo-Nazi activists were able to survive for a long time due to tight connections in the far-right sector, which allowed them to maintain reciprocal links and connections (Caiani and Wagemann 2009). Another study on 157 extremist organizations in the United States (Gerstenfeld et al. 2003) shows that most far-right websites contain external links to other extremist sites. These ties enable such extremist organizations or groups to exchange important information faster and to have access to greater knowledge base related to issues such as bomb-making, weapons training and techniques, or shared objectives. However, the density and communication between individual extremist organizations vary between countries.

A large study on the virtual far-right networks in Europe and the United States show that these networks include various types of organizations with varying ideological tendencies and objectives. Some of them adopt fascistic beliefs and neo-Nazi positions, while others show some sort of flattened, "right-wing conservatism" with anti-globalization and anti-liberalism attitudes. They vary from far-right political parties that aspire to gain political power, to militant neo-Nazi groups that spread fascistic pro-Hitler ideals; from negationist and nostalgic groups that deny the Holocaust, to cultural right-wing organizations that adopt "modern" New-Age beliefs and a kind of Celtic spiritualism. So, too, do right-wing publishers and subcultural youth organizations vary, such as skin heads and far-right rock music or sport clubs (such as soccer hooligans). Beyond "holistic ideologies," some right-wing groups focus solely on a single issue, such as abortion or immigration, and form large organizations on the basis of a specific subject (Caiani and Parenti 2013). In the American context, additional types of organizations exist online that are not common in Europe, such as White supremacist groups, Christian identity organizations, Ku Klux Klan groups, and far-right patriotic groups (e.g., the American Oklahoma Constitutional Militia), which are often armed paramilitary groups with an anti-governmental, conspiracy-laden ideology (Durham 2007).

Alongside the heterogeneity of the far-right sector, the weight and impact of the single groups vary between countries. In the United States, cultural, New Age, and neo-mystical far-right organizations make up the largest part (thirty-five percent), followed by fundamental religious and KKK groups (twenty-two percent), while political right-wing parties account for less than one percent of the whole online sector. But also, neo-Nazi and subcultural organizations represent a significant part in the network (eleven percent). On the opposite, in France political movements constitute the largest part (36.2 percent), followed by nationalistic and patriotic groups (20.7 percent), while political parties (12.1 percent), and subcultural organizations (8.6 percent) are less present in the French right-wing network. In Germany, the online right-wing sector is dominated by neo-Nazi groups (twenty-six percent), political movements (twenty-four percent), as well as subcultural organizations (nineteen percent) and nationalistic groups (thirteen percent). The Italian right-wing landscape is mainly occupied by nostalgic negationist groups (thirty-seven percent) and by subcultural organizations (twenty-four percent). While in the US far-right publishers and cultural/religious New Age groups are very common, they appear very limited in Europe. However, the virtual communities of the extreme right, both in Europe and the United Sates, seem to be fragmented and not focused on some central organizations that have monopolized power. There is no centralized umbrella organization that coordinates the communication within the network (Caiani and Parenti 2013). All the networks do not show high density; however, the German virtual far-right network appear to be the densest, while the American one the loosest. The German and Italian networks seem to communicate largely via well-connected online platforms, while the American network appears to be more "individualistic," where the majority of the websites have no external links to other extreme organizations. The German far-right network tends to be most cohesive, which means that the organizations are very close with each other. On the opposite end, in the United States the majority of the far-right organizations seem to not cooperate extensively with each other and act rather on an individual basis (Caiani et al. 2012). This implies that the far-right network in the US is far more decentralized and horizontal than those in Europe. The French network shows the highest level of centralization, which means that not all organizations show the same level of activity and initiation.

But despite this inequality in activity and approach, the extreme right network in France is organized internally according to a horizontal structure. This means that there are low inequalities between organizations in terms of what concerns receiving support or prestigious contacts from the far-right milieu (Caiani and Parenti 2013).

Recent literature on radical networks suggests that the organizational structure and the network itself are important elements in the process of recruitment, mobilization, information processing, and coordination flows among individual entities. They are also perceived to influence individual behavior and collective decision-making, as close and tight relations have been found to favor participation, even in violent terms (della Porta 1995). This is also true for radical right networks, where individuals form close ties to other ingroup members and use numerous websites to meet like-minded individuals and to mobilize and exchange information. As the previously mentioned, analysis on the various virtual far-right networks in Europe and the United States have shown (Caiani and Parenti 2013) that all of the networks employ a different internal organizational structure. While the Italian radical right network appears to be fragmented and highly diversified, the French[3] and the German networks are more centralized, denser, and focus on some few central actors. The American far-right network is even more fragmented and decentralized than the Italian one, with many isolated and dispersed organizations. The shape of such networks is perceived to be an important determinant of the forms of actions used by organizations. Hadden (2015) argues that organizational decision-making is fundamentally relational because it depends on the actions and decision of other organizations in the sector. Therefore, the ties or the level of embeddedness of an organization tend to determine its strategic choices. The empirical analysis of Hadden (2015) suggests that if an organization has ties with other organizations that use controversial, or even violent, forms of actions, this will increase the likelihood that the organization itself will also draw on violent means in the future. This assumption has been approved by an empirical study, which shows that large organizations with religious or nationalistic ideologies that form and maintain extensive alliance connections with other organizations, and that maintain control over a specific territory, tend to be more disruptive and violent. Even the most ideologically benign organizations tend to engage in homicide if they have enough close alliances. According to the authors, dense ties enable the organization to gain access to the knowledge needed to engage in deadly terrorism. Further, "the more alliances an organization makes the more likely it is to associate with peer organizations that have a permissive attitude toward killing, which may lead to competitive behavior or degradation of existing ethical commitments to avoid killing" (Asal and Rethemeyer 2008, 445).

8.4 The Radical Left Organizations

Despite the significant relationship between the organizational form and the functioning, decision-making, and survival of radical groups, there is only a limited number of empirical studies on this issue. In particular, the organizational differences between left-wing and right-wing organizations lack consistent research. Social movement literature suggests that right-wing groups tend to interact more with similarly ideologically oriented groups than left-wing groups. They also tend to interact more with political institutions and think tanks, and collaborate with political elites and receive sympathetic support in the police or military forces[4] (Caiani and Borri 2013). While previously mentioned studies assume that well-connected organizations with allied ties tend to be more disruptive, opposite studies argue that potential allies can also be detrimental for an organization. In this respect, an empirical analysis based in Italy, Germany, and the United States provides evidence that far-right groups in the US draw more on violent means than far-right groups in the two other countries. This can be explained by the lack of radical right-wing parties in the United States that can "co-determine" the strategic choices of the radical groups and act as institutional allies, which would potentially contribute to a moderation of the action repertoires (Caiani et al. 2012). However, the greater use of violence can also be explained by the available resources of the US's far-right network and the high degree of tolerance in the country toward individual freedom of expression, as well as the rights to possess and use firearms (Caiani and della Porta 2018). These material and symbolic resources leveraged one of the oldest and most violent far-right organizations in the United States, the Aryan Nations, which used to provide an umbrella framework to form and maintain allies with other radical groups, such as the Ku Klux Klan, the Christian Identity Movement, The Order, the Covenant and the Sword, the Arm of the Lord, and so on (Alexander and Pluchinsky 1992).

Radical left-wing groups in the United States do not form a well-organized network, but rather organize themselves in a military "underground" fashion. One of the oldest and most violent left-wing group in the US is the Weatherman organization. The organization was a direct offspring of a peaceful and nonviolent student organization, the Students for a Democratic Society (SDS), that proclaimed itself as a liberal and democratic New Left movement. "Not only did the SDS of the early 1960s reject the traditional solutions of the extreme left of the pre-World War II era, it also refused to grant membership to members of Communist and, in general, 'totalitarian' organizations" (Sprinzak 1998, 71). Despite its dissociation of violence and fundamentalism, the group drifted in their seven years of existence into a radical mass movement and then it split and shrank. At its 1965 national convention, the SDS dropped its "exclusionist" rule and allowed membership to "advocates of totalitarian principles" to recruit individuals to survive the political resistance (Falciola 2013). But their collaboration with the Maoist Progressive Labor party (PLP) led to an ideological and organizational shift of the group, which was now infiltrated by new "Marxist" principles and an ideological framework for a rebellious "groupthink." This led to a split of the SDS in 1969 into three fractions, which all, in fact, adopted different behavioral tactics but adhered commonly to a militant Marxist belief system (Sprinzak 1998). One of them was the Weatherman organization, which adopted a political language of delegitimation of the regime and dehumanization of individuals belonging to the system. It endorsed violence and terrorism to arouse a "socialist revolution" (Falciola 2013). Although the organization was responsible for many bombings in 1970, which took place among others in the Capitol, the Pentagon, and the New Yorker police headquarters, the underground organization failed to succeed. Its inexperienced and untrained members worried about the internal group relations instead of their ideological revolution and goals (Sprinzak 1998). To this, the radical left community didn't provide support for the violent extremist group and questioned their course of actions. Even the Weatherman's relation to the radical group Black Panther was inconsistent and characterized by strong distrust and non-affiliation. "Black constituencies did not dissent on the issue of revolutionary violence, but treated with contempt the idealistic attitude of white revolutionaries and were worried about the repression that, triggered by white radicals' attacks, could have fallen back on black militants" (Falciola 2013, 10). In addition, international allies from Vietnam and Cuba disapproved the Weatherman's violent atrocities, which enhanced its political and psychological isolation in the left-wing community.

Similar disruptions could be observed in the case of other left-wing organizations, such as the Black Panther Party for Self-Defense (BPP), which failed due to intragroup rivalry and inconsistency. The Black Liberation Army (BLA), which split off from the Black Panthers, formed a militant underground group and adopted radical and violent actions. The BLA was responsible for at least twenty fatalities, which were classified as retaliation for injustice and police brutality toward African Americans. According to an

NYPD intelligence report in 1973, the membership size of BLA never numbered more than twenty-five to thirty core members and possibly seventy-five additional supporters. Similar to their parent group, the BPP, the BLA had a disorganized and amorphous organizational structure. It was decentralized and had no common leadership, no central objectives, and no organized patterns. It lacked clear guiding principles, role prescriptions, and a strong group identity (Rosenau 2013). According to FBI documents, BLA was not perceived and classified as a terroristic organization that focuses on a particular grievance, but rather as an underground guerilla that seeks revolution (FBI 1973). However, by the end of 1975, the group's revolution seemed to be over. Thinking about the strategic weaknesses of BLA, a former group member, Russell Shoats, described the group's central weaknesses as political isolation, ideological inconsistency, and a failure to gain support from the left-wing community and the Black masses. Lacking strong ties with other political movements, the group failed in mobilizing and recruiting forces, as well as in integrating grassroots into their activities.

Learning from these miscarriages, in the following years the group's remnant tried to build and enforce ties with the left-wing network and potential supporters. It created a "Coordinating Committee" to spread their beliefs and concrete messages, to maintain ties to former members, and to communicate their collective objectives. The BLA also shifted their focus on Black nationalism, formed their collective identity based on African heritage, and identified itself as part of the Republic of New Africa (RNA), an organization that aimed to establish an independent African American state. However, the new collective identity and the networking initiatives failed to form a strong, new BLA (Rosenau 2013). In addition, the political and ideological climate in the United States had changed by the mid-1970s and popular support for the New Left and Black liberation movements had evaporated. In this time frame ideological militancy declined, which curbed the leftist constituencies. The gradual withdrawal of American forces from Vietnam also changed the attitudes toward militant participation, which particularly affected the recruitment and mobilization process of such groups. To this, the rise of feminism and climate change debate shifted the attention away from imperialism and capitalism to sexual and environmental issues. This process relocated activist's interests and attitudes toward more private concerns, which, especially in the case of feminism, took a clear stance against violence and dogmatic world views (Falciola 2013).

The rise and fall of New Left organizations in the United States has been perceived as a movement of alienated youth with no clear objectives, leadership, and structure. They represented a system of ad hoc leadership, missing communal network and lacking clear ideological messages, which contrasted with the hierarchical organization of the Old Left. The theories and beliefs arose spontaneously, changed fast, and were inconsistent, coupled with unclear and increasingly unrealistic demands for social change. With this inconsistency and instability, the groups couldn't define a clear collective identity, which in turn created a loose membership environment. As result, groups dissolved easily and were not persistent (Young 2019). Adding to this, the decline of public support led to subsequent marginalization and isolation of the groups in the political and social environments. Changing socioeconomic and political conditions diminished the attractiveness and the appeal of left-wing ideologies, which often failed to adapt to changing circumstances (Gvineria 2009).

In comparison, the left-wing network in Europe was extensively connected on a national and international level. The most successful radical left parties for most of the twentieth century in Europe were Communists, who adhered to the Marxist-driven idea of a socialist revolution, and who rejected in the first place the underlying socioeconomic structure of capitalism and its ideological principles. In the post-war period, in many Western European countries, Communist parties gained high electoral victory and were most notably present and active in Italy, France, and Austria. However, with the onset of the Cold War, the status and electoral success of communists changed in the opposite direction—with some exceptions in Finland, France, and Italy, where the Communist parties still received high support and had a high membership size, despite their exclusion from the political environment. This high support has been explained by ideological commitment. "Their exclusion from the governing elite and anti-bourgeois "anti-system" doctrines allowed communists to attract the votes both of those dissatisfied with discrete political issues such as unemployment, and of those disaffected with the political system as a whole—the parties vocalized and organized the interests of those who might otherwise be excluded from political attention" (March and Mudde 2005, 26). However, literature on Western European Communist parties points to the tension between their national and international identities and the absent consistence between them. While on the one hand almost all these parties identified themselves with the so-called World Communist Movement, on the other hand large parties like those in Finland, Italy, and France, which registered political success, were an integral part of the regional politics in their countries. They could participate in national politics and in trade unions, and they could co-determine social aspects in society, all which was denied to smaller communist organizations. The French historians Courtois and Lazar analyzed these tensions in the communist network and introduced a two-dimensional model of the Western European communist identity. They argue that the "teleological" dimension refers to the utopia of world communism and the belief of a necessary global revolution. Here the communist identity is formed by the traditional Leninist-Marxist doctrines, by the idea of avant-gardism, and by the necessity to act. It is goal-driven and marked by the objective to establish a homogeneous and cohesive unity of all Communist groups all over the world. The second, "societal" dimension, on the other hand, identifies social categories of the communist identity, which make it a part of its (local) society. It emphasizes the diversity which arises from various cultural, social, and political conditions in every country that have to be taken into consideration (Bracke and Jorgensen 2002). These two dimensions led to an "identity conflict," in which Western European Communist parties found themselves drawn between the idea of a homogeneous world communism on the one hand and as political actors in pluralist democracies on the other. Following the period of de-Stalinization in 1956, the communists in Western Europe strived for autonomy, for more egalitarianism than Soviet dogmatism in the communist network, and for the re-enforcement of their domestic identity. As result, the communists evolved toward reformism, (national) adaptation, and the abandonment of orthodox and dogmatic ideals. While in the first instance this process of change enhanced the threat of losing the shared identity and the existing power structures, some groups in the Western European communist community managed to successfully transform their organizational structures (Backes and Moreau 2008).

One such group is Partito comunista Italiano (PCI), the Italian Communist Party that adopted the concepts of autonomy and polycentrism. This implied at first a distancing from the Soviet Union and its idealistic visions of socialism by developing instead domestic strategies to gain political success. Further, PCI did not strive for a loose communist network, but rather for decentralized and regionally organized clusters of communist parties or organizations—the so-called polycentrism. The term implies that communist parties and organizations should strengthen their ties in a global network, but also form sub-entities inside the network to act effectively on a regional level. This global network should be thus formed according to a decentralized order and a fragmented power structure (Bracke and Jorgensen 2002). On the opposite, the French Communist Party, PCF, reacted in a different way to the phase of de-Stalinization. Due to severe disputes with the CPSU, the Communist Party of the Soviet Union, the French indeed endorsed the Italian idea of autonomy but rejected the modern vision of a "peaceful coexistence" (Backes and Moreau 2008). PFC criticized the Soviet Union in their abandonment of their leadership role and the idea of a socialist revolution. But the

Soviet Union's invasion of Hungary in 1957 reassured the PFC that the CPSU was still prepared to use whatever means necessary to establish its hegemonic power. To this, Khrushchev's criticism of Mao made him, in the eyes of PFC leaders, trustworthy as the unifier and defender of the communist collective identity and ideological principles. In contrast to the PCI, the PCF endorsed orthodoxy and centralized decision-making and rejected the idea of ideological autonomy, as it was perceived as a loss of discipline and ideological coherence. In this regard, the PCF became the harshest supporter of ideological rigidity and communist unity (especially against Maoism and the revisionism triggered by the PCI), and it aimed to protect its "traditional communist identity" and its influence in the global communist network. However, when, in the 1970s, the Soviet Union loosened their rigid leadership in the global communist network while advocating reformism, the PCF felt constrained to change their position. In these circumstances, the leadership of PCF formed an alliance with PCI to break with the lax policy of the CPSU and comply with PCI's reformistic ideas. As a result, a European communist network grew where smaller organizations and groups could express freely their opinion and idealistic ideas (Bracke and Jorgensen 2002). But despite the increasing polycentrism and the formation of regional networks, the intentions and idealistic perspectives differed among the parties. While PCI, the Spanish PCS, and some other small groups from Belgium, Austria, and Switzerland endorsed polycentrism, PCF, but also the Danish, Norwegian, and Portuguese groups, appealed to traditionality and rigid coherence. Smaller Northern European communist groups, like those in Great Britain, Sweden, and Iceland were only in favor of pure autonomy. Their loyalty toward the world communism decreased steadily and there was no motivation left to construct a strong Western European communist identity. This inconsistency, enhanced ambiguity, and lack of concrete leadership and a shared identity led to decreased support within the global communist network, eventually prompting a crisis of ideology and organization (March and Mudde 2005).

By the 1970s, electoral, intellectual, and membership support of the Communists across Europe experienced a long-term decline. However, at the same time militant underground organizations, which unlike their political counterparts, rejected the democratic system per se, increased in size. Such "fighting communist organizations" have been classified as small, urban, extremist groups that are driven by a Marxist-Leninist ideology and the dream of a socialist revolution. Their main objective was to overthrow the democratic system and to replace it with a vaguely defined "proletarian dictatorship." The most active and significant organizations which operated in Western Europe since the 1970s have been, among others, the Red Army Faction (RAF) in

West Germany, the Red Brigades (RB) in Italy, Direct Action (DA) in France, the Fighting Communist Cells (CCC) in Belgium, the First of October Anti-Fascist Resistance Groups (GRAPO) in Spain, and the Revolutionary Organization 17 November (17N) in Greece.

The RAF, for example, is a small Marxist-Leninist extremist group that is perceived to be rooted in the Baader-Meinhof Gang of 1970, and even goes back to the violent student protests during the late 1960s in West Germany. The goal of the RAF was to destroy the current political, economic, and social regime in West Germany and replace it with a vaguely defined proletarian sovereignty. It considered itself a member of an international network of revolutionaries that reject, or fight against, imperialism, capitalism, and fascism. Of all left-wing extremist groups, the RAF is perceived as being the most pervasive, resilient, and effective organization in Europe. It survived the arrests or deaths of three leadership generations and the arrests of more than 150 of its core members, and it managed to form strong mobilizing propaganda forces even within the prisons (Alexander and Pluchinsky 1992).

Starting with the first generation from 1970–1972, the RAF members were characterized by the drive to mobilize masses to incite a socialist revolution, a people's war (Volkskrieg). The leading figures of the first generation were Andreas Baader and his girlfriend Gudrun Ensslin, as well as Ulrike Meinhof and Horst Mahler.[5] All members of the RAF came from a bourgeois familial background and had a similar level of education. Personality profiles of all RAF members show that almost all of them were young and highly motivated to change the system, and were not greedy nor selfish (Moghadam 2012). The group organized itself as an urban guerrilla, based on the guidelines laid out in Carlos Marighella's *Mini-Handbook of the Urban Guerilla*. The members carried false identification documents, conducted bank-robberies to assure financial subsistence, and carried hand weapons to protect themselves from arrest. They endorsed violence and were willing to draw on radical means to attain their collective objectives. To act effectively and be persistent the group adopted a nonhierarchical cellular structure, in which only members knew the identity of other group members. Despite their goal to incite a "people's war," the ideology of the organization was not strictly defined nor followed. Action was more important than following dogmatic doctrines, and "courage and steely determination" was worth more than theoretical discussions (Alexander and Pluchinsky 1992). Historians thus argue that the ideology of the group lacked consistency, theoretical "justification," and concrete guiding principles. The RAF formed their beliefs around anti-fascistic and anti-imperialistic assumptions, borrowing elements from Marx, Mao, and Marcuse, and from all those who supported their aversion toward the existing order. Their main cause was in fact to eliminate the existing social, political, and economic system, but they failed at the same time to provide concrete ideas of the future order to follow (Moghadam 2012). The several arrests of the core members in 1972, the voluntary drop-outs due to ideological inconsistency, and the decreased support from the German population led to a mitigation of the first generation.

The second generation that endured from 1972 to 1982, and the third generation that continued and declined in 1998, have not been considered as meaningful as the first chapter because of their decreased ideological significance and loss of realism[6] (Von Stetten 2009). Elements such as violence, adventurism, and excitement seemed to play a more important role than ideological discussions and practical guiding solutions. To this, ideological splits within the organization led to intragroup conflicts, while in 1996 some members openly called for the RAF to dissolve. Finally, in 1998 the group openly declared its resolution. In summing up the development and failures of the RAF organization, it becomes clear that interpersonal and organizational dynamics played a significant role in its decline. Differences in ideology, tactics, and strategy within the group, and the lack of a strong collective identity, especially among the last two generations, also contributed to the group's resolution. To this, lack of external support and enhanced isolation increased the number of dropouts and vaulted the group into a chronic shortage of recruits. Former members of the second the third generation also started to feel a general meaninglessness about their actions and ideology (Moghadam 2012).

The collapse of the Soviet Union in 1991 and the fall of the Berlin Wall were additional factors contributing to the group's decay, leading to a general decline of left-wing extremist and communist organizations in Europe. Some political parties decided to change their ideological identity, such as the Italian, the Finnish, and the Swedish communist parties. Some others, such as the French PCF, tried to distance themselves from the past but to maintain their core communist identity, while the Greek KKE remained loyal to its communist past and belief system (Backes and Moreau 2008). While in Western Europe, some of the left-wing organizations moved toward the democratic left, in Eastern Europe nationalistic and authoritarian tendencies remained firm. The success of extreme and communistic parties in Eastern Europe, even after the collapse of the Soviet Union, could be explained by the problems of the socioeconomic transformation and the persistence of a "socialist value culture." Rising unemployment, inflation, and perceived loss of control enhanced the demand for collective solidarity, state welfarism, and governmental protection (March and Mudde 2005).

Departing from Europe, the Shining Path (Sl or Sendero Luminoso) of Peru is by far the most active and violent underground left-wing extremist group, accounting for 3,713 incidents, of which ninety-five percent were carried out domestically (Enders and Sandler 2012). It was founded in 1970 by Abimael Guzmán Reynoso, a former professor of philosophy at the University of Huamanga in Ayachucho. He aimed to incite a rural-based revolt against the Lima regime under a Maoist ideology and spent years on strategic planning, recruitment, and ideological indoctrination (McCormick 2003). In contrast to its European counterparts, the SL had a dogmatic and consistent ideology, a strong and complex organization, with a substantial grass-roots support structure, as well as a strong collective identity. It was directed by the National Central Committee, composed of Abimael Guzmán Reynoso and a few top lieutenants. The Central Committee was responsible for the formation and preservation of the belief system and the elaboration of a strategy and policy for the entire organization. Beneath the National Central Committee, six regional Committees were formed: the Northern, Central, Southern, Eastern, Primary and the Metropolitan, which all functioned independently but complied with guiding principles of the National Committee. Each of these regional Committees consisted of several departments and local branches and was responsible for planning and performing of all regional activities, starting from recruitment and indoctrination to military operations. The Regional Committees were again subdivided into specific zones and cells, each having its own military detachments. These subdivisions enabled the Shining Path to use local resources, such as the knowledge of the local people, and to process information faster to make strategic decisions. Therefore, the National Central Committee granted a certain amount of autonomy to their regional committees and local commanders, which enabled them to react faster and more efficiently to changing circumstances. This organizational form has led to enhanced mobility and fast adaption, which in turn has increased the success rate of Sendero's operations.

In contrast, the Peruvian Army cannot respond in a similarly fast and efficient manner to the group's actions, due to its very hierarchical and centralized command structure. Beyond regional autonomy and efficient adaptation, the organization, as a whole, is able to act as a strong unit due to its shared beliefs and a collective identity. This is also the case for individual cells, independent of their size and impact, which receive operational independence. This autonomy, however, does not imply any level of strategic decision-making, which resides in the hands of the National Central Committee alone. This combination of personal initiative, regional autonomy, and organizational consistence forms one of Sendero's core (success) principles (Tarazona-Sevillano 1994).

One of the few analyses on Sendero's success assumes that the leader–follower relationship was unique in this case (see Ron 2001). The group leader, Abimael Guzmán Reynoso, is believed to have a superior vision of the world and "extraordinary" human qualities, neither of which are questioned by the group followers. The members comply with his beliefs, orders, and guiding principles, and provide the leader strong support and devotion. Political research suggests that such an intra-organizational relationship generates a strong bond of command between the leader of an organization and its rank-and-file membership. The leader is viewed as a heroic figure who motivates the followers to act in the service "of a moral and superior purpose." This generated a high group cohesion, solidarity, and internal discipline, which enabled the organization to remain prevalent, despite several drawbacks throughout the years. Researchers thus argue that the Shining Path exhibits many of the qualities of a religious cult. "It is founded, in a sense, on the revelations of Comrade Gonzalo, has divided the world sharply between good and evil, maintains a highly rigid belief system, and demands absolute commitment on the part of its membership" (McCormick 1987, 119). To this, the organization was "completely isolated from society" and had "no legal or open front that might serve as a source of intra-organizational conflict" (119). The overall success of the Shining Path has thus been attributed to its structural integrity, which is the ability to remain unified, to avoid fragmentation, and to sustain intra-organizational consistency, but also to its rigid and closed belief system and a cohesive shared identity.

The second most-active and violent extremist organization, according to the Global Terrorism Database, is the Farabundo Marti National Liberation Front (FMLN) of El Salvador. It was formed in 1980 as an umbrella organization for five terrorist groups: the Popular Liberation Forces (FPL), the People's Revolutionary Army (ERP), the National Resistance (RN), the Central American Revolutionary Worker's Party (PRTC), and the Salvadoran Communist Party (PCS). These groups are considered as paramilitary organizations that all aimed to overthrow the military junta, which, in the eyes of FMLN, was responsible for social inequality and resource deprivation in the country (Enders and Sandler 2012). FMLN recruited and mobilized members primarily from the rural areas in northern El Salvador, where it established and operated training camps for newcomers and the following generation. However, the majority of the leaders, intermediary cadres, and many of the rank-and-file had previously been professors, rectors, or students at the University of El Salvador (Behlendorf et al. 2012). The FMLN, like other revolutionary left-wing groups in Latin America, adopted a radical belief system, which was their main appeal to attract and mobilize recruits. Therefore, the ideology of the organization was perceived to be the most important part to ensure member's loyalty and coherence. Contrary to Sendero Luminoso, FMLN was formed out of five extremist groups who agreed on the same beliefs, goals, and tactics—in particular, they endorsed socialism and rejected capitalism, shared a Marxist theoretical and analytical framework, and accepted the use of violence and arms to reach their goals. However, differences within the groups remained in force. Each group maintained its own organizational structure, articles of association, procured its own financing, and autonomously elected its leaders. Members maintained their solidarity and discipline to their own individual organization and not to the umbrella organization FMLN. "The groups remained divided over the interpretation of the national reality, the appropriateness of alliances, and the strategy for taking power. They disagreed about whether the FMLN should pursue a prolonged popular war or an insurrection strategy and how much attention to dedicate to political work. The groups had achieved structural integrity, but cohesion[7] remained elusive" (Allison and Alvarez 2012, 95). The consequences of the FMLN's lack of cohesion was first observed during a planned attack in January 1981 that failed, at least partly, due to intra-organizational disputes. There was no common objective related to the planned offensive and no common elaborated strategies. This inconsistency was especially driven by the lack of mutual support and trust among the organizations (Grenier 1991). After its failure, FMLN moved into the countryside and mobilized support from mainly rural communities. However, it still formed informal allies with urban organizations, such as the National Union of Salvadoran Workers (UNTS), and it was strategically linked to the Democratic Revolutionary Front (FDR). Several independent brigades and commanders completed the elusive framework of the organization. Despite the ideological homogeneity (the fate of "revolution"), the decisional and operational power among the different groups, actors, and leaders was not clearly settled. But even the structural integrity, which generated a strong unity between the single groups and individuals, crumbled in the post-war period. Different opinions and attitudes within the FMLN toward the end of the Civil War[8] and the following negotiations generated a long-term ideological divide in the organization. The FMLN's structural integrity soon fractured, but greater cohesion emerged ten years later, after the peace accords in 1992, when FMLN transformed from a revolutionist extremist organization to a political left party (Allison and Alvarez 2012).

In contract to the Shining Path and the FMLN, the Revolutionary Armed Forces of Colombia (FARC) also operated on a transnational level. It is one of the most successful guerrilla organizations in the Americas that has survived decades of international and national counter-insurgency strategies and political pressure campaigns. Beyond the often mentioned weak political and economic structures in Colombia, the ability of FARC to adapt to changing circumstances and a precise organizational restructuring enabled the group to maintain its long-lasting prevalence. FARC's initial organizational structure has often been portrayed as a wheel or a star, encompassing a centralized command structure and a hierarchical system based on a Leninist ideology. This enabled the organization to pursue a clear chain of command and to extend its forces into regions that specialized in certain activities (such as the production of narcotics in one region, trafficking in another, etc.) (Eccarius-Kelly 2012). Although the organizational form of FARC has often been portrayed as being strictly hierarchical, the geographical challenges of the country made it impossible for the Secretariat, the direct command, to exercise control over the whole organization. The Secretariat consists of seven individuals who are responsible for strategic decision-making and for issuing operational orders to the blocs. Despite their geographical distance, all seven members communicate regularly and rule by consensus (Gentry and Spencer 2010).

When FARC was formed in 1964, it collaborated intensively with the Communist Party of Colombia (PCC), which led them to create an overt political movement in the late 1980s—the Popular Unity (UP). But due to deviations in tactics and objectives, FARC and UP broke over irreconcilable differences, followed by FARC's permanent split with the PCC by 1995. Instead, FARC created the Clandestine Colombian Communist Party (PCCC) and established a military-run intelligence organization. The base of FARC was thus formed by "the front—a geographically-based, tactically-oriented, political/military organization, composed mainly of smaller fighting units that primarily conduct military operations consistent with directives they receive from above. Fronts are numbered in chronological order of their creation (up to about 70) and have varying numbers of fighters that range from several dozen to several hundred" (Gentry and Spencer 2010, 457). Most of the fighters are young men, or even children, while women represent an appreciable minority (between twenty to forty percent). The basic combat unit of the front is the company, which is usually composed of two guerilla groups of roughly twenty-five fighters, each having two squads of twelve individuals. The squads imply two "commandos" of six combatants, which comprises two triads of three fighters each. Two or more of such companies form a "column." Beyond these basic combat units, FARC had tactical combat units, composed of eighteen fighters, which were mostly responsible for temporal missions. The fronts are organized into five blocks and two joint commandos. FARC established the blocs in the 1990s to better control and "categorize" the high number of the fronts. Blocs have operational-level military responsibility, but their regional jurisdiction also obliges them to process and collect useful, non-military information. The two geographically largest and operationally most important blocs lie in the East and South of Colombia, where sparsely populated lowlands form the heartland of the organization (Gentry and Spencer 2010).

Despite the significance of the Secretariat, FARC's organizational structure displayed a rather decentralized system based mutual relations instead of control and doctrinal command. The group succeeded because of the organizational discipline, the shared goals and ideals, and the personal relationships that senior leaders had with each other (Saab and Taylor 2009).

8.5 The Radical Religious Organizations

Although political and religious ideologies seem to differ in their organizational structure, research and case studies provide evidence that significant similarities exist (e.g., Whitehouse and McQuinn 2013; Ilardi 2009). Considering the findings in Part II of this book, we saw that religious ideologies can provide viable reconciliation options to serve psychological human needs. These need-serving capabilities are especially enforced through the organizational structure of religious groups—the mostly vertical, centralized order; the prescriptive roles; and the strict adherence to rules, beliefs, and norms generate a consistent and meaningful life for the adherents.[9] However, literature on religions emphasizes that understanding their organizational structure and dynamics requires differentiation among religious groups that display different organizational characteristics. Traditional literature distinguishes between four types of religious organizations: church, denomination, cult, and sect. The church is perceived as the strongest institution, and it bases its structure on a universalistic, vertical, and centralized decision-making. The "ideal-typical" church, irrespective of their type and foundation, demands strict loyalty, norm abidance, firm belief, and rigid adherence to a distinctive lifestyle. Churches predefine a social order, rules, and norms which have to be obeyed and accepted, and disseminate a closed and consistent world view (Iannaccone 1994). However, traditional churches can also imply more lenient and progressive characteristics and favor diversity, tolerance, and dialogue, as well as various sects, denominations, and cults, which can display hierarchical and dogmatic traits, favoring absolutism, conformity, and order (Bromley and Melton 2012).

Historical research reveals that "the mainstream" church attendance has been declining in the US, while "sects" or alternative denominations, such as the Mormons and the Assemblies of God, now outnumber "mainline" denominations, such as the Episcopal Church (Finke and Stark 1992). Such sects or denominations mostly portray a strict order and rigid norms: for example, Mormons, currently the sixth largest religious body in the United States, follow a strict nutritional diet (no caffeine, alcohol, etc.) and show a centralized, patriarchal, and authoritarian organizational structure. Mormons, or Latter-day-Saints, have a single leader (Joseph Smith) for the entire organization—the "prophet, seer and revelator—and the only person entitled to receive divine instruction pertaining to the church as a whole" (Campbell and Monson 2003, 23). Dietary restrictions and other obligations are set up in "the Mormon World of Wisdom," a consistent manifesto written by the leader, which provides guiding principles and establishes identifiable boundaries for the members. The rules and norms governing daily activities and practices, information processing, and collective behavior enable the members to form a shared identity and to set themselves apart from other Americans. They form clear boundaries between those who have "embraced the gospel of Jesus Christ" and who have adopted the ancient faith and traditions, and those who had not. Mormons employ an aggressive missionization in an effort to create "safe havens" for those who want to escape "the dangerous world," and where "the saints" could survive the "coming apocalypse" (Taysom 2011).

Founded in 1830, the religious organization has been governed as a commune, including a bank, which was integrated into local and state politics, and a militia to secure defense of the group. "By 1835, the church is organized into a Presidency, which consisted of Smith and two councilors, the twelve apostles, a group called the seventies, and two high councils. [. . .] In addition, every male was made an elder, and if one demonstrated faith and perseverance, any elder could move up the ranks of the hierarchy. [. . .], this method of promotion practically ensured aged prophets in the future [and] helped the long run viability of the church by raising the cost of becoming a prophet for personal gain" (Allen 1995, 110). It identifies, enforces, and rewards high contributors who are willing to invest personal resources, thereby limiting free riders in the community: by imposing rigid rules and behavioral norms, potential members must decide whether to follow fully such rules and to be a part of the community or not. This means that possible free riders, or those who will not commit fully to the dogmatic beliefs and norms, will select themselves out of the group. Accordingly, the rigidity and dogmatism of such organizations screens out less committed individuals, thereby creating a homogeneous group of coherent and submissive individuals (McBride 2007).

Sociologists (e.g., Benson and Dorsett 1971; Allen 1995) thus assume that the organizational structure of a denomination is closely related to its doctrines and ideology, which also seem to determine its functioning and success. Allen (1995) identified three categories of a church's organizational structures, based on the ability of the clergy to manage and control transactions and wealth. (i) In congregational churches all decisions are made at the congregational level, where all rights, power, and control derive from the community. Usually, these churches adhere to the Bible but allow congregational members for a subjective interpretation of the passages. (ii) In hierarchical churches, power, control, and responsibilities flow from the highest officers down to the members. Usual ingroup members have neither direct influence nor decisional power in the church and must oblige to its propagated doctrines, rules, and beliefs. The Bible is the only source of authority, which can be represented by an earthy prophet or agent who serves as an interpreter of a church's doctrines and beliefs. (iii) Denominational churches are governed by middle-level authority, which consists of both clergy and chosen representatives. The Bible represents the sole authority, which is interpreted by the denomination alone, not the individual. These variations determine the manifestations of religious groups; for example, the decisional power of authorities, the control over religious education curriculum, the ownership of church property, the communication between group members and authorities, recruitment and promotion methods, and so on.

Accordingly, a religious group chooses the organizational form that maximizes group membership and that is consistent with its ideological doctrines. In this regard, an economic study, using a spatial model of structural choices, argues that the organizational structure of a church can be multidimensional, with the attempt to easily adjust to changing circumstances and to ensure membership growth, subject to their ideological constraints. The authors conclude that "a church will maximize its membership when it minimizes the distance between its organizational structure and that preferred by the population, subject to doctrinal constraints" (Mao and Zech 2002, 69).

Considering these results, we may argue that religious organizations choose the organizational form that strongly relates to their ideology and to the needs and preferences of a given society. This means that the chosen organizational form is a "calculated" outcome, where the payoff is measured in the membership size and ideological adherence. In other, and oversimplified, words, the organizational size adjusts to the ideology and the needs of a social group. Churches that are more individualistic in their ideology, which implies a free interpretation of the Bible by its adherents, choose congregational, rather than hierarchical, organizational structure. On the opposite, churches, or religious groups that are Prophetic in their ideology, implying authority, strict order, and rule adherence, will choose a hierarchical organizational form in which congregation members have no direct impact in church matters and must obey the rules from above (e.g., Mormon Church, the Roman Catholic Church)[10] (Mao and Zech 2002).

Another economic study postulates that especially hierarchical religious organizations with rigid beliefs and strict obligations tend to attract more adherents (Iannaccone 1992). As discussed in Part II of this book, individuals choose an ideology that resonates with their underlying needs and preferences. They also decide how many resources to invest in engaging and following that particular ideology. On the other hand, ideological groups can only survive with high levels of commitment and collective actions of their adherents. This means that ideological groups, like churches, sects, cults, or religious extremist groups, want to avoid free riding and instead mobilize individuals to invest personal resources and to contribute to the group's objectives. Iannaccone (1992) suggests that costly demands, such as sacrifice and stigma, can solve this dilemma. Such demands can be dietary restrictions, sexual prohibitions, distinctive dress and grooming, restrictions surrounding modern medicine or Western education, and many more. "Costly demands mitigate the free-rider problems that otherwise undermine a religious group. They do so for two reasons. First, they create a barrier to group entry, a barrier that screens out half-hearted members. No longer is it possible just to drop in and reap the benefits of attendance or membership. To take part, you must pay a price; you must accept the stigmas and sacrifices demanded of all members. Casual members are unwilling to bear these costs. High costs have a second effect. They stimulate participation among those who join the group. They do so, not by somehow transforming human nature, but by increasing the relative value of group activities" (Iannaccone 1992, 127). That said, religious groups with high demands, a strict order, rule abidance, and a supply of exclusive goods and activities, attract individuals whose preferences and needs match these group characteristics. Those who join such religious groups and bear high personal costs are also more willing to engage in group activities, and even risk their lives for the purpose of the group. An empirical study provides evidence that the most lethal and successful extremist organizations are those that are large, control territory, have a wide and well-connected network, and follow a particular religion (Asal and Rethemeyer 2008). This means that organizational structure directly affects the capabilities and viability of religious organizations.

One of those lethal and successful organizations is Al-Qaeda. Al-Qaeda is an international terrorist organization with clear objectives, strict membership, and a hierarchical organizational structure. The origin of the Al-Qaeda organization is believed to lie in the resistance of the Soviet occupation of

Afghanistan, but the ideological roots are more far-reaching. The ideology was inspired by the writings of Ibn Taymiyah, a thirteenth-century Islamic scholar, who first introduced the concept of Dar al-Islam, Dar al-Kufr, and Dar al-Harb. Dar al-Islam, which can be translated as "the house of Islam," describes the region where the Muslim rule is present, and where Sharia law is enforced. Dar al-Kufr, which means "the house of unbelievers," comprises the areas that reject Islam, while Dar al-Harb ("the house of war") describes the regions in which (present or future) conflicts between the Islam and unbelievers take place. These concepts clearly separate those who belong to the Muslim world and live under the Sharia law, and those who do not. Both Al-Qaeda and the Islamic State (IS) adopt these categories, which are enforced by strict Islamic rules (strict adherence to the writings of Quran) (Burke 2004). This segregation between true believers and unbelievers, and the intention to use violence (*jihad*) against unbelievers, is also reflected in the organizational structure of Al-Qaeda. Many scholars have ascribed Al-Qaeda the role of an umbrella organization—"the base" of all Islamic movements around the globe and the center for all operational activities of "global *jihad*." The organization assumes a strict and clear-cut hierarchical structure (Figure 8.3). At the very top is the Amir, the leader, who holds direct responsibility over all operations and activities of Al-Qaeda; for many years, the Amir was Osama bin Laden. The Amir possesses religious, operational, and logistic authority and makes decisions about internal and external operations around the globe. He also oversees and approves the annual financial plan, the annual work plan, and the annual objectives, which are adjusted to changing conditions and developments. He also decides about promotions and all senior positions in the organization.

The Secretary works for the Amir and is responsible for secretarial duties, such as organizing his appointments, work schedule, or external meetings outside the group. The Deputy represents the leader, who delegates to him certain duties. After the unification of several organizations that aimed to "fight against the Jews and the crusaders," which was dominated by Al-Qaeda, Dr. Ayman al-Zawahiri served as the Deputy of Osama bin Laden. The Command Council, which is nominated by the leader every second year, is the highest decision-making body in the organization. The members of the council organize, plan, and supervise all activities; consult the leader by all his decisions; and authorize the organization's regulations, policy, financial, and working plans; and elect the members of the various committees. The council consists of seven to ten members, who are the "top senior managers" of the organization and who are responsible for the every-day business of the organization. The Amir (and his Secretary), the Deputy, and the Council Committee represent the authority and main decision-making unit of the organization.

340 Ideology and the Microfoundations of Conflict

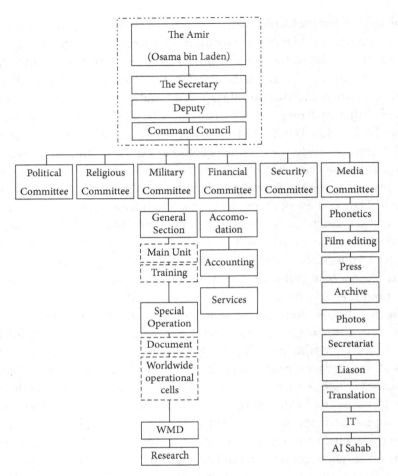

Figure 8.3 The Organizational Structure of Al-Qaeda
Source: Gunaratna and Oreg (2010, 1055).

The subunits consist of various departments that are responsible for different operations of the organization. The military committee trains and prepares, both mentally and physically, the soldiers of the organization, the *Mujahidin*. It is also responsible for the combat and military technical skills of the *Mujahidin*, their success, and mental (ideological) preparedness based on the readings of the Quran. The military committee consists of four main units: the internal general section, the special operations unit, the WMD (nuclear weapons section), and the research unit. The general section is responsible for ongoing wars and conflicts that are fought on a national level (i.e., inside Afghanistan and the Afghanistan–Pakistan border zone). The main unit is responsible for the fight itself and is subdivided according to different geographical regions, each supervised by a senior Al-Qaeda operative, while the training unit is responsible for the training of the soldiers. The special operations unit is responsible for discrete, international operations outside of Afghanistan. Both the WMD (nuclear weapon section) and the research unit are secret units, and there is no information about their responsibilities and activities available.

The political committee establishes relations to other *jihad* movements and is responsible for creating a dense network, while the religious committee decides if particular courses of action conform with Sharia law. The media committee works as a marketing and propaganda unit and is responsible for spreading the ideology in the general Muslim population. The committee, which is one of the most important units in the organization, has several subdepartments that are responsible for the IT, the social media content, the editing of movies and videos, translation, photography, phonetics, the printing press, and so on. The security committee collects and processes important information regarding operational security and forwards the analyses to its senior leaders to prevent information leaks or infiltration. It also observes and classifies each individual who wants to join the organization to prevent espionage. And finally, the financial (and administrative) committee undertakes different administrative tasks for all members of Al-Qaeda and their families. The accommodation subunit welcomes guests at the airport and provides accommodation for them, the accounting subunit is responsible for transferring funds, and the interorganizational services subunit provides members and their families goods and services to assure their well-being, such as health services, groceries, school, cars, hosing, electricity, and water provision (Gunaratna and Oreg 2010).

However, some scholars (Cebrowski and Garstka 1998; Burke 2004) noticed that Al-Qaeda transformed from a centrally controlled and hierarchically organization to a network-centric organization to easily adjust to fast changing circumstances and external conditions. Hence, Al-Qaeda changed its business of warfare; that is, it shifted the view of members as independent and loose beings to the awareness that they are embedded actors who shape the success and functioning of the organization, and it changed their organization into a more fluid and dynamic network to make fast strategic choices to adapt and survive in a fast-changing environment. As a result, Al-Qaeda formed a conglomerate of franchises, which allowed it to establish offshoot organizations in Iraq, Algeria, Yemen, Somalia, Syria, and the Indian Subcontinent.[11] This allowed the organization to operate on a local level, use and process information faster, and target the local population for recruitment.

A similar network-centric structure is displayed by the terrorist organization, the Islamic State (IS), also named ISIS (Islamic State in Iraq and Syria[12]). The bureaucratic organization puts high emphasis on their military operations, ideological propaganda, and finance. Compared to Al-Qaeda, which relied heavily on external funds and donors, IS focuses on maintaining financial independence. In doing so, the organization has developed multiple sources of income, including oil, gas, agriculture, taxation, extortion, kidnapping, black market antique selling, and many more ventures, which has made IS the wealthiest terrorist organization worldwide, earning approximately $2 million per day in 2014. Hence, it was estimated that, in 2014, the Islamic State was worth close to $2 billion (Lister 2014). Beyond ensuring financial independence, IS aimed for establishing a self-organized and governed Islamic state—a combination of strict law, strict order, its own taxation and security systems, and provision of social services to its members. This means that the IS's key objective is not to act mainly as a terrorist organization, but to establish an Islamic state, in both Syria and Iraq, with its own economic, political, social, and legal systems. Providing order and key services to the public living in instability, threat, and harsh conditions enabled the organization to be accepted on a local level. IS employs a strictly hierarchical and bureaucratic organizational structure (Figure 8.4), similar to that of Al-Qaeda, covering a chain of command, the Amir, various committees, deputies, a cabinet, local leaders, military commanders, Sharia commanders, a media department, and local fighters (Antony 2020). Before his accession in 2010, Abu Bakr al-Baghdadi was the Amir of the organization. He had a personal advisor (formerly Haji

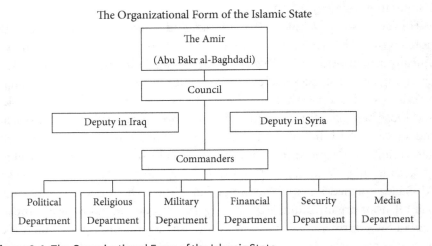

Figure 8.4 The Organizational Form of the Islamic State
Source: Based on various information such as Lister (2014), Antony (2020), Spiegel International (2015)

Bakr), two deputies (one for Syria and one for Iraq), an eight-man cabinet that served him as counselors, and a military council of, at most, thirteen men. While Baghdadi justified his knowledge about Islam by his (apparent) PhD in Islamic Studies from the Islamic University of Baghdad and his work as an imam and preacher in Iraq, his deputies have crucial military and intelligence experience, which contributed significantly to the operational success of the organization. Moreover, in 2014, the organization accounted for more than one thousand medium and top-level field commanders, who held technical, military, and security experience. Next to field commanders, the organization also maintains a cabinet of ministers, who are managing various departments within the organization, such as the media, finance, military, civil duties, or political department (Lister 2014).

Because no official documents about the organizational structure of IS exist so far, researchers rely on unpublished governmental reports or investigations from journals like that from *Spiegel International* (2015). The US Department of Defense, for example, reports in unpublished documents that IS operated as a complex, hierarchical, and bureaucratic organization between 2005 and 2010, which established local branches to make excessive income. "Higher-ranking commanders would examine the revenues and redistribute the funds to provincial or local subsidiaries that were in dire straits or needed additional money to conduct attacks [. . .] Reallocation and payroll costs—compensation to members and the families of deceased members—were by far the largest expenses [. . .] accounting for as much as 56% of all payouts at certain points of time" (Lister 2014, 22). *Spiegel International* (2015) reports that the most critical component of the organization, and possibly the one that leads to its success, is their intelligence operations unit "Emni." "Emni" derives from the Arabic root "amn," which can be translated as "trust," "security," and "safety" (in Farsi, "Amniyat," and in Turkish, "Emniyet," both means "security").

For the Islamic State, "Emni" basically implies an intelligence unit that is responsible for collecting and processing information, as well as planning and executing global attacks. The Emni consists of the regional and district level (Figure 8.5).[13] Both levels are responsible for collecting information for potential territories to acquire and plots in Syria, Iraq, and globally. Further, they collect information about the members inside the organization and about those who want to get in, in particular, those who come without "references." They gather and analyze information about potential threats to the organization but are also responsible for disseminating ideology and fear inside the organization and on a global scale. Moreover, both levels are responsible for recruiting and deploying new foreign fighters, disseminating propaganda

344 Ideology and the Microfoundations of Conflict

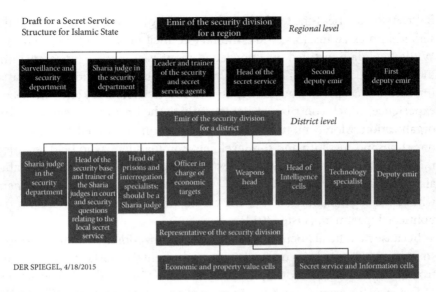

Figure 8.5 The "Emni" Structure of the Islamic State
Source: Spiegel International (2015). https://www.spiegel.de/international/world/islamic-state-files-show-structure-of-islamist-terror-group-a-1029274.html.

and news about the organization of various media channels, sending spies and recruiters in Turkey and other countries, ensuring that there are no leaks, networking with other rival terrorist groups, and making business plans (Speckhard and Yayla 2017). The Emni enjoys a prestigious status in the organization because those who are selected into the intelligence unit have more authority and decisional power than other high-status positions in the organization (e.g., police unit [*hisbah*] or foreign fighters' unit). Members of the Emni also have high financial resources at their disposal, which they use for propaganda and information acquisition. Information is gathered, in particular, about members inside the organization so as to identify potential spies, and about new incoming fighters who want to join the organization. In doing so, the Emni keeps detailed lists and personal files about each member of the organization and the foreign fighters, including cover letters, letters of application with detailed questionnaires about their level of religious knowledge, former military training, and criminal experiences, and also personal information, such as hobbies or telephone numbers (Spiegel International 2015).

This structure enables the organization to have control on a local level, receive fast information, and observe their fighters. Beyond their intelligence unit, IS also possesses considerable territorial control, a number of weapons systems and vehicles, more than thirty-one thousand fighters, as well as an assortment of anti-tank guided missiles, anti-aircraft guns, and air-defense systems. The organization also has a number of training camps, in which new recruits must undergo several weeks of religious and military training, and some "post offices," in which communication and information acquisition take place on a local level. Moreover, the organization uses information and their massive financial resources to gain control in some areas by providing security, food, and social services to encourage popular support. "Local citizens living under IS rule have described its local administration as "fast and efficient" with "everything coordinated [and all] parts of the administration are linked, [they] share information and in general seem good at working together" (Lister 2014, 25).

This implies that IS does not act as an underground terrorist organization but as a "governmental" organization, or even a state, that provides its citizens vital resources, social services, and well-organized local administration. This governance hence serves fundamental needs of individuals: IS provides existential security in terms of money, food, accommodation, and health services, and it provides a structured system that serves the needs for certainty, order, consistency, and control. But also, relational needs are addressed, in particular, of discontent Sunni living in Shia-led governments, who feel deprived of their religious identity and rights. Next to their hierarchical and bureaucratic structure, IS implements strict daily rules and a strict form of Sharia law that all members must follow, including punishments for violations; the enforcement of attendance of the five daily prayers; strict prohibition of drugs, alcohol, gambling, non-Islamic music and tobacco; strict clothing rules; and gender segregation. But also, non-Muslim citizens living in Syria and Iraq receive protection from IS, as long as they regularly pay a poll tax and abide by strict rules, including not consuming or selling pork and alcohol, not building places of worship, not wearing or showing visible signs of faith, and not bearing weapons. However, this form of "protection" implies a degradation to second-class citizens, who were always subject to existential threat and had minimal rights, if any (Lister 2014).

All in all, IS's ultimate goal is to establish a Sunni Islamic state that provides law and order to its citizens, including strict behavioral rules and beliefs; male and female police forces, who control and enforce the abidance of traditional civil and Sharia law; and the establishment of appropriate Sharia courts. Female police forces, in particular, played an important role in maintaining the newly established social order and rules. Several interviews of Syrian IS defectors revealed "that women are the most brutal enforcers and take women who infringe on the dress and moral codes of ISIS to prison to flog and bite them" (Almohammad and Speckhard 2017, 2). Beyond strict law and rules enforcement, the IS spends a significant amount of its financial resources to provide social services to its members, such as electricity, water, and gas supply, food provision, and health care—all what serves the existential needs of a civilian population. "For example, after assuming control of much of Deir Ezzor governorate in July 2014, IS funded the reduction of bread prices from 200 Syrian Pounds to 45 and also made it mandatory for bakeries to provide *zakat* (a charitable obligation in Islam) to the poor. In Mosul, IS established a free hospital a day before capturing the city and later capped monthly rent prices at a more affordable $85. Civilian bus services are frequently established and normally offered for free. Electricity lines, roads, sidewalks, and other critical infrastructure are repaired; postal services are created; free healthcare and vaccinations for children are offered; soup kitchens are established for the poor; construction projects are offered loans; and Islam-oriented schools are opened for boys and girls. In Raqqa, IS even operates a consumer protection office, which has closed shops for selling poor quality products. Put simply, IS attempts to provide the same services that a nation-state offers to its citizens, but, according to the group, in a more ethical manner" (Lister 2014, 28).

Considering this, it becomes apparent that both Al-Qaeda and the Islamic State, provided full-fledged services to their members, which exceeded the standard organizational offers. This enables them to address various fundamental needs of individuals, who in turn accept the established mode of governance. Similar community services have also been provided by other religious extremist organizations, such as Boko Haram or Hamas, which could address a variety of deprived human needs. Especially in environments with a partial government that only follows parochial interests and neglects the interests of the broad society, extremist organizations can gain high resonance among the deprived. This means that factors such as political and economic corruption; lack of social and educational opportunities; inequality; lack of vital resources such as water, gas, food, and health care; and also environmental degradation and human insecurity deprive individuals from serving their fundamental human needs. Extremist organizations, in particular those who can provide such "state-based" goods and services, increase the tendency to be accepted among the broader public. To this, increased rivalries between groups or regions in a country enhance the likelihood of ideological extremism—in Iraq, Sunnis living in Shia-led governments; in Nigeria, the Northern Muslims against the Southern Christian; or the Palestinians against the Israelis. All these rivalries are backed up by religious extremist organizations, such as Al-Qaeda, the Islamic State, Boko Haram, and Hamas, which address with their ideology, organizational structure, and "state-based" goods and services the needs of their adherents.

Religious extremist organizations can be thus conceived as "communities, dedicated to the production of communal goods and the pursuit of communal goals. [. . .] [They] flourish because they provide their members hope for the future, benefits for the present, and insurance against misfortune. They assist those who suffer financial setbacks and ill health. Their social networks help members form joint business ventures, establish long-term friendships, and find suitable marriage partners. As Adam Smith realized, they also provide information about an individual's reliability and creditworthiness, which economically disadvantaged people may otherwise have trouble signaling to financial institutions, prospective employers, and the society at large (Smith, 1965)" (Iannaccone and Berman 2006, 118). This means that those religious extremist organizations that can maintain their credibility and minimize free riding will operate successfully, especially where poor government or civil disorder undermines the provision of vital resources and services. "From Egypt and Palestine to Pakistan, Afghanistan, and Indonesia, radical Islamist groups have enjoyed broad support especially among the poorest segments of society—because they are major suppliers of mutual aid and social services" (Iannaccone and Berman 2006, 119).

Several case studies show that when individuals suffer from a lack of resources, social services, and opportunities to meet their fundamental needs—as was the case in Indonesia due to the currency crisis, in Afghanistan during the Soviet occupation, or in Lebanon during the civil war—the acceptance and participation in Islamic radical networks increase (e.g., Chen 2003; Fritsch 2001). Hence, extremist organizations that provide resources and services to serve human needs, to feed the poor, to educate children, and to protects one's own family increase the likelihood of acceptance and commitment, and decrease potential dropouts. It is thus no coincidence that organizations like Al-Qaeda, the Islamic State, Boko Haram, Hamas, Hezbollah, or the Taliban are lethal, effective, and successful in their operations.

9

Extremist Organizations

Their Recruitment and Mobilization Strategies

9.1 Recruitment and Mobilization from the Need-Serving Perspective

The last chapter showed how various organizational forms can determine the success, lethality, and need-serving capabilities of ideologically radicalized groups. Depending on the group size, complexity, and interactions, a group can assume a horizontal, vertical, or dynamic (networking) organizational structure, in which all members are differentiated according to their specific role and responsibility. Not all members occupy an active position but may act passively and in response to instructions or actions of others. Usually such organizations, which employ a deterministic role structure, are strictly hierarchical, but they also provide the possibility for their members to reach higher positions based on their efficiency and self-assertion (Nance 2016). The empirical evidence and literature suggest that right-wing, left-wing, and religious extremist organizations assume the organizational form that best matches their belief system. Right-wing organizations are more likely to assume a vertical, strictly organized, and hierarchical structure, with centralized, top-down decision-making, strict rule, command, and control, which correspond to their mostly segregating and authoritarian ideology. The organizational form is thus based on the narratives and ideas of superiority, a "natural social hierarchy," collectivity, obedience, and subordination. The membership is propagated as an exclusive form of belongingness, in which the individual is absorbed by the group, and the shared ideals, norms, values, and beliefs.

Right-wing organizations usually establish a well-connected, dense, and internationalized network to receive support from internal members and external public, as well as private institutions. This network enables group members to better communicate and propagate the organizational beliefs and goals; recruit and mobilize members; plan gatherings, events, and potential attacks; collaborate with clergymen and politicians; share information; sustain influence in policy; and for lobbying and funding. The interconnection between right-wing organizations worldwide decreases recruitment and information costs and enhances financing offers. However, the decisional power remains authoritarian and centralized. This hierarchical organizational form, with its top-down decision-making, various departments, and prescribed roles and duties address, in particular, human needs for order, stability, consistency, and control. But also needs for belongingness, social approval, and identification, as well as the need for self-esteem, are addressed in terms of a superior group image, social classifications, distinctive group characteristics, and strong mythological and historical narratives. Usually, such groups have strong and charismatic leaders with good rhetoric skills, who provide orientation and authority.

Similar organizational forms, shaped by vertical and centralized decision-making, are assumed by religious extremist organizations. Churches, sects, or religious extremist groups that are more Prophetic in their ideology, implying strict adherence to the Holy Scripture, authority, order, rules, and restrictions, choose a hierarchical organizational form in which members have no direct impact on governance and decision-making but must obey the rules from above. Such costly rules or demands can include dietary restrictions, sexual prohibitions, distinctive dress and grooming, restrictions against modern medicine or Western education, and many more. These demands reduce the free-rider problem by creating a barrier to group entry and stimulating group participation. Those who accept and follow these rules will be rewarded with exclusive goods and services. Some religious extremist organizations, such as Al-Qaeda, Hamas, IS, the Taliban, or Boko Haram, even provide full-fledged services to their members, which exceed the standard organizational offers and simulate state provision. They all assume a hierarchical organizational form, with a prophetic leader, deputies, counselors, and various departments that are responsible for different operations of the organization, such as marketing and media, human resources, funding and investment, military operations, and political networking. They also form internationalized networks and collaborate intensively with governments, policymakers, businessmen, and clergymen to sustain their position and receive support in terms of funding, information, and mobilization.

In contrast to right-wing and religious extremist organizations that usually assume a vertical organizational structure and establish dense internal and external networks, ("New") left-wing extremist organizations are more horizontally structured. This implies decentralized decision-making, regionally formed small clusters, and a fragmented power structure. Some left-wing groups organize themselves in a more underground, military fashion that plans and executes attacks individually. However, the "Old Left" differs considerably from the "New Left" in its working methods, organizational structure, and ideology. "Old Left," post-war communist groups adopt a vertical and hierarchical organizational form, implying centralized decision-making (e.g., "Soviet dogmatism"), a secretive and elitist membership, strong group homogeneity and cohesion, collectivity instead of individualism, and a dense internationalized network ("World Communist Movement"). The Soviet and Chinese communist organizations assume the same hierarchical structure, dogmatic world view, strict rule adherence, and orthodoxy. They perceive themselves as the main organization that governs, leads, controls, and makes decisions. Each member within the organization adopts a particular role and duty and is responsible for the success and implementation of certain operations.

Left-wing extremist organizations in South America have a similar dogmatic world view; however, they assume a more horizontal and flexible organizational form. Although they clearly support centralized decision-making, regional subgroups and local leaders also receive autonomy and decision-making power to flexibly react to changed circumstances. But here, too, the organizations demand strict rule adherence and commitment, structural integrity (unity and intra-organizational consistency), and role fulfillment. Also, "New Left" extremist organizations assume a rather horizontal or network organizational form that is shaped by decentralized decision-making, various regional subgroups, and no clear and dogmatic leadership. They also do not form internationalized networks united by the same ideology, goals, and identity, but instead act locally and individually. Consequently, the various ideological manifestations are not capable of establishing the common identity, clear role prescriptions, rules, and ideals that are shared by all New-Left extremist groups.

As a result, it may be clear that extremist groups assume the organizational form that best matches and represents their belief system. Extremist groups that adopt a more conservative, status-quo-driven, and authoritarian belief system form an organization that is shaped by hierarchy, rule abidance, clear leadership, and role prescriptions. Those who adopt a revolutionary and change-driven belief system form a more dynamic and polycentric organization, with no clear leadership and roles. Individuals, in turn, adopt a belief system and join an extremist group that best matches or addresses their underlying needs and motives. In Chapter 8 we saw that individuals who score higher on the need for cognitive closure and ambiguity avoidance, and who prefer order, structure, and stability over change and flexibility, are more likely to adopt right-wing or religious extremist ideas (Jost et al. 2003). They hence choose an extremist group that not only disseminates beliefs and ideas that address their needs and preferences, but also that provides particular organizational structures that generate order, stability, and consistency. The world view of right-leaning and religious individuals is derived from perceived threat and established order—the conviction that society is a dangerous place and that individuals must observe strict discipline, self-reliance, obedience, and respect. Adherents of such world views support the idea of law and order; of a moral, just, and beneficial authority; and of a "natural" social hierarchy (e.g., God is above all humans, some "races" are more capable than others, men are above women, etc.). For this reason, feminism, atheism, or homosexuality are perceived as a threat to society because they do not adhere to the perceived "natural order" (Strickland 2008). On the opposite end of the spectrum, individuals who score higher on the need for change and autonomy, and who prefer less traditionalism, conventionalism, and social order, are more likely to adopt left-wing extremist ideas (McAadams et al. 2008). While it is argued that communists and the "Old-Left" adherents have similar psychological needs as right-wing adherents (such as uncertainty and ambiguity avoidance, order, control, and certainty), empirical evidence show that there are significant differences between the West and the East (see Chapter 7, section 7.4 of this book for an extensive discussion).

That said, it becomes clear that individuals adopt an ideology and join an extremist group that tends to best match their underlying needs and preferences. These groups, in turn, use distinct recruitment and mobilization strategies to find and attract in particular those who fit to their group to reduce free-riding and increase commitment. Before discussing the recruitment and mobilization strategies of traditional criminal organizations, like the Mafia, and right-wing, left-wing, and religious extremist groups, a general outlook about recruitment is given. What exactly is recruitment and what are the different strategies that can be applied to successfully recruit matching individuals? How can groups or organizations mobilize individuals to overcome the collective action dilemma?

From the most basic perspective, recruitment is a human resource management function to enlist new members for employment. Recruitment is a significant instrument to acquire and retain qualified individuals, which is thus critical to organization's success. Due to enhanced competition, dynamics, and high fluctuations, recruiters need to be more selective in their choices to identify poor performance and decrease costs of poor recruiting decisions, which can produce negative long-term effects. Recruiting individuals who do not match the organization's objectives, ideals, and morale can impact its functioning, output, and long-term success. This means that recruitment is an active and dynamic process, used to bring organizations and individuals together to match their short-term and long-term interests (Richardson 2012).

The success of a recruitment process is determined by particular recruitment strategies that organizations employ to identify and select the best candidates. The recruitment process consists of several stages, such as vacancy verification, job listing, attraction of potential candidates, interviews, and selection process, and finalizing the job offer. "A company that implements an effective recruitment process is likely to gain competitive advantage in the marketplace, improve returns, and achieve economies of scale. This is possible only through the recruitment of quality candidates into the organizational workforce" (Sangeetha 2010, 93). Usually, individuals can be recruited internally through transfer of existing personnel or promotion, or externally through open vacancies or referrals. While internal recruitment requires higher costs and may not be always efficient in selecting matching candidates, external recruitment, either through referrals, local institutions (headhunters or universities), or social media, represents a low-cost-per-hire way of recruitment (Richardson 2012).

In human resource management, external recruitment is often used to fill lower-level positions, while internal recruitment, in the form of promotions, is granted to individuals with longer tenure in the company. "It is a well-known result in human capital theory that accumulation of firm-specific human capital usually involves joint investment by both the employer and the employee, so that both parties have the incentive to maintain a long-term relationship (see, e.g., Becker 1975). And the longer the tenure of the worker, the more specific human capital accumulated, and the more costly it would be for the firm to find an external candidate who could outperform an existing worker within the setting of the firm. Another possibility is that the abilities of existing employees can be observed with less noise than those of external applicants, so that risk-averse employers may prefer to go with a less uncertain prospect by promoting qualified candidates from within (Greenwald 1979)" (Chan 1996, 556). This form of recruitment reduces monitoring, training, and information costs significantly, and is often applied by large institutions or companies with a mostly bureaucratic and hierarchical organizational structure. Internal recruitment in form of promotions provides an incentive to constantly put effort into the organization, in particular when monitoring costs are high (Chan 1996).

Further recruitment strategies focus on "elitist selection processes." This means that working for a particular organization or company is promoted as being a privilege, which is expressed through a harsh selection process (cognitive ability tests, case studies, work simulation exercises, assessment centers, several rounds with interviewers, assignments, etc.) (Patterson and Lane 2007). A harsh recruitment process aims at addressing only "high-potential" candidates who are willing to invest personal resources to be selected, which in turn affects organizational performance, image, viability, and labor turnout. Investing high personal resources to pass the recruitment process signals to the organization or company that the individual is willing to stay in the organization in the long run, comply with organizational rules and norms, and invest personal resources to advance organizational goals (Iannaccone 1992). Due to increased globalization, complexity, and enhanced job market flexibility, companies or organizations extended their recruitment strategies by attracting potential candidates though social media. Here individuals are recruited through Web database sources, such as career sites or networking platforms, and through networking, resumes and references, direct mail campaigns, job fairs, job advertisements in magazines, newspapers or TV, or through professional hiring agencies (Sangeetha 2010).

A limited number of studies showed that organizational characteristics are associated with the differences in recruitment strategies. The study of Barber and colleagues (1999) revealed that larger organizations were more likely than smaller ones to use more distinctive and sophisticated recruitment strategies; that is, to invest more in their HR staff, train their recruiters properly, allow applicants more time for job acceptance, use campus placement offices, and use more screening devices. This means that larger organizations apply more formal and bureaucratic recruitment practices to reduce hiring costs and increase efficiency (e.g., automate the processing of large numbers of applications). Similar studies confirm that smaller firms are more likely to use informal recruitment strategies (Bartram et al. 1995), relying more on referrals or networks for recruitment (Pritchard and Fidler 1993). Both studies also found that small firms put more emphasis on personality characteristics than hard skills, like academic achievements or work experience, when selecting their candidates. One major reason why large organizations use more distinctive recruitment strategies is the presence of a well-structured HR department. Larger firms have, as a result, well-trained hiring staff that can forecast hiring needs for different departments. In addition, larger organizations can more flexibly react to changed conditions and hiring requests (Barber et al. 1999).

Organizations with more resources can also apply methods to screen personality, values, and preferences of individuals and to assess how well they match the job and the organization. The goal of such efforts is to find recruits who are attracted to the attributes of the organization and are willing to comply with job requirements. Communicating organizational culture and identity, but also promotion possibilities, financial benefits, and social services in advance is related to recruit's attraction and match to the organization, but also their satisfaction and retention once they enter the organization (Reeve et al. 2006). A study (Gardner et al. 2009) examined the relationship between traditional recruitment versus realistic job previews (RJPs), personality characteristics, and the attraction of recruits to organizational culture profiles. RJPs aim to provide individuals with information about positive and negative features of the organization, to help them make a more deliberate decision before accepting the job offer. The authors assume that in contrast to traditional recruitment, where recruits receive only positive information about the organization, RJPs will decrease organizational attraction. To measure the variety of organizational cultures, the study relied on Cameron and Quinn's competing values taxonomy (1999), which includes four basic cultural types: hierarchy, clan, market, and adhocracy. Each cultural type reflects a particular set of organizational effectiveness indicators and defines core values of the organization. The clan, for example, emphasizes cohesion, conformity, morale, participation, and loyalty, which is the exact opposite of the market that focuses more on growth, competition, and achievement. The hierarchy stresses rules, efficiency, control, policies, and strict processes, which opposes the values of adhocracy, such as innovation, creativity, flexibility, and risk. Personality is measured by the horizontal and vertical individualism and collectivism taxonomy (HV-IC). HV-IC identifies two sets and four types of selves: the first set describes the "same" or "different" selves, which are determined by how much one accepts inequality or status quo. The "different self" represents the concept of verticality, whereas the "same self" corresponds to horizontality. The second set outlines the independent and interdependent selves, which relates to individuality and collectivity, respectively. The combination of these two sets creates four types of selves: vertical collectivism, horizontal collectivism, vertical individualism, and horizontal individualism. Vertical collectivism reflects an emphasis on the community, but other than horizontal collectivism, accepts inequality within society. The horizontal individualist strives for equality but is self-reliant and not group oriented, while a vertical individualist accepts social inequality and strives for individual autonomy. The theoretical base for the study is provided by the ASA model (Schneider et al. 1995), which argues that individuals will gravitate toward and be satisfied with organizations that have characteristics consistent with their own. From the other perspective, organizations will choose individuals who possess attributes that are deemed compatible with those of other members and the work environment (Scott et al. 1999). The results show that individuals who score high on horizontal collectivism are more attracted to organizations with a (family-like) clan culture, while those who score high on vertical collectivism prefer hierarchical organizational cultures because they provide security, control, orientation, and tradition. Individuals high on horizontal individualism prefer organizations with an adhocracy culture, which corresponds to their equity-driven and risk-taking character, and those who score high on vertical individualism are more attracted to the market culture because it serves their needs for autonomy and competition. Additionally, the results indicate that respondents exposed to traditional recruitment strategies, rather than to RJPs, were more likely attracted to an organization. Although this seems to be an undesirable outcome, RJPs help individuals to decide whether the organizational culture fits their personality or not. This, in turn, supports organizations in their effective screening and hiring decisions.

Successful recruitment also plays an important role in mobilization because it reduces the costs for collective action. "Mobilization is the process of aggregating or accumulating resources under collective control of a corporate group or entity for the express purpose of engaging in collective action. Collective actions, in turn, are joint actions in the pursuit of the collective goals or ends" (Jenkins 1981, 114). This implies that the process of mobilization also constitutes the process of change; that is, a group of individuals, who share the same understanding of reality, transforms into a corporate group capable of making collective decisions. Mobilization is important in the sense that it creates the conditions of willingness for collective action and reduces the free-rider dilemma (Klandermans 2013). Free-riding is considered a major problem in collective action because the cost of participation is individual, but the benefits of any action are shared by all group members, regardless of the extent of their personal contribution. The subjective rational choice in this case is to "free ride," given the high costs of participation and the expectation that the benefits of a successful collective action are equally shared. Given this collective action dilemma, groups or organizations have to increase the subjective motivation to bear high personal costs of participation, when rational self-interest would rather favor individual non-participation (Bornstein 1992).

Successful recruitment is hence an important "pre-stepm" which can help to identify individuals who match the group's organizational structure, identity, ideology, and goals. After identifying and attracting matching candidates, the group or organization must provide incentives and particular "goods and services" to enhance commitment and participation. Such incentives can be physical (e.g., money, health care, or housing) and psychological (e.g., collective activities, group identification, social approval, self-esteem, and many more). Also, costly demands can be a good and powerful source of mobilization and group coherence. Demanding all group members sacrifice and comply to particular groups norms, such as strict dietary restrictions; sexual prohibition; distinctive dress and grooming; or restrictions on the use of modern technology, education, or medicine; mitigate the free-rider problem in two ways. "First, they create a social barrier that tends to screen out half-hearted members. To take part one must pay a price, bearing the stigma and sacrifice demanded of all members. Second, they increase the relative value of group activities, thereby stimulating participation among those who do join the group. Social stigmas make it costly to engage in activities outside the group, and as the price of external activities rises, the demand for internal substitutes increases" (Iannaccone 2012, 113). Iannaccone (1992, 2012) argues that individuals join groups because they provide valuable goods and services, and thus serve needs and wants through collective action. In particular, extremist groups flourish because they provide trust and hope in the future, benefits in the present, and (palliative) explanations for the past. As described before, extremist groups and organizations offer excludable goods and social networks which assist their members in forming joint business ventures, getting financial funds, establishing social relations, receiving health care, and providing education for the children. All these valuable services and goods create, beyond positive need satisfaction, a strict demand and abidance from their members. It can foster commitment, reduce free-riding, sustain group homogeneity, enforce collective action, and can make it effective in their goal achievements if it does embrace violence, as seen by Al-Qaeda, Hamas, the Taliban, IS, or Boko Haram (Iannaccone and Berman 2006; Iannaccone 2012).

Other researchers, like Klandermans (2002), argue that group identification, in particular, is the key to mobilization success. Identification plays a significant role in how individuals form their social identity, perceive themselves and their social environment, and how they behave and interact with social others. Identifying with a particular ethnic, social, or cultural group, nation, or political party enables individuals to form a concept of oneself (i.e., one's description, perception, and evaluation of oneself) and the social environment (Abrams and Hogg 1990). Identifying with a particular group and its norms, values, and beliefs regulates feelings of attachment and gives a sense of certainty in life. This sense of certainty, in turn, provides orientation and confidence about how to behave and perceive the social environment (Hogg and Adelman 2013). The stronger the identification with the group, the higher the willingness of individuals to adhere to its rules and norms and invest their own personal resources to reach the goals of that group.

Identification in this regard implies two major aspects: first, it creates a shared identity that defines the group or collective (the "we," the ingroup) and second, it identifies those who do not belong to that group ("they," the outgroup). The ingroup and outgroup thinking is a powerful concept to create affinity and contrast and to mobilize individuals to perceive and evaluate the social environment according to this concept. Empirical studies show that identity and identification have a higher impact on collective action than feelings of injustice or grievance, as well as cost–benefit considerations (Mummendey et al. 1999; Kelly and Breinlinger 1996). However, neither laboratory experiments nor field studies could find a direct correlation between ingroup positivity and intergroup attitudes (Hinkle and Brown 1990; Brewer and Campbell 1976). In this regard, Brewer (2001a) argues that the relationship between ingroup formation and intergroup relations is driven by more factors than mere ingroup identification. The organization into discrete ingroup–outgroup categories (the social categorization principle), as well as the tendency of individuals to value their group more positively (ingroup positivity principle), are universal but do not invariably lead to intergroup tensions.

This led researchers to examine the question of which factors can drive individuals to form hostile feelings and attitudes toward an outgroup that can invariably lead to violence and conflict. In many neuroimaging studies, Greene and colleagues showed that the aversion to be violent against someone (or even killing) depends on the emotional part of the brain, in particular on uncertainty (Greene et al. 2004; Greene 2007). Uncertainty is the basic cause of anxiety that, when released, can distract individuals from achieving their goals (McGregor et al. 2008). Individuals who overcome the aversion of being violent or killing are thus capable of reducing this state of uncertainty. Research on extremism and conflict argues that ideological extremist groups use "techniques" to reduce this state of uncertainty and regulate morality to mobilize individuals for goal attainment (Connelly et al. 2016; Bandura 1990; Wahlström et al. 2021). Bandura's (1999) theory of moral disengagement argues that individuals are capable of cognitively separating the moral component from an unmoral act to rationalize it. This means that "there are a number of ways people can bypass self-regulatory processes, resulting in selective disengagement from reflection on unethical behavior and self-sanctioning both before and after the behavior has occurred" (Connelly et al. 2016, 18). Possible ways to frame or cognitively restructure morally reprehensible behavior are moral justification narratives (e.g., killing someone who "threatens our existence"), advantageous comparison of the immoral behavior with other more destructive atrocities, and denial of the consequences (e.g., a group uses violent narratives or destructive language against an outgroup without admitting the violence or rejection that results from it). Furthermore, feelings of uncertainty and moral agency can be weakened by releasing the personal responsibility for one's actions through shifting it to external authority (e.g., a leader or holy figure), or diluting responsibility through division of collective decision-making so that no one feels directly accountable (Connelly et al. 2016).

One of the most powerful techniques, however, is intergroup comparison. Ingroup positivity is emphasized through intergroup comparisons, in which ingroup attributes are evaluated as better than, or even superior to, those of outgroups. This intergroup comparison principle can motivate individuals to perceive outgroup members as less valuable, and can lead, in extreme cases to dehumanization—the denial of humanness to others (Bandura 2011). Dehumanization implies beliefs about negative characteristics attributed to a particular group, with the purpose of excluding it from society and denying it humanity (Haslam 2006). Such beliefs legitimize discrimination and rejection of outgroup members and activate negative emotions, such as hate, contempt, fear, or even disgust, toward them. "According to Kelman (1976), dehumanization involves denying a person 'identity'—a perception of the person 'as an individual, independent and distinguishable from others, capable of making choice' (p. 301)—and 'community'—a perception of the other as 'part of an interconnected network of individuals who care for each other' (p. 301). When people are divested of these agentic and communal aspects of humanness they are deindividuated, lose the capacity to evoke compassion and moral emotions, and may be treated as means toward vicious ends" (Haslam 2006, 254). A typical form of dehumanization is the use of animal metaphors in response to outgroup members, which denies them of having cognitive and mental human abilities (Harris and Fiske 2006). Dehumanization in this regard can lead to moral exclusion of one particular group; that is, placing individuals who belong to this group outside social boundaries of morality, norms, and fairness. This means that individuals who are excluded from the moral and ethnic community, and who are denied humanity and identity, can easily become subject to harsh hostility, violence, and conflict.

One way to exclude individuals from the moral community is the shared belief about the group's value hierarchy. When an outgroup is perceived to have dissimilar values or a different way of living to the ingroup, the outgroup can be perceived to lack shared values and humanity (Struch and Schwartz 1989). One example of such a moral disengagement mechanism is cited by Akins (2006) in his case analysis of the KKK: on its website, the group proclaims that those who do not share the same values or the same way of living to the group—in particular "anti-White, anti-Christian liberals, socialists, feminists, homosexuals, and militant minorities" (129) are regarded as enemies who are destroying the United States. These outgroup members are perceived as a threat to the social order and should be eliminated to "restore law and order to America" (129). Another study shows that the use of dehumanizing narratives, portrayed on a Swedish far-right website, about crimes with (real and imagined) immigrant perpetrators and vulnerable victims, linked to a failed governmental responsibility, spurred negative emotions and mobilized individuals for violent action. The authors argue that the use of violent and dehumanizing rhetoric in social media is key for understanding mobilization and political violence (Wahlström et al. 2021).

All that said, to understand how ideological extremist groups operate and make decisions, we must understand how they recruit individuals and use moral disengagement techniques, among others, to mobilize them. Empirical findings provide considerable support that individuals gravitate toward organizations that show characteristics similar to their own personality and can reconcile their idiosyncratic needs and preferences. To transfer these theoretical and empirical findings to our framework, the following sections will discuss how various extremist organizations—including those with a clan-based mafia structure—adopt distinct recruitment and mobilization strategies to attract, train, and motivate individuals. Understanding the distinct techniques and strategies used enables us to understand why some groups are more lethal and successful in their operations than others. We start with traditional criminal organizations, followed by right-wing, left-wing, and religious extremist organizations.

9.2 Recruitment and Mobilization in Traditional Criminal Organizations

In Chapter 9 we elaborated that criminal organizations, or traditional clan-based Mafia, are usually organized and governed in a rational corporate structure. In most cases, such organizations employ a vertical structure which entails a leader who has executive control, a deputy, senior advisors, a number of members who supervise all members of the organization, and several hundred associates who perform a wide range of operational tasks (Catino 2014). This vertical organizational order is characterized by centralized power and systemic decision-making processes, which allow for better control of decisions and actions. Membership and recruitment processes are strictly regulated with varying degrees of rigidity. Being a member of such an organization, as "a man of honor," implies lifetime obedience, subordination, and loyalty. The mafia brotherhood demands secrecy (omerta), discipline, cohesion, and manhood. It is accompanied by affiliation codes with mystified legends, which serve as symbols to enhance fascination and identification with the group (Ciconte 2014). Despite similar organizational forms, the recruitment practices differ among the different mafias, such as Cosa Nostra, 'Ndrangheta, Camorra, or the Yakuza. Although studies and empirical evidence are both scarce on that issue, those available (e.g., Collins 2008) argue that the major reason why the mafia is lethal, strong, and successful in their operations is their recruitment and mobilization base—the families. Contrastingly, lower-class criminal gangs, youth gangs, or other criminal street groups recruit more from broken, fragmented, lower-class families that cannot be used as a sustainable basis of an organization.

The narrative of "the family" describes a traditionally basic unit of social organization, defined in some combination of kinship, parentage, and coexistence. It represents a naturalistic and closely intertwined social entity that follows certain rules, norms, and values, and that makes collective decisions to survive and sustain internally and externally. The family, at least in some cultures, requires high commitment, loyalty, and moral obligation, and, in case of non-compliance, punishes with social exclusion. Mobilization, in this regard, functions through emotional attachments such as fear, guilt, shame, honor, love, loyalty, or compassion. In the Mafia, these emotions play a significant role in how well a "family" organizes and functions itself. They form a foundation for the mobilization, cohesion, and longevity of a clan. In every Mafia family there are established behavioral codes, norms, and values that must be followed or else there will be punishment or exclusion (Pierce and Pierce 2016). Hence, recruitment, mobilization, and the operations of Mafia clans are largely based on the narrative of the "family" and the values, norms, and duties aligned with it.

The Cosa Nostra, for example, was originally formed on the basis of family ties—a group of individuals with a specific territorial base, which controls a specific zone or city (e.g., the family of Porta Nuova, the family of Villabate, etc.)—to survive and provide an alternative system of justice to the overpowering and corrupt Sicilian government (Dickie 2004). "The term family denotes the fundamental importance given to the concepts of loyalty and honor: actual blood-ties between the members are not necessary. The selection of members is extremely strict, unlike the selection and recruiting mechanisms of the Camorra. The families are organized according to a pyramidal model, a hierarchy with subdivisions of power: from the *picciotto* (the "button man") at the bottom, up to the family heads. This division of power is similar to the "decimal organization" (Keegan 1994) used by the army" (Catino 2014, 189). Before being recruited into "the family," individuals are screened to meet certain strict requirements: members are not allowed to follow a left-wing ideology and they must come from a family with a respectable and pristine reputation. Homosexuals, illegitimate children, and divorcees were eliminated from the pool of recruits, as well as individuals with relatives working at the police or judiciary (Catino 2014). Another precondition for recruitment is gender and national and familial affiliation: only men, born either in Sicily or in Calabria, or already coming from Mafia families were admitted for recruitment.

Before becoming a member of the Mafia family, the recruits must take part in various rituals to pledge oneself to deep commitment, allegiance, and abidance to the Ten Commandments of the Mafia clan. The rituals resemble religious baptism ceremonies, in which the new member becomes "the man of honor" (Gambetta 1993). Similar to the Catholic Church, the recruits choose a godfather as a supervisor and guide, and they swear "with their own blood" to respect and be loyal to the family. During this process, the finger of the new member is picked to draw blood, which is then spilled onto a holy card that is burnt, symbolizing that a person enters and leaves the Mafia family only with blood. During this ceremony, the new member agrees to protect the new family and friends, to be loyal and secretive, and to obey with compassion. The Ten Commandments provide a restrictive guide on how to become a Mafia man of honor: the first rule implies that you are not allowed to present yourself directly to another person, but there must be a third party to do so; the second rule restricts looking at the wives of friends; the third rule is to never be seen with cops; the fourth rule prohibits visiting pubs and clubs; the fifth rule requires one must always be available for the Mafia family, irrespective of personal emergency; the sixth rules commands that each appointment be respected; the seventh rule places importance on respecting one's own wife; the eighth rule demands strict truth and honesty; the ninth rule states that money cannot be appropriated if it belongs to other families; and the tenth, and final, rule lists the conditions that prevent individuals from being a part of Cosa Nostra, such as having close family members who work for the law, having unfaithful family members, showing bad behavior, or not holding oneself to moral values (Gambetta 1993).

Values, rules, and narratives play an important role in the Mafia family. The adherence to them helps the units to organize themselves, to recruit only those who are willing to commit, and to mobilize all members. They provide guidelines about how to perceive the social environment, with whom to cooperate, how to behave, and how to meet the expectations of the family to be "a man of honor." The mobilization and indoctrination thus starts from early childhood, when the children learn that the Mafia family is the only place with which to identify and belong, to support, and to commit to. But also, other members form their identity based on the collectively shared values, norms, and narratives framed by emotions like hate, honor, fear, love, respect, loyalty, and so on. Breaking these rules or behaving in a morally wrong way leads to punishment or social rejection, which holds the members in fear and compliance (Di Maria and Lo Verso 2007). Psychological studies with former Mafia members show that the belonging to a Mafia family and the duty to follow its rules led to moral disengagement; that is, adhering to the norms, values, and rules to be a man of honor and protecting the family justified the illegal, violent, and criminal acts (Lo Verso and Lo Coco 2004).

However, over the years these rigid requirements prevented Cosa Nostra from adding new members to their organization who had skills and experiences necessary to compete in the black markets for drugs, arms, and gold. The rules also prevented the organization from geographical expansion and the formation of international alliances, as Cosa Nostra only recruits from Sicily or Calabria. These self-imposed recruitment rules, which aimed to establish strong homogeneity and cohesion within the organization, have limited the resources needed to compete in the global market, particularly in the international narcotics trade (Paoli 2004).

Being, for the most part, a hierarchical and homogenous organization, the Cosa Nostra, however, was forced to adapt to changing circumstances that had been threatening its own existence. These circumstances and changes, starting in the early 1990s, related to anti-mafia law enforcements that brought many mafia bosses to jail, the choice made by many members to cooperate with the police, and the growth of anti-mafia movements in the civil society. At the same time, the expansion of global markets and increased internationalization led the organization to realign its objectives and investment opportunities, such as in public health, construction, waste disposal, legal and illegal gambling, large scale retail, and even in the market for renewable energies. These changes led Cosa Nostra to form alliances and establish dense networks with other Mafia clans, Italo-American criminal groups, Camorra associations and Calabrian 'ndrine clans. Furthermore, the change in leadership transformed the Mafia clan from an authoritarian, hierarchical, violent organization with centralized power and strict rules, to a more flexible and democratic organizational form. The new "democratic" structure gave districts more autonomy and decision-making power, and allowed each family to individually recruit new members and form its own network of ties. However, Cosa Nostra faced difficulties recruiting younger generations to pass on the traditional rules, values, and culture, which were not highly appreciated by them. As a consequence, high-level managerial positions have been filled with older generations to re-establish reliance and trust within the organization that was particularly harmed by the younger cohort (Dickie 2004).

The biggest organizational change, however, represented the transformed role of women, who have been accepted as full members and who received a status for certain aspects similar to those of the male members (Scaglione 2016). Traditionally, women were not actively recruited into the Mafia clan, which was based on the narrative of the family but dominated by a hierarchical, patriarchal setting. Women were usually obliged to take care of the children and establish values in their sons, who would lead the clan in the next generation. Hence, the "indoctrination and mobilization" within the Mafia families starts already at an early age. Women, in this regard, received a significant role within the basic social unit, namely, to maintain and nourish it. They were the ones to implant the traditional values, behavioral codes, and norms into the next generation, and to make sure that they were followed and respected (Di Maria and Lo Verso 2007). However, the tasks and duties of women were constantly monitored and controlled by men, and in case of non-compliance they were socially punished or physically abused. This submissive role changed with changed external conditions. Women were not merely identified with their traditional roles, but received full-fledged information about organizational operatives and functions, which has never happened in the past. "Within Cosa Nostra, the female role has become crucial. With the arrests of male members, wives and daughters are, in fact, the only ones able to guarantee continuity within the families. In other words, women are fundamentally involved in a wide range of activities: extortion collection, planning of criminal strategies, carrying out damages and the distribution of orders" (Scaglione 2016, 64).

Unlike the Cosa Nostra and Camorra, where blood-ties between the members are not necessary for recruitment, the 'Ndrangheta is formed around blood parentage and intermarital connections. The members are thus recruited on the basis of interfamilial relationships. The organization is strictly regulated by rules and rituals, which guide members from the initiated membership to the next level of criminal ranking, up until the punishment imposed in case of violations or deviant behavior (Serenata 2014). Alternately, Camorra is a decentralized organization consisting of heterogeneous criminal clans that are not formed based on blood-ties or familial relations. Each clan receives decisional power and forms its own network; that is, new members are recruited also outside of the family or town. However, it is not easy to become a member of the Camorra gang: the selection process is cruel—one needs to undergo several tests and those who violate the *Frieno* (a codex made by twenty-six rulers) receive harsh punishments. However, similar to Cosa Nostra, Camorra was forced to change its organizational structure from a decentralized heterogeneous form to a more vertical and centralized structure to adapt to changing circumstances. When Raffeale Cutolo became the new leader of Camorra, both the ideological doctrine and identity of the organization changed along with its recruitment practices. New members were mainly recruited from juvenile jails or from economically poor environments, where young adolescents received the opportunity to gain prestige and approval through membership. This means that Camorra recruited new members also from rural, abandoned areas based on a new regional identity and a (populist) ideology of anti-establishment, justice, and the protection of the poor and weak.

Individuals with lower education and social status were recruited to conduct lower-profile criminal activities, while wealthy, educated, socially respectable individuals assumed top-level management jobs. Similar to Cosa Nostra, each new member had to undergo a ritual: "baptism, legalization, and fidelity." In the first step of the ritual, the place is baptized with an incantation and, in the second step, the new member swears on the code of silence (*omertà*). The ritual continues with historical narratives of Camorra, with particular focus on the founding fathers, who were expelled from Spain in 1771 and went to Sardinia, Sicily, and Calabria to establish Camorra. The new member of the organization will then pledge allegiance to the godfather, who cuts him on the forearm; both men unite their bloody wrists and swear loyalty to the organization. At the end of the ritual, they hug each other and make a cross-shaped cut on their right thumb to promise their loyalty to the organization (Ceci 2018).

Similar procedures can be found in the Japanese mafia, the Yakuza (*bōryokudan*, the official term for Yakuza). In December 2010, the Japanese police counted 78,600 members of the Yakuza, and this number has remained stable over the last two decades. Of the twenty-two designated Yakuza groups, the biggest three—the Yamaguchi-gumi, the Inagawa-kai, and the Sumiyoshi-kai—are the largest and most significant Mafia organizations in Japan, making up seventy-two percent of the total members. The Yamaguchi-gumi, based in western Japan, is the most successful and aggressive of all clans, with a dense network and ties to other clans throughout Japan. "Gangs are based on fictive family ties of father–son (*oyabun–kobun*) and brother–brother (*kyōdai*) relationships. These are cemented through formal ceremonies involving the exchange of sake cups and other Shintō rituals. For important ceremonies, professional quality videos are made for distribution to allied gangs and other non-Yakuza associates as demonstration of the authority of the members" (Hill 2014, 236). The three largest clans usually employ a quasi-feudal, hierarchical, and strictly bureaucratic structure, managed under the principle of *daikazoku* (big family), which resembles modern business organizations in

Japan. Also, the entrance ceremonies have similarities: during the annual entrance ceremony of a big Japanese bank, the new workers are welcomed as new members of the "big family" and receive company badges that, like the Yakuza's, entail the company's logo and list their rank and office within the organization (Kaplan and Dubro 2012). Here again, the narrative of the *family* shapes the functioning, recruitment, and mobilization of the organization and generates one important guiding rule, namely, to work for, protect, and be loyal to the family. It also shapes the understanding of the social environment and guides one about how to behave and which moral values to adopt.

Although the common perception is that only individuals with criminal pasts or outcasts are recruited into the organization, field data show that the background of members varies from former police officers to university graduates, wrestlers, pachinko workers, managers, debt-collectors, and boxers. Before joining the organization, the recruits must undergo certain rituals and training prior to formal acceptance. Trainees are responsible for menial household chores while living in the office of a particular clan; running errands; and learning the norms, values, and behavioral codes of the clan through observation rather than explicit instruction. In the past, the training usually lasted for up to three years, but it has declined to six months. This has led older Yakuza members to complain about the declining standards of the new recruits. While each gang has its own norms and values that are learned during the apprenticeship, there are also general codes that apply to every gang to facilitate communication and identification: *jingi, irezumi*, and *yubetsume*. *Jingi* refers to traditional greetings between Yakuza members, which today consist of name cards and a lapel pin bearing their gang crest. *Irezumi* are traditional gang tattoos that are famous among the members, and *yubetsume* refers to finger amputation, which is usually performed as a punishment, apology, or demonstration of commitment. Hence, the absence of one or more fingertips is a famous and recognizable Yakuza trademark. In addition, special clothing, walking, speech patterns, and hair styles represent the status and membership of a particular gang that all new recruits must adopt. They are also expected to attend several ceremonies, such as weddings, funerals, office openings, succession ceremonies, initiation rites, or jail releases, to demonstrate gang cohesion, control, power, and the importance of community and network. During these ceremonies, the trainees learn how to socialize and network in order to form important channels of information transfer (Hill 2014).

To sum up, the recruitment and mobilization processes of various mafia organizations show similar patterns and cultures, and they seem to attract individuals who prefer a family-like atmosphere, hierarchical order, strict behavioral rules and norms, and strong group cohesion. Empirical evidence (Pacheco 2019) shows that especially individuals with instable or uncertain familial conditions, and with higher needs for approval, belongingness, and identification are more vulnerable to gang recruitment. Joining a Mafia gang represents a new "family," which is more stable, ordered, and consistent. It also provides meaning in life (a sense of contribution to a higher cause), increases self-esteem, and provides a new form of commitment (self-efficacy). Others argue that young adults join gangs to receive protection, safety, order, and control. Belonging to a powerful group that has a high social status and reputation increases one's own self-esteem and decreases self-uncertainty (Hogg 2014). The new "family" gives a sense of mutual support, safety, coherence, order, and trust. Belonging to a Mafia "family" with power and control over a particular territory not only generates a sense of control and self-esteem, but also a sense of purpose to act on behalf of that family.

Various studies provide evidence that Mafia members form their personal identity on the basis of affiliation with the family and the community to which they belong, and that group identification represents a core dimension for explaining their behaviors and moral attitudes (Lo Verso and Lo Coco 2004; Dean et al. 2010; Di Maria 1997). Lo Verso and Lo Coco (2004), for example, show that Mafia families reject individualism and strictly emphasize a collectivistic mindset. "Mafia members are not allowed to gain personal authority without the help of their boss and their family, so they are entirely reliant on the organization for their criminal career development and for receiving social and psychological support. Thus, members may feel virtually incapable of acting against the will of the group: after the individuals join actively in the Mafia organization, they lose the ability to differentiate between their own goals, objectives, friends and enemies and those of their family (Fabj 1998; Bovenkerk 2000)"(Schimmenti et al. 2014, 322). In this regard, the psychological study of Schimmenti and colleagues (2014), with thirty incarcerated Mafia members, showed that group membership is less associated with personality disorder, lack of empathy and morality, or substance abuse, but more with loyalty, rule abidance, and collectivistic thinking. All Mafia members had surprisingly very low personality disorder scores, which means that, compared to the control group, they were less narcissistic, manipulative, Machiavellian, unemotional, parasitic, or impulsive. They explained their criminal and violent actions as acts of loyalty, duty, and "family mission," which can be classified into a "superior orders defense." The superior orders defense promotes a form of moral disengagement, which means that functionaries carry out the orders of superiors by giving up or displacing their personal responsibility. As a result, the morality or uncertainty of carrying out violent or criminal acts is weakened because the link between the action and its consequences is obscured by responsibility diffusion. But also, high justification and collective consensus about the importance and morality of an act release high personal control and enable a member of the Mafia family to conduct his duties without much emotional affect (Bandura 2007).

9.3 Recruitment and Mobilization in Radical Right Organizations

Similar to some Mafia organizations, radical right groups usually adopt a more vertical, hierarchically organized structure with strict rules, command, predefined roles, and duties, where decisions are usually made at the top and transmitted to the bottom. The structure is formed around beliefs in nativism (i.e., states should be governed exclusively by native groups, while non-native elements [people and ideas] threaten the homogeneity and cohesion of society), obedience, and a strictly ordered society in which deviations from prescribed norms and values are punished by authority (Mudde 2010). Because right-wing groups or organizations are usually well-connected, it enables them to better communicate and propagate their group identity, beliefs, and goals; share information; plan gatherings, events, and potential attacks; and recruit new members from the party and non-party sectors.

One major tool to reach potential candidates, share information, and disseminate beliefs is the media. Radical right-wing media, such as books, journals, newspapers and other printed matter, and broadcasting, usually portray themselves as a viable alternative to mainstream media, which is portrayed as a follower of mainstream parties, liberal democracy, and the capitalist economy. Right-wing media platforms adopt a populist appeal by adopting and propagating specific ideological elements and claiming to provide the "alternative truth." They use narratives such as "the homogeneous people, who are the majority but are pushed into the corner" (creating ingroups and outgroups); hostility toward elites in policy and science, as well as institutions of representative democracy (who want to take "people's freedom and autonomy"); and narratives pertaining to moral sentiments (evoking emotions like fear, anxiety, shame, disgust, anger, etc.) (Krämer 2017). In a broader sense, these media outlets claim to represent the broader will of the people and to work toward its implementation. In the United States, publishers like the Social Contract Press or the American Free Press include such narratives by promoting Holocaust negation, conspiracy theories, and opposition to immigration; whereas European publishers, like Arktos in

Great Britain, Krisis in France, or Antaois in Germany, promote and adhere to cultural conservatism, anti-globalization, and admiration for fascism.

"In the United States the New Right[1] and the Christian right of fundamentalist Protestantism overlap considerably. Conservative think tanks such as the Free Congress Foundation, the American Enterprise Institute, and the Heritage Foundation provide a well-funded institutional base for ideologues whose enthusiasm for capitalism is not shared by their counterparts in Europe" (Veugelers and Menard 2018, 288). This means that, given the bipartisan structure of American politics, not only radical right parties support conservative think tanks and media outlets, but also the extreme right fringe of the Republican Party and right-wing independents (Minkenberg 2000; Gross, Medvetz, and Russell 2011). In Europe, (with the exception of Great Britain), radical right-wing parties are not supported by official conservative think tanks or intellectuals. In addition, unlike most of the American counterparts, the European radical right has an inconsistent, and even hostile, view of Christianity—honored, on the one side, as an essential part of the Western tradition, but devalued, on the other side, as a *master–slave morality* (particularly by those inspired by Nietzsche). However, the European radical right also displays greater sympathy toward alternative cults, such as the pagan cults of the Celts and Norsemen (Veugelers and Menard 2018). All that said, the European radical right focuses more on ethnonationalism, "the will of the people," anti-multiculturalism, and anti-globalization by calling for a strong and protective state, which provides security, dampens migration, strengthens the national identity, and curbs international competition, whereas the American radical right adopts more libertarian attitudes by rejecting a powerful and intrusive state.

This means that the national context and the use of different narratives and beliefs have an impact on the recruitment processes; that is, the selection process of matching candidates and the recruitment venues. In Europe, for example, the radical right overlaps with small groups such as fan clubs that support some European football teams, bands of Neo-Nazi skinheads, or even some mystical sects. In Britain, football hooliganism has provided a viable and effective venue for recruitment. But also in France, Portugal, Spain, and Italy, radical right-wing parties reached out to organized fans of football teams, the ultras, and, especially in Italy, the link between the ultras and politics is long-standing. "Inspired by Britain's hooligans and skinheads as well as the tense political climate in their own country, during the 1970s Italian fans adopted distinctive fashions as well as banners and chants modeled after political movements. Although less closed to women than their British counterparts, the ultras show a similar concern with territoriality (down to their seating in stadiums, where they dominate the curved stands behind the goals) and defense of a common space against the encroachments of outsiders (fans for rival teams, supporters of opposing political orientations, and, since the 1990s, non-European migrants). This has led to the orchestrated heckling of nonwhite players on the playing field, violent street clashes between leftists and rightists, and links between the ultras and neofascist groups as well as the radical right Lega Nord (Podaliri and Balestri 1998)" (Veugelers and Menard 2018, 293).

The anti-immigration sentiments increased tremendously after the so called "refugee crisis" in 2015–2016, which led to the formation of vigilante activities across Europe and North America, including street patrols, border patrols, and militias. Vigilantes disseminated the narrative of a weak state that failed to provide safety to their citizens and claimed that they would assume the role and manage the tasks that state authorities and police failed to perform. Hence, their aim was to maintain public safety and secure the streets and borders from the threat—the refugees. Most of these vigilant groups are organized and supervised top-down by local far-right groups and parties. Forza Nuova, for example, an extreme far-right party from Italy, has organized street patrols to take on the responsibility of patrolling local areas that are considered as dangerous. Evidence shows that similar vigilantism groups can be found across Europe in Germany, Greece, Bulgaria, United Kingdom, Hungary, Slovakia, Czech Republic, Sweden, and Finland, but also in the United States, Canada, Norway, Russia, India, and Israel (see Bjorgo and Mares 2019). These street patrols, or vigilantism in general, is thus framed as a necessity to guarantee safety and security that is shaken by the criminal immigrants, but also as a response to the weakness of the state. Such street patrols also served as recruitment and mobilization strategies for far-right groups and parties: concerned or threatened individuals were called out to join the group and "protect the nation." "This is part of their general delegitimization strategy directed against the mainstream political establishment and a consequence of their political agenda based on a notion of existential threats faced by the [. . .] population due to the negligence of the currently ruling elites" (Koehler 2019, 92).

Another example is the Minutemen, a militia group in the United States that is patrolling along the Mexican border, consisting mainly of aging veterans who aim to reclaim their lost sense of purpose and identity. They also frame the state as a failed institution and urge the need for patriots to protect and keep safe the nation. They define the border as a dangerous, threatening place and they dehumanize the people who aim to cross the border. The following recruitment and mobilization campaign serves as an example: "It is unjust to leave law-abiding American citizens helpless to defend themselves against well-organized international crime cartels and violent foreign gangs, rapists, murderers, and drug dealers who are terrorizing our neighborhoods and exploiting the prosperity and generosity of this great nation" (Shapira 2019, 156). This campaign clearly portrays the positive narrative of the ingroup (the law-abiding Americans), that is subject to injustice and threat (helplessness, left alone by the government) and thus has no other option than to defend themselves and protect the whole nation (terror and exploitation) against the dangerous outgroup (the well-organized international crime cartels, violent foreign gangs, rapists, murderers, and drug dealers). The most common narrative used by the Minutemen is that of the "coyote," the savage "macho man" with a tainted masculinity who rapes women, which stands against the American vision of a man as the guardian of the fragile female. The narrative is used to emphasize the inhumane and immoral nature of the Mexican immigrants, and the heroic image of the own group.

The reasons why individuals join such far-right groups are diverse. Life history interviews with 157 activists of extreme right organizations in Belgium, France, Germany, Italy, and the Netherlands provide insight into how and why individuals have been successfully recruited into right-wing organizations. The researchers identified three types of life histories that differ significantly among countries: continuity, conversion, and compliance. Continuity refers to life histories in which recruitment and membership become a natural consequence of proceeding political experiences and socialization. Conversion, however, arises as a consequence of a significant or critical event, which leads to a break with the past. In this regard, the recruitment process and the decision to join a radical right organization is also accompanied by life dissatisfaction and the internal drive for change. The third trajectory, compliance, refers to situations in which individuals were persuaded by their social group to actively participate in a right-wing organization. The emergence of each trajectory depends on the social and political conditions in a country. In Belgium, France, and Italy—with their viable right-wing sectors—continuity seems to be the most frequent trajectory; that is, socialization leads more often to the recruitment of activists. But also in Germany, where the supply side (the right-wing organizations) is not so viable and strong, recruitment into right-wing organizations follows "organically or naturally" as a consequence of socialization; that is, individuals grew up in an extreme right milieu. In the Netherlands, the weak supply and demand for right-wing organizations does not create viable socialization networks for recruitment, which means that individuals are recruited due to compliance or conversion, or through self-education (acquiring more information out of interest). The author argues that a strong demand and/or supply in a country ensures that comparatively many individuals grow up in a rather right-wing social milieu, and therefore define their recruitment and the membership in a right-wing organization as a natural consequence of their socialization. However, a strong demand for right-wing groups, ideas, and narratives alone is not sufficient to create a strong right-wing base. A weak supply of right-wing organizations results in weak recruitment and mobilization (Klandermans 2013). In conclusion, the life history interviews show that, in particular, socialization and a familiar right-wing network enforce recruitment and activism. Individuals who grow up in an extreme right-wing environment tend to join radical groups more often as a "natural" consequence of their upbringing.

These findings seem to be consistent with the networking structure and interconnectedness of right-wing organizations. As shown in the previous chapter, right-wing groups and organizations maintain good relationships with the social, economic, and political public, as well as with the private sector on a national and international level. The dense network structure enables them to plan and execute events, concerts, conferences, and other social gatherings where new members can easily be recruited. The major instrument that is used to connect, plan, and execute these actions is social media. Social media provides platforms through which individuals can access information, share ideas and beliefs, and communicate with sympathizers—all anonymously. Because right-wing organizations receive less support in public and are less socially accepted, the internet provides the opportunity to search and share information, ideas, and beliefs; to express one's own opinion; and to demonstrate one's affiliation with a right-wing party or group without fearing the possibility of being socially excluded. Such virtual communities provide a viable tool for users to interact on a global space and act as "safe places" for supporters of extremist ideologies. They provide a source for social approval, belonging, and identification, but also for information access (Bowman-Grieve 2013).

One of the most widely known and pioneering radical-right virtual community platforms is Stormfront. Stormfront was established in March 1995 by former Alabama KKK leader Don Black. As of May 2015, the group claimed a membership of more than 300,000 registered members (SPLC). The major mission of Stormfront is "to provide information that is not available in the controlled news media and to build a community of White activists working for the survival of our people" (from "Guidelines for Posting" at stormfront.org). Stormfront has grown into the most popular radical-right website in the Western world due to its focus on community building. Whereas usual radical-right websites focus on one-way information access and ideological dissemination, Stormfront is organized as virtual interaction space, enabling members to share beliefs, express their opinions, and participate in discussions. Below their motto "White Pride World Wide" appear racially loaded "news" headlines, such as "Mestizo Rapes White Woman in Elevator" or "Negro Man Stabs Elderly Woman," which can be read, shared, and commented upon by all members of the virtual community. Members of Stormfront's various forums can also open new threads and discuss issues; this allows them to share their personal concerns, questions, or insecurities. The main part of the forum is divided into various subsections of interest, allowing members to discuss topics, ask questions, share concerns, and receive guidance regarding science, culture and customs, technology and race, ideology and philosophy, revisionism, network security and encryption, privacy, business and finance, self-defense, martial arts, strategies, household matters, caretaking, education, home-schooling, and youth issues (Bowman-Grieve 2009). This variety of topics attracts various individuals, even those who seem to not share the main beliefs and ideals but can identify with the community and their concerns. Besides the interactive tools, members also receive access to articles and books published by leading radical-right movement writers, like Willis Carto, publisher of the Holocaust-denying journal *The Barnes Review*, or Sam Dickson, the leader of the Council of Conservative Citizens (SPLC).

Another success factor of Stormfront is that it has tried to maintain a relatively neutral ideological stance to attract people from different backgrounds and with various beliefs, so that each member could identify, and feel approved by, the community. The virtual community itself is divided into different sections and subsections, targeting different fields of interest and people. There is also a specific international section, divided into subsections by region or country, including members from Europe, Australia, North and South America, and Russia. This enables the virtual community to network on a global scale, to plan events, and to recruit and mobilize individuals, thus creating a global support and information sharing system. Overall, the communication style between members is described as familial, emotional, and supportive. "A sense of community is also enhanced by members who encourage each other to express opinions and viewpoints on topics of interest, and the eager challenging of each other's perspectives. For example, a member may request supporting evidence from another in relation to a comment made. Discourses and debates are often initiated with direct questions; however, while debate is recognized as beneficial to the community, disrespectful behavior (such as name calling, flaming, etc.) are seen as unacceptable forms of behavior. Community rules and behavioral norms can be identified, with these often being stipulated and enforced by the community moderators and administrators. [. . .] In addition, community members often construct their own set of community norms through a process of ingroup monitoring. Ingroup monitoring allows community members to construct and maintain their own rules of acceptability in relation to the content and nature of interactions" (Bowman-Grieve 2009, 997).

While Stormfront provides a platform to attract and recruit different types of supporters, some right-wing organizations use social media to target specific minority groups. In Britain, for example, the National Front publishes the magazine *Blood and Honour* and has a website which specifically targets underrepresented groups, such as women. The website promotes the idea of the "National Women's Front," which describes the narrative of a strong and proud British woman who supports the enforcement of a great and strong nation, following their traditional gender task in educating and nurturing the next British generation. Similar to the Mafia, the narrative of the family is used to portray the importance of morality and role abidance of women, who should nurture the nation and transfer the traditional values to the next generation. The English Defense League (EDL) has a YouTube channel to disseminate its right-wing beliefs and, in particular, to attract women by explaining to them why being nationalistic is socially acceptable. Such videos and messages are persistent and globally accessible, and thus have a higher outreach (Dauber 2017). This accessibility and proximity to end-users eases the path to ideological radicalization and recruitment. But also, enhanced skepticism of mainstream media attracts millions of users every day to consume news and opinions on social media like Twitter, Facebook, and YouTube. A quantitative analysis conducted a large-scale audit on user radicalization on YouTube by analyzing 330,925 videos posted on 349 channels. These channels have been classified into four main types: Media, the Alt-lite, the Alt-right, and the Intellectual Dark Web (IDW), which differ in the extremity of their content. While users in IDW discuss controversial ideas about race and IQ without becoming necessarily extreme, users of the Alt-right channels adopt more White supremacist ideas. The Alt-lite channel positions itself in the middle by frequently flirting with ideas and beliefs associated with White supremacy but actively denying it. The result of the analysis shows that user bases for these communities are similar, but over time a significant number of users migrate from "moderate" to more extreme content. They also show that YouTube's recommendation algorithm suggests Alt-lite and IDW content frequently, through which it is possible to find more extreme content of the Alt-right (Ribeiro et al. 2020).

This implies that social media platforms, such as YouTube, Facebook, or Twitter, can accelerate the radicalization process because they provide easily accessible information about right-wing groups, which in turn use these platforms to inform, attract, and recruit individuals. Beyond belief dissemination, interaction, and recruitment, these platforms are also used for mobilization, which can, in extreme cases, result in intergroup violence (Wahlström and Törnberg 2021). Contemporary examples of such violence range from severe attacks against refugee housing facilities across Europe to mass shootings, such as Utøya in Norway in 2011, Christchurch in New Zealand in 2019, or El Paso in Texas in 2019. The influential study by Koopmans and Olzak (2004) argues that the frequency of violent political actions can be partly explained by the discursive opportunities provided by social media. In other words, the operational success of far-right extremist groups is dependent on the extent to which they are visible, easily accessible, frequent in their responses, and receive social support within the public sphere. In this regard, an empirical study (Müller and Schwarz 2021) provides evidence that social media has a high impact on variations in levels of far-right violence. The authors demonstrate geographical and temporal correlations between anti-immigrant comments and violent far-right incidents against immigrants on the social media pages of the AfD (Alternative für Deutschland), a right-wing political party in Germany. Another research study shows that the exposure to violent far-right rhetoric on social media can enhance the willingness to participate in violent political actions (Pauwels and Schils 2016). As noted earlier, to legitimize violent actions, individuals must engage in moral disengagement techniques and decrease their level of uncertainty. They can do so in either establishing collective norms that frame violence as morally right; deny their own responsibility, the severity of the act, or the existence of "true victims"; or appeal to higher loyalty (superior orders defense).

The most significant technique used in social media is the denial of the victim—or dehumanization—which involves denying humanity to an individual or group (Bandura 1999). A typical manifestation of dehumanization in social media is the use of animal metaphors to devalue and dehumanize a particular group, such as "parasites," "pigs," or "apes." These metaphors generate the perception that the other person is lacking features typically associated with humans that distinguish them from animals (e.g., rationality, mental capacities, etc.) (Haslam 2006). In this regard, an empirical study (Wahlström et al. 2021) analyzed the relationship between political violence and the violent and dehumanizing rhetoric of the Swedish Far-Right Facebook group "Stand up for Sweden," which had 170,000 members and was the largest political Facebook group in Sweden in 2018. The topics that were mostly discussed in threads focused on violent and sexual crimes and the failure of the state (and police) to deal with the increasing violence in disadvantaged neighborhoods. They included stories about perpetrators—mostly immigrants—and their victims—often elderly, children, young women, or animals—which evoked strong emotions, shaped attitudes, and called for violent actions. Victimization topics often included words like child, girl, and woman, accompanied with emojis and proclamations filled with anger, disgust, frustration, and aggression, combined with abusive expressions and dehumanizing connotations. Another topic that frequently evoked violent and dehumanizing rhetoric was the deportation of immigrants, who were described as "parasites," "pigs," and "vermin," and who threaten the social security in the country. Some dehumanizing characterizations even portrayed immigrants as monsters which deserved retaliation and did not have the "right to breath oxygen."

Although other, minor topics were also discussed in threads that dealt with international politics, the "corrupt" establishment, or the economy, they were not loaded with negative emotions or dehumanizing rhetoric. The most violent and strongly affective topics were always related to an outgroup. That said, posts that prompted much violent rhetoric in their subsequent comments were typically related to a particular outgroup and its morally condemnable actions. The victim was hereby portrayed as "weak and reputable, with a strong and unknown offender." Personal stories or witnesses of young immigrants assaulting a seal cub or harassing an old lady, as well as victimized teenage girls, generated the strongest responses and were used to legitimize violent revenge. However, the authors show that it was not the posts that created racist, violent, or dehumanizing rhetoric, but the comments related to a post. This means the posts established a diagnostic frame by portraying a social problem, followed by comments either elaborating on this diagnosis (who is responsible for this problem and how can it be integrated into a broader pattern), or moving on to prognostic framing (which actions to take) and legitimization (why is it morally accepted to do it). "In the most violent threads, a prominent diagnostic frame was that immigration had caused increased criminality and a successive Islamization of society. [. . .] The Swedish police were characterized as too meek, or too restrained by excessively restrictive regulations, to contain the rising criminality. The police monopoly on violence in Swedish society was broadly depicted as failing or as having already failed. While the threat was indeed frequently framed in the comments as coming from Islam and Muslims, other categories were also mentioned, such as Arabs and Roma or more vaguely "immigrants." Perpetrators of crimes were always assumed to be immigrants, even when there was no information about this in a news item" (Wahlström et al. 2021, 3305). A technique used to legitimize violence against this threat was the reference to a higher loyalty (to an ethnically homogeneous state) and denial of responsibility (seeing no other options as violence to restore law and order). All in all, the authors conclude that, in particular, the dehumanizing rhetoric in far-right discussion groups evokes negative emotions and calls for retributive actions, hence reinforcing mobilization and indirectly contribute to intergroup violence.

9.4 Recruitment and Mobilization in Radical Left Organizations

Compared to radical right organizations, the radical left does not portray consistent organizational patterns—ranging from vertically and centrally organized forms of the Old Left, to decentralized horizontal militia groups of the New Left. The radical left groups or organizations in the United States, compared to their counterpart, the radial right, do not form a well-organized network but rather organize themselves in a military "underground" fashion. These groups did not form relationships with the public or private sector, but instead carried out small attacks against the state or private companies to demonstrate their will to revolt. According to empirical studies and the reports published by the Department of Homeland Security (DHS), attacks by left-wing groups aimed at sending symbolic signals instead of targeting humans, relying more on means of property destructions, vandalism, or violent protests (Gaibulloev et al. 2012). This implies that leftist violence was less lethal (less mass violence) because the groups aimed at recruiting and mobilizing the masses to induce social change. "While many of the Marxist-Leninist cadres were decidedly vanguardist, they still envisioned a manner of popular revolt that involved the working class (i.e., international proletariat) taking power. For this to occur, the armed units that constitute the vanguard must be loved and cherished by the people, something difficult to achieve of the population is made to feel unsafe due to frequent explosions in sites of leisure, business, and transport. It is for this reason that leftist violence tends to target *property* or *individuals*, while avoiding more indiscriminate forms of mass violence common in rightist, ethno-nationalist, separatist, and other manners of violent politics" (Loadenthal 2018, 40). In this manner, left-wing groups' political protests and revolts served as an expression of their social, economic, and political grievances, and they sought to demonstrate political critique through direct actions. The argument behind this was that attacks directed toward property or single individuals (such as the US industrialist

Henry Clay Frick, or the Haymarket bombing in Chicago in 1886) had more power to propagate the vision of the groups than speeches and pamphlets alone. However, in the twentieth century, pamphlets remained the main media through which to share information between left-wing groups and individuals, as well as for mobilization. For example, the Italian anarchist Luigi Galleani, who came to the US in 1905, published a pamphlet titled "Salute e in Voi" ["The health is within you"], which instructed readers in manufacturing explosives. This pamphlet was secretly disseminated among other anarchist groups, who used it, for example, to manufacture and place explosives at the home of John D. Rockefeller in 1914. Other shootings and bombings followed, which were argued to demonstrate their anti-state and anti-capitalist sentiments, but which also received less public support, and particularly after the Wall Street bombing in 1920, the anarchist groups in the United States almost vanished.

In Europe, the Old Left groups and organizations were more "successful" in their operations, recruitment, and mobilization. Prior and during World War II, the Communist parties in Eastern Europe were mainly operating as underground militia groups due to the repression of right-wing regimes allied with Germany. Many of the members of the underground organizations fled during the Nazi occupation to Moscow, which reduced the membership size of the "home" communists to no more than thirty thousand members. But following the military occupation of Eastern Europe by the Red Army, the emigrated communists returned to their home countries and rejoined organizations with an effort to transform their respective parties into leading political institutions (Hanley 2003). National statistics show that, by 1948, the Communist Party had gained high popular support in many Eastern European countries and evolved into mass parties with thousands, or even millions, of members (Molnar 1978). Especially in these countries, the membership in the Communist Party was, at least partly, a precondition for promotion to higher educational levels and positions of higher office. Because upward mobility was administered centrally, it was granted to those sharing the political beliefs and values of the main party (Walder 1985), which would imply that at least a number of people joined the group only for instrumental reasons.

During the periods of industrialization and modernization, the recruitment of new members into the Communist Party was not merely based on political loyalty, activity, and class background, but increasingly on the basis of educational qualifications. However, empirical evidence on the Party composition remains scarce, and has been only provided by Party officials themselves in the past (Wong 1996). To close this research gap, an empirical study

(Hanley 2003) examined the recruitment strategies used by the Communist Party in five Eastern European countries: Hungary, Poland, Bulgaria, and the Czech and Slovak Socialist Republics. Data have been obtained of nationally representative samples of the adult populations collected in 1993. The author elaborates that, after 1949, "the Communist Party came to function as the real government in the countries that fell behind the Iron Curtain, first by creating a bureaucratic structure that mirrored that of the formal government at the national and local levels and, second by establishing local committees in workplaces, administrative units, villages, and neighborhoods. In addition, an elaborate system of surveillance was established that relied not only on police agents and their networks of informants but also the maintenance of political dossiers on every citizen; these dossiers were reviewed by Party committees when individuals were considered for admission to higher education or job promotions" (Hanley 2003, 1076).

To ensure the smooth operation of the surveillance system, the Party had to occupy positions of authority with Party loyalists. The recruitment strategy thus involved the idea that individuals from underprivileged socioeconomic backgrounds, who received the opportunity of upward mobility as a result of their commitment and loyalty to the Communist Party, were more likely to continue adhering to the rules, beliefs, and demands of the Party (Jowitt 1992). Official statistics provided by the Communist Party show that more than sixty percent of Party members in Poland, Hungary, Czechoslovakia, and Bulgaria were factory and agricultural workers (de Weydenthal 1986). However, in the 1960s, so argued by the "deproletarianization" approach, a shift away from sole party loyalty toward educational and technical competence in the recruitment processes occurred, spurred by the rapid expansion of the educational system of the working class. The change of the recruitment strategy has been associated with the changed goal of the Party—away from the consolidation of power to more economic growth and development (Giddens 1973; Walder 1985). This shift from "loyalty to meritocracy" in Party recruitment also involved changed weights in the characteristics and preconditions of individuals: during the reconstruction period, characteristics like the parent's Party membership or socio-cultural background (lower working class) enhanced the probability of being recruited, while during the post-reconstruction era (from 1960s) individual characteristics like education and proficiency played a more important role. Similar changes in the recruitment system have been observed in China between 1949 and 1996, where education immensely increased the likelihood of becoming a member in the Chinese Communist Party. While professionals and educated people were (violently) excluded by the Party during the Mao regime (1949–1977), in the late reform period they received more opportunities to join the Party. The criterion of family affiliation with the Communist Party was also removed from the recruitment process (Walder et al. 2000).

However, due to lack of clear empirical evidence, there is still much ambiguity about the strategies and preconditions in Communist Party recruitment across Eastern European countries. The results of the empirical analysis mentioned previously (Hanley 2003) indicate clear patterns of recruitment: women were greatly underrepresented in the Communist Party in all observed countries (thirty percent or less in Poland and the Czech and Slovak Socialist Republics); members whose fathers worked in a nonmanual occupations have been overrepresented within the Party, which would imply that having a privileged background would increase the likelihood of membership. Furthermore, respondents whose fathers had an affiliation with the Communist Party (in terms of belongingness) were also overrepresented among Party members across all Eastern European countries. Regarding education, having a university or college degree had a strong and positive effect on the probability of being successfully recruited into the Party, in particular in Poland, Bulgaria, and Hungary, and less in the Czech and Slovak Socialist Republics. The author concludes that the results provide partial support for the established "deproletarianization" approach in the sense that they show declining effects of family background as a recruitment criteria but the results contradict the approach in terms of education. When it comes to occupation, the analysis shows that managers and supervisors were eagerly recruited into the Party, preferably those with a previous position of authority.

Considering these results, many researchers argue that individuals joined the Communist Party in China, Russia, and Eastern Europe because of their monopolistic status in society (i.e., distribution of goods and resources such as jobs, education, housing, or health care, etc.). This would imply that the majority joined the Party not for ideological reasons, but for instrumental reasons. While this may apply to some individuals, the analysis in Chapter 8 showed that Communism also has the capacity to address various psychological needs of individuals. The early stages of industrialization and modernization in these countries produced poverty and unemployment among the working class, which had few political rights of co-determination. Estimates of the unemployment rate in the 1940s and 1950s in Eastern Europe and China were particularly high, totaling twenty to thirty percent of the farm population (Berry and Sabot 1984). The traditional patterns of family and community that were disrupted by economic transition and the cultural implications of modernization created physically and psychologically uprooted individuals. Communism in this sense offered mental stability in form of a closed meaning system and guidance on how to deal with the increased complexity (Salzman 2008). The Communist Party offered loyal members the opportunity of upward mobility, but at the same time it also provided new recruits with a sense of belongingness and orientation. An empirical study (Denver and Bochel 1973) analyzed the political socialization of activists in the British Communist Party in 1966 to understand why individuals joined a party that was not much represented and supported in the city of Dundee. The relatively small number of interviewed communists (n = 43) has been compared with the general Labour voters (n = 279) and Labour activists (n = 31). The results show that the majority of the Communist activists were more likely than either of the other group to have a low working-class background. The authors exemplify that during this period of time, the life of the working-class in Dundee (and in Britain in general) was marked by high unemployment and harsh living conditions. Another factor that tends to explain recruitment into the Communist Party is socialization; that is, the familial voting behavior of the respondents. The data indicate that the majority of the Communist Party activists were raised in a non-conservative and non-religious familial setting where at least one parent affiliated with either a left-wing or Communist party. This is remarkable, given the fact that the support of the Communist Party in Britain was not very high at that time. Another reason for membership that has been mentioned by the Communist Party activists was the lack of order in the post-war and recession period. Some interviewees mentioned the Spanish Civil War, or the increased poverty in other countries, that led to chaos, disorder, and instability, that led them to rethink their political support. Regarding media outlets, most Communist Party activists, but to a lesser extent the Labour voters and activists, stated that regular newspapers, BBC TV, and BBC Radio were not reliable sources of information. While the majority of the Communist Party activists were using the same media outlets as the other two groups, they were also eager to read additional party literature (higher reading habits). This means that the Communist Party offered its own produced newspapers and magazines for information transfer, recruitment, and mobilization (Denver and Bochel 1973).

A similar study (Dickson and Rublee 2000) analyzed the self-recruitment of individuals into the Chinese Communist Party (CCP) during the reform era, which induced market independence from the party for distribution of goods, jobs, housing, and resources. "During the Maoist era, gaining access to the CCP was the sole means of career mobility, but post-Mao reforms created new opportunities for pursuing career goals. Individuals could seek advanced degrees from Chinese or foreign universities and thereby pursue careers on the basis of their technical expertise, or they could engage in entrepreneurial activities to accrue higher incomes" (Dickson and Rublee 2000, 88). Looking at historical recruitment processes at the CCP in 1949, its members were generally young, poorly educated, of peasant background, and more experienced in underground militia operations than in organizational development. The Party thus shifted their recruitment targets to expand its membership nationwide and to recruit more educated, technically skilled individuals. But the recruitment periods were subject to fluctuations: during the Great Leap Forward (1958–1960) the membership size rose by fifty percent, while during the period of recovery (1960–1964), the recruitment of new members stagnated. The Cultural Revolution fueled the recruitment process and the Party recruited members mostly for their ideological adherence rather than professional skills. During this time, the CCP doubled in size, growing from 18.7 million to 35.1 million members (Dickson 1997). However, at the time of Mao's death, the CCP struggled with organizational and personnel problems because their members were too old, too ideologically radical, and too low educated to implement the new reforms of Deng Xiaoping. Consequently, the CCP introduced new recruitment criteria, focusing more on young and well-educated individuals. As result, the average age of Party and government officials at the local, county, and prefecture level decreased from sixty-two to fifty-five, and the number of college or university graduates rose to 73.6 percent among them. The Chinese Household Income Project (CHIP 1988) survey data show that, in 1988, the members of CCP were, in general, male, well educated, and older than non-members (what resembles the Party composition in Eastern Europe), while holding all relevant positions in the public and private sector (eighty-four percent officials, seventy-seven percent factory managers and directors, and only seven percent laborers). Using and analyzing the CHIP data, Dickson and Rublee (2000) confirm that the CCP mostly attracts male, well-educated individuals of old age. Party membership also incurs monetary benefits for an individual's income, including bonuses and subsidies as well as a higher salary, in particular for those with a cadre status. A second incentive to join the party is enhanced access to positions related to officials and factory managers, but less for office work and technical positions. Especially for the younger generation, having a good education and being a party member can increase job market opportunities, in particular, in the public sector.

In the course of globalization and enhanced complexity, the CCP has shifted its target recruitment group to more lawyers and private entrepreneurs, which, the latter, would contradict the history of CCP and their negative attitude toward private entrepreneurship. But to adapt to changed external conditions and the growing private sector in China, CCP enhanced their recruitment of private sector entrepreneurs. But also, foreign-educated returnees, graduating from prestige universities in the United States and Europe, have been gradually recruited into the party. This would imply that the CCP constantly adapts their recruitment strategies to changing global conditions, which created a bipartisanship within the party: the "elitist" and the "populist" coalition. The elitist coalition consists of private entrepreneurs, foreign-educated returnees, or children of high-raking officials, while the populist coalition encounters members from rather low-ranked, working-class backgrounds. The two coalitions represent two different socioeconomic classes and geographical regions, and can hence address, while both united by one party, different concerns, goals, and needs of different social classes. The elitist group emphasizes economic growth, while the populist group strives for social justice and social integration. Both coalitions have equal decisional power, and each has different expertise and skills that complements the other (Li 2009).

The recruitment processes of the New Left radical groups differ significantly from those of the Old Left—the usually clandestine, revolutionary-toned militia groups operated underground and recruited new members through established (underground) networks. In the early 1960s, the United States began to experience a new wave of "New Left" movements, inspired by Marxist-Leninist views and anti-colonial sentiments. But also in Europe, groups like the Red Army Faction in West Germany, the Red Brigades in Italy, or Action Directe in France have been formed to fight against the dehumanizing effects of capitalism and imperialism (Loadenthal 2018). Research on both Old Left and New Left recruitment processes is comparatively low; however, the existing studies show that New Left groups recruit new members within homogeneous groups aggregated on the basis of multiple ties. Della Porta (1988) examined the recruitment processes of the four most important New Left radical groups in Italy: the Red Brigades, the Proletarian Armed Groups, the Front Line, and the Communist Fighting Formation (and some other minor groups) and showed that social ties and networks play an important role in recruitment and mobilization. The decision to join (or self-recruit into) a left-wing underground organization was amplified if the person had at least one friend already involved in that organization. But also, clusters of people or cliques can be jointly recruited into an organization, such as neighbors, colleagues, classmates, or relatives. Della Porta shows that in 289 of the cases in his sample (n = 789), militants had other relatives, such as wife/husband or brother/sister, who shared their commitment. He elaborates that recruitment into left-wing organizations is more likely when it is reinforced by previous social ties, and that one major motivation is social approval. The data show that the majority of the individuals who had been recruited into the Italian left-wing groups were affiliated with the recruiters, and hence knew them before joining the group. Such reciprocal affiliations were essential for reducing the risks a clandestine underground group faces when recruiting new members. Another prerequisite to join an Italian left-wing group was political engagement and knowledge. The data reveal that some of the members of the left-wing radical groups were actively engaged in other legal political organizations, such as the "Worker Power" or "Continuous Struggle" before joining the extremist group, and that these political ties were even more important than social ties in terms of recruitment. This implies that Italian clandestine left-wing organizations recruited new members "from tight-knit networks of social relations in which political ties were strengthened by primary solidarity based on friendship and kinship relations. These networks offered loyalty channels of communication to the underground groups" (Della Porta 1988, 163).

Recruitment and mobilization practices of clandestine New Left radical groups are hardly studied because of their hidden mode of operation. Activists who join underground organizations usually break significant social ties to mainstream institutions, which limits the possibility to recruit from these populations. For that account, many researchers argue that affective ties in clandestine New Left organizations were vital to preserve loyalty and recruit from existing social networks. Social bonds, a shared collective identity, and beliefs have been regarded as the premise for successful mobilization and opposing forces to the individualization of the capitalist system (Zwerman et al. 2000). Life history stories of left-wing militants show that loyalty and solidarity preserved and reinforced personal commitment to the group. In an interview, a German left-wing militant said that "the identity or identification with the group is like an alarm clock that always rings an 'I keep going' . . . when, with a residual spark of self-preservation, you ask yourself 'Why?' . . . You cannot cut the thick bonds the group has covered you with in the course of time. One's whole existence was first of all in the group . . . the entire existence of all of us was first of all the group" (Speitel 1980, 34). Despite this strong group coherence, the New Left movements of the 1960s and 1970s started to decline due to ambiguous ideological beliefs, goals, and fracturing identities, and collapsed entirely after the breakdown of the Soviet Union (Loadenthal 2018). As more and more individuals started to leave the clandestine underground groups, they became more closed without topsider links to above-ground institutions. This state of isolation changed their recruitment sources from political and mainstream institutions like universities to more non-political sources such as runaways, drifters, and criminals who had weak ideological adherence but much knowledge on underground illegal operations (Zwerman et al. 2000).

As the Marxist-Leninist inspired organizations declined over time, new left-wing organizations like the Animal Liberation Front (ALF) and the Earth Liberation Front (ELF) formed, which quickly became internationalized. Unlike the clandestine organizations, they operated, recruited, and mobilized new members in a more visible form. Existing studies, if not many, show that, in particular, the mass media and music play an important role in recruitment and mobilization (Koch 2018; Figeac et al. 2021). ELF, for example, used their aboveground website, NAELFPO, to disseminate training and logistic information, but also to attract and mobilize sympathizers. By paying attention to attacks, strikes, and revolts of the militia group, the mass media disseminated information about this group that might have conditioned some individuals to support its goals and missions. In other words, mass media helped interested individuals to find the group's website, which served as a source for recruitment and technical guidance. Although the website has been banned, some of its communiqués can still be accessed through third-party websites, such as Bite Back Magazine or the North American Animal Liberation Press Office, from which individuals can receive reading material and learn operational skills, such as weapons production, sabotage, and protection (Loadenthal 2013).

However, mass media is not only sharing information. It also communicates through manipulated narratives, symbols, and emotions. The well-established left-wing group the Revolutionary Armed Forces of Colombia (FARC), for example, has its own radio channel, the "Voice of Resistance," that is operated by communications managers who are responsible for the dissemination of ideological beliefs and narratives. "Claiming that they do their shooting from the radio, disk jockeys play traditional Colombian hit songs with one twist: in FARC's adaptation the songs have more radical lyrics and revolutionary titles such as 'We Will Conquer,' 'Ambush Rap' and 'Guerrilla Girls.' Nobody knows for sure the size of FARC radio's audience—mostly impoverished peasants, many of whom cultivate illegal coca leaf, the raw material for the production of cocaine, but in the rugged terrain that is controlled by the group, commercial radio is difficult to receive. Thus the 'Voice of Resistance' fills a void and, at the same time, exploits the airwaves for propaganda messages and recruiting pitches" (Nacos 2016, 49).

With the exception of developing countries, in which the access to the internet and the mass media may be constrained, social media channels like Facebook, YouTube, or Twitter are widely used by modern left-wing radical groups. While the roles of music and social media of right-wing extremist and religious fundamentalist groups are adequately studied, their role in left-wing extremism lack considerable research. Koch (2018), for example, argues that the anarchist's revolt during the G20 summit in Germany in July 2017 has been fueled by militant anti-fascist propaganda videos and anti-fascist music, which portrayed the activists as wild, aggressive, and militant. These videos were distributed under the title "Welcome to Hell," with some of them being posted on the *Autonome Aktion Europe* Facebook page (not available anymore), which informed the viewer about the anarchist activities in Europe. Another website, *Its Going Down*—a popular and well-known webpage among anarchists—shares news, reports, podcasts, and columns, and has an internationally connected Twitter account. The author exemplifies that social media use, and the internet in general, has facilitated recruitment and mobilization tremendously, and is now an essential part of modern anti-fascist, anarchist groups. To date, however, there has been a lack of consistent research addressing these important organizational processes, as well as the role of new tools, which need more attention across academic disciplines.

9.5 Recruitment and Mobilization in Radical Religious Organizations

Similar to their political counterparts, radical religious organizations or groups employ a distinct organizational structure that represents both their goals and their ideological world views. The mostly vertical religious organizations show a centralized order with prescribed roles and duties, and a high demand for strict adherence to rules, beliefs, and norms—which address a variety of psychological human needs. However, we also saw in Chapter 9 that radical religious organizations like the Islamic State, Hamas, or Al-Qaeda provide full-fledged, communal services to their adherents that go beyond the standard organizational offer. Iannaccone and Berman (2006) hence define religious organizations as "communities, dedicated to the production of communal goods and the pursuit of communal goods. [. . .] [They] flourish because they provide their members hope for the future, benefits for the present, and insurance against misfortune" (118). This means that those religious extremist organizations that can maintain their credibility and minimize free riding will operate successfully, especially where poor government or civil disorder undermines the provision of vital resources and services. "From Egypt and Palestine to Pakistan, Afghanistan, and Indonesia, radical Islamist groups have enjoyed broad support especially among the poorest segments of society—because they are major suppliers of mutual aid and social services" (Iannaccone and Berman 2006, 119). These goods and social services are provided under the pretext of the *umma*, the global Islamic religious community, which should be organized under a caliphate. Broadly speaking, this is the narrative that all Islamist organizations agree on, while rejecting the Westphalian nation-state model (Gartenstein-Ross et al. 2016). While different Islamist groups follow their own interests and goals, by operating on a local and regional level, their interconnectedness allows them to communicate, recruit, and mobilize individuals on a global scale.

In Tunisia, for example, the Islamist group Ansar al-Sharia (AST), which was established after the revolution in 2011, operated based on its own immediate interests, but also collaborated intensively with other national radical groups, like the Al-Qaeda in the Islamic Maghrib (AQIM), recruited and trained foreign fighters to support the Islamic State in Syria, and extended its presence in Iraq and Libya by building local AST groups. Although AST and AQIM pursued contradicting goals at the local level, both supported each other in terms of recruitment and mobilization at the regional level. AST helped AQIM, for example, to recruit new members from Tunisia for operations in Mali and assisted with mobilizing individuals in Libya to fight in Syria. This implies that both groups operate under the umbrella of the global Islamic community—by sharing the same fundamental beliefs, interests, and understanding of international relations, the common enemy and regional politics—and at the same time they act individually on a local level by pursuing their own distinct goals.

When AST was active in Tunisia between 2011 and 2013, it recruited and disseminated their beliefs primarily through their official Facebook page and website, which was hosted in Germany and registered to an Abu Usamah al-Muslim in Roubaix, France. The primarily goal of the group was to reeducate the Tunisians about Islam and to establish an Islamic state in Tunisia based on the Sharia law. AST was basically organized in a vertical structure consisting of a leader, an official spokesperson, three committees, and three offices. Similar to Al-Qaeda, it employed a high number of "middle managers," who communicated with both the leadership and the local grass-root supporters, which enabled strategic decision-making at the national level and the implementation at the local level. This means that implementation was decentralized, which allowed local grass-roots supporters (and also new members) to feel a sense of autonomy and self-efficacy. The group also employed its own clerics and callers to the correct interpretation of the Islam, who acted on a local, regional, and national level. To recruit members from rural areas in Tunisia, the group implemented "social service campaigns," in which members drove to impoverished rural areas to provide goods and services, such as food, water, and medical, repair, and construction services. One of these affected regions was Haydrah, where people live in isolation and suffer from resource deprivation. AST's campaign provided goods and services for these people in need—serving sixty families with rice, bread, pasta, canned goods, water, warm clothes, and blankets—all under the guise of Allah, by spreading the narrative of the creation of a strong Islamic state or Caliphate (Zelin 2020).

By providing such goods and services, the group established a changed understanding of the Jihad, shifting the narrative away from pure *fighting* to *enrichment of oneself and one's community* (Gartenstein-Ross et al. 2014). Hence, these activities were symbolic for the formation of a strong Islamic state and aimed at serving individuals' needs—not only their existential and materialistic needs, but also their needs for autonomy, self-efficacy, and self-esteem by giving, in particular, power and resources to individuals who felt left behind by the top-down and bureaucratic government. Instead, AST promoted itself as an inclusive, supportive, young, and less centralized organization where every member has been valued and given opportunities to restore their agency. New recruits have been welcomed warmly to the community, which was built on solidarity, charity, brotherhood, or sisterhood. The group also extensively supported refugees by building temporary housing for them and providing medical health and food to build relationships for future recruitment. One of the main narratives of the group when providing such services to the people in need was "*abna'ukum fi khadamatukum*" ("your sons are at your service"), an attempt to illustrate that those in AST were working on Tunisians' behalf and that they are members of the community and not people from a distant faceless entity like the central government. AST promoted the message that, while the central government overpromises and underdelivers, "'we' in AST were working hard to improve your health and the broader community. By ingratiating itself to a particular town or community, AST bought goodwill and an opening to perform ideological outreach to facilitate its broader project of building an Islamic state" (Zelin 2020, 146).

The case of AST implies that individuals may join a radical group not primarily because of its ideology but because of its provision of resources and opportunities, in particular for young people and those who feel left behind by the government, to address their fundamental human needs. Other cases, however, show that ideology indeed plays the major role in recruitment and mobilization, as seen with the Hizb al-Tahrir al-Islami (Islamic Liberation Party). The group was founded in 1952 in Jerusalem by Taqi al-Din al-Nabhani, with the central aim to restore the Islamic Caliphate. Over the years it has transformed itself into a transnational Islamic organizations, covering a chain of commands in the Middle East, Central Asia, Western Europe, the United States, South-East Asia, and Australia (Gross 2012). When the group started to operate, it created several study circles in which new members were recruited only in terms of ideological beliefs. Only fully committed members, who embraced the ideology and adhered consequently to its rules, were admitted to the group (Taji-Farouki 1996).

Shifting their base to Beirut, Lebanon, in 1960, the group initiated a campaign to enhance their membership size and gain popular support among the Lebanese public. To fulfil this goal, members communicated directly with the people, and went from door to door to establish personal relationships with them, as well as propagate the ideology and the offered study circles. This educational approach expected to intensively indoctrinate new members in study circles, who were then trained to disseminate their beliefs and knowledge to the public. A field study (Gross 2012) with female members of Hizb al-Tahrir al-Islami shows that the indoctrination process, or the formation of ideological knowledge, was a sequential learning process. The ideology was not disseminated in a fast and efficient way, but rather slowly and consistently to form sound and unwavering ideological knowledge. But what motivated women to join the study circles and continue to visit the weekly meetings in the first place? The author argues that none of the women who joined the group were deprived or had a low-income background; they came from middle-class families, were well educated, and were integrated into society. Instead, their motive was social justice; that is, to change the social and political institutions and create an egalitarian society based on solidarity and equality. The ideological manifesto of Hizb al-Tahrir al-Islami proclaimed to reduce social inequality in the highly divided Lebanon, guided by the principle to address people's needs and implement a just Islamic State (see Taji-Farouki 1996, appendix IV). This means that individual grievances did not motivate the women to join the group, but instead they were motivated by the collective grievances of disadvantaged individuals in society.

This is consistent with the empirical work done by Mueller (2021), who observed that individuals (especially young males) whose needs for identification with the social value system and collective existential security had gone unsatisfied were highly likely to join extremist organizations that espoused religiously fundamentalist (Islamic) ideology. Similar to the women in Lebanon, the young individuals were neither socioeconomically deprived nor uneducated, but instead, they could not identify with the society they lived in and experienced an intense grievance pertaining to group-level threats and injustices. This implies that individuals may join radical groups not because of individual grievances, but because of their disagreements with society. Feeling attached to a particular group that is believed to be under threat or has been subject to injustice (real or imagined), increases an individual's willingness to retaliate. This means that individuals' perceptions and experiences of grievance are significantly shaped by the social context in which they are embedded (Akerlof and Kranton 2010). Hence, individuals who may have a good social standing but feel that their social group is under threat or treated unfairly can feel compelled to retaliate injustices committed against their ingroup (McCauley and Moskalenko 2011).

Although felt collective injustice was a strong motivation of Lebanese women to join Hizb al-Tahrir al-Islami, the author (Gross 2012) expands upon the major reason why they joined the group; namely, identity and group belongingness. The group didn't offer social services or material goods to their adherents but it portrayed itself as the "receiver and owner of the truth." The selective and elitist image of the group, paired with the emphasis on intellect and knowledge, attracted those who wanted to belong to a "chosen" and secretive group that stood out among the plethora of other Islamic organizations. The group demanded strict rule abidance and rejected individuals based on non-conformity. Only the adoption of its shared identity and adherence to the guiding principles generated the symbolic reward of *wa'y*, the high awareness and knowledge which clearly distinguished the members from other Islamists. To maintain its image of exclusiveness, the group used their informal networks and recruited intensively among family, friends, and relatives. Another mobilization factor was ingroup monitoring. If women missed study circles or group meetings, other ingroup members contacted them immediately and urged them, in a caring and empathic way, to not miss any sessions. This generated, on the one hand, a sense of importance and belonging to the group (which enhanced their sense of self-esteem), and, on the other hand, reduced the free-rider problem. This emotional attachment to the group was a precondition for being willing to fully adopt and follow the group's ideology and political goals.

A major recruitment tool that has been used by radical religious groups and organizations, in particular in developed nations, is social media. Social media enable organizations to overcome physical and cultural barriers to spread information and to recruit and mobilize individuals all over the world. Especially after the 9/11 attacks, it has become difficult for religious radical groups, particularly Islamists, to cultivate operatives and travel across borders as Western security agencies have started to closely observe their behavioral patterns and organizational networks. To continue their operations, recruit new members, radicalize and mobilize their target audiences, and carry out attacks, these religious extremist groups have shifted their *modus operandi* to the internet. The internet is an efficient, decentralized, and anonymous method for propaganda, recruitment, and mobilization because it neither requires many resources nor a face-to-face interaction. In essence, it enables the groups and organizations to reach out to their target audience—young men in aged sixteen to twenty-two, which is the largest demographic population online in the West. In the US, these groups spend, on average, thirty-two hours per month online playing games, using messengers, or watching music videos (Gruen 2006). Most recently, this time has included almost seven hours of social media use per day (Rogers 2019).

According to the Pew Research Center, YouTube (eighty-one percent) and Facebook (sixty-nine percent) were the dominant social media tools that have been used by American citizens in 2021, followed by Instagram, TikTok, and Snapchat, which have an especially strong following among eighteen- to twenty-nine-year-olds (PEW 2021). Another tool that has been extensively used for propaganda is Twitter. A social network analysis of the Islamist Twitter account @shamiwitness shows that it interacted with more than 877 other Twitter users to form a dynamic social network through tweet exchanges. The network shows that @shamiwitness interacted with four distinct populations of Twitter users, namely international media, national Arabic media, IS sympathizers, and IS fighters. Fake news and propaganda were disseminated through this network to increase support among individuals, but active solicitations were also sent to each individual for recruitment and mobilization purposes (Chatfield et al. 2015). "The comprehensive online propaganda campaign includes truth mixed with exaggeration and also some blatant deception. A steady stream of testimonials from well-known persons respected by the target subject, and from those he regards as peers, transforms his thinking about the world. Adversaries' positions are ridiculed. The target will be overwhelmed with literature that threatens grave consequences for not following the extremist's objectives. Finally, the target is bombarded with material that forces him to question his beliefs and persuades him that the radical's way of life is better for him and his loved ones" (Gruen 2006, 14).

A case analysis (Gruen 2006) of the political organization Hizb ut-Tahrir (HT), which supports Al-Qaeda and uses its worldwide presence to overthrow Western governments through nonviolent means, shows how the organization developed its own pop culture by producing video games and promoting hip-hop artists to spread its radical ideology. HT uses message boards to reach out to Muslim individuals living in the United States, especially second-generation Muslims, who feel vulnerable in terms of their beliefs and belongingness. The link to the board can be found by interested individuals on other websites or through search engines, where they will be slowly introduced to other members and the goals of the organization. Those who are already members of HT share positive information about the organization and its beliefs, goals, and successful operations, as well as convince newcomers why joining the group would change their lives for the better. Contrasting viewpoints are not accepted on the board, which enables HT to create a unified and homogeneous group that supposedly shares the same beliefs, identity, and intentions. This full-fledged online community generates a sense of empowerment, belongingness, and mutual understanding, that puts high social pressure on dissidents. Hence, an individual who may not fully agree with the group's ideology or who had no inclination to become a member, may do so because he has developed an intense relationship to this online peer group. Once the subject has become more deeply involved in the online community, the organization switches to a direct communication by sending an individual constant emails filled with information about other group-sponsored websites. The direct emails will not only question the individual's previous way of thinking and believing, but they will also ridicule authorities in the individual's direct social environment. Guidelines about how to behave, think, and perceive the environment will be introduced, and a radical group leader will be presented as a wise and benevolent authority to follow. Having had their previous life shattered, the already vulnerable individual is offered a social role in the organization and a purpose, both of which may have been lacking in their previous life.

Beyond social media, music seems to play a significant part in recruitment and mobilization across all ideological radical groups. In his book, *Radicalism and Music*, Jonathan Pieslak (2015) examines the music cultures of Al-Qaeda, racist skinheads, Christian-affiliated radicals, and Eco-Animal Rights Activists, and he shows how music can facilitate the formation of social bonds, identity, and self-expression while mobilizing for actions. One of the examples he includes in the book is the case of Arid Uka, a twenty-one-year-old of Kosovo-Albanian descent living in Frankfurt, Germany, who attacked a group of American soldiers at the airport, killing two of them. This act of retaliation was, in part, fueled by YouTube videos the perpetrator watched the day before committing the crime. One video, titled "Americans raping our sisters! Wake up ummah!" shows a rape scene from the movie *Redacted*, which fictionalizes a real-life case of US military soldiers who raped a girl and killed an Iraqi family in 2006. The YouTube video had been disseminated on an Islamist website, which had been propagated on a Facebook Islamist group. But his last doubts, according to Uka, had been eradicated by music—Islamic *jihad*-themed songs (*anashid*) that he shared on YouTube and Facebook with his Islamist community. According to the German police investigation, the perpetrator was also indirectly mobilized by the ex-rapper Deso Dogg, who converted to Islam and now calls himself Abu Malik. Abu Malik has created *anashid* songs that praise *jihad* and martyrdom, and he commented on Arid

Uka's actions, depicting them as an active defense against the American threat ("who aims to kill Muslims"). "Uka's use of song to sustain a violent course of action, with a specific socioreligious and sociopolitical purpose, is as old as music itself. Throughout the history of war, men have continually employed music to inspire themselves for combat. Before and during battle, music has been a catalyst to heighten anger, aggression, and the appetite for violence. Religious organizations have consistently found music an expedient tool to assert or maintain control over congregations and to inspire the violent fervor of religious defense" (Pieslak 2015, 17).

Both ex-rappers like Abu Malik in Germany and Islamist hip-hop bands in the United States aim to promote political awareness and mobilize for retaliation. For example, the hip-hop band Arab Legion is closely linked to Hizb ut-Tahrir, and often expresses anger over the US interventions in Muslim countries to shape the political beliefs and attitudes of its listeners. Although the lyrics do not call for insurgency, they clearly address the feelings of target subjects, particularly those who are vulnerable in terms of their own beliefs. Listening to such lyrics that reduce one's own uncertainty and guide one as to how to think and perceive external events increases emotional attachment and compliance with that group. But lyrics can also be brutal and extreme, calling for violence and glorifying terrorism. The British hip-hop band Soul Salah Crew produces "Terror Rap," covering simple words in which extremist organizations, like Hamas and Hizballah, but also the 9/11 attack, are glorified, and politicians like Tony Blair and George W. Bush get insulted as dirty *Kuffar* (disbelievers) who should be thrown on fire. Usually, the lyrics are easy to memorize, aer catchy, and are meant to be repeated like a mantra. Such videos are released directly over the internet, which enables free and unlimited accessibility (Gruen 2006).

However, the identity and the level of extremism of such groups are sometimes difficult to identify. Groups such as Hizb ut-Tahrir use "honeypot" sites that do not appear extreme at first glance, but which are used to introduce unsuspecting individuals to their radical ideology. After the group was banned from university campuses at the United Kingdom, it launched a website called *www.muslimstudent.org*. The website neither appeared extreme on the surface nor was linked to the extremist group, and thus it attracted many Muslim students who were searching for a community and student activities. Only after a student has participated in one of the offered activities, would the connection to the group be revealed. Similar websites have been also launched in the United States. In Los Angeles, for example, the hip-hop band Soldiers of Allah (SOA) hosts a professional and modern website, which does not reveal any information about its linkage to Hizb ut-Tahrir, unless the target subjects join the band's fan community. The band promotes the ideology of HT, proclaiming that *Kuffar* (disbelievers) cause harm to Muslim nations and that the only solution would be the establishment of an Islamic state that unites all Muslims around the globe. The lyrics also highlight that the true will of all Muslims is oppressed by corrupt governments and alerts all listeners to take action to incite change (Gruen 2006). This form of manipulation creates the impression that all Muslims strive for one cause but feel oppressed to do so, and therefore mobilizes listeners to "rise up and be strong." Although all forms of music are forbidden under the radical interpretation of Islam, such songs are perceived as a passive (and sacred) recitation of radical doctrines (Pieslak 2015).

Radical Christian groups, like the Westboro Baptist Church (WBC), also use media and music for recruitment and mobilization. The WBC was founded in 1931 as a branch of the East Side Baptist Church of Topeka, Kansas, which follows the five-point Calvinist teachings. The group is relatively small, consisting of around seventy people who are mostly the relatives and children of its founder, Pastor Phelps (Pieslak 2015). The ideology of the WBC is based on anti-homosexuality, anti-abortion, and anti-sin. The Bible serves as the literal and unquestionable law of God and as a guiding source of their behavior, perception, and beliefs. Every action, tragedy, or external event is explained as God's predetermined plan and is accepted uncontestably (Barrett-Fox 2016). The WBC became prominent in the media because of its radical and violent language and protests, as well as its creation of memes and mocking videos that are spread through its numerous websites, blogs, and thirty-six Twitter accounts. They receive, on average, two thousand to three thousand visitors per day and the group spends more than $200,000 per year to travel to picket sites to promote its beliefs and convictions (Pieslak 2015). Although the group emphasizes following the Bible uncontestably, it deconstructs and reinterprets the content of the Bible by rejecting the view that "God loves everyone." Only those who follow their rules and beliefs receive love from God, which creates an exclusive form of belonging. This exclusivity is underscored by the lack of ties or alliances with other religious groups, the rejection of outside donations, and the low intake of new members. The group members see publishing and releasing the word and "hatred" of God as their duty and have referred themselves as the "Weapons of Mass Publication." Their most popular argument revolves around tragic external events, such as the 9/11 attack or Hurricane Katrina, which are seen as the result of God's hate for Americans' sinful behavior, in particular homosexuality.

Conducting interviews with fifty-one WBC members and analyzing their protests and two thousand artifacts disseminated by the group, an empirical study (Powell-Williams and Powell-Williams 2017) observed the WBC's tactics and the mechanisms responsible for their mobilization success. The authors argue that the WBC contrasts significantly with other religious groups by their unusual and intentional coupling of feelings that are otherwise considered culturally and even morally oppositional. "The two most common forms of this practice are the verbal and written assertions that the Christian God is capable of hatred and an emasculation of traditionally masculine and/or conservative individuals" (1445). During protests and picket lines, and within their media presence, the group uses sentiments to provoke intense responses, which is very effective in their continued mobilization (e.g., laughing at funerals while holding signs like "God Hates Your Tears" or "You Cry, God Laughs"; ridiculing tragic events while blaming the victims, such as "Thank God for Dead Soldiers"; arguing that the 9/11 attack was a gift from God to finally "wake up and turn back to the ways of God," etc.). Another mobilizing tactic is the denigration of individuals, symbols, or groups that are deemed sacred in the American society (e.g., the desecration of the American flag, soldiers, and national holidays; condemnation of victims; counting tragedies and deaths happening every day on their website as a result of "God's wrath," etc.). To implement these tactics and spread their messages, the members of the group engage in a neutralization mechanism; that is, denial of responsibility, harm, and victims. In this sense, they deny their responsibility and justify their actions as an inevitable consequence of being "God's Elect" and as the pure will of God. "[W]hen interviewed, congregants claim that they themselves do not hate anyone nor desire to harm others but are simply *messenger*, charged with the *duty* of informing the public of *God's* hatred toward the world and most of its habitants" (1450). When asked about their involvement, group members insist that their membership and participation are not "about them or their wants" but that they only obey the will of God and there is "nothing that they can do about." Members also vehemently denied that their actions caused harm or were responsible for real victimization, arguing that those who experience tragedy or suffering deserve condemnation. The authors conclude that, in particular, these unusual mobilization techniques are what makes the group so effective and successful in their operations, and that they strategically use the negative reactions from the public to form and maintain a deviant and hatred-filled collective identity.

However, among all the radical religious groups, the Islamic State (IS) is believed to have revolutionized the use of social media to recruit and mobilize individuals. The majority of the research output on IS thus focuses on their extensive use of various digital media channels to reach out to target subjects on the regional, local, and global level to disseminate their ideological beliefs. IS created a sophisticated media campaign and established media suborganizations, such as *al-Furqan Foundation for Media Production*, *al-Hayat Media Center*, *Dabiq* magazine, and *al-Naba* newspaper, which focus only on information distribution. These media outlets usually disseminated speeches by the leader, Abu Bakr al-Baghdadi, who often spoke about the *jihad* and its physical component. He emphasized the righteousness of the organization to form an Islamic State, and he described the *jihad* as a "struggle between the people of faith and the nonbelievers." Hence, he postulated that IS was fighting for the cause of Allah and that was the responsibility of every Muslim to join the organization. The operations of IS are propagated as the war against disbelief and the enemies of Allah, and every Muslim worldwide is called out to pursue *hijrah*—the immigration of all Muslims to the new Islamic State, which is compared to the historical narrative of the Prophet and his companions moving from Mecca to Medina. Those who join the organization are portrayed in the media as fighters for the holy cause and true believers, and are promised a "reward from Allah," whereas those who reject their participation are disobeying Allah and will be punished by him. In essence, all information about the group, be it newspapers, speeches, articles, and videos, are framed by means of contrast, legitimacy, and requirements. Contrast implies an ingroup and outgroup imaging (us vs. them), in which IS is portrayed in a mostly positive light, as holy fighters that support the right cause, and its opponents are degraded as infidels who believe in false Gods and adopt wrong ideologies (democracy, secularism, nationalism, etc.). To legitimize the group's self-proclaimed "Islamic *khilafah*" (leader), a specific terminology and historic narrative are used, as well as honorable characteristics, such as "holy warrior," "scholar," "worshipper," and "descendent from the family of the Prophet," which would imply the attempt to compare its leader to the Rightly Guided Caliphs, who were the first four successors of the Prophet. Using the term "Rightly Guided" emphasizes that IS knows the right path to follow and that its actions are accepted by all Muslims as being the closest to the Prophet's example. Therefore, the major requirement is that all Muslims follow the call of IS to collectively build an Islamic State, the "dream for all true Muslims." IS, as the savior of the people, thus aims to "enlighten," "educate," and "spread knowledge" to them by means of guiding them toward the truth path. This presupposes that without IS there will be no enlightenment, no experience of the truth, and no knowledge, but only ignorance, deception, and darkness (Abdulmajid 2021).

In this chapter we elaborated how radical groups and organizations recruit and mobilize individuals by adopting different, sometimes unusual, modes of operation. Their aim is to attract those whose underlying need structure fits to the ideology, goals, and form of the organization to reduce free-riding and increase commitment. After identifying and attracting matching candidates, the group or organization must provide incentives and particular "goods and services" to enhance commitment and participation. Especially in environments with a partial government that only follows parochial interests and neglects the interests of the broad society or a minority group, extremist organizations like Hamas, the Taliban, Boko Haram, IS, or Al-Qaeda can gain high resonance among the deprived because of their provision of full-fledged services. This means that factors such as political and economic corruption; lack of social and educational opportunities; inequality; lack of vital resources, such as water, gas, food, and health care; and also environmental degradation and human insecurity deprive individuals from serving their fundamental human needs. Extremist organizations, in particular those who can provide such "state-based" goods and services, increase the tendency to be accepted among the broader public. To this, increased rivalries between groups or regions in a country enhance the likelihood of ideological extremism; for example, in Iraq, Sunnis living in Shia-led governments; in Nigeria, the Northern Muslims against the Southern Christian; or the Palestinians against the Israelis. All these rivalries are backed up by some religious extremist organizations, which address with their ideology, organizational structure and "state-based" goods and services for the needs of their adherents. This means that, for potential recruits, the organization's ideology and goals may be secondary to the perceived opportunities and goods of joining the organization. While particular recruitment rhetoric may influence this choice, some individuals may view such organizations as offering services and options that would be otherwise unattainable.

But this is only one way of recruiting and mobilizing individuals. Recruitment and mobilization can be fully executed through ideologization. As discussed throughout this book, all ideologies, irrespective of their content, provide a mental meaning-making system—a predictable, reliable, and relatively stable mental representation of reality that helps individuals to reduce complexity, understand their environment, integrate their own self into this environment (own social role), and make decisions. This means that organizations and groups, irrespective of their beliefs and values, recruit individuals by portraying themselves as the "receiver and owner of the truth," as a selective and elitist entity "chosen" to disseminate knowledge and reveal the true reality. They provide information, narratives, beliefs, and values to the "seekers" who aim to understand the environment and their role in it, and to find stable integration in society. Such groups demand strict rule abidance and reject individuals on the basis of non-conformity. They usually recruit individuals through kinship and social networks and they aim to address the needs and emotions of individuals on a local, regional, and global level. To do so, they form sophisticated media campaigns to reach as many individuals as possible, consisting of professionally produced propaganda videos, video games, music, websites, newspapers, publishers and magazines, TV and radio channels, and multiple social media accounts. Their mobilizing messages usually entail images of contrast (us vs. them), justification (we know the sole truth and we are chosen to spread it), and requirements (individuals must wake up and fight for the truth). The fact that social media has become an increasing source for recruitment and mobilization is challenging for governments and security agencies because it's hardly regulated or observed. This enables radical groups and organizations to freely communicate and anonymously spread information, goals, and beliefs, which are constantly available and accessible to all individuals in the world. Governments and policies face the complex task of reducing the activities of these organizations without constraining the free flow of information, speech, and privacy.

10
Real-life Cases and the Link between Needs, Ideology, and Conflict

In this book we combined insights from various academic disciplines to explain the interrelations between the following three layers: (i) fundamental (psychological) human needs, (ii) ideologies, and (iii) the (mostly radical and dogmatic) groups or organizations that recruit and mobilize individuals and decide between violent and nonviolent alternatives. We aimed at understanding the microfoundations of ideologies; that is, why individuals are motivated to adopt particular ideologies; how ideologies function on an individual level; and how they can influence, or degenerate, into violent behavior. Understanding these microfoundations of ideologies allowed us to explain how they can influence political outcomes and exacerbate violence and conflict. We defined ideologies as mental meaning-making systems that offer individuals alternative interpretations and explanations of reality which allow them to understand and evaluate the social, economic, and political systems of a given society. They provide narratives that enable individuals to link the past, present, and potential future, and integrate this coherent story with their lives and identities. Having consistent, predictable narratives and beliefs that explain and restore order to a complex world and that assist individuals as to how to perceive and make decisions, generates a sense of meaning in life. Because ideologies vary in content and demand, they address different human needs and preferences, so that individuals adopt ideologies that tend to "best" address their underlying need systems. All that implies that ideologies are not only capable of addressing and reconciling fundamental needs, desires, and emotions, but also of shaping operational intent, decision-making, and mobilizing political actors.

While some researchers, especially in political science, question the focus on the seemingly "blurry" concept of needs, we argued throughout the book that the consideration of human needs is of utmost importance because they provide a basis for understanding society and human behavior, in particular, during conflict onset. Human needs define important elements of humanity ("what it means to be a human being") and show the deficiencies of society and politics. In other words, human beings can be defined in terms of their

Ideology and the Microfoundations of Conflict. Veronika Müller and Thomas Gries, Oxford University Press.
© Oxford University Press 2024. DOI: 10.1093/oso/9780197670187.003.0010

capacity to feel, reason, evoke emotions, or attach to social others, which they express, among other ways, in their underlying need structure—needs to secure their existence, needs to process information and understand their environment, needs to form social relations and make autonomous decisions. If these needs are thwarted—if individuals feel threatened in their existence, cannot make autonomous choices, don't feel belonged to a group, and don't feel approved by their group or society, or even feel rejected because of their identity—and if society fails to reconcile these needs, individuals will search for alternative options for their need reconciliation. This means conflicts are not only an expression of unresolved interests between two political actors striving for power, sovereignty, or territory, they can also be an expression of inappropriate social structures and political institutions to which individuals have problems adjusting.

However, the argument that grievance, or the lack of options and resources to serve one's own needs, will exacerbate violence and aggression—as expressed by the well-known frustration-aggression theory—is somewhat short-sighted. Need deprivation is not invariably the direct cause of conflict but is the primary motive to start searching for alternative reconciliation options. Opinion leaders, elites, or politicians can exploit these needs for their own ends and disseminate ideologies and narratives to develop a loyal following. So, there is only an incentive to strategically use ideology if there is a target group that feels aligned with the ideas and beliefs in question. Hence, focusing only on grievance and deprivation would not fully explain the whole picture. Organizational networks, structure, recruitment and mobilization techniques, and the collective interplays within the organization itself play a crucial role in conflict onset. These organizations can only be successful in their operations to the extent that they are able to address the underlying needs of individuals, reduce free-riding, and adopt efficient management and mobilization techniques. However, we also take into account that certain environments and institutional conditions influence ideological choices: people who are exposed to threats, food and water shortages, or a lack of health care or education are more likely to accept the ideas that are spread by radical organizations that provide physical goods and services to them.

This implies that ideological narratives and beliefs can be combined with instrumental mechanisms. In situations where states and governments fail to provide resources and opportunities to serve one's own needs, extremist groups, such as IS, Al-Qaeda, Hamas, or Boko Haram, provide full-fledged services to their adherents and address in particular the physical needs of individuals who either truly adopt their belief system or just accept the established mode of governance in return for the benefits. Especially in environments with a failing government that only follows parochial interests and neglects the interests of society at large or discriminates against minority groups, extremist organizations and its leaders can gain high resonance among the deprived. All that being said, individuals can be clearly motivated to join a group not by a deep ideological commitment but because the organizations offer structural opportunities to reconcile their fundamental needs, environmental constraints, and economic incentives. In the following, we will apply our framework to analyze and explain, in a compact manner, real-life ideological conflicts that happened in the past. We will first consider the socioeconomic and political conditions in a country that may deprive individuals from resources and opportunities to serve their physical and psychological human needs. Next, we focus on one particular group or organization and its leader, who disseminate particular beliefs to address the deprived needs of individuals. Here we shortly portray the ideology and the goals of the organization, and move on, in the next step, to its recruitment and mobilization techniques. This approach allows us to explain within each case how radical organizations were able to address the needs, emotions, and desires of the deprived. However, we will also see that deprivation in terms of lacking resources are not always the primary motive to join a radical organization. Identity, the sense of belonging, and emotions do also play a role in this regard. Ideology and cultural/historical narratives can also have an independent structural power. The framing and wording can address different needs and emotions and has a powerful mobilization effect. Even if people live under the same socioeconomic conditions and constraints, different narratives can resonate with different needs and emotions. Our analysis should not be considered as holistic. It provides one consistent and compact way to explain why individuals adopt certain ideologies; how ideologies function on an individual level; and how they can influence, or degenerate, into violent behavior.

10.1 Case: FARC in Colombia

10.1.1 Socioeconomic and Political Conditions that Deprived Human Needs

The history of regional guerrilla movements in Colombia began with peasant struggles in the 1920s and 1930s. Peasant and indigenous groups were exposed to the harsh working conditions imposed on day laborers by coffee plantation owners and conflicts over land ownership (Angrist and Kugler 2008). The country was subject to severe vertical inequality as a small group of privileged and wealthy landowners controlled the political, social, and economic sphere, as well as ninety-nine percent of the land in the country. The peasants had no other option than renting or sharecropping some land from the wealthy, and hence becoming very dependent on them to secure their existence. This created an inegalitarian and unequal society, with a lack of opportunities for social mobility or autonomy, which induced the creation of the Communist Party that first organized armed militias that fought to resist the military and the conservative government (Rinehart 2013).

At this time, in 1948, the Conservatives, the Communists, and the military were killing thousands of people, leading peasants into existential crisis and creating the first civil war in the country—*La Violencia*. While economic inequality and social injustice were the main reasons for the dispute, the civil war sparked with the assassination of leftist Liberal Party leader Jorge Eliécer Gaitán. Gaitán supported the peasants in their struggle against landowner oppression and was thus regarded as an enemy by the Conservative and Liberal Parties (Flores 2014). The brutal civil war divided the country between radical supporters of Conservative, Liberal, and Communist Parties that fought for power at the local, regional, and national levels (Angrist and Kugler 2008). *La Violencia* gave the elites of the Conservative and Liberal political parties a pretense to use violence to evict individuals from public land. "By 1958, Conservative and Liberal elites, fearing that further violence would challenge their shared hegemony, had agreed to the National Front, in which the parties would alternate control of the presidency" (Flores 2014, 19).

The National Front, in particular, was formed to fight against the communism that was perceived as the main enemy of the country, an idea which was also backed up by the US government. Although the aim of the coalition was to improve the lives of the poorest citizens, it still followed parochial interests by neglecting the needs of the majority while using violence and military power to remove oppositional political groups and demobilized guerillas (Rinehart 2013). This sense of injustice, a violent and inconsistent political environment, and the thwarted needs of particular deprived groups not only increased the motivation to use violence but also led to the formation of armed *campesino* groups. They felt pleasure and pride in changing unjust conditions through intentional action. Despite political efforts to democratize access to land, the opposition of large landowners and unreliable support from political elites limited these reforms' effectiveness, resulting in a continued concentration in land ownership (Flores 2014). Data from 1960 show that one-third of the Colombian population was accounted for by one million peasant families with farms smaller than twenty hectares. The bottom 62.5 percent of farms had only 4.5 percent of the farmland, while the top 0.2 percent of farms owned

30.4 percent of the farmland (Zamosc 1986). This continuing unequal land distribution was reinforced by a governmentally initiated operation known as *Marquetalia*, which aimed to retake the territory possessed by a guerilla group. "The severity of Operation Marquetalia also finalized the slow transformation of agrarian groups seeking land reforms into insurgent groups seeking the overthrow of the State. The next year, guerrillas who had survived Operation Marquetalia formed the Bloqué Sur (Southern Bloc), a completely mobile force, and in 1966, the FARC was officially born" (Flores 2014, 23).

10.1.2 Extremist Organization—Ideology and Goal

The initial goal of the Southern Bloc, and later FARC, was to initiate land reforms and to fight for all marginalized Colombians. They adopted a Marxist-Leninist ideology, and its military approach was derived from Maoist and Vietnamese "people's war" doctrine. They called together all citizens to *fight for a country that unites all Colombians* based on social equality and sovereignty, with wealth redistribution and equal opportunities for all (Stanski 2006). Beyond generating security for the rural population, the FARC provided full-fledged services to their adherents, such as education, health care, and food provision (Gus 2011), which attracted a large number of new recruits who aimed to escape the poor living conditions across the country (Leech 2011). While hardships and extreme poverty faced by peasants have been argued to be the major reason for the success of the violent organization, others imply that governmental failure led to increased support of FARC (Vargas 1999). All in all, state violence, political instability (i.e., the constant disputes between the Conservatives and Liberals and the Communist Party), and economic inequality created a feasible environment for the FARC to strive (Stafford and Palacios 2002; Osterling 1989; Rinehart 2013). The existing government indeed failed to establish a state apparatus and functioning institutions to provide resources and opportunities for individuals to serve their fundamental human needs (Holmes and de Pineres 2011).

However, Rinehart (2013) argues that the combination of persistent violence, grievances, and a charismatic leadership in form of Pedro Antonio Marin, later known as Manuel Marulanda Vélez, may better explain the creation of the organization. According to Max Weber's criteria for charismatic leadership, Marulanda fulfills all the qualities, and that enabled him to act on behalf of the organization. Because the organization strictly rejects spirituality in form of religious beliefs, the higher being referring to a god-like entity was replaced by the common people. "For Marxists, the Proletariat Revolution is for the good of the people to break down class inequalities and to create an atmosphere where every citizen has enough resources. The people or the welfare of the people replace a spiritual entity. It can then be said that Marulanda believed that he had the permission of the people to start a Marxist revolution in Colombia" (Rinehart 2013, 84).

10.1.3 Extremist Organization—Its Structure, Recruitment, and Mobilization

FARC's initial organizational structure has been often portrayed as a wheel or a star, encompassing a centralized command system and a hierarchical structure. This enabled the organization to pursue a clear chain of command and to extend its forces into regions that specialized in certain activities (such as the production of narcotics in one region, trafficking in another, etc.) (Eccarius-Kelly 2012). Although the organizational form of FARC has been often portrayed as being strictly hierarchical (Rinehart 2013), the geographical challenges of the country made it impossible for the Secretariat, the direct command, to exercise control over the whole organization. The Secretariat consists of seven individuals who are responsible for strategic decision-making and for issuing operational orders to the blocs. Despite their geographical distance, all seven members communicate regularly and rule by consensus (Gentry and Spencer 2010). Under the Secretariat is the Estado Mayor Central, which consists of twenty-five members who are in charge of different blocs. The blocs are divided according to Colombia's geography into the South Bloc, Center Bloc, East and West Bloc, Middle Magdalena, Caribbean, and Cesar. Each of the blocs are then in charge of and coordinate the fronts (Rinehart 2013). The fronts are organized into five blocks and two joint commandos. FARC established the blocs in the 1990s to better control and "categorize" the high number of the fronts. Blocs have operational-level military responsibility but their regional jurisdiction also obliges them to process and collect useful non-military information. The two geographically largest and operationally most important blocs lie in the East and South of Colombia, where sparsely populated lowlands form the heartland of the organization (Gentry and Spencer 2010).

In its early stages, the FARC was financially supported by poor *campesinos* and external ideological partners, such as Russian and Cuban communist groups. To enhance its feasibility, the group entered the drug market, first by controlling the cultivation areas and then moving into the drug trade itself. The economic benefits of the coca plant were straightforward, as it not only generated the most revenues that funded the organizational operations, but it also allowed for territorial control in the countryside. The coca plant could be easily cultivated in the rural areas due to its robustness, its ability to thrive in poor soils, and its ease of processing into nonperishable paste. Also, for poor Colombian farmers without land titles and without access to complex irrigation and modern fertilizers, coca was the most economically lucrative crop (Cook 2011).

Most of the fighters that have been recruited into the organization were young men from rural areas, but also children and women represented a large minority group in the organization. The FARC's call for "a Colombia for Colombians" indicated their rural origin, as it was founded and led on the basis of deprived peasants; and as Marulanda had peasant origin as well, the organization declared that it understood the needs of the people (Rabasa et al. 2011). Hence, those who joined the organization received (or were promised to receive) economic and social goods and services, such as education, health care, a stable income, clothes, and food. The recruiters usually went from community to community to convince individuals of all ages to join the group. To reach more individuals and disseminate their ideology and mission, FARC had its own radio channel, the "Voice of Resistance," which was managed and operated by the organization's communication managers. Disc jockeys played traditional Colombian hit songs that were known by everyone, but which were adapted to the mission and narratives of FARC: with more radical lyrics and revolutionary titles, such as "We Will Conquer," "Ambush Rap," and "Guerrilla Girls." Because commercial radio was difficult to receive in rural areas, where mostly impoverished peasants were living and who were also the target group of the organization, the radio's sphere of influence is difficult to define. However, "Voice of Resistance," which had also been used by Marulanda, who spoke at least one hour a day to disseminate his message to the public and his eighteen thousand soldiers, was an efficient tool for propaganda and recruitment (Nacos 2007).

All new members received extensive training, irrespective of age and gender, which involved, beyond armed training and self-defense, also ideological indoctrination, adherence to authority, prestige, and identity of the group. The training required discipline and responsibility, while the military uniforms helped to decrease uncertainty of new members, accelerate self-esteem, and even serve as a form of empowerment. Because men and women were demanded to fulfill the same physical and psychological training, it has been perceived as a way to create gender equality within the group, which was one of the pillars of their belief system. If members did not fulfill the orders, or if they outright disobeyed, they received harsh physical punishment.

All members were obliged to follow the rules and orders of the organization and to expect immediate consequences for breaking established rules. Despite FARC's attempt to create gender equality, the hierarchy of power and authority also led to the sexual abuse of women and girls. According to Human Rights Watch, some male commanders used their authority to arrange sexual relationships with women, and even under-age girls. However, sexual and romantic relationships were strongly controlled by the organization, leading to birth control and multiple abortions. This means that the FARC controlled every aspect of its members' lives and was even willing to impose strict rules of conduct on them (Stanski 2006).

10.1.4 How FARC Addressed the Needs of the Deprived

The extreme left-wing, communist-inspired organization aimed at reducing poverty, inequality, privatization, and injustice, while generating wealth redistribution and employment opportunities. The ideology of FARC served as a mental meaning-making system that offered interpretations and explanations of the harsh reality, explained the unjust socioeconomic and political conditions, and offered narratives how to perceive the past, the present, and the future. It provided guidance and an anchor point in life, particularly for those who felt neglected and left behind by the parochial and corrupt government. Because all members of the organization were peasants themselves, the inner creed was that they can understand and fulfill the needs of the Colombia's poor, especially the peasants and the indigenous people who lived in remote rural areas. Those who obeyed the rules and norms of the organization received economic and social services and goods. FARC members were mostly better paid than members of the Colombian Army. They not only received food and clothes, but also social approval and respect from both their ingroup members and common peasants, who idealized and praised them for their commitment (Rinehart 2013).

An empirical study using the PAHD database, which contains 15,308 interviews with former group members, examined the reasons why individuals joined the extremist organization. The preliminary analysis with 535 interviews with children (those under eighteen years of age) who demobilized between 2002 and 2008 shows that the primary motive to join the organization was the desire to their change their lives and living conditions. "Interviewees cited the tediousness of their former lives, family ties to armed groups, and the desire for a better quality of life rather than coercion as principal reasons for joining the armed struggle. What emerged from these interviews is the sense that these children were not simply passive victims, but quasi-independent agents faced with a limited menu of unpalatable options" (Rosenau et al. 2014, 282). Hence, FARC promised to provide full-fledged services and goods to those who were largely neglected by the government, and an "unlimited" menu of opportunities, not only for existential security but also for self-realization. The rigid and hierarchical organizational structure served the needs for order and consistency and provided guidance and a sense of control of one's own life (and conditions). Also, relational and agency needs have been addressed by the organization—the shared group's identity and goals, and the discipline and commitment to the group generated a sense of belonging and identification. Adhering to the group's norms and behavioral rules not only generated stability in a mostly instable life, but it also provided social approval from other ingroup members, the authority, and the public. They were praised by others for their courage and combat readiness and were looked upon as heroes. This, in turn, enhanced their self-esteem and served their need for self-efficacy, as members received the impression that they could finally be active and change their lives.

10.2 Case: Sri Lanka and LTTE

10.2.1 Socioeconomic and Political Conditions that Deprived Human Needs

Sri Lanka, a small island at the southern tip of India, is home to two major ethnic groups: the Sinhalese majority and the Tamil minority.[1] Although both groups developed their own sense of group identity based on different beliefs[2] about their ethnic origin, language, and religion, they enjoyed a mostly peaceful ethno-pluralistic co-existence during the pre-colonial period (Manogaran 1987). During British colonial rule (1815–1948), however, the previously separate nationalist entities were merged to form a highly centralized colonial state. The Colebrooke–Cameron Reforms of 1832 organized the country into five artificially created administrative provinces, which were governed by a combination of British-imposed direct and indirect rule.[3] To assert control and organize the communities, the British adopted separate legal codes for each ethnic group and promoted an essentialist approach which ascribed ethnic groups their substantial distinctness (divide and rule policy) (Bandarage 2009). This social antagonism became even more prominent when the British imported low-caste Tamils from South India into predominantly Sinhalese areas as a cheap workforce for their tea and coffee plantations, excluding Sinhalese peasantry from this work opportunity in the process. As more Tamils of Sri Lankan and Indian origin moved into Sinhalese areas, the ancient fear of a cultural and existential (Tamil) threat was revived (Manogaran 1987).

Given the lack of resources in the water-deficient northern and eastern regions, the Tamils were forced to find alternative comparative advantages, which resulted in greater appropriation of the English language. This enabled the Jaffna Vellalar Tamils (a dominant caste in the North) to secure a disproportionate number of well-paid jobs in the public sector and the British-run government, as well as in the legal, medical, and engineering fields. Furthermore, the British-loyal Jaffna Tamils received greater opportunities for political participation and were given more seats in the first Legislative Council in 1833. This privileged access to education, political representation, and employment of the Tamil elites enhanced the threat and resentment felt by the Sinhalese majority, which sparked a resurgence of Sinhalese (ethnic) nationalism (Bandarage 2009). But the Tamils' political overrepresentation came to a dramatic end after the adoption of the Donoughmore Constitution of 1931, which allowed for territorial elections of State Council members. The minorities, especially the Tamils, feared losing their political representation given a territorial domination of the Sinhalese majority group. After the 1936 elections, Tamil representatives found themselves without cabinet representation for the first time and a Sinhalese-dominated ministry was formed (Manogaran 1987). After independence in 1948, the cultural and existential threat felt by the Tamils was reinforced by the nationalistic approach of the Sinhalese to pass citizenship legislation. The citizenship legislation restricted Sri Lankan citizenship to those who could claim it by descent, which mainly affected the South Indian Tamils who were imported as workers by the British government. As a result, they were denied Sri Lankan citizenship and were excluded from the electoral poll (Bandarage 2009).

Furthermore, the Sinhalese-dominated ministry aimed to restore Buddhism as the main national religion and designate Sinhala as the official language for administrative purposes. These changes were implemented through the passing of legislation in 1956, as well as a constitution in 1972, that made Sinhala the official language of the country and gave Buddhism special status as the state religion. Sinhalese domination led to feelings of discrimination, social disapproval, and deprivation on the part of the largest ethnic minority group, the Tamils, who pleaded for the establishment of an independent and sovereign state (Cooray 2014). The dominance of the Sinhala majority over all aspects of the private and public life in Sri Lanka decreased the resources and opportunities for the Tamils to address their fundamental human needs—needs for securing one's own existence (security/stability), having the feeling that one can control one's life (and the living conditions), participating in and having an impact on society (control), being able to identify with the norms and values of a society (identification), feeling belongingness and accepted for one's identity (belongingness and social approval), being able to make autonomous decisions (self-determination), and feeling positive about oneself (self-esteem) and one's achievements (self-efficacy).

This severe form of deprivation, the enhanced nationalism of the Sinhala majority, and the failed attempt of the government to protect the Tamil minority, induced enhanced nationalistic feelings by the threatened group. The intensification of Tamil (ethnic) nationalism was promoted by Tamil militants—many of whom were young adults who were barred from entering university or government service—who formed underground groups to express their grievances. The most prominent and violent of these groups was the Liberation Tigers of Tamil Eelam (LTTE), which was founded in 1976 by the leader Vellupillai Prabhakaran.

10.2.2 Extremist Organization—Ideology and Goal

Vellupillai Prabhakaran, born in 1954 in the Jaffa Peninsula, experienced a childhood full of poverty, violence, and Sinhalese dominance. In one of his rare interviews he explained that his motivation to form LTTE had been based on his early experiences as a witness to the Sinhalese atrocities. Feeling the grievances, injustices, and threats experienced by his ingroup, he felt compelled to start armed struggle for the recognition of the identity, rights, and independent homeland of the Tamil people. The ideology of the group was inspired by the Marxist-Leninist revolutionary appeal and nationalist-separatist doctrines, which aimed to establish an independent state for the Tamils based on socialism and nationalism. Hence the overall goal of the group was to reduce class and national struggle at the same time, by creating national independence and a socialist transformation of all social, economic, and political institutions. The attempt of the Sinhalese government to marginalize and oppress the Tamil ethnic identity contributed to the urge to revive, consolidate, and assert peoples' identity. "Throughout the 1970s and into the early 1980s, violence and ethnic tension throughout the country led ethnic Tamils who had lived among the Sinhalese to migrate north and east. A strong sense of identity formed as the Tamil population became geographically concentrated in the north, increasing LTTE membership exponentially. This collective identity provided a need for a nationalistic leader to emerge and champion the movement for an independent Tamil homeland" (Post 2007, 86). Hence, the goals of LTTE grew around the recognition of (i) Tamil's identity and its distinct nationality; (ii) the national sovereignty of the eastern and northern provinces of Sri Lanka, which should be regarded as the traditional and historical homeland of the Tamil people; and (ii) the rights of the Tamils for self-determination (Rinehart 2013).

10.2.3 Extremist Organization—Its Structure, Recruitment, and Mobilization

LTTE was officially led by Prabhakaran, but governed by a five-member central committee, which was responsible for both the military operations and the political decisions. The constitution of the organization, which was written by Prabhakaran in 1976, stated that all members agree to invest their personal resources to fight for the cause of the group—to establish an independent Tamil Eelam, a sovereign and socialist democratic peoples' government, and a just and social mode of production; to abolish all forms of marginalization (in particular the unequal caste system); and to continue revolutionary struggle to transform guerrilla warfare into a strategic war of liberation. To reach these goals, the activities of the organization were divided into three main divisions: the first division was responsible for dealing with opponents and the Sri Lankan police intelligence unit, while the second division aimed at manipulating the administration of the government. The third division was charged with the task of demobilizing the Sri Lankan army camps and the establishment of a surrogate administrative structure, which would form a basis for a sovereign and autonomous Tamil Eelam state (Richards 2014).

To realize its goals and missions, the organization recruited mainly educated Tamil youth who had been rejected and discriminated against by the Sinhalese government, and lower-caste rural peasants, who aimed at changing their poor and unfair living conditions (Biziouras 2012). The recruitment strategies were based on selective historical narratives about the Tamil history and culture, which were decontextualized and reinterpreted to legitimize armed struggle. Hence, LTTE claimed that their ideology was rooted in the tradition and culture of the Tamils, which should create ingroup and outgroup thinking. "Prabhakaran saw the LTTE ideology and struggle as continuing in a long historical martial tradition. The name and logo of the insurgency, the 'Tigers,' is an example. LTTE members would generally explain that the 'Tiger' refers to the old royal emblem of the Chola Kings (Hellmann-Rajanayagam 1994, 56). In the collective memory, those were great imperial

Kings under whom Tamil culture and Tamil power expanded and flourished. Songs about the LTTE connected the greatness of Prabhakaran with these Kings. The LTTE created an image of Prabhakaran as able to step into their footsteps and conquer the north-east of Sri Lanka. The geographical borders for the imagines Eelam, the 'historical' homeland of the Tamil population, coincided with the areas where the Tamil-speaking community historically lives (Hellmann-Rajanayagam 1994, 57, Sitrampalam 2005b). In that sense, the LTTE presented the 'greatness' and 'sanctity' of these ancient Tamil Kingdoms in order to legitimize its claim to liberate and govern the Tamil population" (Terpstra and Frerks 2017, 292). The greatness of the Tamil population has been contrasted to the evil of the Sri Lankan government. Propaganda videos produced by the organization portrayed soldiers of the Sri Lankan military as alcohol abusers and rapists, who enjoyed their life while the Tamil people suffered. They also showed the historical struggle of the Tamil people, the achievements of group, and the atrocities against the Tamils carried out by the Sri Lankan government (Terpstra and Frerks 2017).

New members have been thus recruited and mobilized under the directory to dedicate life to a "cause," namely, to liberate and protect the Tamil people, and a moral doctrine of discipline, that is, following the rules and norms of the group. Members of LTTE usually attended festivals and memorials to revive and remember the "history," and were taught to bow down to the rules and guiding principles of the leader. Prabhakaran has been perceived as a charismatic leader who could easily convince individuals to adopt his nationalistic ideas and follow the interests of the organization. He demanded complete obedience from all members of LTTE, who were not allowed to question his authority and orders. All members were obliged to follow strict organizational rules (e.g., abstaining from alcohol, drugs, and tobacco), and were forbidden to have premarital and extramarital affairs. Furthermore, all new members received extensive training and were forced to wear a cyanide vial around their necks, which they had to swallow to avoid potential capture to protect the group. This willingness to die for the group served as a strong mobilizing factor and has been understood as a part of the Tamil national identity. The death of the martyrs generated a sense of solidarity and national pride. However, beyond ideological narratives, new members would receive social and material rewards from the organization: they would work collectively on a farm and grow vegetables, chili, and peanuts; hunt wild animals; receive clothes, a salary, personal care, and (restrictive) entertainment (access to TV, radio). Those who joined the group had suffered from resource deprivation and, often, the only meals they would receive in a day would be supplied by LTTE.

10.2.4 How LTTE Addressed the Needs of the Deprived

The Marxist-inspired, (ethnic) nationalistic organization aimed to protect and liberate the Tamil population while generating an independent Tamil state and a strong national identity. The organization served the needs of the people by several means: on the one side, they received social goods, services, protection, and monetary rewards for their commitment and loyalty. On the other hand, the nationalistic ideology served the psychological needs of the adherents. Because many Tamils suffered discrimination and abuse by the Sri Lankan security forces, LTTE provided the means to secure their existence and to reduce their existential threat. In other words, staying within the LTTE territory served not only their need for existential safety and security, but it also reduced real or imagined threat and uncertainty. The hierarchical organizational structure, which demanded strict rule-following, generated order and consistency in a complex and uncertain environment. LTTE predetermined the consumption habits of their members; that is, they decided what they were allowed to eat, to watch, and to listen to. Only limited goods and media access was available, which was fully controlled by the organization. This allowed them to control the information flow within the organization. The limited access to external sources of information and constant ideological indoctrination served the needs for ambiguity avoidance and reduced cognitive complexity. The nationalistic ideology provided a mental framework about how to understand the social environment (the evil Sri Lankan government vs. us, the threatened Tamils), and their own role within it (subject to discrimination and marginalization), explained the unjust socioeconomic and political conditions, and offered historical and cultural narratives how to perceive the past, present, and the future. It provided an anchor point in life and "a cause for existence," in particular for those who felt threatened and left behind by the parochial and brutal government.

However, participation in the organization also served relational and agency needs. The LTTE members received high social approval for their loyalty, commitment, and sacrifice. Heroes Week was held every November to remember and show respect for killed Tiger soldiers. Euphemisms like "Eternally, your remembrance is deep in our heart" (Rinehart 2013, 128) marked building entrances that were decorated with flowers and colorful ribbons. The highest honor was to be killed during a battle or an order for the group and the whole community pays empathic attention to those who have been lost. Beyond serving the need for belonging and social approval, the organization placed much emphasis on the national identity of the Tamil population. They shared historical and cultural narratives that highlighted the unique identity of the group. According to that, the Tamils, who were usually discriminated against and abused by the Sri Lankan government, were praised and respected for their identity and their commitment within the group. All members received the opportunity to show their self-efficacy; that is, the capability to perform tasks and reach particular goals. All in all, being accepted and loved for who one is, feeling belongingness and safe within a community, and having the opportunity to prove oneself has a high and positive impact on one's sense of self-esteem.

10.3 Case: Boko Haram

10.3.1 Socioeconomic and Political Conditions that Deprived Human Needs

Even though Nigeria became the richest nation in Sub-Saharan Africa in 2014, it is still facing severe inequalities, corruption, political instability, poverty, and socioeconomic deprivation. Despite resource wealth, 60.9 percent of the population live in absolute poverty, especially in the northern part of the country, where seventy-five percent suffer from severe resource deprivation. In Borno state, the birthplace of Boko Haram, eighty-three percent of young people are illiterate, and seventy-two percent of children aged six to sixteen have never attended a school (Rogers 2012). The northeastern and northwestern states have the highest unemployment rates in the country at around forty percent, compared to the southwest and southeast with rates of around ten percent (NBS 2010). Furthermore, the 2010 National Bureau of Statistics (NBS) data show that 64.8 percent of people living in the northeast region suffer from severe poverty and resource deprivation, followed by 61.2 percent in the northwest—representing the highest numbers in the country. On the other hand, the lowest poverty rate of 31.2 percent has been recorded in the southeast, followed by 40.2 percent in the southwest. This implies that the poorest regions in the country are all in the northern areas (UNDP 2009).

In addition, the state security forces—originally established to protect colonial interests—remained a structured force after decolonialization and now serves elite groups rather than the average Nigerian, and they have been accused of war crimes, rape, and violence (Comolli 2015). The severely unequal resource distribution between the north and the south, grievances resulting from poor governance, elite delinquency, and discrimination, has caused alienation and frustration among the northern population on a scale that has led them to refuse to cooperate with state security forces and an untrustworthy government (Asfura-Heim and McQuaid 2015). Adding to that, the situation has been exacerbated by the perception of the north that "the wealthy elite throughout the country tend to be Christian, while the most impoverished communities in the country are found among the Hausa, Fulani, Kanuri, and other northers groups—all of them primarily Muslim" (Forest 2012, 56). In particular, the Kanuri tribe, living predominantly in Borno and northern Cameroon, was affected by the Fulani–Hausa tribal domination and climate-affected environmental changes. Lake Chad, which was traditionally the living environment of the Kanuri tribe, decreased tremendously in size, accounting for only 5.4 percent of what it was in 1963. The north of Nigeria, and in particular the Sahel region, experienced severe desertification due to water redirection of all neighboring countries (Cook 2014). Hence it is assumed that members of Boko Haram were initially drawn from the Kanuri tribe, which represents roughly four percent of the Nigerian population and that were predominantly living under harsh living conditions in the north. Although most members were unemployed and deprived, some were also graduates, university lecturers, bankers, members of the political elite, and migrants from neighboring countries. As Ucha (2010) notes, "the fact that you are an educated Nigerian is no guarantee that you will be employed. [...] Many graduates in Nigeria wander the streets without anything reasonable to do for a living. The government is capable but unwilling to provide jobs for them. Employment in Nigeria is usually not based on merit but depends on how connected you are with people that have power. This leaves many highly qualified people in poverty as seemingly no one cares to know what they are capable of achieving" (127).

The communities that fueled Boko Haram's existence have been thus destroyed by severe poverty, high youth unemployment, educational backwardness, ecological degradation, lack of social services and infrastructure, a high number of unemployed graduates, and a lack of assistance and governmental care. Feeling deprived, abandoned, powerless, and insignificant, individuals found solace in their religious identity, guided by religious actors that are visible and commonly accessible at even the most grassroots levels[4] (Agbiboa 2013).

10.3.2 Extremist Organization—Ideology and Goal

"Jama'atul Alhul Sunnah Lidda'wati wal Jihad," which can be translated to "People committed to the Propagation of the Prophet's Teaching and Jihad," is the official name of the jihadi-Salafistic organization, which was initially formed and introduced by Mohammed Yusuf. Its jihadi-Salafistic ideology, which railed against Western culture and institutions, led to its internationally known name of "Boko Haram," literally "Western education is forbidden" (Onuoha 2014). But the radical group rejects this implication, arguing that it does not reject Western formal education per se, but rather the cultural values, beliefs, and norms that seem to "undermine" the supremacy of Islamic culture. It rejects and resists the system of colonial organization and the elites in the northern part of Nigeria who received Western education and training and who are blamed for the country's corruption and economic collapse (Agbiboa 2013). Since 2009, Boko Haram has committed many violent attacks in Nigeria involving brutality, kidnapping, sexual violence against women, and decapitation. The group was previously led by Mohammed Yusuf, who was killed by Nigerian security forces in November 2009 after a sectarian mass killing involving more than one thousand fatalities. The core objective of the group is to replace Nigeria's secular government, which is viewed as a counterpart of a corrupt, Christian-dominated federal government, with a religious regime that strictly adheres to Islamic Sharia law (Onuoha 2014).

The basic narrative of the organization hence grew from the idea that poverty, corruption, and discrimination in Nigeria are the result of failed behavior and attitudes of the Western-affiliated elites, who received secular education and training. The system represented by these elites is perceived as unjust, secular, and of no divine origin, which must be replaced by Islamic-shaped institutions and mindsets (Agbiboa 2013). According to that, the radical organization postulates that only the introduction of the Sharia law will dissolve the complex problems of social injustice, poverty, and corruption. They follow strictly the beliefs and teachings of Jihadi Salafism,[5] which postulates a total rejection of religious modernization and the return to the Sunni orthodoxy; that is, the unquestioning abidance to the Quranic orders, the Prophetic traditions, and the consensus of the "true" predecessors of Prophet Muhammad, who are regarded as the followers of pristine Islam. Jihadi Salafism perceives *jihad* (warfare) as a legitimate method to establish the Islamic state and follow the doctrines of *takfir*. *Takfir* implies the declaration of infidelity on a Muslim, who refuses to follow the rigid Salafi code of conduct. This allows the radical organization to strictly draw boundaries or a clear distinction between "true believers and infidels," which also includes non-jihadi-Salafis co-religionists, who adopt different beliefs and religious practices that do not conform to the jihadi-Salafi interpretation of Islam. To emphasize this distinction, the Salafi creed agrees on a principle, which implies that those who do not identify infidels (make *takfir*) are also considered as infidels. The major unbelievers are considered those who replace the Sharia law with secular law, in particular, political rulers who govern by non-Islamic laws. These doctrines and the interpretation that ruling by other than God's law is a major disbelief, legitimized Boko Haram to use violent means (*jihad*) to overthrow the political leaders and establish an Islamic state (Kassim 2015).

10.3.3 Extremist Organization—Its Structure, Recruitment, and Mobilization

Due to the secretive nature of Boko Haram, and the lack of extensive research on the group, its internal structure and modus operandi remain largely unknown. Some researchers argue that Boko Haram is a centralized, highly hierarchical organization that is governed by Abubaker Shekau (Zenn 2020), while others perceive it as a decentralized organization, organized into a loose federation of operating cells and governed under the umbrella headship of the Islamic standard, the "Shura Council" (Anugwom 2019). The latter implies that Boko Haram operates in a cell-like structure, in which each autonomous cell receives decisional and operational power and control. To reduce this inconsistency and uncover the organizational structure and fragmentation of the group, Prieto Curiel and colleagues (2020) used data from the Armed Conflict Location and Event Data Project (ACLED). The authors exemplify that Boko Haram has been most active around Lake Chad, which almost dried out due to ecological degradation. The mostly swampy region has poorly constructed roads, which leads to limited and costly mobility. The data show that the highest number of attacks took place in January (covering almost two events on each day of the month since 2016) and the highest number of casualties was recorded in February (with 12.3 casualties each day of the month since 2016). To have the capacity to implement this high number of attacks, Boko Haram must have established numerous cells across the region. The data confirm and suggest that the radical organization is constructed of approximately fifty to sixty cells, which operate along specific routes around Lake Chad. Each cell travels, at most, sixty kilometers a day on average, while one-third of the routes cross international borders. In this regard, it has been argued that in recent years the radical organization managed to relocate to remote and regional places that are difficult to access by governmental forces, such as the Mandara mountains in Cameroon, the Sambisa Forest in Nigeria, and small islands around Lake Chad.

To mobilize and legitimize its actions, Boko Haram, in particular its leaders like Shekau, used religious and historical rhetoric backed with narratives that seek to explain organizational goals to justify its existence. Such narratives usually revolved around the lost power of Islam in Nigeria, and the marginalization of the Muslim population, which should activate grievances and the fear of losing grounds to the forces of "immorality and secularism" (Thurston 2016). In a 2014 speech, Abubaker Shekau proclaimed that Boko Haram was not pursuing nationalistic goals, such as the establishment of an inclusive Nigerian state for all the disadvantaged, but rather the creation of an Islamic state across the African continent in which all share the same values, beliefs, and codes of conduct. Shekau even refused to acknowledge the legitimacy of Nigeria as a sovereign state. He portrayed himself as the leader and authority that adheres only to God, as the hero of the Muslim people and the fighter for the "real Islam" who can stand against every opponent. Although Shekau constantly refers to the will of God, in his speeches he barely quotes from the Quran, which contradicts the speeches of Al-Qaeda or IS (Cook 2014). The narratives and messages should reach every Muslim in Nigeria, even those who are not religious or have little knowledge of the Quran (because a high number of northern Nigerians are illiterate). This implies that every individual could join the group, without having prior knowledge of Islam, which attracted many from both Nigeria and the surrounding region.

10.3.4 How Boko Haram Addressed the Needs of the Deprived

Order, stability, and personal significance are among the factors that seem to play an important role in explaining why a vast number of young adults joined the radical Islamist group. A field survey in Nigeria of 1,607 respondents from three northern and two non-northern cities found that, beyond mental support, financial incentives paid by Boko Haram played an important role in attracting members to the group. Former members explained that financial resources, respect, solidarity, social approval, and feelings of belongingness were primary motivators for joining the radical group. By contrast, factors such as religion, education, or unemployment have been found to play a less significant role in the decision to join Boko Haram (Ewi and Salifu 2017). Considering the data and the multifaced analyses, it is evident that social, political, economic, and psychological factors played a role in the successful operation and subsistence of Boko Haram. The unmet human needs of the population, especially of that in the northern part of Nigeria, explain, at least in part, the growth and successful persistence of the group.

The subjective faith, or religion, seemed to be not the driving force behind individuals joining the group; instead, psychological factors like stability, order, control, power, and self-significance drove membership. The radical ideology provided a mental framework that provided guidance about how to perceive the unjust social environment and one's own role in society and offered historical and cultural narratives how to perceive the past, present, and the future. It provided an anchor point in life and "a cause for existence," particularly for those who felt threatened and left behind by the parochial government. Individual group members were connected through a shared fate, goal, enemy, and struggle. The shared group identity and negative experiences and feelings created a strong bond between the members, which in turn enforced mutual solidarity and group cohesion. The young adults, who felt desperate, worthless, and powerless, could suddenly make choices, take actions, and experience a sense of self-efficacy, even in the negative sense. They received the opportunity to express themselves politically and to air their grievances and perceived injustice; in other words, they felt finally seen and heard (Dim 2017).

10.4 Case: Niger–Delta Resource Abundance, Grievance, and Conflict

10.4.1 Socioeconomic and Political Conditions that Deprived Human Needs

The discovery of oil in 1956 transformed the Nigerian economy from an agrarian to an essentially petroleum-dependent economy.[6] Over the past fifty years, oil output has increased tremendously, from just over 5,100 barrels a day to about 2.68 million barrels per day, with oil accounting for forty percent of national GDP and eighty-three percent of governmental revenue in 2012. Despite its oil wealth, per capita income in Nigeria fell from $250 USD to $212 USD over the period of 1965–2004, and the number of people living on less than $1 USD a day grew from thirty-six percent to more than seventy percent. The reason behind this was a highly unequal income distribution, with ninety percent of oil revenue in the hands of only one percent of the population (Watts 2007). Added to this, widespread corruption and mismanagement disrupted the appropriate reinvestment of oil revenues in the public sector, precipitating the country into severe poverty, violent disorder, and military dictatorship.

This unequal resource redistribution was fueled primarily by the policy of ethnic competitive communalism (federal system), which invariably led to the political and economic marginalization of ethnic minorities (Idemudia 2009). Conservative estimates show that in oil-rich states, such as Delta and Bayelsa, there is only one doctor for every 150,000 citizens and that Delta is one of the most polluted places on earth (Okonta 2005). The Niger Delta Human Development Report (UN 2006) revealed poor-quality infrastructure; severe poverty; lack of adequate social, political, and educational institutions; and a severe increase in HIV and AIDS cases. In this deprived region, several ethnic groups coexist, including the Andoni, Efik, Ogoja, Annang, Ibibio, Ijaw, Itsekiri, Ikwere, Kalabari, Ogoni, and Okrika. These ethnic communities live close to the numerous oilfields and pipelines that intersect their landscapes and generate severe health, environmental, and socioeconomic problems. In particularly, the Ogoni and Ijaw ethnic groups have voiced their concerns and dissatisfaction in the past, which went unheard by the government. Exploitation, dispossession, governmental neglect, and environmental degradation in the region have thus provoked political and social struggles, especially in local communities at whose cost the oil has been extracted. Consequently, the Ogoni ethnic group demanded more control of their resources, which was laid out in the form of an Ogoni Bill of Rights in 1990, which addressed the deprivation of the Ogoni group, questioned the federalism and ethnic marginalization in Nigeria, and called for more involvement in governmental affairs (Watts 2004).

Similarly, the Ijaw ethnic group, and in particular the deprived youth from five hundred different communities, addressed their claim to the ownership of the land and resources within their communities in 1998 in the Kaiama declaration (Ikelegbe 2005). Many of the young generation's grievances, such as poverty, unemployment, and lack of educational opportunities, have been widely shared across the region, which was additionally fueled by the perception that the oil wealth is controlled by the ethnic-majority ruling elites from other, non-oil-extracting regions of the country (Watts 2007). This was possible due to the abandonment of the revenue allocation principle of derivation, which required that national revenues should be distributed in line with contribution. The timing of this political shift coincided with a period during which oil became the main source of national revenues, which generated anger and resentment among citizens of the oil-extracting Niger Delta who received nothing in return (Obi 2010).

10.4.2 Extremist Organization—Ideology and Goal

The ongoing grievance and deprivation sparked violent disputes in February 1966, with an attempt to assert regional autonomy over the Niger Delta, led by an Ijaw militant, Isaac Adaka Boro. Boro was the leader of the youth movement named the Niger Delta Volunteer Force (NDVF), which pursued secession goals and feared the domination of the Igbo ethnic-majority group (Obi 2010). On the other side, the Ogoni ethnic group reacted differently to the grievances and choose, under the leadership of Ken Saro-Wiwa, a rather peaceful approach. Even though both communities have lived under the exact same conditions and precarity, different narratives and approaches of the leaders led to different decisional outcomes of the groups. Ogoni based their belief system largely on ecologism and human rights, spurring a debate about internal colonialism, minority rights, and human agency, while the Ijaw followed the beliefs of constant threat and victimhood of deliberate and calculated neglect (Mai-Bornu 2019). Ken Saro-Wiwa, the leader of Ogoni, talked in his powerful speeches about the historical neglect and marginalization of the Ogoni group in the past, the present precarious conditions, and how the group should work collectively to create a better future. Narratives of a collective identity help individuals to understand who they are, where they belong, and where they are headed—all which create social categorizations of identification and belongingness (Mai-Bornu 2020). Saro-Wiwa also used narratives about Ogoni's inheritance and land in the past, which was endowed with rich resources and agricultural blessings. He used expressions like "blessed land," "rich soil," "fresh water streams," "seas full of fish," and "forests with an abundance of animals and hard woods." Using such narratives, he created an image of a paradise, an idyllic existence, that has been created by God, combining the sacral land and its resources with ethnic rituals and religious procedures. But this holy place has been destroyed by greedy and scrupulous oil companies, which urged the Ogoni people to unite and cooperate with each other based on the Ogoni agenda. This agenda postulates the equality of all ethnic groups within the Nigerian federalism, as well as the formation of a fair and transparent national political, economic, and social system. "Although Saro-Wiwa challenged the damage caused by the activities of oil exploration, which, he claimed had destroyed the spiritual connection the Ogoni shared with the land, he opted pragmatically to lay revenues gained from the oil, as both a right and a way to redress the people's suffering. [He further claimed that] the achievement of political autonomy and the right to use a fair proportion of Ogoni resources for regional development was a responsibility of all Ogoni, but he clarified that this was not a call to violent action" (Mai-Bornu 2020, 830).

Similar to Ogoni, the Ijaw group also expressed their grievances about environmental degradation and lack of rights but explained its marginalization as a result of British discriminatory and anti-Ijaw policies, rather than internal colonialism. The narrative of internal colonialism, which was widely used by the Ogoni group, suggested a sense of agency; that is, that institutions and the Nigerian federalist system need to be reshaped. The narrative of historical oppression by external forces, however, implied helplessness, frustration, and lack of potential actions (Mai-Bornu 2019). The Ijaw leader, Adaka Boro blamed the British colonial government of failing to mitigate political and ethnic domination and failing to take the fears of the ethnic minority groups seriously. In his speeches he used expressions such as "tyrannical chains," "dark alley of perpetual political and social deprivation," "strangers in our country," "long denied right of self-determination," while proclaiming that there will be "no point of return," if the Nigerian government refuses to improve "drastically" the conditions of the people. Some Ijaw leaders also accused the three major ethnic groups—the Hausa, Yoruba, and Igbo—of controlling and dominating all institutions and resource flows in the country. The narratives were thus filled with accusations and emotions, addressing anger, frustration, and a sense of mental fatigue of the people. While the Ogoni demonstrated a strong culture of mutual and peaceful cooperation and collective agency, the Ijaw claimed that the government suppressed their agency needs, which left them no other option than resorting to violence.

10.4.3 Extremist Organization—Its Structure, Recruitment, and Mobilization

Beyond narratives, the role of the leadership and mobilization strategies played a large role in the different decisional outcomes of both groups. Ken Saro-Wiwa was the leader of the Ogoni group, and he also became president of the Movement for the Survival of the Ogoni People (MOSOP)—the umbrella organization of the Ogoni movement. His concerns evolved around the political insignificance of the Ogoni people, their lack of agency, and their harsh exclusion from formal institutions, which decreased the meaningful self-representation of the group. As a result, in his speeches he spoke about the "real identity" of the Ogoni people that the British colonizers sought to dilute, followed by the goal to evoke this authentic self, in terms of an intellectual approach that is based on theories, ideas, and thoughts rather than violence (Saro-Wiwa 1993). His methods of operation were considered to be diplomatic and thoughtful, carefully considering all outcomes and strategies prior of application. He elaborated that during his travels and visits to Ogoni villages, he understood the needs of the people and made their concerns his political priority. Applying tools of nonviolent advocacy, Saro-Wiwa mobilized individuals through philosophical resolutions to Nigeria's problems, clear observations and understanding of international politics, and his foresight in advancing agency to all ethnic groups to allow for personal fulfillment.

The slogan he used to mobilize individuals was "Alo be, iko be, nale begin," meaning "we will fight with our brains, not with a knife" (Hunt 2005, 64). He connected ethnic autonomy to resource and environmental control as well as the importance of ecological justice and sustainability in the international setting. He rejected a unitary political system in a multi-ethnic state and proclaimed instead that the rights of all minority groups in Nigeria should be respected. To voice his concerns, he extensively collaborated with international organizations, such as the United Nations and Greenpeace, where he received much support for his peaceful approach (Mai-Bornu 2019, 2020).

On the other end of the spectrum, the Ijaw leadership displayed a much more aggressive and unpredictable approach. Isaac Adako Boro claimed the secession of the Ijaw community from the Nigerian state and the formation of an independent state of the Niger Delta. To reach this goal, he led the Niger Delta Volunteer Force (NDVF) in a "12-day revolution." This rebellion represented the peak of the grievances, frustrations, and felt injustices of the people, and, differing from the Ogoni, the Ijaw group opted for violence to voice this issues. To mobilize individuals, particularly the abandoned and deprived youth, Boro used narratives and words pertaining to the continuing state of oppression and poverty, to emotions like anger and frustration and the urge to "fight for freedom." "Boro emerged as a political figure determined to lead the region out of the terrible situation of neglect in which it found itself. For Boro, calling the attention of the world to the situation of the Ijaw represented success, even if it was achieved through violence" (Mai-Bornu 2020, 837).

10.4.4 How Both Organizations Addressed the Needs of the Deprived

The failure of the Nigerian government to address the needs of the people, in particular those living in the Niger Delta region, aggravated the conflicts, which have turned violent since 1997. The reasons for rebellion and protests were centered on demands for justice, ethnic minority rights, employment opportunities, payment of compensation for damages caused by oil extraction, and environmental protection. The communities suffered from governmental neglect, underdevelopment, and ecological degradation. Youth, in particular, have been confronted with high unemployment, lack of agency, and material deprivation. Instead of supporting the people in need, the government exploited the oil-rich regions without any compensation. Additionally, since 1960, public policy was not inclusionary; that is, citizens did not receive the opportunity to actively participate in and have impact on the policies affecting their lives. This created local and national policies that neglected the needs and preferences of the citizens, which was most evident in the deprived Niger Delta region. The subsequent distrust of the government translated in anti-government movements that have been hijacked by several militant (youth) organizations, which addressed the deprived needs of the people in a different way. Although both the Ogoni and Ijaw movements propagated a similar belief system that guided people about how to perceive the unjust social environment and offered historical and cultural narratives about how to understand the past, present, and the future, they addressed different emotions and needs of the people. The Ogoni focused on justice, agency, and human rights by using narratives and proclamations pertaining to cohesion, peace, and intellectuality. They addressed, in particular, the agency needs of the people, but also pro-sociality needs, as the belief system and the goals of the movement aimed at improving the conditions of all the ethnic groups in the country. The belief system did not focus on negative emotions like threat, anger, and frustration, but rather on the chances and possibilities of improvement. The Ogoni neither perceived themselves as superior nor as victims, but they chose the peaceful and intellectual path to voice their grievances and receive international support. Alternately, the Ijaw addressed negative emotions like threat, anger, frustration, a sense of helplessness, and lack of control by focusing more on existential and agency needs. In particular, youth, who had felt desperate and powerless, could suddenly make autonomous choices, take actively actions, shape their environment, have an impact on policies, and experience a sense of self-efficacy. They could air their grievances and perceived injustices and felt finally seen and heard. The Ijaw focused on their own ethnic group and demanded secession to establish an independent Niger Delta state, where they could control resources, reduce domination and threat, and establish stability. Other than the Ogoni, the Ijaw perceived themselves as victims, who were deprived of opportunities and resources, and who had no other option as to regain back control with violence and aggression.[7]

10.5 Case: Muslim Youth in Europe and the Islamic State

10.5.1 Socioeconomic and Political Conditions that Deprived Human Needs

Because groups are fundamental to identity and social life, individuals strive to belong to and be accepted by a certain group. Naturally, individuals like to perceive themselves in a positive light and thus prefer it if their group reflects positively on themselves. Identification processes have important intragroup implications because one's ingroup serves as a key reference point in everyday life—it guides how to perceive oneself and others, how to act, and how to evaluate and process information (Verkuyten and Martinovic 2012). However, immigrants with different cultural backgrounds often face uncertainty and negative appraisal regarding their groups and their social identity. Accordingly, members of such groups tend to search for psychological ways to reduce uncertainty and maintain their sense of self-worth and that of the group as a whole (Koomen and Van der Pligt 2016). A study on Dutch citizens with a Turkish background shows that these individuals identify more with their Turkish identity than their Dutch identity and more with their Turkish culture and its values, beliefs, and norms. They were also found to put more emphasis on their cultural ethnicity than the ethnic Dutch citizens on theirs (Verkuyten and Reijerse 2008). A similar study on 602 Turkish Muslims living in Germany and the Netherlands examined ingroup pressure to maintain one's ethnoreligious culture and identity. The more the Muslim individuals felt this ingroup pressure or norm, the stronger they identified with their cultural and religious group, regardless of outgroup behavior (such as discrimination). This finding confirms research that shows that within ingroups and ethnic communities there is often normative pressure to sustain the ingroup culture, values, and norms and to adapt to given roles and customs (Martinovic and Verkuyten 2012). However, strong ingroup identification can also result in ethnic separation, which involves rejecting the mainstream culture or dominant ethnic group (Berry 1990). An empirical study on second-generation Indian and Pakistani adolescents living in Britain showed that those who felt socially rejected by society tended to identify more strongly with their ethnic identity. Mainly Pakistani adolescents reported they felt discriminated in British society, which in turn had a negative impact on their willingness to adapt (Robinson 2009). This implies that feelings of rejection, discrimination, or non-acceptance by society or the major ethnic group strengthen identification with highly entitative groups or, in severe cases, with extremist groups (Hogg and Adelman 2013). One of those extremist groups is IS. Recent German government data on 910 individuals who traveled to Syria and Iraq to join IS show that the majority (seventy-eight percent), aged eighteen to twenty-five, had German or dual citizenship. The theory on dual-identity conflict argues that those who experience a strong identity incompatibility have more sympathy for radical beliefs. A study on Russian and Turkish individuals in Germany confirmed this theory and showed that neither grievance nor lack of opportunities fostered radicalism but only perceived identity incompatibility (Simon et al. 2013).

10.5.2 Extremist Organization—Ideology and Goal

The Islamic State (IS), also named the Islamic State in Iraq and Syria (ISIS), is one of the most brutal and effective Salafi-Jihadist organizations to date. The organization embraces doctrines that reject modernization in religion, Western cultural influence (secularism), and liberalism. It stresses the importance of monotheism—or the holiness of only one God, by rejecting the variety of different denominations—and *jihad*, as the holy war to fight disbelief (Byman 2016). The aim of the organization is to establish a self-organized and governed Islamic state—a combination of Sharia law, strict order, its own taxation and security systems, and the provision of social services to its members. This means that IS's key objective was not to act mainly as a terrorist organization, but to establish an Islamic state, in both Syria and Iraq, with its own economic, political, social, and legal systems. This would entail the replacement of all human-made laws and state sovereignty with Allah's rule through the establishment of Sharia law and a Quranic-based state, in which all "true believers" are unified (Abdulmajid 2021).

10.5.3 Extremist Organization—Its Structure, Recruitment, and Mobilization

The success of IS is explained by many researchers and politicians as a combination of its radical ideology, international networking structure, financial autonomy, the provision of state-based services and goods, military power, strategic social media campaigns, and ruthlessness (Abdulmajid 2021). To remain financially independent, the organization developed multiple sources of income, including oil, gas, agriculture, taxation, extortion, kidnapping, black market antique selling, and many more, which made IS the wealthiest terrorist organization worldwide, with approximately $2 million in earnings per day in 2014 (Lister 2014). The IS employs a strictly hierarchical and bureaucratic organizational structure, covering a chain of command, the Amir, various committees, deputies, a cabinet, local leaders, military commanders, Sharia commanders, a media department, and local fighters (Antony 2020). Before his accession in 2010, Abu Bakr al-Baghdadi was the Amir, the leader, of the organization. He had a personal advisor (formerly Haji Bakr), two deputies (one for Syria and one for Iraq) an eight-man cabinet that served as counselors, and a military council of at most thirteen men. While Baghdadi justifies his knowledge about the Islam by his (apparent) PhD in Islamic Studies from the Islamic University of Baghdad and his work as an imam and preacher in Iraq, his deputies have crucial military and intelligence experiences, which contributed significantly to the operational success of the organization. Moreover, in 2014, the organization accounted for more than one thousand medium and top-level field commanders, who held technical, military, and security experience. Next to field commanders, the organization also maintains a cabinet of ministers, who are managing various departments within the organization, such as the media, finance, military, civil duties, or political departments (Lister 2014).

The media department is argued to play a crucial role in recruitment and mobilization, in particular of Muslim youth living in the West. The youth in Iraq and Syria joined IS because it supplied them with state-based services and goods, financial resources, and power. They were mainly driven by severe socioeconomic conditions, such as poverty, high unemployment, rapid demographic growth, and governmental failure, and were thus seeking the opportunity to reach a transformation from marginalization to power, and to find a cause in life, receive social approval, reduce their frustration toward ruling regimes, and oppose Western secularism (Abdulmajid 2021).

To recruit and mobilize individuals, IS has created a sophisticated media campaign and established media sub-organizations, such as al-Furqan Foundation for Media Production, al-Hayat Media Center, *Dabiq* magazine, and *al-Naba* newspaper, which only focuses on information distribution. These media outlets usually disseminated speeches by the leader Abu Bakr al-Baghdadi, who often spoke about the *jihad* and its physical component. He emphasized the righteousness of the organization to form an Islamic state and described the *jihad* as a "struggle between the people of faith and the nonbelievers." He postulated that IS was fighting for the cause of Allah and that it was the responsibility of *every Muslim* to join the organization. The operations of IS are propagated as the war against disbelief and the enemies of Allah, and every Muslim worldwide is called out to pursue *hijrah*—the immigration of all Muslims to the new Islamic state, which is compared to the historical narrative of the Prophet and his companions moving from Mecca to Medina. Those who join the organization are portrayed in the media as fighters for the holy cause and true believers, and they are promised a "reward from Allah," whereas those who reject their participation are disobeying Allah and will be punished by him. In essence, all information about the group—be it newspapers, speeches, articles, and videos—were framed by means of contrast, legitimacy, and requirements. Contrast implies an ingroup and outgroup imaging (us vs. them), in which IS portrayed itself in a mostly positive light, merely as holy fighters that support the right cause, and its opponents are degraded as infidels who believe in false Gods and adopt wrong ideologies (democracy, secularism, nationalism, etc.). To legitimize the group's self-proclaimed "Islamic khilafah" (leader), a specific terminology and historic narratives are used, as well as honorable characteristics, such as "holy warrior," "scholar," "worshipper," and "descendent from the family of the Prophet," which would imply the attempt to compare its leader to the Rightly Guided Caliphs, who were the first four successor of the Prophet. Using the term "Rightly Guided" emphasizes that IS knows the right path to follow and that its actions are accepted by all Muslims as being the closest to the Prophet's example. Therefore, the major requirement is that all Muslims follow the call of IS to collectively build an Islamic state, the "dream for all true Muslims." IS, as the savior of the people, thus aims to "enlighten," "educate," and "spread knowledge" to them by means of guiding the truth path. This presupposes that without IS there will be no enlightenment, no experience of the truth, and no knowledge, but instead ignorance, deception, and darkness (Abdulmajid 2021). With such cultural and historical narratives about the "real Muslim heritage and identity" and the promise of finding meaning in life, IS could recruit more than five thousand foreign fighters from the West. While most of them were male, a vast number of women, aged between eighteen and twenty-five years, were also willing to join the radical organization (Saltman and Smith 2015). To address in particular the female adherents, IS published a high number of online videos showing the "real role and identity" of Muslim women, namely giving birth and raising the next generation of Muslim fighters. They were also obliged to support the *jihad* and make sure that all strict rules and norms were abided by all adherents. Women hence received a crucial role in the organization, as promoter, supporter, and guardian (Cunningham 2007).

10.5.4 How IS Addressed the Needs of the Deprived

Many young individuals traveled to Iraq and Syria to join IS, not because of socioeconomic grievances or lack of opportunities in life, but because of their need for self-significance and meaning in life. The significance quest theory indicates that "extremist behavior is seen as a means to gaining or restoring an individuals' sense of personal significance, importance, or effectiveness; that is, the sense of mattering in the eyes of oneself and others who matter"

(Webber et al. 2018, 271). Increased feelings of self-insignificance, social disapproval, and personal randomness can be triggered by shattering events which may entail social rejection, discrimination, humiliation of one's own social group, or the denigration of personal characteristics that define one's own identity. Such incidents can lead to social disintegration and identity vulnerability and induce negative feelings about oneself (Anhut 2005; Sageman 2008). A radical ideology, as in the case of IS, can be a viable reconciliation option to satisfy one's own needs and thus provide a sense of meaningful existence, in particular to those with a dual-identity vulnerability. Muslims living in the West are confronted with opposing cultural norms and values, and feel torn between their traditional, mostly conservative cultural heritage, and the liberal and secular social environment. But also experiences of social exclusion, feelings of discrimination and lack of power and agency can enhance the desire to belong to a strong group that appears to be powerful and influential. Paradoxically, in the Islamic organization women acquired power and autonomy to act, which they were otherwise denied in their conservative traditional environments. The mental framework provided guidance about how to perceive the Western world and their own role within it (which reduced the uncertainty and ambiguity); delivered cultural and historical narratives to link the past, present, and potential future (generated a sense of shared identity and belonging); and explained the obligations of each individual (duty and agency). The *jihadist* ideology offered alternatives to Western life and gender roles, which provided individuals who felt otherwise ostracized or not accepted a sense of social approval, orientation, and stability in life. "The Islamic way of life" is a way to show resistance—an act of rebellion and retaliation. Identifying with and adhering to ingroup customs, values, rules, and norms generate consistency and stability in life. It reduces self-uncertainty because it guides the individual about how to perceive the self and others and how to behave and interact with one another. "Social categorization of self and others generates a sense of ingroup identification and belonging, and regulates perception, inference, feelings, behavior, and interaction to conform to prototype-based knowledge one has about one's own group and relevant outgroups. Furthermore, because group prototypes are shared ('we' agree 'we' are like this, 'they' are like that) one's world view and self-concept are consensually validated by the overt and verbal behavior of fellow group members" (Hogg and Adelman 2013, 439). Those experiencing an identity vulnerability, or a dual-identity conflict, find a clear definition of one's own self-concept and a consistent image of oneself. The ability to act autonomously with the constant reassurance from ingroup members endows the individual with confidence, self-significance, and a high self-esteem.

10.6 Case: Right-Wing Populism in (Post-Soviet) Eastern European Nations

10.6.1 Socioeconomic and Political Conditions that Deprived Human Needs

After the collapse of the Soviet Union and its ideological-backed communist system, post-Soviet states found themselves in a vulnerable, ambiguous state marked with uncertainty about its future existence. Their ideological foundation, which formed their identity, values, and norms had been shattered and resulted in a fragmented society and people. The 2004 entrance of Poland, Hungary, the Czech Republic, and Slovakia to the European Union was celebrated heartedly and seen as a hopeful path to form a democratic, fair, and trustful state that would establish stable socioeconomic conditions and anti-corrupt systems. However, the integration of post-Soviet states, and their communist-shaped mindsets, turned out to be more challenging than previously expected. A study (Schwartz et al. 2014) examined the relationship between personal values and core political values in Western and Eastern European nations. The eight core political values are blind patriotism (no questioning and adherence), traditional morality (preservation of traditions in society and family), law and order (the government should generate order and rules), free enterprise (no governmental intervention in economic market), equality (equal opportunities for all citizens), civil liberties (freedom of speech), foreign military intervention, and immigration. The basic personal values are power (control and dominance over resources and people), achievement, hedonism, stimulation (excitement and novelty in life), self-direction (autonomy), universalism (welfare for all), benevolence, tradition, conformity, and security. The authors argue that individuals' personal values should match political values consistently; that is, power and security, for example, should match military intervention, but less benevolence or universalism. The results show clear differences between Western and post-communist nations. Universalism, for example, correlated with traditional morality positively in post-communist countries, but negatively in non-communist countries. Caring for the community and nature is perceived as a traditional and moral value in post-communist countries, but not in non-communist countries. The three conservation values (security, conformity, and tradition) correlated positively with military intervention and equality and negatively with free enterprise in post-communist countries. In this regard, the authors reason that governmental intervention (military power, equal opportunities for all, and intervention in the economy) enhances the sense of security and certainty in post-communist countries, while the negative correlation in non-communist countries implies that they prefer a rather limited role of the government. The authority and strong role of the government, which is perceived as the main caregiver and supplier of social and economic security, thus correlates positively with conservation values in post-communist countries. This implies that the state apparatus is seen as a moral authority, a source of security, and a social caregiver—a strong and powerful unit that produces and sustains security, conformity, and tradition.

After the collapse of the Communist system, numerous scholars assumed that the shift to democracy and capitalism would effect a change in the general belief system from egalitarianism to meritocratic, market-based principles. However, the negative implications of the economic transition, including high unemployment and high inflation, dampened the enthusiasm for the new system. Instead, increased perception of economic inequality and market unfairness arose, which in turn led to distrust against globalization and the democratic free-market system (Smith and Mateju 2012). This uncertainty about the newly established social, economic, and political systems was also fueled by identity vulnerability. The communist ideology propagated, beyond the role of an authoritarian government, the importance of a strong, unified, and homogeneous nation that shared the same values, norms, and identity. Unlike in China, where communism was homegrown, communism in Eastern Europe was imposed by a foreign authority, which suppressed their traditional national identities (Bunce 2005). The disintegration of the communist system resulted not only in economic and political turmoil, but also in alienated individuals who lacked a shared national identity. Oppositional forces thus used the momentum, and the insecurities of the people, to establish new anti-communist and nationalistic sentiments.

10.6.2 Extremist Organization—Ideology and Goal

In Poland, the right-leaning Poland's Law and Justice Party (PiS), founded in 2001 by the twin brothers Lech and Jarosław Kaczyński, successfully integrated its anti-communist, anti-migration, and ultra-ethnic-nationalistic narratives into the broad society. The belief system of PiS revolves around the sovereignty of the Polish people, who are considered to be homogeneous and strictly catholic. It uses patriotic sentiments, traditional moral values, and Catholicism to establish a shared understanding of a Polish national identity and how society should look (Ding and Hlavac 2017). The focus on Catholicism and a national identity received much appeal in a society that was forced to abandon their religious and national identity during the communist era. In their founding manifesto, the Kaczyński brothers highlighted their disapproval of communism and its pathological implications, linking the past regime to massive corruption and clientelism. "On the one hand, PiS supported private ownership, small and medium-sized enterprises, and tax decreases for physical and legal persons. On the other, the party was critical of banks, calling their greater regulation, as well as regulation of the stock market and large enterprises [. . .]. The party also wanted to maintain state influence in crucial businesses, e.g. the PKN Orlen petrochemicals company, the Polish State Railways and the Polish Post (PiS 2006), and sharply criticised neoliberal approaches (PiS 2014a). The party continuously expressed support for Polish businesses and argued that there was a need to 'rationalise foreign investment' (PiS 2001b) and introduce sectoral taxes. Both measures were evidently largely aimed against the influx of foreign capital" (Folvarčný and Kopeček 2020, 170). PiS also aimed at supporting, in particular, the socially disadvantaged, providing free healthcare for those over seventy-five-years-old and an extensive family care package, and lowering the retirement age, which filled the gap of the communist social system. In a 2019 manifesto, the social care package was enlarged by free healthcare for pregnant women, income tax waivers for the those younger than twenty-six, and a minimum wage increase—the goal is to establish a social welfare state for the Polish people.

The party not only aimed to introduce economic regulations, but also to maintain state influence in the private sphere of the citizens. Faith was not seen as a private matter, but as a national, collectivistic duty—the foundation of the Polish nation and society. In this regard, PiS enforces the traditional marriage and gender roles and a "moral order of society." It vehemently rejects LGBTQIA rights and abortion, which, in their perception, lead to "social demoralization." Beyond the family and religion, the homogeneous nation is seen as the fundamental base of the Polish identity and society. To establish "a Poland for the Poles," the party adopts a harsh anti-immigration political stance and antisemitic positions of some segments of the party. To secure national sovereignty, provide security, order, regulation, and ethnic homogeneity, the party demands strong and clear authority and the "removal of corrupt and dishonest elites." It wants to centralize power and control the judiciary, and the output of public service radio and television (Folvarčný and Kopeček 2020). PiS gained control of the presidency, premiership, and the Sejm (parliament) in the 2015 election and it continues to receive much control and influence over the state.

A similar mental framework is provided by the Alliance of Young Democrats–Hungarian Civic Alliance (Fiatal Demokraták Szövetsége–Magyar Polgári

Szövetség, or Fidesz) under the leadership of Viktor Orbán. The right-leaning party disregards the principles of liberalism and democracy and aims to establish their vision of "illiberal democracy" in Hungary, which rejects free and government-critical media, independent and non-politicized judiciary, and liberal and autonomous universities that support politically independent critical knowledge (Hellström et al. 2020). Fidesz, similar to PiS, adopted anti-communist, anti-liberal, and ultra-nationalistic views, rejected immigration and LGBTQIA rights, and aimed at establishing an ethnically homogeneous, Christian society based on traditional gender roles, marriage, and religious morality. In his popular speech in 1997, Orbán contrasted a liberal and open society to a wealthy and growing nation by attacking globalization, cosmopolitanism, and those who expect Hungarians to apologize for alleged historical crimes. In his view, an "open society" creates a weak nation that is shaken in its morals and identity, and leads to decreased self-esteem, enhanced feelings of guilt, and deprived national confidence. Instead, he urged Hungarians to be proud of the nation and to come out in opposition against foreign influence (Enyedi 2015). This means that nationalistic feelings of pride and a shared collectivistic identity should replace the materialistic, meritocratic, and individualistic values of the liberal, modern democracy. Orbán's early legal initiatives attacked the independence of crucial public institutions, such as the judiciary, media, education, tax authority, and the election commission with the overall goal to centralize power. Previously independent institutions have been filled with party loyalists by removing opposition figures and neutral experts. The constitution has been changed to establish vertical power; that is, to give the national leader, Viktor Orbán, "a direct line into the local government to exercise detailed control of their actions without going through the national parliament" (Scheppele 2018, 551). Overall, Fidesz adopts an authoritarian, anti-communism, anti-liberalism, anti-immigration, and ultra-nationalistic belief system that aims to centralize power, establish a homogeneous nation based on traditional gender roles, and control all public institutions and media outlets.

10.6.3 Extremist Organization—Its Structure, Recruitment, and Mobilization

The greatest PiS electoral support comes from the eastern and southeastern parts of Poland, which are more rural, religious, and traditionalist. The countryside exemplifies the conservative vision of the party—tradition, faith, and traditional family—and is used as an instrument to position itself in opposition to their rival parties, which are portrayed as left-leaning proponents who only concern about the metropolitan areas (Folvarčný and Kopeček 2020). In its founding manifesto, PiS used historical and cultural narratives about the "heroic" actions and periods of Poland, such as the interwar Second Polish Republic (1918–1939) and the struggle against German and Soviet dominance. Ding and Hlavac (2017) argue that both Poland and Hungary evolved their ideology around what they call restorative nationalism. "Restorative nationalism is shaped by historical circumstances, and embodied in political memories that are passed down from one generation to another (e.g., through the education system). It can be activated and animated by rhetorical and cultural symbols, and has a lasting impact on public opinion and political behavior. Restorative nationalism often reflects on a historical period of perceived greatness and glory, often juxtaposed with an ensuing period of trauma and humiliation, and calls for the restoration of a glorious past" (429). Hence, during their campaigns, PiS often adopted narratives of the "nationhood" and patriotism, and used media platforms, such as the widely circulated Polish magazine *Wprost*, to propagate their anti-EU attitudes: on one cover, five leading EU politicians and then German Chancellor Angela Merkel were portrayed in Nazi uniforms leaning over a map, with the headline "these people want to control Poland again (Zno'w chca ͺ nadzorowac' Polske)." The strong alliance with the Catholic Church was not only an important source for financial support, but also as the most important source for recruitment and mobilization. The influential Radio Maryja, whose director is Father Tadeusz Rydzyk, disseminated PiS's beliefs, visions, and narratives, and made clear that the Church approved them. The Church served as national identifier, as a pillar of Polishness and, so argued by the party, as a substitute for the non-existent sovereign state during the Communist era. The national and religious identity of oneness, together with patriotism and tradition, defined the concept of the national identity (Ding and Hlavac 2017; Folvarčný and Kopeček 2020).

Orbán also used cultural and historical narratives to portray the great Hungarian nation that should be protected against "foreign domination." In the beginning, the party addressed its rhetoric to the middle class, showing little interests in the working class, and adjusting its speeches and policy to the *polgári* (civic/bourgeois). Their loss during the 2002 election led them to rethink their strategy and discourse, and they turned toward more radical forms of populism, anti-communism, illiberalism, and nationalism. The rhetoric shifted away from *polgár* to *emberek* (the people) by attacking opponents to create a segregating environment ("we" vs. "them"). "The people" have been portrayed as a hard-working, suffering group, while "the aristocrats" were described as weak individuals who never really worked or suffered in their lives, and who lived in their privileged, artificial bubbles away from reality. The normal people, who "try to live in dignity, raise their children and take care of each other" are deprived from resources and options to live a good life, while "the millionaire swindlers, conmen protected by the state" take all the resources that people work for and treat them "as fools." The grievances of people have been interpreted as a criticism of the pluralistic political arena and a demand for a strong government that does not debate but forcefully acts (Enyedi 2005). To propagate their visions, Fidesz used extensively various media platforms, adopted viral marketing techniques for voter mobilization, used vehemently historic national symbols, and applied narratives that identified the party with the whole nation (Szilágy and Bozóki 2015). Orbán also formed a loose network of informal clubs, initiatives, and associations—the Civic Circles—which "provided an ideal frame for populist politics because its amorphous structure served the prevailing anti-party sentiments well and because it lacked internal formal procedures for accountability" (Enyedi 2005, 232). Fidesz organized huge party rallies which were broadcasted live by the Hungarian Public Television. Popular artists performed at the rallies, followed by speeches of political leaders, and a closing with a speech by Viktor Orbán, who was celebrated as a star: participants enthusiastically waved national flags and support banners and chanted "Viktor, Viktor." These rallies attracted many participants (and TV viewers) because they offered an experience of collective belongingness and an identification with the nation and the social others. Those who came received approval from the group, coupled with positive emotions during chanting and flag waving. The sense of pride, solidarity, and a shared national identity were reasons, among others, why these rallies received much attention and enhanced appeal among the public (Szilágyi and Bozóki 2015).

10.6.4 How Both Organizations Addressed the Needs of the Deprived

The collapse of the Soviet Union resulted not only in political, social, and economic turmoil, but also vulnerable individuals who were once held together by a centralized, authoritarian power and a shared ideology and identity but who now found themselves alienated and insecure about their own self-concept and belonging. Parties like PiS in Poland and Fidesz in Hungary used the uncertain times to propagate their anti-communist and ultra-nationalist beliefs and to address the needs of those who were longing for a strong and powerful authority. In Poland, PiS described itself as the alternative to a communist and "post-communist" regime that sought to redefine the foundations of a Polish nation. By disseminating cultural and historical narratives, the party linked the glorious (pre-communist) past, present, and bright future of the nation together, which generated both a sense of a shared history and culture and a newly framed national identity. The focus on Catholicism, which was banned during the Communist era, and on traditional gender roles, family, and traditions, generated a new definition of the Polish self-concept. The homogeneous society, and the exclusion of dissidents, ethnic minorities, and otherness, provided guidance how to perceive the social environment, social others, and one's own role, and how to make decisions and behave (e.g., adhere to the rules and norms to be accepted and belonged). The anti-communist, anti-immigration, anti-LGBTQIA and ultra-nationalist beliefs reduced uncertainty and ambiguity, and generated order and control, serving the existential needs of the adherents.

In Hungary, Fidesz and the twinned anti-communist, anti-immigration, anti-LGBTQIA, illiberal, and ultra-nationalist belief system served, in particular, the existential and relational needs of the Hungarians. Portraying the liberal and pluralistic society as a threat and globalization as uncontrollable force that would destroy the nation, the social order, and the societal norms, guided the individuals in how to understand the world, perceive the social environment, and one's own role in it. Identifying with Christianity, in the otherwise secular Hungary, traditions and national symbols provided a source for identity and orientation in life. Big rallies with national flags, chanting, and heroic speeches created collectivistic experiences that enhanced positive emotions of solidarity and a sense of belongingness. The party provided, in authoritarian terms, a sense of certainty, order, and control in the lives of the people who were longing for a strong and powerful leader capable of making decisions, prevailing, and defending the nation. Various surveys provide evidence that nostalgia and positive attitudes toward the old communist system have not entirely disappeared in post-communist nations. A Polish survey in 2010 found that sixty-four percent of respondents evaluated their lives before the transition to capitalism more positively, whereas only seven percent indicated the opposite (Prusik and Lewicka 2016). Also, in other Eastern European countries, individuals revealed their demand for a strong and powerful state that is responsible for the economic situation, job status, and welfare of each citizen (Cernat 2010), but also for a dominant leader, who is able to protect the nation, even in aggressive and offensive terms (Laustsen and Petersen 2017). Both parties, PiS and Fidesz, served these needs of the people by means of an authoritarian regime and right-leaning, ultra-nationalistic belief system.

Notes

Chapter 2

1. There are other well-known need classifications, such as Maslow (1943, 1954), Burton (1990), Deci and Ryan (2000), and Jost (2017). While these already give clear insights, in the context of social conflict we slightly adjust the existing schemes and suggest, portray, and refer to the need categorizations of Figure 2.1, namely existential, relational, and agency needs.
2. Our focus here is on psychological needs. However, consumption and physical goods are obviously relevant and can be included if required (Gries et al. [2022]; Burs et al. [2022]).
3. Most studies assign belief systems or ideologies along a more or less definite left-to-right ideological scale, or alternatively along the liberal–conservative scale that dominates in the United States. While this classification is generally seen as a viable instrument for ideological orientation and self-identification in a complex political environment, it can also be misleading given that ideologies can manifest differently depending on the cultural, social, and geographical context, which makes it more difficult to place them along the spectrum (e.g., feminism or ecologism are present in both liberal and conservative ideologies).
4. Liberalism is a powerful ideology of the industrialized West. However, since the nineteenth century different factors have reshaped its nature. Classic liberalism, or libertarianism as it is termed in the United States, was formed in the early nineteenth century to reduce state intervention and allow for personal and economic freedom. Liberalism adopted a more anti-governmental and free market-supporting appeal. Modern liberalism emerged during industrialization due to the changed view that government should help to reduce negative consequences or obstacles of industrialization, such as poverty, discrimination, or poor access to education (Heywood 2017).
5. We do not want to call this a "rational choice" because the term "rational choice" is linked to a particular economic modeling (mostly including perfect information). Further, the term "rational" is often positively connotated. However, here it can be subjectively logically consistent that an individual is attracted to an ethically "bad" ideology and turns into a follower. In our view, this cannot be termed "rational" because, at least collectively from a societal point of view, this will not be rational. Further, if someone is considered rational it often means they only had one logical decision. However, this is too simple. There may be subjectively logical decisions which may lead to some more benefits, but when they violate fundamental rules, such as human rights, we cannot regard that as ultimately rational.
6. That said, individuals may choose and stick to a belief system despite bad decisional outcomes or a biased representation of reality. This choice is guided by self-serving and identity-maintaining motives (Benabou 2015). Individuals hold beliefs that generate a positive self-view and are even willing to invest resources to avoid information that contradicts their beliefs (Eil and Rao 2011; Ganguly and Tasoff; Golman et al. 2017). Such a preservation of a belief system can be surely regarded as irrational. In our analysis, however, we focus on the logic behind choosing a particular belief system.

7. A more poetic description of this meritocratic ideological narrative may be: "But there has been also the American Dream, that dream of a land in which life should be better and richer and fuller for every man, with opportunity for each according to ability or achievement. . . . regardless of the fortuitous circumstances of birth or position" (Adams 1931, 404).
8. The categorization of a narrative as "good" or "bad" employs a simple benchmark—compatibility with human rights. We consider a narrative "bad" if it conceptually violates human rights. There is no other particular concept involved because we do not want to open up an ethical debate at this point, even if this is important as a next step.
9. Passive recruitment is more focused on presenting information about the group's goals, beliefs, and interests violence (e.g., via a website) rather than openly calling for violence. Active recruitment encourages participation in and support for the group's causes, directly addresses potential members, and in extreme cases openly calls for violence. But individuals, too, may also actively reach out to certain groups that seem appealing to them and request to become a member.

Part I

1. We refrain from reviewing all the theories and models dealing with human needs, especially in the psychological discipline, and instead focus on our own framework. For a review see, among others, Pittman and Zeigler (2007).

Chapter 3

1. The resource curse is widely discussed in both economic and political science literature. At least two excellent surveys describe the major strands of the resource curse debate. For a deeper and more detailed discussion we recommend van der Ploeg (2011).

Chapter 4

1. Personality consists of two components: traits and states. Traits are perceived as relatively stable and static, while states can change in response to changing situations and environmental conditions (Fontana 1983).
2. According to the *APA Dictionary of Psychology*, a dissociative identity disorder is "characterized by the presence in one individual of two or more distinct identities or personality states that each recurrently take control of the individual's behavior" (American Psychological Association 2019a).
3. The Need to Belong Scale is a ten-item measure of individual differences in the need to belong (Leary et al. 2013).

Chapter 5

1. Identity can be understood as a subjective sense of self defined by a set of physical, psychological, and interpersonal characteristics, as well as social identifications and roles. It involves a sense of continuity and stability; that is, the feeling that one is the same person

today that one was yesterday (self-sameness) (APA 2019b), which is derived, among other things, by a clear and consistent self-concept. Identity thus expresses a mutual relationship between self-persistence and individuality and the sharing of similar characteristics with significant others (Erikson 1956).
2. If, for example, you are at a party and you are the only person who has dressed up, this social circumstance (especially if it is self-relevant) at a given time will possibly change your perception or evaluation of yourself, without changing your stable self-knowledge stored in long-term memory.
3. In the identity development process, the individual explores and commits; that is, the individual explores a set of potential options and chooses to move forward (commitment). For instance, an individual has a wide choice of study subjects (exploration of possible alternatives). By examining the options, the individual decides which option fits in with their overall sense of self and what they can identify most. In the end they decide to study economics and integrate this choice in their identity (commitment). However, if after a certain amount of time, they realize that studying economics does not fit with their self-concept after all, they may reconsider this commitment.
4. Personality consists of two components: traits and states. Traits are perceived as relatively stable and static, while states can change in response to changing situations and environmental conditions (Fontana 1983).
5. We do not provide an extensive discussion of these measurements, which are all based on self-reports to assess greed as a personality trait. The scales differ in length, ranging from six items to twelve, but have substantial similarities in terms of item content.
6. This would correspond to our need system, yet we use different terms: need for self-determination for autonomy, need for self-efficacy for competence, and need for belongingness for relatedness.
7. Other researchers and clinicians argue that high levels of self-efficacy can also have negative treatment outcomes because it can lead to an overconfidence in one's abilities to overcome drug dependency (Mayer and Koeningsmark 1992). However, we abstain from a deeper discussion on this issue and continue with the positive outcomes enhanced self-efficacy beliefs can have.

Chapter 6

1. Economists such as Khalil (2010) would argue that such biased and self-serving beliefs are non-Bayesian because they are subject to internal motivations. They are self-beliefs that are based on context information, which affords meaning or a level of desire that are non-empirical (mind dependent). For example, by engaging in wishful thinking or a self-serving bias, the agent is not updating their beliefs correctly because they are letting the wish, rather than the evidence, update their belief.
2. To clarify, beliefs do not always address the self. Here we are talking about need-serving beliefs which address subjective needs and preferences. A belief can, for example, serve the "need for ambiguity avoidance." If an individual is subjectively threatened by ambiguity and wants to reduce it, a belief can help them to do so and thus becomes a mean for need reconciliation. In this case, the belief indeed addresses the self, in particular the structure of the preferences of the individual.
3. Jacobin radicals sat to the left of the King, moderates sat in the center, and royalists and clerics sat to the right (Oxford Dictionary of Social Sciences 2002).

4. Liberalism, in simplified terms, implies a belief system that advocates the right of individuals, each of equal worth, to make decisions. Conservatism, to the contrary, draws on political order based on law and tradition and seeks to preserve the continuity of society's social structure and institutions (Oxford Dictionary of Social Sciences 2002). These definitions, however, are very simplified and do not address the whole discussion and variability of these terms.
5. Egalitarianism is characterized by a belief that equality is the primary value politics should strive for. However, ideologies differ in their perspectives on equality. While liberalism believes that all individuals are born "equal" and thus should have the same legal, social, and political rights, conservatism view society as naturally hierarchical and thus reject the idea of equality (Heywood 2017).
6. Individuals who score high on Extraversion are sociable, talkative, energetic, and gregarious. Traits associated with high Agreeableness include cooperation, trust, generosity, and lenience. High Neuroticism describes individuals who are emotionally unstable, worried, anxious, and uncertain, whereas individuals who score high on Conscientiousness are well-organized, punctual, ambitious, responsible, and persevering. Openness to experience describes individuals who are broad-minded, flexible, curious, and creative (Okun and Finch 1998).

Chapter 7

1. Between 1860 and 1930, nationalist and racist ideologies implied a "natural" or biological concept of belonging which was inflected by social Darwinism or Lamarckian thinking. During this time race and nationality were viewed through the lens of evolutionary biology (Vincent 2013).
2. The term first coined by Mussolini in 1919 was derived from the Italian plural form *fasci*, meaning political unions, and is etymologically linked to *fasces*, the axe-bound-with-rods symbol of authority in Ancient Rome. Later movements, such as Georges Valois's French Faisceau or the British Union of Fascism (BUF) adopted the Italian interpretation of fascism, while others, such as Falange in Spain or the Iron Guard in Romania, openly denied that their party was fascist in nature (Eatwell 2013).
3. In the Hawk–Dove game, participants receive a certain lump sum at the beginning of the game and "fight" over certain resources like food or money. Players can choose between two behavioral strategies to "fight" for this lump sum: claiming (the Hawkish strategy) or not claiming (the Dovish strategy) the other player's money. When the Hawkish strategy is adopted, the player's payout is either doubled (if the other player chooses the Dovish strategy) or zeroed (if the coplayer also chooses the Hawkish strategy). On the other hand, if the player follows the Dovish strategy, the payout is either untouched (if the coplayer plays Dove) or halved (if the coplayer plays Hawk). In other words, the Hawkish strategy involves aggression and a selfish high-risk, high-gain strategy, while the Dovish strategy is more submissive and low-risk and no-gain in nature.
4. In his famous work, *Evolutionary Socialism* (1898), the German socialist politician Eduard Bernstein proposed the first revision of Marxism, criticizing the urge to withdraw from capitalism and start a revolution. Instead, he called for collaboration with the liberal middle class and the peasantry (cross-class alliances) and effecting a peaceful gradual transition

to democratic socialism (Heywood 2015). Bernstein was influenced by Kantian socialism, which emphasized empirical evidence that constructs scientific knowledge rather than theoretical and prescriptive claims (clear distinction between facts and values).
5. In Britain, Germany, Sweden, and France, the social and political environment, marked by rapid industrialization and a slow formation of liberal constitutionalism and democracy, allowed for the emergence of labor movements that differed from those in southern and eastern Europe. "In this relatively liberal environment, the politicized elements of the working class could build powerful political parties and trade unions to represent and protect their interests" (Jackson 2013, 411).
6. In the years that followed, the dominant communist model of the Soviet Union paved the way for the establishment of communist regimes in Eastern Europe in 1945 and in China in 1949, from where it subsequently spread further into Asia to countries, such as Vietnam, North Korea, and Cambodia. More moderate forms of socialism were adopted in India, while modified anti-colonial, religiously adjusted socialist models emerged in African and Arab countries. In the 1960s and 1970s, socialist revolutionaries in Latin America waged war against military dictatorships, commencing with the Cuban revolution in 1959 (Heywood 2017).
7. Empirical studies on post-communist countries provide evidence that after the collapse of communism, these countries struggled to find a new shared identity and value system (by experiencing rather the perception of disparity) (e.g., Bringa 2002; Schöpflin 1993).
8. The primatologist Frans de Waal provides evidence that nonhuman primates, too, display moral behavior, indicating morality has a shared evolutionary background (e.g., Killen and de Waal 2000).
9. Extremism "characterizes an ideological position embraced by those anti-establishment movements, which understand politics as struggle for supremacy rather than as peaceful competition between parties with different interests [. . .]. Extremism exists at the periphery of societies and seeks to conquer its center by creating fear of enemies within and outside society. They divide fellow citizens and foreigners into friends and foes, with no room for diversity of opinions and alternative lifestyles. Extremism is, due to its dogmatism, intolerant and unwilling to compromise" (Bötticher 2017, 74).

Chapter 8

1. Traditional literature on right-wing groups recognizes the importance of organizational structure and development, but it does not discuss it in detail and mostly takes it as a given, by focusing rather on the effects and consequences of the group's activities (e.g., Berman 1997)
2. However, contrasting studies argue that higher interconnectivity among groups may enhance intergroup conflict, and thus decrease operational effectiveness (Chermak et al. 2013).
3. An empirical cross-national study on right-wing mobilization shows that the level of mobilization in France diminishes drastically if the political extreme right parties are excluded, most notably the largest one—the Front National. This implies that this big political actor tends to determine the overall actions and decisions of the far-right sector and is detrimental to the mobilization of other far-right organizations (Giugni et al. 2005).

4. This is surprising because usually radical right groups (especially populist radical right) reject representative politics in the electoral channel, but, on the other hand, use the same channel to mobilize individuals and communicate their ideology (Hutter and Kriesi 2013).
5. Andreas Baader, a high-school dropout with a weakness for cars, motorcycles, and weapons was the leader of the group until his suicide in 1977. Gudrun Ensslin grew up in a religious family and was a doctoral student at the University of Tübingen. Ulrike Meinhof was a writer and Horst Mahler a successful lawyer (Moghadam 2012). After dropping out of the group, Horst Mahler adopted radical right-wing beliefs and joined the leading neo-Nazi group NPD in the late 1990s. After distancing himself from the political arena, he founded a far-right think tank, where he incorporated his extremist left-wing and right-wing beliefs into a nationalistic, far-right ideology that featured anti-Americanism, anti-capitalism, nationalism, and antisemitism (Michael 2009).
6. Historians and sociologists assume that both, right-wing and left-wing extremism in Germany were shaped by the socioeconomic transformation that mitigated traditional norms and values, by leading to an uncertain, disintegrated, and instable sense of self. This fragility and instability in turn was filled with simple and radical beliefs and theories that offered "solutions" and guiding principles to confused individuals (Moghadam 2012).
7. Cohesion implies here the formation and preservation of cooperative efforts to achieve collective goals. An organization can show organizational unity and strong hierarchical patterns, but in fact individuals may join the group for subjective self-interest or may not fight for the same collective reason. This would result in disintegration. At the same time an organization can be fragmented and decentralized, but still be cohesive (Kenny 2010).
8. The aim of this elaboration is not to go deeper into the historical facts and reasons of the Civil War of El Salvador, which would go beyond the scope of this project, but rather to provide an overview of the organizational patterns of FMLN.
9. We do not claim that every religion has the same organizational structure and the same foundations. We are aware of the differences implying the uniqueness of every religion.
10. We do not claim a strict typology here, as one finds a great deal of variety among churches, their ideologies, and their organizational forms.
11. For detailed elaboration about Al-Qaeda's influence in the specific regions see Burke (2004), Forest (2011), Green (2014), Fishman (2006)
12. Although initial roots of the Islamic State lie in Afghanistan and Jordan, most operations took place in Iraq and, recently, in Syria (Lister 2014).
13. Information about the existence of Emni were revealed in documents found in 2014, owned by Haji Bakr, a former colonel in the intelligence service of Saddam Hussein's Air Defense Force (Speckhard and Yayla 2017). According to *Spiegel International* (2015), Haji Bakr was the designer of the "Islamic Intelligence State," the "Emni," who has created the draft shown above.

Chapter 9

1. The New Right is a term that gained usage in 1970s and 1980s, in particular in the wake of the economic crisis (1973–1974) and after the electoral success of Ronald Reagan (1980) in the United States and Margaret Thatcher (1979) in the UK. The New Right ideas revolve around libertarianism and conservatism, the former around the beliefs of free market dominance and minimal government: privatization of the public sector, deregulation, and

reduction of the welfare state. The latter promotes conservative values and beliefs of social inequality, social hierarchy, traditional moralism, role abidance, group homogeneity, anti-abortion, and anti-immigration (*The Oxford Companion to Politics of the World* 2004).

Chapter 10

1. There are not only these two ethnic groups, but also a substantial number of Muslims (referred to "Ceylon Moors") and Malay in Sri Lanka. Although the relationship between Muslims and the Sinhalese and Tamils is important, we refrain here from going into detail.
2. "Sinhalese, the majority of whom are Buddhists, consider themselves to be descendants of the fair-skinned Aryan people of North India, pointing out that the Sinhala language is related to the refined and widely used Indo-European group of languages rather than to the Dravidian language of the Tamils, the darker-skinned largely Hindu people of South India" (Manogaran 1987, 1).
3. Colonial powers introduced two modes of control over their colonies: direct rule, mainly practiced by France, Belgium, and Portugal, which featured centralization and cultural assimilation; or an indirect style of rule, preferred mainly by the British, which involved more decentralized decision-making and the establishment of local "intermediaries" who were loyal to the colonial powers. For example, France discouraged local decision-making; established a political authority that governed from Paris; perceived its culture, language, and colonial officers as superior; and thus eliminated indigenous structures and identity groups. By contrast, the British did not aim to import their culture or political system, but instead located "legitimate" local leaders, strengthened their power and authority, and brought the communities under these leaders' control to reinforce their own (Crowder 1968).
4. There are certainly other arguments explaining the resurrection of Boko Haram, which, in particular, focus on the historic traditions of Islam in Nigeria and the loss of power of Islamic traditions due to the British colonial rule. This loss of power spurred a reaction to modernization and liberalism, the rejection of European Enlightenment (secularism), and the growth of opposing Islamic groups that aimed to "protect" fading puritan Islamic traditions and beliefs from the threat of secularism (Kassim 2015).
5. Nesser (2013) defines jihadi-Salafism as "the ideology of al-Qaida and likeminded movements, mixing Wahhabi-inspired Sunni fundamentalism (Salafism) with a revolutionary program of overthrowing unjust and un-Islamic regimes in the Muslim world, as well as irredentism aiming at expelling non-Muslim military presence and influences from Muslim lands" (417).
6. Nigeria experienced several conflicts after its independence from Great Britain in 1960 regarding three areas: territory, resources, and politics. As Africa's most populous country, it is made up of 250 ethno-linguistic groups and thirty-six states, which additionally caused several ethnic and ideological disputes. Here, we only observe the resource-based conflicts and disputes in Niger Delta in the 1960s and 1970s.
7. This violent approach sparked the first disputes in February 1966. A military coup in July 1966, led by military officers from the northern states, resulted in a regime change and a new federal military government. Within a year, the new government under General Yakubu Gowen created twelve new states, which contributed partly to the outbreak of the Biafra Civil War in 1967. Biafra, a region where the dominant Igbo group controlled the

eastern region and the Niger Delta, attempted to secede from Nigeria and retain control over the oil-rich eastern parts of the country (Garba and Garba 2005). At this time, marginalized ethnic minority groups in the Niger Delta fought in the civil war on the federal side to defend their interests from Igbo domination. But several developments after the end of the civil war in 1970 compounded the situation of the Niger Delta ethnic minorities. Despite their support of the government during the war, the control of oil revenues shifted from the regions to the federal military government, and the vast expansion in local oil production accelerated the environmental degradation of the fragile Niger Delta. The situation remained unchanged even after the democratization process in 1999 (Obi 2010).

References

Abadie, A. 2006. "Poverty, political freedom, and the roots of terrorism." *American Economic Review* 96, no. 2: 50–56.

Abdulmajid, A. 2021. *Extremism in the Digital Era: The Media Discourse of Terrorist Groups in the Middle East*. London: Palgrave Macmillan. https://doi.org/10.1007/978-3-030-74833-3.

Abels, H. 2006. *Identität: Lehrbuch*. Wiesbaden: VS Verlag für Sozialwissenschaften. https://doi.org/10.1007/978-3-531-90437-5.

Abelson, R. P. 1979. "Differences between Belief and Knowledge Systems." *Cognitive Science* 3, no. 4: 355–366. https://doi.org/10.1207/s15516709cog0304_4.

Abrams, D., and M. A. Hogg. 1990. "Social Identification, Self-categorization and Social Influence." *European Review of Social Psychology* 1, no. 1: 195–228. https://doi.org/10.1080/14792779108401862.

Abu-Rayya, M. H., R. Walker, F. A. White, and H. M. Abu-Rayya. 2016. "Cultural Identification and Religious Identification Contribute Differentially to the Adaptation of Australian Adolescent Muslims." *International Journal of Intercultural Relations* 54: 21–33. https://doi.org/10.1016/j.ijintrel.2016.07.002.

Achterberg, P., and D. Houtman. 2009. "Ideologically Illogical? Why Do the Lower-educated Dutch Display So Little Value Coherence?" *Social Forces* 87, no. 3: 1649–1670. https://doi.org/10.1353/sof.0.0164.

Adams, James T. 1931. *Epic of America*. Boston: Little, Brown, and Company.

Adorno, T., E. Frenkel-Brenswik, D. J. Levinson, and R. N. Sanford. 1950. *The Authoritarian Personality*. New York: Harper & Row, Inc.

Agassi, J. 1960. "Methodological Individualism." *British Journal of Sociology* 11: 144–170.

Agassi, J. 1975. "Institutional Individualism." *British Journal of Sociology* 26, no. 2: 144–155. https://doi.org/10.2307/589585.

Agbiboa, D. E. 2013. "Why Boko Haram Exists: The Relative Deprivation Perspective." *African Conflict and Peacebuilding Review* 3, no. 1: 144–157. https://doi.org/10.2979/africonfpeacrevi.3.1.144.

Akbarzadeh, S., and A. Saeed. 2001. *Muslim Communities in Australia*. Sydney: UNSW Press.

Akerlof, G. A., and R. E. Kranton. 2010. *Identity Economics: How Our Identities Shape Our Work, Wages, and Well-being*. Princeton, NJ: Princeton University Press.

Akins, J. K. 2006. "The Ku Klux Klan: America's Forgotten Terrorists." *Law Enforcement Executive Forum* 5, no. 7: 127–144.

Alarcón, R. D., and E. F. Foulks. 1995. "Personality Disorders and Culture: Contemporary Clinical Views (Part A)." *Cultural Diversity and Mental Health* 1, no. 1: 3–17. https://doi.org/10.1037/1099-9809.1.1.3.

Albarello, F., E. Crocetti, and M. Rubini. 2018. "I and Us: A Longitudinal Study on the Interplay of Personal and Social Identity in Adolescence." *Journal of Youth and Adolescence* 47, no. 4: 689–702. https://doi.org/10.1007/s10964-017-0791-4.

Alesina, A., and N. Fuchs-Schündeln. 2005. "Goodbye Lenin (or not)? The Effect of Communism on People's Preferences." NBER Working Paper, no. 11700. https://doi.org/10.3386/w11700.

References

Alesina, A., and P. Giuliano. 2011. "Preferences for Redistribution." In *Handbook of Social Economics (Vol. 1)*, edited by J. Bahnabib, A. Bisin, and O. M. Jackson, 93–131. Amsterdam: Elsevier. https://doi.org/10.1016/B978-0-444-53187-2.00004-8.

Alesina, A., and R. Perotti. 1996. "Income Distribution, Political Instability, and Investment." *European Economic Review* 40, no. 6: 1203–1228. https://doi.org/10.1016/0014-2921(95)00030-5.

Alesina, A., R. Baqir, and W. Easterly. 1999. "Public Goods and Ethnic Divisions." *The Quarterly Journal of Economics* 114, no. 4: 1243–1284. https://doi.org/10.1162/003355399556269.

Alesina, A., G. Cozzi, and N. Mantovan. 2012. "The Evolution of Ideology, Fairness and Redistribution." *The Economic Journal* 122, no. 565: 1244–1261. https://doi.org/10.1111/j.1468-0297.2012.02541.x.

Alesina, A., and E. L. Glaeser. 2004. *Fighting Poverty in the US and Europe: A World of Difference*. New York: Oxford University Press. https://doi.org/10.1093/0199267669.001.0001.

Alesina, A., S. Stantcheva, and E. Teso. 2018. "Intergenerational Mobility and Preferences for Redistribution." *American Economic Review* 108, no. 2: 521–554. https://doi.org/10.1257/aer.20162015.

Alexander, Y., and D. A. Pluchinsky. 1992. *Europe's Red Terrorists: The Fighting Communist Organizations*. London: Routledge. https://doi.org/10.4324/9780203043769.

Ali, S. R., E. H. McWhirter, and K. M. Chronister. 2005. "Self-efficacy and Vocational Outcome Expectations for Adolescents of Lower Socioeconomic Status: A Pilot Study." *Journal of Career Assessment* 13, no. 1: 40–58. https://doi.org/10.1177/1069072704270273.

Alizadeh, M., I. Weber, C. Cioffi-Revilla, S. Fortunato, and M. Macy. 2017. "Psychological and Personality Profiles of Political Extremists." *arXiv preprint arXiv*: 1704.00119. https://doi.org/10.48550/arXiv.1704.00119.

Allen, D. W. 1995. "Order in the Church: A Property Rights Approach." *Journal of Economic Behavior & Organization* 27, no. 1: 97–117. https://doi.org/10.1016/0167-2681(94)00026-B.

Allison, M. E., and A. M. Alvarez. 2012. "Unity and Disunity in the FMLN." *Latin American Politics and Society* 54, no. 4: 89–118. https://doi.org/10.1111/j.1548-2456.2012.00174.x.

Allport, F. H. 1954. "The Structuring of Events: Outline of a General Theory with Applications to Psychology." *Psychological Review* 61, no. 5: 281.

Almohammad, A. 2018. "ISIS Child Soldiers in Syria: The Structural and Predatory Recruitment, Enlistment, Pre-training Indoctrination, Training, and Deployment." *The International Centre for Counter-Terrorism–The Hague* 8, no. 14. http://doi.org/10.19165/2018.1.02.

Almohammad, A. H., and A. Speckhard. 2017. "The Operational Ranks and Roles of Female ISIS Operatives: From Assassins and Morality Police to Spies and Suicide Bombers." International Center for the Study of Violent Extremism. https://www.icsve.org/the-operational-ranks-and-roles-of-female-isis-operatives-from-assassins-and-morality-police-to-spies-and-suicide-bombers/.

Almond, Gabriel A., R. Scott Appleby, and Emmanuel Sivan. 2003. *Strong Religion: The Rise of Fundamentalisms Around the World*. Chicago, IL: University of Chicago Press.

Altemeyer, B. 1981. *Right Wing Authoritarianism*. Winnipeg: University of Manitoba Press.

Altemeyer, B. 1998. "The Other 'Authoritarian Personality.'" In *Advances in Experimental Social Psychology (Vol. 30)*, edited by M. Zanna, 47–92. San Diego: Academic Press. https://doi.org/10.1016/S0065-2601(08)60382-2.

Amat, J., M. V. Baratta, E. Paul, S. T. Bland, L. R. Watkins, and S. F. Maier. 2005. "Medial Prefrontal Cortex Determines How Stressor Controllability Affects Behavior and Dorsal Raphe Nucleus." *Nature Neuroscience* 8, no. 3: 365–371. https://doi.org/10.1038/nn1399.

American Psychological Association. 2019a. "Dissociative Identity Disorder." *APA Dictionary of Psychology*. https://dictionary.apa.org/dissociative-identity-disorder.

American Psychological Association. 2019b. "Identity." *APA Dictionary of Psychology*. https://dictionary.apa.org/identity.
American Psychological Association. 2019c. "Need." *APA Dictionary of Psychology*. https://dictionary.apa.org/need.
American Psychological Association. 2019d. "Personality." *APA Dictionary of Psychology*. https://dictionary.apa.org/personality.
American Psychological Association. 2019e. "Posttraumatic Stress Disorder (PTSD)." *APA Dictionary of Psychology*. https://dictionary.apa.org/posttraumatic-stress-disorder.
Amichai-Hamburger, Y., A. Fine, and A. Goldstein. 2004. "The Impact of Internet Interactivity and Need for Closure on Consumer Preference." *Computers in Human Behavior* 20, no. 1: 103–117. https://doi.org/10.1016/S0747-5632(03)00041-4.
Amnesty International. 2014. "Central African Republic: Time for Accountability." https://www.amnesty.org/en/documents/afr19/006/2014/en/.
Andersen, S. M., S. Chen, and C. Carter. 2000. "Fundamental Human Needs: Making Social Cognition Relevant." *Psychological Inquiry* 11, no. 4: 269–275. https://doi.org/10.1207/S15327965PLI1104_02.
Anderson, C. J., and M. M. Singer. 2008. "The Sensitive Left and the Impervious Right: Multilevel Models and the Politics of Inequality, Ideology, and Legitimacy in Europe." *Comparative Political Studies* 41, no. 4–5: 564–599. https://doi.org/10.1177/0010414007313113.
Angrist, J. D., and A. D. Kugler. 2008. "Rural Windfall or a New Resource Curse? Coca, Income, and Civil Conflict in Colombia." *The Review of Economics and Statistics* 90, no. 2: 191–215. https://doi.org/10.1162/rest.90.2.191.
Anhut, R. 2005. "Die Konflikttheorie der Desintegrationstheorie." In *Sozialwissenschaftliche Konflikttheorien (Vol. 5)*, edited by T. Bonacker, 381–407. Opladen: VS Verlag für Sozialwissenschaften.
Anhut, R., and W. Heitmeyer. 2005. "Desintegration, Anerkennungsbilanzen und die Rolle sozialer Vergleichsprozesse für unterschiedliche Verarbeitungsmuster." In *Integrationspotenziale einer modernen Gesellschaft. Analysen zu gesellschaftlicher Integration und Desintegration*, edited by W. Heitmeyer and P. Imbusch, 75–100. Wiesbaden: VS Verlag für Sozialwissenschaften. https://doi.org/10.1007/978-3-322-80502-7_2.
Antony, A. N. 2020. "National Intelligence Assessment: ISIS." Georgetown University. https://doi.org/10.13140/RG.2.2.31799.55205.
Anugwom, E. E., ed. 2019. "Origin, Growth and Ideology of Boko Haram." In *The Boko Haram Insurgence in Nigeria*, 45–65. Cham: Palgrave Macmillan. https://doi.org/10.1007/978-3-319-96959-6_4.
Argiolas, A., and M. R. Melis. 2004. "The Role of Oxytocin and the Paraventricular Nucleus in the Sexual Behaviour of Male Mammals." *Physiology & Behavior* 83, no. 2: 309–317. https://doi.org/10.1016/j.physbeh.2004.08.019.
Aries, E., and K. Moorehead. 1989. "The Importance of Ethnicity in the Development of Identity of Black Adolescents." *Psychological Reports* 65, no. 1: 75–82. https://doi.org/10.2466/pr0.1989.65.1.75.
Aron, A., H. Fisher, D. J. Mashek, G. Strong, H. Li, and L. L. Brown. 2005. "Reward, Motivation, and Emotion Systems Associated with Early-stage Intense Romantic Love." *Journal of Neurophysiology* 94, no. 1: 327–337. https://doi.org/10.1152/jn.00838.2004.
Aron, A., M. Paris, and E. N. Aron. 1995. "Falling in Love: Prospective Studies of Self-concept Change." *Journal of Personality and Social Psychology* 69, no. 6: 1102–1112. https://doi.org/10.1037/0022-3514.69.6.1102.
Arzheimer, K. 2018. "Explaining Electoral Support for the Radical Right." In *The Oxford Handbook of the Radical Right*, edited by J. Rydgren, 143–165. Oxford, UK: Oxford University Press. https://doi.org/10.1093/oxfordhb/9780190274559.013.8.

References

Asal, V., and R. K. Rethemeyer. 2008. "The Nature of the Beast: Organizational Structures and the Lethality of Terrorist Attacks." *The Journal of Politics* 70, no. 2: 437–449. https://doi.org/10.1017/S0022381608080419.

Asfura-Heim, P., and J. McQuaid. 2015. *Diagnosing the Boko Haram conflict: Grievances, Motivations, and Institutional Resilience in Northeast Nigeria*. Alexandria, VA: Center for Naval Analyses. https://www.cna.org/archive/CNA_Files/pdf/dop-2014-u-009272-final.pdf.

Ashmore, R. D., K. Deaux, and T. McLaughlin-Volpe. 2004. "An Organizing Framework for Collective Identity: Articulation and Significance of Multidimensionality." *Psychological Bulletin* 130, no. 1: 80–114. https://doi.org/10.1037/0033-2909.130.1.80.

Atkins, S. E. 2011. *Encyclopedia of Right-wing Extremism in Modern American History*. Santa Barbara, CA: ABC-CLIO.

Augustyn, B. D., T. W. Hall, D. C. Wang, and P. C. Hill. 2017. "Relational Spirituality: An Attachment-based Model of Spiritual Development and Psychological Well-being." *Psychology of Religion and Spirituality* 9, no. 2: 197. https://doi.org/10.1037/rel0000100.

Avenanti, A., A. Sirigu, and S. M. Aglioti. 2010. "Racial Bias Reduces Empathic Sensorimotor Resonance with Other-Race Pain." *Current Biology* 20, no. 11: 1018–1022. https://doi.org/10.1016/j.cub.2010.03.071.

Aydin, N., P. Fischer, and D. Frey. 2010. "Turning to God in the Face of Ostracism: Effects of Social Exclusion on Religiousness." *Personality and Social Psychology Bulletin* 36, no. 6: 742–753. https://doi.org/10.1177/0146167210367491.

Azevedo, R. T., E. Macaluso, A. Avenanti, V. Santangelo, V. Cazzato, and S. M. Aglioti. 2013. "Their Pain Is Not Our Pain: Brain and Autonomic Correlates of Empathic Resonance with the Pain of Same and Different Race Individuals." *Human Brain Mapping* 34, no. 12: 3168–3181. https://doi.org/10.1002/hbm.22133.

Backes, U., and P. Moreau, eds. 2008. *Communist and Post-communist Parties in Europe (Vol. 36)*. Göttingen: Vandenhoeck & Ruprecht.

Baldwin, J. 2017. Culture, Prejudice, Racism, and Discrimination. In *Oxford Research Encyclopedia of Communication*, edited by M. Powers. New York: Oxford University Press. https://doi.org/10.1093/acrefore/9780190228613.013.164.

Ball, T., R. Dagger, and D. I. O'Neill. 2019. *Political Ideologies and the Democratic Ideal* 11th ed.. New York: Routledge. https://doi.org/10.4324/9780429286551.

Ballentine, K., and J. Sherman, eds. 2003. *The Political Economy of Armed Conflict: Beyond Greed and Grievance*. Boulder, CO: Lynne Rienner. https://doi.org/10.1515/9781685853402.

Banai, E., M. Mikulincer, and P. Shaver. 2005. "Self-object Needs in Kohut's Self Psychology: Links with Attachment, Self-cohesion, Affect Regulation and Adjustment." *Psychoanalytic Psychology* 22, no. 2: 224–260. https://doi.org/10.1037/0736-9735.22.2.224.

Bandarage, A. 2009. *The Separatist Conflict in Sri Lanka: Terrorism, Ethnicity, Political Economy*. London: Routledge. https://doi.org/10.4324/9780203886311.

Bandura, A. 1977. "Self-efficacy: Toward a Unifying Theory of Behavioral Change." *Psychological Review* 84, no. 2: 191–215. https://doi.org/10.1037/0033-295X.84.2.191.

Bandura, A. 1986. *Social Foundations of Thought and Action: A Social Cognitive Theory*. Englewood Cliffs, NJ: Prentice Hall.

Bandura, A. 1990. "Selective Activation and Disengagement of Moral Control." *Journal of Social Issues* 46, no. 1: 27–46. https://doi.org/10.1111/j.1540-4560.1990.tb00270.x.

Bandura, A. 1997. *Self-efficacy: The Exercise of Control*. New York: W.H. Freeman.

Bandura, A. 1998. "Mechanisms of Moral Disengagement." In *Origins of Terrorism: Psychologies, Ideologies, Theologies, States of Mind*, edited by W. Reich, 161–191. Cambridge: Cambridge University Press.

Bandura, A. 1999. "Moral Disengagement in the Perpetration of Inhumanities." *Personality and Social Psychology Review* 3, no. 3: 193–209. https://doi.org/10.1207/s15327957pspr0303_3.

Bandura, A. 2000. *Self-efficacy: The Foundation of Agency.*
Bandura, A. 2007. "Impeding Ecological Sustainability through Selective Moral Disengagement." *International Journal of Innovation and Sustainable Development* 2, no. 1: 8–35.
Bandura, A. 2011. "Moral Disengagement." *The Encyclopedia of Peace Psychology.* https://onlinelibrary.wiley.com/doi/full/10.1002/9780470672532.wbepp165.
Bandura, A., C. Barbaranelli, G. V. Caprara, and C. Pastorelli. 2001. "Self-efficacy Beliefs as Shapers of Children's Aspirations and Career Trajectories." *Child Development* 72, no. 1: 187–206. https://doi.org/10.1111/1467-8624.00273.
Bangura, Y. 1994. The Search for Identity: Ethnicity, Religion and Political Violence (No. 6). UNRISD Occasional Paper: World Summit for Social Development.
Banton, M. 1998. *Racial Theories.* Cambridge: Cambridge University Press.
Bao, X. H., and S. F. Lam. 2008. "Who Makes the Choice? Rethinking the Role of Autonomy and Relatedness in Chinese Children's Motivation." *Child Development* 79, no. 2: 269–283. https://doi.org/10.1111/j.1467-8624.2007.01125.x.
Barber, A. E., M. J. Wesson, Q. M. Roberson, and M. S. Taylor. 1999. "A Tale of Two Job Markets: Organizational Size and Its Effects on Hiring Practices and Job Search Behavior." *Personnel Psychology* 52, no. 4: 841–868. https://doi.org/10.1111/j.1744-6570.1999.tb00182.x.
Barlow, D. H. 2000. "Unraveling the Mysteries of Anxiety and Its Disorders from the Perspective of Emotion Theory." *American Psychologist* 55, no. 11: 1247–1263. https://doi.org/10.1037/0003-066X.55.11.1247.
Barnes, C. D., R. P. Brown, J. Lenes, J. Bosson, and M. Carvallo. 2014. "My Country, My Self: Honor, Identity, and Defensive Responses to National Threats." *Self and Identity* 13, no. 6: 638–662. https://doi.org/10.1080/15298868.2014.892529.
Barni, D., A. Vieno, and M. Roccato. 2016. "Living in a Non-communist versus in a Post-communist European Country Moderates the Relation between Conservative Values and Political Orientation: A Multilevel Study." *European Journal of Personality* 30, no. 1, 92–104. https://doi.org/10.1002/per.2043.
Barrett-Fox, R. 2016. *God Hates: Westboro Baptist Church, American Nationalism, and the Religious Right.* Lawrence: University Press of Kansas.
Bartels, L. M. 2005. "Homer Gets a Tax Cut: Inequality and Public Policy in the American Mind." *Perspectives on Politics* 3, no. 1: 15–31. https://doi.org/10.1017/S1537592705050036.
Bartram, D., P. A. Lindley, L. Marshall, and J. Foster. 1995. "The Recruitment and Selection of Young People by Small Businesses." *Journal of Occupational and Organizational Psychology* 68, no. 4: 339–358. https://doi.org/10.1111/j.2044-8325.1995.tb00592.x.
Bartusevičius, H. 2014. "The Inequality–Conflict Nexus Re-examined: Income, Education, and Popular Rebellions." *Journal of Peace Research* 51, no. 1, 35–50. https://doi.org/10.1177/0022343313503179.
Basedau, M., and J. Lay. 2009. "Resource Curse or Rentier Peace? The Ambiguous Effects of Oil Wealth and Oil Dependence on Violent Conflict." *Journal of Peace Research* 46, no. 6: 757–776. https://doi.org/10.1177/0022343309340500.
Basedau, M., J. Fox, J. H. Pierskalla, G. Strüver, and J. Vüllers. 2017. "Does Discrimination Breed Grievances—and Do Grievances Breed Violence? New Evidence from an Analysis of Religious Minorities in Developing Countries." *Conflict Management and Peace Science* 34, no. 3: 217–239. https://doi.org/10.1177/0738894215581329.
Baten, J., and C. Mumme. 2013. "Does Inequality Lead to Civil Wars? A Global Long-Term Study Using Anthropometric Indicators (1816–1999)." *European Journal of Political Economy* 32: 56–79. https://doi.org/10.1016/j.ejpoleco.2013.06.007.
Bateson, M., D. Nettle, and G. Roberts. 2006. "Cues of Being Watched Enhance Cooperation in a Real-world Setting." *Biology Letters* 2, no. 3: 412–414. https://doi.org/10.1098/rsbl.2006.0509.

References

Batson, C. D., and L. L. Shaw. 1991. "Evidence for Altruism: Toward a Pluralism of Prosocial Motives." *Psychological Inquiry* 2, no. 2: 107–122. https://doi.org/10.1207/s15327965pli0202_1.

Batson, C. D., J. G. Batson, C. A. Griffitt, S. Barrientos, J. R. Brandt, P. Sprengelmeyer, and M. J. Bayly. 1989. "Negative-state Relief and the Empathy—Altruism Hypothesis." *Journal of Personality and Social Psychology* 56, no. 6: 922–933. https://doi.org/10.1037/0022-3514.56.6.922.

Batson, C. D., J. G. Batson, J. K. Slingsby, K. L. Harrell, H. M. Peekna, and R. M. Todd. 1991. "Empathic Joy and the Empathy-Altruism Hypothesis." *Journal of Personality and Social Psychology* 61, no. 3: 413.

Batson, C. D., B. D. Duncan, P. Ackerman, T. Buckley, and K. Birch. 1981. "Is Empathic Emotion a Source of Altruistic Motivation?" *Journal of Personality and Social Psychology* 40, no. 2: 290.

Batthyany, A., and P. Russo-Netzer, eds. 2014. *Meaning in Positive and Existential Psychology*. New York: Springer. https://doi.org/10.1007/978-1-4939-0308-5.

Baumeister, R. F. 1991. *Meanings of Life*. New York: Guilford Press.

Baumeister, R. F. 1993. "Understanding the Inner Nature of Low Self-Esteem: Uncertain, Fragile, Protective, and Conflicted." In *Self-Esteem: The Puzzle of Low Self-Regard*, edited by R. F. Baumeister, 208–218. The Plenum Series in Social/Clinical Psychology. Boston: Springer. https://doi.org/10.1007/978-1-4684-8956-9_11.

Baumeister, R. F. 1997. "Identity, Self-concept, and Self-esteem: The Self Lost and Found." In *Handbook of Personality Psychology*, edited by R. Hogan, J. A. Johnson, and S. R. Briggs, 681–710. Cambridge, MA: Academic Press. https://doi.org/10.1016/B978-012134645-4/50027-5.

Baumeister, R. F. 2010. "The Self." In *Advanced Social Psychology: The State of the Science*, edited by R. F. Baumeister and E. J. Finkel, 139–175. New York: Oxford University Press.

Baumeister, R. F., ed. 2012. *Public Self and Private Self*. Berlin: Springer Science & Business Media.

Baumeister, R. F., and J. M. Boden. 1998. "Aggression and the Self: High Self-esteem, Low Self-control, and Ego Threat." In *Human Aggression*, 111–137. Academic Press.

Baumeister, R. F., and M. R. Leary. 1995. "The Need to Belong: Desire for Interpersonal Attachments as a Fundamental Human Motivation." *Psychological Bulletin* 117, no. 3: 497–529. https://doi.org/10.1037/0033-2909.117.3.497.

Baumeister, R. F., T. F. Heatherton, and D. M. Tice. 1993. "When Ego Threats Lead to Self-regulation Failure: Negative Consequences of High Self-esteem." *Journal of Personality and Social Psychology* 64, no. 1: 141–156. https://doi.org/10.1037/0022-3514.64.1.141.

Baumeister, R. F., L. Smart, and J. M. Boden. 1996. "Relation of Threatened Egotism to Violence and Aggression: The Dark Side of High Self-esteem." *Psychological Review* 103, no. 1: 5–33. https://doi.org/10.1037/0033-295X.103.1.5.

Baumgardner, A. H. 1990. "To Know Oneself is to Like Oneself: Self-certainty and Self-affect." *Journal of Personality and Social Psychology* 58, no. 6: 1062–1072. https://doi.org/10.1037/0022-3514.58.6.1062.

Baumgartner, T., M. Heinrichs, A. Vonlanthen, U. Fischbacher, and E. Fehr. 2008. "Oxytocin Shapes the Neural Circuitry of Trust and Trust Adaptation in Humans." *Neuron* 58, no. 4: 639–650. https://doi.org/10.1016/j.neuron.2008.04.009.

Bazenguissa-Ganga, R. 1998. "The Political Militia in Brazzaville." *African Issues* 26, no. 1: 37–40. https://doi.org/10.2307/1166551.

Beatty, T. K., and D. E. Sommervoll. 2012. "Discrimination in Rental Markets: Evidence from Norway." *Journal of Housing Economics* 21, no. 2: 121–130. https://doi.org/10.1016/j.jhe.2012.03.001.

Beck, U. 1996. *Risikogesellschaft: Auf dem Weg in eine andere Moderne*. Einmalige Sonderausgabe.

Becker, B. E., and S. S. Luthar. 2007. "Peer-perceived Admiration and Social Preference: Contextual Correlates of Positive Peer Regard among Suburban and Urban Adolescents."

References 449

Journal of Research on Adolescence 17, no. 1: 117–144. https://doi.org/10.1111/j.1532-7795.2007.00514.x.
Becker, G. S. 1965. "A Theory of the Allocation of Time." *The Economic Journal* 75, no. 299: 493–517. https://doi.org/10.2307/2228949.
Becker, G. S. 1973. "A Theory of Marriage: Part I." *Journal of Political Economy* 81, no. 4: 813–846. https://doi.org/10.1086/260084.
Becker, G. S. 1985. "Human Capital, Effort, and the Sexual Division of Labor." *Journal of Labor Economics* 3, no. 1: 33–58. https://doi.org/10.1086/298075.
Becker, G. S., and R. J. Barro. 1986. "Altruism and the Economic Theory of Fertility." *Population and Development Review* 12: 69–76. https://doi.org/10.2307/2807893.
Becker, J. C., and U. Wagner. 2009. "Doing Gender Differently—The Interplay of Strength of Gender Identification and Content of Gender Identity in Predicting Women's Endorsement of Sexist Beliefs." *European Journal of Social Psychology* 39, no. 4: 487–508. https://doi.org/10.1002/ejsp.551.
Behlendorf, B., G. LaFree, and R. Legault. 2012. "Microcycles of Violence: Evidence from Terrorist Attacks by ETA and the FMLN." *Journal of Quantitative Criminology* 28, no. 1: 49–75. https://doi.org/10.1007/s10940-011-9153-7.
Bell, D. 1960. *The End of Ideology: On the Exhaustion of Political Ideas in the Fifties*. Glencoe, IL: Free Press.
Beller, J., and C. Kröger. 2017. "Is Religious Fundamentalism a Dimensional or a Categorical Phenomenon? A Taxometric Analysis in Two Samples of Youth from Egypt and Saudi Arabia." *Psychology of Religion and Spirituality* 9, no. 2: 158–164. https://doi.org/10.1037/rel0000085.
Bénabou, R. 2015. "The Economics of Motivated Beliefs." *Revue d'économie Politique* 125, no. 5: 665–685. https://doi.org/10.3917/redp.255.0665.
Bénabou, R., and E. A. Ok. 2001. "Social Mobility and the Demand for Redistribution: The POUM Hypothesis." *The Quarterly Journal of Economics* 116, no. 2: 447–487. https://doi.org/10.1162/00335530151144078.
Bénabou, R., and J. Tirole. 2016. "Mindful Economics: The Production, Consumption, and Value of Beliefs." *Journal of Economic Perspectives* 30, no. 3: 141–164. https://doi.org/10.1257/jep.30.3.141.
Bénabou, R., A. Falk, and J. Tirole. 2018. *Narratives, Imperatives, and Moral Reasoning* (No. w24798). National Bureau of Economic Research.
Bennett, D. H. 1988. *The Party of Fear: From Nativist Movements to the New Right in American History*. Chapel Hill: UNC Press Books.
Benson, J. K., and J. H. Dorsett. 1971. "Toward a Theory of Religious Organizations." *Journal for the Scientific Study of Religion* 10, no. 2: 138–151. https://doi.org/10.2307/1385302.
Benuzzi, F., F. Lui, D. Duzzi, P. F. Nichelli, and C. A. Porro. 2008. "Does It Look Painful or Disgusting? Ask Your Parietal and Cingulate Cortex." *Journal of Neuroscience* 28, no. 4: 923–931. https://doi.org/10.1523/JNEUROSCI.4012-07.2008.
Berezin, M. 2017. "On the Construction Sites of History: Where Did Donald Trump Come From?" *American Journal of Cultural Sociology* 5, no. 3: 322–337. https://doi.org/10.1057/s41290-017-0045-7.
Berman, S. 1997. "The Life of the Party." *Comparative Politics* 30, no. 1: 101–122. https://doi.org/10.2307/422195.
Bernhard, H., E. Fehr, and U. Fischbacher. 2006. "Group Affiliation and Altruistic Norm Enforcement." *American Economic Review* 96, no. 2: 217–221.
Bernholz, P., ed. 2017. "Ideologies of National Socialism, Communism, Christianity, and Islam." In *Totalitarianism, Terrorism and Supreme Values. Studies in Public Choice*, vol 33, 7–21. Cham: Springer. https://doi.org/10.1007/978-3-319-56907-9_2.

Berns, G. S., S. M. McClure, G. Pagnoni, and P. R. Montague. 2001. "Predictability Modulates Human Brain Response to Reward." *Journal of Neuroscience* 21, no. 8: 2793–2798. https://doi.org/10.1523/JNEUROSCI.21-08-02793.2001.

Berry, A., and R. H. Sabot. 1984. "Unemployment and Economic Development." *Economic Development and Cultural Change* 33, no. 1: 99–116. https://doi.org/10.1086/451445.

Berry, J. W. 1990. "Acculturation and Adaptation: A General Framework." In *Mental Health of Immigrants and Refugees*, edited by W. H. Holtzman and T. H. Bornemann, 90–102. Austin, TX: Hogg Foundation for Mental Health.

Bertrand, M., and S. Mullainathan. 2004. "Are Emily and Greg More Employable than Lakisha and Jamal? A Field Experiment on Labor Market Discrimination." *American Economic Review* 94, no. 4: 991–1013. https://doi.org/10.3386/w9873.

Bhanji, J. P., and M. R. Delgado. 2014. "The Social Brain and Reward: Social Information Processing in the Human Striatum." *Wiley Interdisciplinary Reviews: Cognitive Science* 5, no. 1: 61–73. https://doi.org/10.1002/wcs.1266.

Bhugra, D., and M. A. Becker. 2005. "Migration, Cultural Bereavement and Cultural Identity." *World Psychiatry* 4, no. 1: 18–24.

Bhui, K., N. Warfa, and E. Jones. 2014. "Is Violent Radicalisation Associated with Poverty, Migration, Poor Self-reported Health and Common Mental Disorders?" *PloS One* 9, no. 3: e90718. https://doi.org/10.1371/journal.pone.0090718.

Bierhoff, H. W., and E. Rohmann. 2004. "Altruistic Personality in the Context of the Empathy–Altruism Hypothesis." *European Journal of Personality* 18, no. 4: 351–365. https://doi.org/10.1002/per.523.

Billig, M., and H. Tajfel. 1973. "Social Categorization and Similarity in Intergroup Behaviour." *European Journal of Social Psychology* 3, no. 1: 27–52. https://doi.org/10.1002/ejsp.2420030103.

Birdwell, A. E. 1968. "A Study of the Influence of Image Congruence on Consumer Choice." *The Journal of Business* 41, no. 1: 76–88. https://doi.org/10.1086/295047.

Bischoff, K., and S. F. Reardon. 2014. "Residential Segregation by Income, 1970–2009." *Diversity and Disparities: America Enters a New Century*, edited by J. R. Logan, 208–234. New York: Russell Sage Foundation.

Biziouras, N. 2012. "The Formation, Institutionalization and Consolidation of the LTTE: Religious Practices, Intra-Tamil Divisions and a Violent Nationalist Ideology." *Politics, Religion & Ideology* 13, no. 4: 547–559. https://doi.org/10.1080/21567689.2012.732016.

Bjørgo, T., and M. Mareš, eds. 2019. *Vigilantism Against Migrants and Minorities*. New York: Routledge.

Blair, I. V. 2002. "The Malleability of Automatic Stereotypes and Prejudice." *Personality and Social Psychology Review* 6, no. 3: 242–261. https://doi.org/10.1207/S15327957PSPR0603_8.

Blanchard, F. A., C. S. Crandall, J. C. Brigham, and L. A. Vaughn. 1994. "Condemning and Condoning Racism: A Social Context Approach to Interracial Settings." *Journal of Applied Psychology* 79, no. 6: 993–997. https://doi.org/10.1037/0021-9010.79.6.993.

Block, J., and J. H. Block. 2006. "Nursery School Personality and Political Orientation Two Decades Later." *Journal of Research in Personality* 40, no. 5: 734–749. https://doi.org/10.1016/j.jrp.2005.09.005.

Blumenthal, M. 2006. "Hell of a Times." *The Nation*. September 20. https://www.salon.com/2003/05/22/vigilante_3/.

Blustein, D. L., and D. E. Palladino. 1991. "Self and Identity in Late Adolescence: A Theoretical and Empirical Integration." *Journal of Adolescent Research* 6, no. 4: 437–453. https://doi.org/10.1177/074355489164005.

BMI Bund. 2018. The Brief Summary of the 2018 Report on the Protection of the Constitution: Facts and Trends. Federal Ministry of the Interior, Building and Community.

https://www.bmi.bund.de/SharedDocs/downloads/EN/publikationen/2019/vsb-2018-en.pdf?__blob=publicationFile&v=2.

Boardman, J. D., and S. A. Robert. 2000. "Neighborhood Socioeconomic Status and Perceptions of Self-efficacy." *Sociological Perspectives* 43, no. 1: 117–136. https://doi.org/10.2307/1389785.

Bodenhausen, G. V. 1988. "Stereotypic Biases in Social Decision Making and Memory: Testing Process Models of Stereotype Use." *Journal of Personality and Social Psychology* 55, no. 5: 726–737. https://doi.org/10.1037/0022-3514.55.5.726.

Bornstein, G. 1992. "The Free-rider Problem in Intergroup Conflicts Over Step-level and Continuous Public Goods." *Journal of Personality and Social Psychology* 62, no. 4: 597–606. https://doi.org/10.1037/0022-3514.62.4.597.

Bosch, O. J., S. L. Meddle, D. I. Beiderbeck, A. J. Douglas, and I. D. Neumann. 2005. "Brain Oxytocin Correlates with Maternal Aggression: Link to Anxiety." *Journal of Neuroscience* 25, no. 29: 6807–6815. https://doi.org/10.1523/JNEUROSCI.1342-05.2005.

Bosma, H. A., and E. S. Kunnen. 2001. "Determinants and Mechanisms in Ego Identity Development: A Review and Synthesis." *Developmental Review* 21, no. 1: 39–66. https://doi.org/10.1006/drev.2000.0514.

Bötticher, A. 2017. "Towards Academic Consensus Definitions of Radicalism and Extremism." *Perspectives on Terrorism* 11, no. 4: 73–77. https://www.jstor.org/stable/26297896.

Bouhana, N., and P. O. H. Wikstrom. 2011. Al Qa'ida Influenced Radicalisation: A Rapid Evidence Assessment Guided by Situational Action Theory. UK Home Office, Office for Security and Counter Terrorism. http://www.homeoffice.gov.uk/publications/science-research-statistics/research-statistics/counter-terrorism-statistics/occ97?view=Binary.

Bowler, R., S. Rauch, and R. Schwarzer. 1986. "Self-esteem and Interracial Attitudes in Black High School Students: A Comparison with Five Other Ethnic Groups." *Urban Education* 21, no. 1: 3–19. https://doi.org/10.1177/004208598602100101.

Bowman-Grieve, L. 2009. "Exploring 'Stormfront': A Virtual Community of the Radical Right." *Studies in Conflict & Terrorism* 32, no. 11: 989–1007. https://doi.org/10.1080/10576100903259951.

Bowman-Grieve, L. 2013. "A Psychological Perspective on Virtual Communities Supporting Terrorist & Extremist Ideologies as a Tool for Recruitment." *Security Informatics* 2, no. 1: 1–5. https://doi.org/10.1186/2190-8532-2-9.

Bozóki, A., and J. T. Ishiyama. 2002. *The Communist Successor Parties of Central and Eastern Europe*. Armonk, NJ: M.E. Sharpe.

Bracke, M., and T. Ekman Jorgensen. 2002. "West European Communism after Stalinism: Comparative Approaches." EUI Working Paper No. 2002/4. https://cadmus.eui.eu/bitstream/handle/1814/63/HEC02-04.pdf.

Braithwaite, A., N. Dasandi, and D. Hudson. 2016. "Does Poverty Cause Conflict? Isolating the Causal Origins of the Conflict Trap." *Conflict Management and Peace Science* 33, no. 1: 45–66. https://doi.org/10.1177/0738894214559673.

Brand, B. L., R. J. Loewenstein, and R. A. Lanius. 2014. "Dissociative Identity Disorder." In *Gabbard's Treatments of Psychiatric Disorders*, edited by G. O. Gabbard, 439–458. Washington: American Psychiatric Publishing.

Brandt, M. J., and C. Reyna. 2010. "The Role of Prejudice and the Need for Closure in Religious Fundamentalism." *Personality and Social Psychology Bulletin* 36, no. 5: 715–725. https://doi.org/10.1177/0146167210366306.

Brandt, M. J., C. Reyna, J. R. Chambers, J. T. Crawford, and G. Wetherell. 2014. "The Ideological-Conflict Hypothesis: Intolerance among both Liberals and Conservatives." *Current Directions in Psychological Science* 23, no. 1: 27–34. https://doi.org/10.1177/0963721413510932.

Brandt, P. Y. 2013. "Psychological Aspects of the Role of Religion in Identity Construction." *Integrative Psychological and Behavioral Science* 47, no. 2: 299–303. https://doi.org/10.1007/s12124-013-9237-z.

Branscombe, N. R., M. T. Schmitt, and R. D. Harvey. 1999. "Perceiving Pervasive Discrimination among African Americans: Implications for Group Identification and Well-being." *Journal of Personality and Social Psychology* 77, no. 1: 135–149. https://doi.org/10.1037/0022-3514.77.1.135.

Brewer, M. B. 1991. "The Social Self: On Being the Same and Different at the Same Time." *Personality and Social Psychology Bulletin* 17, no. 5: 475–482. https://doi.org/10.1177/0146167291175001.

Brewer, M. B. 2001a. "Ingroup Identification and Intergroup Conflict: When Does Ingroup Love Become Outgroup Hate?" In *Social Identity, Intergroup Conflict, and Conflict Reduction*, edited by R. D. Ashmore, L. Jussim, and D. Wilder, 17–41. New York: Oxford University Press.

Brewer, M. B. 2001b. "The Many Faces of Social Identity: Implications for Political Psychology." *Political Psychology* 22, no. 1: 115–125. https://doi.org/10.1111/0162-895X.00229.

Brewer, M. B., and D. T. Campbell. 1976. *Ethnocentrism and Intergroup Attitudes: East African Evidence*. Thousand Oaks, CA: SAGE.

Bringa, T. 2002. "Islam and the Quest for Identity in Post-Communist." In *Islam and Bosnia: Conflict Resolution and Foreign Policy in Multi-Ethnic States*, edited by M. Schatzmiller, 24–56. Montreal: McGill-Queen's University Press. https://www.jstor.org/stable/j.ctt80trg.

Brito, N. H., and K. G. Noble. 2014. "Socioeconomic Status and Structural Brain Development." *Frontiers in Neuroscience* 8: 276. https://doi.org/10.3389/fnins.2014.00276.

Brodbeck, M. 1958. "Methodological Individualisms: Definition and Reduction." *Philosophy of Science* 25, no. 1: 1–22. https://doi.org/10.1086/287573.

Bromley, D. G., and J. G. Melton. 2012. "Reconceptualizing Types of Religious Organization: Dominant, Sectarian, Alternative, and Emergent Tradition Groups." *Nova Religio: The Journal of Alternative and Emergent Religions* 15, no. 3: 4–28. https://doi.org/10.1525/nr.2012.15.3.4.

Brothers, L. 1990. "The Neural Basis of Primate Social Communication." *Motivation and Emotion* 14, no. 2: 81–91. https://doi.org/10.1007/BF00991637.

Brown, A. 2013. "Communism." In *The Oxford Handbook of Political Ideologies*, edited by M. Freeden, T. L. Sargent, and M. Stears, 175–196. Oxford: Oxford University Press http://dx.doi.org/10.1093/oxfordhb/9780199585977.013.007.

Brown, B. B., and J. Larson. 2009. "Peer Relationships in Adolescence." In *Handbook of Adolescent Psychology: Contextual Influences on Adolescent Development*, edited by R. Lerner and L. Steinberg, 74–103. New York: John Wiley & Sons, Inc. https://doi.org/10.1002/9780470479193.adlpsy002004.

Brown-Iannuzzi, J. L., K. B. Lundberg, A. C. Kay, and B. K. Payne. 2015. "Subjective Status Shapes Political Preferences." *Psychological Science* 26, no. 1: 15–26. https://doi.org/10.1177/0956797614553947.

Brubaker, R. 2004. *Ethnicity Without Groups*. Cambridge, MA: Harvard University Press.

Brunnschweiler, C. N., and E. H. Bulte. 2008. "The Resource Curse Revisited and Revised: A Tale of Paradoxes and Red Herrings." *Journal of Environmental Economics and Management* 55, no. 3: 248–264. https://doi.org/10.1016/j.jeem.2007.08.004.

Bui, A. L., J. L. Dieleman, H. Hamavid, M. Birger, A. Chapin, H. C. Duber, C. Horst, A. Reynolds, E. Squires, P. J. Chung, and C. J. Murray. 2017. "Spending on Children's Personal Health Care in the United States, 1996–2013." *JAMA Pediatrics* 171, no. 2: 181–189. https://doi.org/10.1001/jamapediatrics.2016.4086.

Bunce, V. 2005. "The National Idea: Imperial Legacies and Post-communist Pathways in Eastern Europe." *East European Politics and Societies* 19, no. 3: 406–442. https://doi.org/10.1177/0888325405277963.

Burgoon, B. 2006. "On Welfare and Terror: Social Welfare Policies and Political-Economic Roots of Terrorism." *Journal of Conflict Resolution* 50, no. 2: 176–203. https://doi.org/10.1177/0022002705284829.

Burke, B. L., S. Kosloff, and M. J. Landau. 2013. "Death Goes to the Polls: A Meta-analysis of Mortality Salience Effects on Political Attitudes." *Political Psychology* 34: 183–200. https://doi.org/10.1111/pops.12005.

Burke, J. 2004. "Al qaeda." *Foreign Policy* 142: 18–26. https://doi.org/10.2307/4147572.

Burklund, L. J., N. I. Eisenberger, and M. D. Lieberman. 2007. "The Face of Rejection: Rejection Sensitivity Moderates Dorsal Anterior Cingulate Activity to Disapproving Facial Expressions." *Social Neuroscience* 2, no. 3–4: 238–253. https://doi.org/10.1080/17470910701391711.

Burraston, B., J. C. McCutcheon, and S. J. Watts. 2018. "Relative and Absolute Deprivation's Relationship with Violent Crime in the United States: Testing an Interaction Effect between Income Inequality and Disadvantage." *Crime & Delinquency* 64, no. 4: 542–560. https://doi.org/10.1177/0011128717709246.

Burs, C., and T. Gries. 2022. Decision-making under Imperfect Information with Bayesian Learning or Heuristic Rules. Working Papers CIE 149. Paderborn University, CIE Center for International Economics.

Burs, C., T. Gries, and V. Mueller. 2022. "The Choice of Ideology and Everyday Decisions." *APSA Preprints*. https://doi.org/10.33774/apsa-2022-0m7t5-v2.

Burton, J. 1990. *Conflict: Human Needs Theory*. London: Palgrave Macmillan. https://doi.org/10.1007/978-1-349-21000-8.

Burton, J. W. 1972. *World Society*. London: Cambridge University Press.

Byman, D. 2016. "ISIS Goes Global: Fight the Islamic State by Targeting its Affiliates." *Foreign Affairs* 95, no. 2: 76–85. https://www.jstor.org/stable/43948181.

Cacioppo, J. T., L. C. Hawkley, and G. G. Berntson. 2003. "The Anatomy of Loneliness." *Current Directions in Psychological Science* 12, no. 3: 71–74. https://doi.org/10.1111/1467-8721.01232.

Caiani, M., and R. Borri. 2013. "The Extreme Right, Violence and Other Action Repertoires: An Empirical Study on Two European Countries." *Perspectives on European Politics and Society* 14, no. 4: 562–581. https://doi.org/10.1080/15705854.2013.793532.

Caiani, M., and D. Della Porta. 2018. "The Radical Right as Social Movement Organizations." In *The Oxford Handbook of the Radical Right*, edited by J. Rydgren, 327–347. New York: Oxford University Press.

Caiani, M., and L. Parenti. 2013. *European and American Extreme Right Groups and the Internet*. London: Routledge. https://doi.org/10.4324/9781315580845.

Caiani, M., and C. Wagemann. 2009. "Online Networks of the Italian and German Extreme Right: An Explorative Study with Social Network Analysis." *Information, Communication & Society* 12, no. 1: 66–109. https://doi.org/10.1080/13691180802158482.

Caiani, M., D. Della Porta, and C. Wagemann. 2012. *Mobilizing on the Extreme Right: Germany, Italy, and the United States*. New York: Oxford University Press. https://doi.org/10.1093/acprof:oso/9780199641260.001.000.

Cameron, K. S., and R. E. Quinn. 1999. *Diagnosing and Changing Organizational Culture based on the Competing Values Framework*. Reading, MA: Addison-Wesley.

Campbell, D. E., and J. Q. Monson. 2003. "Following the Leader? Mormon Voting on Ballot Propositions." *Journal for the Scientific Study of Religion* 42, no. 4: 605–619. https://doi.org/10.1046/j.1468-5906.2003.00206.x.

Campbell, J. D. 1986. "Similarity and Uniqueness: The Effects of Attribute Type, Relevance, and Individual Differences in Self-esteem and Depression." *Journal of Personality and Social Psychology* 50, no. 2: 281–294. https://doi.org/10.1037/0022-3514.50.2.281.

Campbell, J. D. 1990. "Self-esteem and Clarity of the Self-concept." *Journal of Personality and Social Psychology* 59, no. 3: 538–549. https://doi.org/10.1037/0022-3514.59.3.538.

Campbell, J. D., and L. F. Lavallee. 1993. "Who Am I? The Role of Self-concept Confusion in Understanding the Behavior of People with Low Self-esteem." In *Self-esteem*, edited by R. F. Baumeister, 3–20. Boston, MA: Springer. https://doi.org/10.1007/978-1-4684-8956-9_1.

Campbell, J. D., and A. Tesser. 1983. "Motivational Interpretations of Hindsight Bias: An Individual Difference Analysis." *Journal of Personality* 51, no. 4: 605–619. https://doi.org/10.1111/j.1467-6494.1983.tb00868.x.

Campbell, J. D., S. Assanand, and A. D. Paula. 2003. "The Structure of the Self-concept and Its Relation to Psychological Adjustment." *Journal of Personality* 71, no. 1: 115–140. https://doi.org/10.1111/1467-6494.t01-1-00002.

Campbell, J. D., P. D. Trapnell, S. J. Heine, I. M. Katz, L. F. Lavallee, and D. R. Lehman. 1996. "'Self-concept Clarity: Measurement, Personality Correlates, and Cultural Boundaries': Correction." *Journal of Personality and Social Psychology* 70, no. 6: 1114. https://doi.org/10.1037/0022-3514.70.6.1114.

Campbell-Meiklejohn, D. K., D. R. Bach, A. Roepstorff, R. J. Dolan, and C. D. Frith. 2010. "How the Opinion of Others Affects our Valuation of Objects." *Current Biology* 20, no. 13: 1165–1170. https://doi.org/10.1016/j.cub.2010.04.055.

Candee, D. 1974. "Ego Developmental Aspects of New Left Ideology." *Journal of Personality and Social Psychology* 30, no. 5: 620–630. https://doi.org/10.1037/h0037437.

Caplin, A., and J. Leahy. 2001. "Psychological Expected Utility Theory and Anticipatory Feelings." *The Quarterly Journal of Economics* 116, no. 1: 55–79. https://doi.org/10.1162/003355301556347.

Carlsson, K., J. Andersson, P. Petrovic, K. M. Petersson, A. Öhman, and M. Ingvar. 2006. "Predictability Modulates the Affective and Sensory-discriminative Neural Processing of Pain." *Neuroimage* 32, no. 4: 1804–1814. https://doi.org/10.1016/j.neuroimage.2006.05.027.

Carney, D. R., J. T. Jost, S. D. Gosling, and J. Potter. 2008. "The Secret Lives of Liberals and Conservatives: Personality Profiles, Interaction Styles, and the Things They Leave Behind." *Political Psychology* 29, no. 6: 807–840. https://doi.org/10.1111/j.1467-9221.2008.00668.x.

Carod-Artal, F. J., and C. Vázquez-Cabrera. 2013. "Burnout Syndrome in an International Setting." In *Burnout for Experts*, edited by S. Bährer-Kohler, 15–35. Boston, MA: Springer. https://doi.org/10.1007/978-1-4614-4391-9_2.

Carr, L. G. 1997. *"Colorblind" Racism*. Thousand Oaks, CA: SAGE.

Carvacho, H., A. Zick, A. Haye, R. González, J. Manzi, C. Kocik, and M. Bertl. 2013. "On the Relation between Social Class and Prejudice: The Roles of Education, Income, and Ideological Attitudes." *European Journal of Social Psychology* 43, no. 4: 272–285. https://doi.org/10.1002/ejsp.1961.

Carvallo, M., and S. Gabriel. 2006. "No Man is an Island: The Need to Belong and Dismissing Avoidant Attachment Style." *Personality and Social Psychology Bulletin* 32, no. 5: 697–709. https://doi.org/10.1177/0146167205285451.

Casale, S., and G. Fioravanti. 2018. "Why Narcissists are At Risk for Developing Facebook Addiction: The Need to be Admired and the Need to Belong." *Addictive Behaviors* 76: 312–318. https://doi.org/10.1016/j.addbeh.2017.08.038.

Caspi, D. J., J. D. Freilich, and S. M. Chermak. 2012. "Worst of the Bad: Violent White Supremacist Groups and Lethality." *Dynamics of Asymmetric Conflict* 5, no. 1: 1–17. https://doi.org/10.1080/17467586.2012.679664.

Catino, M. 2014. "How Do Mafias Organize? Conflict and Violence in Three Mafia Organizations." *European Journal of Sociology/Archives Européennes de Sociologie* 55, no. 2: 177–220. https://doi.org/10.1017/S0003975614000095.

Cebrowski, A. K., and J. J. Garstka. 1998. "Networks Centric Warfare: Its Origins and Future." *Proceedings* 124, no. 1/1: 139. U.S. Naval Institute. http://www.usni.org/proceedings/Articles98/PROcebrowski.html.

Ceci, E. 2018. "Analysis of Organized Crime: CAMORRA." *CRIMEN* 3: 285–302.

Cederman, L. E., K. S. Gleditsch, and H. Buhaug. 2013. *Inequality, Grievances, and Civil War*. New York: Cambridge University Press.

Cederman, L. E., A. Wimmer, and B. Min. 2010. "Why Do Ethnic Groups Rebel? New Data and Analysis." *World Politics* 62, no. 1: 87–119. https://doi.org/10.1017/S0043887109990219.

Çelebi, E., M. Verkuyten, and S. C. Bagci. 2017. "Ethnic Identification, Discrimination, and Mental and Physical Health among Syrian Refugees: The Moderating Role of Identity Needs." *European Journal of Social Psychology* 47, no. 7: 832–843. https://doi.org/10.1002/ejsp.2299.

Celinska, K. 2007. "Individualism and Collectivism in America: The Case of Gun Ownership and Attitudes toward Gun Control." *Sociological Perspectives* 50, no. 2: 229–247. https://doi.org/10.1525/sop.2007.50.2.229.

Cernat, V. 2010. "Intergroup Contact in Romania: When Minority Size is Positively Related to Intergroup Conflict." *Journal of Community & Applied Social Psychology* 20, no. 1: 15–29. https://doi.org/10.1002/casp.1001.

Cernat, V. 2010. "Socio-economic Status and Political Support in Post-communist Romania." *Communist and Post-Communist Studies* 43, no. 1: 43–50. https://doi.org/10.1016/j.postcomstud.2010.01.001.

Chan, W. 1996. "External Recruitment versus Internal Promotion." *Journal of Labor Economics* 14, no. 4: 555–570. https://doi.org/10.1086/209822.

Chandler, M. J., C. E. Lalonde, B. W. Sokol, D. Hallett, and J. E. Marcia. 2003. "Personal Persistence, Identity Development, and Suicide: A Study of Native and Non-native North American Adolescents." *Monographs of the Society for Research in Child Development* 68, no. 2: vii–viii, 1–130; discussion 131–138.

Chatfield, A. T., C. G. Reddick, and U. Brajawidagda. 2015. "Tweeting Propaganda, Radicalization and Recruitment: Islamic State Supporters Multi-sided Twitter Networks." In *Proceedings of the 16th Annual International Conference on Digital Government Research*, edited by J. Zhang and Y. Kim, 239–249. New York: ACM. https://doi.org/10.1145/2757401.2757408.

Chen, D. 2003. Economic Distress and Religious Intensity: Evidence from Islamic Resurgence during the Indonesian Financial Crisis. *American Economic Review*. https://users.nber.org/~dlchen/papers/Club_Goods_and_Group_Identity_slides.pdf.

Chen, E., S. Cohen, and G. E. Miller. 2010. "How Low Socioeconomic Status Affects 2-year Hormonal Trajectories in Children." *Psychological Science* 21, no. 1: 31–37. https://doi.org/10.1177/0956797609355566.

Chen, E., D. A. Langer, Y. E. Raphaelson, and K. A. Matthews. 2004. "Socioeconomic Status and Health in Adolescents: The Role of Stress Interpretations." *Child Development* 75: 1039–1052.

Chermak, S., and J. A. Gruenewald. 2015. "Laying a Foundation for the Criminological Examination of Right-wing, Left-wing, and Al Qaeda-inspired Extremism in the United States." *Terrorism and Political Violence* 27, no. 1: 133–159. https://doi.org/10.1080/09546553.2014.975646.

Chermak, S., J. Freilich, and M. Suttmoeller. 2013. "The Organizational Dynamics of Far-right Hate Groups in the United States: Comparing Violent to Nonviolent Organizations." *Studies in Conflict & Terrorism* 36, no. 3: 193–218. https://doi.org/10.1080/1057610X.2013.755912.

Chiao, J. Y., V. A. Mathur, T. Harada, and T. Lipke. 2009. "Neural Basis of Preference for Human Social Hierarchy versus Egalitarianism." *Annals of the New York Academy of Sciences* 1167, no. 1: 174–181. https://doi.org/10.1111/j.1749-6632.2009.04508.x.

Chinese Household Income Project. 1988. Survey Data and Summary. http://www.ciidbnu.org/chip/chips.asp?year=1988.

Chirumbolo, A. 2002. "The Relationship between Need for Cognitive Closure and Political Orientation: The Mediating Role of Authoritarianism." *Personality and Individual Differences* 32, no. 4: 603–610. https://doi.org/10.1016/S0191-8869(01)00062-9.

References

Chirumbolo, A., and L. Leone. 2010. "Personality and Politics: The Role of the HEXACO Model of Personality in Predicting Ideology and Voting." *Personality and Individual Differences* 49, no. 1: 43–48. https://doi.org/10.1016/j.paid.2010.03.004.

Chow, R. M., L. Z. Tiedens, , and C. L. Govan. 2008. "Excluded Emotions: The Role of Anger in Antisocial Responses to Ostracism." *Journal of Experimental Social Psychology* 44, no. 3: 896–903. https://doi.org/10.1016/j.jesp.2007.09.004.

Chowanietz, C. 2010. "Politics in Extraordinary Times: A Study of the Reaction of Political Parties and Elites To Terrorism." PhD diss., Université de Montréal. https://papyrus.bib.umontreal.ca/xmlui/bitstream/handle/1866/3716/chowanietz_christophe_2009_these.pdf?sequence=4&isAllowed=y.

Christakis, N. A., and J. H. Fowler. 2007. "The Spread of Obesity in a Large Social Network Over 32 Years." *New England Journal of Medicine* 357, no. 4: 370–379. https://doi.org/10.1056/NEJMsa066082.

Chung-Hall, J., and X. Chen. 2010. "Aggressive and Prosocial Peer Group Functioning: Effects on Children's Social, School, and Psychological Adjustment." *Social Development* 19, no. 4: 659–680. https://doi.org/10.1111/j.1467-9507.2009.00556.x.

Cialdini, R. B., and N. J. Goldstein. 2004. "Social Influence: Compliance and Conformity." *Annual Review of Psychology* 55, no. 1: 591–621. https://doi.org/10.1146/annurev.psych.55.090902.142015.

Cialdini, R. B., S. L. Brown, B. P. Lewis, C. Luce, and S. L. Neuberg. 1997. "Reinterpreting the Empathy–Altruism Relationship: When One Into One Equals Oneness." *Journal of Personality and Social Psychology* 73, no. 3: 481–494. https://doi.org/10.1037/0022-3514.73.3.481.

Cialdini, R. B., M. Schaller, D. Houlihan, K. Arps, J. Fultz, and A. L. Beaman. 1987. "Empathy-based Helping: Is It Selflessly or Selfishly Motivated?" *Journal of Personality and Social Psychology* 52, no. 4: 749–758. https://doi.org/10.1037/0022-3514.52.4.749.

Cialdini, R. B., M. R. Trost, and J. T. Newsom. 1995. "Preference for Consistency: The Development of a Valid Measure and the Discovery of Surprising Behavioral Implications." *Journal of Personality and Social Psychology* 69, no. 2: 318–328. https://doi.org/10.1037/0022-3514.69.2.318.

Cichocka, A., and J. T. Jost. 2014. "Stripped of illusions? Exploring System Justification Processes in Capitalist and Post-communist Societies." *International Journal of Psychology* 49, no. 1: 6–29. https://doi.org/10.1002/ijop.12011.

Ciconte, E. 2014. "Origins and Development of the 'Ndrangheta." In *The 'Ndrangheta and Sacra Corona Unita*, edited by N. Serenata, 33–50. Vol. 12 of *Studies of Organized Crime*. Cham: Springer. https://doi.org/10.1007/978-3-319-04930-4_3.

Cilliers, P. 2010. "Difference, Identity and Complexity." In *Complexity, Difference and Identity*, edited by P. Cilliers and R. Preiser, 3–18. Volume 26 of Issues in Business Ethics. Dordrecht: Springer. https://doi.org/10.1007/978-90-481-9187-1_1.

Cohen, A. B. 2011. "Religion and Culture." *Online Readings in Psychology and Culture* 4, no. 4: 1–13. http://dx.doi.org/10.9707/2307-0919.1108.

Coleman, P. K., and K. H. Karraker. 1997. "Self-efficacy and Parenting Quality: Findings and Future Applications." *Developmental Review* 18, no. 1: 47–85. https://doi.org/10.1006/drev.1997.0448.

Collier, P. 2000. *Economic Causes of Civil Conflict and Their Implications for Policy*.

Collier, P. 2003. *Breaking the Conflict Trap: Civil War and Development Policy*. Washington, DC: World Bank and Oxford University Press. https://openknowledge.worldbank.org/handle/10986/13938.

Collier, P., and A. Hoeffler. 2004. "Greed and Grievance in Civil War." *Oxford Economic Papers* 56, no. 4: 563–595. https://doi.org/10.1093/oep/gpf064.

Collier, P., and A. Hoeffler. 2005. "Resource Rents, Governance, and Conflict." *Journal of Conflict Resolution* 49, no. 4: 625–633. https://doi.org/10.1177/0022002705277551.

Collins, R. 2008. *Violence: A Microsociological Theory*. Princeton: Princeton University Press.

Comolli, V. 2015. *Boko Haram: Nigeria's Islamist Insurgency*. New York: Oxford University Press.

Compton, W. M., Y. F. Thomas, F. S. Stinson, and B. F. Grant. 2007. "Prevalence, Correlates, Disability, and Comorbidity of DSM-IV Drug Abuse and Dependence in the United States: Results from the National Epidemiologic Survey on Alcohol and related Conditions." *Archives of General Psychiatry* 64, no. 5: 566–576. https://doi.org/10.1001/archpsyc.64.5.566.

Connelly, S., N. E. Dunbar, M. L. Jensen, J. Griffith, W. D. Taylor, G. Johnson, M. Hughes, and M. D. Mumford. 2016. "Social Categorization, Moral Disengagement, and Credibility of Ideological Group Websites." *Journal of Media Psychology: Theories, Methods, and Applications* 28, no. 1: 16–31. https://doi.org/10.1027/1864-1105/a000138.

Constantino, M. J., K. R. Wilson, L. M. Horowitz, and E. C. Pinel. 2006. "The Direct and Stress-buffering Effects of Self-organization on Psychological Adjustment." *Journal of Social and Clinical Psychology* 25, no. 3: 333–360. https://doi.org/10.1521/jscp.2006.25.3.333.

Cook, D. 2014. "Boko Haram: A New Islamic State in Nigeria." James A. Baker III Institute for Public Policy. https://www.bakerinstitute.org/media/files/files/5f1f63c4/BI-pub-BokoHaram-121114.pdf.

Cook, T. R. 2011. "The Financial Arm of the FARC: A Threat Finance Perspective." *Journal of Strategic Security* 4, no. 1: 19–36. http://doi.org/10.5038/1944-0472.4.1.2.

Cooray, A. 2014. "Ethnic or Political Fractionalisation? A District Level Analysis of the Provision of Public Goods in Sri Lanka." *Growth and Change* 45, no. 4: 640–666. https://doi.org/10.1111/grow.12060.

Copsey, N. 2018. "The Radical Right and Fascism." In *The Oxford Handbook of the Radical Right*, edited by J. Rydgren, pp. 105–121. New York: Oxford University Press.

Cosgrove, L., and S. Krimsky. 2012. "A Comparison of DSM-IV and DSM-5 Panel Members' Financial Associations with Industry: A Pernicious Problem Persists." *PLoS Medicine* 9, no. 3: e1001190. https://doi.org/10.1371/journal.pmed.1001190.

Crenshaw, M. 1998. "The Logic of Terrorism: Terrorist Behavior as a Product of Choice." *Terrorism and Counter Terrorism* 2, no. 1: 54–64.

Crocker, J., and R. K. Luhtanen. 2003. "Level of Self-esteem and Contingencies of Self-worth: Unique Effects on Academic, Social, and Financial Problems in College Students." *Personality and Social Psychology Bulletin* 29, no. 6: 701–712. https://doi.org/10.1177/0146167203029006003.

Crocker, J., and L. E. Park. 2004. "The Costly Pursuit of Self-esteem." *Psychological Bulletin* 130, no. 3: 392–414. https://doi.org/10.1037/0033-2909.130.3.392.

Croissant, A. 2007. "Muslim Insurgency, Political Violence, and Democracy in Thailand." *Terrorism and Political Violence* 19, no. 1: 1–18. https://doi.org/10.1080/09546550601054485.

Crooker, R. A. 2007. "Ecological Marginalization and Hill Tribe Security in Northern Thailand." *The Geographical Bulletin* 48, no. 1: 15–40.

Crowder, M. 1968. *West Africa Under Colonial Rule*. London: Hutchinson.

Cummins, D. D. 2000. "How the Social Environment Shaped the Evolution of Mind." *Synthese* 122, no. 1: 3–28. https://doi.org/10.1023/A:1005263825428.

Cummins, R. A. 1998. *Directory of Instruments to Measure Quality of Life and Cognate Areas*. Melbourne: Deakin University, School of Psychology.

Cunningham, D. 2004. *There's Something Happening Here: The New Left, the Klan, and FBI Counterintelligence*. University of California Press.

Cunningham, K. J. 2007. "Countering Female Terrorism." *Studies in Conflict & Terrorism* 30, no. 2: 113–129. https://doi.org/10.1080/10576100601101067.

Curley, S. P., J. F. Yates, and R. A. Abrams. 1986. "Psychological Sources of Ambiguity Avoidance." *Organizational Behavior and Human Decision Processes* 38, no. 2: 230–256. https://doi.org/10.1016/0749-5978(86)90018-X.

Cutts, D., R. Ford, and M. J. Goodwin. 2011. "Anti-immigrant, Politically Disaffected or Still Racist After All? Examining the Attitudinal Drivers of Extreme Right Support in Britain in the 2009 European Elections." *European Journal of Political Research* 50, no. 3: 418–440. https://doi.org/10.1111/j.1475-6765.2010.01936.x.

Dalal, F. 2006. "Racism: Processes of Detachment, Dehumanization, and Hatred." *The Psychoanalytic Quarterly* 75, no. 1: 131–161. https://doi.org/10.1002/j.2167-4086.2006.tb00035.x.

Daly, T. 2019. Populism, public law, and democratic decay in Brazil: Understanding the rise of Jair Bolsonaro. Paper presented at The 14th International Human Rights Researchers' Workshop: "Democratic Backsliding and Human Rights." *The Law and Ethics of Human Rights (LEHR) Journal* 2-3. https://papers.ssrn.com/sol3/papers.cfm?abstract_id=3350098.

Damon, W. 2008. *The Path to Purpose: Helping our Children Find Their Calling in Life*. New York: Simon and Schuster.

Dantschke, C. 2017. "Attraktivität, Anziehungskraft und Akteure des politischen und militanten Salafismus in Deutschland." In *Salafismus in Deutschland*, edited by A. Toprak und G. Weitzel, 61–76. Wiesbaden: VS Springer.

Darley, J. M., and R. H. Fazio. 1980. "Expectancy Confirmation Processes Arising in the Social Interaction Sequence." *American Psychologist* 35, no. 10: 867–881. https://doi.org/10.1037/0003-066X.35.10.867.

Dasgupta, P. 2005. "Economics of Social Capital." *Economic Record* 81, no. S1: S2–S21. https://doi.org/10.1111/j.1475-4932.2005.00245.x.

Dashwood, H. S. 2000. *Zimbabwe: The Political Economy of Transformation*. Toronto: University of Toronto Press. https://doi.org/10.3138/9781442683792.

Dauber, A. S. 2017. "The Increasing Visibility of Right-Wing Extremist Women in Contemporary Europe: Is Great Britain an Exception?" In *Gender and Far Right Politics in Europe. Gender and Politics*, edited by M. Köttig, R. Bitzan, and A. Petö, 49–64. Cham: Palgrave Macmillan. https://doi.org/10.1007/978-3-319-43533-6_4.

Davies, M., and Stone, T. 1995. *Mental Simulation: Evaluations and Applications-reading in Mind and Language*. New York: John Wiley & Sons.

Davis, B. J. 2003. *The Theory of the Individual in Economics*. London: Routledge. https://doi.org/10.4324/9780203457689.

Davis, C. G., and J. M. McKearney. 2003. "How Do People Grow from Their Experience with Trauma or Loss?" *Journal of Social and Clinical Psychology* 22, no. 5: 477. https://doi.org/10.1521/jscp.22.5.477.22928.

Deci, E. L., and R. M. Ryan. 2008. "Self-determination Theory: A Macrotheory of Human Motivation, Development, and Health." *Canadian Psychology / Psychologie canadienne* 49, no. 3: 182–185. https://doi.org/10.1037/a0012801

De Cremer, D., and M. Van Vugt. 1999. "Social Identification Effects in Social Dilemmas: A Transformation of Motives." *European Journal of Social Psychology* 29, no. 7: 871–893. https://doi.org/10.1002/(SICI)1099-0992(199911)29:7<871::AID-EJSP962>3.0.CO;2-I.

De Donder, L., N. De Witte, T. Buffel, S. Dury, and D. Verté. 2012. "Social Capital and Feelings of Unsafety in Later Life: A Study on the Influence of Social Networks, Place Attachment, and Civic Participation on Perceived Safety in Belgium." *Research on Aging* 34, no. 4: 425–448. https://doi.org/10.1177/0164027511433879.

de Jong, J. T. V. M. 2002. "Public Mental Health, Traumatic Stress and Human Rights Violations in Low-income Countries: A Culturally Appropriate Model in Times of Conflict, Disaster and Peace." In *Trauma, War, and Violence: Public Mental Health in Socio-cultural Context*, edited by J. de Jong, 1–91. New York: Kluwer Academic/Plenum Publishers. https://doi.org/10.1007/0-306-47675-4_1.

De Jong, J. T., I. H. Komproe, M. Van Ommeren, M. El Masri, M. Araya, N. Khaled, W. van De Put, and D. Somasundaram. 2001. "Lifetime Events and Posttraumatic Stress Disorder in 4 Postconflict Settings." *JAMA* 286, no. 5: 555–562. https://doi.org/10.1001/jama.286.5.555.

De Koster, W., P. Achterberg, and J. Van der Waal. 2013. "The New Right and the Welfare State: The Electoral Relevance of Welfare Chauvinism and Welfare Populism in the Netherlands." *International Political Science Review* 34, no. 1: 3–20. https://doi.org/10.1177/0192512112455443.

De Lange, S. L., and D. Art. 2011. "Fortuyn versus Wilders: An Agency-based Approach to Radical Right Party Building." *West European Politics* 34, no. 6: 1229–1249. https://doi.org/10.1080/01402382.2011.616662.

De Matas, J. 2017. "Making the Nation Great Again: Trumpism, Euro-scepticism and the Surge of Populist Nationalism." *Journal of Comparative Politics* 10, no. 2: 19–36.

De Neve, J. E. 2015. "Personality, Childhood Experience, and Political Ideology." *Political Psychology* 36, no. 1: 55–73. https://doi.org/10.1111/pops.12075.

De Soysa, I. 2002. "Paradise is a Bazaar? Greed, Creed, and Governance in Civil War, 1989–99." *Journal of Peace Research* 39, no. 4: 395–416. https://doi.org/10.1177/0022343302039004002.

De Soysa, I., and E. Neumayer. 2007. "Resource Wealth and the Risk of Civil War Onset: Results from a New Dataset of Natural Resource Rents, 1970—1999." *Conflict Management and Peace Science* 24, no. 3: 201–218. https://doi.org/10.1080/07388940701468468.

De Waal, F. 1996. *Good Natured: The Origins of Right and Wrong in Humans and Other Animals*. Cambridge, MA: Harvard University Press.

De Waal, F. B. 1998. "No Imitation Without Identification." *Behavioral and Brain Sciences* 21, no. 5: 689–689.

De Waal, F. B. 2008. "Putting the Altruism Back into Altruism: The Evolution of Empathy." *Annual Review of Psychology* 59: 279–300. https://doi.org/10.1146/annurev.psych.59.103006.093625.

De Waal, F. B. 2012. "The Antiquity of Empathy." *Science* 336, no. 6083: 874–876. https://doi.org/10.1126/science.1220999.

de Weydenthal, J. B. 1986. *The Communists of Poland: An Historical Outline*. Stanford, CA: Hoover Institution Press.

De Zavala, A. G., A. Cichocka, R. Eidelson, and N. Jayawickreme. 2009. "Collective Narcissism and Its Social Consequences." *Journal of Personality and Social Psychology* 97, no. 6: 1074–1096. https://doi.org/10.1037/a0016904.

Dean, G., P. Gottschalk, and I. Fahsing. 2010. *Organized Crime: Policing Illegal Business Entrepreneurialism*. New York: Oxford University Press. https://doi.org/10.1093/acprof:osobl/9780199578436.001.0001.

Deci, E. L. 1980. *The Psychology of Self-Determination*. New York: Lexington Books.

Deci, E. L., and R. M. Ryan. 1986. "The Dynamics of Self-determination in Personality and Development." In *Self-related Cognitions in Anxiety and Motivation*, edited by R. Schwarzer, 171–194. New York: Psychology Press.

Deci, E. L., and R. M. Ryan. 1995. "Human Autonomy." In *Efficacy, Agency, and Self-esteem*, edited by M. H. Kernis, 31–49. Boston, MA: Springer. https://doi.org/10.1007/978-1-4899-1280-0_3.

Deci, E. L., and R. M. Ryan. 2000. "The 'What' and 'Why' of Goal Pursuits: Human Need and the Self-determination of Behavior." *Psychological Inquiry* 11, no. 4: 227–268. https://doi.org/10.1207/S15327965PLI1104_01.

Deci, E. L., and R. M. Ryan. 2002. "Overview of Self-determination Theory: An Organismic Dialectical Perspective." In *Handbook of Self-determination Research*, edited by E. L. Deci and R. M. Ryan, 3–33. New York: University of Rochester Press.

Deci, E. L., and R. M. Ryan. 2012. "Self-determination Theory." In *Handbook of Theories of Social Psychology*, edited by P. A. Van Lange, A. W. Kruglanski, and E. T. Higgins, 416–436. Thousand Oaks, CA: Sage Publications Ltd. https://doi.org/10.4135/9781446249215.n21.

Degner, J., and D. Wentura. 2010. "Automatic Prejudice in Childhood and Early Adolescence." *Journal of Personality and Social Psychology* 98, no. 3: 356–374. https://doi.org/10.1037/a0017993.

Della Porta, D. 1988. "Recruitment Processes in Clandestine Political Organizations." *International Social Movement Research* 1: 155–169.

della Porta, D. 1995. *Social Movements, Political Violence and the State*. Cambridge: Cambridge University Press. https://doi.org/10.1017/CBO9780511527555.

Demo, D. H. 1992. "The Self-concept Over Time: Research Issues and Directions." *Annual Review of Sociology* 18, no. 1: 303–326. https://doi.org/10.1146/annurev.so.18.080192.001511.

Denny, E. K., and B. F. Walter. 2014. "Ethnicity and Civil War." *Journal of Peace Research* 51, no. 2: 199–212. https://doi.org/10.1177/0022343313512853.

Denver, D. T., and J. M. Bochel. 1973. "The Political Socialization of Activists in the British Communist party." *British Journal of Political Science* 3, no. 1: 53–71. https://doi.org/10.1017/S0007123400007699.

Deraniyagala, S. 2005. "The Political Economy of Civil Conflict in Nepal." *Oxford Development Studies* 33, no. 1: 47–62. https://doi.org/10.1080/13600810500099659.

Deutsch, F. M., and D. M. Lamberti. 1986. "Does Social Approval Increase Helping?" *Personality and Social Psychology Bulletin* 12, no. 2: 149–157. https://doi.org/10.1177/0146167286122001.

Devine, P. G., and S. M. Baker. 1991. "Measurement of Racial Stereotype Subtyping." *Personality and Social Psychology Bulletin* 17, no. 1: 44–50. https://doi.org/10.1177/0146167291171007.

De Waal, F. B. M. 2010. "Morality and its Relation to Primate Social Instincts." In *Human Morality and Sociality: Evolutionary and Comparative Perspectives*, edited by H. Høgh-Olesen, 31–57. New York, NY: Palgrave Macmillan.

de-Wit, L., B. Machilsen, and T. Putzeys. 2010. "Predictive Coding and the Neural Response to Predictable Stimuli." *Journal of Neuroscience* 30, no. 26: 8702–8703. https://doi.org/10.1523/JNEUROSCI.2248-10.2010.

Di Maria, F., and G. Lo Verso. 2007. "Women in Mafia Organizations." In *Women and the Mafia: Female Roles in Organized Crime Structures*, edited by G. Fiandaca, 87–102. New York: Springer.

Dickerson, S. S. 2011. "Physiological Responses to Experiences of Social Pain." In *Social Pain: Neuropsychological and Health Implications of Loss and Rejection*, edited by G. MacDonald and L. A. Jensen-Campbell, 79–94. Washington: American Psychological Association.

Dickerson, S. S., T. L. Gruenewald, and M. E. Kemeny. 2004. "When the Social Self is Threatened: Shame, Physiology, and Health." *Journal of Personality* 72, no. 6: 1191–1216. https://doi.org/10.1111/j.1467-6494.2004.00295.x.

Dickie, J. 2004. *Cosa Nostra: A History of the Sicilian Mafia*. London: Hodder & Stoughton.

Dickson, B. J. 1997. *Democratization in China and Taiwan: The Adaptability of Leninist Parties*. New York: Oxford University Press.

Dickson, B. J., and M. R. Rublee. 2000. "Membership Has Its Privileges: The Socioeconomic Characteristics of Communist Party Members in Urban China." *Comparative Political Studies* 33, no. 1: 87–112. https://doi.org/10.1177/0010414000033001004.

Diener, E., and R. Biswas-Diener. 2002. "Will Money Increase Subjective Well-being?" *Social Indicators Research* 57, no. 2: 119–169. https://doi.org/10.1023/A:1014411319119.

Dim, E. E. 2017. "An Integrated Theoretical Approach to the Persistence of Boko Haram Violent Extremism in Nigeria." *Journal of Peacebuilding & Development* 12, no. 2: 36–50. https://doi.org/10.1080/15423166.2017.1331746.

Dinas, E., V. Georgiadou, I. Konstantinidis, and L. Rori. 2016. "From Dusk to Dawn: Local Party Organization and Party Success of Right-wing Extremism." *Party Politics* 22, no. 1: 80–92. https://doi.org/10.1177/1354068813511381.

Ding, I., and M. Hlavac. 2017. "'Right' Choice: Restorative Nationalism and Right-Wing Populism in Central and Eastern Europe." *Chinese Political Science Review* 2, no. 3: 427–444. https://doi.org/10.1007/s41111-017-0069-8.

Do, Q. T., and L. Iyer. 2010. "Geography, Poverty and Conflict in Nepal." *Journal of Peace Research* 47, no. 6: 735–748.

Doosje, B., A. Loseman, and K. Van Den Bos. 2013. "Determinants of Radicalization of Islamic Youth in the Netherlands: Personal Uncertainty, Perceived Injustice, and Perceived Group Threat." *Journal of Social Issues* 69, no. 3: 586–604. https://doi.org/10.1111/josi.12030.

Douglas, J., G. A. Field, and L. X. Tarpey. 1967. *Human Behavior in Marketing*. New York: CE Merrill Books.

Dovidio, J. F., and S. L. Gaertner. 1998. "On the Nature of Contemporary Prejudice." In *Confronting Racism: The Problem and the Response*, edited by J. L. Eberhardt and S. T. Fiske, 3–32. Thousand Oaks, CA: SAGE.

Dovidio, J. F., and S. L. Gaertner. 2004. "Aversive Racism." In *Advances in Experimental Social Psychology (Vol. 36)*, edited by M. P. Zanna, 1–52. 67 vols. New York: Elsevier Academic Press. https://doi.org/10.1016/S0065-2601(04)36001-6.

Dovidio, J. F., N. Evans, and R. B. Tyler. 1986. "Racial Stereotypes: The Contents of Their Cognitive Representations." *Journal of Experimental Social Psychology* 22, no. 1: 22–37. https://doi.org/10.1016/0022-1031(86)90039-9.

Dovidio, J. F., S. L. Gaertner, and T. Saguy. 2007. "Another View of 'We': Majority and Minority Group Perspectives on a Common Ingroup Identity." *European Review of Social Psychology* 18, no. 1: 296–330. https://doi.org/10.1080/10463280701726132.

Dowlah, A. F. 1993. "Soviet Socialism: The Era of War Communism." *International Journal of Social Economics* 20, no. 5/6/7: 57–83. https://doi.org/10.1108/EUM0000000000526.

Doxsee, C., S. G. Jones, G. Hwang, and K. Halstead. 2022. *Pushed to Extremes, Domestic Terrorism amid Polarization and Protest*. CSIS Briefs. Washington DC: Center for Strategic and International Studies. https://www.csis.org/analysis/pushed-extremes-domestic-terrorism-amid-polarization-and-protest.

Doyal, L., and I. Gough. 1991. *A Theory of Human Need*. London: Macmillan.

Duckitt, J. 1989. "Authoritarianism and Group Identification: A New View of an Old Construct." *Political Psychology* 10, no. 1: 63–84. https://doi.org/10.2307/3791588.

Duckitt, J. 2006. "Differential Effects of Right-wing Authoritarianism and Social Dominance Orientation on Outgroup Attitudes and their Mediation by Threat from and Competitiveness to Outgroups." *Personality and Social Psychology Bulletin* 32, no. 5: 684–696. https://doi.org/10.1177/0146167205284282.

Duckitt, J., and K. Fisher. 2003. "The Impact of Social Threat on Worldview and Ideological Attitudes." *Political Psychology* 24, no. 1: 199–222. https://doi.org/10.1111/0162-895X.00322.

Duckitt, J., and C. G. Sibley. 2007. "Right-wing Authoritarianism, Social Dominance Orientation and the Dimensions of Generalized Prejudice." *European Journal of Personality: Published for the European Association of Personality Psychology* 21, no. 2: 113–130. https://doi.org/10.1002/per.614.

Duckitt, J., C. Wagner, I. Du Plessis, and I. Birum. 2002. "The Psychological Bases of Ideology and Prejudice: Testing a Dual Process Model." *Journal of Personality and Social Psychology* 83, no. 1: 75–93. https://doi.org/10.1037/0022-3514.83.1.75.

Duflo, E., and A. Banarjee. 2019. *Good Economics for Hard Times*. New York: PublicAffairs.

Dumont, M., and M. A. Provost. 1999. "Resilience in Adolescents: Protective Role of Social Support, Coping Strategies, Self-esteem, and Social Activities on Experience of Stress and

Depression." *Journal of Youth and Adolescence* 28, no. 3: 343–363. https://doi.org/10.1023/A:1021637011732.

Dunlop, W. L. 2017. "Situating Self-concept Clarity in the Landscape of Personality." In *Self-concept Clarity*, edited by J. Lodi-Smith and K. G. DeMarree, 19–41. Cham: Springer. https://doi.org/10.1007/978-3-319-71547-6_2.

Dunn, K. M. 2004. "Racism in Australia: Findings of a Survey on Racist Attitudes and Experiences of Racism." Working paper. ANU Centre for European Studies. Retrieved from: https://openresearch-repository.anu.edu.au/handle/1885/41761.

Dunning, D. 2007. "Self-image Motives and Consumer Behavior: How Sacrosanct Self-beliefs Sway Preferences in the Marketplace." *Journal of Consumer Psychology* 17, no. 4: 237–249. https://doi.org/10.1016/S1057-7408(07)70033-5.

Dunphy, R. 2004. *Contesting Capitalism? Left Parties and European Integration*. Manchester: Manchester University Press.

Durham, M. 2007. *White Rage: The Extreme Right and American Politics*. London: Routledge. https://doi.org/10.4324/9780203012581.

Easterly, W. 2007. "Inequality Does Cause Underdevelopment: Insights From a New Instrument." *Journal of Development Economics* 84, no. 2: 755–776. https://doi.org/10.1016/j.jdeveco.2006.11.002.

Eatwell, R. 2006. "The Concept and Theory of Charismatic Leadership." *Totalitarian Movements and Political Religions* 7, no. 2: 141–156. https://doi.org/10.1080/14690760600642156.

Eatwell, R. 2013. "Fascism." In *The Oxford Handbook of Political Ideologies*, edited by M. Freeden, L. Tower Sargent, and M. Stears, 474–492. New York: Oxford University Press.

Eaves, L. J., and P. K. Hatemi. 2008. "Transmission of Attitudes toward Abortion and Gay Rights: Effects of Genes, Social Learning and Mate Selection." *Behavior Genetics* 38, no. 3: 247–256. https://doi.org/10.1007/s10519-008-9205-4.

Eccarius-Kelly, V. 2012. "Surreptitious Lifelines: A Structural Analysis of the FARC and the PKK." *Terrorism and Political Violence* 24, no. 2: 235–258. https://doi.org/10.1080/09546553.2011.651182.

Eccles, J. S., C. A. Wong, and S. C. Peck. 2006. "Ethnicity as a Social Context for the Development of African-American Adolescents." *Journal of School Psychology* 44, no. 5: 407–426. https://doi.org/10.1016/j.jsp.2006.04.001.

Edensor, T. 2002. *National Identity, Popular Culture and Everyday Life*. New York: Routledge.

Edmondson, D., S. R. Chaudoir, M. A. Mills, C. L. Park, J. Holub, and J. M. Bartkowiak. 2011. "From Shattered Assumptions to Weakened Worldviews: Trauma Symptoms Signal Anxiety Buffer Disruption." *Journal of Loss and Trauma* 16, no. 4: 358–385. https://doi.org/10.1080/15325024.2011.572030.

Eil, D., and J. M. Rao. 2011. "The Good News–Bad News Effect: Asymmetric Processing of Objective Information about Yourself." *American Economic Journal: Microeconomics* 3, no. 2: 114–138. https://doi.org/10.1257/mic.3.2.114.

Eilam, G., and B. Shamir. 2005. "Organizational Change and Self-concept Threats: A Theoretical Perspective and a Case Study." *The Journal of Applied Behavioral Science* 41, no. 4: 399–421. https://doi.org/10.1177/0021886305280865.

Eisenberg, N., N. D. Eggum-Wilkens, and T. L. Spinrad. 2015. "The Development of Prosocial Behavior." In *The Oxford Handbook of Prosocial Behavior*, edited by D. A. Schroeder and W. G. Graziano, 114–136. New York: Oxford University Press.

Eisenberg, N., T. L. Spinrad, and A. Sadovsky. 2006. "Empathy-related Responding in Children." In *Handbook of Moral Development*, edited by M. Killen and J. G. Smetana, 517–549. New York: Lawrence Erlbaum Associates Publishers.

Eisenberger, N. I. 2011. "The Neural Basis of Social Pain: Findings and Implications." In *Social Pain: Neuropsychological and Health Implications of Loss and Exclusion*, edited by G.

References

MacDonald and L. A. Jensen-Campbell, 53–78. Washington, DC: American Psychological Association. https://doi.org/10.1037/12351-002.

Eisenberger, N. I., M. D. Lieberman, and K. D. Williams. 2003. "Does Rejection Hurt? An fMRI Study of Social Exclusion." *Science* 302, no. 5643: 290–292. https://doi.org/10.1126/science.1089134.

Ekins, E. 2017. "The Five Types of Trump voters." Democracy Fund Voter Study Group, June. https://www.voterstudygroup.org/reports/2016-elections/the-five-types-trump-voters.

Ekman, J., and J. Linde. 2005. "Communist Nostalgia and the Consolidation of Democracy in Central and Eastern Europe." *Journal of Communist Studies and Transition Politics* 21, no. 3: 354–374. https://doi.org/10.1080/13523270500183512.

Elder Jr., G. H.. 1995. "Life Trajectories in Changing Societies." In *Self-efficacy in Changing Societies*, edited by A. Bandura, 46–68. New York: Cambridge University Press.

Ellenbroek, M., M. Verkuyten, J. Thijs, and E. Poppe. 2014. "The Fairness of National Decision-making Procedures: The Views of Adolescents in 18 European Countries." *Journal of Community & Applied Social Psychology* 24, no. 6: 503–517. https://doi.org/10.1002/casp.2189.

Ellinas, A. A., and I. Lamprianou. 2017. "How Far Right Local Party Organizations Develop: The Organizational Buildup of the Greek Golden Dawn." *Party Politics* 23, no. 6: 804–820. https://doi.org/10.1177/1354068816641337.

Ellison, C. G., Q. Fang, K. J. Flannelly, and R. A. Steckler. 2013. "Spiritual Struggles and Mental Health: Exploring the Moderating Effects of Religious Identity." *International Journal for the Psychology of Religion* 23, no. 3: 214–229. https://doi.org/10.1080/10508619.2012.759868.

El-Mafaalani, A. 2017. "Provokation und Plausibilität–Eigenlogik und soziale Rahmung des jugendkulturellen Salafismus." In *Salafismus in Deutschland*, edited by Ahmet Toprak and Gerrit Weitzel, 77–90. Wiesbaden: Springer VS.

Emerson, M. O., and D. Hartman. 2006. "The Rise of Religious Fundamentalism." *Annual Review of Sociology* 32: 127–144. https://doi.org/10.1146/annurev.soc.32.061604.123141.

Enders, W., and T. Sandler. 2012. *The Political Economy of Terrorism*. 2nd ed. New York: Cambridge University Press. https://doi.org/10.1017/CBO9780511791451.

Englebert, P., and J. Ron. 2004. "Primary Commodities and War: Congo-Brazzaville's Ambivalent Resource Curse." *Comparative Politics* 37, no. 1: 61–81. https://doi.org/10.2307/4150124.

Enyedi, Z. 2005. "The Role of Agency in Cleavage Formation." *European Journal of Political Research* 44, no. 5: 697–720.

Enyedi, Z. 2015. "Plebeians, Citoyens and Aristocrats or Where is the Bottom of Bottom-up? The Case of Hungary." In European Populism in the Shadow of the Great Recession, edited by H. Kriesi and T. S. Pappas, 235–250. Colchester, UK: ECPR Press.

Epstein, S. 1973. "The Self-concept Revisited: Or a Theory of a Theory." *American Psychologist* 28, no. 5: 404–416. https://doi.org/10.1037/h0034679.

Erikson, E. 1956. "The Problem of Ego Identity." *Journal of the American Psychoanalytic Association* 4, no. 1: 56–121. https://doi.org/10.1177/000306515600400104.

Erikson, E. 1968. *Identity: Youth and Crisis*. New York: W. W. Norton.

Essed, P. 1991. *Understanding Everyday Racism: An Interdisciplinary Theory (Vol. 2)*. Thousand Oaks, CA: SAGE.

Esteban, J. M., and D. Ray. 1994. "On the Measurement of Polarization." *Econometrica* 62, no. 4: 819–851. https://doi.org/10.2307/2951734.

Esteban, J., and G. Schneider. 2008. "Polarization and Conflict: Theoretical and Empirical Issues." *Journal of Peace Research* 45, no. 2: 131–141. https://doi.org/10.1177/0022343307087168.

Esteban, J., L. Mayoral, and D. Ray. 2012. "Ethnicity and Conflict: An Empirical Study." *American Economic Review* 102, no. 4: 1310–1342. https://doi.org/10.1257/aer.102.4.1310.

Evans, G. W., C. Gonnella, L. A. Marcynyszyn, L. Gentile, and N. Salpekar. 2005. "The Role of Chaos in Poverty and Children's Socioemotional Adjustment." *Psychological Science* 16, no. 7: 560–565. https://doi.org/10.1111/j.0956-7976.2005.01575.x.

Ewi, M. A., and U. Salifu. 2017. "Money Talks—A Key Reason Youths Join Boko Haram." Institute for Security Studies. https://www.africaportal.org/publications/money-talks-a-key-reason-youths-join-boko-haram/.

Eyber, C., and A. Ager. 2003. "Poverty and Youth." In *Poverty and Psychology: From Global Perspective to Local Practice*, edited by S. C. Carr and T. S. Sloan, 229–250. Boston, MA: Springer.

Eysenck, H. J. 1954. *The Psychology of Politics*. London: Routledge & Kegan Paul.

Fair, C. C., and B. Shepherd. 2006. "Who Supports Terrorism? Evidence from Fourteen Muslim Countries." *Coastal Management* 29, no. 1: 51–74. https://doi.org/10.1080/10576100500351318.

Falciola, L. 2013. "Pathways of an 'Early' De-Escalation: The Case of the Weather Underground Organization." In ECPR General Conference, 4–7. Sciences Po Bordeaux.

Falkinger, J., E. Fehr, S. Gächter, and R. Winter-Ember. 2000. "A Simple Mechanism for the Efficient Provision of Public Goods: Experimental Evidence." *American Economic Review* 90, no. 1: 247–264. https://doi.org/10.1257/aer.90.1.247.

FAO. 2018. "Central African Republic: Situation Report - May 2018." Food and Agriculture Organization of the United Nations. https://www.fao.org/3/ca7372en/ca7372en.pdf.

Farfan-Vallespin, A., and M. Bonick. 2016. "On the Origins and Consequences of Racism." Paper presented at Jahrestagung des Vereins für Socialpolitik 2016: Demographischer Wandel. ZBW—Deutsche Zentralbibliothek für Wirtschaftswissenschaften, Leibniz-Informationszentrum Wirtschaft, Kiel und Hamburg.

FBI. 1973. *Black Liberation Army*. Washington, DC: FBI archives/BLA.

Feagin, J. R., and R. Hohle. 2017. *Racism in the Neoliberal Era: A Meta History of Elite White Power*. New York: Routledge.

Fearon, J. D. 2005. "Primary Commodity Exports and Civil War." *Journal of Conflict Resolution* 49, no. 4: 483–507. https://doi.org/10.1177/0022002705277544.

Fearon, J. D., and D. D. Laitin. 2000. "Violence and the Social Construction of ETHNIC IDENTIty." *International Organization* 54, no. 4: 845–877. https://doi.org/10.1162/002081800551398.

Fearon, J. D., and D. D. Laitin. 2003. "Ethnicity, Insurgency, and Civil War." *American Political Science Review* 97, no. 1: 75–90. https://doi.org/10.1017/S0003055403000534.

Feather, N. T. 2006. *Values, Achievement, and Justice: Studies in the Psychology of Deservingness*. New York: Kluwer Academic Publishers.

Fehr, E., and S. Gächter. 2000. "Cooperation and Punishment in Public Goods Experiments." *American Economic Review* 90, no. 4: 980–994. https://doi.org/10.1257/aer.90.4.980.

Fehr, E., and B. Rockenbach. 2004. "Human Altruism: Economic, Neural, and Evolutionary Perspectives." *Current Opinion in Neurobiology* 14, no. 6: 784–790. https://doi.org/10.1016/j.conb.2004.10.007.

Feinberg, T. E. 2009. *From Axons to Identity: Neurological Explorations of the Nature of the Self*. New York: W. W. Norton & Company.

Ferris, D. L., D. J. Brown, and D. Heller. 2009. "Organizational Supports and Organizational Deviance: The Mediating Role of Organization-based Self-esteem." *Organizational Behavior and Human Decision Processes* 108, no. 2: 279–286. https://doi.org/10.1016/j.obhdp.2008.09.001.

Festinger, L. 1957. *A Theory of Cognitive Dissonance*. Stanford, CA: Stanford University Press.

Field, S., and A. Hoffman. 1994. "Development of a Model for Self-determination." *Career Development and Transition for Exceptional Individuals* 17, no. 2: 159–169. https://doi.org/10.1177/088572889401700205.

Field, S., A. Hoffman, and M. Posch. 1997. "Self-determination during Adolescence: A Developmental Perspective." *Remedial and Special Education* 18, no. 5: 285–293. https://doi.org/10.1177/074193259701800504.

Figeac, J., N. Paton, A.Peralva, A. C.Bezerra, G. Cabanac, H. Prévost, P. Ratinaud, and T. Salord. 2021. "Digital Participation of Left-wing Activists in Brazil: Cultural Events as a Cement to Mobilization and Networked Protest." *Brasiliana: Journal for Brazilian Studies* 10, no. 1: 261–284.

Finke, R., and R. Stark. 1992. *The Churching of America, 1776–1990: Winners and Losers in Our Religious Economy*. New Brunswick: Rutgers University Press.

Finlayson, A. 1998. "Psychology, Psychoanalysis and Theories of Nationalism." *Nations and Nationalism* 4, no. 2: 145–162. https://doi.org/10.1111/j.1354-5078.1998.00145.x.

Fishman, B. 2006. "After Zarqawi: The Dilemmas and Future of al Qaeda in Iraq." *Washington Quarterly* 29, no. 4: 19–32. https://doi.org/10.1162/wash.2006.29.4.19.

Fiske, S. T., and S. E. Taylor. 1991. *Social Cognition*. New York: McGraw-Hill Book Company.

Flanagan, C. A., B. Campbell, L. Botcheva, J. Bowes, B. Csapo, P. Macek, and E. Sheblanova. 2003. "Social Class and Adolescents' Beliefs about Justice in Different Social Orders." *Journal of Social Issues* 59, no. 4: 711–732. https://doi.org/10.1046/j.0022-4537.2003.00086.x.

Flannelly, K. J. 2017. "Religion and Death Anxiety." In Religious Beliefs, Evolutionary Psychiatry, and Mental Health in America, 153–164. Cham: Springer.

Flannelly, K. J., and K. Galek. 2010. "Religion, Evolution, and Mental Health: Attachment Theory and ETAS theory." *Journal of Religion and Health* 49, no. 3: 337–350. https://doi.org/10.1007/s10943-009-9247-9.

Flannelly, K. J., C. G. Ellison, K. Galek, and H. G. Koenig. 2008. "Beliefs about Life-After-Death, Psychiatric Symptomology and Cognitive Theories of Psychopathology." *Journal of Psychology and Theology* 36, no. 2: 94–103. https://doi.org/10.1177/009164710803600202.

Flores, T. E. 2014. "Vertical Inequality, Land Reform, and Insurgency in Colombia." *Peace Economics, Peace Science and Public Policy* 20, no. 1: 5–31. https://doi.org/10.1515/peps-2013-0058.

Folvarčný, A., and L. Kopeček. 2020. "Which Conservatism? The Identity of the Polish Law and Justice Party." *Politics in Central Europe* 16, no. 1: 159–188. https://doi.org/10.2478/pce-2020-0008.

Fontana, D. 1983. "Individual Differences in Personality: Trait Based versus State Based Approaches." *Educational Psychology* 3, no. 3–4: 189–200. https://doi.org/10.1080/0144341830030304.

Forest, J. J. 2011. "Al-Qaeda's Influence in Sub-Saharan Africa: Myths, Realities and Possibilities." *Perspectives on Terrorism* 5, no. 3–4: 63–80. https://www.jstor.org/stable/26298524.

Forest, J. J. 2012. "Confronting the Terrorism of Boko Haram in Nigeria." Joint Special Operations University. https://cco.ndu.edu/Portals/96/Documents/Articles/Confronting_the_terrrorism_of_%20Boko_Haram_JSOU-Report-2012.pdf.

Fosu, A. K., and P. Collier. 2005. *Post-conflict Economies in Africa*. New York: Palgrave Macmillan.

Fowler, J. H., L. A. Baker, and C. T. Dawes. 2008. "Genetic Variation in Political Participation." *American Political Science Review* 102, no. 2: 233–248. https://doi.org/10.1017/S0003055408080209.

Fowler, J. H., P. J. Loewen, J. Settle, and C. T. Dawes. 2011. *Genes, Games, and Political Participation. Man Is By Nature a Political Animal: Evolution, Biology, and Politics*. Chicago: University of Chicago Press. https://doi.org/10.7208/chicago/9780226319117.001.0001.

Francis, L. J., and T. E. Evans. 1996. "The Relationship Between Personal Prayer and Purpose in Life Among Churchgoing and Non-Churchgoing Twelve-to-Fifteen-Year-Olds in the UK." *Religious Education* 91, no. 1: 9–21. https://doi.org/10.1080/0034408960910102.

Franck, E., and R. De Raedt. 2007. "Self-esteem Reconsidered: Unstable Self-esteem Outperforms Level of Self-esteem as Vulnerability Marker for Depression." *Behaviour Research and Therapy* 45, no. 7: 1531–1541. https://doi.org/10.1016/j.brat.2007.01.003.

Freeden, M. 2003. *Ideology: A Very Short Introduction (Vol. 95)*. New York: Oxford University Press.

Freeden, M., L. T. Sargent, and M. Stears, eds. 2013. *The Oxford Handbook of Political Ideologies*. New York: Oxford University Press.

Frenkel-Brunswik, E. 1949. "Intolerance of Ambiguity as an Emotional and Perceptual Personality Variable." *Journal of Personality* 18: 108–143. https://doi.org/10.1111/j.1467-6494.1949.tb01236.x.

Friedland, N., G. Keinan, and Y. Regev. 1992. "Controlling the Uncontrollable: Effects of Stress on Illusory Perceptions of Controllability." *Journal of Personality and Social Psychology* 63, no. 6: 923–931. https://doi.org/10.1037/0022-3514.63.6.923.

Friedman, M., and W. S. Rholes. 2007. "Successfully Challenging Fundamentalist Beliefs Results in Increased Death Awareness." *Journal of Experimental Social Psychology* 43, no. 5: 794–801. https://doi.org/10.1016/j.jesp.2006.07.008.

Friesen, J. P., A. C. Kay, R. P. Eibach, and A. D. Galinsky. 2014. "Seeking Structure in Social Organization: Compensatory Control and the Psychological Advantages of Hierarchy." *Journal of Personality and Social Psychology* 106, no. 4: 590–609. https://doi.org/10.1037/a0035620.

Fritsch, P. 2001. "Religious Schools in Pakistan Fill Void—and Spawn Warriors." *Wall Street Journal*, October 2: A1, A24.

Fuchs, T. 2014. "The Virtual Other: Empathy in the Age of Virtuality." *Journal of Consciousness Studies* 21, no. 5–6: 152–173.

Fulton, B. D., R. M. Scheffler, and S. P. Hinshaw. 2015. "State Variation in Increased ADHD Prevalence: Links to NCLB School Accountability and State Medication Laws." *Psychiatric Services* 66, no. 10: 1074–1082. https://doi.org/10.1176/appi.ps.201400145.

Fukuyama, F. 1992. *The End of History and the Last Man* (Reprint 2006). New York: Free Press.

Gächter, S., and E. Fehr. 1999. "Collective Action as a Social Exchange." *Journal of Economic Behavior & Organization* 39, no. 4: 341–369. https://doi.org/10.1016/S0167-2681(99)00045-1.

Gaertner, S. L., and J. F. Dovidio. 1986. "The Aversive Form of Racism." In *Prejudice, Discrimination, and Racism* edited by J. F. Dovidio and S. L. Gaertner, 61–89. Orlando, FL: Academic Press.

Gaertner, L., C. Sedikides, and K. Graetz. 1999. "In Search of Self-definition: Motivational Primacy of the Individual Self, Motivational Primacy of the Collective Self, or Contextual Primacy?" *Journal of Personality and Social Psychology* 76, no. 1: 5–18. https://doi.org/10.1037/0022-3514.76.1.5.

Gaibulloev, K., and T. Sandler. 2019. "What We Have Learned about Terrorism since 9/11." *Journal of Economic Literature* 57, no. 2: 275–328.

Gaibulloev, K., T. Sandler, and C. Santifort. 2012. "Assessing the Evolving Threat of Terrorism." *Global Policy* 3, no. 2: 135–144. https://doi.org/10.1111/j.1758-5899.2011.00142.x.

Galek, K., K. J. Flannelly, C. G. Ellison, N. R. Silton, and K. R. Jankowski. 2015. "Religion, Meaning and Purpose, and Mental Health." *Psychology of Religion and Spirituality* 7, no. 1: 1–12. https://doi.org/10.1037/a0037887.

Gallese, V., C. Keysers, and G. Rizzolatti. 2004. "A Unifying View of the Basis of Social Cognition." *Trends in Cognitive Sciences* 8, no. 9: 396–403. https://doi.org/10.1016/j.tics.2004.07.002.

Gallo, L. C., T. W. Smith, and C. M. Cox. 2006. "Socioeconomic Status, Psychosocial Processes, and Perceived Health: An Interpersonal Perspective." *Annals of Behavioral Medicine* 31, no. 2: 109–119. https://doi.org/10.1207/s15324796abm3102_2.

Gambetta, D. 1993. *The Sicilian Mafia: The Business of Private Protection*. Cambridge: Harvard University Press.

Ganguly, A., and J. Tasoff. 2017. "Fantasy and Dread: The Demand for Information and the Consumption Utility of the Future." *Management Science* 63, no. 12: 4037–4060. https://doi.org/10.1287/mnsc.2016.2550.

Garba, A. G., and P. K. Garba. 2005. "The Nigerian Civil War: Causes and the Aftermath." In *Post-Conflict Economies in Africa*, edited by A. K. Fosu and P. Collier, 91–108. London: Palgrave Macmillan. https://doi.org/10.1057/9780230522732_6.

Gardner, W. L., B. J. Reithel, R. T. Foley, C. C. Cogliser, and F. O. Walumbwa. 2009. "Attraction to Organizational Culture Profiles: Effects of Realistic Recruitment and Vertical and Horizontal Individualism—Collectivism." *Management Communication Quarterly* 22, no. 3: 437–472. https://doi.org/10.1177/0893318908327006.

Garfield, Z. H., C. von Rueden, and E. H. Hagen. 2019. "The Evolutionary Anthropology of Political Leadership." *The Leadership Quarterly* 30, no. 1: 59–80. https://doi.org/10.1016/j.leaqua.2018.09.001.

Gartenstein-Ross, D., N. Barr, and B. Moreng. 2016. "The Islamic State's Global Propaganda Strategy." *The International Centre for Counter-Terrorism—The Hague* 7, no. 1: 1–84. http://doi.org/10.19165/2016.1.01.

Gartenstein-Ross, D., B. Moreng, and K. Soucy. 2014. "Raising the Stakes: Ansar al-Sharia in Tunisia's Shift to Jihad. *The International Centre for Counter-Terrorism—The Hague* 5, no. 3: 1–23. http://dx.doi.org/10.19165/2014.1.03.

Gawronski, B. 2012. "Back to the Future of Dissonance Theory: Cognitive Consistency as a Core Motive." *Social Cognition* 30, no. 6: 652–668. https://doi.org/10.1521/soco.2012.30.6.652.

Geary, R. 2002. *Hitler and Nazism*. New York: Routledge.

Gebhardt, W. A., and J. F. Brosschot. 2002. "Desirability of Control: Psychometric Properties and Relationships with Locus of Control, Personality, Coping, and Mental and Somatic Complaints in Three Dutch Samples." *European Journal of Personality* 16, no. 6: 423–438. https://doi.org/10.1002/per.463.

Gecas, V. 1989. "The Social Psychology of Self-efficacy." *Annual Review of Sociology* 15, no. 1: 291–316. https://doi.org/10.1146/annurev.so.15.080189.001451.

Gelfand, D. M., D. P. Hartmann, C. C. Cromer, C. L. Smith, and B. C. Page. 1975. "The Effects of Instructional Prompts and Praise on Children's Donation Rates." *Child Development* 46, no. 4: 980–983. https://doi.org/10.2307/1128408.

Gelfand, M. J., H. C. Triandis, and D. K. S. Chan. 1996. "Individualism versus Collectivism or versus Authoritarianism?" *European Journal of Social Psychology* 26, no. 3: 397–410. https://doi.org/10.1002/(SICI)1099-0992(199605)26:3<397::AID-EJSP763>3.0.CO;2-J.

Gentry, J. A., and D. E. Spencer. 2010. "Colombia's FARC: A Portrait of Insurgent Intelligence." *Intelligence and National Security* 25, no. 4: 453–478. https://doi.org/10.1080/02684527.2010.537024.

Geoghegan, V., ed. 2003. *Political Ideologies: An Introduction*. 3rd ed. New York: Routledge. https://doi.org/10.4324/9780203402498.

Georgiadou, V. 2013. "Right-wing Populism and Extremism: The Rapid Rise of 'Golden Dawn' in Crisis-ridden Greece." In *Right-wing in Europe*, edited by R. Melzer and S. Serafin, 75–101. Berlin: Friedrich-Ebert Stiftung.

Gerber, A. S., G. A. Huber, D. Doherty, C. M. Dowling, and S. E. Ha. 2010. "Personality and Political Attitudes: Relationships across Issue Domains and Political Contexts." *American Political Science Review* 104, no. 1: 111–133. https://doi.org/10.1017/S000305541000031.

Gerber, J., and L. Wheeler. 2009. "On Being Rejected: A Meta-analysis of Experimental Research on Rejection." *Perspectives on Psychological Science* 4, no. 5: 468–488. https://doi.org/10.1111/j.1745-6924.2009.01158.x.

References

Gerring, J. 1997. "Ideology: A Definitional Analysis." *Political Research Quarterly* 50, no. 4: 957–994. https://doi.org/10.1177/106591299705000412.

Gerstenfeld, P., D. Grant, and C. Chiang. 2003. "Hate Online: A Content Analysis of Extremist Internet Sites." *Analyses of Social Issues and Public Policy* 3, no. 1: 29–44. https://doi.org/10.1111/j.1530-2415.2003.00013.x.

Gethin, A., and M. Morgan. 2018. "Brazil Divided: Hindsights on the Growing Politicisation of Inequality." *WID. World Issue Brief* 3: 1–8.

Giddens, A. 1973. *The Class Structure of the Advanced Societies*. London: Hutchinson.

Giddens, A. 2008. *The Third Way: The Renewal of Social Democracy*. Cambridge, UK: Polity Press.

Gilbert, P. 2001. "Evolution and Social Anxiety. The Role of Attraction, Social Competition, and Social Hierarchies." *The Psychiatric Clinics of North America* 24, no. 4: 51–72. https://doi.org/10.1016/S0193-953X(05)70260-4.

Gill, P., J. Horgan, and P. Deckert. 2014. "Bombing Alone: Tracing the Motivations and Antecedent Behaviors of Lone-actor Terrorists." *Journal of Forensic Sciences* 59, no. 2: 425–435. https://doi.org/10.1111/1556-4029.12312.

Giugni, M., R. Koopmans, F. Passy, and P. Statham. 2005. "Institutional and Discursive Opportunities for Extreme-right Mobilization in Five Countries." *Mobilization: An International Quarterly* 10, no. 1: 145–162. https://doi.org/10.17813/maiq.10.1.n40611874k23l1v7.

Giuliano, P., and A. Spilimbergo. 2008. *Growing Up in Bad Times: Macroeconomic Volatility and the Formation of Beliefs*. Los Angeles, CA: UCLA mimeo.

Glasford, D. E., and J. F. Dovidio. 2011. "E pluribus unum: Dual Identity and Minority Group Members' Motivation to Engage in Contact, as well as Social Change." *Journal of Experimental Social Psychology* 47, no. 5: 1021–1024. https://doi.org/10.1016/j.jesp.2011.03.021.

Gollwitzer, P. M., and G. B. Moskowitz. 1996. "Goal Effects on Action and Cognition." In *Social Psychology: Handbook of Basic Principles*, edited by E. T. Higgins and A. W. Kruglanski, 361–399. New York: Guilford.

Golman, R., and G. Loewenstein. 2018. "Information Gaps: A Theory of Preferences regarding the Presence and Absence of Information." *Decision* 5, no. 3: 143–164. https://doi.org/10.1037/dec0000068.

Golman, R., D. Hagmann, and G. Loewenstein. 2017. "Information Avoidance." *Journal of Economic Literature* 55, no. 1: 96–135. https://doi.org/10.1257/jel.20151245.

Golman, R., G. Loewenstein, K. O. Moene, and L. Zarri. 2016. "The Preference for Belief Consonance." *Journal of Economic Perspectives* 30, no. 3: 165–188. http://dx.doi.org/10.1257/jep.30.3.165.

Gomez, R., L. Morales, and L. Ramiro. 2016. "Varieties of Radicalism: Examining the Diversity of Radical Left Parties and Voters in Western Europe." *West European Politics* 39, no. 2: 351–379. https://doi.org/10.1080/01402382.2015.1064245.

Graham, J., and J. Haidt. 2010. "Beyond Beliefs: Religions Bind Individuals into Moral Communities." *Personality and Social Psychology Review* 14, no. 1: 140–150. https://doi.org/10.1177/1088868309353415.

Graham, J., J. Haidt, and B. A. Nosek. 2009. "Liberals and Conservatives Rely on Different Sets of Moral Foundations." *Journal of Personality and Social Psychology* 96, no. 5: 1029–1046. https://doi.org/10.1037/a0015141.

Graham, S., A. Z. Taylor, and C. Hudley. 1998. "Exploring Achievement Values Among Ethnic Minority Early Adolescents." *Journal of Educational Psychology* 90, no. 4: 606.

Grasmick, H. G., and D. E. Green. 1980. "Legal Punishment, Social Disapproval and Internalization as Inhibitors of Illegal Behavior." *Journal of Criminal Law and Criminology* 71, no. 3: 325–335. https://doi.org/10.2307/1142704.

Green, B. L., L. A. Goodman, J. L. Krupnick, C. B. Corcoran, R. M. Petty, P. Stockton, and N. M. Stern. 2000. "Outcomes of Single versus Multiple Trauma Exposure in a Screening Sample." *Journal of Traumatic Stress* 13, no. 2: 271–286. https://doi.org/10.1023/A:1007758711939.

Green, D. R. 2014. "A New Strategy to Defeat Al-Qaeda in Yemen." *Orbis* 58, no. 4: 521–539. https://doi.org/10.1016/j.orbis.2014.08.005.

Greenaway, K. H., S. A. Haslam, T. Cruwys, N. R. Branscombe, R. Ysseldyk, and C. Heldreth. 2015. "From 'We' to 'Me': Group Identification Enhances Perceived Personal Control with Consequences for Health and Well-being." *Journal of Personality and Social Psychology* 109, no. 1: 53. https://doi.org/10.1037/pspi0000019.

Greenberg, J., and T. Pyszczynski. 1985. "Compensatory Self-inflation: A Response to the Threat to Self-regard of Public Failure." *Journal of Personality and Social Psychology* 49, no. 1: 273–280. https://doi.org/10.1037/0022-3514.49.1.273.

Greene, J. D. 2007. "Why are VMPFC Patients More Utilitarian?: A Dual-process Theory of Moral Judgment Explains." *Trends in Cognitive Sciences* 11, no. 8: 322–323. https://doi.org/10.1016/j.tics.2007.06.004.

Greene, J. D., L. E. Nystrom, A. D. Engell, J. M. Darley, and J. D. Cohen. 2004. "The Neural Bases of Cognitive Conflict and Control in Moral Judgment." *Neuron* 44, no. 2: 389–400. https://doi.org/10.1016/j.neuron.2004.09.027.

Greenier, K. D., M. H. Kernis, and S. B. Waschull. 1995. "Not All High (or Low) Self-Esteem People Are the Same." In *Efficacy, Agency, and Self-Esteem*, edited by M. H. Kernis, 51–71. Boston, MA: Springer. https://doi.org/10.1007/978-1-4899-1280-0_4.

Greenwald, A. G., C. T. Smith, N. Sriram, Y. Bar-Anan, and B. A. Nosek. 2009. "Implicit Race Attitudes Predicted Vote in the 2008 US Presidential Election." *Analyses of Social Issues and Public Policy* 9, no. 1: 241–253. https://doi.org/10.1111/j.1530-2415.2009.01195.x.

Grenier, S., A. M. Barrette, and R. Ladouceur. 2005. "Intolerance of Uncertainty and Intolerance of Ambiguity: Similarities and Differences." *Personality and Individual Differences* 39, no. 3: 593–600. https://doi.org/10.1016/j.paid.2005.02.014.

Grenier, Y. 1991. "Understanding the FMLN: A Glossary of Five Words." *Journal of Conflict Studies* 11, no. 2: 51–5.

Gries, T., V. Mueller, J. T. Jost. 2022. "The Market for Belief Systems: A Formal Model of Ideological Choice." *Psychological Inquiry* 33, no. 2: 65–83. https://doi.org/10.1080/1047840X.2022.2065128.

Griffin, R. 2018. *Fascism*. Cambridge, UK: Polity Press.

Gross, A. 2012. *Reaching Wa'y: Mobilization and Recruitment in Hizb Al-Tahrir Al-Islami. A Case Study Conducted in Beirut (Vol. 20)*. Berlin: Klaus Schwarz Verlag.

Gross, N., T. Medvetz, and R. Russell. 2011. "The Contemporary American Conservative Movement." *Annual Review of Sociology* 37: 325–354. https://doi.org/10.1146/annurev-soc-081309-150050.

Gruen, M. 2006. "Innovative Recruitment and Indoctrination Tactics by Extremists: Video Games, Hip-Hop, and the World Wide Web." In *The Making of a Terrorist: Recruitment, Training, and Root Causes*, edited by J. J. F. Forest, 11–22. Westport, CT: Praeger.

Gruenewald, T. L., M. E. Kemeny, N. Aziz, and J. L. Fahey. 2004. "Acute Threat to the Social Self: Shame, Social Self-esteem, and Cortisol Activity." *Psychosomatic Medicine* 66, no. 6: 915–924. https://doi.org/10.1097/01.psy.0000143639.61693.ef.

Gubler, J. R., and J. S. Selway. 2012. "Horizontal Inequality, Crosscutting Cleavages, and Civil War." *Journal of Conflict Resolution* 56, no. 2: 206–232. https://doi.org/10.1177/0022002711431416.

Gump, B. B., K. A. Matthews, and K. Räikkönen. 1999. "Modeling Relationships among Socioeconomic Status, Hostility, Cardiovascular Reactivity, and Left Ventricular Mass in African American and White Children." *Health Psychology* 18, no. 2: 140–150. https://doi.org/10.1037/0278-6133.18.2.140.

Gunaratna, R., and A. Oreg. 2010. "Al Qaeda's Organizational Structure and Its Evolution." *Studies in Conflict & Terrorism* 33, no. 12: 1043–1078. https://doi.org/10.1080/1057610X.2010.523860.

Gurr, T. R. 1970. "Sources of Rebellion in Western Societies: Some Quantitative Evidence." *Annals of the American Academy of Political and Social Science* 391, no. 1: 128–144.

Gurr, T. R. 1970. *Why Men Rebel*. Princeton, NJ: Princeton University Press.

Gus, M. 2011. *The Sage Encyclopedia of Terrorism*. 2nd ed. Thousand Oaks, CA: SAGE Publications.

Gutierrez Sanın, F., and E. J. Wood. 2014. "Ideology in Civil War: Instrumental Adoption and Beyond." *Journal of Peace Research* 51, no. 2: 213–226. https://doi.org/10.1177/0022343313514073.

Gutsell, J. N., and M. Inzlicht. 2010. "Empathy Constrained: Prejudice Predicts Reduced Mental Simulation of Actions during Observation of Outgroups." *Journal of Experimental Social Psychology* 46, no. 5: 841–845. https://doi.org/10.1016/j.jesp.2010.03.011.

Gvineria, G. 2009. "How Does Terrorism End?" In *Social Science for Counterterrorism*, edited by P. K. Davis and K. Cragin, 257–291. Santa Monica, CA: RAND Corporation.

Hadden, J. 2015. *Networks in Contention*. Cambridge: Cambridge University Press. https://doi.org/10.1017/CBO9781316105542.

Hagendoorn, L. 1995. "Intergroup Biases in Multiple Group Systems: The Perception of Ethnic Hierarchies." *European Review of Social Psychology* 6, no. 1: 199–228. https://doi.org/10.1080/14792779443000058.

Haidt, J., and J. Graham. 2007. "When Morality Opposes Justice: Conservatives Have Moral Intuitions that Liberals May Not Recognize." *Social Justice Research* 20, no. 1: 98–116. https://doi.org/10.1007/s11211-007-0034-z.

Haidt, J., J. Graham, and C. Joseph. 2009. "Above and Below Left–Right: Ideological Narratives and Moral Foundations." *Psychological Inquiry* 20, no. 2–3: 110–119. https://doi.org/10.1080/10478400903028573.

Halvorsen, K. 2002. *Solidarity and the Legitimacy of the Welfare State: Attitudes to Abuse of Welfare Benefits in Scandinavian Countries*. Florence: COST13 Working Group II Meeting.

Hamilton, D. L. 1981. "Stereotyping and Intergroup Behavior: Some Thoughts on the Cognitive Approach." In *Cognitive Processes in Stereotyping and Intergroup Behavior*, edited by D. L. Hamilton, 333–353. Hillsdale, NJ: Erlbaum.

Hamlin, J. K., K. Wynn, and P. Bloom. 2007. "Social Evaluation by Preverbal Infants." *Nature* 450, no. 7169: 557–559. https://doi.org/10.1038/nature06288.

Handler, J. S. 1990. "Socioeconomic Profile of an American Terrorist: 1960s and 1970s." *Terrorism* 13, no. 3: 195–213. https://doi.org/10.1080/10576109008435831.

Hanley, E. 2003. "A Party of Workers or a Party of Intellectuals? Recruitment into Eastern European Communist Parties, 1945–1988." *Social Forces* 81, no. 4: 1073–1105. https://doi.org/10.1353/sof.2003.0056.

Hansen, D. M., and N. Jessop. 2017. "A Context for Self-Determination and Agency: Adolescent Developmental Theories." In *Development of Self-Determination Through the Life-Course*, edited by M. Wehmeyer, K. Shogren, T. Little and S. Lopez, 27–46. Dordrecht: Springer. https://doi.org/10.1007/978-94-024-1042-6_3.

Hare, R. D. 1999. "Psychopathy as a Risk Factor for Violence." *Psychiatric Quarterly* 70, no. 3: 181–197. https://doi.org/10.1023/A:1022094925150.

Harris, L. T., and S. T. Fiske. 2006. "Dehumanizing the Lowest of the Low: Neuroimaging Responses to Extreme Out-groups." *Psychological Science* 17, no. 10: 847–853. https://doi.org/10.1111/j.1467-9280.2006.01793.x.

Harrison, N. A., T. Singer, P. Rotshtein, R. J. Dolan, and H. D. Critchley. 2006. "Pupillary Contagion: Central Mechanisms Engaged in Sadness Processing." *Social Cognitive and Affective Neuroscience* 1, no. 1: 5–17. https://doi.org/10.1093/scan/nsl006.

Hargreaves Heap, S. H. 2001. "Expressive Rationality: Is Self- Worth Just Another Kind of Preference?" In *The Economic World View*, edited by U. Mäki, 98–113. Cambridge: Cambridge University Press.

Hartling, L. 2007. "Humiliation: Real Pain, a Pathway to Violence." *RBSE* 6: 276–290.

Haslam, C., A. Holme, S. A. Haslam, A. Iyer, J. Jetten, and W. H. Williams. 2008. "Maintaining Group Memberships: Social Identity Continuity Predicts Well-being After Stroke." *Neuropsychological Rehabilitation* 18, no. 5–6: 671–691. https://doi.org/10.1080/0960201070 1643449.

Haslam, N. 2006. "Dehumanization: An Integrative Review." *Personality and Social Psychology Review* 10, no. 3: 252–264. https://doi.org/10.1207/s15327957pspr1003_4.

Haslam, N., and A. Pedersen. 2007. "Attitudes Towards Asylum Seekers: The Psychology of Prejudice and Exclusion." In Yearning to Breathe Free: Seeking Asylum in Australia, edited by D. Lusher and N. Haslam, 208–218. Sydney: Federation Press.

Haslam, S. A., J. Jetten, T. Postmes, and C. Haslam. 2009. "Social Identity, Health and Wellbeing: An Emerging Agenda for Applied Psychology." *Applied Psychology* 58, no. 1: 1–23. https://doi.org/10.1111/j.1464-0597.2008.00379.x.

Hastings, P. D., K. E. McShane, R. Parker, and F. Ladha. 2007. "Ready to Make Nice: Parental Socialization of Young Sons' and Daughters' Prosocial Behaviors with Peers." *Journal of Genetic Psychology* 168, no. 2: 177–200. https://doi.org/10.3200/GNTP.168.2.177-200.

Hastings, P. D., K. H. Rubin, and L. DeRose. 2005. "Links among Gender, Inhibition, and Parental Socialization in the Development of Prosocial Behavior." *Merrill-Palmer Quarterly* 51, no. 4: 467–493. https://doi.org/10.1353/mpq.2005.0023.

Hatemi, P. K., and R. McDermott. 2012. "The Genetics of Politics: Discovery, Challenges, and Progress." *Trends in Genetics* 28, no. 10: 525–533. https://doi.org/10.1016/j.tig.2012.07.004.

Hatemi, P. K., S. E. Medland, R. Klemmensen, S. Oskarsson, L. Littvay, C. T. Dawes, . . . and N. G. Martin. 2014. "Genetic Influences on Political Ideologies: Twin Analyses of 19 Measures of Political Ideologies from Five Democracies and Genome-wide Findings from Three Populations." *Behavior Genetics* 44, no. 3: 282–294. https://doi.org/10.1007/s10519-014-9648-8.

Hauge, W., and T. Ellingsen. 1998. "Beyond Environmental Scarcity: Causal Pathways to Conflict." *Journal of Peace Research* 35, no. 3: 299–317. https://doi.org/10.1177/00223433 98035003003.

Headey, B., R. Muffels, and G. G. Wagner. 2010. "Long-running German Panel Survey Shows that Personal and Economic Choices, Not Just Genes, Matter for Happiness." *Proceedings of the National Academy of Sciences* 107, no. 42: 17922–17926. https://doi.org/10.1073/pnas.1008612107.

Heath, J. 2000. "Ideology, Irrationality and Collectively Self-defeating Behavior." *Constellations* 7, no. 3: 363–371. https://doi.org/10.1111/1467-8675.00193.

Hegre, H., J. Karlsen, H. M. Nygård, H. Strand, and H. Urdal. 2013. "Predicting Armed Conflict, 2010–2050." *International Studies Quarterly* 57, no. 2: 250–270. https://doi.org/10.1111/isqu.12007.

Heidelberg Institute for International Conflict Research. 2019. "Conflict Barometer 2018." https://hiik.de/konfliktbarometer/bisherige-ausgaben/.

Heidelberg Institute for International Conflict Research. 2020. "Conflict Barometer 2019." https://hiik.de/konfliktbarometer/bisherige-ausgaben/.

Heine, S. J., and D. R. Lehman. 1997. "Culture, Dissonance, and Self-affirmation." *Personality and Social Psychology Bulletin* 23, no. 4: 389–400. https://doi.org/10.1177/014616729 7234005.

Heinke, D. H. 2017. "German Foreign Fighters in Syria and Iraq: The Updated Data and Its Implications." *CTC Sentinel* 10, no. 3: 17–22.

Heitmeyer, W. 1991. "Politische Orientierungen bei westdeutschen Jugendlichen und die Risiken von deutsch-deutschen Vergleichsuntersuchungen." In *Aufwachsen hüben und *drüben*, edited by Peter Büchner, Heinz-Hermann Krüger, 243–253. Wiesbaden: VS Verlag für Sozialwissenschaften.

Heitmeyer, W. 2003. "Right-Wing Extremist Violence." In *International Handbook of Violence Research*, edited by W. Heitmeyer and J. Hagan, 399–436. Dordrecht: Springer. https://doi.org/10.1007/978-0-306-48039-3_22.

Heitmeyer, W. 2005a. "Gruppenbezogene Menschenfeindlichkeit. Die theoretische Konzeption und empirische Ergebnisse aus 2002, 2003 und 2004." In *Deutsche Zustände (Vol. 3)*, edited by W. Heitmeyer, 13–34. Dordrecht: Springer.

Heitmeyer, W. 2005b. "Right-wing Terrorism." In *Root Causes of Terrorism*, edited by T. Bjørgo, 141–153. London: Routledge.

Hellbeck, J. 2009. "Galaxy of Black Stars: The Power of Soviet Biography." *The American Historical Review* 114, no. 3: 615–624. https://doi.org/10.1086/ahr.114.3.xvi.

Hellmann-Rajanayagam, D. 1994. *The Tamil Tigers: Armed Struggle for Identity*. Stuttgart: Franz Steiner Verlag.

Hellström, A., O. C. Norocel, and M. B. Jørgensen. 2020. "Nostalgia and Hope: Narrative Master Frames Across Contemporary Europe." In *Nostalgia and Hope: Intersections between Politics of Culture, Welfare, and Migration in Europe*, edited by O. Norocel, A. Hellström, and M. Jørgensen, 1–16. Cham: Springer. https://doi.org/10.1007/978-3-030-41694-2_1.

Hendrix, C., and H. J. Brinkman. 2013. "Food Insecurity and Conflict Dynamics: Causal Linkages and Complex Feedbacks." *Stability: International Journal of Security and Development* 2, no. 2: 26. http://doi.org/10.5334/sta.bm.

Henry, P. J., and A. Saul. 2006. "The Development of System Justification in the Developing World." *Social Justice Research* 19, no. 3: 365–378. https://doi.org/10.1007/s11211-006-0012-x.

Heppner, W. L., C. A. Spears, J. I. Vidrine, and D. W. Wetter. 2015. "Mindfulness and Emotion Regulation." In *Handbook of Mindfulness and Self-regulation*, edited by B. Ostafin, M. Robinson, and B. Meier, 107–120. New York: Springer. https://doi.org/10.1007/978-1-4939-2263-5_9.

Hermans, H. J., and G. Dimaggio. 2007. "Self, Identity, and Globalization in Times of Uncertainty: A Dialogical Analysis." *Review of General Psychology* 11, no. 1: 31–61. https://doi.org/10.1037/1089-2680.11.1.31.

Hertel, A. W. 2017. "Sources of Self-Concept Clarity." In *Self-Concept Clarity*, edited by J. Lodi-Smith and K. DeMarree, 43–66. Cham: Springer. https://doi.org/10.1007/978-3-319-71547-6_3.

Heywood, A. 2015. *Political Theory: An Introduction*. New York: Macmillan International Higher Education.

Heywood, A. 2017. *Political Ideologies: An Introduction*. New York: Macmillan International Higher Education.

Heywood, A. 2003. *Political Ideologies*. 3rd ed. New York: Macmillan.

Hick, J. 2006. *The New Frontier Of Religion And Science: Religious Experience, Neuroscience, and the Transcendent*. Boston: Springer.

HIIK. 2018. https://hiik.de/download/conflict-barometer-2018/.

Hill, P. 2014. "The Japanese Yakuza." In *The Oxford Handbook of Organized Crime*, edited by L. Paoli, 234–253. New York: Oxford University Press. https://doi.org/10.1093/oxfordhb/9780199730445.013.027.

Hindriks, P., M. Verkuyten, and M. Coenders. 2014. "Dimensions of Social Dominance Orientation: The Roles of Legitimizing Myths and National Identification." *European Journal of Personality* 28, no. 6: 538–549. https://doi.org/10.1002/per.1955.

Hinkle, S., and R. Brown. 1990. "Intergroup Comparisons and Social Identity: Some Links and Lacunae." In *Social Identity Theory: Constructive and Critical Advances*, edited by D. Abrams, and M. A. Hogg, 48–70. New York: Springer Verlag.

Hinshaw, S. P. 2018. "Attention Deficit Hyperactivity Disorder (ADHD): Controversy, Developmental Mechanisms, and Multiple Levels of Analysis." *Annual Review of Clinical Psychology* 14: 291–316. https://doi.org/10.1146/annurev-clinpsy-050817-084917.

Hirschfeld, L. A. 1996. *Race in the Making: Cognition, Culture, and the Child's Construction of Human Kinds*. Cambridge, MA: MIT Press. https://doi.org/10.2307/2654625.

Hirshleifer, J. 1994. "The Dark Side of the Force." *Economic Inquiry* 32: 1–10. https://doi.org/10.1111/j.1465-7295.1994.tb01309.x.

Hixson, W. L. 2008. *The Myth of American Diplomacy*. New Haven, CT: Yale University Press.

Ho, A. K., J. Sidanius, N. S. Kteily, J. Sheehy-Skeffington, F. Pratto, K. E. Henkel, . . . A. L. Stewart. 2015. "The Nature of Social Dominance Orientation: Theorizing and Measuring Preferences for Intergroup Inequality Using the New SDO7 Scale." *Journal of Personality and Social Psychology* 109, no. 6: 1003. https://doi.org/10.1037/pspi0000033.

Ho, A. K., J. Sidanius, F. Pratto, S. Levin, L. Thomsen, N. Kteily, and J. Sheehy-Skeffington. 2012. "Social Dominance Orientation Revisiting the Structure and Function of a Variable Predicting Social and Political Attitudes." *Personality and Social Psychology Bulletin* 38, no. 5: 583–606. https://doi.org/10.1177/0146167211432765.

Hoffman, M. L. 1987. "The Contribution of Empathy to Justice and Moral Judgment." In *Empathy and Its Development*, edited by N. Eisenberg and J. Strayer, 47–80. New York: Cambridge University Press.

Hoffman, M. L. 2008. "Empathy and Prosocial Behavior." In *Handbook of Emotions*, edited by M. Lewis, J. M. Haviland-Jones, and L. F. Barrett, 440–455. New York: Guilford Press.

Hogan, R. 1969. "Development of an Empathy Scale." *Journal of Consulting and Clinical Psychology* 33, no. 3: 307–316. https://doi.org/10.1037/h0027580.

Hogg, M. A. 2000. "Social Identity and Social Comparison." In *Handbook of Social Comparison*, edited by J. Suls and L. Wheeler, 401–421. Boston, MA: Springer. https://doi.org/10.1007/978-1-4615-4237-7_19.

Hogg, M. A. 2004. "Social Categorization, Depersonalization, and Group Behavior." In *Self and Social Identity*, edited by M. B. Brewer and M. Hewstone, 203–231. London: Blackwell Publishing.

Hogg, M. A. 2007. "Uncertainty–Identity Theory." *Advances in Experimental Social Psychology* 39: 69–126. https://doi.org/10.1016/S0065-2601(06)39002-8.

Hogg, M. A. 2010. "Human Groups, Social Categories, and Collective Self: Social Identity and the Management of Self-uncertainty." In *Handbook of the Uncertain Self*, edited by R. M. Arkin, K. C. Oleson, and P. J. Carroll, 401–420. Hove, East Sussex: Psychology Press.

Hogg, M. A. 2014. "From Uncertainty to Extremism: Social Categorization and Identity Processes." *Current Directions in Psychological Science* 23, no. 5: 338–342. https://doi.org/10.1177/0963721414540168.

Hogg, M. A. 2016. "Social Identity Theory." In *Understanding Peace and Conflict Through Social Identity Theory*, edited by S. McKeown, R. Haji and N. Ferguson, 3–17. Cham: Springer. https://doi.org/10.1007/978-3-319-29869-6_1.

Hogg, M. A., and J. Adelman. 2013. "Uncertainty–Identity Theory: Extreme Groups, Radical Behavior, and Authoritarian Leadership." *Journal of Social Issues* 69, no. 3: 436–454. https://doi.org/10.1111/josi.12023.

Hogg, M. A., J. R. Adelman, and R. D. Blagg. 2010. "Religion in the Face of Uncertainty: An Uncertainty-Identity Theory Account of Religiousness." *Personality and Social Psychology Review* 14, no. 1: 72–83. https://doi.org/10.1177/1088868309349692.

Hogg, M. A., C. Meehan, and J. Farquharson. 2010. "The Solace of Radicalism: Self-uncertainty and Group Identification in the Face of Threat." *Journal of Experimental Social Psychology* 46, no. 6: 1061–1066. https://doi.org/10.1016/j.jesp.2010.05.005.

Hogg, M. A., D. K. Sherman, J. Dierselhuis, A. T. Maitner, and G. Moffitt. 2007. "Uncertainty, Entitativity, and Group Identification." *Journal of Experimental Social Psychology* 43, no. 1: 135–142. https://doi.org/10.1016/j.jesp.2005.12.008.

Hohman, Z. P., and M. A. Hogg. 2015. "Fearing the Uncertain: Self-uncertainty Plays a Role in Mortality Salience." *Journal of Experimental Social Psychology* 57: 31–42. https://doi.org/10.1016/j.jesp.2014.11.007.

References

Holländer, H. 1990. "A Social Exchange Approach to Voluntary Cooperation." *The American Economic Review* 80, no. 5: 1157–1167. https://www.jstor.org/stable/2006767.

Holmes, J. S., and S. A. G. De Piñeres. 2011. "Conflict-induced Displacement and Violence in Colombia." *Studies in Conflict & Terrorism* 34, no. 7: 572–586. https://doi.org/10.1080/1057610X.2011.578552.

Homer-Dixon, T. 1999. *Environment, Scarcity, and Violence*. Princeton, NJ: Princeton University Press.

Homer-Dixon, T. F. 1994. "Environmental Scarcities and Violent Conflict: Evidence from Cases." *International Security* 19, no. 1: 5–40. https://doi.org/10.2307/2539147.

Homer-Dixon, T., and J. Blitt, eds. 1998. *Ecoviolence: Links among Environment, Population, and Security*. New York: Rowman & Littlefield Publishers.

Hood Jr, R. W., P. C. Hill, and B. Spilka. 2018. *The Psychology of Religion: An Empirical Approach*. New York: Guilford Publications.

Horgan, J. 2003. "The Search for the Terrorist Personality." In *Terrorists, Victims and Society: Psychological Perspectives on Terrorism and Its Consequences*, edited by A. Silke, 3–27. Chichester, UK: John Wiley & Sons Ltd.

Hornsey, M. J. 2008. "Social Identity Theory and Self-categorization Theory: A Historical Review." *Social and Personality Psychology Compass* 2, no. 1: 204–222. https://doi.org/10.1111/j.1751-9004.2007.00066.x.

Horowitz, M. C. 2010. "Nonstate Actors and the Diffusion of Innovations: The Case of Suicide Terrorism." *International Organization* 64, no. 1: 33–64. https://doi.org/10.1017/S0020818309990233.

Howell, R. T., and G. Hill. 2009. "The Mediators of Experiential Purchases: Determining the Impact of Psychological Needs Satisfaction and Social Comparison." *Journal of Positive Psychology* 4, no. 6: 511–522. https://doi.org/10.1080/17439760903270993.

Howell, R. T., M. Kurai, and L. Tam. 2013. "Money Buys Financial Security and Psychological Need Satisfaction: Testing Need Theory in Affluence." *Social Indicators Research* 110, no. 1: 17–29. https://doi.org/10.1007/s11205-010-9774-5.

HRW. 2018. "World Report 2018: Central African Republic." Human Rights Watch. https://www.hrw.org/world-report/2018/country-chapters/central-african-republic.

Hsu, M., M. Bhatt, R. Adolphs, D. Tranel, and C. F. Camerer. 2005. "Neural Systems Responding to Degrees of Uncertainty in Human Decision-making." *Science* 310, no. 5754: 1680–1683. https://doi.org/10.1126/science.1115327.

Huddy, L., and S. Feldman. 2011. "Americans Respond Politically to 9/11: Understanding the Impact of the Terrorist Attacks and Their Aftermath." *American Psychologist* 66, no. 6: 455. https://doi.org/10.1037/a0024894.

Hudson, D. L., H. W. Neighbors, A. T. Geronimus, and J. S. Jackson. 2016. "Racial Discrimination, John Henryism, and Depression among African Americans." *Journal of Black Psychology* 42, no. 3: 221–243. https://doi.org/10.1177/0095798414567757.

Huettel, S. A., and R. E. Kranton. 2012. "Identity Economics and the Brain: Uncovering the Mechanisms of Social Conflict." *Philosophical Transactions of the Royal Society B: Biological Sciences* 367, no. 1589: 680–691. https://doi.org/10.1098/rstb.2011.0264.

Huettel, S. A., C. J. Stowe, E. M. Gordon, B. T. Warner, and M. L. Platt. 2006. "Neural Signatures of Economic Preferences for Risk and Ambiguity." *Neuron* 49, no. 5: 765–775. https://doi.org/10.1016/j.neuron.2006.01.024.

Hui, E. K. P., R. C. Sun, S. S.-Y. Chow, and M. H.-T. Chu. 2011. "Explaining Chinese Students' Academic Motivation: Filial Piety and Self-determination." *Educational Psychology* 31, no. 3: 377–392. https://doi.org/10.1080/01443410.2011.559309.

Humphreys, M. 2005. "Natural Resources, Conflict, and Conflict Resolution: Uncovering the Mechanisms." *Journal of Conflict Resolution* 49, no. 4: 508–537. https://doi.org/10.1177/0022002705277545.

Hunt, T. 2005. *The Politics of Bones: Dr. Owens Wiwa and the Struggle for Nigeria's Oil.* Toronto: McClelland & Stewart.

Hunter, W., and T. J. Power. 2019. "Bolsonaro and Brazil's Illiberal Backlash." *Journal of Democracy* 30, no. 1: 68–82. https://doi.org/10.1353/jod.2019.0005.

Huntington, S. P. 1996. "The West Unique, Not Universal." *Foreign Affairs* 75, no. 6: 28–46.

Hur, Y. M., and J. P. Rushton. 2007. "Genetic and Environmental Contributions to Prosocial Behaviour in 2-to 9-Year-Old South Korean Twins." *Biology Letters* 3, no. 6: 664–666. https://doi.org/10.1098/rsbl.2007.0365.

Hurlemann, R., A. Patin, O. A. Onur, M. X. Cohen, T. Baumgartner, S. Metzler, I. Dziobek, J. Gallinat, M. Wagner, W. Maier, and K. M. Kendrick. 2010. "Oxytocin Enhances Amygdala-dependent, Socially Reinforced Learning and Emotional Empathy in Humans." *Journal of Neuroscience* 30, no. 14: 4999–5007. https://doi.org/10.1523/JNEUROSCI.5538-09.2010.

Hutter, S., and H. Kriesi. 2013. "Movements of the Left, Movements of the Right Reconsidered." In *The Future of Social Movement Research: Dynamics, Mechanisms, and Processes,* edited by J. von Stekelenburg, C. Roggeband, and B. Klandermans, 281–298. Minneapolis: University of Minnesota Press. https://doi.org/10.5749/minnesota/9780816686513.003.0016.

Iannaccone, L. R. 1992. "Sacrifice and Stigma: Reducing Free-riding in Cults, Communes, and Other Collectives." *Journal of Political Economy* 100, no. 2: 271–291. https://doi.org/10.1086/261818.

Iannaccone, L. R. 1994. "Why Strict Churches are Strong." *American Journal of Sociology* 99, no. 5: 1180–1211. https://doi.org/10.1086/230409.

Iannaccone, L. R. 2012. "Extremism and the Economics of Religion." *Economic Record* 88, no. s1: 110–115. https://doi.org/10.1111/j.1475-4932.2012.00803.x.

Iannaccone, L. R., and E. Berman. 2006. "Religious Extremism: The Good, the Bad, and the Deadly." *Public Choice* 128, no. 1: 109–129. https://doi.org/10.1007/s11127-006-9047-7.

Idemudia, U. 2009. "Oil Extraction and Poverty Reduction in the Niger Delta: A Critical Examination of Partnership Initiatives." *Journal of Business Ethics* 90, no. 1: 91–116. https://doi.org/10.1007/s10551-008-9916-8.

Idemudia, U. 2012. "The Resource Curse and the Decentralization of Oil Revenue: The Case of Nigeria." *Journal of Cleaner Production* 35: 183–193. https://doi.org/10.1016/j.jclepro.2012.05.046.

Ikelegbe, A. 2005. "The Economy of Conflict in the Oil Rich Niger Delta Region of Nigeria." *Nordic Journal of African Studies* 14, no. 2: 208–234. https://doi.org/10.53228/njas.v14i2.276.

Ilardi, G. J. 2009. "The 9/11 Attacks—A Study of Al Qaeda's Use of Intelligence and Counterintelligence." *Studies in Conflict & Terrorism* 32, no. 3: 171–187. https://doi.org/10.1080/10576100802670803.

Ilgen, M., J. McKellar, and Q. Tiet. 2005. "Abstinence Self-efficacy and Abstinence 1 Year After Substance Use Disorder Treatment." *Journal of Consulting and Clinical Psychology* 73, no. 6: 1175–1180. https://doi.org/10.1037/0022-006X.73.6.1175.

Inglehart, R. 1977. "Values, Objective Needs, and Subjective Satisfaction among Western Publics." *Comparative Political Studies* 9, no. 4: 429–458. https://doi.org/10.1177/001041407700900403.

Inglehart, R., and W. E. Baker. 2000. "Modernization, Cultural Change, and the Persistence of Traditional Values." *American Sociological Review* 65, no. 1: 19–51. https://doi.org/10.2307/2657288.

Inglehart, R., and D. Oyserman. 2004. "Individualism, Autonomy, Self-expression: The Human Development Syndrome." In *Comparing Cultures,* edited by H. Vinken, J. Soeters, and P. Ester, 73–96. Leiden: Brill. https://doi.org/10.1163/9789047412977_008.

Isaksson, A. S., and A. Lindskog. 2007. "Preferences for Redistribution—A Cross-country Study in Fairness." *Working Papers in Economics* 258: 1–37.

476 References

Ivtzan, I., C. P. Chan, H. E. Gardner, and K. Prashar. 2013. "Linking Religion and Spirituality with Psychological Well-being: Examining Self-actualisation, Meaning in Life, and Personal Growth Initiative." *Journal of Religion and Health* 52, no. 3: 915–929. https://doi.org/10.1007/s10943-011-9540-2.

Izuma, K., and R. Adolphs. 2013. "Social Manipulation of Preference in the Human Brain." *Neuron* 78, no. 3: 563–573. https://doi.org/10.1016/j.neuron.2013.03.023.

Izuma, K., D. N. Saito, and N. Sadato. 2010. "Processing of the Incentive for Social Approval in the Ventral Striatum during Charitable Donation." *Journal of Cognitive Neuroscience* 22, no. 4: 621–631. https://doi.org/10.1162/jocn.2009.21228.

Jackson, B. 2013. "Social Democracy." In *The Oxford Handbook of Political Ideologies*, edited by M. Freeden, T. L.Sargent, and M. Stears, 175–196. Oxford: Oxford University Press. http://dx.doi.org/10.1093/oxfordhb/9780199585977.013.007.

Jackson, P. L., A. N. Meltzoff, and J. Decety. 2005. "How Do We Perceive the Pain of Others? A Window into the Neural Processes Involved in Empathy." *NeuroImage* 24, no. 3: 771–779. https://doi.org/10.1016/j.neuroimage.2004.09.006.

Jackson, S. 2019. "A Schema of Right-wing Extremism in the United States." International Centre for Counter-Terrorism. https://doi.org/10.19165/2019.2.06.

Janoff-Bulman, R. 1992. *Shattered Assumptions: Towards a New Psychology of Trauma.* New York: Free Press.

Janssen M. C. W. 2008. "Microfoundations." In *The New Palgrave Dictionary of Economics*, edited by S. N. Durlauf and L. E. Blume. London: Palgrave Macmillan. https://doi.org/10.1007/978-1-349-58802-2_1093.

Jarjoura, G. R., and R. Triplett. 1997. "The Effects of Social Area Characteristics on the Relationship between Social Class and Delinquency." *Journal of Criminal Justice* 25, no. 2: 125–139. https://doi.org/10.1016/S0047-2352(96)00056-6.

Jasko, K., G. LaFree, and A. Kruglanski. 2017. "Quest for Significance and Violent Extremism: The Case of Domestic Radicalization." *Political Psychology* 38, no. 5: 815–831. https://doi.org/10.1111/pops.12376.

Jenkins, J. C. 1981. "Sociopolitical Movements." In *The Handbook of Political Behavior*, edited by S. L. Long, 81–135. Boston, MA: Springer. https://doi.org/10.1007/978-1-4684-3878-9_2.

Jenkins, R. 2008. *Rethinking Ethnicity*. London: Sage Publications. https://doi.org/10.4135/9781446214855.

Jenssen, A. T., and H. Engesbak. 1994. "The Many Faces of Education: Why Are People with Lower Education More Hostile towards Immigrants than People with Higher Education?" *Scandinavian Journal of Educational Research* 38, no. 1: 33–50. https://doi.org/10.1080/0031383940380103.

Jetten, J., N. R. Branscombe, M. T. Schmitt, and R. Spears. 2001. "Rebels With a Cause: Group Identification as a Response to Perceived Discrimination from the Mainstream." *Personality and Social Psychology Bulletin* 27, no. 9: 1204–1213. https://doi.org/10.1177/0146167201279012.

Jewell, A. 2010. "The Importance of Purpose in Life in an Older British Methodist Sample: Pastoral Implications." *Journal of Religion, Spirituality & Aging* 22, no. 3: 138–161. https://doi.org/10.1080/15528030903321170.

Johnson, H., and A. Thompson. 2008. "The Development and Maintenance of Post-traumatic Stress Disorder (PTSD) in Civilian Adult Survivors of War Trauma and Torture: A Review." *Clinical Psychology Review* 28, no. 1: 36–47. https://doi.org/10.1016/j.cpr.2007.01.017.

Johnson, J. G., P. Cohen, B. P. Dohrenwend, B. G. Link, and J. S. Brook. 1999. "A Longitudinal Investigation of Social Causation and Social Selection Processes Involved in the Association between Socioeconomic Status and Psychiatric Disorders." *Journal of Abnormal Psychology* 108, no. 3: 490–499. https://doi.org/10.1037/0021-843X.108.3.490.

Jonas, E., S. Schulz-Hardt, D. Frey, and N. Thelen. 2001. "Confirmation Bias in Sequential Information Search After Preliminary Decisions: An Expansion of Dissonance Theoretical Research on Selective Exposure to Information." *Journal of Personality and Social Psychology* 80, no. 4: 557–571. https://doi.org/10.1037/0022-3514.80.4.557.

Jones, R. M., L. H. Somerville, J. Li, E. J. Ruberry, V. Libby, G. Glover, H. U. Voss, D. J. Ballon, and B. J. Casey. 2011. "Behavioral and Neural Properties of Social Reinforcement Learning." *Journal of Neuroscience* 31, no. 37: 13039–13045. https://doi.org/10.1523/JNEUROSCI.2972-11.2011.

Jones, S. G. 2018. "The Rise of Far-Right Extremism in the United States." *CSIS Briefs*. https://www.csis.org/analysis/rise-far-right-extremism-unitedstates.

Jones, S. G., and M. C. Libicki. 2008. *How Terrorist Groups End: Lessons for Countering Al Qa'ida*. Santa Monica: RAND Cooperation.

Joseph, S., and P. A. Linley, eds. 2008. *Trauma, Recovery, and Growth: Positive Psychological Perspectives on Posttraumatic Stress*. Hoboken, NJ: John Wiley & Sons.

Jost, J. T. 1995. "Negative Illusions: Conceptual Clarification and Psychological Evidence Concerning False Consciousness." *Political Psychology* 16, no. 2: 397–424. https://doi.org/10.2307/3791837.

Jost, J. T. 2006. "The End of the End of Ideology." *American Psychologist* 61, no. 7: 651. https://doi.org/10.1037/0003-066X.61.7.651.

Jost, J. T. 2009. "'Elective Affinities': On the Psychological Bases of Left–Right Differences." *Psychological Inquiry* 20, no. 2–3: 129–141. https://doi.org/10.1080/10478400903028599.

Jost, J. T. 2017. "Ideological Asymmetries and the Essence of Political Psychology." *Political Psychology* 38, no. 2: 167–208. https://doi.org/10.1111/pops.12407.

Jost, J. T. 2021. *Left & Right: The Psychological Significance of a Political Distinction*. New York: Oxford University Press.

Jost, J. T., and D. M. Amodio. 2012. "Political Ideology as Motivated Social Cognition: Behavioral and Neuroscientific Evidence." *Motivation and Emotion* 36, no. 1: 55–64. https://doi.org/10.1007/s11031-011-9260-7.

Jost, J. T., and O. Hunyady. 2005. "Antecedents and Consequences of System-justifying Ideologies." *Current Directions in Psychological Science* 14, no. 5: 260–265. https://doi.org/10.1111/j.0963-7214.2005.00377.x.

Jost, J. T., M. R. Banaji, and B. A. Nosek. 2004. "A Decade of System Justification Theory: Accumulated Evidence of Conscious and Unconscious Bolstering of the Status Quo." *Political Psychology* 25, no. 6: 881–919. https://doi.org/10.1111/j.1467-9221.2004.00402.x.

Jost, J. T., V. Chaikalis-Petritsis, D. Abrams, J. Sidanius, J. Van Der Toorn, and C. Bratt. 2012. "Why Men (and Women) Do and Don't Rebel: Effects of System Justification on Willingness to Protest." *Personality and Social Psychology Bulletin* 38, no. 2: 197–208. https://doi.org/10.1177/0146167211422544.

Jost, J. T., C. M. Federico, and J. L. Napier. 2009. "Political Ideology: Its Structure, Functions, and Elective Affinities." *Annual Review of Psychology* 60, no. 1: 307–337. https://doi.org/10.1146/annurev.psych.60.110707.163600.

Jost, J. T., C. M. Federico, and J. L. Napier. 2013. "Political Ideologies and Their Social Psychological Functions." In *The Oxford Handbook of Political Ideologies*, edited by M. Freeden, T. L. Sargent, and M. Stears, 232–250. Oxford: Oxford University Press.

Jost, J. T., J. Glaser, F. Sulloway, and A. W. Kruglanski. 2003. "Political Conservatism as Motivated Social Cognition." *Psychological Bulletin* 129: 339–375. https://doi.org/10.1037/0033-2909.129.3.339.

Jost, J. T., J. L. Napier, H. Thorisdottir, S. D. Gosling, T. P. Palfai, and B. Ostafin. 2007. "Are Needs to Manage Uncertainty and Threat Associated with Political Conservatism or Ideological Extremity?" *Personality and Social Psychology Bulletin* 33, no. 7: 989–1007. https://doi.org/10.1177/0146167207301028.

References

Jost, J. T., B. A. Nosek, and S. D. Gosling. 2008. "Ideology: Its Resurgence in Social, Personality, and Political Psychology." *Perspectives on Psychological Science* 3, no. 2: 126–136. https://doi.org/10.1111/j.1745-6916.2008.00070.x.

Jost, J. T., C. Stern, N. O. Rule, and J. Sterling. 2017. "The Politics of Fear: Is There an Ideological Asymmetry in Existential Motivation?" *Social Cognition* 35, no. 4: 324–353. https://doi.org/10.1521/soco.2017.35.4.324.

Jowitt, K. 1992. *New World Disorder: The Leninist Extinction*. Berkeley: University of California Press. https://doi.org/10.1525/9780520913783.

Jugert, P., J. C. Cohrs, and J. Duckitt. 2009. "Inter- and Intrapersonal Processes Underlying Authoritarianism: The Role of Social Conformity and Personal Need for Structure." *European Journal of Personality* 23, no. 7: 607–621. https://doi.org/10.1002/per.735.

Jung, J. H. 2015. "Sense of Divine Involvement and Sense of Meaning in Life: Religious Tradition as a Contingency." *Journal for the Scientific Study of Religion* 54, no. 1: 119–133. https://doi.org/10.1111/jssr.12170.

Kaddor, L. 2017. "Vom Klassenzimmer in den Heiligen Krieg–Warum Jugendliche islamistische Fundamentalisten werden." In *Salafismus in Deutschland*, edited by Ahmet Toprak and Gerrit Weitzel, 91–102. Wiesbaden: Springer Fachmedien Wiesbaden. https://doi.org/10.1007/978-3-658-15097-6_6.

Kahan, D. M. 2014. "Making Climate-science Communication Evidence-based: All the Way Down." *Culture, Politics and Climate Change*, edited by Deserai Crow and Maxwell Boykoff, 203–220. Routledge https://doi.org/10.1111/pops.12244.

Kahan, D. M. 2012. "Ideology, Motivated Reasoning, and Cognitive Reflection: An Experimental Study." *Judgment and Decision Making* 8, no. 4: 407–424. http://doi.org/10.2139/ssrn.2182588.

Kahan, D. M., D. Braman, J. Gastil, P. Slovic, and C. K. Mertz. 2007. "Culture and Identity-protective Cognition: Explaining the White-male Effect in Risk Perception." *Journal of Empirical Legal Studies* 4, no. 3: 465–505. https://doi.org/10.1111/j.1740-1461.2007.00097.x.

Kahl, C. H. 2006. *States, Scarcity, and Civil Strife in the Developing World*. Princeton, NJ: Princeton University Press. https://doi.org/10.1515/9780691188379.

Kaiser, C. R., and C. T. Miller. 2001. "Stop Complaining! The Social Costs of Making Attributions to Discrimination." *Personality and Social Psychology Bulletin* 27, no. 2: 254–263. https://doi.org/10.1177/0146167201272010.

Kakkar, H., and N. Sivanathan. 2017. "When the Appeal of a Dominant Leader is Greater than a Prestige Leader." *Proceedings of the National Academy of Sciences* 114, no. 26: 6734–6739. https://doi.org/10.1073/pnas.161771111.

Kallis, A. A. 2004. "Studying Inter-war Fascism in Epochal and Diachronic Terms: Ideological Production, Political Experience and the Quest for 'Consensus.'" *European History Quarterly* 34, no. 1: 9–42. https://doi.org/10.1177/0265691404040007.

Kanagaratnam, P., M. Raundalen, and A. E. Asbjørnsen. 2005. "Ideological Commitment and Posttraumatic Stress in Former Tamil Child Soldiers." *Scandinavian Journal of Psychology* 46, no. 6: 511–520. https://doi.org/10.1111/j.1467-9450.2005.00483.x.

Kandler, C., W. Bleidorn, and R. Riemann. 2012. "Left or Right? Sources of Political Orientation: The Roles of Genetic Factors, Cultural Transmission, Assortative Mating, and Personality." *Journal of Personality and Social Psychology* 102, no. 3: 633. https://doi.org/10.1037/a0025560.

Kaplan, D. E., and A. Dubro. 2012. *Yakuza: Japan's Criminal Underworld*. Berkeley: University of California Press. https://doi.org/10.1525/9780520953819.

Karl, T. L. 2007. "Ensuring Fairness: The Case for a Transparent Fiscal Social Contract." In *Escaping the Resource Curse*, edited by M. Humphreys, J. D. Sachs, and J. E. Stiglitz, 256–285. New York: Columbia University Press.

Karsh, N., and B. Eitam. 2015. "I Control Therefore I Do: Judgments of Agency Influence Action Selection." *Cognition* 138: 122–131. https://doi.org/10.1016/j.cognition.2015.02.002.

Kasser, T. 2002. *The High Price of Materialism*. Cambridge, MA: MIT Press.

Kasser, T. 2009. "Psychological Need Satisfaction, Personal Well-being, and Ecological Sustainability." *Ecopsychology* 1, no. 4: 175–180. https://doi.org/10.1089/eco.2009.0025.

Kassim, A. 2015. "Defining and Understanding the Religious Philosophy of Jihādī-Salafism and the Ideology of Boko Haram." *Politics, Religion & Ideology* 16, no. 2–3: 173–200. https://doi.org/10.1080/21567689.2015.1074896.

Kater, M. H. 2006. *Hitler Youth*. Cambridge, MA: Harvard University Press.

Katsiaficas, G. N. 1987. *The Imagination of the New Left: A Global Analysis of 1968*. Cambridge, MA: South End Press.

Kay, A. C., and R. P. Eibach. 2013. "Compensatory Control and Its Implications for Ideological Extremism." *Journal of Social Issues* 69, no. 3: 564–585. https://doi.org/10.1111/josi.12029.

Kay, A. C., and J. Friesen. 2011. "On Social Stability and Social Change: Understanding When System Justification Does and Does Not Occur." *Current Directions in Psychological Science* 20, no. 6: 360–364. https://doi.org/10.1177/0963721411422059.

Kay, A. C., and J. T. Jost. 2003. "Complementary Justice: Effects of 'Poor but Happy' and 'Poor but Honest' Stereotype Exemplars on System Justification and Implicit Activation of the Justice Motive." *Journal of Personality and Social Psychology* 85, no. 5: 823–837. https://doi.org/10.1037/0022-3514.85.5.823.

Kay, A. C., D. Gaucher, J. L. Napier, M. J. Callan, and K. Laurin. 2008. "God and the Government: Testing a Compensatory Control Mechanism for the Support of External Systems." *Journal of Personality and Social Psychology* 95, no. 1: 18–35. https://doi.org/10.1037/0022-3514.95.1.18.

Kay, A. C., D. Gaucher, J. M. Peach, K. Laurin, J. Friesen, M. P. Zanna, and S. J. Spencer. 2009. "Inequality, Discrimination, and the Power of the Status Quo: Direct Evidence for a Motivation to See the Way Things Are as the Way They Should Be." *Journal of Personality and Social Psychology* 97, no. 3: 421–434. https://doi.org/10.1037/a0015997.

Kay, A. C., J. A. Whitson, D. Gaucher, and A. D. Galinsky. 2009. "Compensatory Control: Achieving Order through the Mind, Our Institutions, and the Heavens." *Current Directions in Psychological Science* 18, no. 5: 264–268. https://doi.org/10.1111/j.1467-8721.2009.01649.x.

Keeley, M. C. 1977. "The Economics of Family Formation." *Economic Inquiry* 15, no. 2: 238–250. https://doi.org/10.1111/j.1465-7295.1977.tb00468.x.

Kelly, R. J. 1999. *The Upperworld and the Underworld: Case Studies of Racketeering and Business Infiltrations in the United States*. New York, NY: Springer. https://doi.org/10.1007/978-1-4615-4883-6.

Kelly, C., and S. Breinlinger. 1996. *The Social Psychology of Collective Action: Identity, Injustice and Gender*. New York: Taylor & Francis US.

Kelman, H. C. 2008. "Reconciliation from a Social-psychological Perspective." In The Social Psychology of Intergroup Reconciliation, edited by A. Nadler, T. E. Malloy, and J. D. Fisher, 15–32. New York: Oxford University Press https://doi.org/10.1093/acprof:oso/9780195300314.003.0002.

Kenny, P. D. 2010. "Structural Integrity and Cohesion in Insurgent Organizations: Evidence from Protracted Conflicts in Ireland and Burma." *International Studies Review* 12, no. 4: 533–555. https://doi.org/10.1111/j.1468-2486.2010.00959.x.

Kernberg, O. 1975. *Borderline Conditions and Pathological Narcissism*. New York: Jason Aronson.

Kernis, M. H. 1995. "Efficacy, Agency, and Self-Esteem." In *Efficacy, Agency, and Self-Esteem*, edited by M. H. Kernis, 237–253. Boston, MA: Springer. https://doi.org/10.1007/978-1-4899-1280-0_12.

References

Kernis, M. H. 2005. "Measuring Self-esteem in Context: The Importance of Stability of Self-esteem in Psychological Functioning." *Journal of Personality* 73, no. 6: 1569–1605. https://doi.org/10.1111/j.1467-6494.2005.00359.x.

Kernis, M. H., ed. 2006. *Self-esteem Issues and Answers: A Sourcebook of Current Perspectives*. New York: Psychology Press. https://doi.org/10.4324/9780203759745.

Kernis, M. H., B. D. Grannemann, and L. C. Barclay. 1989. "Stability and Level of Self-esteem as Predictors of Anger Arousal and Hostility." *Journal of Personality and Social Psychology* 56, no. 6: 1013–1022. https://doi.org/10.1037/0022-3514.56.6.1013.

Kertzer, J. D. 2017. "Microfoundations in International Relations." *Conflict Management and Peace Science* 34, no. 1: 81–97.

Keysers, C., and V. Gazzola. 2007. "Integrating Simulation and Theory of Mind: From Self to Social Cognition." *Trends in Cognitive Sciences* 11, no. 5: 194–196. https://doi.org/10.1016/j.tics.2007.02.002.

Khalil, E. L. 2010. "The Bayesian Fallacy: Distinguishing Internal Motivations and Religious Beliefs from Other Beliefs." *Journal of Economic Behavior & Organization* 75, no. 2: 268–280. https://doi.org/10.1016/J.JEBO.2010.04.004.

Khalil, E. L. 2011. "Rational, Normative and Procedural Theories of Beliefs: Can They Explain Internal Motivations?" *Journal of Economic Issues* 45, no. 3: 641–664. https://doi.org/10.2753/JEI0021-3624450307.

Kibria, N. 2008. "The 'New Islam' and Bangladeshi Youth in Britain and the US." *Ethnic and Racial Studies* 31, no. 2: 243–266. https://doi.org/10.1080/01419870701337593.

Kiesler, S. B. 1973. "Preference for Predictability or Unpredictability as a Mediator of Reactions to Norm Violations." *Journal of Personality and Social Psychology* 27, no. 3: 354–359. https://doi.org/10.1037/h0034934.

Killen, M., and F. B. de Waal. 2000. "Development of Morality." In *Natural Conflict Resolution*, edited by F. Aureli and F. B. M. de Waal, 352–372. University of California Press.

King, V., and G. H. Elder Jr. 1998. "Perceived Self-efficacy and Grandparenting." *The Journals of Gerontology Series B: Psychological Sciences and Social Sciences* 53, no. 5: S249–S257. https://doi.org/10.1093/geronb/53B.5.S249.

Kirsch, P., C. Esslinger, Q. Chen, D. Mier, S. Lis, S. Siddhanti, H. Gruppe, V. S. Mattay, B. Gallhofer, and A. Meyer-Lindenberg. 2005. "Oxytocin Modulates Neural Circuitry for Social Cognition and Fear in Humans." *Journal of Neuroscience* 25, no. 49: 11489–11493. https://doi.org/10.1523/JNEUROSCI.3984-05.2005.

Kirsch, P., A. Schienle, R. Stark, G. Sammer, C. Blecker, B. Walter, U. Otta, J. Burkart, and D. Vaitl. 2003. "Anticipation of Reward in a Nonaversive Differential Conditioning Paradigm and the Brain Reward System: An Event-related fMRI Study." *NeuroImage* 20, no. 2: 1086–1095. https://doi.org/10.1016/S1053-8119(03)00381-1.

Klafter, A. 2015. "Greed, Greediness and Greedy Patients." In Greed: Developmental, Cultural, and Clinical Realms, edited by S. Akhtar, chapter 9, 179–206. New York: Routledge.

Klandermans, B. 2002. "How Group Identification Helps to Overcome the Dilemma of Collective Action." *American Behavioral Scientist* 45, no. 5: 887–900. https://doi.org/10.1177/0002764202045005009.

Klandermans, B. 2013. "The Dynamics of Demand." In *The Future of Social Movement Research: Dynamics, Mechanisms, and Processes*, edited by J. von Stekelenburg, C. Roggeband and B. Klandermans, 3–16. Minneapolis: University of Minnesota Press. https://doi.org/10.5749/minnesota/9780816686513.003.0001.

Klare, M. T. 2001. *Resource Wars: The New Landscape of Global Conflict*. New York: Metropolitan Books.

Klimecki, O. M., S. V. Mayer, A. Jusyte, J. Scheeff, and M. Schönenberg. 2016. "Empathy Promotes Altruistic Behavior in Economic Interactions." *Scientific Reports* 6, no. 1: 1–5. https://doi.org/10.1038/srep31961.

Klinger, E. 2012. "The Search for Meaning in Evolutionary Goal-theory Perspective and Its Clinical Implications." In *The Human Quest for Meaning: Theories, Research, and Application*, 2nd ed., edited by P. T. P. Wong, 23–56. New York, NY: Routledge; Taylor & Francis.

Kluegel, J. R., and D. S. Mason. 2004. "Fairness Matters: Social Justice and Political Legitimacy in Post-communist EUROPE." *Europe-Asia Studies* 56, no. 6: 813–834. https://doi.org/10.1080/0966813042000258051.

Kluegel, J. R., and P. M. Smith. 1986. *Beliefs about Inequality: Americans' Views of What is and What Ought To Be*. Hawthorne, NY: Aldine de Gruyter.

Kluegel, J. R., D. S. Mason, and B. Wegener, eds. 1995. *Social Justice and Political Change. Public Opinion in Capitalist and Post-Communist States*. New York: Aldine De Gruyter. https://doi.org/10.1515/9783110868944.

Kly, Y. N. 1998. "The Meaning of Racism: Societal Proclivity to Conflict." *The Black Scholar* 28, no. 2: 48–58. https://doi.org/10.1080/00064246.1998.11430915.

Knafo, A., C. Zahn-Waxler, C. Van Hulle, J. L. Robinson, and S. H. Rhee. 2008. "The Developmental Origins of a Disposition toward Empathy: Genetic and Environmental Contributions." *Emotion* 8, no. 6: 737–752. https://doi.org/10.1037/a0014179.

Knapton, H. 2014. "The Recruitment and Radicalisation of Western Citizens: Does Ostracism have a Role in Homegrown Terrorism?" *Journal of European Psychology Students* 5, no. 1: 38–48. http://doi.org/10.5334/jeps.bo.

Knight, K. 2006. "Transformations of the Concept of Ideology in the Twentieth Century." *American Political Science Review* 100, no. 4: 619–626. https://doi.org/10.1080/00064246.1998.11430915.

Knowles, M. L., G. M. Lucas, D. C. Molden, W. L. Gardner, and K. K. Dean. 2010. "There's No Substitute for Belonging: Self-affirmation Following Social and Nonsocial Threats." *Personality and Social Psychology Bulletin* 36, no. 2: 173–186. https://doi.org/10.1177/0146167209346860.

Knutson, J. N. 1974. *Psychological Variables in Political Recruitment: An Analysis of Party Activists*. Berkeley, CA: Wright Institute.

Knutson, K. M., J. N. Wood, M. V. Spampinato, and J. Grafman. 2006. "Politics on the Brain: An fMRI Investigation." *Social Neuroscience* 1, no. 1: 25–40. https://doi.org/10.1080/17470910600670603.

Koch, A. 2018. "Trends in Anti-Fascist and Anarchist Recruitment and Mobilization." *Journal for Deradicalization* 14: 1–51.

Koehler, D. 2016. "Right-wing Extremism and Terrorism in Europe." *Prism* 6, no. 2: 84–105. https://www.jstor.org/stable/26470450.

Koehler, D. 2019. "Anti-Immigration Militias and Vigilante Groups in Germany." In *Vigilantism against Migrants and Minorities*, edited by T. Bjørgo and M. Mareš, 86–103. New York: Taylor & Francis.

Kohut, H. 1971. *The Analysis of the Self: A Systematic Approach to the Psychoanalytic Treatment of Narcissistic Personality Disorders*. New York: International Universities Press.

Kohut, H. 1984. *How Does Analysis Cure?* Chicago: University of Chicago Press.

Kolář, P. 2012. "The Party as a New Utopia: Reshaping Communist Identity after Stalinism." *Social History* 37, no. 4: 402–424. https://doi.org/10.1080/03071022.2012.732734.

Koomen, W., and J. Van Der Pligt. 2016. *The Psychology of Radicalization and Terrorism*. London: Routledge. https://doi.org/10.4324/9781315771984.

Koopmans, R. 2013. "Multiculturalism and Immigration: A Contested Field in Cross-national Comparison." *Annual Review of Sociology* 39: 147–169. https://doi.org/10.1146/annurev-soc-071312-145630.

Koopmans, R. 2014. "Religious Fundamentalism and Out-group Hostility among Muslims and Christians in Western Europe." (No. SP VI 2014-101). WZB Discussion Paper.

Koopmans, R. 2015. "Religious Fundamentalism and Hostility against Out-groups: A Comparison of Muslims and Christians in Western Europe." *Journal of Ethnic and Migration Studies* 41, no. 1: 33–57. https://doi.org/10.1080/1369183X.2014.935307.

Koopmans, R., and S. Olzak. 2004. "Discursive Opportunities and the Evolution of Right-wing Violence in Germany." *American journal of Sociology* 110, no. 1: 198–230. https://doi.org/10.1086/386271.

Kőszegi, B. 2010. "Utility from Anticipation and Personal Equilibrium." *Economic Theory* 44, no. 3: 415–444. https://doi.org/10.1007/s00199-009-0465-x.

Koubi, V., and T. Böhmelt. 2014. "Grievances, Economic Wealth, and Civil Conflict." *Journal of Peace Research* 51, no. 1: 19–33. https://doi.org/10.1177/0022343313500501.

Krämer, B. 2017. "Populist Online Practices: The Function of the Internet in Right-wing Populism." *Information, Communication & Society* 20, no. 9: 1293–1309. https://doi.org/10.1080/1369118X.2017.1328520.

Krause, N. 2011. "Religion and Health: Making Sense of a Disheveled Literature." *Journal of Religion and Health* 50, no. 1: 20–35. https://doi.org/10.1007/s10943-010-9373-4.

Krause, N. 2015. "Assessing the Relationships among Race, Religion, Humility, and Self-forgiveness: A Longitudinal Investigation." *Advances in Life Course Research* 24: 66–74. https://doi.org/10.1016/j.alcr.2015.02.003.

Krauss, S. W. 2002. "Romanian Authoritarianism 10 Years After Communism." *Personality and Social Psychology Bulletin* 28, no. 9: 1255–1264. https://doi.org/10.1177/01461672022812010.

Krieger, T., and D. Meierrieks. 2011. "What Causes Terrorism?" *Public Choice* 147, no. 1: 3–27. https://doi.org/10.1007/s11127-010-9601-1.

Krueger, A. B., and J. Malečková. 2003. "Education, Poverty and Terrorism: Is There a Causal Connection?" *Journal of Economic Perspectives* 17, no. 4: 119–144. https://doi.org/10.1257/089533003772034925.

Kruglanski, A. W., and T. Freund. 1983. "The Freezing and Unfreezing of Lay-inferences: Effects on Impressional Primacy, Ethnic Stereotyping, and Numerical Anchoring." *Journal of Experimental Social Psychology* 19, no. 5: 448–468. https://doi.org/10.1016/0022-1031(83)90022-7.

Kruglanski, A. W., and G. Shteynberg. 2012. "Cognitive Consistency as Means to an End: How Subjective Logic Affords Knowledge." In *Cognitive Consistency: A Fundamental Principle in Social Cognition*, edited by B. Gawronski and F. Strack, 245–264. New York: Guilford Press.

Kruglanski, A. W., M. J. Gelfand, J. J. Bélanger, A. Sheveland, M. Hetiarachchi, and R. Gunaratna. 2014. "The Psychology of Radicalization and Deradicalization: How Significance Quest Impacts Violent Extremism." *Political Psychology* 35, no. S1: 69–93. https://doi.org/10.1111/pops.12163.

Kunovich, R. M. 2004. "Social Structural Position and Prejudice: An Exploration of Cross-national Differences in Regression Slopes." *Social Science Research* 33, no. 1: 20–44. https://doi.org/10.1016/S0049-089X(03)00037-1.

Kuppens, T., and R. Spears. 2014. "You Don't Have to Be Well-educated to Be an Aversive Racist, but It Helps." *Social Science Research* 45: 211–223. https://doi.org/10.1016/j.ssresearch.2014.01.006.

Küpper, B., C. Wolf, and A. Zick. 2010. "Social Status and Anti-immigrant Attitudes in Europe: An Examination from the Perspective of Social Dominance Theory." *International Journal of Conflict and Violence* 4, no. 2: 205–219. https://doi.org/10.4119/ijcv-2826.

Kurzban, R., P. DeScioli, and E. O'Brien. 2007. "Audience Effects on Moralistic Punishment." *Evolution and Human Behavior* 28, no. 2: 75–84. https://doi.org/10.1016/j.evolhumbehav.2006.06.001.

Lambert, N. M., T. F. Stillman, J. A. Hicks, S. Kamble, R. F. Baumeister, and F. D. Fincham. 2013. "To Belong is to Matter: Sense of Belonging Enhances Meaning in Life." *Personality* and *Social Psychology Bulletin* 39, no. 11: 1418–1427. https://doi.org/10.1177/0146167213499186.

Lammers, J., A. Koch, P. Conway, and M. J. Brandt. 2017. "The Political Domain Appears Simpler to the Politically Extreme than to Political Moderates." *Social Psychological and Personality Science* 8, no. 6: 612–622. https://doi.org/10.1177/1948550616678456.

Landau, M. J., J. Greenberg, and D. Sullivan. 2009. "Defending a Coherent Autobiography: When Past Events Appear Incoherent, Mortality Salience Prompts Compensatory Bolstering of the Past's Significance and the Future's Orderliness." *Personality and Social Psychology Bulletin* 35, no. 8: 1012–1020. https://doi.org/10.1177/0146167209336608.

Landon Jr., E. L. 1974. "Self Concept, Ideal Self Concept, and Consumer Purchase Intentions." *Journal of Consumer Research* 1, no. 2: 44–51. https://doi.org/10.1086/208590.

Langer, A., and G. K. Brown. 2008. "Cultural Status Inequalities: An Important Dimension of Group Mobilization." In *Horizontal Inequalities and Conflict*, edited by F. Stewart, 41–53. London: Palgrave Macmillan. https://doi.org/10.1057/9780230582729_3.

Langford, D. J., S. E. Crager, Z. Shehzad, S. B. Smith, S. G. Sotocinal, J. S. Levenstadt, M. L. Chanda, D. J. Levitin, and J. S. Mogil. 2006. "Social Modulation of Pain as Evidence for Empathy in Mice." *Science* 312, no. 5782: 1967–1970. https://doi.org/10.1126/science.1128322.

Langman, L. 2006. "The Social Psychology of Nationalism: To Die for the Sake of Strangers." In *The SAGE Handbook of Nations and Nationalism*, edited by G. Delanty and K. Kumar, 66–83. London: SAGE Publications Ltd. https://dx.doi.org/10.4135/9781848608061.n7.

Larrick, R. P. 1993. "Motivational Factors in Decision Theories: The Role of Self-protection." *Psychological Bulletin* 113, no. 3: 440–450. https://doi.org/10.1037/0033-2909.113.3.440.

Larsen, S. 2007. "The Anti-immigration Movement: From Shovels to Suits." *NACLA Report on the Americas* 40, no. 3: 14–18. https://doi.org/10.1080/10714839.2007.11722307.

Latin American Public Opinion Project (LAPOP). 2016–2017. Americas Barometer. https://www.vanderbilt.edu/lapop/ab2016.php.

Laurin, K., A. C. Kay, and D. A. Moscovitch. 2008. "On the Belief in God: Towards an Understanding of the Emotional Substrates of Compensatory Control." *Journal of Experimental Social Psychology* 44, no. 6: 1559–1562. https://doi.org/10.1016/j.jesp.2008.07.007.

Lauriola, M., R. Foschi, O. Mosca, and J. Weller. 2016. "Attitude toward Ambiguity: Empirically Robust Factors in Self-report Personality Scales." *Assessment* 23, no. 3: 353–373. https://doi.org/10.1177/1073191115577188.

Laustsen, L., and M. B. Petersen. 2016. "Winning Faces Vary by Ideology: How Nonverbal Source Cues Influence Election and Communication Success in Politics." *Political Communication* 33, no. 2: 188–211. https://doi.org/10.1080/10584609.2015.1050565.

Laustsen, L., and M. B. Petersen. 2017. "Perceived Conflict and Leader Dominance: Individual and Contextual Factors behind Preferences for Dominant Leaders." *Political Psychology* 38, no. 6: 1083–1101. https://doi.org/10.1111/pops.12403.

Laustsen, L., and M. B. Petersen. 2017. "Perceived Conflict and Leader Dominance: Individual and Contextual Factors Behind Preferences for Dominant Leaders." *Political Psychology* 38, no. 6: 1083–1101. https://doi.org/10.1111/pops.12403.

Leader Maynard, J. 2019. "Ideology and Armed Conflict." *Journal of Peace Research* 56, no. 5: 635–649. https://doi.org/10.1177/0022343319826629.

Le Billon, P. 2001. "The Political Ecology of War: Natural Resources and Armed Conflicts." *Political Geography* 20, no. 5: 561–584. https://doi.org/10.1016/S0962-6298(01)00015-4.

Leary, M. R., and R. F. Baumeister. 2000. "The Nature and Function of Self-esteem: Sociometer Theory." In *Advances in Experimental Social Psychology (Vol. 32)*, edited by M. P. Zanna, 1–62. San Diego: Academic Press. https://doi.org/10.1016/S0065-2601(00)80003-9.

Leary, M. R., and G. MacDonald. 2003. "Individual Differences in Self-esteem: A Review and Theoretical Integration." In *Handbook of Self and Identity*, edited by M. R. Leary and J. P. Tangney, 401–418. New York: The Guilford Press.

Leary, M. R., C. A. Cottrell, and M. Phillips. 2001. "Deconfounding the Effects of Dominance and Social Acceptance on Self-esteem." *Journal of Personality and Social Psychology* 81, no. 5: 898–909. https://doi.org/10.1037/0022-3514.81.5.898.

Leary, M. R., K. M. Kelly, C. A. Cottrell, and L. S. Schreindorfer. 2013. "Construct Validity of the Need to Belong Scale: Mapping the Nomological Network." *Journal of Personality Assessment* 95, no. 6: 610–624. https://doi.org/10.1080/00223891.2013.819511.

Leary, M. R., R. M. Kowalski, L. Smith, and S. Phillips. 2003. "Teasing, Rejection, and Violence: Case Studies of the School Shootings." *Aggressive Behavior* 29, no. 3: 202–214. https://doi.org/10.1002/ab.10061.

Ledyard, J. O. 1995. "Is There a Problem with Public Goods Provision." In *The Handbook of Experimental Economics*, edited by J. H. Kagel and A. E. Roth, 111–194. Princeton, NJ: Princeton University Press.

Lee, E. J. 2014. "The Relationship between Unstable Self-esteem and Aggression: Differences in Reactive and Proactive Aggression." *Journal of Early Adolescence* 34, no. 8: 1075–1093. https://doi.org/10.1177/0272431613518973.

Lee, R. M., and S. B. Robbins. 1998. "The Relationship between Social Connectedness and Anxiety, Self-esteem, and Social Identity." *Journal of Counseling Psychology* 45, no. 3: 338–345. https://doi.org/10.1037/0022-0167.45.3.338.

Leech, G. 2011. *The FARC: The Longest Insurgency*. London, UK: Bloomsbury Publishing. https://doi.org/10.5040/9781350223127.

Leininger, M. M. 1984. *Care: The Essence of Nursing and Health*. Thorofare, NJ: Charles B. Slack.

Leotti, L. A., C. Cho, and M. R. Delgado. 2015. "The Neural Basis Underlying the Experience of Control in the Human Brain." In *The Sense of Agency*, edited by P. Haggard and B. Eitam, 145–176. Oxford, UK: Oxford University Press. https://doi.org/10.1093/acprof:oso/9780190267278.003.0006.

Leotti, L. A., S. S. Iyengar, and K. N. Ochsner. 2010. "Born to Choose: The Origins and Value of the Need for Control." *Trends in Cognitive Sciences* 14, no. 10: 457–463. https://doi.org/10.1016/j.tics.2010.08.001.

Levitsky, S., and K. M. Roberts. 2011. *The Resurgence of the Latin American Left*. Baltimore: JHU Press.

Levy, I., J. Snell, A. J. Nelson, A. Rustichini, and P. W. Glimcher. 2010. "Neural Representation of Subjective Value Under Risk and Ambiguity." *Journal of Neurophysiology* 103, no. 2: 1036–1047. https://doi.org/10.1152/jn.00853.2009.

Levy, S. J. 1981. "Interpreting Consumer Mythology: A Structural Approach to Consumer Behavior." *Journal of Marketing* 45, no. 3: 49–61. https://doi.org/10.1177/002224298104500304.

Li, C. 2009. "The Chinese Communist Party: Recruiting and Controlling the New Elites." *Journal of Current Chinese Affairs* 38, no. 3: 13–33. https://doi.org/10.1177/186810260903800302.

Licata, L., M. Sanchez-Mazas, and E. G. Green. 2011. "Identity, Immigration, and Prejudice in Europe: A Recognition Approach." In *Handbook of Identity Theory and Research*, edited by S. Schwartz, K. Luyckx, and V. Vignoles, 895–916. New York: Springer. https://doi.org/10.1007/978-1-4419-7988-9_38.

Lichter, S. R., and S. Rothman. 1982. "The Radical Personality: Social Psychological Correlates of New Left Ideology." *Political Behavior* 4, no. 3: 207–235. https://doi.org/10.1007/BF00990106.

Lieberman, M. D. 2007. "Social Cognitive Neuroscience: A Review of Core Processes." *Annual Review of Psychology* 58: 259–289. https://doi.org/10.1146/annurev.psych.58.110405.085654.

Light, A. E., and P. S. Visser. 2013. "The Ins and Outs of the Self: Contrasting Role Exits and Role Entries as Predictors of Self-concept Clarity." *Self and Identity* 12, no. 3: 291–306. https://doi.org/10.1080/15298868.2012.667914.

Linde, J. 2012. "Why Feed the Hand that Bites You? Perceptions of Procedural Fairness and System Support in Post-communist Democracies." *European Journal of Political Research* 51, no. 3: 410–434. https://doi.org/10.1111/j.1475-6765.2011.02005.x.
Lister, C. 2014. "Profiling the Islamic state." Brookings Doha Center Analysis Paper (No. 13). Washington DC: The Brookings Institution.
Little, L. M., B. L. Simmons, and D. L. Nelson. 2007. "Health among Leaders: Positive and Negative Affect, Engagement and Burnout, Forgiveness and Revenge." *Journal of Management Studies* 44, no. 2: 243–260. https://doi.org/10.1111/j.1467-6486.2007.00687.x.
Little, T. D., W. A. Cunningham, G. Shahar, and K. F. Widaman. 2002. "To Parcel or Not to Parcel: Exploring the Question, Weighing the Merits." *Structural Equation Modeling* 9, no. 2: 151–173. https://doi.org/10.1207/S15328007SEM0902_1.
Lo Verso, G., and G. Lo Coco. 2004. "Working With Patients Involved in the Mafia: Considerations From Italian Psychotherapy Experiences." *Psychoanalytic Psychology* 21, no. 2: 171–182. https://doi.org/10.1037/0736-9735.21.2.171.
Loadenthal, M. 2013. "The Earth Liberation Front: A Movement Analysis." *Radical Criminology* 2: 15–46.
Loadenthal, M. 2018. "Leftist Political Violence: From Terrorism to Social Protest." In *Terrorism in America*, edited by R. M. Valeri and K. Borgeson, 36–74. New York: Routledge.
Locke, J. 1690. "An Essay on Human Understanding." http://www.ilt.columbia.edu/projects/digitexts/locke/understanding/title.html.
Lodi-Smith, J., and K. G. DeMarree, eds. 2017. *Self-Concept Clarity: Perspectives on Assessment, Research, and Applications*. Cham: Springer. https://doi.org/10.1007/978-3-319-71547-6.
Lodi-Smith, J., and E. Crocetti. 2017. "Self-concept Clarity Development across the Lifespan." In *Self-Concept Clarity*, edited by J. Lodi-Smith and K. G. DeMarree, 67–84). Cham: Springer. https://doi.org/10.1007/978-3-319-71547-6_4.
Lodi-Smith, J., A. C. Geise, B. W. Roberts, and R. W. Robins. 2009. "Narrating Personality Change." *Journal of Personality and Social Psychology* 96, no. 3: 679–689. https://doi.org/10.1037/a0014611.
Long, D. E. 1990. *The Anatomy of Terrorism*. New York: Free Press.
Lott, B. 2002. "Cognitive and Behavioral Distancing from the Poor." *American Psychologist* 57, no. 2: 100–110. https://doi.org/10.1037/0003-066X.57.2.100.
Lott, B. 2012. "The Social Psychology of Class and Classism." *American Psychologist* 67, no. 8: 650–658. https://doi.org/10.1037/a0029369.
Lott, B. 2016. "Relevance to Psychology of Beliefs about Socialism: Some New Research Questions." *Analyses of Social Issues and Public Policy* 16, no. 1: 261–277. https://doi.org/10.1111/asap.12092.
Lott, J. R. 2000. *More Guns, Less Crime: Understanding Crime and Gun Control Laws*. 2nd ed. Chicago: University of Chicago Press.
Louis, W. R., V. M. Esses, and R. N. Lalonde. 2013. "National Identification, Perceived Threat, and Dehumanization as Antecedents of Negative Attitudes toward Immigrants in Australia and Canada." *Journal of Applied Social Psychology* 43, no. S2: E156–E165. https://doi.org/10.1111/jasp.12044.
Lubbers, M., M. Gijsberts, and P. Scheepers. 2002. "Extreme Right-wing Voting in Western Europe." *European Journal of Political Research* 41, no. 3: 345–378. https://doi.org/10.1111/1475-6765.00015.
Luby, J., A. Belden, K. Botteron, N. Marrus, M. P. Harms, C. Babb, T. Nishino, and D. Barch. 2013. "The Effects of Poverty on Childhood Brain Development: The Mediating Effect of Caregiving and Stressful Life Events." *JAMA Pediatrics* 167, no. 12: 1135–1142. https://doi.org/10.1001/jamapediatrics.2013.3139.
Lüders, A., E. Jonas, I. Fritsche, and D. Agroskin. 2016. "Between the Lines of Us and Them: Identity Threat, Anxious Uncertainty, and Reactive In-Group Affirmation: How Can

Antisocial Outcomes be Prevented?" In *Understanding Peace and Conflict Through Social Identity Theory*, edited by S. McKeown, R. Haji, and N. Ferguson, 33–53. Cham: Springer. https://doi.org/10.1007/978-3-319-29869-6_3.

Lujala, P., N. P. Gleditsch, and E. Gilmore. 2005. "A Diamond Curse? Civil War and a Lootable Resource." *Journal of Conflict Resolution* 49, no. 4: 538–562. https://doi.org/10.1177/0022002705277548.

Luttmer, E. F. 2001. "Group Loyalty and the Taste for Redistribution." *Journal of Political Economy* 109, no. 3: 500–528. https://doi.org/10.1086/321019.

Ly, M., M. R. Haynes, J. W. Barter, D. R. Weinberger, and C. F. Zink. 2011. "Subjective Socioeconomic Status Predicts Human Ventral Striatal Responses to Social Status Information." *Current Biology* 21, no. 9: 794–797. https://doi.org/10.1016/j.cub.2011.03.050.

MacDonald, G., J. L. Saltzman, and M. R. Leary. 2003. "Social Approval and Trait Self-esteem." *Journal of Research in Personality* 37, no. 2: 23–40. https://doi.org/10.1016/S0092-6566(02)00531-7.

Macedo, D., and P. Gounari. 2016. *Globalization of Racism*. New York: Routledge.

MacKenzie, M. J., and R. F. Baumeister. 2014. "Meaning in Life: Nature, Needs, and Myths." In *Meaning in Positive and Existential Psychology*, edited by A. Batthyany and P. Russo-Netzer, 25–37. New York, NY: Springer. https://doi.org/10.1007/978-1-4939-0308-5_2.

Macrae, C. N., and G. V. Bodenhausen. 2000. "Social Cognition: Thinking Categorically." *Annual Review of Psychology* 51: 93–120. https://doi.org/10.1146/annurev.psych.51.1.93.

Maddux, J. E. 1995. "Self-Efficacy Theory." In Self-Efficacy, Adaptation, and Adjustment: Theory, Research, and Application, edited by J. E. Maddux, 3–33. Boston, MA: Springer. https://doi.org/10.1007/978-1-4419-6868-5_1.

Maddux, J. E. 2002. "Self-efficacy: The Power to Believing You Can." In *Handbook of Positive Psychology*, edited by C. R. Snyder and S. Lopez, 277–287. New York: Oxford University Press.

Mai-Bornu, Z. 2019. "Oil, Conflict, and the Dynamics of Resource Struggle in the Niger Delta: A Comparison of the Ogoni and Ijaw Movements." *The Extractive Industries and Society* 6, no. 4: 1282–1291. https://doi.org/10.1016/j.exis.2019.10.002.

Mai-Bornu, Z. L. 2020. "Dynamics of Leadership Styles within the Ogoni and Ijaw Movements in the Niger Delta." *Journal of Social and Political Psychology* 8, no. 2: 823–850. https://doi.org/10.5964/jspp.v8i2.1075.

Majid, A., and J. Pragasam. 1997. "Interactions of Intolerance of Ambiguity and of Contingent Liability on Auditors' Avoidance of Litigation." *Psychological Reports* 81, no. 3: 935–944. https://doi.org/10.2466/pr0.1997.81.3.935.

Makwana, A. P., K. Dhont, P. Akhlaghi-Ghaffarokh, M. Masure, and A. Roets. 2018. "The Motivated Cognitive Basis of Transphobia: The Roles of Right-wing Ideologies and Gender Role Beliefs." *Sex Roles: A Journal of Research* 79, no. 3–4: 206–217. https://doi.org/10.1007/s11199-017-0860-x.

Malešević, S. 2006a. *Identity as Ideology: Understanding Ethnicity and Nationalism*. New York: Springer.

Malešević, S. 2006b. "Nationalism and the Power of Ideology." In *The SAGE Handbook of Nations and Nationalism*, edited by G. Delanty and K. Kumar, 307–322. London: SAGE Publications Ltd.

Malešević, S. 2013. "Is Nationalism Intrinsically Violent?" *Nationalism and Ethnic Politics* 19, no. 1: 12–37. https://doi.org/10.1080/13537113.2013.761894.

Malešević, S. 2015. "War and Nationalism." *The Wiley Blackwell Encyclopedia of Race, Ethnicity, and Nationalism*, edited by John Stone, Rutledge M. Dennis, Polly S. Rizova, Anthony D. Smith, and Xiaoshou Hou, 1–5. https://doi.org/10.1002/9781118663202.wberen372.

Manogaran, C. 1987. *Ethnic Conflict and Reconciliation in Sri Lanka*. Honolulu: University of Hawaii Press. https://doi.org/10.1515/9780824844981.

Mannheim, K. 1936. *Ideology and Utopia*. Routledge.
Mansouri, F. 2012. "Muslim Migration to Australia and the Question of Identity and Belonging." *Muslims in the West and the Challenges of Belonging*, edited by F. Mansouri and V. Marotta, 13–33. Melbourne: Melbourne University Press.
Manstead, A. S. 2018. "The Psychology of Social Class: How Socioeconomic Status Impacts Thought, Feelings, and Behaviour." *British Journal of Social Psychology* 57, no. 2: 267–291. https://doi.org/10.1111/bjso.12251.
Mao, W., and C. Zech. 2002. "Choices of Organizational Structures in Religious Organizations: A Game Theoretic Approach." *Journal of Economic Behavior & Organization* 47, no. 1: 55–70. https://doi.org/10.1016/S0167-2681(01)00168-8.
Maoz, I., and C. McCauley. 2008. "Threat, Dehumanization, and Support for Retaliatory Aggressive Policies in Asymmetric Conflict." *Journal of Conflict Resolution* 52, no. 1: 93–116. https://doi.org/10.1177/0022002707308597.
Mapping Militant Organizations (MMP). 2021. "The Islamic State." Stanford University. https://cisac.fsi.stanford.edu/mappingmilitants/profiles/islamic-state.
March, L., and C. Mudde. 2005. "What's Left of the Radical Left? The European Radical Left after 1989: Decline and Mutation." *Comparative European Politics* 3, no. 1: 23–49. https://doi.org/10.1057/palgrave.cep.6110052.
Marcia, J. E. 2002. "Identity and Psychosocial Development in Adulthood." *Identity: An international Journal of Theory and Research* 2, no. 1: 7–28. https://doi.org/10.1207/S1532706XID0201_02.
Maria, F. D. 1997. "The 'Mafia Feeling': A Transcultural Theme of Sicily." *Group Analysis* 30, no. 3: 361–367. https://doi.org/10.1177/0533316497303005.
Markus, H. R., and S. Kitayama. 1991. "Cultural Variation in the Self-concept." In *The Self: Interdisciplinary Approaches*, edited by J. Strauss and G. R. Goethals, 18–48. New York: Springer. https://doi.org/10.1007/978-1-4684-8264-5_2.
Markus, H., and Z. Kunda. 1986. "Stability and Malleability of the Self-concept." *Journal of Personality and Social Psychology* 51, no. 4: 858–866. https://doi.org/10.1037/0022-3514.51.4.858.
Markus, H., and E. Wurf. 1987. "The Dynamic Self-concept: A Social Psychological Perspective." *Annual Review of Psychology* 38, no. 1: 299–337. https://doi.org/10.1146/annurev.ps.38.020187.001503.
Martinez, R., and R. L. Dukes. 1991. "Ethnic and Gender Differences in Self-esteem." *Youth & Society* 22, no. 3: 318–338. https://doi.org/10.1177/0044118X91022003002.
Martinovic, B., and M. Verkuyten. 2012. "Host National and Religious Identification among Turkish Muslims in Western Europe: The Role of Ingroup Norms, Perceived Discrimination and Value Incompatibility." *European Journal of Social Psychology* 42, no. 7: 893–903. https://doi.org/10.1002/ejsp.1900.
Masclet, D., C. Noussair, S. Tucker, and M. C. Villeval. 2003. "Monetary and Nonmonetary Punishment in the Voluntary Contributions Mechanism." *American Economic Review* 93, no. 1: 366–380. https://doi.org/10.1257/000282803321455359.
Maslach, C., W. B. Schaufeli, and M. P. Leiter. 2001. "Job Burnout." *Annual Review of Psychology* 52, no. 1: 397–422. https://doi.org/10.1146/annurev.psych.52.1.397.
Maslow, A. H. 1943. "A Theory of Human Motivation." *Psychological Review* 50, no. 4: 370–396. https://doi.org/10.1037/h0054346.
Maslow, A. H. 1954. *Motivation and Personality*. New York: Harper & Row.
Mason, D. 1985. "Public Opinion and Political Change in Poland, 1980–1982." Butler University. https://digitalcommons.butler.edu/facsch_papers/901.
Mason, D. S. 1995. "Attitudes Toward the Market and Political Participation in the Postcommunist States." *Slavic Review* 54, no. 2: 385–406. http://dx.doi.org10.2307/2501627.

Matsuba, M. K., and L. J. Walker. 2004. "Extraordinary Moral Commitment: Young Adults Involved in Social Organizations." *Journal of Personality* 72, no. 2: 413–436. https://doi.org/10.1111/j.0022-3506.2004.00267.x.

Max-Neef, M. 1992. "Development and Human Needs." In *Real life Economics: Understanding Wealth Creation*, edited by P. Ekins and M. Max-Neef, 97–213. London: Routledge.

Mayer, J. E., and C. P. S. Koeningsmark. 1992. "Self efficacy, Relapse and the Possibility of Posttreatment Denial as a Stage in Alcoholism." *Alcoholism Treatment Quarterly* 8, no. 4: 1–16. https://doi.org/10.1300/J020V08N04_01.

Mazzocco, P. J., and R. P. Brunner. 2012. "An Experimental Investigation of Possible Memory Biases Affecting Support for Racial Health Care Policy." *American Journal of Public Health* 102, no. 5: 1002–1005. https://doi.org/10.2105/AJPH.2011.300556.

McAdams, D. P. 1995. "What Do We Know When We Know a Person?" *Journal of Personality* 63, no. 3: 365–396.

McAdams, D. P., M. Albaugh, E. Farber, J. Daniels, R. L. Logan, and B. Olson. 2008. "Family Metaphors and Moral Intuitions: How Conservatives and Liberals Narrate Their Lives." *Journal of Personality and Social Psychology* 95, no. 4: 978. https://doi.org/10.1037/a0012650.

McAdams, D. P., S. Rothman, and S. R. Lichter. 1982. "Motivational Profiles: A Study of Former Political Radicals and Politically Moderate Adults." *Personality and Social Psychology Bulletin* 8, no. 4: 593–603. https://doi.org/10.1177/0146167282084002.

McBride, M. 2007. "Why Churches Need Free-riders: Religious Capital Formation and Religious Group Survival." Working Papers 060722. Irvine: University of California-Irvine.

McCarthy, C. 2003. "Contradictions of Power and Identity: Whiteness Studies and the Call of Teacher Education." *International Journal of Qualitative Studies in Education* 16, no. 1: 127–133. https://doi.org/10.1080/0951839032000033572.

McCauley, C., and S. Moskalenko. 2011. *Friction: How Radicalization Happens to Them and Us*. New York: Oxford University Press.

McCormick, G. H. 1987. "The Shining Path and Peruvian Terrorism." *The Journal of Strategic Studies* 10, no. 4: 109–126. https://doi.org/10.1080/01402398708437317.

McCormick, G. H. 2003. "Terrorist decision making." *Annual Review of Political Science* 6, no. 1: 473–507. https://doi.org/10.1146/annurev.polisci.6.121901.085601.

McCrae, R. R., and P. T. Costa. 1982. "Self-concept and the Stability of Personality: Cross-sectional Comparisons of Self-reports and Ratings." *Journal of Personality and Social Psychology* 43, no. 6: 1282–1292. https://doi.org/10.1037/0022-3514.43.6.1282.

McElwee, S., and J. McDaniel. 2017. "Economic Anxiety Didn't Make People Vote Trump, Racism Did." *The Nation* 8.

McFarland, S. G., V. S.Ageyev, and M. A. Abalakina-Paap. 1992. "Authoritarianism in the Former Soviet Union." *Journal of Personality and Social Psychology* 63, no. 6: 1004–1010. https://doi.org/10.1037/0022-3514.63.6.1004.

McFarland, S., V. Ageyev, and M. Abalakina. 1993. "The Authoritarian Personality in the United States and the Former Soviet Union: Comparative Studies." In *Strength and Weakness*, edited by W. F. Stone, G. Lederer, and R. Christie, 199–225. New York: Springer. https://doi.org/10.1007/978-1-4613-9180-7_10.

McGregor, I., and D. C. Marigold. 2003. "Defensive Zeal and the Uncertain Self: What Makes You So Sure?" *Journal of Personality and Social Psychology* 85, no. 5: 838–852. https://doi.org/10.1037/0022-3514.85.5.838.

McGregor, I., R. Haji, K. A. Nash, and R. Teper. 2008. "Religious Zeal and the Uncertain Self." *Basic and Applied Social Psychology* 30, no. 2: 183–188. https://doi.org/10.1080/01973530802209251.

McGregor, I., M. Prentice, and K. Nash. 2013. "Anxious Uncertainty and Reactive Approach Motivation (RAM) for Religious, Idealistic, and Lifestyle Extremes." *Journal of Social Issues* 69, no. 3: 537–563. https://doi.org/10.1111/josi.12028.

McGregor, I., M. P. Zanna, J. G. Holmes, and S. J. Spencer. 2001. "Compensatory Conviction in the Face of Personal Uncertainty: Going to Extremes and Being Oneself." *Journal of Personality and Social Psychology* 80, no. 3: 472. https://doi.org/10.1111/josi.12028.

McGuire, W. J. 1966. "The Current Status of Cognitive Consistency Theories." In *Cognitive Consistency: Motivational Antecedents and Behavioral Consequents*, edited by S. Feldman, 1–26. New York: Academic Press.

McKay, R., and H. Whitehouse. 2015. "Religion and Morality." *Psychological Bulletin* 141, no. 2: 447–473. https://doi.org/10.1037/a0038455.

McLean, K. C., M. Pasupathi, and J. L. Pals. 2007. "Selves Creating Stories Creating Selves: A Process Model of Self-development." *Personality and Social Psychology Review* 11, no. 3: 262–278. https://doi.org/10.1177/1088868307301034.

McNamara, P. 2001. "Religion and the Frontal Lobes." In *Religion in Mind: Cognitive Perspectives on Religious Belief, Ritual, and Experience*, edited by A. Andresen, 237–256. Cambridge, UK: Cambridge University Press. https://doi.org/10.1017/CBO9780511586330.

Mellor, D., M. E. Merino, J. L. Saiz, and D. Quilaqueo. 2009. "Emotional Reactions, Coping and Long-term Consequences of Perceived Discrimination among the Mapuche People of Chile." *Journal of Community & Applied Social Psychology* 19, no. 6: 473–491. https://doi.org/10.1002/casp.996.

Mellor, D., M. Stokes, L. Firth, Y. Hayashi, and R. Cummins. 2008. "Need for Belonging, Relationship Satisfaction, Loneliness, and Life Satisfaction." *Personality and Individual Differences* 45, no. 3: 213–218. https://doi.org/10.1016/j.paid.2008.03.020.

Mercer, N., E. Crocetti, S. Branje, P. Van Lier, and W. Meeus. 2017. "Linking Delinquency and Personal Identity Formation across Adolescence: Examining Between- and Within-person Associations." *Developmental Psychology* 53, no. 11: 2182–2194. https://doi.org/10.1037/dev0000351.

MHA. n.d. "Black and African American Communities and Mental Health." Mental Health America. https://www.mhanational.org/issues/black-and-african-american-communities-and-mental-health.

Michael, G. 2009. "The Ideological Evolution of Horst Mahler: The Far Left–Extreme Right Synthesis." *Studies in Conflict & Terrorism* 32, no. 4: 346–366. https://doi.org/10.1080/10576100902743997.

Middleton, K. L., and J. L. Jones. 2000. "Socially Desirable Response Sets: The Impact of Country Culture." *Psychology & Marketing* 17, no. 2: 149–163. https://doi.org/10.1002/(SICI)1520-6793(200002)17:2<149::AID-MAR6>3.0.CO;2-L.

Mieriņa, I. 2014. "Political Alienation and Government–Society Relations in Post-communist Countries." *Polish Sociological Review* 185, no. 1: 3–24.

Mikulincer, M. 1997. "Adult Attachment Style and Information Processing: Individual Differences in Curiosity and Cognitive Closure." *Journal of Personality and Social Psychology* 72, no. 5: 1217–1230. https://doi.org/10.1037/0022-3514.72.5.1217.

Miller, S. M. 1979. "Controllability and Human Stress: Method, Evidence and Theory." *Behaviour Research and Therapy* 17, no. 4: 287–304. https://doi.org/10.1016/0005-7967(79)90001-9.

Minkenberg, M. 2000. "The Renewal of the Radical Right: Between Modernity and Anti-modernity." *Government and Opposition* 35, no. 2: 170–188. https://doi.org/10.1111/1477-7053.00022.

Mirza, M., A. Senthilkumaran, and Z. Ja'far. 2007. *Living Apart Together: British Muslims and the Paradox of Multiculturalism*. London: Policy Exchange.

Mitchell, J. P., C. N. Macrae, and M. R. Banaji. 2006. "Dissociable Medial Prefrontal Contributions to Judgments of Similar and Dissimilar Others." *Neuron* 50, no. 4: 655–663. https://doi.org/10.1016/j.neuron.2006.03.040.

Möbius, M. M., M. Niederle, P. Niehaus, and T. S. Rosenblat. 2014. "Managing Self-confidence." NBER Working paper, 17014.

Moghadam, V. M. 2012. *Globalization and Social Movements: Islamism, Feminism, and the Global Justice Movement*. New York: Rowman & Littlefield.

Moir, N. L. 2017. "ISIL Radicalization, Recruitment, and Social Media Operations in Indonesia, Malaysia, and the Philippines." *PRISM* 7, no. 1: 90–107. https://www.jstor.org/stable/26470500.

Molenberghs, P., R. Cunnington, and J. B. Mattingley. 2012. "Brain Regions with Mirror Properties: A Meta-analysis of 125 Human fMRI Studies." *Neuroscience & Biobehavioral Reviews* 36, no. 1: 341–349. https://doi.org/10.1016/j.neubiorev.2011.07.004.

Moller, A. C., R. Friedman, and E. L. Deci. 2006. "A Self-determination Theory Perspective on the Interpersonal and Intrapersonal Aspects of Self-esteem." In *Self-esteem Issues and Answers: A Sourcebook of Current Perspectives*, edited by H. M. Kernis, 188–195. New York: Psychology Press.

Mollica, R. F., K. Donelan, S. Tor, J. Lavelle, C. Elias, M. Frankel, and R. J. Blendon. 1993. "The Effect of Trauma and Confinement on Functional Health and Mental Health Status of Cambodians Living in Thailand–Cambodia Border Camps." *JAMA* 270, no. 5: 581–586. https://doi.org/10.1001/jama.1993.03510050047025.

Molnar, M. 1978. *A Short History of the Hungarian Communist Party*. Boulder, CO: Westview Press. https://doi.org/10.4324/9780429306006.

Morrison, I., M. V. Peelen, and P. E. Downing. 2007. "The Sight of Others' Pain Modulates Motor Processing in Human Cingulate Cortex." *Cerebral Cortex* 17, no. 9: 2214–2222. https://doi.org/10.1093/cercor/bhl129.

Mortimer, J. T., M. D. Finch, and D. Kumka. 1982. "Persistence and Change in Development: The Multidimensional Self-concept." *Life-span Development and Behavior* 4: 263–313.

Moskowitz, G. B. 1993. "Individual Differences in Social Categorization: The Influence of Personal Need for Structure on Spontaneous Trait Inferences." *Journal of Personality and Social Psychology* 65, no. 1: 132–142. https://doi.org/10.1037/0022-3514.65.1.132.

Mossakowski, K. N. 2003. "Coping with Perceived Discrimination: Does Ethnic Identity Protect Mental Health?" *Journal of Health and Social Behavior* 44, no. 3: 318–331. https://doi.org/10.2307/1519782.

Moulding, R., and M. Kyrios. 2006. "Anxiety Disorders and Control Related Beliefs: The Exemplar of Obsessive–Compulsive Disorder (OCD)." *Clinical Psychology Review* 26, no. 5: 573–583. https://doi.org/10.1016/j.cpr.2006.01.009.

Mousseau, M. 2011. "Urban Poverty and Support for Islamist Terror: Survey Results of Muslims in Fourteen Countries." *Journal of Peace Research* 48, no. 1: 35–47. https://doi.org/10.1177/0022343310391724.

Mouzon, D. M., R. J. Taylor, V. M. Keith, E. J. Nicklett, and L. M. Chatters. 2017. "Discrimination and Psychiatric Disorders among Older African Americans." *International Journal of Geriatric Psychiatry* 32, no. 2: 175–182. https://doi.org/10.1002/gps.4454.

Moyo, S. 2005. "Land and Natural Resource Redistribution in Zimbabwe: Access, Equity and Conflict." *African and Asian Studies* 4, no. 1–2: 187–224. https://doi.org/10.1163/1569209054547283.

Mudde, C. 2000. "Extreme-right Parties in Eastern Europe." *Patterns of Prejudice* 34, no. 1: 5–27. https://doi.org/10.1080/00313220008559132.

Mudde, C. 2002. *The Ideology of the Extreme Right*. Manchester: Manchester University Press. https://doi.org/10.7228/manchester/9780719057939.001.0001.

Mudde, C. 2007. *Populist Radical Right Parties in Europe*. Cambridge: Cambridge University Press. https://doi.org/10.1017/CBO9780511492037.

Mudde, C. 2010. "The Populist Radical Right: A Pathological Normalcy." *West European Politics* 33, no. 6: 1167–1186. https://doi.org/10.1080/01402382.2010.508901.

Muller, E.N., and M. A. Seligson. 1987. "Inequality and Insurgency." *The American Political Science Review* 81, no. 2: 425–452.

Mueller, J. C. 2013. "Tracing Family, Teaching Race: Critical Race Pedagogy in the Millennial Sociology Classroom." *Teaching Sociology* 41, no. 2: 172–187. https://doi.org/10.1177/0092055X12455135.

Mueller, V. 2021. "Searching for Alternative Worldviews—How Need Thwarting, Group Characteristics and the Social Environment Determine Ideological Extremism." *APSA Preprints.* https://doi.org/10.33774/apsa-2021-rd67h.

Mughan, A., and P. Paxton. 2006. "Anti-immigrant Sentiment, Policy Preferences and Populist Party Voting in Australia." *British Journal of Political Science* 36, no. 2: 341–358. https://doi.org/10.1017/S0007123406000184.

Müller, K., and C. Schwarz. 2021. "Fanning the Flames of Hate: Social Media and Hate Crime." *Journal of the European Economic Association* 19, no. 4: 2131–2167. https://doi.org/10.1093/jeea/jvaa045.

Mummendey, A., T. Kessler, A. Klink, and R. Mielke. 1999. "Strategies to Cope with Negative Social Identity: Predictions by Social Identity Theory and Relative Deprivation Theory." *Journal of Personality and Social Psychology* 76, no. 2: 229–245. https://doi.org/10.1037/0022-3514.76.2.229.

Murshed, S. M., and S. Gates. 2005. "Spatial–Horizontal Inequality and the Maoist Insurgency in Nepal." *Review of Development Economics* 9, no. 1: 121–134. https://doi.org/10.1111/j.1467-9361.2005.00267.x.

Muscatell, K. A., S. A. Morelli, E. B. Falk, B. M. Way, J. H. Pfeifer, A. D. Galinsky, M. D. Lieberman, M. Dapretto, and N. I. Eisenberger. 2012. "Social Status Modulates Neural Activity in the Mentalizing Network." *Neuroimage* 60, no. 3: 1771–1777. https://doi.org/10.1016/j.neuroimage.2012.01.080.

Mussel, P., and J. Hewig. 2016. "The Life and Times of Individuals Scoring High and Low on Dispositional Greed." *Journal of Research in Personality* 64: 52–60. https://doi.org/10.1016/j.jrp.2016.07.002.

Mussel, P., A. M. Reiter, R. Osinsky, and J. Hewig. 2015. "State- and Trait-greed, Its Impact on Risky Decision-making and Underlying Neural Mechanisms." *Social Neuroscience* 10, no. 2: 126–134. https://doi.org/10.1080/17470919.2014.965340.

Mussel, P., J. Rodrigues, S. Krumm, and J. Hewig. 2018. "The Convergent Validity of Five Dispositional Greed Scales." *Personality and Individual Differences* 131: 249–253. https://doi.org/10.1016/j.paid.2018.05.006.

Nacos, B. L. 2007. *Mass-mediated Terrorism: The Central Role of the Media in Terrorism and Counterterrorism.* New York: Rowman & Littlefield.

Nacos, B. L. 2016. *Mass-mediated Terrorism: Mainstream and Digital Media in Terrorism and Counterterrorism.* New York: Rowman & Littlefield.

Nafziger, E. W., and J. Auvinen. 2002. "Economic Development, Inequality, War, and State Violence." *World Development* 30, no. 2: 153–163. https://doi.org/10.1016/S0305-750X(01)00108-5.

Nafziger, E. W., F. Stewart, and R. Väyrynen, eds. 2000. *War, Hunger, and Displacement: The Origins of Humanitarian Emergencies (Vol. 1).* Oxford: Oxford University Press. http://doi.org/10.1093/acprof:oso/9780198297390.001.0001.

Nagel, J. 1994. "Constructing Ethnicity: Creating and Recreating Ethnic Identity and Culture." *Social Problems* 41, no. 1: 152–176. https://doi.org/10.1525/sp.1994.41.1.03x0430n.

Nance, M. 2016. *Defeating ISIS: Who They Are, How They Fight, What They Believe.* New York: Simon and Schuster.

Nangle, D. W., C. A. Erdley, and J. A. Gold. 1996. "A Reflection on the Popularity Construct: The Importance of Who Likes or Dislikes a Child." *Behavior Therapy* 27, no. 3: 337–352. https://doi.org/10.1016/S0005-7894(96)80021-9.

Napier, J. L., and J. T. Jost. 2008. "Why Are Conservatives Happier Than Liberals?" *Psychological Science* 19, no. 6: 565–572. https://doi.org/10.1111/j.1467-9280.2008.02124.x.

References

National Bureau of Statistics (NBS). 2010. "Nigeria Poverty Profile, 2010." National Bureau of Statistics. https://www.nigerianstat.gov.ng/pdfuploads/Nigeria%20Poverty%20Profile%202010.pdf.

National Survey on Drug Use and Health. 2016. "Methodological Summary and Definitions." SAMHSA. https://www.samhsa.gov/data/sites/default/files/NSDUH-MethodSummDefs-2016/NSDUH-MethodSummDefs-2016.html.

Nesser, P. 2013. "Abū Qatāda and Palestine." *Die Welt des Islams* 53, no. 3–4: 416–448.

Neuberg, S. L., and J. T. Newsom. 1993. "Personal Need for Structure: Individual Differences in the Desire for Simpler Structure." *Journal of Personality and Social Psychology* 65, no. 1: 113–131. https://doi.org/10.1037/0022-3514.65.1.113.

Neville, H. A., V. P. Poteat, J. A. Lewis, and L. B. Spanierman. 2014. "Changes in White College Students' Color-blind Racial Ideology Over 4 Years: Do Diversity Experiences Make a Difference?" *Journal of Counseling Psychology* 61, no. 2: 179–190. https://doi.org/10.1037/a0035168.

Nichols, S. 2001. "Mindreading and the Cognitive Architecture Underlying Altruistic Motivation." *Mind & Language* 16, no. 4: 425–455. https://doi.org/10.1111/1468-0017.00178.

Nikelly, A. 2006. "The Pathogenesis of Greed: Causes and Consequences." *International Journal of Applied Psychoanalytic Studies* 3, no. 1: 65–78. https://doi.org/10.1002/aps.50.

Noble, K. G., S. M. Houston, E. Kan, and E. R. Sowell. 2012. "Neural Correlates of Socioeconomic Status in the Developing Human Brain." *Developmental Science* 15, no. 4: 516–527. https://doi.org/10.1111/j.1467-7687.2012.01147.x.

NSPCC. 2019. "ChildLine Annual Review 2018/19." National Society for the Prevention of Cruelty to Children. https://learning.nspcc.org.uk/research-resources/childline-annual-review.

O'Leary, A., and S. Brown. 1995. "Self-efficacy and the Physiological Stress Response." In *Self-efficacy, Adaptation, and Adjustment*, edited by J. E. Maddux, 227–246. Boston, MA: Springer. https://doi.org/10.1007/978-1-4419-6868-5_8.

Obi, C. I. 2010. "Oil Extraction, Dispossession, Resistance, and Conflict in Nigeria's Oil-rich Niger Delta." *Canadian Journal of Development Studies/Revue canadienne d'études du développement* 30, no. 1–2: 219–236. https://doi.org/10.1080/02255189.2010.9669289.

Odmalm, P., and E. Hepburn. 2017. *The European Mainstream and the Populist Radical Right*. New York: Routledge.

O'Doherty, J., H. Critchley, R. Deichmann, and R. J. Dolan. 2003. "Dissociating Valence of Outcome from Behavioral Control in Human Orbital and Ventral Prefrontal Cortices." *Journal of Neuroscience* 23, no. 21: 7931–7939. https://doi.org/10.1523/JNEUROSCI.23-21-07931.2003.

OECD. 2016. "States of Fragility 2016: Understanding Violence." OECD Publishing. https://doi.org/10.1787/9789264267213-en.

Oesch, D. 2008. "Explaining Workers' Support for Right-wing Populist Parties in Western Europe: Evidence from Austria, Belgium, France, Norway, and Switzerland." *International Political Science Review* 29, no. 3: 349–373. https://doi.org/10.1177/0192512107088390.

Okonta, I. 2005. "Nigeria: Chronicle of a Dying State." *Current History* 104, no. 682: 203–208. https://doi.org/10.1525/curh.2005.104.682.203.

Okun, M. A., and J. F. Finch. 1998. "The Big Five Personality Dimensions and the Process of Institutional Departure." *Contemporary Educational Psychology* 23, no. 3: 233–256. https://doi.org/10.1006/ceps.1996.0974.

Olson, J. M. 1995. "Behind the Recent Tragedy in Rwanda." *GeoJournal* 35, no. 2: 217–222. https://doi.org/10.1007/BF00814068.

Onuoha, F. C. 2014. "A Danger Not to Nigeria Alone: Boko Harams's Transnational Reach and Regional Responses." Peace and Security Series (No. 17). Friedrich-Ebert Stiftung.

O'Reilly, J. X. 2013. "Making Predictions in a Changing World—Inference, Uncertainty, and Learning." *Frontiers in Neuroscience* 7, no. 105: 1–10. https://doi.org/10.3389/fnins.2013.00105.

Osborne, D., and C. G. Sibley. 2013. "Through Rose-colored Glasses: System-justifying Beliefs Dampen the Effects of Relative Deprivation on Well-being and Political Mobilization." *Personality and Social Psychology Bulletin* 39, no. 8: 991–1004. https://doi.org/10.1177/0146167213487997.

Osborne, D., and B. Weiner. 2015. "A Latent Profile Analysis of Attributions for Poverty: Identifying Response Patterns Underlying People's Willingness to Help the Poor." *Personality and Individual Differences* 85: 149–154. https://doi.org/10.1016/j.paid.2015.05.007.

Ostapczuk, M., J. Musch, and M. Moshagen. 2009. "A Randomized-response Investigation of the Education Effect in Attitudes towards Foreigners." *European Journal of Social Psychology* 39, no. 6: 920–931. https://doi.org/10.1002/ejsp.588.

Østby, G. 2008. "Polarization, Horizontal Inequalities and Violent Civil Conflict." *Journal of Peace Research* 45, no. 2: 143–162. https://doi.org/10.1177/0022343307087169.

Østby, G., R. Nordås, and J. K. Rød. 2009. "Regional Inequalities and Civil Conflict in Sub-Saharan Africa." *International Studies Quarterly* 53, no. 2: 301–324. https://doi.org/10.1111/j.1468-2478.2009.00535.x.

Osterling, J. P. 1989. *Democracy in Colombia: Clientelist Politics and Guerrilla Warfare*. New York: Routledge. https://doi.org/10.4324/9780429336881.

Ottaway, M., and A. Hamzawy. 2011. *Protest Movements and Political Change in the Arab World (Vol. 28)*. Washington, DC: Carnegie Endowment for International Peace.

Oxford Companion to Philosophy. 2005. "Belief." https://www.oxfordreference.com/view/10.1093/acref/9780199264797.001.0001/acref-9780199264797-e-234.

Oxford Dictionary of Social Sciences. 2002. "Liberalism." https://www.oxfordreference.com/view/10.1093/acref/9780195123715.001.0001/acref-9780195123715-e-962?rskey=1FG28R&result=4.

Oxford Dictionary of Social Sciences. 2002. "Right-wing and Left-Wing." https://www.oxfordreference.com/view/10.1093/acref/9780195123715.001.0001/acref-9780195123715-e-1448?rskey=elLrt9&result=8.

Oxford Dictionary of the Social Sciences. 2002. "Social Democracy." https://www.oxfordreference.com/view/10.1093/acref/9780195123715.001.0001/acref-9780195123715-e-1547.

Oxford Dictionary of World History. 2015. "Race." https://www.oxfordreference.com/view/10.1093/acref/9780199685691.001.0001/acref-9780199685691-e-3036?rskey=jc4S93&result=1.

Oyserman, D. 2007. "Social Identity and Self-regulation." In *Social Psychology: Handbook of Basic Principles*, edited by A. W. Kruglanski and E. T. Higgins, 432–453. New York: The Guilford Press.

Oyserman, D., and M. Destin. 2010. "Identity-based Motivation: Implications for Intervention." *The Counseling Psychologist* 38, no. 7: 1001–1043. https://doi.org/10.1177/0011000010374775.

Pacheco, C. 2019. *Reducing Recidivism in Gang Affiliated Offenders: An Interpretative Phenomenological Approach*. Minneapolis, MN: Walden University.

Page, B. I., and L. R. Jacobs. 2009. *Class War? What Americans Really Think about Economic Inequality*. Chicago: University of Chicago Press.

Paoli, L. 2004. "Italian Organised Crime: Mafia Associations and Criminal Enterprises." *Global Crime* 6, no. 1: 19–31. https://doi.org/10.1080/1744057042000297954.

Papini, D. R., and L. A. Roggman. 1992. "Adolescent Perceived Attachment to Parents in Relation to Competence, Depression, and Anxiety: A Longitudinal Study." *The Journal of Early Adolescence* 12, no. 4: 420–440. https://doi.org/10.1177/0272431692012004005.

Paradise, A. W., and M. H. Kernis. 2002. "Self-esteem and Psychological Well-being: Implications of Fragile Self-esteem." *Journal of Social and Clinical Psychology* 21, no. 4: 345–361. https://doi.org/10.1521/jscp.21.4.345.22598.

Park, C. L., and D. Edmondson. 2012. "Religion as a Source of Meaning." In *Meaning, Mortality, and Choice: The Social Psychology of Existential Concerns*, edited by P. R. Shaver and M. Mikulincer, 145–162. Washington, DC: American Psychological Association. https://doi.org/10.1037/13748-008.

Patterson, F., and P. Lane. 2007. "Assessment for Recruitment." In *Assessment in Medical Education and Training*, edited by N. Jackson, F. Jamieson, and A. Khan, 62–73. Oxford: Radcliffe Publishing.

Paulus, M. P., N. Hozack, B. Zauscher, J. E. McDowell, L. Frank, G. G. Brown, and D. L. Braff. 2001. "Prefrontal, Parietal, and Temporal Cortex Networks Underlie Decision-making in the Presence of Uncertainty." *NeuroImage* 13, no. 1: 91–100. https://doi.org/10.1006/nimg.2000.0667.

Pauwels, L., and N. Schils. 2016. "Differential Online Exposure to Extremist Content and Political Violence: Testing the Relative Strength of Social Learning and Competing Perspectives." *Terrorism and Political Violence* 28, no. 1: 1–29. https://doi.org/10.1080/09546553.2013.876414.

Payne, A. J., S. Joseph, and J. Tudway. 2007. "Assimilation and Accommodation Processes Following Traumatic Experiences." *Journal of Loss and Trauma* 12, no. 1: 75–91. https://doi.org/10.1080/15325020600788206.

Payzan-LeNestour, É., and P. Bossaerts. 2012. "Do Not Bet On the Unknown versus Try to Find Out More: Estimation Uncertainty and 'Unexpected Uncertainty' both Modulate Exploration." *Frontiers in Neuroscience* 6, no. 150: 1–6. https://doi.org/10.3389/fnins.2012.00150.

Pears, K. C., H. K. Kim, and P. A. Fisher. 2008. "Psychosocial and Cognitive Functioning of Children with Specific Profiles of Maltreatment." *Child Abuse & Neglect* 32, no. 10: 958–971. https://doi.org/10.1016/j.chiabu.2007.12.009.

Pearson, A. R., J. F. Dovidio, and S. L. Gaertner. 2009. "The Nature of Contemporary Prejudice: Insights from Aversive Racism." *Social and Personality Psychology Compass* 3, no. 3: 314–338. https://doi.org/10.1111/j.1751-9004.2009.00183.x.

Pehrson, S., R. Brown, and H. Zagefka. 2009b. "When Does National Identification Lead to the Rejection of Immigrants? Cross-sectional and Longitudinal Evidence for the Role of Essentialist In-group Definitions." *British Journal of Social Psychology* 48, no. 1: 61–76. https://doi.org/10.1348/014466608X288827.

Pehrson, S., V. L. Vignoles, and R. Brown. 2009a. "National Identification and Anti-immigrant Prejudice: Individual and Contextual Effects of National Definitions." *Social Psychology Quarterly* 72, no. 1: 24–38. https://doi.org/10.1177/019027250907200104.

Pellicer, M., P. Piraino, and E. Wegner. 2016. *Is Inequality Inevitable? A Survey Experiment on Demand for Redistribution in South Africa*. German Institute of Global and Area Studies. Unpublished manuscript.

Peluso, N. L., and M. Watts, eds. 2001. Violent Environments. Ithaca, NY: Cornell University Press.

Perry, E. 2002. "Moving the Masses: Emotion Work in the Chinese Revolution." *Mobilization: An International Quarterly* 7, no. 2: 111–128. https://doi.org/10.17813/MAIQ.7.2.70RG70L202524UW6.

Pervin, L. A. 1963. "The Need to Predict and Control under Conditions of Threat." *Journal of Personality* 31, no. 4: 570–587. https://doi.org/10.1111/j.1467-6494.1963.tb01320.x.

Petersen, L. E., and J. Dietz. 2006. "Social Discrimination in a Personnel Selection Context: The Effects of an Authority's Instruction to Discriminate and Followers' Authoritarianism." *Journal of Applied Social Psychology* 30, no. 1: 206–220. https://doi.org/10.1111/j.1559-1816.2000.tb02312.x.

Pettigrew, T. F., O. Christ, U. Wagner, and J. Stellmacher. 2007. "Direct and Indirect Intergroup Contact Effects on Prejudice: A Normative Interpretation." *International Journal of Intercultural Relations* 31, no. 4: 411–425. https://doi.org/10.1016/j.ijintrel.2006.11.003.

Pew Research Center. 2014. "Worldwide, Many See Belief in God as Essential to Morality." Survey Report. https://www.pewresearch.org/global/2014/03/13/worldwide-many-see-belief-in-god-as-essential-to-morality/.

Pew Research Center. 2017. "Christians Remain World's Largest Religious Group, but They are Declining in Europe." https://www.pewresearch.org/fact-tank/2017/04/05/christians-remain-worlds-largest-religious-group-but-they-are-declining-in-europe/.

Pew Research Center. 2019. "Key Findings on Americans' Views of Race in 2019." https://www.pewresearch.org/fact-tank/2019/04/09/key-findings-on-americans-views-of-race-in-2019/.

Pew Research Center. 2017. "America's Complex Relationship with Guns." https://www.pewresearch.org/social-trends/2017/06/22/americas-complex-relationship-with-guns/.

Pew Research Center. 2021. "Social Media Use in 2021." https://www.pewresearch.org/internet/2021/04/07/social-media-use-in-2021/.

Phillips III, R. E., and G. G. Ano. 2015. "A Re-examination of Religious Fundamentalism: Positive Implications for Coping." *Mental Health, Religion & Culture* 18, no. 4: 299–311. https://doi.org/10.1080/13674676.2015.1022521.

Phinney, J. S., and L. L. Alipuria. 1990. "Ethnic Identity in College Students from Four Ethnic Groups." *Journal of Adolescence* 13, no. 2: 171–183. https://doi.org/10.1016/0140-1971(90)90006-s.

Phinney, J. S., and V. Chavira. 1992. "Ethnic Identity and Self-esteem: An Exploratory Longitudinal Study." *Journal of Adolescence* 15, no. 3: 271–281. https://doi.org/10.1016/0140-1971(92)90030-9.

Phinney, J. S., C. L. Cantu, and D. A. Kurtz. 1997. "Ethnic and American Identity as Predictors of Self-esteem among African American, Latino, and White Adolescents." *Journal of Youth and Adolescence* 26, no. 2: 165–185. https://doi.org/10.1023/A:1024500514834.

Piazza, J. A. 2006. "Rooted in Poverty? Terrorism, Poor Economic Development, and Social Cleavages." *Terrorism and Political Violence* 18, no. 1: 159–177. https://doi.org/10.1080/09546550590944578.

Piazza, J. A. 2011. "Poverty, Minority Economic Discrimination, and Domestic Terrorism." *Journal of Peace Research* 48, no. 3: 339–353. https://doi.org/10.1177/0022343310397404.

Pickett, C. L., W. L. Gardner, and M. Knowles. 2004. "Getting a Cue: The Need to Belong and Enhanced Sensitivity to Social Cues." *Personality and Social Psychology Bulletin* 30, no. 9: 1095–1107. https://doi.org/10.1177/0146167203262085.

Pierce, J., and B. Pierce. 2016. "For the Love of Family: A Mafia Lens on Love and Commitment." In *The Contribution of Love, and Hate, to Organizational Ethics*, edited by M. Schwartz, H. Harris, and D. R. Comer, 139–159. Bingley, UK: Emerald Group Publishing Limited. https://doi.org/10.1108/S1529-209620160000016005.

Pieslak, J. 2015. Radicalism and Music: An Introduction to the Music Cultures of Al-Qa'ida, Racist Skinheads, Christian-affiliated Radicals, and Eco-animal Rights Militants. Middletown, CT: Wesleyan University Press.

Piliavin, J. A., and H. W. Charng. 1990. "Altruism: A Review of Recent Theory and Research." *Annual Review of Sociology* 16, no. 1: 27–65. https://doi.org/10.1146/annurev.so.16.080190.000331.

Pinstrup-Andersen, P., and S. Shimokawa. 2008. "Do Poverty and Poor Health and Nutrition Increase the Risk of Armed Conflict Onset?" *Food Policy* 33, no. 6: 513–520. https://doi.org/10.1016/j.foodpol.2008.05.003.

Pittman, T. S., and K. R. Zeigler. 2007. "Basic Human Needs." In *Social Psychology: Handbook of Basic Principles*, edited by A. W. Kruglanski and E. T. Higgins, 473–489. New York: Guilford Press.

Piurko, Y., S. H. Schwartz, and E. Davidov. 2011. "Basic Personal Values and the Meaning of Left-Right Political Orientations in 20 Countries." *Political Psychology* 32, no. 4: 537–561. https://doi.org/10.1111/j.1467-9221.2011.00828.x.

Ploghaus, A., L. Becerra, C. Borras, and D. Borsook. 2003. "Neural Circuitry Underlying Pain Modulation: Expectation, Hypnosis, Placebo." *Trends in Cognitive Sciences* 7, no. 5: 197–200. https://doi.org/10.1016/S1364-6613(03)00061-5.

Ploghaus, A., I. Tracey, J. S. Gati, S. Clare, R. S. Menon, P. M. Matthews, and J. N. P. Rawlins. 1999. "Dissociating Pain from Its Anticipation in the Human Brain." *Science* 284, no. 5422: 1979–1981. https://doi.org/10.1126/science.284.5422.1979.

Plomin, R., K. Asbury, and J. Dunn. 2001. "Why are Children in the Same Family So Different? Nonshared Environment a Decade Later." *The Canadian Journal of Psychiatry* 46, no. 3: 225–233. https://doi.org/10.1177/070674370104600302.

Pokorny, J. J., and F. B. de Waal. 2009. "Monkeys Recognize the Faces of Group Mates in Photographs." *Proceedings of the National Academy of Sciences* 106, no. 51: 21539–21543. https://doi.org/10.1073/pnas.0912174106.

Poleshuck, E. L., and C. R. Green. 2008. "Socioeconomic Disadvantage and Pain." *Pain* 136, no. 3: 235–238. https://doi.org/10.1016/j.pain.2008.04.003.

Polivy, J., and C. P. Herman. 2002. "Causes of Eating Disorders." *Annual Review of Psychology* 53, no. 1: 187–213. https://doi.org/10.1146/annurev.psych.53.100901.135103.

Pop-Eleches, G., and J. A. Tucker. 2010. "After the Party: Legacies and Left-Right Distinctions in Post-communist Countries." Working paper Series. Available at SSRN 1670127. http://dx.doi.org/10.2139/ssrn.1670127.

Post, J. M. 2007. *The Mind of the Terrorist: The Psychology of Terrorism from the IRA to al-Qaeda*. New York: Palgrave Macmillan.

Poteat, V. P., and L. B. Spanierman. 2010. "Do the Ideological Beliefs of Peers Predict the Prejudiced Attitudes of Other Individuals in the Group?" *Group Processes & Intergroup Relations* 13, no. 4: 495–514. https://doi.org/10.1177/1368430209357436.

Poutvaara, P., and M. F. Steinhardt. 2018. "Bitterness in Life and Attitudes towards Immigration." *European Journal of Political Economy* 55: 471–490. https://doi.org/10.1016/j.ejpoleco.2018.04.007.

Powdthavee, N., and Y. E. Riyanto. 2015. "Would You Pay for Transparently Useless Advice? A Test of Boundaries of Beliefs in the Folly of Predictions." *Review of Economics and Statistics* 97, no. 2: 257–272. https://doi.org/10.1162/REST_a_00453.

Powell-Williams, T., and M. Powell-Williams. 2017. "'God Hates Your Feelings': Neutralizing Emotional Deviance within the Westboro Baptist Church." *Deviant Behavior* 38, no. 12: 1439–1455. https://doi.org/10.1080/01639625.2016.1257887.

Pratto, F., J. Sidanius, L. M. Stallworth, and B. F. Malle. 1994. "Social Dominance Orientation: A Personality Variable Predicting Social and Political Attitudes." *Journal of Personality and Social Psychology* 67, no. 4: 741–763. https://doi.org/10.1037/0022-3514.67.4.741.

Prehn-Kristensen, A., C. Wiesner, T. O. Bergmann, S. Wolff, O. Jansen, H. M. Mehdorn, R. Ferstl, and B. M. Pause. 2009. "Induction of Empathy by the Smell of Anxiety." *PloS One* 4, no. 6: e5987. https://doi.org/10.1371/journal.pone.0005987.

Preston, S. D., and F. B. De Waal. 2002. "Empathy: Its Ultimate and Proximate Bases." *Behavioral and Brain Sciences* 25, no. 1: 1–20. https://doi.org/10.1017/S0140525X02000018.

Price, R. B., D. Rosen, G. J. Siegle, C. D. Ladouceur, K. Tang, K. B. Allen, . . . and J. S. Silk. 2016. "From Anxious Youth to Depressed Adolescents: Prospective Prediction of 2-Year Depression Symptoms via Attentional Bias Measures." *Journal of Abnormal Psychology* 125, no. 2: 267–278. https://doi.org/10.1037/abn0000127.

Pridemore, W. A. 2011. "Poverty Matters: A Reassessment of the Inequality–Homicide Relationship in Cross-national Studies." *The British Journal of Criminology* 51, no. 5: 739–772. https://doi.org/10.1093/bjc/azr019.

Prieto Curiel, R., O. Walther, and N. O'Clery. 2020. "Uncovering the Internal Structure of Boko Haram through Its Mobility Patterns." *Applied Network Science* 5, no. 1: 1–23. https://doi.org/10.1007/s41109-020-00264-4.

Pritchard, C. J., and P. P. Fidler. 1993. "What Small Firms Look for in New-Graduate Candidates." *Journal of Career Planning and Employment* 53, no. 3: 45–50.

Pronin, E., D. Y. Lin, and L. Ross. 2002. "The Bias Blind Spot: Perceptions of Bias in Self versus Others." *Personality and Social Psychology Bulletin* 28, no. 3: 369–381. https://doi.org/10.1177/0146167202286008.

Proulx, T., M. Inzlicht, and E. Harmon-Jones. 2012. "Understanding All Inconsistency Compensation as a Palliative Response to Violated Expectations." *Trends in Cognitive Sciences* 16, no. 5: 285–291. https://doi.org/10.1016/j.tics.2012.04.002.

Prusik, M., and M. Lewicka. 2016. "Nostalgia for Communist Times and Autobiographical Memory: Negative Present or Positive Past?" *Political Psychology* 37, no. 5: 677–693. https://doi.org/10.1111/pops.12330.

Purves, T., A. Middlemas, S. Agthong, E. B. Jude, A. J. Boulton, P. Fernyhough, and D. R. Tomlinson. 2001. "A Role for Mitogen-activated Protein Kinases in the Etiology of Diabetic Neuropathy." *FASEB Journal* 15, no. 13: 2508–2514. https://doi.org/10.1096/fj.01-0253hyp.

Putnam, R. 1993. "The Prosperous Community: Social Capital and Public Life." In *CrossCurrents: Cultures, Communities, Technologies*, edited by L. K. Blair, J. Almjeld, and M. R. Murphy, 249–258. Boston, MA: Wadsworth.

Putnam, R. D. 1971. "Studying Elite Political Culture: The Case of 'Ideology.'" *The American Political Science Review* 65, no. 3: 651–681.

Pyszczynski, T., A. Abdollahi, S. Solomon, J. Greenberg, F. Cohen, and D. Weise. 2006. "Mortality Salience, Martyrdom, and Military Might: The Great Satan versus the Axis of Evil." *Personality and Social Psychology Bulletin* 32, no. 4: 525–537. https://doi.org/10.1177/0146167205282157.

Pyszczynski, T., J. Greenberg, and S. Solomon. 1997. "Why Do We Need What We Need? A Terror Management Perspective on the Roots of Human Social Motivation." *Psychological Inquiry* 8, no. 1: 1–20. https://doi.org/10.1207/s15327965pli0801_1.

Pyszczynski, T., J. Greenberg, and S. Solomon. 1999. "A Dual-process Model of Defense against Conscious and Unconscious Death-related Thoughts: An Extension of Terror Management Theory. *Psychological Review* 106, no. 4: 835–845. https://doi.org/10.1037/0033-295X.106.4.835.

Rabasa, A., I. V. Gordon, P. Chalk, A. K. Grant, K. S. McMahon, S. Pezard, C. Reilly, D. Ucko, and S. R. Zimmerman. 2011. *From Insurgency to Stability: Volume II: Insights from Selected Case Studies*. Santa Monica, CA: Rand National Defense Research Institute.

Raleigh, C., and H. Urdal. 2007. "Climate Change, Environmental Degradation and Armed Conflict." *Political Geography* 26, no. 6: 674–694. https://doi.org/10.1016/j.polgeo.2007.06.005.

Rasmussen, B., and D. Salhani. 2010. "A Contemporary Kleinian Contribution to Understanding Racism." *Social Service Review* 84, no. 3: 491–513. https://doi.org/10.1086/656401.

Reeve, C. L., S. Highhouse, and M. E. Brooks. 2006. A Closer Look at Reactions to Realistic Recruitment Messages." *International Journal of Selection and Assessment* 14, no. 1: 1–15. https://doi.org/10.1111/j.1468-2389.2006.00330.x.

Rege, M., and K. Telle. 2004. "The Impact of Social Approval and Framing on Cooperation in Public Good Situations." *Journal of Public Economics* 88, no. 7–8: 1625–1644. https://doi.org/10.1016/S0047-2727(03)00021-5.

Rein, M. 2001. "Dominance, Contest and Reframing." In *Into the Promised Land: Issues Facing the Welfare State*, edited by A. Ben-Arieh and J. Gal, 175–192. Westport, CT: Praeger Publishers.

Reitz, A. K., J. Zimmermann, R. Hutteman, J. Specht, and F. J. Neyer. 2014. "How Peers Make a Difference: The Role of Peer Groups and Peer Relationships in Personality Development." *European Journal of Personality* 28, no. 3: 279–288. https://doi.org/10.1002/per.1965.

Reniers, R. L., R. Corcoran, R. Drake, N. M. Shryane, and B. A. Völlm. 2011. "The QCAE: A Questionnaire of Cognitive and Affective Empathy." *Journal of Personality Assessment* 93, no. 1: 84–95. https://doi.org/10.1080/00223891.2010.528484.

Renno, L. R. 2020. "The Bolsonaro Voter: Issue Positions and Vote Choice in the 2018 Brazilian Presidential Elections." *Latin American Politics and Society* 62, no. 4: 1–23.

Rhee, S. H., and I. D. Waldman. 2002. "Genetic and Environmental Influences on Antisocial Behavior: A Meta-analysis of Twin and Adoption Studies." *Psychological Bulletin* 128, no. 3: 490–529. https://doi.org/10.1037/0033-2909.128.3.490.

Ribeiro, M. H., R. Ottoni, R. West, V. A. Almeida, and W. Meira Jr. 2020. "Auditing Radicalization Pathways on YouTube." In *Proceedings of the 2020 Conference on Fairness, Accountability, and Transparency, Barcelona, Spain*, 131–141. Association for Computing Machinery. https://doi.org/10.1145/3351095.3372879.

Richards, J. 2014. "An Institutional History of the Liberation Tigers of Tamil Eelam (LTTE)." CCDP Working Paper (No. 10).

Richardson, J. 2012. *War, Science and Terrorism: From Laboratory to Open Conflict*. New York: Routledge.

Riek, B. M., E. W. Mania, and S. L. Gaertner. 2006. "Intergroup Threat and Outgroup Attitudes: A Meta-analytic Review." *Personality and Social Psychology Review* 10, no. 4: 336–353. https://doi.org/10.1207/s15327957pspr1004_4.

Rinehart, C. S. 2013. *Volatile Social Movements and the Origins of Terrorism: The Radicalization of Change*. Blue Ridge Summit, PA: Lexington Books.

Riordan, J. 1980. *Sport in Soviet Society: Development of Sport and Physical Education in Russia and the USSR (Vol. 22)*. Cambridge, UK: Cambridge University Press.

Riva, P., K. D. Williams, A. M. Torstrick, and L. Montali. 2014. "Orders to Shoot (a Camera): Effects of Ostracism on Obedience." *The Journal of Social Psychology* 154, no. 3: 208–216. https://doi.org/10.1080/00224545.2014.883354.

Rizzolatti, G., L. Fogassi, and V. Gallese. 2001. "Neurophysiological Mechanisms Underlying the Understanding and Imitation of Action." *Nature Reviews Neuroscience* 2, no. 9: 661–670. https://doi.org/10.1038/35090060.

Roberts, B. W., and W. F. DelVecchio. 2000. "The Rank-order Consistency of Personality Traits from Childhood to Old Age: A Quantitative Review of Longitudinal Studies." *Psychological Bulletin* 126, no. 1: 3–25. https://doi.org/10.1037/0033-2909.126.1.3.

Roberts, D. 2005. *The Totalitarian Experiment in Twentieth Century Europe: Understanding the Poverty of Great Politics*. 1st ed. New York: Routledge. https://doi.org/10.4324/9780203087848.

Robinson, L. 2009. "Cultural Identity and Acculturation Preferences among South Asian Adolescents in Britain: An Exploratory Study." *Children & Society* 23, no. 6: 442–454. https://doi.org/10.1111/j.1099-0860.2008.00179.x.

Rodin, J., and E. J. Langer. 1977. "Long-term Effects of a Control-relevant Intervention with the Institutionalized Aged." *Journal of Personality and Social Psychology* 35, no. 12: 897–902. https://doi.org/10.1037/0022-3514.35.12.897.

Rodriguez-Bailon, R., B. Bratanova, G. B. Willis, L. Lopez-Rodriguez, A. Sturrock, and S. Loughnan. 2017. "Social Class and Ideologies of Inequality: How They Uphold Unequal Societies." *Journal of Social Issues* 73, no. 1: 99–116. https://doi.org/10.1111/josi.12206.

Roets, A., and A. Van Hiel. 2011. "The Role of Need for Closure in Essentialist Entitativity Beliefs and Prejudice: An Epistemic Needs Approach to Racial Categorization." *British Journal of Social Psychology* 50, no. 1: 52–73. https://doi.org/10.1348/014466610X491567.

Rogers, K. 2019. "US Teens Use Screens More than Seven Hours a Day on Average—And That's Not Including School Work." *CNN Health*, October 29. https://edition.cnn.com/2019/10/29/health/common-sense-kids-media-use-report-wellness/index.html.

Rogers, P. 2012. "Nigeria: The Generic Context of the Boko Haram Violence." In *Oxford Research Group, Monthly Global Security Briefing*, April 30, 1–5.

Rokeach, M. 1960. *The Open and Closed Mind: Investigations into the Nature of Belief Systems and Personality Systems*. New York: Basic Books. https://doi.org/10.1126/science.132.3420.142.b.

Rolison, J. J., Y. Hanoch, and M. Gummerum. 2013. "Characteristics of Offenders: The HEXACO Model of Personality as a Framework for Studying Offenders' Personality." *Journal of Forensic Psychiatry & Psychology* 24, no. 1: 71–82. https://doi.org/10.1080/14789949.2012.752024.

Ron, J. 2001. "Ideology in Context: Explaining Sendero Luminoso's Tactical Escalation." *Journal of Peace Research* 38, no. 5: 569–592. https://doi.org/10.1177/0022343301038005002.

Rose, R. 2008. *Understanding Post-Communist Transformation: A Bottom-Up Approach*. 1st ed. New York: Routledge. https://doi.org/10.4324/9780203884935.

Rosenau, W. 2013. "'Our Backs Are Against the Wall': The Black Liberation Army and Domestic Terrorism in 1970s America." *Studies in Conflict & Terrorism* 36, no. 2: 176–192. https://doi.org/10.1080/1057610X.2013.747074.

Rosenau, W., R. Espach, R. D. Ortiz, and N. Herrera. 2014. "Why They Join, Why They Fight, and Why They Leave: Learning from Colombia's Database of Demobilized Militants." *Terrorism and Political Violence* 26, no. 2: 277–285. https://doi.org/10.1080/09546553.2012.700658.

Ross, M. 2006. "A Closer Look at Oil, Diamonds, and Civil War." *Annual Review of Political Science* 9: 265–300. https://doi.org/10.1146/annurev.polisci.9.081304.161338.

Ross, M. L. 2004. "What Do We Know about Natural Resources and Civil War?" *Journal of Peace Research* 41, no. 3: 337–356. https://doi.org/10.1177/0022343304043773.

Rotter, J. 1966. "Generalized Expectancies for Internal versus External Control of Reinforcement." *Psychological Monographs* 80, no. 1: 1–28. https://doi.org/10.1037/h0092976.

Rousseau, D. M. 1998. "Why Workers Still Identify with Organizations." *Journal of Organizational Behavior* 19, no. 3: 217–233. https://doi.org/10.1002/(SICI)1099-1379(199805)19:3<217::AID-JOB931>3.0.CO;2-N.

Russell, C. A., and B. H. Miller. 1977. "Profile of a Terrorist." *Studies in Conflict & Terrorism* 1, no. 1: 17–34. https://doi.org/10.1080/10576107708435394.

Ryan, R. M., and E. L. Deci. 2000. "Self-determination Theory and the Facilitation of Intrinsic Motivation, Social Development, and Well-being." *American Psychologist* 55, no. 1: 68–78. https://doi.org/10.1037/0003-066X.55.1.68.

Ryan, R. M., and P. H. Hawley. 2017. "Naturally Good? Basic Psychological Needs and the Proximal and Evolutionary Bases of Human Benevolence." In *The Oxford Handbook of Hypo-egoic Phenomena*, edited by K. W. Brown, and R. M. Leary, 205–223. New York: Oxford University Press.

Saab, B. Y., and A. W. Taylor. 2009. "Criminality and Armed Groups: A Comparative Study of FARC and Paramilitary Groups in Colombia." *Studies in Conflict & Terrorism* 32, no. 6: 455–475. https://doi.org/10.1080/10576100902892570.

Sageman, M. 2008. "The Next Generation of Terror." *Foreign Policy* 165: 37.

Saito, M., K. Kondo, N. Kondo, A. Abe, T. Ojima, and K. Suzuki. 2014. "Relative Deprivation, Poverty, and Subjective Health: JAGES Cross-sectional Study." *PloS One* 9, no. 10: e111169. https://doi.org/10.1371/journal.pone.0111169.

Saltman, E. M., and M. Smith. 2015. "'Till Martyrdom Do Us Part': Gender and the ISIS Phenomenon." Institute for Strategic Dialogue. https://www.isdglobal.org/isd-publications/till-martyrdom-do-us-part-gender-and-the-isis-phenomenon/.

Salzman, M. B. 2008. "Globalization, Religious Fundamentalism and the Need for Meaning." *International Journal of Intercultural Relations* 32, no. 4: 318–327. https://doi.org/10.1016/j.ijintrel.2008.04.006.

Sambanis, N. 2001. "Do Ethnic and Nonethnic Civil Wars have the Same Causes? A Theoretical and Empirical Inquiry (Part 1)." *Journal of Conflict Resolution* 45, no. 3: 259–282. https://doi.org/10.1177/0022002701045003001.

Sambanis, N. 2002. "A Review of Recent Advances and Future Directions in the Quantitative Literature on Civil War." *Defence and Peace Economics* 13, no. 3: 215–243. https://doi.org/10.1080/10242690210976.

Sampson, R. J., and J. H. Laub. 1995. *Crime in the Making: Pathways and Turning Points through Life*. Cambridge, MA: Harvard University Press.

Sanbonmatsu, D. M., and R. H. Fazio. 1990. "The Role of Attitudes in Memory-based Decision Making." *Journal of Personality and Social Psychology* 59, no. 4: 614–622. https://doi.org/10.1037/0022-3514.59.4.614.

Sangeetha, K. 2010. "Effective Recruitment: A Framework." *IUP Journal of Business Strategy* 7, no. 1–2: 93–107.

Saro-Wiwa, K. 1993. "They are killing my people." *The News*, May 17.

Sarraj, E. E., R. L. Punamäki, S. Salmi, and D. Summerfield 1996. "Experiences of Torture and Ill-treatment and Posttraumatic Stress Disorder Symptoms among Palestinian Political Prisoners." *Journal of Traumatic Stress* 9, no. 3: 595–606. https://doi.org/10.1007/BF02103668.

Scaglione, A. 2016. "Cosa Nostra and Camorra: Illegal Activities and Organisational Structures." *Global Crime* 17, no. 1: 60–78. https://doi.org/10.1080/17440572.2015.1114919.

Schaffner, B. F., M. MacWilliams, and T. Nteta. 2017. "Hostile Sexism, Racism Denial, and the Historic Education Gap in Support for Trump." In *The 2016 Presidential Election: The Causes and Consequences of a Political Earthquake*, edited by A. Cavari, R. J. Powell, and K. R. Mayer, 99–116. New York: Rowman and Littlefield.

Schwank, N. 2014. "Ideologie und Konflikt, Bundeszentrale für politische Bildung." https://www.bpb.de/themen/kriege-konflikte/dossier-kriege-konflikte/186896/ideologie-und-konflikt/

Schein, E. H. 1992. *Organizational Culture and Leadership*. 2nd ed. San Francisco, CA: Jossey-Bass.

Schellenberg, B. 2013. *Die Rechtsextremismus-Debatte: Charakteristika, Konflikte und ihre Folgen*. Cham: Springer.

Scheppele, K. L. 2018. "Autocratic Legalism." *The University of Chicago Law Review* 85, no. 2: 545–584.

Schildkraut, D. J. 2011. "National Identity in the United States." In *Handbook of Identity Theory and Research*, edited by S. Schwartz, K. Luyckx, and V. Vignoles, 845–865. New York: Springer. https://doi.org/10.1007/978-1-4419-7988-9_36.

Schimmenti, A., C. Caprì, D. La Barbera, and V. Caretti. 2014. "Mafia and Psychopathy." *Criminal Behaviour and Mental Health* 24, no. 5: 321–331. https://doi.org/10.1002/cbm.1902.

Schlenker, B. R., J. R. Chambers, and B. M. Le. 2012. "Conservatives are Happier than Liberals, But Why? Political Ideology, Personality, and Life Satisfaction." *Journal of Research in Personality* 46, no. 2: 127–146. https://doi.org/10.1016/j.jrp.2011.12.009.

Schmid, A. A. 2004. *Conflict and Cooperation: Institutional and Behavioral Economics*. Blackwell Publishing Ltd.

Schmitt, D. P., and J. Allik. 2005. "Simultaneous Administration of the Rosenberg Self-Esteem Scale in 53 Nations: Exploring the Universal and Culture-specific Features of Global Self-esteem." *Journal of Personality and Social Psychology* 89, no. 4: 623–642. https://doi.org/10.1037/0022-3514.89.4.623.

Schneider, B., H. W. Goldstiein, and D. B. Smith. 1995. "The ASA Framework: An Update." *Personnel Psychology* 48, no. 4: 747–773. https://doi.org/10.1111/j.1744-6570.1995.tb01780.x.

Schopflin, G. 1993. "The Road from Post Communism." In *The New Institutional Architecture of Eastern Europe. Studies in Russia and East Europe*, edited by S. Whitefield, 183–200. London: Palgrave Macmillan. https://doi.org/10.1007/978-1-349-23075-4_10.

Schore, A. N. 2001. "The Effects of Early Relational Trauma on Right Brain Development, Affect Regulation, and Infant Mental Health." *Infant Mental Health Journal* 22, no. 1–2: 201–269. https://doi.org/10.1002/1097-0355(200101/04)22:1<201::AID-IMHJ8>3.0.CO;2-9.

Schrock-Jacobson, G. 2012. "The Violent Consequences of the Nation: Nationalism and the Initiation of Interstate War." *Journal of Conflict Resolution* 56, no. 5: 825–852. https://doi.org/10.1177/0022002712438354.

Schulz-Hardt, S., D. Frey, C. Lüthgens, and S. Moscovici. 2000. "Biased Information Search in Group Decision Making." *Journal of Personality and Social Psychology* 78, no. 4: 655–669. https://doi.org/10.1037/0022-3514.78.4.655.

Schwartz, B. 2000. "Self-determination: The Tyranny of Freedom." *American Psychologist* 55, no. 1: 79–88. https://doi.org/10.1037/0003-066X.55.1.79.

Schwartz, S. H., and J. A. Fleishman. 1982. "Effects of Negative Personal Norms on Helping Behavior." *Personality and Social Psychology Bulletin* 8, no. 1: 81–86. https://doi.org/10.1177/014616728281013.

Schwartz, S. H., G. V. Caprara, and M. Vecchione. 2010. "Basic Personal Values, Core Political Values, and Voting: A Longitudinal Analysis." *Political Psychology* 31, no. 3: 421–452. https://doi.org/10.1111/j.1467-9221.2010.00764.x.

Schwartz, S. H., G. V. Caprara, M. Vecchione, P. Bain, G. Bianchi, M. G. Caprara ... Z. Zaleski. 2014. "Basic Personal Values Underlie and Give Coherence to Political Values: A Cross National Study in 15 Countries." *Political Behavior* 36, no. 4: 899–930. https://doi.org/10.1007/s11109-013-9255-z.

Schwartz, S. J., A. Meca, and M. Petrova. 2017. "Who Am I and Why Does It Matter? Linking Personal Identity and Self-concept Clarity." In *Self-concept Clarity*, edited by J. Lodi-Smith and K. DeMarree, 145–164. Cham: Springer. https://doi.org/10.1007/978-3-319-71547-6_8.

Scott, C. R., S. L. Connaughton, H. R. Diaz-Saenz, K. Maguire, R. Ramirez, B. Richardson, S. P. Shaw, and D. Morgan. 1999. "The Impacts of Communication and Multiple Identifications on Intent to Leave: A Multimethodological Exploration." *Management Communication Quarterly* 12, no. 3: 400–435. https://doi.org/10.1177/0893318999123002.

Sears, D. O., and P. J. Henry. 2003. "The Origins of Symbolic Racism." *Journal of Personality and Social Psychology* 85, no. 2: 259–275. https://doi.org/10.1037/0022-3514.85.2.259.

Sechrist, G. B., and C. Stangor. 2001. "Perceived Consensus Influences Intergroup Behavior and Stereotype Accessibility." *Journal of Personality and Social Psychology* 80, no. 4: 645–654. https://doi.org/10.1037/0022-3514.80.4.645.

Sechrist, G. B., J. K. Swim, and C. Stangor. 2004. "When Do the Stigmatized Make Attributions to Discrimination Occurring to the Self and Others? The Roles of Self-presentation and Need for Control." *Journal of Personality and Social Psychology* 87, no. 1: 111–122. https://doi.org/10.1037/0022-3514.87.1.111.

Seiffge-Krenke, I. 1984. "Formen der Problembewältigung bei besonders belasteten Jugendlichen." In *Probleme des Jugendalters*, edited by E. Olbrich and E. Todt, 353–386. Berlin, Heidelberg: Springer. https://doi.org/10.1007/978-3-642-69128-7_17.

Seiffge-Krenke, I. 1990. "Developmental Processes in Self-Concept and Coping Behaviour." In *Coping and Self-Concept in Adolescence*, edited by H. A Bosma, A. E. S. Jackson, 49–68. Berlin, Heidelberg: Springer. https://doi.org/10.1007/978-3-642-75222-3_4.

References

Seligson, M. A. 2006. "The Measurement and Impact of Corruption Victimization: Survey Evidence from Latin America." *World Development* 34, no. 2: 381–404. https://doi.org/10.1016/j.worlddev.2005.03.012.

Sen, A. 1992. *Inequality Reexamined*. Cambridge, MA: Harvard University Press and Russell Sage Foundation.

Sen, A. 2017. *Collective Choice and Social Welfare*. Cambridge, MA: Harvard University Press.

Serenata, N. 2014. *The 'Ndrangheta and Sacra Corona Unita (Vol. 12)*. Cham: Springer. https://doi.org/10.1007/978-3-319-04930-4_3.

Seul, J. R. 1999. "'Ours Is the Way of God': Religion, Identity, and Intergroup Conflict." *Journal of Peace Research* 36, no. 5: 553–569. https://doi.org/10.1177/0022343399036005004.

Seuntjens, T. G., N. Van de Ven, M. Zeelenberg, and S. M. Breugelmans. 2019. "Greedy Bastards: The Desire for More as a Motivator for Unethical Behavior." *Personality and Individual Differences* 138, no. 1: 147–156. https://doi.org/10.1016/j.paid.2018.09.027.

Seuntjens, T. G., M. Zeelenberg, N. Van de Ven, and S. M. Breugelmans. 2015. "Dispositional Greed." *Journal of Personality and Social Psychology* 108, no. 6: 917–933. https://doi.org/10.1037/pspp0000031.

Shapira, H. 2019. "The Minutemen: Patrolling and Performativity along the U.S./Mexico Border." In *Vigilantism Against Migrants and Minorities*, edited by T. Bjørgo and M. Mareš, 151–164. New York: Taylor & Francis.

Shapiro Jr., D. H., C. E. Schwartz, and J. A. Astin. 1996. "Controlling Ourselves, Controlling Our World: Psychology's Role in Understanding Positive and Negative Consequences of Seeking and Gaining Control." *American Psychologist* 51, no. 12: 1213–1230. https://doi.org/10.1037/0003-066X.51.12.1213.

Sharma, K. 2006. "The Political Economy of Civil War in Nepal." *World Development* 34, no. 7: 1237–1253. https://doi.org/10.1016/j.worlddev.2005.12.001.

Shay, L. 2015. "A Nazi Childhood: Hitler's Germany, 1939–1945." *Saber & Scroll Historical Journal* 1, no. 2: 28452.

Shaykhutdinov, R., and B. Bragg. 2011. "Do Grievances Matter in Ethnic Conflict? An Experimental Approach." *Analyses of Social Issues and Public Policy* 11, no. 1: 141–153. https://doi.org/10.1111/j.1530-2415.2011.01240.x.

Sheldon, K. M. 2004. "The Benefits of a 'Sidelong' Approach to Self-esteem Need Satisfaction: Comment on Crocker and Park (2004)." *Psychological Bulletin* 130, no. 3: 421–424. https://doi.org/10.1037/0033-2909.130.3.421.

Sheldon, K. M. 2011. "Integrating Behavioral-motive and Experiential-requirement Perspectives on Psychological Needs: A Two Process Model." *Psychological Review* 118, no. 4: 552–569. https://doi.org/10.1037/a0024758.

Sherif, M., O. J. Harvey, B. J. White, W. R. Hood, and C. W. Sherif. 1961. *Intergroup Conflict and Cooperation: The Robbers Cave Experiment*. Norman: University of Oklahoma Book Exchange.

Shogren, K. A., M. L. Wehmeyer, and S. B. Palmer. 2017. "Causal Agency Theory." In *Development of Self-determination through the Life-course*, edited by L. M. Wehmeyer, A. K. Shogren, D. T. Little, and J. S. Lopez, 55–67. Dordrecht: Springer. https://doi.org/10.1007/978-94-024-1042-6_5.

Schore, A. N. 2001. "The Effects of Early Relational Trauma on Right Brain Development, Affect Regulation, and Infant Mental Health." *Infant Mental Health Journal: Official Publication of The World Association for Infant Mental Health* 22, no. 1–2: 201–269.

Schwartz, S. H. 1992. "Universals in the Content and Structure of Values: Theoretical Advances and Empirical Tests in 20 Countries." In *Advances in Experimental Social Psychology*, edited by M. P. Zanna, 25, 1–65. New York: Academic Press.

Schwartz, B., and A. Ward. 2004. "Doing Better but Feeling Worse: The Paradox of Choice." *Positive Psychology in Practice*, 86–104.

Shrum, L. J., N. Wong, F. Arif, S. K. Chugani, A. Gunz, T. M. Lowrey, A. Nairn, M. Pandelaere, S. M. Ross, A. Ruvio, K. Scott, and J. Sundie. 2013. "Reconceptualizing Materialism as Identity Goal Pursuits: Functions, Processes, and Consequences." *Journal of Business Research* 66, no. 8: 1179–1185. https://doi.org/10.1016/j.jbusres.2012.08.010.

Sicherman, N., G. Loewenstein, D. J. Seppi, and S. P. Utkus. 2016. "Financial Attention." *The Review of Financial Studies* 29, no. 4: 863–897. https://doi.org/10.1093/rfs/hhv073.

Sidanius, J., and F. Pratto. 1993. "The Inevitability of Oppression and the Dynamics of Social Dominance." In *Prejudice, Politics, and the American Dilemma*, edited by P. M. Sniderman, P. E. Tetlock, and E. G. Carmines, 173–211. Redwood City, CA: Stanford University Press.

Sidanius, J., and F. Pratto. 1999. *Social Dominance: An Intergroup Theory of Social Hierarchy and Oppression*. Cambridge: Cambridge University Press. https://doi.org/10.1017/CBO9781139175043.

Sidanius, J., S. Cotterill, J. Sheehy-Skeffington, N. Kteily, and H. Carvacho. 2017. "Social Dominance Theory: Explorations in the Psychology of Oppression." In *The Cambridge Handbook of the Psychology of Prejudice*, edited by C. G. Sibley and F. K. Barlow, 149–187. Cambridge, MA: Cambridge University Press. https://doi.org/10.1017/9781316161579.008.

Sidanius, J., N. Kteily, S. Levin, F. Pratto, and M. Obaidi. 2016. "Support for Asymmetric Violence among Arab Populations: The Clash of Cultures, Social Identity, or Counterdominance?" *Group Processes & Intergroup Relations* 19, no. 3: 343–359. https://doi.org/10.1177/1368430215577224.

Siegfried, D. 2006. *Time Is On My Side: Konsum und Politik in der westdeutschen Jugendkultur der 60er Jahre (Vol. 41)*. Göttingen: Wallstein Verlag.

Silke, A. 2008. "Holy Warriors: Exploring the Psychological Processes of Jihadi Radicalization." *European Journal of Criminology* 5, no. 1: 99–123. https://doi.org/10.1177/1477370807084226.

Simon, B., and R. Brown. 1987. "Perceived Intragroup Homogeneity in Minority–Majority Contexts." *Journal of Personality and Social Psychology* 53, no. 4: 703–711. https://doi.org/10.1037/0022-3514.53.4.703.

Simon, B., and O. Grabow. 2010. "The Politicization of Migrants: Further Evidence that Politicized Collective Identity is a Dual Identity." *Political Psychology* 31, no. 5: 717–738. https://doi.org/10.1111/j.1467-9221.2010.00782.x.

Simon, B., and D. L. Hamilton. 1994. "Self-stereotyping and Social Context: The Effects of Relative In-group Size and In-group Status." *Journal of Personality and Social Psychology* 66, no. 4: 699–711. https://doi.org/10.1037/0022-3514.66.4.699.

Simon, B., F. Reichert, and O. Grabow. 2013. "When Dual Identity Becomes a Liability: Identity and Political Radicalism among Migrants." *Psychological Science* 24, no. 3: 251–257. https://doi.org/10.1177/0956797612450889.

Sinclair, S., E. Dunn, and B. Lowery. 2005. "The Relationship between Parental Racial Attitudes and Children's Implicit Prejudice." *Journal of Experimental Social Psychology* 41, no. 3: 283–289. https://doi.org/10.1016/j.jesp.2004.06.003.

Singer, P. 2020. "Reflections on Socialism." In *Reflections on Socialism in the Twenty-First Century*, edited by C. Brundenius, 149–155. Cham: Springer. https://doi.org/10.1007/978-3-030-33920-3_6.

Singer, T., B. Seymour, J. O'Doherty, H. Kaube, R. J. Dolan, and C. D. Frith. 2004. "Empathy for Pain Involves the Affective but Not Sensory Components of Pain." *Science* 303, no. 5661: 1157–1162. https://doi.org/10.1126/science.1093535.

Sıradağ, A. 2016. "Explaining the Conflict in Central African Republic: Causes and Dynamics." *Epiphany: Journal of Transdisciplinary Studies* 9, no. 3: 86–103. http://doi.org/10.21533/epiphany.v9i3.246.

Skinner, B. F. 1971. *Beyond Freedom and Dignity*. New York: Bantam Books.

References

Slavich, G. M., A. O'Donovan, , E. S. Epel, , and M. E. Kemeny. 2010. "Black Sheep Get the Blues: A Psychobiological Model of Social Rejection and Depression." *Neuroscience & Biobehavioral Reviews* 35, no. 1: 39–45. https://doi.org/10.1016/j.neubiorev.2010.01.003.

Slotter, E. B., and W. L. Gardner. 2014. "Remind Me Who I Am: Social Interaction Strategies for Maintaining the Threatened Self-concept." *Personality and Social Psychology Bulletin* 40, no. 9: 1148–1161. https://doi.org/10.1177/0146167214537685.

Slotter, E. B., L. Winger, , and N. Soto. 2015. "Lost Without Each Other: The Influence of Group Identity Loss on the Self-concept." *Group Dynamics: Theory, Research, and Practice* 19, no. 1: 15–30. https://doi.org/10.1037/gdn0000020.

Smart Richman, L., and M. R. Leary. 2009. "Reactions to Discrimination, Stigmatization, Ostracism, and Other Forms of Interpersonal Rejection: A Multimotive Model." *Psychological Review* 116, no. 2: 365–383. https://doi.org/10.1037/a0015250.

Smith, A. 2010. *Nationalism: Theory, Ideology, History*. Cambridge, UK: Polity Press.

Smith, B. L., K. R. Damphousse, and P. Roberts. 2006. *Pre-incident Indicators of Terrorist Incidents: The Identification of Behavioral, Geographic, and Temporal Patterns of Preparatory Conduct*. Arkansas: Arkansas University Fayetteville Terrorism Research Center, Fulbright College.

Smith, H. J., T. F. Pettigrew, G. M. Pippin, and S. Bialosiewicz. 2012. "Relative Deprivation: A Theoretical and Meta-analytic Review." *Personality and Social Psychology Review* 16, no. 3: 203–232. https://doi.org/10.1177/1088868311430825.

Smith, M. L., and P. Matějů. 2012. "Two Decades of Value Change: The Crystallization of Meritocratic and Egalitarian Beliefs in the Czech Republic." *Social Justice Research* 25, no. 4: 421–439.

Smith, T. W., and J. Son. 2017. *Trends in National Spending Priorities, 1973–2016*. Chicago, IL: National Opinion Research Center, University of Chicago.

Snyder, R., and R. Bhavnani. 2005. "Diamonds, Blood, and Taxes: A Revenue-centered Framework for Explaining Political Order." *Journal of Conflict Resolution* 49, no. 4: 563–597. https://doi.org/10.1177/0022002705277796.

Sollberger, D. 2013. "On Identity: From a Philosophical Point of View." *Child and Adolescent Psychiatry and Mental Health* 7, no. 1: 1–10. https://doi.org/10.1186/1753-2000-7-29.

Somasundaram, D. J., and S. Sivayokan. 1994. "War Trauma in a Civilian Population." *The British Journal of Psychiatry* 165, no. 4: 524–527. https://doi.org/10.1192/bjp.165.4.524.

Sommer, K. L., K. D. Williams, N. J. Ciarocco, and R. F. Baumeister. 2001. "When Silence Speaks Louder than Words: Explorations into the Intrapsychic and Interpersonal Consequences of Social Ostracism." *Basic and Applied Social Psychology* 23, no. 4: 225–243. https://doi.org/10.1207/153248301753225694.

Southern Poverty Law Center. 2013. "Hate and Extremism." http://www.splcenter.org/what-we-do/hate-and-extremism.

Spanierman, L. B., E. Oh, V. P. Poteat, A. R. Hund, V. L. McClair, A. M. Beer, and A. M. Clarke. 2008. "White University Students' Responses to Societal Racism: A Qualitative Investigation." *The Counseling Psychologist* 36, no. 6: 839–870. https://doi.org/10.1177/0011000006295589.

Spears, R. 2011. "Group Identities: The Social Identity Perspective." In Handbook of Identity Theory and Research, edited by S. Schwartz, K. Luyckx, and V. Vignoles, 201–224. New York: Springer. https://doi.org/10.1007/978-1-4419-7988-9_9.

Speckhard, A., and A. S. Yayla. 2017. "The ISIS Emni: Origins and Inner Workings of ISIS's Intelligence Apparatus." *Perspectives on Terrorism* 11, no. 1: 2–16. https://www.jstor.org/stable/26297733.

Speitel, V. 1980. "Wir Wollten Alles und Gleichzeitig Nichts III." *Der Spiegel* 33, 30–36.

Spencer, S. J., R. A. Josephs, and C. M. Steele. 1993. "Low Self-esteem: The Uphill Struggle for Self-integrity." In *Self-esteem*, edited by R. F. Baumeister, 21–36. Boston, MA: Springer. https://doi.org/10.1007/978-1-4684-8956-9_2.

Spiegel International. 2015. "Secret Files Reveal the Structure of Islamic State." https://www.spiegel.de/international/world/islamic-state-files-show-structure-of-islamist-terror-group-a1029274.html.

Spiegler, O., R. Wölfer, and M. Hewstone. 2019. "Dual Identity Development and Adjustment in Muslim Minority Adolescents." *Journal of Youth and Adolescence* 48, no. 10: 1924–1937. https://doi.org/10.1007/s10964-019-01117-9.

Spisak, B. R., P. H. Dekker, M. Krüger, and M. Van Vugt. 2012. "Warriors and Peacekeepers: Testing a Biosocial Implicit Leadership Hypothesis of Intergroup Relations Using Masculine and Feminine Faces." *PloS One* 7, no. 1: e30399.

Sprinzak, E. 1998. "The Psychological Formation of Extreme Left Terrorism in a Democracy: The Case of the Weatherman." In *Origins of Terrorism: Psychologies, Ideologies, Theologies, States of Mind*, edited by W. Reich, 65–86. Washington, DC: Woodrow Wilson Center Press.

Sprunger, J. G., A. Hales, M. Maloney, K. Williams, and C. I. Eckhardt. 2020. "Alcohol, Affect, and Aggression: An Investigation of Alcohol's Effects Following Ostracism." *Psychology of Violence* 10, no. 6: 585–593. https://doi.org/10.1037/vio0000341.

Staebler, K., E. Helbing, C. Rosenbach, and B. Renneberg. 2011. "Rejection Sensitivity and Borderline Personality Disorder." *Clinical Psychology & Psychotherapy* 18, no. 4: 275–283. https://doi.org/10.1002/cpp.705.

Stafford, F., and M. Palacios. 2002. *Colombia: Fragmented Land, Divided Society*. New York: Oxford University Press.

Stanski, K. 2006. "Terrorism, Gender, and Ideology: A Case Study of Women Who Join the Revolutionary Armed Forces of Colombia (FARC)." In *The Making of a Terrorist: Recruitment, Training, and Root Causes*, edited by J. J. F. Forest, 148–149. Westport, CT: Praeger Security International.

Staub, E. 1993. "Individual and Group Selves: Motivation, Morality, and Evolution." In *The Moral Self*, edited by G. G. Noam, T. E. Wren, G. Nunner-Winkler, and W. Edelstein, 337–358. Cambridge, MA: The MIT Press.

Staub, E. 2001. "Individual and Group Identities in Genocide and Mass Killing." In *Social Identity, Intergroup Conflict, and Conflict Reduction*, edited by R. D. Ashmore, L. Jussim, and D. Wilder, 159–184. New York: Oxford University Press.

Staub, E., B. Tursky, and G. E. Schwartz. 1971. "Self-control and Predictability: Their Effects on Reactions to Aversive Stimulation." *Journal of Personality and Social Psychology* 18, no. 2: 157–162. https://doi.org/10.1037/h0030851.

Steel, Z., T. Chey, D. Silove, C. Marnane, R. A. Bryant, and M. Van Ommeren. 2009. "Association of Torture and Other Potentially Traumatic Events with Mental Health Outcomes among Populations Exposed to Mass Conflict and Displacement: A Systematic Review and Meta-analysis." *JAMA* 302, no. 5: 537–549. https://doi.org/10.1001/jama.2009.1132.

Steele, C. M., S. J. Spencer, and M. Lynch. 1993. "Self-image Resilience and Dissonance: The Role of Affirmational Resources." *Journal of Personality and Social Psychology* 64, no. 6: 885–896. https://doi.org/10.1037/0022-3514.64.6.885.

Steger, M. F. 2009. "Meaning in Life." In *Oxford Handbook of Positive Psychology*, edited by S. J. Lopez and C. R. Snyder, 679–687. New York: Oxford University Press.

Steger, M. B. 2013. "Political Ideologies in the Age of Globalization." In *The Oxford Handbook of Political Ideologies*, edited by M. Freeden, T. L. Sargent, and M. Stears, 214–231. Oxford: Oxford University Press. http://dx.doi.org/10.1093/oxfordhb/9780199585977.013.007.

Stellar, J. E., V. M. Manzo, M. W. Kraus, and D. Keltner. 2012. "Class and Compassion: Socioeconomic Factors Predict Responses to Suffering." *Emotion* 12, no. 3: 449–459. https://doi.org/10.1037/a0026508.

Stephan, W. G., and C. W. Stephan. 2000. "An Integrated Threat Theory of Prejudice." In *Reducing Prejudice and Discrimination*, edited by S. Oskamp, 23–45. Mahwah, NJ: Lawrence Erlbaum Associates Publishers.

References

Stephan, W. G., C. L. Renfro, and M. D. Davis. 2008. "The Role of Threat in Intergroup Relations." In *Improving Intergroup Relations: Building on the Legacy of Thomas F. Pettigrew*, edited by U. Wagner, L. R. Tropp, G. Finchilescu and C. Tredoux, 55–72. London: Blackwell Publishing. https://doi.org/10.1002/9781444303117.ch5.

Stephan, W. G., O. Ybarra, and R. K. Morrison. 2009. "Intergroup Threat Theory." In *Handbook of Prejudice, Stereotyping, and Discrimination*, edited by D. T. Nelson, 43–55. New York: Psychology Press.

Steptoe, A. E., and A. E. Appels. 1989. *Stress, Personal Control and Health*. New York: John Wiley & Sons.

Stets, J. E., and P. J. Burke. 2000. "Identity Theory and Social Identity Theory." *Social Psychology Quarterly* 63, no. 3: 224–237. https://doi.org/10.2307/2695870.

Stewart, F. 2002. "Horizontal Inequalities: A Neglected Dimension of Development." (Working Paper No. 81). University of Oxford. http://www.qeh.ox.ac.uk/pdf/qehwp/qehwps81.pdf.

Stewart, F. 2008. "Horizontal Inequalities and Conflict: An Introduction and some Hypotheses." In *Horizontal Inequalities and Conflict: Understanding Group Violence in Multiethnic Societies*, edited by F. Stewart, 3–23. London: Palgrave Macmillan. https://doi.org/10.1057/9780230582729_1.

Stewart, F., M. Barrón, G. Brown, and M. Hartwell. 2006. "Social Exclusion and Conflict: Analysis and Policy Implications." CRISE Policy Paper. Oxford, UK.

Stinson, D. A., C. Logel, J. G. Holmes, J. V. Wood, A. L. Forest, D. Gaucher, G. M. Fitzsimons, and J. Kath. 2010. "The Regulatory Function of Self-Esteem: Testing the Epistemic and Acceptance Signaling Systems." *Journal of Personality and Social Psychology* 99, no. 6: 993–1013. https://doi.org/10.1037/a0020310.

Strentz, T. 1988. "A Terrorist Psychosocial Profile: Past and Present." *FBI Law Enforcement Bulletin* 57, no. 4: 13–19.

Strickland, A. A. 2008. "Conservative Mind: A Focus on Introspection and Worldview." (Publication No. 433). MSc diss., Georgia Southern University. https://digitalcommons.georgiasouthern.edu/etd/433.

Strickland, A. A., C. S., Taber, and M. Lodge. 2011. "Motivated Reasoning and Public Opinion." *Journal of Health Politics, Policy and Law* 36, no. 6: 935–944. https://doi.org/10.1215/03616878-1460524.

Struch, N., and S. H. Schwartz. 1989. "Intergroup Aggression: Its Predictors and Distinctness from In-group Bias." *Journal of Personality and Social Psychology* 56, no. 3: 364–373. https://doi.org/10.1037/0022-3514.56.3.364.

Suliman, M. 1998. "Resource Access: A Major Cause of Armed Conflict in the Sudan. The Case of the Nuba Mountains." In *International Workshop on Community-Based Natural Resource Management*, 10–14. Washington DC: World Bank.

Sullivan, M. W., and M. Lewis. 2003. "Contextual Determinants of Anger and Other Negative Expressions in Young Infants." *Developmental Psychology* 39, no. 4: 693–705. https://doi.org/10.1037/0012-1649.39.4.693.

Sumner, W. G. 1906. *Folkways: A Study of Mores, Manners, Customs and Morals*. New York: Dover Publications, Inc.

Sun, J., K. Zhuang, H. Li, D. Wei, Q. Zhang, and J. Qiu. 2018. "Perceiving Rejection by Others: Relationship between Rejection Sensitivity and the Spontaneous Neuronal Activity of the Brain." *Social Neuroscience* 13, no. 4: 429–438. https://doi.org/10.1080/17470919.2017.1340335.

Suor, J. H., M. L. Sturge-Apple, P. T. Davies, and D. Cicchetti. 2017. "A Life History Approach to Delineating How Harsh Environments and Hawk Temperament Traits Differentially Shape Children's Problem-Solving Skills." *Journal of Child Psychology and Psychiatry* 58, no. 8: 902–909. https://doi.org/10.1111/jcpp.12718.

Sutherland, S. 2014. *Greed: From Gordon Gekko to David Hume*. London: Haus Publishing.

Swann Jr., W. B., and C. Seyle. 2005. "Personality Psychology's Comeback and Its Emerging Symbiosis with Social Psychology." *Personality and Social Psychology Bulletin* 31, no. 2: 155–165. https://doi.org/10.1177/0146167204271591.

Swindle Jr., R., K. Heller, B. Pescosolido, and S. Kikuzawa. 2000. "Responses to Nervous Breakdowns in America Over a 40-year Period: Mental Health Policy Implications." *American Psychologist* 55, no. 7: 740–749. https://doi.org/10.1037/0003-066X.55.7.740.

Szilágyi, A., and A. Bozóki. 2015. "Playing It Again in Post-communism: The Revolutionary Rhetoric of Viktor Orbán in Hungary." *Advances in the History of Rhetoric* 18, no. Sup1: S153–S166. https://doi.org/10.1080/15362426.2015.1010872.

Tajfel, H. 1982. "Social Psychology of Intergroup Relations." *Annual Review of Psychology* 33, no.1: 1–39.

Tajfel, H., and J. C. Turner. 1979. "An Integrative Theory of Intergroup Conflict." In *The Social Psychology of Intergroup Relations*, edited by W. G. Austin and S. Worchel, pp. 33–48. Monterey, CA: Brooks/Cole.

Taji-Farouki, S. 1996. *A Fundamental Quest: Hizb al-Tahrir and the Search for the Islamic Caliphate*. London: Grey Seal.

Tamir, Y. 1993. *Liberal Nationalism*. Princeton, NJ: Princeton University Press.

Tarazona-Sevillano, G. 1994. "The Organization of Shining Path." In *The Shining Path of Peru*, edited by D. S. Palmer, 189–208. New York: Palgrave Macmillan. https://doi.org/10.1007/978-1-137-05210-0_9.

Taylor, D. M. 1997. "The Quest for Collective Identity: The Plight of Disadvantaged Ethnic Minorities." *Canadian Psychology/Psychologie canadienne* 38, no. 3: 174–190. https://doi.org/10.1037/0708-5591.38.3.174.

Taylor, L. D., P. Davis-Kean, and O. Malanchuk. 2007. "Self-esteem, Academic Self-concept, and Aggression at School." *Aggressive Behavior* 33, no. 2: 130–136. https://doi.org/10.1002/ab.20174.

Taysom, S. 2011. *Dimensions of Faith: A Mormon Studies Reader*. Salt Lake City, UT: Signature Books.

Tennen, H., and G. Affleck. 1993. "The Puzzles of Self-Esteem a Clinical Perspective." In *Self-Esteem: The Puzzle of Low Self-Regard*, edited by R. F. Baumeister, 241–262. Boston, MA: Springer. https://doi.org/10.1007/978-1-4684-8956-9_13.

Terpstra, N., and G. Frerks. 2017. "Rebel Governance and Legitimacy: Understanding the Impact of Rebel Legitimation on Civilian Compliance with the LTTE Rule." *Civil Wars* 19, no. 3: 279–307. https://doi.org/10.1080/13698249.2017.1393265.

Testas, A. 2004. "Determinants of Terrorism in the Muslim World: An Empirical Cross-sectional Analysis." *Terrorism and Political Violence* 16, no. 2: 253–273. https://doi.org/10.1080/09546550490482504.

Thagard, P., and J. V. Wood. 2015. "Eighty Phenomena about the Self: Representation, Evaluation, Regulation, and Change." *Frontiers in Psychology* 6, no. 334: 1–15. https://doi.org/10.3389/fpsyg.2015.00334.

The Oxford Companion to Politics of the World. 2004. "New Right." https://www.oxfordreference.com/view/10.1093/acref/9780195117394.001.0001/acref-9780195117394-e-0519?rskey=0I5UMj&result=1.

Theisen, O. M. 2008. "Blood and Soil? Resource Scarcity and Internal Armed Conflict Revisited." *Journal of Peace Research* 45, no. 6: 801–818. https://doi.org/10.1177/0022343308096157.

Theisen, O. M. 2012. "Climate Clashes? Weather Variability, Land Pressure, and Organized Violence in Kenya, 1989–2004." *Journal of Peace Research* 49, no. 1: 81–96. https://doi.org/10.1177/0022343311425842.

Thompson, M. M., M. E. Naccarato, K. C. Parker, and G. B. Moskowitz. 2013. "The Personal Need for Structure and Personal Fear of Invalidity Measures: Historical Perspectives,

Current Applications, and Future Directions." *Cognitive Social Psychology: The Princeton Symposium on the Legacy and Future of Social Cognition*, 25–45.

Thorbecke, E., and C. Charumilind. 2002. "Economic Inequality and Its Socioeconomic Impact." *World Development* 30, no. 9: 1477–1495. https://doi.org/10.1016/S0305-750X(02)00052-9.

Thorisdottir, H., J. T. Jost, I. Liviatan, and P. E. Shrout. 2007. "Psychological Needs and Values Underlying Left–Right Political Orientation: Cross-national Evidence from Eastern and Western Europe." *Public Opinion Quarterly* 71, no. 2: 175–203. https://doi.org/10.1093/poq/nfm008.

Thurston, A. 2016. "'The Disease is Unbelief': Boko Haram's Religious and Political Worldview." Africa Portal. Brookings Institution. https://www.africaportal.org/publications/the-disease-is-unbelief-boko-harams-religious-and-political-worldview/.

Tice, D. M. 1993. "The Social Motivations of People with Low Self-esteem." In *Self-Esteem: The Puzzle of Low Self-Regard*, edited by R. F. Baumeister, 37–53. Boston, MA: Springer. https://doi.org/10.1007/978-1-4684-8956-9_3.

Timmer, M., M. I. Cordero, Y. Sevelinges, and C. Sandi. 2011. "Evidence for a Role of Oxytocin Receptors in the Long-term Establishment of Dominance Hierarchies." *Neuropsychopharmacology* 36, no. 11: 2349–2356. https://doi.org/10.1038/npp.2011.125.

Tomasello, M., M. Carpenter, J. Call, T. Behne, and H. Moll. 2005. "Understanding and Sharing Intentions: The Origins of Cultural Cognition." *Behavioral and Brain Sciences* 28, no. 5: 675–691. https://doi.org/10.1017/S0140525X05000129.

Toner, K., M. R. Leary, M. W. Asher, and K. P. Jongman-Sereno. 2013. "Feeling Superior is a Bipartisan Issue: Extremity (Not Direction) of Political Views Predicts Perceived Belief Superiority." *Psychological Science* 24, no. 12: 2454–2462. https://doi.org/10.1177/0956797613494848.

Topik, S. 1978. "Middle-Class Brazilian Nationalism, 1889–1930: From Radicalism to Reaction." *Social Science Quarterly* 59, no. 1: 93–104.

Toprak, A., and G. Weitzel. 2017. *Salafismus in Deutschland. Jugendkulturelle Aspekte, pädagogische Perspektiven*. Wiesbaden, DE: Springer VS. https://doi.org/10.1007/978-3-658-15097-6.

Townsend, K. C., and B. T. McWhirter. 2005. "Connectedness: A Review of the Literature with Implications for Counseling, Assessment, and Research." *Journal of Counseling & Development* 83, no. 2: 191–201. https://doi.org/10.1002/j.1556-6678.2005.tb00596.x.

Tricomi, E. M., M. R. Delgado, and J. A. Fiez. 2004. "Modulation of Caudate Activity by Action Contingency." *Neuron* 41, no. 2: 281–292. https://doi.org/10.1016/S0896-6273(03)00848-1.

Trope, Y. 1983. "Self-assessment in Achievement Behavior." In *Psychological Perspectives on the Self (Vol. 2)*, edited by J. Suls, and A. G. Greenwald, 402–425. Hillsdale, NJ: Erlbaum.

Turner, J. C. 1987. "A Self-categorization Theory." In *Rediscovering the Social Group: A Self-categorization Theory*, edited by J. C. Turner, M. A. Hogg, P. J. Oakes, S. D. Reicher, and M. S. Wetherell, 42–67. Oxford: Blackwell.

Tusche, A., A. Böckler, P. Kanske, F. M. Trautwein, and T. Singer. 2016. "Decoding the Charitable Brain: Empathy, Perspective Taking, and Attention Shifts Differentially Predict Altruistic Giving." *Journal of Neuroscience* 36, no. 17: 4719–4732. https://doi.org/10.1523/JNEUROSCI.3392-15.2016.

Twenge, J. M., and W. K. Campbell. 2002. "Self-esteem and Socioeconomic Status: A Meta-analytic Review." *Personality and Social Psychology Review* 6, no. 1: 59–71. https://doi.org/10.1207/S15327957PSPR0601_3.

Twenge, J. M., and W. K. Campbell. 2003. "'Isn't It Fun to Get the Respect that We're Going to Deserve?' Narcissism, Social Rejection, and Aggression." *Personality and Social Psychology Bulletin* 29, no. 2: 261–272. https://doi.org/10.1177/0146167202239051.

Twenge, J. M., and Im, C. 2007. "Changes in the Need for Social Approval, 1958–2001." *Journal of Research in Personality* 41, no. 1: 171–189. https://doi.org/10.1016/j.jrp.2006.03.006.

Tyler, T. R., R. M. Kramer, and O. P. John, eds. 1999. *The Psychology of the Social Self*. Mahwah, NJ: Lawrence Erlbaum Associates Publishers.

Tyson, K., D. R. Castellino, and W. Darity. 2005. "It's Not 'a Black Thing': Understanding the Burden of Acting White and Other Dilemmas of High Achievement." *American Sociological Review* 70, no. 4: 582–605. https://doi.org/10.1177/000312240507000403.

Ucha, C. 2010. "Poverty in Nigeria: Some Dimensions and Contributing Factors." *Global Majority E-Journal* 1, no. 1: 46–56.

UNESCO. 2018. "UNESCO Report 2017." UNESCO Digital Library. https://unesdoc.unesco.org/ark:/48223/pf0000261971.

United Nations. 2006. *The Niger Delta Human Development Report*. Abuja: UNDP. https://digitallibrary.un.org/record/600794.

United Nations Development Programme (UNDP). 2009. *Human Development Report Nigeria, 2008–2009*. Abuja: UNDP.

United Nations Development Programme (UNDP). 2018. *Human Development Indices and Indicators: 2018 Statistical Update: Nepal*. New York: United Nations Development Programme. https://un.org.np/sites/default/files/doc_publication/2018-09/NPL%281%29.pdf.

Unkelbach, C., J. P. Forgas, and T. F. Denson. 2008. "The Turban Effect: The Influence of Muslim Headgear and Induced Affect on Aggressive Responses in the Shooter Bias Paradigm." *Journal of Experimental Social Psychology* 44, no. 5: 1409–1413. https://doi.org/10.1016/j.jesp.2008.04.003.

Uppsala Conflict Data Program (UCDP). 2022. Uppsala University, Department of Peace Research. https://ucdp.uu.se/.

Usborne, E., and R. de la Sablonnière. 2014. "Understanding My Culture Means Understanding Myself: The Function of Cultural Identity Clarity for Personal Identity Clarity and Personal Psychological Well-being." *Journal for the Theory of Social Behaviour* 44, no. 4: 436–458. https://doi.org/10.1111/jtsb.12061.

Usó-Doménech, J. L., and J. Nescolarde-Selva. 2016. "What Are Belief Systems?" *Foundations of Science* 21, no. 1: 147–152. https://doi.org/10.1007/s10699-015-9409-z.

Vadlamannati, K. C. 2011. "Why Indian Men Rebel? Explaining Armed Rebellion in the Northeastern States of India, 1970–2007." *Journal of Peace Research* 48, no. 5: 605–619. https://doi.org/10.1177/0022343311412409.

Van Bavel, J. J., D. J. Packer, and W. A. Cunningham. 2008. "The Neural Substrates of In-group Bias: A Functional Magnetic Resonance Imaging Investigation." *Psychological Science* 19, no. 11: 1131–1139. https://doi.org/10.1111/j.1467-9280.2008.02214.x.

Van den Bos, K., and M. Maas. 2009. "On the Psychology of the Belief in a Just World: Exploring Experiential and Rationalistic Paths to Victim Blaming." *Personality and Social Psychology Bulletin* 35, no. 12: 1567–1578. https://doi.org/10.1177/0146167209344628.

Van der Brug, W., M. Fennema, and J. Tillie. 2000. "Anti-immigrant Parties in Europe: Ideological or Protest Vote?" *European Journal of Political Research* 37, no. 1: 77–102. https://doi.org/10.1111/1475-6765.00505.

Van der Ploeg, F. 2011. "Natural Resources: Curse or Blessing?" *Journal of Economic Literature* 49, no. 2: 366–420. https://doi.org/10.1257/jel.49.2.366.

Van Der Waal, J., W. De Koster, and W. Van Oorschot. 2013. "Three Worlds of Welfare Chauvinism? How Welfare Regimes Affect Support for Distributing Welfare to Immigrants in Europe." *Journal of Comparative Policy Analysis: Research and Practice* 15, no. 2: 164–181. https://doi.org/10.1080/13876988.2013.785147.

Van Dijk, M., S. Branje, L. Keijsers, S. T. Hawk, W. W. Hale, and W. Meeus. 2014. "Self-concept Clarity across Adolescence: Longitudinal Associations with Open Communication with Parents and Internalizing Symptoms." *Journal of Youth and Adolescence* 43, no. 11: 1861–1876. https://doi.org/10.1007/s10964-013-0055-x.

van Dijk, T. 2013. "Ideology and Discourse." In *The Oxford Handbook of Political Ideologies*, edited by M. Freeden, T. L. Sargent, and M. Stears, 175–196. Oxford: Oxford University Press http://dx.doi.org/10.1093/oxfordhb/9780199585977.013.007.

van Harreveld, F., B. T. Rutjens, I. K. Schneider, H. U. Nohlen, and K. Keskinis. 2014. "In Doubt and Disorderly: Ambivalence Promotes Compensatory Perceptions of Order." *Journal of Experimental Psychology: General* 143, no. 4: 1666–1676. https://doi.org/10.1037/a0036099.

Van Hiel, A. 2012. "A Psycho-political Profile of Party Activists and Left-wing and Right-wing Extremists." *European Journal of Political Research* 51, no. 2: 166–203. https://doi.org/10.1111/j.1475-6765.2011.01991.x.

Van Hiel, A., I. Cornelis, and A. Roets. 2007. "The Intervening Role of Social Worldviews in the Relationship between the Five-factor Model of Personality and Social Attitudes." *European Journal of Personality: Published for the European Association of Personality Psychology* 21, no. 2: 131–148. https://doi.org/10.1002/per.618.

Van Hiel, A., B. Duriez, and M. Kossowska. 2006. "The Presence of Left-wing Authoritarianism in Western Europe and Its Relationship with Conservative Ideology." *Political Psychology* 27, no. 5: 769–793. https://doi.org/10.1111/j.1467-9221.2006.00532.x.

Van Hiel, A., I. Mervielde, and F. De Fruyt. 2004. "The Relationship between Maladaptive Personality and Right-wing Ideology." *Personality and Individual Differences* 36, no. 2: 405–417. https://doi.org/10.1016/S0191-8869(03)00105-3.

Van Leeuwen, F., and J. H. Park. 2009. "Perceptions of Social Dangers, Moral Foundations, and Political Orientation." *Personality and Individual Differences* 47, no. 3: 169–173. https://doi.org/10.1016/j.paid.2009.02.017.

Van Leeuwen, K. G., I. Mervielde, B. J. De Clercq, and F. De Fruyt. 2007. "Extending the Spectrum Idea: Child Personality, Parenting and Psychopathology." *European Journal of Personality* 21, 63–89. https://doi.org/10.1002/per.598.

Van Oorschot, W. 2000. "Who Should Get What, and Why? On Deservingness Criteria and the Conditionality of Solidarity among the Public." *Policy & Politics* 28, no. 1: 33–48. https://doi.org/10.1332/0305573002500811.

Van Oorschot, W. 2006. "Making the Difference in Social Europe: Deservingness Perceptions among Citizens of European Welfare States." *Journal of European Social Policy* 16, no. 1: 23–42. https://doi.org/10.1177/0958928706059829.

van Prooijen, J. W., and A. P. Krouwel. 2017. "Extreme Political Beliefs Predict Dogmatic Intolerance." *Social Psychological and Personality Science* 8, no. 3: 292–300. https://doi.org/10.1177/1948550616671403.

Van Prooijen, J. W., and A. P. Krouwel. 2019. "Psychological Features of Extreme Political Ideologies." *Current Directions in Psychological Science* 28, no. 2: 159–163. https://doi.org/10.1177/0963721418817755.

van Prooijen, J. W., A. P. Krouwel, M. Boiten, and L. Eendebak. 2015. "Fear among the Extremes: How Political Ideology Predicts Negative Emotions and Outgroup Derogation." *Personality and Social Psychology Bulletin* 41, no. 4: 485–497. https://doi.org/10.1177/0146167215569706.

Vansteenkiste, M., and R. M. Ryan. 2013. "On Psychological Growth and Vulnerability: Basic Psychological Need Satisfaction and Need Frustration as a Unifying Principle." *Journal of Psychotherapy Integration* 23, no. 3: 263–280. https://doi.org/10.1037/a0032359.

Vargas, R. 1999. "The Revolutionary Armed Forces of Colombia (FARC) and the Illicit Drug Trade." TNI. https://www.tni.org/en/publication/the-revolutionary-armed-forces-of-colombia-farc-and-the-illicit-drug-trade.

Vasilopoulos, P., G. E. Marcus, and M. Foucault. 2018. "Emotional Responses to the Charlie Hebdo Attacks: Addressing the Authoritarianism Puzzle." *Political Psychology* 39, no. 3: 557–575. https://doi.org/10.1111/pops.12439.

Vasilopoulou, S., and D. Halikiopoulou. 2015. *The Golden Dawn's "Nationalist Solution": Explaining the Rise of the Far Right in Greece*. New York: Palgrave Pivot.

Vásquez, M. A. 2011. *More Than Belief: A Materialist Theory of Religion*. New York: Oxford University Press.

Vedder, P., D. L. Sam, and K. Liebkind. 2007. "The Acculturation and Adaptation of Turkish Adolescents in North-Western Europe." *Applied Development Science* 11, no. 3: 126–136. https://doi.org/10.1080/10888690701454617.

Verhulst, B., L. J. Eaves, , and P. K. Hatemi. 2012. "Correlation Not Causation: The Relationship between Personality Traits and Political Ideologies." *American Journal of Political Science* 56, no. 1: 34–51. https://doi.org/10.1111/j.1540-5907.2011.00568.x.

Verkuyten, M. 2001. "Global Self-esteem, Ethnic Self-esteem, and Family Integrity: Turkish and Dutch Early Adolescents in The Netherlands." *International Journal of Behavioral Development* 25, no. 4: 357–366. https://doi.org/10.1080/01650250042000339.

Verkuyten, M. 2004a. "Emotional Reactions To and Support For Immigrant Policies: Attributed Responsibilities to Categories of Asylum Seekers." *Social Justice Research* 17, no. 3: 293–314. https://doi.org/10.1023/B:SORE.0000041295.83611.dc%20.

Verkuyten, M. 2004b. *The Social Psychology of Ethnic Identity*. Hove, East Sussex: Psychology Press. https://doi.org/10.4324/9780203338704.

Verkuyten, M. 2009. "Self-esteem and Multiculturalism: An Examination among Ethnic Minority and Majority Groups in the Netherlands." *Journal of Research in Personality* 43, no. 3: 419–427. https://doi.org/10.1016/j.jrp.2009.01.013.

Verkuyten, M. 2011. "Assimilation Ideology and Outgroup Attitudes among Ethnic Majority Members." *Group Processes & Intergroup Relations* 14, no. 6: 789–806. https://doi.org/10.1177/1368430211398506.

Verkuyten, M. 2018. "Religious Fundamentalism and Radicalization among Muslim Minority Youth in Europe." *European Psychologist* 23, no. 1: 21. https://doi.org/10.1027/1016-9040/a000314.

Verkuyten, M., and B. Martinovic. 2012. "Immigrants' National Identification: Meanings, Determinants, and Consequences." *Social Issues and Policy Review* 6, no. 1: 82–112. https://doi.org/10.1111/j.1751-2409.2011.01036.x.

Verkuyten, M., and A. Reijerse. 2008. "Intergroup Structure and Identity Management among Ethnic Minority and Majority Groups: The Interactive Effects of Perceived Stability, Legitimacy, and Permeability." *European Journal of Social Psychology* 38, no. 1: 106–127. https://doi.org/10.1002/ejsp.395.

Vermetten, E., C. Schmahl, S. Lindner, R. J. Loewenstein, and J. D. Bremner. 2006. "Hippocampal and Amygdalar Volumes in Dissociative Identity Disorder." *American Journal of Psychiatry* 163, no. 4: 630–636. https://doi.org/10.1176/ajp.2006.163.4.630.

Veselka, L., E. A. Giammarco, and P. A. Vernon. 2014. "The Dark Triad and the Seven Deadly Sins." *Personality and Individual Differences* 67: 75–80. https://doi.org/10.1016/j.paid.2014.01.055.

Veugelers, J., and G. Menard. 2018. "The Non-party Sector of the Radical Right." In *The Oxford Handbook of the Radical Right*, edited by J. Rydgren, 285–304. Oxford: Oxford University Press.

Vincent, A. 2013. "Nationalism." In *The Oxford Handbook of Political Ideologies*, edited by M. Freeden, T. L. Sargent, and M. Stears, 175–196. Oxford: Oxford University Press http://dx.doi.org/10.1093/oxfordhb/9780199585977.013.007.

Viola, W. E., E. S. Mankowski, and M. E. Gray. 2015. "The Moderating Effect of Within-group Similarity on Change in a Strengths-based Programme for Incarcerated Young Men." *Journal of Community & Applied Social Psychology* 25, no. 2: 95–109. https://doi.org/10.1002/casp.2196.

Vlachos, S. 2016. *The Legacy of War Exposure on Political Radicalization*. Lausanne: Université de Lausanne, Faculté des hautes études commerciales (HEC), Département d'économétrie et économie politique.

Von Geldern, J. 1998. "Putting the Masses in Mass Culture: Bolshevik Festivals, 1918–1920." *Journal of Popular Culture* 31, no. 4: 123–144. https://doi.org/10.1111/j.0022-3840.1998.3104_123.x.

von Soest, T., J. Wagner, T. Hansen, and D. Gerstorf. 2018. "Self-esteem across the Second Half of Life: The Role of Socioeconomic Status, Physical Health, Social Relationships, and Personality Factors." *Journal of Personality and Social Psychology* 114, no. 6: 945–958. https://doi.org/10.1037/pspp0000123.

Von Stetten, M. 2009. "Recent Literature on the Red Army Faction in Germany: A Critical Overview." *Critical Studies on Terrorism* 2, no. 3: 546–554. https://doi.org/10.1080/17539150903306279.

Wachtel, P. L. 2003. "Full Pockets, Empty Lives: A Psychoanalytic Exploration of the Contemporary Culture of Greed." *The American Journal of Psychoanalysis* 63, no. 2: 103–122. https://doi.org/10.1023/A:1024037330427.

Wade, R. 2010. "Bridging Christianity, Islam, and Buddhism with Virtue Ethics." In *International Handbook of Inter-religious Education*, edited by K. Engebretson, M. de Souza, G. Durka, L. Gearon, 313–324. Dordrecht: Springer. https://doi.org/10.1007/978-1-4020-9260-2_19.

Wade, W. C. 1998. *The Fiery Cross: The Ku Klux Klan in America*. New York: Oxford University Press.

Wahlström, M., and A. Törnberg. 2021. "Social Media Mechanisms for Right-wing Political Violence in the 21st century: Discursive Opportunities, Group Dynamics, and Co-ordination." *Terrorism and Political Violence* 33, no. 4: 766–787. https://doi.org/10.1080/09546553.2019.1586676.

Wahlström, M., A. Törnberg, and H. Ekbrand. 2021. "Dynamics of Violent and Dehumanizing Rhetoric in Far-right Social Media." *New Media & Society* 23, no. 11: 3290–3311. https://doi.org/10.1177/1461444820952795.

Walder, A. G. 1985. "The Political Dimension of Social Mobility in Communist States: China and the Soviet Union." *Research in Political Sociology* 1: 101–117.

Walder, A. G., B. Li, and D. J. Treiman. 2000. "Politics and Life Chances in a State Socialist Regime: Dual Career Paths into the Urban Chinese Elite, 1949 to 1996." *American Sociological Review* 65, no. 2: 191–209. https://doi.org/10.2307/2657437.

Waldmann, P. 2005. "The Radical Community: A Comparative Analysis of the Social Background of ETA, IRA, and Hezbollah." *Sociologus* 55, no. 2: 239–257. https://www.jstor.org/stable/43645553.

Waller, G., and S. Hodgson. 1996. "Body Image Distortion in Anorexia and Bulimia Nervosa: The Role of Perceived and Actual Control." *Journal of Nervous and Mental Disease* 184, no. 4: 213–219. https://doi.org/10.1097/00005053-199604000-00003.

Walter B. F. 2017. "The Extremist's Advantage in Civil Wars." *International Security* 42, no. 2: 7–39.

Warburton, W. A., K. D. Williams, and D. R. Cairns. 2006. "When Ostracism Leads to Aggression: The Moderating Effects of Control Deprivation." *Journal of Experimental Social Psychology* 42, no. 2: 213–220. https://doi.org/10.1016/j.jesp.2005.03.005.

Warburton, W. A., K. D. Williams, and D. R. Cairns. 2006. "When Ostracism Leads to Aggression: The Moderating Effects of Control Deprivation." *Journal of Experimental Social Psychology* 42, no. 2: 213–220. https://doi.org/10.1016/j.jesp.2005.03.005.

Ward, M. D., B. D. Greenhill, and K. M. Bakke. 2010. "The Perils of Policy By p-Value: Predicting Civil Conflicts." *Journal of Peace Research* 47, no. 4: 363–375. https://doi.org/10.1177/0022343309356491.

Warneken, F., and M. Tomasello. 2008. "Extrinsic Rewards Undermine Altruistic Tendencies in 20-Month-Olds." *Developmental Psychology* 44, no. 6: 1785–1788. https://doi.org/10.1037/a0013860.

Waska, R. 2003. "The Impossible Dream and the Endless Nightmare: Clinical Manifestations of Greed." *Canadian Journal of Psychoanalysis* 11, no. 2: 379–397.

Watanabe, S., and K. Ono. 1986. "An Experimental Analysis of 'Empathic' Response: Effects of Pain Reactions of Pigeon upon other Pigeon's Operant Behavior." *Behavioural Processes* 13, no. 3: 269–277. https://doi.org/10.1016/0376-6357(86)90089-6.

Watkins, D. C., D. L. Hudson, C. Howard Caldwell, K. Siefert, and J. S. Jackson. 2011. "Discrimination, Mastery, and Depressive Symptoms among African American Men." *Research on Social Work Practice* 21, no. 3: 269–277. https://doi.org/10.1177/1049731510385470.

Watts, M. 2004. "Resource Curse? Governmentality, Oil and Power in the Niger Delta, Nigeria." *Geopolitics* 9, no. 1: 50–80. https://doi.org/10.1080/14650040412331307832.

Watts, M. 2007. "Petro-insurgency or Criminal Syndicate? Conflict and Violence in the Niger Delta." *Review of African Political Economy* 34, no. 114: 637–660. https://doi.org/10.1080/03056240701819517.

Webber, D., M. Babush, N. Schori-Eyal, A. Vazeou-Nieuwenhuis, M. Hettiarachchi, J. J. Bélanger, M. Moyano, H. M. Trujillo, R. Gunaratna, A. W. Kruglanski, and M. J. Gelfand. 2018. "The Road to Extremism: Field and Experimental Evidence that Significance Loss-induced Need for Closure Fosters Radicalization." *Journal of Personality and Social Psychology* 114, no. 2: 270–285. https://doi.org/10.1037/pspi0000111.

Webber, D., K. Klein, A. Kruglanski, A. Brizi, and A. Merari. 2017. "Divergent Paths to Martyrdom and Significance among Suicide Attackers." *Terrorism and Political Violence* 29, no. 5: 852–874. https://doi.org/10.1080/09546553.2015.1075979.

Webber, D., R. Zhang, J. Schimel, and J. Blatter. 2016. "Finding Death in Meaninglessness: Evidence that Death-thought Accessibility Increases in Response to Meaning Threats." *British Journal of Social Psychology* 55, no. 1: 144–161. https://doi.org/10.1111/bjso.12118.

Weber, B. J., and W. P. Tan. 2012. "Ambiguity Aversion in a Delay Analogue of the Ellsberg Paradox." *Judgment and Decision Making* 7, no. 4: 383–389.

Weber, C. R., and C. M. Federico. 2013. "Moral Foundations and Heterogeneity in Ideological Preferences." *Political Psychology* 34, no. 1: 107–126. https://doi.org/10.1111/j.1467-9221.2012.00922.x.

Webster, D. M. 1993. "Motivated Augmentation and Reduction of the Overattribution Bias." *Journal of Personality and Social Psychology* 65, no. 2: 261–271. https://doi.org/10.1037/0022-3514.65.2.261.

Webster, D. M., and A. W. Kruglanski. 1994. "Individual Differences in Need for Cognitive Closure." *Journal of Personality and Social Psychology* 67, no. 6: 1049–1062. https://doi.org/10.1037/0022-3514.67.6.1049.

Webster, D. M., and A. W. Kruglanski. 1997. "Cognitive and Social Consequences of the Need for Cognitive Closure." *European Review of Social Psychology* 8, no. 1: 133–173. https://doi.org/10.1080/14792779643000100.

Wechselblatt, T., G. Gurnick, and R. Simon. 2000. "Autonomy and Relatedness in the Development of Anorexia Nervosa: A Clinical Case Series using Grounded Theory." *Bulletin of the Menninger Clinic* 64, no. 1: 91–123.

Wehmeyer, M. L., K. A. Shogren, T. D. Little, and S. J. Lopez. 2017. "Introduction to the Self-determination Construct." In *Development of Self-determination Through the Life-course*, edited by L. M. Wehmeyer, A K. Shogren, D. T. Little, and J. A. Lopez, 3–16. Dordrecht: Springer. https://doi.org/10.1007/978-94-024-1042-6_1.

Weinstein, N., and D. N. Stone. 2018. "Need Depriving Effects of Financial Insecurity: Implications for Well-being and Financial Behaviors." *Journal of Experimental Psychology: General* 147, no. 10: 1503–1520. https://doi.org/10.1037/xge0000436.

References

Wekerle, C., E. Leung, A. M. Wall, H. MacMillan, M. Boyle, N. Trocme, and R. Waechter. 2009. "The Contribution of Childhood Emotional Abuse to Teen Dating Violence among Child Protective Services-involved Youth." *Child Abuse & Neglect* 33, no. 1: 45–58. https://doi.org/10.1016/j.chiabu.2008.12.006.

Welz, M. 2014. "Briefing: Crisis in the Central African Republic and the International Response." *African Affairs* 113, no. 453: 601–610. https://doi.org/10.1093/afraf/adu048.

Wennerhag, M., C. Fröhlich, , and G. Piotrowski, eds. 2018. *Radical Left Movements in Europe*. Abingdon: Routledge.

Werff, J. V. D. 1990. "The Problem of Self-conceiving." In *Coping and Self-concept in Adolescence*, edited by H. A. Bosma and A. E. S. Jackson, 13–33. Heidelberg: Springer. https://doi.org/10.1007/978-3-642-75222-3_2.

Wesselmann, E. D., D. Ren, and K. D. Williams. 2015. "Motivations for Responses to Ostracism." *Frontiers in Psychology* 6: article 40. https://doi.org/10.3389/fpsyg.2015.00040.

Weyns, Y., L. Hoex, and S. Spittaels. 2014. *Mapping Conflict Motives: The Central African Republic*. Antwerp: IPIS. http://ipisresearch.be/wp-content/uploads/2014/11/IPIS-CAR-Conflict-Mapping-November2014.pdf.

Wheeler, E. A. 2017. "On the Stability of Identity Interacting with the Impermanence of Time." In *Identity Flexibility During Adulthood*, edited by J. Sinnott, 3–17. Cham: Springer. https://doi.org/10.1007/978-3-319-55658-1_1.

Whitehead, A. L., S. L. Perry, and J. O. Baker. 2018. "Make America Christian Again: Christian Nationalism and Voting for Donald Trump in the 2016 Presidential Election." *Sociology of Religion* 79, no. 2: 147–171. https://doi.org/10.1093/socrel/srx070.

Whitehouse, H., and B. McQuinn. 2013. "Ritual and Violence: Divergent Modes of Religiosity and Armed Struggle." In *Oxford Handbook of Religion and Violence*, edited by M. Jerryson, M. Juergensmeyer and M. Kitts, 597–619. New York: Oxford University Press.

Whitley Jr, B. E. 1999. "Right-wing Authoritarianism, Social Dominance Orientation, and Prejudice." *Journal of Personality and Social Psychology* 77, no. 1: 126–134. https://doi.org/10.1037/0022-3514.77.1.126.

WHO. 2008. "mhGAP Mental Health Gap Action Programme." World Health Organization. https://www.who.int/publications/i/item/9789241596206.

WHO. 2018. "Youth Violence: Key Facts." World Health Organization. https://www.who.int/news-room/fact-sheets/detail/youth-violence.

Wiedenfeld, S. A., A. O'Leary, A. Bandura, S. Brown, S. Levine, and K. Raska. 1990. "Impact of Perceived Self-efficacy in Coping with Stressors on Components of the Immune System." *Journal of Personality and Social Psychology* 59, no. 5: 1082–1094. https://doi.org/10.1037/0022-3514.59.5.1082.

Wiklund, M., E. B. Malmgren-Olsson, A. Öhman, E. Bergström, and A. Fjellman-Wiklund. 2012. "Subjective Health Complaints in Older Adolescents are Related to Perceived Stress, Anxiety and Gender—A Cross-sectional School Study in Northern Sweden." *BMC Public Health* 12, no. 1: 1–13. https://doi.org/10.1186/1471-2458-12-993.

Williams, K. D. 2001. *Ostracism: The Power of Silence*. New York: Guilford Press.

Williams, K. D. 2007. "Ostracism: The kiss of social death." *Social and Personality Psychology Compass* 1, no. 1: 236–247. https://doi.org/10.1111/j.1751-9004.2007.00004.x.

Williams, K. D., F. J. Bernieri, S. L. Faulkner, N. Gada-Jain, and J. E. Grahe. 2000. "The Scarlet Letter Study: Five Days of Social Ostracism." *Journal of Personal & Interpersonal Loss* 5, no. 1: 19–63. https://doi.org/10.1080/10811440008407846.

Williams, R., R. Nesiba, and E. D. McConnell. 2005. "The Changing Face of Inequality in Home Mortgage Lending." *Social Problems* 52, no. 2: 181–208. https://doi.org/10.1525/sp.2005.52.2.181.

Williamson, W. P., and R. W. Hood Jr. 2014. "Religious Fundamentalism and Perceived Threat: A Report from an Experimental Study." *Mental Health, Religion & Culture* 17, no. 5: 520–528. https://doi.org/10.1080/13674676.2013.857297.

Wohl, M. J., N. R. Branscombe, and S. Reysen. 2010. "Perceiving Your Group's Future to be in Jeopardy: Extinction Threat Induces Collective Angst and the Desire to Strengthen the Ingroup." *Personality and Social Psychology Bulletin* 36, no. 7: 898–910. https://doi.org/10.1177/0146167210372505.

Wolf, J. B., ed. 1981. "Organization and Management Practices of Urban Terrorist Groups." In *Fear of Fear*, 25–42. Boston, MA: Springer. https://doi.org/10.1007/978-1-4684-3995-3_3.

Wong, R. S. K. 1996. "The Social Composition of the Czechoslovak and Hungarian Communist Parties in the 1980s." *Social Forces* 75, no. 1: 61–89. https://doi.org/10.1093/sf/75.1.61.

World Food Program. 2018. "Food Security Monitoring System." https://www.wfp.org/publications/sudan-food-security-monitoring.

Wright, M. O. D., E. Crawford, and D. Del Castillo. 2009. "Childhood Emotional Maltreatment and Later Psychological Distress among College Students: The Mediating Role of Maladaptive Schemas." *Child Abuse & Neglect* 33, no. 1: 59–68. https://doi.org/10.1016/j.chiabu.2008.12.007.

Xu, X., X. Zuo, X. Wang, and S. Han. 2009. "Do You Feel My Pain? Racial Group Membership Modulates Empathic Neural Responses." *Journal of Neuroscience* 29, no. 26: 8525–8529. https://doi.org/10.1523/JNEUROSCI.2418-09.2009.

Yang, Y. C., C. Boen, and K. Mullan Harris. 2015. "Social Relationships and Hypertension in Late Life: Evidence from a Nationally Representative Longitudinal Study of Older Adults." *Journal of Aging and Health* 27, no. 3: 403–431. https://doi.org/10.1177/0898264314551172.

Yongnian, Z. 2009. *The Chinese Communist Party as Organizational Emperor: Culture, Reproduction, and Transformation*. New York: Routledge. https://doi.org/10.4324/9780203863213.

Young, N. 2019. *An Infantile Disorder? The Crisis and Decline of the New Left: The Crisis and Decline of the New Left*. New York: Routledge. https://doi.org/10.4324/9780429051326.

Yurchak, A. 2006. *Everything Was Forever, Until It Was No More: The Last Soviet Generation*. Princeton, NJ: Princeton University Press. https://doi.org/10.1515/9781400849109

Yzerbyt, V., and S. Demoulin. 2010. "Intergroup Relations." In *Handbook of Social Psychology*, edited by S. T. Fiske, D. T. Gilbert, and G. Lindzey, 1024–1083. New York: John Wiley & Sons, Inc. https://doi.org/10.1002/9780470561119.socpsy002028.

Zahn-Waxler, C., and M. Radke-Yarrow. 1990. "The Origins of Empathic Concern." *Motivation and Emotion* 14, no. 2: 107–130. https://doi.org/10.1007/BF00991639.

Zahn-Waxler, C., S. L. Friedman, and E. M. Cummings. 1983. "Children's Emotions and Behaviors in Response to Infants' Cries." *Child Development* 54, no. 6: 1522–1528. https://doi.org/10.2307/1129815.

Zak, P. J., A. A. Stanton, and S. Ahmadi. 2007. "Oxytocin Increases Generosity in Humans." *PloS One* 2, no. 11: e1128. https://doi.org/10.1371/journal.pone.0001128.

Zaki, J., and J. P. Mitchell. 2013. "Intuitive Prosociality." *Current Directions in Psychological Science* 22, no. 6: 466–470. https://doi.org/10.1177/0963721413492764.

Zamosc, L. 1986. *The Agrarian Question and the Peasant Movement in Colombia: Struggles of the National Peasant Association 1967–1981*. New York: United Nations Research Institute for Social Development.

Zelin, A. Y. 2020. *Your Sons are at Your Service: Tunisia's Missionaries of Jihad*. New York: Columbia University Press.

Zenn, J. 2020. *Unmasking Boko Haram: Exploring Global Jihad in Nigeria*. Boulder, CO: Lynne Rienner Publishers.

Zhang, W., and M. Chen. 2014. "Psychological Distress of Older Chinese: Exploring the Roles of Activities, Social Support, and Subjective Social Status." *Journal of Cross-Cultural Gerontology* 29, no. 1: 37–51. https://doi.org/10.1007/s10823-013-9219-0.

Zheng, Z., S. Gu, Y. Lei, S. Lu, W. Wang, Y. Li, and F. Wang. 2016. "Safety Needs Mediate Stressful Events Induced Mental Disorders." *Neural Plasticity* 2016, no. 1: 1–6. https://doi.org/10.1155/2016/8058093.

Zhou, M., and C. C. S. Kam. 2018. "Self-determination and Personal Identity in University Students: The Mediating Role of Future Orientation." *The Spanish Journal of Psychology* 21: E14.

Zick, A. 2021. "Hinführung zur Mitte-Studie 2020/21." In *Die geforderte Mitte*, edited by A. Zick and B. Küpper, 17–43. Bonn: Friedrich-Ebert-Stiftung (Friedrich-Ebert Foundation).

Zuckerman, P. 2009. "Atheism, Secularity, and Well-being: How the Findings of Social Science Counter Negative Stereotypes and Assumptions." *Sociology Compass* 3, no. 6: 949–971. https://doi.org/10.1111/j.1751-9020.2009.00247.x.

Zwerman, G., P. G. Steinhoff, and D. Porta. 2000. "Disappearing Social Movements: Clandestinity in the Cycle of New Left Protest in the United States, Japan, Germany, and Italy." *Mobilization* 5, 85–104. https://doi.org/10.17813/maiq.5.1.0w068105721660n0.

Index

For the benefit of digital users, indexed terms that span two pages (e.g., 52–53) may, on occasion, appear on only one of those pages.

Figures and boxes are indicated by *f*, and *b* following the page number

Ação Social Nationalista, 235–36
Action Directe (France), 270–71, 382–83
adolescence, 114–15, 149–52, 163–64, 172, 178–79
Adorno, T. E., 214–15
affiliation, 101, 143
Afghanistan, 57–58
aggression–frustration theory (Gurr), 62–63, 66
agreeableness, 154–55, 209–12
alienation, 63
Alliance of Young Democrats–Hungarian Civic Alliance (FiatalDemokratakSzovetsege–Magyar PolgariSzovetseg, or Fidesz), 430–31, 433–34
al-Qaeda, 29–30, 338–43, 346, 347, 349, 385–86, 395–96
Alternative fur Deutschland (AfD), 374
altruism, 133, 140–41
ambiguity avoidance, 42, 84*b*, 84–89
amygdala, 99–100
anarchism, 200–1
Angola, 56
Animal Liberation Front (ALF), 384
Ansar al-Sharia (AST, Tunesia), 386–88
anterior cingulate cortex (dACC), 16–17, 44, 70–71, 185–86
anterior insula (AI), 70–71, 137
antisemitism, 36–37
appraisal theory, 77
approval (social), 16, 101–2, 115–16, 130–31, 131*b*, 134–38
Arab Legion, 392
Arktos (Great Britain), 367–68
Arm of the Lord, 323
Aryan Nation, 229–30, 323
assimilation, 94–95, 111–12, 218–19, 243, 244–45, 246
assumptions (shattered), 92*b*

attachment, 113–14, 119, 133–34
autonomy, 21, 168, 170–73
Azerbaijan, 68

Baader-Meinhof Gang, 329
Baghdadi, Abu Bakr al-, 342–43, 394–95, 424–25
Bandura, Albert, 175–76, 178, 179, 357–58
Bangladesh, 68
Baumeister, R. F., 8, 186–87, 194
behavior, 53–54, 109–10
belief systems
  decision making and, 22
  defined
    Müller and Gries, 9–10, 187–88, 191–92
    Steger, Freeden, Heywood, 8
    traditionally, 18
  functions / purpose of, 18, 41, 194–95, 304, 398
  ideology and, 10–11, 13, 18–26
  imperfect information and, 18–19
  organizations and, 22–23
beliefs
  Bayesian "evidential," 189–90
  defined, 189
  formation of, 189
  motivated, 189
belongingness, 16–17, 42, 50–51, 109–10, 113–14, 125*b*, 143, 185, 242, 247
  relational need for, 121–27
  self-esteem and, 122–23
Big Five/Five Factor Personality Model (FFM), 154–55, 209–11
bin Laden, Osama, 338–39
Black Legion, 229
Black Liberation Army (BLA), 324–25
Black Panther Party for Self-Defense (BPP), 323–25
Boko Haram (Nigeria), 29–30, 305, 347, 349, 395–96, 399–400, 412–15

Boro, Isaac Adaka, 418–20, 421
Botswana, 54
Brazil, 275*b*
British National Party (BNP), 312–13

Camorra, 308–11, 359–60, 363–64
campesino groups, 401–2, 403–4
capitalism. *See* socialism
Castro, Fidel, 260–61
Central African Republic, 62–63, 65*b*
Central American Revolutionary Worker's Party (PRTC, El Salvador), 332–33
certainty, 116–17
Chad, 57–58
Chiapas, 13, 52–53
Chile, 54
choice, 12, 16, 18–19
Christianity, 429–31, 433–34
  Christian Identity, 229–30, 323
church, 335, 336–38
civil rights, 67–68
Clandestine Colombian Communist Party (PCCC), 334–35
closure (cognitive), 84–89
coherence, 4, 24, 194–95. *See also* meaning
Combatant Communist Cells (Belgium), 270–71
communism, 38*b*, 254–70, 326–29
  assumptions and characteristics of, 260–70
  Communist Fighting Formation (Italy), 382–83
  Communist Manifesto (Marx), 258–59
  Communist Party, in Eastern Europe, 377–79
  Communist Party (CCP), in China, 378–82
  Communist Party (PCC), in Colombia, 334–35
  Communist Party (PCF), in France, 274, 327–28, 330
  Communist Party (PCS), in El Salvador, 332–33
  "revolutionary," 258–60
Comparative Manifesto Project (CMP), 274
complexity, 16
conflict. *See also specific country or incident*
  armed, by number and type, 1946-2020, 2*f*
  economic risk factors in, 55
  ethnicities and, 66–69
  frequency of, by conflict item, 6*f*
  global trajectory of, 1, 5
  ideology and, 9, 11, 32

intrastate, 1, 6*f*
religious, 5–7, 68
Russian-Ukrainian, 1, 3, 36–37
Congo, 51*b*, 68
conscientiousness, 154–55, 192, 209–12
conservatism, 19–20, 200–1, 206, 277–78, 367–68
consistency, 42, 194–95
  epistemic need for, 89–92
conspiracy theory, 26
contagion (emotional), 135–36
control, 16, 42–43, 81–83, 185
  asserting, 81–82
  compensatory control model (CCT), 197–98
  existential need for, 80–83
  illusion of, 81–82
  loci of, 80–81
  neural basis of need for, 83*b*
cooperation, 101–2, 143
coping strategies / dimensions, 164–66, 297–98
cortisol, 36, 70–71, 81
Cosa Nostra, La. 360–61, *See* Mafia
Cote d'Ivoire, 68
Cultural Revolution (China), 380–81

Dansk Folkeparti (Denmark), 315
decision-making, subjective, 107–8, 108*b*, 109–10
dehumanization, 358, 374–75
democracy, social, 256–58
Democratic Revolutionary Front (FDR, El Salvador), 332–33
Deng Xiaoping, 380–81
deprivation, 186–88
  absolute, 56. *See also* poverty
  fundamental needs and, 194
  group-based, 58–60
  personal, 58–60
  relative, 58–60, 60*b*
"deservingness principle" (criteria of), 206–7
dictatorship, 258
discrimination, 119–20
disengagement (moral)
  Mafia and, 361–62
  theory of (Bandura), 357–58
disinformation, 26
disintegration, 298–99
Dispositional Greed Scale, 159
dissonance, cognitive (Festinger), 89–92

dominance, 214–15
dorsal anterior cingulate cortex (dACC), 123–24, 137
Dutch Party for Freedom (Netherlands), 316

Earth Liberation Front (ELF), 384
egalitarianism, 205–6, 214–15
empathy, 134–38, 143
 -altruism hypothesis, 138–42
 developmental, 135–36, 139–42
Engels, Friedrich, 192, 258–59, 260–61, 268–69
English Defense League (EDL), 373
English First, 318–19
Erikson, E., 109–10, 149–50
Ethiopia, 68
ethnicity, 240–41
European Social Survey (ESS), 292–93
Euroscepticism, 237–38
Evolutionary Threat Assessment Systems (ETAS) theory, 285
exclusion ("targeted"), 70
extraversion, 154–55, 209–12
extremism. *See also* groups / organizations, extremist
 differences and similarities, 290–99
 Extremist Crime Database (ECDB), 317–18
 far-left, 291–94
 far-right, 291–94, 370–71
 shared characteristics of extremists, 290–91, 294–97

Farabundo Marti National Liberation Front (FMLN, El Salvador), 332–34
fascism, 248–53
 defined, 248
 Italian versus German, 248–49
Fidesz. *See* Alliance of Young Democrats–Hungarian Civic Alliance (FiatalDemokratakSzovetsege–Magyar PolgariSzovetseg, or Fidesz)
Forza Nuova (Italy), 315–16, 369
Freedom Party (Austria), 251
free-rider, 338, 355–56
frustration-aggression theory, 399
functional magnetic resonance imaging (fMRI), 94–95, 128–29, 137–38
fundamentalism (religious), 287–89

Gaitán, Jorge Eliécer, 399–400

General Social Survey, 233–34
German Socio-Economic Panel (SOEP), 226
Global Corruption Barometer, 268
Golden Dawn (Greece), 315–16
GR€€D Scale, 159
greed, 156–60
 Greed Trait Measure, 159
grievance, 399
groups / organizations. *See also* terrorism; *specific groups*
 characteristics of, 4
 extremist, 198–200, 335–47. *See also* extremism
  conservative, 30–31
  far-left, 323–35, 349–50
  far-right, 7, 311–24, 348–49
  functions of, 399–400
  Old versus New Left, 349–50
  radical, 30–31
  religious, 349–50
  "state based" goods / services and, 29–30, 346, 395–96, 424–25
 "hate" groups, 312–17
 identification with, 63, 243–47, 356–57
 ingroup, 21–22, 55–56, 58–60, 63, 101, 103–9, 115–21, 130, 133, 139–40, 215–16, 221–23, 242–46, 286–90, 356–58
 leftist/terrorist, 5–7
 liberal, 30–32
 nationalist, 5–7
 outgroup, 21–22, 58–62, 103–9, 115, 117–18, 119–20, 214–15, 221–22, 224–28, 235–36, 243–44, 247, 357–59, 375–76
 religious
  "state based" goods / services and, 385–88
  types of, 335
Guevara, Che, 260–61
gun culture (United States), 79*b*

Hamas, 29–30, 347, 349, 385–86, 395–96, 399–400
Hawk-Dove game, 251–52
Heritage Foundation, 368
HEXACO model, 154–55, 159, 211–12
Hezbollah, 347
hierarchy / hierarchies, 30–31, 99–51, 350–51
hippocampus, 52–53
Hitler, Adolf, 248
Hitler Youth, 311–12

Hizb al-Tahrir al-Islami (Islamic Liberation Party), 387–89
Hizbut-Tahrir (HT), 390–91, 392–93
honesty-humility, 154–55, 211–12
human rights, universal, 35
hypothalamic-pituitary-adrenal (HPA) axis, 70–71

identification, 101–2, 116–21, 143
identity, 42, 240–41
    concept of, 102–8
    cultural, and religion, 279–81
    cultural and ethnic, 67–68
    defined
        in psychology, 53, 102, 103
        in social psychology, 102–3
    ethnic, 240–47
    group/organization, 196–97
    social, 16, 25–26, 36, 103–4, 104*b*, 144–54, 234, 241
    "utility," 54, 108*b*
ideologization, 304, 396–97
ideology, 19–20. *See also* communism; nationalism; New Left; racism; socialism
    adopting an, 23
    belief systems and, 18–26
    concept of, 188–93
    conflict and, 32
    defined
        Knight, 4
        MacKenzie and Baumeister, 8
        Müller and Gries, 192–93
        Steger, Freeden, Heywood, 8
    functions of, 18, 41, 194–95
    individual choice and, 13
    needs deprivation and, 27
    needs reconciliation and, 27–29
    populist, 26
        right-wing, in Eastern Europe, 428–34
    religious, 278–90
    rightist/conservative, 217–53
    "traditional left," 254–78
immigration, 120–21, 317, 318–19, 369
imperialism, 36–37
India, 67–68
individualism (methodological), 3
Indonesia, 68
inequality
    horizontal, 62–64
    income, 58–60, 63–64
    social, 202
information, 16

information avoidance, 87–89
Iraq, 57–58, 62–63
Islamic Maghrib (AQIM), 386
Islamic State in Iraq and Syria (ISIS), 424. *See also* Islamic State (IS)
Islamic State (IS), 29–30, 198–99, 338–39, 342–47, 349, 385–86, 394–96, 399–400, 422–27
Israel, 68

Jaffna Vellalar Tamils, 407
jihad, 29, 338–39, 394–95, 424, 425–27
Jihadi Salafism (Propagation of the Prophet's Teaching and Jihad), 413–15

Kaczynski, Lech and Jaroslaw, 429–30
Kenya, 13
KKE (Communist Party, Greece), 274, 330
Komsomol, 262–63
Ku Klux Klan, 228–30, 311–13, 320–23, 358–59. *See also* racism

Labour Party (Great Britain), 256–58
Latter-Day Saints (Mormons), 335–37
Law and Justice Party (PiS, Poland), 429–30
Le Pen, Jean-Marie, 251
leadership
    authoritarian, 315–16
    autocratic, 65–66
    charismatic, 402–3
    directive, 30–31
    dogmatic, 31–32, 350
    dominance and prestige models of authoritarian, 252
learning processes (Bayesian), 23–24
Left Party (Die Linke, Germany), 274
Lenin, Vladimir, 260–61
liberalism, 200–1, 212–13
    classical versus modern, 20–21
Liberation Tigers of Tamil Eelam (LTTE, Sri Lanka), 406–12
LPF (Lijst Pin Fortuyn, Pin Fortuyn List, Netherlands), 313–14

Mafia, 307–11
"Make America Great Again," 236–37
Malaysia, 67
Mali, 57–58
Mao Zedong, 260–62, 268–69, 329–30
Maoist Progressive Labor Party (PLP), 323–24
marginalization, ecological, 13, 49–50

Marquetalia, 401–2
Marulanda Velez, Manuel, 402–3, 404
Marx, Karl, 37b–38, 177, 192, 256–59, 268–69, 329–30
Maslow, A., 76–100
meaning, 19–20, 42, 198–99, 240–41. *See also* coherence
   defined, 194
   systems, and ideology, 24–26
media, 111–12, 373, 379–80, 384–85, 393–97, 425–26, 431–33
   Islamic groups and, 313, 342–43
   Islamic State (IS) and, 425–26
   Law and Justice Party (PiS, Poland) and, 431–33
   social, 352–53, 358–59, 367–69, 371–75, 389–90
medial prefrontal cortex (mPFC), 126–27
Meeus-Crocetti model, 110
mentalization, defined (Zick), 34
meritocracy, 25–26
microfoundations (in economics), 3
migration, 55
Militia Movement, 229–30
minorities, 66–69, 119–21
Minutemen (U. S.), 369–70
mirror neurons, 136–37
mirroring, 111
mortality, 2f, 56–57
Movement for the Survival of the Ogoni People (MOSOP, Nigeria), 420–22
Mussolini, Benito, 248–49

Nepal, 17–18, 60b
narratives
   defined, 191
   functions of, 398
   ideological, 8–11, 13–14, 18–19, 26, 32–33, 34, 191, 201–2, 399–400, 410
   populist, 26
National Alliance (NA, U. S.), 312–13
National Democratic Party (NDP)
   Canada, 256–58
   Germany, 312–13, 315–16
National Front
   France, 251, 316
   Great Britain, 373
National Front (Colombia), 399–401
National Resistance (RN, El Salvador), 332–33
National Socialist Front (NSF, Sweden), 312–13

nationalism, 230–39
   Black, 325
   Christian, 236–37
   defined, 231
   ethnic, 238–39, 240–47
   ethno-, 368
   functions of, 239
   manifestations of, 234–35
'Ndrangheta, 308–11
Need to Belong Scale, 124–25
needs
   agency, 15–16, 42, 43, 160–79, 185
   belonging, 16–17, 44
   deprivation, 399
   essential, 8–9
   existential and epistemic, 15–16, 42, 43, 185
   relational, 15–16, 30–31, 42, 43, 185
neuroticism, 154–55, 209–11
New Left, 323–24, 325–26, 349–50, 376–77, 382–84. *See also* Old Left
Niger, 57–58
Niger Delta Human Development Report (UN 2006), 417–18
Niger Delta Volunteer Force (NDVF), 418–19, 421–22
Nigeria, 30
Northern Ireland, 62–63
Norway, 54

Old Left, 325–26, 349–51, 376–77, 382–83. *See also* New Left
openness (to experience), 154–55, 209–12
Orbán, Viktor, 430–33
order, 1, 96b, 96–100
Order, the Covenant and the Sword, The, 323
ostracism, 70, 242
oxytocin, 36–37, 138–39

"paradox of plenty." *See* resource, abundance
parochialism, 139–40
PartitoComunista Italiano (PCI, Italy), 327–28
peace, 33–34, 35–36
People's Revolutionary Army (ERP, El Salvador), 332–33
Perestroika, 263
personality, 154–60
   defined, 145, 154
   ideology and, 4
   psychology and, 214, 224–25
   traits, 209–16

Philippines, 13, 68
Podemos (Spain), 274
polarization, 63–64
polycentralism/heterogeneity, 30–32
Popular Liberation Forces (FPL, El Salvador), 332–33
Popular Unity (UP, Colombia), 334–35
poverty, 25–26, 48, 55–58, 60b
Prabhakaran, Vellupillai, 408–9
predictability, 42, 93–95, 95b, 195
prefrontal cortex (PFC), 81–82
   right ventral (RVPFC) of, 123–24
prejudice, 70, 214, 219–20, 226
Proletarian Armed Groups (Italy), 382–83
pro-sociality, 16, 42, 101–2, 133–42, 143, 185
Prospects of Upward Mobility (POUM) hypothesis, 203–4
"protest vote," 252–53
PVV (Partij voor de Vrijheid, Party for Freedom, Netherlands), 313–14

racism, 36–37, 218–30. *See also* Ku Klux Klan
radicalism/radicalization, 200, 246–47
rebellion, 17–18
reconciliation
   concept of, 194–209
   defined (Müller and Gries), 17–18, 186–87, 194
   ideological, 196–203
recruitment/mobilization, 351–67
   Boko Haram (Nigeria), 415–16
   criminal organizations and, 359–67
   FARC and, 403–5
   ideological groups/organizations and, 27–28, 28f
   Islamic State (IS) and, 424–26
   Law and Justice Party (PiS, Poland) and, 431–33
   Liberation Tigers of Tamil Eelam (LTTE, Sri Lanka), 410
   Mafia and, 359–67
   New and Old Left, 381–84
   radical organizations and, 367–97
   social vehicles for, 389–96
Red Army Faction (RAF, West Germany), 28–29, 270–71, 328–30, 382–83

Red Army (Japan), 270–71
Red Brigades (Italy), 270–71, 382–83
Red-Green Unity Lits (Denmark), 274
redistribution, 203–9
rejection, 185–86
religion, 279–80, 281–90
Republic of New Africa (RNA), 325
resource
   abundance, 50–54, 51b
   capture, 13
   "curse," 14
   scarcity, 49–50, 57–58
Revolutionary Armed Forces of Colombia (FARC), 333–35, 384, 400–6
reward, 128–30
Reynoso, Abimael Guzmán, 331, 332
Right-Wing Authoritarianism Scale (RWA), 214, 215–16, 251–52
Rosenberg Self-Esteem Scale, 166
Rwanda, 13

safety/existential security, 21, 42, 78, 185
Salafist, 198–99
SAP (Sveriges socialdemokratska arbetareparti, Social Democratic Party, Sweden), 256–58
Saro-Wiwa, Ken, 418–19, 420–21
scarcity (structural), 13
Schwartz Value Theory (personal values of), 293–94
sect, 335–36
self
   -awareness, 50–51
   -categorization theory, 103
   -concept, 53, 144, 149–50, 185
      clarity, 150–53, 156
      culture and, 147–48
      defined, 145
      intrapersonal process and, 144–54
   -continuity, 150
   -determination, 8–9, 42, 115, 144, 145, 185
      agency need for, 168–73
      defined, 168–70
      theory (SDT), 296–97
   -devaluation, 123
   -efficacy, 16, 42, 144, 145, 185, 186–87
      agency need for, 175–79
      meaning and, 179b
      theory, 175–76

-esteem, 16, 42–43, 116–17, 122–23, 143–44, 145
   agency need for, 160–66
   culture and, 166
   darker side of, 166*b*
   defined, 153, 160–61
   self-concept and, 162
   state, 152–53, 160–61
   trait, 152–53, 160–61
-evaluation, 153
-knowledge, 153–54
-perception, 109–10, 111
-reflection, 126–27
Sharia law, 288–89, 338–39, 414–15, 424
Shekau, Abubaker, 415–16
Shining Path (Sendero Luminoso, SL, Peru), 331–32
Sierra Leone, 53
significant quest theory, 198–99
social dominance
   orientation (SDO), 208, 214–16, 251–52
   theory (SDT), 220–21
socialism, 254–70
   basic assumptions and characteristics of, 254–60, 268–70
   Socialist Party
      France, 256–58
      Netherlands, 274
society, 125
   socio-economic status (SES), 202, 207
Soldiers of Allah (SOA), 392–93
Somalia, 57–58
South America, 275*b*
SPD (Germany), 256–58
stability, 19
Stalin, Joseph, 260–62, 268–69
"Stand up for Sweden," 374–76
stereotypes/heuristics, 89–90, 99–100, 194–95
stigmatization, 70, 165–66
Stormfront (U. S.), 371–72
striatum, 81–82, 128–30
Students for a Democratic Society (SDS), 323–24
Sudan, 13, 57–58, 68
supremacy, White, 317–18
survival, 185–86
sympathetic-adrenalmedullary (SAM) axis, 70–71

Syria, 62–63
Syriza (Greece), 274
system justification theory, 201–2

Taliban, 28–29, 347, 349, 395–96
terrorism, 313. *See also* group/organization, extremist
Thailand, 13, 67
threat, 185–86, 277–78, 285, 288–89. *See also* competition, poverty, resource scarcity; Evolutionary Threat Assessment Systems (ETAS) theory
   consequences of, 47–48
   information processing and, 77
   intergroup, 61–62, 65*b*
   perceived, 12, 76
   psychological implications of, 69–71, 71*b*
   socio-economic status (SES) and, 73*b*
totalitarianism, 250–53
trait (dispositional), 154–55, 165–66
Trump, Donald, 236–37
trust, 35–36

Uganda, 68
uncertainty-identity theory (Hogg), 30, 152–53, 196–97, 282
Union of Soviet Socialist Republics, 62–63
United Klan of America (UCA), 229–30
United Liberation Front of Asom, 67–68
universalism (welfare), 205–6

V (Vansterpariet, Sweden), 274
values, 35–36, 186–87
   Schwartz Value Theory and, 293–94
VAS (Vasemmistoliitto, Socialist Party, Finland), 274
Venezuela, 57–58
ventromedial prefrontal cortex (vmPFC), 76–77, 81–82, 127
Vices and Virtues Scale (VAVS), 159
vigilantism, 369
violence
Violencia, La (Colombia), 401
voting, majority, 21

Weatherman, 323–24
Weber, Max, 402–3
Westboro Baptist Church (WBC), 393–94
White Power Movement (WPM), 317–18

Wilders, Geert, 314–15
women
　Boko Haram and, 413–14
　Eastern European Communit parties and, 379
　empathy and, 137
　FARC and, 404–5
　fascism and, 248–49
　Hizb al-Tahrir al-Islami and, 388–89
　Islamic State (IS), 345–46, 425–27
　left-wing, 290–91
　Mafia and, 363
　National Women's Front, 373
　racism and, 223–24
World Communist Movement, 326–27, 349–50
World Value Survey, 233–34

Yakuza (*boryokudan*), 359–60, 364–65
Yemen, 57–58
Yugoslavia, 62–63

Zenga Kuren, 270–71